SOUTH AFRICAN PARTIES AND POLICIES

SOUTH AFRICAN PARTIES AND POLICIES

1910-1960

A SELECT SOURCE BOOK

Edited with an introduction by

D. W. KRÜGER, M.A., D.LITT.

Professor of History at the Potchefstroom University for Christian Higher Education, South Africa.

HUMAN & ROUSSEAU
CAPE TOWN

PRINTED IN THE UNION OF SOUTH AFRICA
BY CAPE TIMES LIMITED • CAPE TOWN

ACKNOWLEDGEMENTS

THE PUBLICATION of this book is due to the enterprise and initiative of the publishers who thus sought to commemorate the Union's first half century. For that and the many ways in which they facilitated my task, I express my appreciation. My thanks are also due to the librarian and staff of the South African Railways Library in Johannesburg who gave me access to sources which were not available elsewhere. Particular mention must in this regard be made of the parliamentary debates of the period 1915-1923 in the form of cuttings from the *Cape Times,* one of the few copies, as the official Hansard was not published during that period.

I wish further to thank the *Cape Times* and the Johannesburg *Star* for generous permission to republish speeches as reported in their newspaper files. My thanks are also due to Mrs. Margaret Creswell for leave to quote from her biography of Colonel Creswell.

To Colonel C. F. Stallard I am indebted for a copy of the Dominion Party Programme, and to Mr. C. M. Tatz, of Johannesburg, for several political pamphlets.

I also wish to thank the Speaker of the House of Assembly for his communication, through the Clerk of the House, regarding quotations from the *House of Assembly Debates.*

I must mention, finally, the assistance I have received from the librarian and staff of the Potchefstroom University library, the librarian and staff of the Johannesburg public library and the head office of the National Party in the Transvaal.

D. W. K.

INTRODUCTION

1. *The growth of Political Consciousness and the forming of Parties.*

Up to the beginning of the nineteenth century the Boer or Afrikaner people had little incentive and less occasion towards political grouping. These people, the great majority of whom were cattle and sheep farmers, were thinly spread out over a vast extent of country. Geographical circumstances led them into isolation both in regard to the centre of government, far removed in Cape Town, and in respect of political intercourse amongst themselves. A rugged individualism developed which adversely affected any co-operative tendency. Grievances there were, of course, but most people were satisfied when left alone as much as possible.

The Great Trek of the thirties of the nineteenth century was the culmination of steadily increasing dissatisfaction with the colonial authorities. It was the only outlet, excepting armed resistance, which politically minded colonists had. The Cape Colony had no representative government to which they could air their grievances and they themselves had few traditions of representative institutions and none in respect of party politics. Theirs was the choice of opposing the government by force of arms or trekking away. They chose the latter.

In Boer republican exclusiveness they sought the answer to the tacitly accepted idea and the fairly widespread practice of British superiority. The Great Trek was a form of political expression and it had important political results. With it began the balkanisation of South Africa which ended only with the fall of the Boer republics in 1902. The Great Trek and the South African War were the two poles which marked the separate republican existence of a large part of Afrikanerdom. The republics of the Transvaal and the Orange Free State which resulted from the Trek provided the Afrikaners in that part of the country with the opportunity of gaining experience in self-government long before their brethren in the Cape Colony, but there was a singular absence of party political feeling. The White population of the republics had a homogeneous character, their interests were the same and there was little incentive towards political grouping. The only exception was during the last years of the Kruger régime in the Transvaal when there was a tendency towards group-forming round the persons of presidential candidates. The absence of class differences also explain circumstances to a certain extent. A unifying factor was undoubtedly the continuous threat of British imperial expansionism and the presence of the Uitlander[1] element on the goldfields during the nineties.

---

[1] Historical Afrikaans term literally meaning " foreigners ".

The first conscious attempt towards political grouping in the northern provinces was made after the South African War when the Boer leaders of the two new provinces began to organise their defeated people. It was not their aim to regain the lost independence but to ensure for their people a proper share in the political life of the country. It was at once a symptom of growing political consciousness and a deliberate attempt to foster it still further. The Boer leaders candidly accepted British rule but they wanted to regain at the polls the substance of what had been lost by the peace treaty of 1902.

As early as July, 1903, General Louis Botha, the last Commander-in-Chief of the republican forces of the Transvaal, held a great popular meeting at Heidelberg. It was followed by others at which he urged the holding of a people's congress in order to consolidate the ranks of his followers. The congress, held at Pretoria in May of the following year, decided to form an organisation called " Het Volk " (The People). Its main principles were conciliation between Dutch and English with a view to forming a united nation, religious and mother tongue instruction in schools, and the rejection of the policy to import Chinese labour for the gold mines. Whatever his original intention may have been, Botha did not want his party to represent Afrikaans sectional interests only, although at first it was a strong motive force. In practice he co-operated with the well-disposed English.

In the Orange River Colony, as the Free State was now called, there was a similar development. Immediately after the war the Boer population had little time for anything but agricultural reconstruction, and was politically apathetic. But as in the Transvaal, circumstances made some sort of political action imperative. In this case it was the education of the new authorities. The Afrikaans people were afraid that as a result of the anglicising policy in the schools their children would be lost to them. Congresses at Brandfort in December, 1904, and at Bloemfontein in July, 1905, led by General J. B. M. Hertzog, decided to form a political organisation, the " Orangia Unie ". The cultural motive was strongly stressed.

English-speaking citizens of the two new colonies likewise showed a renewed interest in politics. Whilst many of the " moderate " English joined the Afrikaner political organisations, the more " British " section hived off to form its own party. In 1904 the Transvaal Progressive Association, led by Sir George Farrar, Sir Percy Fitzpatrick and Sir Abe Bailey, all of them ex-Uitlander opponents of the old Kruger régime and representatives of mining interests, came into being. In the same year E.P. and Harry Solomon formed the Responsible Government Party which, as the name indicated, aimed at the early granting of responsible government to the Transvaal. English White labour stood aside and a few years later formed the Independent Labour Party, led by H. W. Sampson, which with small parties of like principles were amalgamated in January, 1910, as the South African Labour Party, with Colonel F. H. P. Creswell as leader.

In the Orange River Colony the British-minded English in January, 1907, formed the Constitutional Party. Its leader was Mr. (later Sir) John Fraser. It was opposed to the granting of responsible government but it represented only a negligible minority and never amounted to much.

Meanwhile in the settled Western Province of the Cape Colony a development had been taking place which resulted in much more political maturity than elsewhere. White political consciousness in that part of South Africa had been slow in awakening. It was as late as the beginning of the eighties of the nineteenth century before there were any signs of it. Influenced by the Transvaal struggle against Britain during the first Boer War (1880-1881) the Reverend S. J. du Toit of Paarl, leader of the Afrikaans language movement, made an attempt to organise the Afrikaners of the Western Province politically. He aimed at an organisation exclusively Dutch in character and called it the Farmers Protection Association. His ultimate object was a united South Africa independent of Great Britain, but he did not receive wide-spread support from his fellow Afrikaners. The leadership of the movement was taken over by J. H. Hofmeyr of the Cape and thus in 1883 the Afrikaner Bond came into being. It had a broad South African basis on which both Dutch (Afrikaans) and English could agree. In the bond both elements of the White population found political expression. It was the outcome of an awareness of the necessity of establishing some sort of political organisation in the common interest. Not unnaturally, in a community largely agricultural and pastoral, it at first stressed farming interests. Gradually, however, broader colonial and even national interests gained prominence in the councils of the party as the instinct or zest for politics was sharpened and as the voting public gained more experience of representative parliamentary government. In this regard it must be remembered that the official use of the Dutch language in Parliament was admitted only since 1881 and then for the first time most Afrikaner colonists began to take a serious interest in politics.

The Afrikaner Bond, according to its constitution of 1883, had lofty ideals and the term " Afrikaner " was interpreted in its widest sense. Art. 1 of its programme expressly stated that the Bond considered everybody to be an Afrikaner, whatever his origin, who aimed at the welfare of South Africa. It wanted a South African nationality based on true patriotism with a united South Africa as the ultimate ideal. For that purpose it encouraged Afrikaners to take part in political life. In 1907 Hofmeyr expressed its principles as encouraging a feeling of national unity, self-respect and pride as British South Africans. He thought that without a strong feeling of nationality which should bind both English- and Dutch-speaking people as an indivisible South African nation, the union of colonies, about to be consummated, would be in danger of disruption.

In the peculiar political situation of the later nineties when Paul Kruger was fighting to preserve the separate identity of his people, the Bond instinctively became linked up with Afrikaner sentiment in the north, at the same time proclaiming its loyalty to the Queen. In preaching and practising broad South African principles, it still placed Cape colonial interests first and tacitly assumed the political superiority of the older colony which would one day take the lead in unifying South Africa. That was the basis of its co-operation with Cecil Rhodes. The sentimental link with the narrower Afrikaner nationalism of the north was strengthened as the result of the South African War, which was accompanied by a flare-up of anti-British feeling. But the outcome of the war had demonstrated at the same time that the ideal of an exclusive Afrikaner (in the narrower sense) nationhood was doomed. Afrikaners in the ex-republics were perceptibly inclined to accept the Bond's broader interpretation of nationhood notwithstanding their own conservative traditions and the Bond's liberal principles in regard to the non-White population. The tendency towards political co-operation increased on the eve of Union.

The Afrikaner Bond was the first conscious political organisation embodying a South African national spirit. It was the forerunner of Botha's South African Party of 1911 as well as of Hertzog's National Party of 1914, and even now its spiritual heritage has not been exhausted. Nearly all parties have tried to adapt its general principles to the needs of the nation.

In the Progressives of the Cape and the Transvaal the followers of Hofmeyr, Botha and Hertzog had a common enemy. The Bond hated the Progressive Party of the Cape, led by Dr. L. S. Jameson, for its part in the movement to suspend the Cape constitution after the South African War. In the same way both " Het Volk " and the " Orangia Unie " considered the ex-Uitlanders of the Transvaal as their mortal enemies, representing those forces which had led to the fall of the Boer republics, British extremists and opponents of true South Africanism. Instinctively they closed their ranks. Notwithstanding the fact that John X. Merriman, Hofmeyr's successor and Cape premier, was overlooked by the Governor-General in favour of Botha as the first Prime Minister of the Union, members of the Bond in the Cape forgot their disappointment and followed Botha to the polls at the first Union general election in September 1910. The allied parties warmly supported the unification of the colonies on the broad South African basis of English and Afrikaans sharing alike as expressed in Article 137 of the constitution which provided for the equality of the two languages. The outward expression of the new idealism was the South African Party, a name already adopted by the Bond in 1908 and generally accepted by the new unified party under Botha in 1911.

Afrikanerdom in the broad sense was prepared to abide by the political results of the Anglo-Boer war, but Afrikaners in the narrower sense refused to acquiesce in the loss of their cultural identity or to accept an inferior constitutional status. That was the background of what used to be known as " Hertzogism ". It found its political expression in the National Party formed by Hertzog in January 1914. It had a close affinity to the Afrikaans cultural movement and it gave great impetus to the constitutional development of South Africa.

Everywhere in opposition were the Progressives which with Fraser's small Constitutional Party on the eve of Union formed the Unionist Party with Jameson as leader. This party, first and foremost, represented industrial interests and openly stood for British supremacy. As viewed by many of its opponents it was the embodiment of imperialism and capitalism at the same time. In 1921, led by Sir Thomas Smartt, it merged with the South African Party and lost its separate identity but its spirit survived for a considerable time.

Natal in 1910 was in the unique position of having no party political traditions nor affiliations. That province at the first general election elected mostly independent candidates who more or less supported Botha in Parliament.

Nearly all parties in 1910 were more or less conservative but from the beginning some of them contained a considerable liberal element. Liberals were not represented as such in Parliament but the liberal viewpoint always had champions except in the National Party. The Liberal Party itself came into being at a much later date.

Federal and similar parties of lesser consequence were never represented in Parliament and were rooted mostly in Natal's particularism. The Dominion Party, formed in 1934, and reminding to some extent of the old Unionist Party, acted as a counter to Dr. D. F. Malan's (Purified) National Party of that year, leaving the United Party, like the South African Party of 1911, holding the centre position.

The Labour Party played a considerable part in its heyday but since 1953 it has been a spent force and at the moment it is not at all represented in Parliament. Its loss of influence may be ascribed to the circumstances that through the pact with the Nationalists it had since 1924 achieved several of its major aims with the result that many of its Afrikaans supporters thereafter voted Nationalist. In other words, it had lost its *raison d'être*. Moreover, since 1943 it had been changing its character gradually until under new leadership after the war it took a liberal course.

2. *Note on election results.*

1910: S.A. Party 68 members in the House of Assembly, Unionists 37, Labour 5, Independents 11.

1915: S.A. Party 54, Unionists 39, Nationalists 27, Labour 4, Independents 6.

1920: National Party 44, S.A. Party 41, Unionists 25, Labour 21, Independents 3.

1921: S.A. Party 79, National Party 45, Labour 9, Independent 1.

1924: National Party 63, S.A. Party 53, Labour 18, Independent 1.

1929: National Party 78, S.A. Party 61, Labour 8, Independent 1.

1933: National Party 75, S.A. Party 61, Labour 4, Roos Party 2, Home Rule 2, Independents 6.

1938: United Party 111, National Party 27, Dominion Party 8, Labour 3, Socialist 1.

1943: United Party 89, National Party 43, Labour 9, Dominion Party 7, Independents 2.

1948: National Party 70, United Party 65, Afrikaner Party 9, Labour 6.

1953: National Party 94, United Party 57, Labour 5.

1958: National Party 103, United Party 53.

PRIME MINISTERS

General L. Botha (S.A. Party) 1910-1919.

General J. C. Smuts (S.A. Party) 1919-1924.

General J. B. M. Hertzog (National Party) 1924-1933.

General Hertzog (Coalition) 1933-1934; (United Party) 1934-1939.

General Smuts (United Party) 1939-1948.

Dr. D. F. Malan (National Party) 1948-1954.

Mr. J. G. Strijdom (National Party) 1954-1958.

Dr. H. F. Verwoerd (National Party) 1958—.

3. *Racial Policy.*

Nearly from the outset South African political parties had to formulate policy in regard to two main issues. On the one hand there was the problem of the position of the Union relative to Great Britain and the Empire and on the other the problem in regard to race relations within the Union. Both problems threaded their way through the history of the Union side by side, sometimes tending to confuse and obscure party political differences.

Of all aspects of South Africa's racial problem the Indian question has caused least dissension amongst White political parties. During the period up to the Second World War the major parties were in principle agreed that the Indian population constituted a distinct and " foreign " element. Since the war, however, there has been a significant change in the attitude of many White people who, as the 1946 and 1948 Parliamentary debates show, are prepared to concede considerable political rights to people of Indian extraction.

Of the vast available literature on the subject it has been found impossible to include for publication more than a few extracts from major speeches high-lighting the attitude of political parties in regard to some aspects of the problem. The student is further referred to C. F. Andrews, *Documents relating to the new Asiatic Bill* (1926) and C. F. Andrews, *Documents relating to the Indian question* (1926); also the report of a commission under the chairmanship of Mr. Justice Richard Feetham (published as Blue Books U.G. 7 of 1934 and 22 of 1935); the reports of two commissions headed by Mr. Justice Broome, 1941 and 1943 (U.G. 39/41 and U.G. 21/43); the various Acts and the full Parliamentary debates, published in Hansard.

A few salient facts may be of some assistance. Indians were first imported into Natal in 1860 as indentured Coolies on the sugar plantations and they have been largely responsible for developing the industry to its subsequent flourishing state. At the expiration of his service contract an Indian could renew his indenture but after five years he was free to take up other employment as a free labourer or to start on his own in any other walk of life. After a further five years he was entitled to a free passage to India or to a grant of Crown land to the same value. Most of the Indians elected to stay and, joined by their womenfolk, they multiplied rapidly. They even overflowed to the Transvaal where the republican authorities in the eighties imposed restrictions in regard to land ownership and occupation. Neither there nor in Natal were Indians granted equal political rights and there were other civil disabilities also. Natal levied a personal tax of £3 on every Indian who refused to re-indenture or to be repatriated.

By 1910 Indians in Natal outnumbered the White people and, particularly in the commercial field, their competition was keenly felt. With the unification of the South African colonies all political parties were committed to a policy of restricting further Indian immigration.

On their side the Indians had various grievances. They objected to the £3 tax and to a fingerprint test on registration, they objected to restrictions on trading licences, they demanded freedom of movement to the other provinces, particularly the Transvaal, and the removal of restrictions in regard to ownership and occupation of land. They were also raising the issue of political rights. In M. K. Gandhi, an able British-trained Indian lawyer, they found a clever and astute leader who in South Africa first preached the practice of civil disobedience and passive resistance. During 1913-1914 he was involved in a severe struggle with General Smuts, the Minister responsible for Indian affairs, in order to get the civil disabilities removed.

Gandhi obtained small concessions, but in 1913 Parliament passed an Immigration Act[1] which on economic and social grounds severely restricted immigration from India. Gandhi continued his campaign, strikes occurred, and after investigation by a commission, headed by Sir William Solomon, and assisted by Sir Benjamin Robertson, an Anglo-Indian official, Parliament passed the Indian Relief Act.[2] It abolished the £3 tax and made some concession in regard to the admission to South Africa of Indians' wives. Gandhi accepted the Act and Smuts agreed with him to administer the laws " in a just manner and with due regard to vested interests ".

But the problem was not solved, for Indians still complained of civil disabilities and White interests still objected to Indian commercial and residential encroachment. Acting on the report of a Parliamentary Select Committee in 1919, Parliament[3] forbade the issue of new trading licences

---

[1] Act 22 of 1913.
[2] Act 22 of 1914.
[3] Act 37 of 1919.

in the Witwatersrand area of the Transvaal and stopped loopholes by which Indians had managed to evade the law. Indians in South Africa, supported by the Indian Government, objected to the Act as imposing fresh limitations in violation of the Smuts-Gandhi agreement of 1914, which was liable of a wide interpretation.

On the other hand, White public opinion was stiffening and early in 1924 the South African Party Government was preparing to introduce a Class Areas Bill to restrict Indian trading and occupation of land to certain defined areas. Relations between India and the Union deteriorated. The succeeding National Party Government, with Dr. Malan as the responsible Minister, took up the matter after a strong anti-Indian election campaign and relations with India did not improve. Negotiations with the Indian Government were initiated in 1926, the Bill was withdrawn and after agreement was reached, the result was embodied in a new Act.[4]

The repatriation scheme was not successful, however, and for several years thereafter Parliament passed further Acts dealing particularly with Indian Land Tenure in the Transvaal. As a result of strong representations from Natal, Parliament in 1943 passed a temporary Pegging Act[5] restricting Indian land holdings in certain areas. All political parties more or less concurred on the general principles underlying these restrictions. The Pegging Act lapsed in 1946 and the Smuts Government proposed new legislation, making the restrictions on occupation and ownership of land permanent, but at the same time making considerable political concessions. Both Opposition groups, the National and the Dominion Parties, led by Dr. Malan and Colonel C. F. Stallard respectively, opposed the political clauses of the Bill which was nevertheless passed by Parliament.[6] Two years later the Malan Government caused the repeal of this part of the Act.[7] The situation has, since then, remained virtually unchanged.

As regards the Cape Coloured problem it should be kept in mind that the Cape Coloured people include the descendants of the original slave population who were imported from East and West Africa, Madagascar and the Indian archipelago during the seventeenth and eighteenth centuries. They represented races widely separated from one another racially and culturally. At the Cape they became mixed and, in addition, they mixed with the indigenous Hottentots as well as with White people. Their descendants include half-castes as well as almost pure Malays, and the racial variety becomes even more colourful when other groups, including Griquas, officially classed as Coloured, are included.

4 The Immigration and Relief Act 37 of 1927.
5 Trading and Occupation of Land (Transvaal and Natal) Restriction Act, No. 35 of 1943.
6 The Asiatic Land Tenure and Indian Representation Act, 28 of 1946.
7 The Asiatics Laws Amendment Act, 47 of 1948.
   It should be pointed out that Dr. Malan's statement of 20 January 1948 on the Indian question (Section IV, No. 6) deals also with Colour policy in general. It has not been possible to break up this document into its component parts.

When the Cape was granted representative government in 1853 those of them (the slaves were freed in 1834) who qualified for the franchise were placed on a common roll with the Whites. It was the policy of the Afrikaner Bond to keep them there and up to 1934 the parties did not differ from one another in regard to the matter. Since that year the National Party changed its programme and advocated placing the Coloured people on a separate voters' roll. The problem during the past few decades has had practically only one political facet, that of representation in the Union's legislature.

The Native (African) question has to do with many more aspects. The word " Native " covers the indigenous Bantu people of the Union. Since 1910 a large number of Acts have been passed by Parliament specially applying to this section of the population. A policy of racial separation has been followed, but since 1948 it has been applied more systematically as a policy of parallel development under the slogan " Apartheid ". The following is a list of the more important Acts relating to Natives:

1911: Mines and Works Act No. 12.
1913: Natives Land Act No. 27.
1920: Native Affairs Act No. 23.
1923: Native (Urban Areas) Act No. 21.
1926: Mines and Works Amendment Act No. 25.
1927: Immorality Act No. 5.
Native Administration Act No. 38.
1932: Native Service Contract Act No. 24.
1936: Representation of Natives Act No. 12.
Native Trust and Land Act No. 18.
1945: Native (Urban Areas) Consolidation Act No. 25.
1949: Prohibition of Mixed Marriages Act No. 55.
1950: Population Registration Act No. 30.
Group Areas Act No. 41.
1951: Native Building Workers Act No. 27.
Bantu Authorities Act No. 68.
1952: Natives (Abolition of Passes and Co-ordination of Documents) Act No. 67.
1953: Bantu Education Act No. 47.
Reservation of Separate Amenities Act No. 49.
1955: Group Areas Development Act No. 69.
1957: Group Areas Act No. 77.
1959: Bantu Investment Corporation Act No. 34.
Extension of University Education Act No. 45.
Promotion of Bantu Self-Government Act No. 46.

4. *The Sources.*

A collection of sources of this kind must necessarily be incomplete. The vastness of the available printed subject material and the limitation of space imposed severe restrictions on the editor and it has been possible

to consider documents of a representative character only. The programmes of only those parties who were represented in Parliament have been included. An exception was made in the case of the Liberal Party. That is also the reason why it has not been possible to include the programmes of the various non-White organisations. For these the reader is referred to Gwendolen Carter, *The Politics of Inequality,* p. 481 ff. Others have been omitted as having had very little influence or significance.

In regard to the papers of political parties it has been very difficult sometimes to trace important documents owing to the fact that parties keep no proper archives or libraries. Their own collections are very incomplete and even the bigger South African public libraries are not well provided with printed political matter. For the first decade after 1910 the daily newspapers present the best printed source material. Reporting of political speeches was very complete and often verbatim. But gradually the picture changed. By the twenties speeches were condensed more and more, so much so that they became hardly worth using as source material. The best complete source remain the officially recorded debates in Parliament. It should be remembered though that even Hansard is not free from mistakes; sometimes whole sentences have been left out. For financial reasons Hansard was not published from 1915 to 1923. Fortunately the *Cape Times* during those years printed a practically verbatim record of parliamentary proceedings.

Other sources which should be mentioned are select committee reports (indicated S.C.) and special commission reports (indicated U.G.).

In some cases parts of speeches have been omitted. Irrelevant interjections as well as asides by the speaker himself, having no real bearing on the subject, have been cut out. But generally the material published here, is a true and verbatim record.

This source book is primarily and obviously intended for the student who already has some general knowledge of the history of the Union. It should prove to be a guide to other source material and stimulate further research. There are, unfortunately, few published historical works devoted to the history of the Union only. For general reading in regard to the period up to 1948 the reader is referred to D. W. Krüger, *The Age of the Generals, 1910–1948.* (Johannesburg, 1958.) Of a more specialised nature is Gwendolen Carter, *The Politics of Inequality; South Africa since 1948.* (London, 1958.)

The documents published here reflect the prevailing spirit of the times and illuminate the attitude of the various parties towards the great questions of the day. They should serve to provide some sort of image of South African politics and give some insight into the minds of men who thought and acted and helped to make history, illustrating reason and passion at work.

D. W. KRÜGER.

CONTENTS

xvii

2

SECTION III

The Development of Constitutional Independence
and the Symbols of Nationhood

SECTION IV

The Indian Problem

xviii

SECTION V

Cape Coloured Representation

SECTION VI

The Native Problem

SECTION I
THE NEW SOUTH AFRICA

LEADERS' VIEWS, 1910

1

GENERAL LOUIS BOTHA[1]

UP TO THE present I have never addressed a large meeting in any other language than the language I am in the habit of speaking. But as I understand that it is generally expected that I should address you in your own language — and convince you of my willingness even at a great disadvantage to make use of this magnificent opportunity of making my remarks in the English language, I trust that the sporting instinct for which you are so famous and well known will help you to overlook whatever shortcomings I may display in expressing myself. It is indeed a great pleasure to me to see this splendid gathering here tonight. This conclusively proves to me that you continue as you have always done in the past, to take a lively interest in State affairs, and this I appreciate very sincerely. This is the first time in the history of the land that Ministers of a United South Africa have had the pleasure of the opportunity of addressing you in this hall of historic associations. Mr. Chairman, ladies and gentlemen, the first point I want to deal with tonight is the education question. (Applause, and a voice: "What about Hertzog?") Criticism has brought the education question so much more than anything else before the public that we can hardly read a newspaper without reading about what has been called Hertzogfontein. The controversy about the Orange River Colony Act[2] is steadily being pressed on the public of the Province, and I am very sorry to see it. In the Transvaal, gentlemen, we have no controversy upon education — and I tell you tonight to stand together, and do not make it a controversy in the Transvaal. There has been the best co-operation on education in the Transvaal — and I hope that that will continue in the future. I ask you, gentleman, do not let us be misled by any party feeling to abandon the good spirit that exists today upon education in the Transvaal — but rather let us live and try to bring about that good spirit for the Union of South Africa.

Now, Mr. Chairman, ladies and gentlemen, there are three points in the education policy which I want to lay before you tonight as being the expression of my Government. It has been said in the papers that my Government ought to speak out upon this education question. Now, gentlemen, the policy, not only my policy, but my Cabinet's policy, is

[1] Leader of Het Volk in the Transvaal and last Prime Minister of the Transvaal. Speech held at the Wanderers, Johannesburg, as reported in the *Star*, 13 July 1910.
[2] Act 35 of 1908, introduced by General Hertzog as Minister of Education in the Orange River Colony.

3

as follows: (1) Equal opportunities of language. (2) Medium in the mother tongue — even if it costs the State a little more money. (3) No compulsion. These are the three educational points, and if we carry them out in a conciliatory and co-operative spirit I have great hopes that the question of education will be settled in an acceptable way for all parties in South Africa. When I first made this statement in Standerton certain papers criticised. In the first instance they said: " This is acceptable, but still, General Botha, it is not enough. General Botha must give something more." The paper said General Botha must pledge himself at once to repeal the Orange River Colony Education Act. That was the first demand. The second demand was, I must promise a Union Act to be passed to make that Act of the Orange River Colony illegal. And now again they say that I must force the Orange Free State people, whenever they require more money for expansion, to change that Act. I appeal to all fair-minded people; is it a just demand — yes or no? Allow me to say that all these demands are most unfair and impossible — and absolutely against our Constitution, as I will point out to you. If I was foolish enough to make such a promise I can assure you it would be an idle one and misleading, and if Dr. Jameson[3] — my friend Dr. Jameson — were today Prime Minister of South Africa it would be impossible for him to make that promise.

Let me tell you that there is today in South Africa nobody in authority to repeal the Orange River Colony Act. According to the Constitution the only body that can alter or repeal that Act is the Provincial Council of that Province. This question of education was one of our most difficult questions during the Convention, and you will find that if one day the history of that Conventon is written you will agree with me it was not only one of the most difficult, but it was the most difficult question of the convention. The arrangement we have today is a compromise. Dr. Jameson and my Progressive friends are bound by this compromise made at the Convention. Personally I regret that it did not prove possible for the Convention to have primary education in the power of the Union Parliament. But there it is and it would be a breach of faith and of the spirit of the Constitution for the Union Parliament deliberately to pass legislation about matters expressively left within the domain of the Provincial Councils during a certain term of years. Therefore I can assure you that the people today who say I can repeal that Act know that to say so is to speak nothing less than nonsense. Now take for instance Natal. What would Natal say if we were to endeavour to impose any other Act upon the Natalians but their own? They have the privilege and right by the Constitution that their Act must remain in Natal and that they are the only people who can change it for the next five years. What would you say if I had the power to repeal or enforce Acts, if I were to force the Orange River Colony Act upon you? The knife cuts both ways. If I had the

3 Leader of the Unionist Opposition.

power to do this today, which certain Press organs and certain parties say I have, it would be unconstitutional. It is impossible for me to do so constitutionally. I know what Natal would say if I did. It would at once say that it had insisted upon primary education being left to the Provinces and " now you are breaking faith, the spirit and the letter of the Constitution, and you are playing us false ". And they will rightly say so, because it was made an essential point in the Convention that education must be left to the Provinces. Every fair-minded man will see that it is impossible to make such a promise. Now, I want to say it again. I will not stand up here before you and tell you a lie or try to mislead you. I have a great responsibility today, and it is my duty to see contentment in South Africa. I say again that it is impossible even for Dr. Jameson or the editor of any of these papers to undertake it. I see a great movement today in the direction of establishing private schools.

Now I can only as a friend warn you not to do so. Rather than start a movement to separate ourselves from each other, let us co-operate together and put our acts together and try to get an Education Act in the whole South Africa acceptable to both parties. I do not believe in compulsion, I hate it; and, gentlemen, there was a time when I stood up against compulsion in this country, and when it was in the power of my Government to co-operate with the Progressive Party, we did so. Therefore, gentlemen, we fell into line and spirit, and that was a good spirit, and let us stand together and keep that spirit for our children's sake, and for the unity of South Africa. Now, gentlemen, do not let us divide on such a vital question. Let us divide on all other questions, but not on the education question. Do not let us make a party question of this, and I ask you for God's sake do not let us make this an electioneering cry. Mr. Chairman, ladies and gentlemen, this is all I have to say about education. I want to say again that what I said on these points is not my policy but the policy of the Government of the United South Africa. Now, Gentlemen, you remember Sir Percy Fitzpatrick.[4] Sir Percy was reported to have said that the Government consisting of ten members was due to him; in fact that was his proposal. It is not desirable to discuss matters which have taken place in the Convention, but if mention is made at all it should be done correctly. I have looked up the records of the Convention, and I can assure you that Sir Percy Fitzpatrick was not the mover of that proposal. The man who proposed it was General Smuts. Therefore I am afraid that Sir Percy Fitzpatrick's vivid imagination has played him tricks upon this occasion.

Now the second point I would like to touch upon is the question of immigration and closer settlement. A great deal has been said about this subject. I can only say, gentlemen, that I am in favour of a carefully worked out scheme of immigration and closer settlement. In the first place I think the first step that ought to be taken is that thousands of people

4 Unionist Party.

5

in the biggest cities of South Africa ought to be brought back on the land where they can make a livelihood. Especially you know that there are thousands of these people both English and Dutch who are poor today and without livelihood, and not through their own fault, but through unfortunate circumstances. Also, gentlemen, I think that the one thing to be encouraged with regard to this immigration and closer settlement scheme is that the Government in the future must provide that when the labourer has finished his work he should stay on the land and not leave the country, so that if any man has worked for a certain time at the mines and has earned some money the Government can assist him with a small plot of land where he can go and become a good farmer and citizen of the country. Then also there is the Civil Service. If members of the Service want to settle after leaving the Service they also should be encouraged to go to the land, and the Government ought to supply them and help them in certain ways. If men must be imported from other parts of the world I think you will agree with me they must be carefully selected, so that we can get the right class of man and make a success of the farmer wherever you put him. Settlement in itself is a most difficult question, and we shall have to go slowly and steadily and work the thing out properly. We have seen that settlement in the past has cost a great deal of money, and I can assure you to an extent it was a failure. My Government, after they took office to assist poor settlers, had to write off certain responsibilites, and 42 per cent off the debt and liabilities. The settlers had a long time to pay up the balance. Just to show you what settlement can do. There was the White River settlement started here just after peace.[5] A big sum of money was spent on the settlement, and it was a hopeless failure. Over £20,000 were spent alone on furrows in bringing water to certain places, and today the settlers have gone and there is nobody left on the settlement.

The Dutch-speaking South Africans welcome a stream of White labour, and I hope that the mine-owners will encourage White immigration to the mines. The best way to encourage immigration is to use less Native labour and more White labour in South Africa. Whether you are a farmer or a mine-owner, I say to you again that if we want a White population, and if we want to make South Africa a White man's country, we ought, every one of us, to encourage White labour. I see that my friend Sir Aubrey Wools-Sampson[6] says that the Boers are jealous and do not want English settlers. Now I can assure you that that is untrue. The Boer people welcome English settlers in this country, and I can assure you that if you go today to the various settlements you will find the Boers and English on the farms to be the best of friends. Therefore the only thing we want is to make a success of farming in South Africa. The White labour question is a question which must go hand in hand with the closer settlement in South Africa. I sincerely hope that such

5 The peace ending the Anglo-Boer War.
6 Unionist Party.

facilities will be forthcoming so that miners may bring their wives from other countries to settle here.

At the last general election the majority of votes in Johannesburg went with my party. I taxed myself with one thing, and that was if I was returned to power I would do away with the Chinese in the Transvaal. Three years ago the papers were full of the Chinese question. There was no room for anything else. Not a speech was made but it was full of the Chinese question, and in those speeches it was distinctly stated that our prosperity depended on the Chinese as our backbone. It was said that everything would be ruined if the Chinese were sent out of the country. I stood firm on the pledge I made, and I want to prove tonight that it was the best thing that was ever done in Transvaal. I think we are all thankful they are gone. The men who referred to the Chinese in those days are silent about the Chinese today. They said in those days that they would clear out of the country if the Chinese were expelled. Today there is greater prosperity than ever there was in South Africa. For the year ended 30 June 1907, the amount of the profits assessable for the Profits Tax was £6,807,844, and for the year ended last month, notwithstanding the Chinese have left, it was £11,480,000.

That was the time when we said the Chinamen must go, and they said thank you for the service you have done to South Africa and the Transvaal. If you look through the programme of a certain party that was in favour of Chinese — they say today the Indians must also go. Gentlemen, they are perfectly converted and today, gentlemen, you find that there is more confidence than there has ever been in business in the Transvaal — there is greater stability and there is magnificent prosperity on the goldfields. Gentlemen, I say that never again shall a British workman's future rest on the so-called British backbone or yellow backbone of the Far East. There is one point I hope you will allow me to explain in connection with my Pretoria speech. I hoped that the Church and State would work together hand in hand in the future. It has been brought to my notice that people are saying that I meant the Dutch Church — that I meant to make the Dutch Church the State Church and give it more privileges than any other church in South Africa. Allow me to state to you tonight that such a thing was never in my mind. Gentlemen, those people who say that are telling nothing else but a falsehood to the people. What I said and the words I used were " Church and State ". I personally, gentlemen, have always been against a State Church — and I will fight against giving one church more privileges than another.

Allow me to say a few words about racialism. If we look at the history of the Transvaal we can see a most unfortunate state of affairs, and, gentlemen, may I say here again to you tonight that during the last war, where I was convinced that it was wrong to go on with that war, I advised as Commander-in-Chief of my Government straight away that they ought to make peace at once. Peace was signed and from that very moment I preached on all occasions, whether in the country or in

Johannesburg or in England, I spoke for co-operation and conciliation. I have read from time to time the criticism that the people are getting sick of this everlasting sound. But, gentlemen, I cannot desist from this work as long as my opposition friends will persist in raising the racial cry. I do not refer to the Leader of the Opposition, my friend Dr. Jameson. I have always found that he is as anxious as I am that racialism should be avoided and I cannot accuse him of having endeavoured to raise the racial cry; on the contrary. But, gentlemen, what about the first lieutenant in the Transvaal, Sir George Farrar?[7] Sir George said in Braamfontein on June 18 that if the British people would stick together they were numerically strong enough to rule the country, and that if they did not rule this country, it would be the fault of the British people. For rank unadulterated racialism nothing can surely surpass this. What would you say, and what would Sir George Farrar say himself, if I had made the same speech and simply substituted the word Dutch every time for British? Would not I have been called a traitor and a rebel and a hundred other unpleasant names? Therefore, I say that such a policy is a most objectionable policy. If I were to make one speech like that it would cause tremendous harm and put the clock back for many years. Why should, therefore, the second most prominent man in the Unionist Party be allowed to make such a statement? What must the Dutch feel when they read such a speech? Do you think it will fill them with confidence? If Sir George were to gain a victory at the poll, and were to have a say in the Government, what confidence does he foreshadow? Will he treat the Dutch equitably? Therefore, gentlemen, it is not on my side that racialism is raised. I have given up my all for peace and co-operation and shall continue to urge the people of South Africa on every possible occasion not to be misled. You, as an English community here tonight, I ask what right has any Englishman today to say that he is a better man to the British Empire than I am myself. I have done everything I could for South Africa, and therefore I won't stand back for any man in South Africa. And my first duty is to see that we have a contented people in South Africa and thereby strengthen the Crown and the British Empire at large. Today there is a better spirit of co-operation between the British and the Dutch than there has ever been before in South Africa. Let us differ on all sorts of points, but now we belong to one King and one Empire. Therefore let us work together and stand together for our King and the Empire. And now, ladies and gentlemen, I thank you most heartily for the hearing which you have accorded me.

7 Unionist Party.

2

GENERAL J. C. SMUTS[1]

GENERAL SMUTS, who was loudly cheered, said the meeting reminded him of the meeting four years ago in the same hall, when the great anti-Chinese campaign was started. That fight had been taken to a successful issue and whereas there were then 53,000 Chinese in this country, now there was not a single one. Similarly he hoped that this fight would lead to a not less great victory. In that election they had been warned against them, and all sorts of terrible things had been prophesied, but he asked them straightly whether they had forfeited the trust which had been placed in them. Sir George Farrar had said they must fight for British principles. What did that mean? Did they think Sir George Farrar had any British principles to teach them? They would hear the same old cries from the other side, but they were sensible men who had been through the mill in South Africa, and they knew how to take these statements. He noticed that the Unionist Party had dropped the name Progressive, and he could well understand it. It would be a parody of things to call this the Progressive Party. It was rapidly becoming the Remschoen[2] Party in South Africa. Sir George Farrar was the great missionary of British principles, and he (Mr. Smuts) was amused to see the other week that Sir George's one convert was Mr. C. A. Lane. At a meeting in Braamfontein they saw C. A. Lane at a meeting between Sir George Farrar and Mr. Lionel Phillips[3] — in the character of convert. The tremendous meetings being held up and down the Rand would have no effect on the temper of the people. The people of this country had learned to know in the very hard school of the past what the real fundamental facts of the situation were, and no chaff or nonsense such as they had heard at recent meetings of the Unionist Party would divide them from the great issue. He knew people in this country were sick of all this nonsense, and they wanted to move on to see progress made. There was an enormous work before the people of South Africa. They had no time for idle criticisms. They wanted to do constructive work. The Nationalists[4] wanted to forge ahead and leave all remschoens behind. He would not go into the party platform that evening because General

---

[1] Colonial Secretary of the Transvaal, 1907-1910, and Minister in Botha's first Union Cabinet. Speech held at the Wanderers, Johannesburg, as reported by the *Star*, 13 July 1910.
[2] Dutch for brake.
[3] Unionist Party.
[4] Botha's followers.

Botha had probably spoken upon that whilst he (General Smuts) was addressing an equally as large overflow meeting.

But he would like to touch upon the important question of national defence. It was recently said at some " remschoen " meeting: " How is it possible for a party government in South Africa to establish a national system of defence to which both English and Dutch will agree?" That question did not trouble him; it only troubled those who day and night had before them the nightmare of English and Dutch. Once that issue was dead the question of national defence could be dealt with on its merits. There was splendid material in the country; the best material in the world. The people of the country had heroic traditions, and from whatever race they had sprung they were ever ready to do their duty and to die for South Africa. Now South Africa was a nation, and if it wanted to be worthy of the status it had attained, then the time had come for a system of national defence. He hoped they would have a system which every part of the population would agree to. He wanted the youngsters to grow up through the schools, to learn their drills, and to learn discipline. He wanted the young men without exception, before they went into life, to become thoroughly efficient and disciplined. They did not want to have soldiers. South Africa did not want to have a standing army. What was required was that the young men should be trained from year to year so that when the day came and an appeal was made there would be a noble response. He hoped that whatever race they sprang from, English or Dutch, German or Jew, they would take part in such a system as he had indicated in the best spirit, and thus create a system which would be worthy of the best traditions of this country. There was another question which was of very great importance. Behind all their political problems lay the deeper question, the national and social question. Was it going to be a White man's land? That was the question which dominated every other question in South Africa. There were many people who were already despairing of South Africa's future. There was no need to despair. If the Government of South Africa did their duty the White race in this country would occupy a position as proud as it was possible for them to occupy. There was much to make them feel diffident about the future. They had seen of recent years more and more of the Asiatic flood towards South Africa. They had tried their best in this country to stem the flood, but it had swept round the shore of the neighbouring Colonies, and it was a great menace to the future of the South African nation. They could not blink the fact that the Native races were moving forward, and it was a matter of the greatest interest and astonishment to him to see in his short lifetime how the Native races had pushed forward and were more and more occupying the position which in bygone days White men had occupied. If they wished to reap the fruits of Union and see South Africa a permanent success they would have to keep that great issue before them. There were many ways in which they were warned of the trend of events

10

in this country. Four years ago the country was full of unemployed and there were deputations and demonstrations. Now that was one of the gravest symptoms in this country. Whilst people were clamouring for Native labour and importing Chinese here, there were thousands of White men who wanted work and could not get it. They had tackled the question, and had decided to strive earnestly against the policy of allowing the Whites to sink lower than the Blacks. Where, he asked, were the unemployed today? He claimed that the policy of the late Transvaal Government had absorbed them, and he defended a policy which had paid 3s. 4d. a day to unemployed who were almost entirely unskilled workers or unable to work. The measure was one of temporary relief, and had led to a position which enabled thousands of people who might otherwise have been walking the streets of Johannesburg and other South African towns to make an honest livelihood.

Ultimately they would get unemployment out of the way, and they would solve the problem of the poor Whites, which was one of the blackest problems in South Africa. If they had to consult their feelings they might have given a much different wage, but it was not a case for consulting their feelings. It was a case for doing the best thing under difficult circumstances, and he was certain they had done the best that could be done with the problem. Alluding to the Mining Regulations Commission,[5] he said he had spoken to some of the Commissioners, who told him that some of the questions that affected the men on the Rand, such as ventilation and miners' phthisis, had been most thoroughly gone into and recommendations had been made which he hoped would be of the greatest value. He hoped that when the recommendations came before the Government it would be possible to deal with those regulations and to improve in every way possible the condition of the skilled White labourers on the goldfields. He did not think that anybody could accuse the late Government of apathy in the matter. It had always strived to improve the conditions of the White workers on the goldfields. It had also passed a Workmen's Compensation Act,[6] which he heard was working satisfactorily all over the country. The late Government had passed an Industrial Disputes Act[7] which would contribute largely to the prevention of strikes and lock-outs and the miseries which followed in their wake. The present Government would do its best, irrespective of party politics, to solve the problems before the country and to improve the conditions of the White workers of the Witwatersrand. In the future the Government would have to devote more time to industrial questions than the late Government had done in the past three or four years, when most of the time had been taken up in dealing with matters of constitutional importance and Union. Now the decks were clear, and it was now possible for the Government to go thoroughly into the matter. He sincerely

[5] Appointed by the Transvaal Government.
[6], [7] Acts passed by the Transvaal Parliament.

hoped — and he spoke in a non-party spirit — that more and more the mine-owners in South Africa would also feel their responsibility. More and more he hoped that they would co-operate with the Government to bring about improved conditions. (A voice: "What about the land-owners?") He was not dealing with the land-owners at present. He thought it would be possible to make a great step in the advance of the country. If the experiment was fairly tried in this country it would be proved that the mines could be worked better and more effectively with White labour than with Coloured labour. He hoped the day was coming, and coming soon, when that experiment could be fairly tried.

The mine-owners might not have the courage to try the experiment, but after all the State had valuable mining properties, and the day might come, and that soon, when the Government of the country might have to start an all-White mine in order to prove that it was possible to work a mine more efficiently and better with White labour, decent, good White labour, than with kaffir labour. They knew that some time ago the Government started a labour bureau in connection with the Mines Depart-ment. Within the last couple of weeks, since the new Union Government was started, he, as Minister of Mines, had extended the scope of that Department all over South Africa. (Laughter.)

General Smuts: They meet us with laughter; that is all they have to meet a serious point with.

Continuing, he said that all over South Africa they had people who wanted work of one kind or another, skilled or unskilled, and he had thought it would be a good system to enlist the sympathy of every magis-trate, mining commissioner and immigration officer in South Africa, and make them all part and parcel of the labour bureau so that all necessary information could be obtained in every part of South Africa and published monthly. He hoped it would be possible to prevent the enormous wastage of White labour which had been going on to the detriment of the country. If they resolutely pushed forward day by day and year by year the time was coming when nobody would despair in this country of the position of the White man, and when everyone would admit that it was a White man's country. He believed there was no scope for party politics in South Africa. There was a great work before all of them. They were all wanted, whether they were following the Unionist or the Nationalist Party — they were all wanted for that work which had to be done.

3

THE LABOUR CAMPAIGN

MR. F. H. P. CRESWELL[1]

MR. CRESWELL, who was received with applause, said in opening his election campaign he did so with a deep sense of the responsibilities with which he asked them to invest him. He stood pledged to the Labour Party programme and would fight for every item in it. Het Volkers[2] had stated they were willing to support his candidature, but it was because they had no candidate of their own, and preferred him to Mr. Feetham.[3] They may have been told that the Labour Party was only concerned with the interests of one small section. Let them study the party's manifesto; they would see then that that was not so. He contradicted the statement that their party would plunge into rash adventures. The party who took them into wild adventures was the one which introduced the Chinese. They regarded as the only solid foundation for the country a well-educated, prosperous, independent class of men who did the work of the country. The whole of our industrial development had been based on a system of Coloured[4] labour closely resembling the old slave system. The effect on the White population was evil in the present and must be disastrous in the future. At present we were approaching the end of a period of capital expenditure and a number of men were being employed on work which would soon be completed. Twenty or 30 per cent more work was being done now than two years ago. Then 4,000 miners were actually breaking rock and they received £4,780 in daily wages. In December 1909, although 30 per cent more work was being done, the number of miners was 100 less, and the aggregate daily income was £700 less. That meant that the spending power of their customers was diminished to that extent. There was an increase of 1,700 White men underground on the mines, but in the grades earning 15s. a day and over there was a decrease of 500 men. In the grades earning under 15s. a day there had been an increase of over 20,000 men. What did that mean?

So long as the system of indentured Coloured labour was continued the people of this country were between the nether millstone of that mass

---

[1] Speech by Mr. Creswell, leader of the newly formed Labour Party, at the Masonic Hall, Jeppe, as reported in the *Star*, 22 July 1910.
[2] Leaders of " Het Volk " Party.
[3] Opposing Botha's Party.
[4] Meaning Black.

13

of Coloured labour and the other millstone of the great corporations, who had to grind out dividends for oversea shareholders. The Unionist Party would bring back the Chinese tomorrow if they could. If they did not find sufficient Coloured labour here they would try and introduce the cheapest labourers from Europe. Mr. Feetham had told them he did not favour such drastic steps as he (the speaker) did, because he was afraid of dislocating the industry. They had seen enough of that old scarecrow whose dilapidated rags had been stripped by the Mining Industry Commission report. Again, it was as difficult to frighten away capital from a 7 dwt. reef as to keep flies off a pot of jam. If they trusted the Unionist Party they would have to take the pickings which the great corporations chose to leave them.

The Labour Party did not believe in the closed door. But would people have been attracted to Canada in such large numbers as at present if that country had been controlled by a few large corporations? The Unionist Party would rejoice at the tremendous rate at which dividends were being turned out on the mines, and would point to a healthier condition of affairs if the number of men employed in the lower ranks were increasing, and they would say that the remedy was not to remove Government aid in the importation of Natives, but for working men to work at practically the same wage as they would in England. Men came out here to better themselves. Proceeding, the speaker referred to miners' phthisis. Industrial diseases should be brought into the Workmen's Compensation Act. That would result in every effort being made to reduce the high insurance rate that would follow. The speaker made comparisons between the programmes of the Labour and Unionist Parties in the matter of land legislation. In regard to women's suffrage, he said he had never heard an argument against it worth answering.

The speaker then outlined his party's policy on the Native question, which was to lead the Natives into a separate line of development in their own reserves. As regards Asiatics, their policy was prohibition of immigration and State-aided Asiatic emigration. As regards education, they objected to parents being coerced as much as any party. Concluding, he said the standpoint from which they regarded every matter that came before them was that the interest of the people of the country should be the supreme consideration of the Government. Every other interest should be subordinate to that, however powerful and however financially strong it might appear to be. The principle on which they would proceed was first that they would examine things for themselves, and, last, that they would not be scared by any bogeys. They would go forward boldly, not rashly, and insist on the adoption of measures which would truly assist the people of the country.

Mr. Wybergh[5] also spoke, and said the Unionist Party was going to be governed by a few kaffirs in the Cape.

Several questions were asked, in reply to which Mr. Creswell said all

[5] Labour Party.

14

mine work should be stopped on Sundays. Native labour should be abolished by degrees and mine benefit funds be subject to Government control. Undermeasuring of miners' work should be punished by imprisonment.

4

THE UNIONIST CAMPAIGN

DR. L. S. JAMESON[1]

IT HAS BEEN said that big causes inspire big ideals. Mr. Rhodes used to add to that in his case it was big surroundings that added to that inspiration and instancing in his own case, first the initiation of the big ideals and then the carrying of them out, he used to say that he largely attributed his success to the fact that his early manhood was spent in the desert-like expanses outside Kimberley and under the majestic shadow of Table Mountain. Well, we have a big cause, we have big surroundings, and, applying the simile to humanity, we have a great audience. We have that inspiration, I say, because this audience does not represent the interests of Johannesburg alone, but it is duplicated and triplicated by people from outside. I think that that being so we ought to be able to take a larger and broader view of the future of this country.

Now, gentlemen, speaking for the first time to a Johannesburg audience, and after long years of political life in the Cape Colony, I must say at once that I am conscious of a difference in the political and, I would say, the intellectual atmosphere of the two places. I know that in your eyes I, representing the Southern Colony, have practically some-what emphasised in me the old proverb of slow but sure. You, in this new country as compared with us, with its enormous natural wealth 6,000 feet above (sic) us, I know you live life much quicker than we do in the south. But I would ask in remembering this difference that these two characteristics, taken together, may actually achieve the best unity in this new country. Unity — that is what we want. The ideal, of course, is — and I believe it is an ideal which will be realised — that all provincialism, all provincial borders will ultimately disappear. We shall be one united homogeneous people. That will come. The only possible division — and it is a sentimental one, and a sentimental one that is thoroughly justified — is that one may be proud of which of the four Colonies one originally came from, by reason of the history of that Colony. That is purely sentimental, and the material interests of the four Colonies must be amalgamated.

Still, that is a slow process and will take time. The individual interests

---

[1] Speech by Dr. Jameson, leader of the Unionist (formerly Progressive) Opposition, at the Wanderers, Johannesburg, as reported by the *Star*, 4 August 1910.

must act and react against each other for a time. That, we know, must be so until, through time, through increased facilities of communication, or whatever it may be, we begin to recognise that we are one people, and the interests of the people have become so intermingled that we only realise that we are one South African nation. Still, that leads me to another thought — even in things as in people all is not bad. There is always some good. So this division may be a factor, and a great factor, in doing away with what I am sorry to acknowledge has been a recrudescence of during the past few months. I mean that these divisions among the people's material interests will blend the people in the various Colonies, so that in fighting for those interests they may forget that there was ever a racial factor in this country.

Well, it is on that very line that I have said now, of taking the best characteristics not only of the Transvaal and the Cape Colony, but of all the four Colonies, and uniting the best characteristics, that we shall get the greatest success in Union; so it is on the same line of thought that we, in the idea of the future government of this country, based our position on getting together a Government formed of the best men from all Colonies, irrespective of race and of party position. It was in running on the same lines of thought that we put forward what has been called by Sir Percy Fitzpatrick " a fresh start ". Well, you all know that we have failed for the present. I say advisedly for the present, because we are not going to abandon the ideal — I stand here for that ideal now. We are not entering into this party fight with that idea, because the present Government has been created out of what has been called the Bond-Het Volk-cum-Unie Parties in the three Colonies[2] — we are not entering into the fight with the idea of ousting them and putting in what has been called the Unionist-Progressive-Constitutional Opposition.[3] We stick to our position, and, even if we could gain on these lines, we would do harm to this country by emphasising the original party lines which we all know — and there is no use denying it — have been racial in this country. We do not want that.

The basis of the formation of our party is to get the best-men Government in this country, and that is what I am standing on this platform tonight to advocate to you. Well, as I said, we have failed for the present. The party forces have been too strong for us. We are back in the old party rut, and you will ask me why? Well, I will premise my answer by saying I believe that the present Prime Minister is absolutely at one with me and with the whole Progressive or Unionist Party as to the policy that should be followed in this country. I will begin with that. I then say the reason we have failed is because the Prime Minister has refused at the last fence. The Prime Minister after taking many

[2] The reference is to the Afrikaner Bond, Het Volk and the Orangia Unie in the Cape, the Transvaal and the Orange River Colony respectively.
[3] Referring to the respective Opposition Parties in the above Colonies.

fences, after, I know, an arduous time in trying to persuade the reactionary colleagues he has with him now, at the last moment has failed. Why? For want of moral pluck. We do not need to read between the lines of the Pretoria speech to know that the Prime Minister would not have surrounded himself with the colleagues that he would have chosen if he had exercised his own free will. We know what the record of those colleagues has been in the past. We know that there has been no recantation of that record from any of those colleagues. We know that those colleagues are in a majority in the Prime Minister's Cabinet, and therefore surely the Prime Minister, having chosen the majority of his colleagues, who, by their past record, by want of later recantation, are inimical to the policy which he announced, surely, I say, we are entitled to say that the Prime Minister no longer leads, and that he has abandoned the role of leader and is being led by the reactionaries. Then, taking up that position, what inference are we to draw from the Pretoria speech? What security have we that the programme annunciated by the Premier, that policy with which we agree, which is our policy (because the same policy was published by us three weeks before the Prime Minister's announcement) — what security, I say, have we that it will be carried out? I say none and that answer gives the root source why it was necessary for us to form a party and to do our utmost to see that that party is as large as possible so as to help the Premier against his reactionaries.

What does the present position mean to this country? It means, absolutely, the negation of righteous, clean honest government where the absolutely vital necessity is that power should go hand in hand with responsibility. But if this is persisted in, what are we in for? What are we starting our new career upon? (A voice: "God only knows.") I won't appeal to the Deity, but I believe that the electors have made up their minds that this policy shall not be persisted in, and that we shall not have a repetition of what happened during the last two sessions of the Cape Parliament — responsibility divorced from power. Now the Government and their friends will say to me: "What proof have you?" My answer is the best proof possible — the words of the Prime Minister in his Pretoria speech. How did he begin it? He first apologised for his long silence and then he gave the reason for his long silence. And what was it? That he did not like to pronounce his policy for fear of breaking the truce which had been brought about at the National Convention. What truce, gentlemen? If there is to be a breaking of a truce then there must at least be two hostile parties after the truce is broken. And what was that party which was hostile? Not the Progressives of the Transvaal or the Cape, or the Constitutionists of the Free State! Why, the Prime Minister and everybody else knows that months before I had announced — without contradiction from any of those parties, but on behalf of those parties — that the present Prime Minister and I could sign the same manifesto. Then where must we look for the other adversary? Where but in the present colleagues of the Prime Minister, and their inspirers, remember — because there are many of their way of thinking outside the Cabinet, and a very powerful many it is. That is my proof of what I say, that the present colleagues of the Prime Minister are inimical to his announced policy in Pretoria. Then, gentlemen, what is the next plank taken up by the Prime Minister which falls under my criticism as to the relative importance of measures and men in forming the present Ministry of the South African Union? He goes back upon the old overworked plank of coalition. Now, I am not going to repeat what I have said on the question of coalition, but I would just say that coalition was a wilful misconception of our ideal of the best-men government. A great portion of the people of this country has been hoodwinked by this name applied to our ideal and the best proof of this is the adoption of Hertzog himself. That is why on May 31 a Government was formed that absolutely answers Mr. Hertzog's requirements, and gives us a ministry which sacrifices its principles for the sake of hanging together. And so I am justified in saying that we never had a better example of a coalition Ministry than that which at present governs South Africa. I go on — I am rather hammering this point because it is the essence of our position as a political party desirous of forming a strong opposition — I go on to examples innumerable of the absolute hostility of the majority (and remember it is a majority of the Cabinet) against the Prime Minister's policy.

There are other examples I shall touch upon, but the solid centre of proof is in the present educational impasse in this country. The Prime Minister, in his Pretoria speech announced to us that he would pursue an educational policy acceptable to all, with, later on, in connection with something else, an absence of coercion. Gentlemen, is that the position in the Orange Free State, is that the policy publicly pronounced by General Hertzog? What does General Hertzog say on the education question in the Orange Free State, subsequent, remember, to the passing of the South Africa Act? That bilingualism, that the double medium shall be compulsory throughout the South African Union. And remember that this does not stop at the Orange Free State. Those of you who take an interest in education, I dare say, have read the proceedings during the last couple of years of the Cape Parliament. An identical amendment to Colonel Crewe's Education Bill was brought in in the first session of the last Bond Government in the Cape Parliament, and it was only defeated by the strenuous opposition of my friends in that Parliament, aided, too, by a few enlightened people on the other side, who refused to be dictated to on this question. I specially mention those enlightened few because I know that the English, the vast majority of the people of this country, of the Orange Free State itself, are not in favour of this policy of General Hertzog. It is a question of the leaders and not of the people. Well, how does that policy of General Hertzog compare with the policy laid down by the Prime Minister? Surely, looking at those two policies, I am justified in saying what the Prime Minister objected to —

that men, and not measures, were the basis of the formation of the present Government. What really happened, I am quite sure, is that a threat was held out to the Prime Minister, and what was that threat? " Form your Ministry from our party, and we will see about the policy afterwards." And that is being proved every day, and during the next few weeks you will have enough proof to say, I am sure: " We will not trust this Government, and we will not only have the Opposition, but we will have such a return at the polls that this immoral Government shall disappear." Still, the Prime Minister, I believe, honestly thinks that he will be able, even on the education question, to coerce his followers. I wait for proof. But are we justified in trusting that the Prime Minister will? Well, after the next few words I say, I think I shall agree with you. A gentleman says " Certainly ". Give me five minutes and I am perfectly certain, if he is an honest man, he will say " No ".

Well, let us follow General Botha, In Pretoria, at a speech there, as I said just now there was the promise of an educational policy which would have been acceptable to all of us. Afterwards, in another sentence, begging for toleration and co-operation, he said, " in which there shall be no room for coercion ". Otherwise the thorny subject of education was no further touched upon. But during the interval between that speech and when he addressed you here in Johannesburg, the public began to think, as they have a way of doing. They began to realise what this policy of Hertzogism really meant. They were waiting anxiously for some repudiation, some explanation, and what did they get? From General Hertzog nothing. From Mr. Sauer nothing, another of those Ministers in the Cape responsible for that amendment — the Hertzog amendment, I will call it — of the Cape Act. What did you get from Mr. Sauer? Nothing but a remark that there was something in Hertzogism. And what from Mr. Malan, the Minister of Education — of higher education? Nothing. It is very significant, though in itself perfectly laudable. No allusion to the primary education question, no allusion to the Prime Minister's policy of education, not even to General Hertzog. Presiding at a meeting of the Taal Academy[4] — where? At that place General Botha (it is his expression, not mine) calls Hertzogfontein.[5] In these circumstances, in the presence of whom is this speech made? In the presence of President Steyn, the most powerful voice in the Free State. It is significant in connection with his silence on the main issue, though laudable in his desire to spread his language and the literature of the language — significant when combined with his silence on the question which is before every individual who cares for the future of the country.

Then you have within the last few days the late Premier of the Colony, Mr. Fischer, and what does he say? He says that his

---

[4] The South African Academy for Language (Dutch) and Literature was formed at Bloemfontein in 1909.
[5] Apparently Bloemfontein, the Free State capital.

Prime Minister has not said anything against General Hertzog's policy. I leave it at that. Now, in the vulgar parlance, it is up to the Premier to answer the Minister of Lands on the question of the education policy of the Minister of Education. Still, on the Pretoria speech, how does General Botha make his position out? Three cardinal principles — no compulsion, mother-tongue medium, equality of opportunity. That is our policy and our interpretation of the language clause, and General Botha's interpretation of the language clause, and that was the interpretation, mark me, of every member of the Convention when that language clause was passed. And then, seeing the impasse, what does General Botha do next? He entrenches himself behind the Constitution Act. He further says that if I were there, I could do nothing else. Well, on the abstract question of the Constitution Act the right of the Union Parliament to interfere with any act of a Provincial Council, I say that in the abstract the Prime Minister is right, provided always that Clause 79 of the South Africa Act is satisfied. This clause reads:

" Any Ordinance made by a Provincial Council shall have effect in and for the Province so long and as far as only as it is not repugnant to any Act of Parliament."

Surely, gentlemen, that applies in the widest sense to our greatest Act of Parliament, the South Africa Act. Well, then they will say, " Oh, it is only a question of interpretation ". Quite true. Almost every clause in the Act is a question of interpretation. I hope that the Union Parliament will use that right to interprete the Act as we interpreted it, as the Prime Minister interprets it, as every member of the Convention when the clause was passed, interpreted it, and doing so they will further have the right — and if the extreme case comes I hope they will exercise that right — to withhold financial assistance, until that interpretation is complied with.

If we go into the past, and General Botha puts to me the same question, " What would I do in his place?" I have a very simple answer. He knows it already. I would not have included in my Ministry any Minister who had made this speech in the Orange Free State. That is, without a public recantation. And I would not have voluntarily put in the position of Chairman of the Executive of the Provincial Council a man who was pledged to carry out that violation of the interpretation put by the Convention upon the language clause. Well, gentlemen, there are the first and second chapters of this education question. The first, the Pretoria speech, the second the Johannesburg speech, and there is still a third chapter. General Botha had to acknowledge that in the Orange Free State the clause of the Convention was violated, and must remain violated for the next five years. The children in the Orange Free State and in the Cape, if there were a sufficient majority in the Provincial Council, were to be handicapped in the race of life against all the other children of the Union — that is the position. And supposing the Orange Free State persist in this policy for five years, and the Cape Colony begins and persists for five years, are you certain that the poison won't permeate into the Transvaal?

Wait until we see. Remember, unless you roll up to the polls and give us a majority, unless you take the thing seriously and see how vital it is to the children that you should give us a majority that will make the Union Government act as I have said — I will not limit it to the Transvaal or Natal, this interpretation of ours — it is quite possible that once the snowball has started you will have the Union Government legislating in the same direction as the Orange Free State.

We come now to the third chapter of the speech. As I said, General Botha had to acknowledge to you that the South Africa Act was at present violated in the Orange Free State, and he could not help it. Agitation still goes on: the snowball is rolling and threatens to overwhelm his party. He must give an explanation, a justification: he must take it in hand. The elections are coming on in six weeks, and this snowball is growing and growing. What explanation does he give in the Yeoville speech of this impasse? Remember, the Prime Minister is obsessed with the idea — he has been so much to the front — he is obsessed with the idea that he can do anything, no matter what the composition of his Cabinet. We know, as practical politicians, what a large majority means, and I say that the power is in the majority. The responsibility only is in the hands of the minority. What is his explanation in getting out of this impasse? He says that the Convention knew, that the Orange Free State knew, that this Act was in existence when the clause was passed. He speaks the truth. No member of the Convention would have been fit to be there unless he knew the Orange Free State Act by heart and also every Education Act in the country. It is for that very reason that there was that long discussion, that frequent proposal, that change and change as to what that clause should be, until we got the clause as it stands now, with the agreement of every member of the Convention to our interpretation of that clause.

There has been a great deal said about giving away Convention secrets. I am giving away none. I preached this on the Grahamstown platform a year ago. I think, at all events, many months ago. But the Prime Minister with this horrible impasse growing and growing, has got bewildered; he has got mixed up in his times; he does not remember the stages at which this clause was passed. As I say, it was at the very earliest stage of the Convention, and why? Because we knew it was a most thorny question, and that if we got agreement on that question other things would run smoothly, as they did. But it is a most preposterous explanation to say that the Convention was responsible for the violation of its own Act for the next five years, for that is what it comes to.

Then, lastly, we have Mr. Fischer's construction in the Orange Free State, which requires no comment and only requires a denial from the Prime Minister; and subsequent to that the Prime Minister, the Minister of Justice, the Minister of Lands, and the four Ministers from the Cape should sit on the same platform and give us their absolute consent to the three cardinal principles announced by the Prime Minister here on this platform — no compulsion, mother-tongue medium and equality of opportunity. Well, of course, gentlemen, that is a standing example of what I have said. Surely, then, I am entitled to call this a coalition Government. Surely, I am entitled to make the criticism which General Botha objects to — that this Government was formed on the basis of men and not measures, and that further, since the Prime Minister yielded to his friends, it was reasonable they should suppose that there was no security, and that measures would follow the men.

There are others on the programme, and my friend is anxious to hear about labour. I should think that on White labour you would have been satisfied with a really brilliant exposition from my friend, Mr. Quinn, the other day. I will still make a few comments on it. With regard to the programme, there has been criticism of both programmes, and it is only natural programmes must deal with generalities. The difference between the two programmes is in their formation. On the face of it we claim that our party is a democratic party. It was built up on a democratic basis. As I dare say you know, delegates from every part of the Union assembled in Bloemfontein. There was no dictation. The whole matter was discussed by these delegates, and not until it was unanimously agreed to, did we put it in our programme. Let us compare that programme with the programme from Pretoria, which on the face of it shows autocracy, not democracy. I suggest that to carry it out, the following should be done. Our programme is that we have met together, and we agree to do certain things. We pledge ourselves to do them, and not only to oppose anything else but to attempt to legislate on those lines, whether in office or out of it.

In that programme I say, we have still further evidence that it is men and not measures, that weigh with the Government. Let me give a few examples. I have dealt with education. Now, for the Native question. We both say we will exercise strict justice and fairness to the Natives. Of course we will. What else is in the Pretoria programme? Nothing. What else is in ours? The essence of everything is dealing with the Native — the drink traffic. We have said that we are in favour of maintaining the present restrictions on the liquor traffic, and that we absolutely go for total prohibition to the aboriginal Natives. I believe the Premier is in favour of that, but I want to see it in his programme. Why don't I see it in his programme? (Voices: "Cape wine!") Yes; you've hit it first time. There are four members of the late Cape Ministry, and what did that Ministry do? It abolished the right of the people to have a voice in the liquor traffic. What they have had for years and years — local option — was abolished by the Ministry of which those four members are representatives. And remember it is not limited to that. These wine farmers in the Cape Colony are a very powerful party in the Bond. Not the National Party, mind you, because there isn't one in the Cape. These wine farmers control 11 seats: but they control much more than that, I can assure you. I have had a very bitter exercise of them during the past ten years. They are the most powerful factor of the whole of the Bond bureaucracy. General Botha invited us to join the National Party. He said that the other parties should be broken up, and of course, today the people who don't think, imagine that there are only two parties — the Unionist and the National. But those who think, know that the Unionist Party is represented in every Colony, whereas the National Party is represented in the Transvaal only, and there only by a few branches of Het Volk, who have adopted General Botha's suggestion to turn themselves into the National Party. In the Cape and the Free State there are still the Bond and the Unie; and I say that this question of Native policy has been deliberately omitted by the so-called National Party because of these members of the Ministry, and because of the fact that this conglomerate party depend very greatly for their majority on their wine farmers.

Now I saw in the paper this morning a request to answer another question, and that is on the franchise. I did not intend to mention the franchise question at all for a very simple reason. The Native franchise question is protected by a two-thirds majority. This is very useful, but it is protected infinitely more by an honourable understanding that it shall not come into party politics at all. It is also understood that we shall not interfere with the Cape franchise, and that the Cape people shall not agitate or try to coerce the other Colonies. (A voice; " What about Colonel Harris?"[6]) Colonel Harris is a candidate for Beaconsfield, in the Kimberley division, and I think, unfortunately, he has evidently put forward his personal opinion; but I, as Leader of the Party, repudiate absolutely any suggestion from the Cape Colony on the subject. I may throw a sidelight upon it by the way, and that is that if Colonel Harris does not entirely agree with us, I hope that is the only question of which he does not agree, because he is standing as an independent.

The next question we come to is that of land. Let us look at the Pretoria programme with regard to the land question. There the same thing is creeping in — measures to suit the men, rather than the men to suit the measures. We all agree with the Prime Minister's cry of " Back to the land!" We also appreciate the way in which the Prime Minister has continued the admirable agricultural policy laid down by Lord Milner. The Prime Minister deserves every credit for the way in which he has enlarged the Agricultural Department of the Transvaal and we hope that he will continue, and I believe he will. He is a broadminded man. If only we had the Prime Minister without some of his supporters! I am told that in Johannesburg — it was a surprise to me — this question of closer settlement is more anxiously discussed than even your own mining matters. I am glad to hear it. It is a splendid sign for the future that the people who come here for supposed temporary occupation are looking to becoming land-owners — true citizens — with that goal always in front

6 Unionist Party.

of them. Well, the Prime Minister evidently recognises that, and knew it even before I did, and he alludes also to the miner and the clerk in the Civil Service, with this bright idea of putting them on the land in front of him.

But how is he going to satisfy it with his programme? How is he going to satisfy it if he endorses the negation of land settlement which has been produced by Mr. Fischer and other members of the Cabinet? Because we all know the crux of land settlement is to give the power to the Government to acquire land. The kernel of the problem is that right to acquire. We know that in Australia they had the right to acquire. I was just reading in a speech of Mr. Hershensohn last night figures which showed that out of 71,000,000 acres of land in the Transvaal 50,000,000 acres were in the hands of private owners and companies, and the balance left in the hands of the Government was not fit to put a dog upon until improvements had taken place — buildings, drainage, etc. Where then are you to get land settlement unless you give the power to the Government to acquire land for settlement? That we have put in our programme. Not only that, but at the present moment there is a committee of our party sitting to draw up a practical scheme for land settlement, which will be produced in the Union Parliament, whether we are in power or not.

As I said, the omission by the Pretoria Government had a reason. The reason has already been given by Mr. Fischer and Mr. Smuts. Mr. Smuts said tentatively that he must recognise vested rights, and secondly, that it might raise the price of land, and the companies would get the benefit. Raise the price of land if the Government acquires by compulsion at a reasonable value? That is what we want, and that is what we must have before our aspirations for closer settlement are realised. Now we come to my friend's labour question. Here again we have the cloven hoof. We have the ordinary platitudes in the Pretoria programme —pure platitudes. In our programme this labour question at the democratic congress in Bloemfontein, to which I have alluded, was thrashed out by every section of the party, and I am glad to say that one of the most important sections of the party was the labour members at the congress. Not only the details given here were thrashed out — but it was fairly ample in our programme — but all these other questions of miners' phthisis and the eight-hour day, were all thrashed out, and I can give you some further tentative results besides what you see in our programme.

This miners' phthisis question, I am very glad to see, is becoming more and more agitated on every day, because there is not the least doubt it is the worst curse from which this place suffers. It is a preventable curse, and the employers have a great responsibility in ousting that curse from among you. Perhaps we have been remiss in not taking it in hand sooner. Rome was not built in a day. The mine-owners are busy men, but I will say that they are awake to the fact now, and the crux before us at the present moment is represented by the two theories. There is one advocated by Mr. Lionel Phillips, Mr. Drummond Chaplin,[7] and others, which seems to me as an outsider to be the natural solution. It goes further than the other suggestion, because miners' phthisis is not the only trouble from which you suffer here. Mr. Phillips, Mr. Chaplin, Sir George Farrar, and others think the best solution would be State insurance, to include not only miners' phthisis, but other disabilities — and old age. The other suggestion is that it should be included under the Workmen's Compensation Act. Mr. Lionel Phillips has given his reasons for not approving of that, which practically means that he thinks it would be detrimental to the workmen themselves; he is against it, but only on that ground. Between these two it is difficult to decide. It ought to be tackled at once; that it should have been tackled long ago I quite agree, but it must be tackled by experts, not only medical men, workmen and employers, but actuaries too. That shows how complicated a question it is. And that is our policy, and it shall be tackled. It is not because of this agitation, or because it does not appear in our programme, that we say that it must be tackled. You know from the labouring men who came to the conference that there was nothing more debated than that was.

Now on the general question of labour. It seems to me that there is no need for a Labour Party in a democratic Government. There is no room for class legislation in the democratic Government. (A voice: "We are all labourers.") Yes, quite right, we are all labourers. It has been said by someone, I forget who, that in England there was a Labour Party because it was necessitated in order to secure the conversion of the Government from an aristocratic form to a democratic. And so you have got a Labour Party in England, but labour is now merging itself into one of the great parties in the State. The actual position in this country is that Labour should form the most advanced wing of the most progressive party in this country. I am speaking now of the labouring men who require their wants attending to. I am not speaking to those gentlemen who whether in the Senate — I do not think probably in the Assembly — will become members of Parliament. I am speaking to the labouring men themselves. If they want their wants attended to by a large party surely they are much more likely to get these wants accomplished than if they send a few men to become either Senators — or, as a separate party, members of the House of Assembly. Now, do not mistake me. I do not say that there should not be Labour representatives. We welcome Labour representatives — in our party. I know at that Congress there was one labouring man there who was as good a debater as I have ever known during my seven years in the Cape Assembly, and I shall welcome him as one of the Unionist Party of South Africa.

Now on White labour: that is a more difficult problem. I may offend some of you, but I must be candid. I believe in every word Mr. Quinn said the other night.

I have many personal friends who take what I call the idealistic view

7 Unionist Party.

of the White labour problem. I respect them for it. They have ideals which they are determined to work out. Some I have talked to I find hopeless. They are idealists and nothing else. The others are idealists who are also practical conditions (*sic*), and they say: " We believe in it and will work for it, but at present we have not the proper scheme to work it out." I was talking to one of the unpractical ones last night, and I told him that my idea was that the White labour question was in the missionary stage, to be dealt with in learned magazines and in lectures, but not to be brought on to the political platform at the present moment. I said that if he went among working constituencies in Johannesburg and preached White labour and got a unanimous vote of confidence, I would guarantee that on the night before the elections I would go on the same platform and put the practical facts before the same people and I would carry the election at the polls.

Now, I don't want to discourage the gentleman with the big ideal. It is pure idealism, and though ideals are fine things to have, in politics practical work alone appeals to electors. And the gist of the reason why this ideal of White labour would not appeal at the present moment is because you cannot deny the fact that if it were carried out it means a lowering of the wages at the present moment. That is practical politics. It means in the future — I hope you will be out of it — it means a competition between the Coloured and the White labourer till we get a scheme by which those things can be got over. I don't say you cannot, but I say that the White labour problem is not practical politics at the present moment. I will just say that this Labour Party question, of course, is one of the dangers we have to face in these coming elections. I notice that every Labour member — every official Labour leader — protests that he has nothing to do with the National Party. Methinks they protest a little too much. You know, where there is a Labour member down goes a National member. Where there is a National member, down goes a Labour member; and I think it is a policy, as Colonel Crewe[8] was saying the other day, of " Divide and conquer ". General Smuts, who is one of the protestors, absolutely denies that there is any compact between the Labour Party and the Nationalist Party. He repudiates the idea that they were a wing of the Nationalist Party. All I can say is that I hope he is right. I don't repudiate it, but I welcome them as a wing of the Unionist Party.

Now I think I have done. I hope I have made it clear to you tonight that I am not arguing that the Prime Minister does not honestly desire to carry out his policy — his policy, which is our policy — but that he has surrounded himself with people who make it impossible for him to carry out that policy; that was the root reason for the formation of our party — to help the Prime Minster to coerce his colleagues, in order that the policy could be carried on. What, unfortunately, the Prime Minister has done is to resign himself to the line of least resistance, so

[8] Unionist Party.

27

attractive to most people; and I think it possible there is the further excuse that, having adopted that line, the Prime Minister may have been influenced by past history in the Transvaal. We all remember the charming National Party at the last elections. What happened? We know that immediately it was understood which was the winning side they flocked to it when there was something to be won. We have had the same people — twin brethren — in the Cape, the so-called Independents. And the only difference I have noticed between them and the Bond was that they had farther to walk when the bell rang for the division. Then we have another class of Independent — a rarer bird, but equally useless — the gentleman who puts himself on a pedestal, worships his own image, is a law to himself, says "I am not as other men are", the real old Biblical Pharisee. You have got some of them here — two got tired of their lonely position on the pedestal and have joined the only party where they could have what is called a top-dog position — the Labour Party. Avoid them all; they are useless, and I am sorry that General Botha has been led away by thinking that history would repeat itself because now they had bigger issues and bigger causes among them, and I feel absolutely certain that the electors will have none of it.

The position is this, gentlemen, that we have a coalition Government in the worst sense of the word, because even in General Hertzog's definition a coalition Government determines to work together, but from the day it was formed the Government has not worked together. There has been no combination at all. It has been a fight between the majority of the reactionaries against the minority of the enlightened followers of the Premier. Surely I am justified in calling it a coalition Ministry and in saying that our only security that the measures will not follow the men is that we, at the worst, shall return a strong minority that will be able to say to the Prime Minister, "You shall not, because of the opposition". The best we should try for — it is quite possible. We have six weeks yet and we have not done badly in the last two months. Our party is growing and the moderate elector is beginning to realise the true position.

At the best, I say, it is possible that we shall get what we desire, what our party is based on — a best-men Government — and get rid of this coalition Government which, in the Prime Minister's own words, according to the history of the world, is the weakest form of Government known. It can do no good, and its life must be short.

5

GENERAL J. B. M. HERTZOG[1]

GENERAL HERTZOG addressed a large public meeting in the Town Hall tonight. He read the greater part of his speech from typed manuscript, a proceeding very unusual with this Minister. The General was very warm and cheerfully vitriolic. After he had exausted his written speech he went ahead extemporaneously, and exhausted every adjective in condemnation of the Unionists.

General Hertzog at the outset referred to the changes which Union had brought and to the differences which Union made in connection with the Imperial Government. They could not, said General Hertzog, be free Republicans any longer, but they could and would remain a free people under the British flag. He then proceeded to deal with the policy of Dr. Jameson and his party, which he described as a policy of lies and misrepresentation, calculated to arouse the bitterest race feeling. Referring to immigration General Hertzog condemned oversea immigration as a cry of the capitalists. What was wanted was the relief of the congestion in the towns and the placing of the people of South Africa on the land. He referred in strong terms to the need for a stricter policy in regard to mining labour in view of the state of affairs revealed by the recent Commission's report.

He said Dr. Smartt[2] had asked at Bloemfontein what was the record of the Unionists. He (General Hertzog) would answer the question. They recognised under the title "Unionists" the old wolf the "Progressives". It would be impossible to get together a greater number of racialists than they. The Unionists had with Transvaal money and by the aid of the Transvaal Press tried to raise racial feeling in the Orange Free State. It was only a few years ago that Dr. Jameson tried to get the British Government to withdraw the Constitution.[3] Not a year ago there was made by members of his party a shameful attempt to get the British Government to interfere with the affairs of the Free State. There they had the record of the Unionists. Imagine the Government of the Union being entrusted to people like that. Notwithstanding the contemptible efforts of the Unionists to influence the English-speaking people by rais-

---

[1] Speech by General Hertzog (Minister in Botha's Cabinet, formerly Minister in the Orange River Colony) at Smithfield, as reported in the *Star*, 20 August 1910.
[2] Dr. (later Sir) Thomas Smartt, one of the leaders of the Unionist Party.
[3] The reference is to the attempt made at the end of the Anglo-Boer War to suspend the constitution of the Cape Colony.

4

ing race hatred, he felt convinced that both sections of the community would work and co-operate together.

Continuing, he denied that he had approved of the coalition idea. Since the war (proceeded General Hertzog) no more contemptible policy had been followed than by the Jameson Party in regard to the education question in the Free State. Lies, gross misrepresentation and prostitution of journalism had all been employed to further the agitation.

Referring to his speech at the Industrial School, General Hertzog said that what he had said there was his conviction, that the sound principles of the Free State Education Act would be maintained throughout South Africa. He denied that he had said that the Free State Act would be imposed upon the other Colonies against their will. He had never said that. He would say, however, with regard to the teaching of both languages, that provision was made in the Free State law with the consent and agreement of Colonel Byron,[4] Mr. Drew[4] and Mr. Browne.[4] General Hertzog then read extracts from Hansard, in which Colonel Byron said that he did not object to the teaching of Dutch, but to the medium. It was pure imagination to say that there was a difference between the Cabinet on the education policy. He (General Hertzog) agreed entirely with General Botha's declaration at the Wanderers. He had never regarded it as right to compel the English people to learn Dutch against their will, though he thought that those who did not compel the teaching of both languages to their children were doing a grave injustice to their children.

The General then proceeded dramatically to quote Mr. Drew's earlier speeches in favour of the Free State Act. The Transvaal Law was held up as the ideal law, which it was said, contained no compulsion. The speaker read a clause from the Transvaal Act in which, after Standard III, English as the medium is prescribed. Under that law the Dutch children would only have mother-tongue instruction up to Standard III, after that English. With what right could any man who praised the Transvaal Law as a model law express his disagreement with the Free State Law? He characterised the policy of the Unionists as a policy of lies and misrepresentation.

Continuing, General Hertzog referred to a letter in *The New Age*, in which it was stated that General Hertzog's intention was to banish the English language from South Africa. Never had he said that such was his intention and never he had entertained such a thought. It was disgusting to find that there was no more honourable way of fighting than that adopted.

Proceeding, General Hertzog referred to the creation of separate schools in the Free State, in which Sir John Fraser explained that mother-tongue instruction would be employed in the preparatory classes, which (said the speaker) meant kindergarten, thereafter only one medium. And yet these

[4] Constitutional Party members in the Legislative Council of the Orange River Colony.

30

people (he continued) spoke of mother-tongue instruction as a sacred principle. Speaking of the Convention spirit, which was a praiseworthy spirit, he said that at the Convention personal and parochial matters were set aside. What did they hear from their Unionist friends? That the spirit was one of bargaining, and because the Unionists did not get three seats in the Ministry they considered themselves justified in doing everything which was contrary to the Convention spirit. General Hertzog reiterated his statement that there was no disunion in the Ministry. There had not been from the very first day any disunion in the Ministry.

If (said General Hertzog in conclusion) they wished to be a great people they could only be so by remaining true to themselves. Their language, their traditions must be preserved. He said the same to the English-speaking people. The language and the traditions of the two people were the basis of their national life. What was great and noble in both would belong to each. The day was not very far off when the traditions and languages of the two peoples would be regarded by the two peoples as their joint possession, and then there would be unity. No one could have too great a contempt for the efforts being made to sow division and racialism in South Africa.

6

MR. JOHN X. MERRIMAN[1]

TODAY YOU HAVE done me the greatest honour it is possible to confer upon a citizen, and that is to elect me as your representative without asking me for any formal expression of my views, without calling upon me to make a series of those somewhat dismal performances, election speeches, in which it is difficult to know who deceive themselves the most, the people who make the speeches or those who listen to them. You have been kind enough to give me a blank cheque, trusting in my honour and discretion to use it to the best possible advantage. But I think it is not only proper and right, but it is very fitting that I should attempt to give you some idea of my views on the present political situation, and I am very glad of the opportunity of doing so, because I speak to you, my friends — who have shown yourselves my friends by many associations — I can speak to you in perfect confidence and put you in possession of my feelings without feeling that you are going to prick holes in what I say and without trying to deceive you in any possible way.

Since I last had the pleasure in addressing you in this hall, very great changes have come over South Africa, changes affecting this Colony to the very greatest extent, and affecting the future of every man whose interest is bound up in South Africa. The last time I was here you were kind enough and flattering enough to express the hope that I should be called to direct the affairs of the Union Government. Well, I am not going to assert that I was not pleased with your wish, or that it would not be satisfactory to me to undertake the business, not, I hope, only on personal grounds, but also on the ground of the interests of our old Colony. I wished most earnestly and desired to start Union upon Cape Colonial lines rather than upon Transvaal lines. I thought the Cape Colony lines were safer. I thought that the Cape, as having more than half the White populaton of the whole Union, had the right to stand at the head of affairs in carrying out the principles of South African affairs. I thought that we in the Cape had a longer parliamentary experience. I thought that our way of looking at financial matters — perhaps taught by the bitter uses of adversity — was safer than what obtained elsewhere. And I felt from the bottom of my heart that it would have been better for the Union had it been started on Cape rather than Transvaal lines. I formed the opinion after many months sitting in the conversation of statesmen

---

[1] Speech by Mr. Merriman, leader of the Afrikaner Bond and last Prime Minister of the Cape, at Victoria West, as reported in the *Star*, 20 August 1910.

from all parts of South Africa, and it was strengthened in my mind by parliamentary actions in other parts of the Union. I am not going to particularise or pick out little holes, because people who live in glass houses should not throw stones. I am now expressing generally my opinion.

Unfortunately, as I think, there was a strong current of opinion in the other direction; the newspapers of this Colony shouted in favour of the Transvaal; and some of my colleagues, I am sorry to say, were in the same direction. The Progressive Party and the magnates were entirely in favour of starting on Transvaal lines, and, of course, the opinion of these worthies was bound to have great weight with the Liberal Government in England; and, above all, Cape Town, the metropolitan city of South Africa, also expressed in most unmistakable terms their desire that the Transvaal interest, and not the Cape interest, should head the Union Government.

I suppose there never was a more unanimous expression of dislike and distrust of a public man than at that anxious meeting in Cape Town, at which my particular friend, Mr. Jagger, took the Chair, and which was addressed by Dr. Jameson in a speech brimful of personalities. Well, at that time it was difficult for me to say what provoked the outburst on that occasion; but there it was. I had simply expressed in some speeches I made in this constituency and at Worcester what I knew to be the views held by those with whom I was working in the Transvaal and in the Free State. I knew it. I did not speak in the dark. I knew what I was talking about. I knew that those were their views, because they have told me so. So I thought I was on perfectly safe ground. Well, I am not going to enlarge upon this. These gentlemen got what they wanted. They got all they shouted for. I will do them justice to say that they were the party of brains; they knew very well that by getting what they were shouting for they meant that the future of the Union was to be started not upon Cape lines, but upon Transvaal lines; that the headship, the hegemony of South Africa, was going to depart from the Cape Colony and to be transferred to Pretoria and the Transvaal. Well, as I say, they got what they wanted, although it was against their own personal material interests; and that shows what high-minded fellows they were when they made a sacrifice of their own material interests rather than entrust the affairs of the Union to a politician whom they dislike! That is the plain English of it. Well that is past and gone; I only refer to it here for the purpose of bringing home the present position to you.

Now, is it not remarkable — and I do think it is very remarkable — that these people who laboured so hard and who shouted so loud to get this state of affairs are the very people who, now that they have put General Botha and his friends in power, turn round and abuse them as hard as they can? These very people are the very foremost in denouncing General Botha. Now, compare that with our action; compare that with the action of myself and the party to which I belong. Although we may have been disappointed, we do not go crying and complaining. Our policy is to make the best of things as they are. The policy of the other people is, having got what they wanted, having cried for the moon and got the moon, to turn round and denounce it. That is very funny.

Many hints have been thrown out to me during the last couple of months about the desirability of forming a third party, but I have steadily discountenanced all ideas of that kind, because I believe it would be most deterimental to the interest of South Africa. Party is not a queston of persons; it is a question of principles; and, having got our principles maintained, what we have to do is to make the best of what we have got, and to try to shape the affairs of the country in the best possible way we can. But how different is that from the policy of those gentlemen to whom I alluded just now. Before the Union Government was formed they were always holding up General Botha as a strong constructive man; now they are all shouting out that he is a very weak man, and they say, "We must get rid of him as soon as possible". While General Botha is trying as far as he can to bring the two sections of the population together, these people are doing the very best they can to try to stir up racial feeling by raking up all sorts of side issues. Yes, it is a shame. They have raised the ridiculous cry of Hertzogism, to which I shall allude by and by. They pick out every little action and every little deed and every foolish little word, and unfortunately there are a good many foolish words spoken at election times. They pick out every foolish little utterance, hold it up, and tear it to pieces — utterances of the very men they were supporting a few months ago. They go so far that one of their leaders, who is so often talking about the spirit of the Convention, has had the bad taste to sneer at General Botha's English. I allude to that because I think it is in the worst possible taste, and another thing is that it is contrary to that universal courtesy which I and others like myself, who speak the Dutch language imperfectly, are always met with when we attempt to make a Dutch speech. I do say that if you want a united people in this country, sneers of that kind are the very last thing to which we should resort. My dear friend Mr. Jagger, one of the cleverest men in Cape Town, certainly one of the cleverest men in the Progressive Party, is now shouting at the Government. He was chairman of the meeting that nearly brought the roof of the City Hall down with shouting and cheering for General Botha. "We must get a party together and turn him out as soon as possible," now says Mr. Jagger.

It has been reserved for the Leader of the Party, who is going about on a sort of peregrination round South Africa, to make the most astounding proposal ever heard, coming from a leader of a party. The other day at Durban he said, after going through a lot of talk of how they should get together a Government of best men and that kind of thing, that the reason why there must be an Opposition should be strong enough, was to allow General Botha to turn round on people in his own Cabinet, whom he (Dr. Jameson) is pleased to call reactionaries. That, he said, was the object of the Opposition, and he (Dr. Jameson) said: "I want to say just one word more, and that is that we must work most strenuously in every possible way in this election not to turn out the Prime Minister, but to revolutionise his Cabinet." Well I think that is the most astounding declaration of policy I have ever heard from the leader of a great party — that they must work to create a split in the Government for the purpose of what we call revolutionising it. Just imagine for one single moment if Mr. Balfour, the Leader of the Opposition in England, were to say, " We must work for one thing and that is to turn some of Mr. Asquith's colleagues out and to keep Mr. Asquith there ". I wonder who does not see what gross reflection that is on General Botha himself, to suppose that a man of honour would sit for one moment in a Cabinet with the object of working with the Opposition. To revolutionise the Cabinet in that way is a contemptible policy and gives the reason why people who wish well to South Africa and wish to show that they do not countenance a despicable policy of that kind should endeavour to keep the present Government in office by their votes.

A great deal has been said about the formation of a best-man Ministry. When it was found that coalition did not go down with the people it was transformed first into " a new start " and then into " a best-man Ministry ". I want to ask any sensible person how you are going to get the best men. Who is going to say who they are? There is one simple way, and that is to have the people whom the majority of the electors put into power. Does any person in his sound or sober senses presume that the electors are going to turn out, let us assume for example, Mr. Sauer[2] from the management of the railways for the purpose of putting Dr. Smartt there? Do they suppose they are going to get that eminent politician and financier, Mr. Walton,[3] and put him in the place of Mr. Hull,[4] who has been successful? I will give what humble assistance and support I can and induce my friends to give to those people who are placed in the position of trust and who have a most difficult and arduous task thrown on them. So long as they continue to conduct the Government on the three cardinal principles — clean government, economical financial administration, and sound party traditions — so long shall they have my support. I have no doubt whatever, when those gentlemen from the north come down, away from the land of the steamroller and the land of the secret caucus, into the free air of party discussion, that they will also find that there is a great deal to be said for the Cape parliamentary system and methods. I believe they will learn a wholesome lesson, and that they will profit by it. More I shall not say, because you must remember it is no light and easy task that these people have to perform. The government of this country by the Union Act is one of the most complicated and difficult machines to set in order. There is no other country that has the same Constitution that we have, and has to bring into one whole various

2 Minister in General Botha's Cabinet.
3 Unionist Party.
4 Minister of Finance in General Botha's Cabinet.

varying interests. Union is for the benefit of South Africa, but I thought its carrying out was difficult when we framed the Act. I think it is ten times more difficult when I see the administration beginning to be put into working order. We as a people, wishing well to the country, must not go about " seeking stones of stumbling and rocks of offence ", but we must try to be patient and considerate and willing to make allowances for people who have to perform a difficult task; and we must try to assist them as much as possible.

We are now in a transition stage. We have only to wait long enough and parties will form on new lines, but we must wait and be patient and see what Parliament has to say. After all, the forming of parties on mere platitudinous programmes will never do. It never has succeeded and it never will succeed. Parties are formed in Parliament first of all, and in our Parliament I have not the slightest doubt that parties will emerge on true lines. I think, first of all, that the great dividing line is the South African Party; the people who are wedded to South Africa, the people who believe in it, who think that South Africans must govern themselves.

And then there are the exotics who, under one name or another, are always looking elsewhere. I believe that division will be accentuated in the future. Englishmen and Dutchmen who make their homes in this country and who have common interests will unite. Those people who belong to the order of men who, when they have made their fortune, go to the other side of the water, will form a party, too. I believe there is a distinct dividing line between the people who have to live their lives out in this country — who have to make their living and not their fortunes out of South Africa — and the capitalists. I believe that is a very strong dividing line, and I believe there is always a natural dividing line, which there is in every country, and that is between what you may call the " pasops "[5] and the " push ups ". The " pasops ", the fellows who have to pay the taxes and the fellows who have got fixed property in this country, and who cannot run away if anything goes wrong, these are the people who are naturally inclined, if they are wise, in my opinion, to the " pasop " policy; that is, not to stop still, but to proceed slowly, to see where they are going, and not to dash into all sorts of wild schemes by dint of huge loans, which have been a burden on this country, and from which we in the Cape Colony have only just emerged after great struggles.

But having said this much about what I call the party aspects of the thing, do let me try to recall to your minds and to the minds of those in this country who may really be interested, not in this man or in that man, not in this party or in that party, but in the welfare of South Africa — let me try to recall to them what are some of the tasks that lay before us in embracing Union. I am a diligent student of those remarkable orations which we see now daily in the Press, and I do not see to my mind sufficient attention given to what I call the essentials which lie before us. There is a great deal made up about parties and " best men ", and things of that

5 Dutch for " be careful ".

sort, which will pass away like a cloud and be forgotten in another two or three years. But I see not enough notice taken of the great things which are before us.

Now, the first great task which I should like to point to is this: we have got to see that there is established in this country what we managed after many years to get in the Cape, and that is sound parliamentary control of finance. Without that we are bound to get on the rocks sooner or later. I do not want to criticise our former neighbours who are now our fellow-citizens, but I must say some of their methods do not seem to me to be exactly admirable. There does not seem to have been that right hold of Parliament on financial matters, but it has been left too much to Ministers to manage. Well, the first thing we have got to see is that the representatives of the people are the men who shall have control of the finances of the country.

A second task, and a gigantic one, is the assimilation of the different laws of the country. Take, for instance, the laws regarding the administration of Crown lands. We, as you know, in this country are bound hand and foot by laws which Parliament sees in the most rigid way are observed. Well, we want to put that system all over South Africa, so that Crown lands shall not be at the disposal of any particular government, but shall be disposed of only with the consent of the representatives of the people. In the same way we have got to harmonise our irrigation system. We have done good work in the matter of irrigation in the Cape, work for which we have not got the credit we should have; for there are people who only look at what is going on outside. I must say I do not think I ever came across anything more cheering than the reports made by the Transvaal expert who was sent down to examine our irrigation systems in the Colony, and who at the Irrigation Congress at Potchefstroom said that he had seen more lucerne growing on one farm at Robertson than was grown in the whole Transvaal. Let me tell you people have a very small idea of how irrigation is progressing in the south-western districts. I hope to see the same energy which is shown there exhibited in our north-western districts. Already the Oudtshoorn people are coming in, and I think by and by irrigation will do as much for this north-west as it has done for Oudtshoorn and Robertson.

Then another great question, and a difficult one, is to assimilate the taxation of all the various Colonies. We all of us have different taxes. Take the question, for instance, of the transfer duty. It is $1\frac{1}{2}$ per cent in the Transvaal, 4 per cent in the Cape Colony and the Free State, and, I think, 2 per cent in Natal. Well, these anomalies can't go on for long. We have to assimilate these things, and in the same way we shall have to deal with every kind of tax. We shall have to bring it down so that the man living in one part of the Union shall not be taxed on a different scale to a man living in another part. But when we are trying to pick holes in what has been done, people should think of the enormously difficult job this is, and they should realise that any government when it has undertaken it, deserves not the objurgations of the public, but its hearty assistance and co-operation.

Then, take the Civil Service. A most important thing is to try to get all civil servants of the Union upon some uniform basis. The salaries and the conditions are different now in every part of South Africa. Well, that cannot go on for long, because it is not fair that a civil servant living in the Cape Colony be put on a totally different scale to that which his junior is paid who happens to be living across the Vaal River. Just think what it means when you have to deal with 20,000 or 30,000 men whose interests are bound up in that question.

One of the questions which will require our greatest attention, and which touches every man in this country, is the devolution of the central control upon local bodies and local governments, so that you keep the main thread of government in the hands of the central Parliament, but at the same time you do not attempt to administer all your local affairs that touch the interests of each locality from one centre miles away, which cannot possibly give the minute attention which is required; to carry that out in a way which will give satisfaction, and in a way which will not raise up what we are trying to destroy, and dealing with the civil rights of people in a different way in different localities — when you come to sit down and think over that problem you will see what a great difficulty it presents.

The same thing must be said about our Native affairs. We have got to had (*sic*) some means of government, and I have no doubt we shall find some satisfactory means. We have already done much in the Cape Legislature on that most important subject (which I remember some 20 or 25 years ago used to occupy the attention of Parliament and which used to drive people into a passion and into quarrelling about it). We have already tried as far as possible to secure that you should take that question altogether out of the arena of politics. We have done that to a great extent in the Cape Colony by means of Native commissions, profiting by the bitter experience of the other state of affairs. Now we have got to try to provide under Union for bodies of Natives of totally different stages of advancement, from the mere barbarian to the civilised and industrious Native in this Colony, the Native who goes out by ten of thousands to work, and who had accumulated great wealth, and who had obtained a certain outlook of advancement — we have got (to) try to harmonise and bring under some common control these Natives and the barbarians who hardly know what government is. If the Government had to do that alone it would be a task enough to break down almost any man.

Now I come to another subject, which I shall be obliged to say something about, because it is so much discussed, and that is education. I am not one of those who consider that a centralised uniform form of education for a vast country like this is altogether practicable or desirable. In England it has been found necessary to give to the country councils who manage education, very vast powers with regard to the curriculum.

In a country like this, to attempt to run this into one mould will rather lessen the benefit we are going to get from education than encourage it. It was for that reason partly that elementary education for the first five years was entrusted under the Act of Union to the Provincial Councils because it was felt that we were not yet ripe to have a central control of elementary education. I see some of our sapient legislators who have been orating in Natal are trying to enforce a uniform system of education on the whole of South Africa. That would be the very greatest possible mistake, and would create nothing but trouble.

There has been a very great deal of talk about the Act passed by my good friend, General Hertzog. If ever a man has been unjustly maligned it is General Hertzog. I am not going to say whether the Orange Free State Act is right or wrong because I have not studied it sufficiently, and I am not certain that all the people who have criticised it have understood it. It is quite sufficient for them to shout about "Hertzogism" and try to create racial and party feeling. There is not in this country a more cultivated or more honest man, or a man who has more brains than General Hertzog. To know him is to like him and to trust him. What is more, you may be perfectly certain, whether his system is absolutely wrong — and it does seem to me, as explained from the papers, to be a somewhat clumsy one — but I am perfectly sure it has been taken up by him after careful study, and he would be the last man in the world to force on any particular section of the people any scheme of his own which he did not consider fair to them. But if you take a strong and firm man, who has done something which you think is wrong — and it may be wrong — and you want to get him to alter it, would you kick his shins and pull his nose? No; you would argue with him and wait until a full and free discussion could be had, and then, if there was anything wrong about it, would be the time to alter it. I am sadly afraid this matter is got hold of just as a party cry, and we are dragging education down to the party arena. Just as for many hundreds of years in Europe untold miseries were brought on by the mistake of making religion a party question, just in the same way some good-natured friends of ours are trying to make education a party question in South Africa. If the educational Act in the Free State is wrong and absurd, the majority is there, and from what I know of the Free State people, they are the last people in the whole world to countenance any Act which is prejudicial to the educational welfare of their children.

What would be the dire result of making a party squabble of this matter? The children of the poor men will suffer, but not those of the rich men, because the latter put their children in other schools. It is the poor man that will suffer if education is once allowed to be made the subject of party squabbles. Education is a thing I view as one great question, and we should be extremely careful how we deal with it.

I could go on a long while, but I have been too long already by telling you of a number of difficult questions there are before this country.

I have mentioned some of them tonight in order to try to bring to people's minds the fact that there is something a little more serious in this election than that mere cry whether so-and-so or somebody else is to be put in power; and also I have endeavoured to show you what an extraordinarily difficult task lies before the people of this country, and the persons who will, as the representatives of the people, have to decide upon these matters.

I should like to allude to some of what I consider are the dangers that beset us in this Union. I have already referred to some of the difficulties. The first danger I should say is the habit which some people have got into of what polite people call megalomania, and what more vulgar people like myself call " swelled head ". We are all of us very fond of talking about national aspirations and a nation and so forth, but we seem to lose sight of the fact that a nation is not made by loud talking, or wealth, nor by a habit of despising other people. A nation is known by the qualities of the individuals constituting it and, above all, by the ideals which those individuals hold. If your ideals are high and lofty, your nation is built on a sound foundation. If your ideals are that wealth is the great thing to look for and advancement, personal or political, the thing to be achieved, be very sure that a nation with the latter ideals is resting on a rotten foundation.

I throw my recollection back about six or seven years ago, and I re-member when a distinguished High Commissioner of this country made a speech in which he talked about there being in a few years a White population of 5,000,000 on the Rand. Well, the few years have gone, the 5,000,000 have not come, and are not likely for a long time. I may just put before those people who talk so glibly about South Africa the bare figures. Do let us come down to practical facts. They do not fit well in with an election speech. I know they do not tickle people's ears. We have got in this Union of ours 5,000,000 Coloured people and 1,250,000 White people, and the true problem which lies before us, is how we have got to keep the White people on the top; not by putting the Native down and tramping on him. That day is past. They are advancing; they have a large share in the material wealth of this country. What we have got to ask when we talk about a White South Africa is what are you going to do with your 5,000,000 Natives? It is idle to talk in the way some people do. What we have got to try to have, as far as possible in this country, is a White aristocracy of people, of people who have had great advantages, educational and otherwise, people who started miles ahead of these others in civilisation. We have to keep them in front. That is our great problem. It is a curious fact that the centre of the anti-Native feeling in this country is not the poor Bond, as it has always supposed to be, and it still supposed to be in England, but the White people at Johannesburg. They are the violent anti-Native people, the people of Johannesburg and the British Colony of Natal. The people there make a great mistake when they talk in the random manner they do of never extending the franchise to the Black man. You are never going to keep this country as long as you hold doctrines of that sort. You may go on for a few years, but sooner or later nature will have its own way and these people who have advanced in civilisation and wealth will not be kept out of their rights. Don't let us have the sentimental doctrine that one man is as good as another, because it is not the case.

The doctrine which I profess, and which I hope all sensible people profess in this country, is "Don't lower down people, but give every man, if he has reached a certain state of civilisation and of wealth, a chance. Do not deny him his chance, simply because his skin happens to be a little darker than somebody else's". (A voice: "No! No!") That "No! No!" has been the ruin of nations. The downfall of nations has been caused by the "No! No!" and the happiness and prosperity of nations have been built upon the true liberalism of not debasing the Native, but of giving every man who has raised himself to a certain pitch the right to partake of the privileges enjoyed by others.

Is it not absurd to think of doing otherwise when at this time, at this very moment you have Coloured men in possession of large wealth, employing servants and keeping White men on charity. I am sorry to say so, but I am speaking of what I know, because I have administered Native Affairs in this country. Those people who talk in that way deny these men the vote, and yet they give it to every rascal who comes to this country and follows the trade, say of illicit liquor selling on the Rand. Is that fair? It is not the way to build up a nation. Believe me, we must now try to shape our politics carefully and judiciously in this matter. Do not let us be in a hurry, as some people are, and these people are doing more harm to their cause than anything else could do when they talk about the Black man being equal to the White man and say that you should give all sorts of rights to all sorts of people These men, I say, are doing incalculable harm to their cause. I do not say that we should go with them, but where a man by reason of his industry has acquired wealth, and by education has raised himself in civilisation, I say you should not withhold from him the rights which you give to other people.

I wish all the people who talk about this could have the opportunity of studying the question that members of Parliament have who have been on committees which sat to deal with the subject. I always remember, and remember with deep gratitude, a speech delivered by my old friend Mr. Andries du Plessis, a man whom I am extremely sorry will not be in the Union Parliament. I remember how at the close of the last Parliament Mr. Du Plessis held up a bluebook containing a report of Native Affairs Commission, on which he had been sitting, and said: "I recommend every candidate for Parliament to study this little book, because it will show every candidate how well the Cape system has worked and what advances we have made."

Now, enough about the question, because it fills me with the greatest alarm when I hear people with these highflown notions, and when I know

41

what causes nations to endure in this world. It is righteousness that exalteth a people and maintains a people, and righteousness, translated into politics, means fair play for all sections of the community.

There is another danger I should like to allude to, and that is not quite an illusionary one. There are many people because of some fancied injustice the Cape has experienced here and there — perhaps getting a little pinch through the civil servants being moved and so on — go about with long faces and say they wonder whether Union was not a mistake after all. Now, that is a dangerous feeling, which ought to be put down at the earliest possible moment. I never question whether Union was right or not. I know it was right. It was not only right, but it was the only safety for this country. Some people ask whether it would not have been wise to wait longer. Well I say you would never have got Union if you had waited. It would have been impossible to bring the people together, and we should have been plunged into a series of disagreements and quarrels throughout the whole of South Africa which would have made Union impossible. Just cast your eyes back upon the last 100 years. A 100 years ago there were only 26,000 White people in the whole of South Africa. Fifty years ago we had 250,000 White people here, and now we have a 1,250,000. Fifty years ago we had nothing but barbarians in South Africa. Now we have a large mass of educated and industrious folk, who are a credit to any country, the results of our management and the spread of our civilisation. When you look on that, take courage and look forward and don't, because this or that little thing offends you, imagine that the whole thing is wrong. Believe me, we are going to advance and have a bright future before us in this country. I am optimistic about it, because it is my duty to be optimistic, and God help this country if on a great national question we are going to be pessimistic. We must take courage and go forward. Do lay to heart the motto " Geduld en Moed " (" Patience and Courage "). If you think things are going wrong, have patience. You have free discussion and free government, and they are bound to right themselves. Above all have courage and don't think because today the clouds may gather the sun is not behind and will not shine on a great, united and prosperous South Africa.

SECTION II
PARTY PRINCIPLES AND
PROGRAMMES

1

UNIONIST PARTY OF SOUTH AFRICA

PROGRAMME[1]

THE OBJECT of the Unionist Party is to bring to completion the Union of South Africa in accordance with the spirit and intention of the Constitution, to work for the advancement of every section of the people; for the promotion of agricultural, commercial and industrial prosperity; for the settlement in the country of a permanent and contented population; to build up in South Africa a strong and united nation, morally, mentally and physically equipped for the task before it; working out its own domestic problems according to its own needs and aspirations, and taking its share in the defence of the Empire and in all movements leading to more effective participation by the different portions of the Empire in its common benefits and obligations.

With these general objects in view, the party adopts the policy set forth below on the chief questions now before South Africa, and will endeavour, whether in or out of power, to promote legislation giving practical effect to such policy.

1. *To Make South Africa Strong Within Her Own Borders and Within The Empire*

By the adoption of a comprehensive scheme of national defence, including the recognition of our Imperial obligations by largely increased support of the Imperial Navy, and by furthering all movements calculated to unite the peoples of the Union, and to draw closer the ties which bind the various portions of the Empire.

2. *To Secure an Efficient and Impartial Public Service*

By upholding the status of the public service and its freedom from all political influences, and the payment of liberal compensation to any public servant who may not be retained in the service on account of Union.

3. *To Improve the Social Conditions of the People*
   (a) By a vigorous education policy, including provision for compulsory education wherever possible, and the extension of free education where required, as well as a liberal system of technical education applied to agriculture, industries, mining and commerce;

---

[1] Printed in pamphlet form, Johannesburg, 1910.

5

(*b*) By opposing the introduction of Asiatics into South Africa, while securing fair treatment for those now lawfully settled in the country; a commission to be appointed as soon as possible to investigate and report upon the special labour conditions prevailing in Natal, in order to bring them into harmony at the earliest possible date with this principle without detriment to established industries;

(*c*) By a Native policy, admitting of the treatment of questions relating to Natives, in accordance with the degree of civilisation attained by them, and with the different and local conditions under which they live and work;

(*d*) By the maintenance of an excise, of the restrictions on the sale of intoxicating liquor, and of the prohibition of the sale of drink to Natives;

(*e*) By the effective supervision and improvement of the conditions under which miners, artisans, railway servants, factory hands and other workers are employed. By the introduction of legislation where necessary (and particularly in cases where the nature of the occupation may have any injurious effect upon health), to regulate the hours of labour and the conditions of employment — such legislation to make provision in particular for:

    1. Workmen's compensation.
    2. Conciliation Boards.
    3. A fair wage clause in all Government contracts or where Government money is given in aid, and in all contracts of Public Bodies whose funds are raised wholly or in part by assessment.
    4. Adequate ventilation of mines, factories and workrooms.

4. *To Promote Closer Settlement and Increase the Productive Capacity of the Land by*

(*a*) The encouragement of closer settlement coupled with State acquisition on payment of land for settlement by suitable settlers whether from South Africa or from oversea.

(*b*) State aid to desirable immigrants.

(*c*) The taxation of unimproved land values.

(*d*) Improved means of distribution.

(*e*) Irrigation schemes.

(*f*) Provision in any land settlement scheme, for the settlement, where practicable, of miners' phthisis sufferers debarred from following their calling.

(*g*) The systematic development of the agricultural resources of the country, by legislation and otherwise with special attention to water conservation, the arresting of veld denudation, irrigation and afforestation as well as by the vigorous suppression of animal diseases and other plagues to which South Africa is subject.

5. *To Encourage Industrial Development and Expansion*
   (*a*) By the administration of the railways, ports and harbours, in accordance with the spirit as well as the letter of the South Africa Act, with a view to the early reduction of the cost of living, the systematic development of the country, and the encouragement of an export trade;
   (*b*) By the fostering of mining in all its branches, and the immediate extension of facilities for prospectors and small workers;
   (c) By the adoption of a moderate Customs Tariff primarily for revenue purposes, but providing for adequate encouragement of legitimate South African industries and products, together with the maintenance and extension of the principle of preferential tariffs within the Empire.

6. *To Maintain the Principles of Local Government*
   By the retention of the Provincial Councils and the delegation of more power to these Councils, so that as far as possible all matters of purely local concern shall come under their jurisdiction.

2

THE SOUTH AFRICAN NATIONAL PARTY

GENERAL LOUIS BOTHA'S MANIFESTO[1]

THE POLITICAL Union of South Africa is no longer an ideal, but has under the guidance of Providence become an accomplished fact through the joint labours and sacrifices of the White races and of all parts of British South Africa. A work has been accomplished which it is fervently hoped will bring lasting peace and happiness to this country, but a task of enormous difficulty and responsibility still lies ahead of the people and the Government of South Africa.

The public and railway services of the various Colonies absorbed by the Union will have to be co-ordinated, their railway policies will have to be recast, their financial systems will have to be assimilated, a fiscal policy will have to be inaugurated which will lead to the rapid development of the resources of the country, the closer settlement of the land will have to be promoted, a defence organisation will have to be created worthy of the heroic traditions of South Africa, the expanding educational requirements will have to be met, and above all a Native question of unexampled complexity requiring the utmost patience and the fairest judgment, will have to be dealt with.

But behind and beyond these grave matters lies the greater national problem of welding into one South African nation the various peoples who have made this country their permanent home.

In order that these matters may be dealt with successfully it is essential to secure the co-operation of all South Africans, of whatever race, and to eliminate racialism from all political and national questions, and it is further essential that political parties should rest upon differences of principle on practical questions, and not upon differences of race.

I feel certain that a great majority of South Africans are in favour of the formation of a political party whose fundamental object shall be to make the Union a real and abiding force in our future development, fully recognising South Africa as an integral part of the Empire. It is with the object of forming such a party that I appeal to my fellow-countrymen in whatever part of South Africa they may live.

As it is our primary object to form a South African nation, I would

---

[1] Read in English and Dutch by Dr. Bok, General Botha's private secretary, during the Prime Minister's address at Pretoria, 2 June 1910. Published by the *Star*, 3 June 1910.

48

suggest that the name of our party shall be the South African National Party, and that it shall undertake:

(a) To use its utmost endeavours to make a success of Union throughout South Africa and among all sections of its people.
(b) To promote a healthy South African spirit in dealing with our political and national problems.

I would also suggest that to secure these objects the party adopt the following principles:

1. The just and equal treatment of all parts of the Union.
2. The maintenance of the equality provisions contained in the South Africa Act, and the avoidance of all causes of estrangement and misunderstanding between the various sections of the people.
3. The placing of the Native question above party politics, and the fair and sympathetic treatment of the Coloured races in a broad and liberal spirit.
4. The encouragement of European, and the prevention of Asiatic, immigration into South Africa.
5. An expanding education policy to meet the growing requirements of South Africa.
6. The improvement of the conditions of labour, and the securing to White labour of its proper share in the industrial and agricultural expansion of South Africa.
7. The establishment for South Africa, as part of the Empire, of an adequate system of national defence which will recognise the obligation of the citizen to take part in the defence of the country.
8. The efficient organisation of the State departments, with due regard to the vested rights of civil servants.
9. The development of economic and railway policy along lines which will give greater freedom of expansion to South African industries and commerce.
10. The fostering of stable conditions in connection with the mining industries of South Africa, so as to encourage the investment of additional capital therein, and vigorous development of the mineral resources of the country.
11. The promotion of agricultural expansion and land settlement by means of improved methods of production, the diffusion of agriculture knowledge, and the opening up of foreign markets for South African products.

These are the objects and principles which I have endeavoured to carry out during my period of office in the Transvaal, and which I and my colleagues desire to carry out to the best of our ability in the Government of South Africa, and I appeal to all South Africans to strengthen our hands by co-operating on these lines.

GENERAL LOUIS BOTHA, 21 NOVEMBER 1911[1]

IN OPENING the Congress, General Botha spoke as follows: Friends, it is to me the greatest honour of my life to be the chairman of this meeting. It is an agreeable task to me to welcome you here most heartily. When one looks round this gathering and sees who are represented here then one must admit that never in the history of South Africa has such a representative meeting been held anywhere and therefore, gentlemen, it is my greater privilege than ever to be chairman of this gathering, where moderate men like these here have come together. If one sees how the invitations to this Congress have been universally accepted, then one is the more proud to be a resident of South Africa. I am particularly thankful for the interest which the two sections of the community are showing in this meeting, and particularly is it a matter for extreme thankfulness and congratulation that members from Natal have seen fit to turn up in such large numbers, and I think that the influence which will go out from this meeting will sweep South Africa clean of racialism.

Never before in the history of South Africa have Englishmen and Boers been able to meet in a gathering such as this, and I must say that I feel small when looking all round at the faces in this meeting to think that I am in the chair. But I shall do my best in acquitting myself of my duty and with a commando like the one before me the position of the chairman will not be endangered. Every corner of South Africa is represented here today and everyone is here with the same object, viz. of forming one great South African Party on the principles laid down in our programme. That such a meeting as this is possible at all is to be ascribed to a fact for which we are thankful to God, that both sections of the community are imbued with a spirit of mutual approach and toleration.

This stream of mutual approach has become, and is becoming from day to day and from year to year, stronger and stronger, and I am convinced that that stream will become so strong and so resistless[2] that it will sweep ruthlessly out of its way everything that stands in the way of mutual approach and conciliation of the two White sections of our inhabitants, and out of that will be born a young but very promising nationality. This Congress is a living proof of the existence of the powerful current. I am convinced that when in the history of our country 18 months ago Union became an established fact, since then our party has been at the helm of affairs. The General Election was fought on a platform and a programme laid down by me in consultation with the other leaders of my party.

1 Speech by General Botha at the Inaugural Congress, Bloemfontein, November 1911, as reported in the *Star,* 21 November 1911.
2 Read: irresistible.

Considerably before this our position in South Africa another party under the leadership of Sir Starr Jameson was formed. We have gone slowly because we believe in the old saying " Go slowly ". Not until now, after 18 months have passed, has the spirit arisen for having this National Congress at which our new party shall take prominent shape and organisation. I trust we shall succeed in these our deliberations — and that the organisation born out of this Congress will remain a permanent blessing in and for South Africa.

What, then, is our chief aim? The co-operation of the two White races in order that along these lines there may be formed a South African nation. That indeed was the chief aim of the existing organisaton, but its realisation is easier now that the way has been cleared by the political union of the country, of the two great political ideals. The political union of the States of South Africa has been attained.

The other and the greater ideal remains to be realised, the national union of the inhabitants, the peoples of South Africa — that is a great and a difficult task, certainly far more difficult than was the political union established by our statesmen. But with determination and with mutual toleration and patience this national union also will be accomplished. To my mind, gentlemen, there are two roads open to our people, and very much more depends on the road that is taken. First, there is the road which leads to co-operation and the formation of a single South African nationality of the White population of our country. There is not the slightest doubt that this is the proper road to take. After the bitter experiences we have gone through along the other road — the road of division — and after the wonderful Union of the South African States which followed this unhappy history, it is clear to me and to every lover of South Africa, clear as daylight, that it is the will of Providence that we shall become one people in South Africa, and that out of the weakness and divisions of the past a great and strong nation shall be born.

But, gentlemen, let us be earnest; let us not only talk of co-operation with the view only of political advantage — let it be our honest, true and absolute endeavour to grasp the hand and keep it. Let us not try to quibble with words, but let us bind each other together for good and all. Then we shall have peace and quietness, and the South African nation will have a bright future before it. There is a second road, the road leading to isolation, the separation of the White races. Some people still desire to take that road and think that along that road language and traditions would better be kept live. I for my part think that along these lines South Africa will remain divided among itself. Brothers, let us recognise God's finger in these things during the past 12 years. Let us work with united strength for a better understanding and co-operation between the White races. Let us stick absolutely to equality on the free basis as laid down in the Constitution, and let us respect each other's language and traditions. In this manner political co-operation will be absolute. There will be toleration and broad-mindedness, and there will be no room left for exploitation and small-mindedness in the minds of the people of South Africa. This Congress is so strongly representative of both White races of South Africa that it is a sure sign that our party has adopted the proper road. We have already got one fatherland under one flag; we also want one people to make a great White man's land of South Africa for ourselves and for generations to come.

I have somewhat laboured this point, but it is the basis and the foundation of our party. It has for its object the consolidation of all South Africans, no matter what their origin may be. When I look about me and I ask myself what is there still remaining that is still separating and tends to separate the two races in South Africa, I see nothing in our Constitution. The great question of equal rights for both languages has been settled for ever and all that now requires to be done is honourably to carry this into effect.

But one thing of great importance has not been settled by the Constitution, and was left to the future. I refer to the education question. I must say that I attach the very slightest importance to the shrieks of the Opposition and the Opposition papers on this question. It seems to me that it is their intention most to keep passion alive to such an extent, and to cause so much bitterness that no solution of this delicate question can be possible. But here I say again I think they are a bit late in this. There are some people who are not disinclined to stir up the water so that it is dirty, so that in that way they may be able to fish in it. I can come to no other conclusion, especially in view of recent speeches delivered by some of the members of the Opposition party. To my regret I must say these are particularly shameful, because it tends to reduce the whole question to racial lines and to house the racial question. The stream of mutual approach will sweep it away. It is of the greatest interest to us to see that this question is solved. We desire to build up good South Africans from the youngsters on the school benches — because we expect they will co-operate in future. Our party is formed of both races and we want to do all in our power to remove all causes of offence, misunderstanding and suspicion. How this is to be carried into effect has already been indicated by the Select Committee[3] appointed by Parliament, and already adopted by the Transvaal Provincial Council.

I have already written to the Provincial Councils about this matter, and I trust with the strong support of public feeling behind us, the Provincial Councils will ere long in this way do a great service to South Africa. The Union of South Africa will stand firmer on this principle of equality and freedom when it is adopted in the schools over the whole of South Africa. You will see, therefore, gentlemen, that where the Government has been accused by the Opposition of breach of faith with reference to this question of education there is not a tittle of justificaton. We have not brought the matter on public platforms in the endeavour to solve this intricate and delicate question. But we have been silently

[3] S.C. 2-1911.

52

using our influence to get this question properly adjusted, and it is today a particularly pleasing duty to mention to you that to the letters addressed by me to the Administrators replies have been received by me which are highly satisfactory. That is to say, that at the first session of the Provincial Councils of the Cape, the Free State and Natal a modification of the laws will be proposed on the language question, either in the spirit of the majority report of the Select Committee, or with the addition of the stipulation adopted by the Transvaal Provincial Council. Therefore, gentlemen, when these laws are passed, as I hope they will be passed, there will be nothing in South Africa to divide the White races. The last obstacles will then be removed and the racialistic question in its full form will then cease to exist in South Africa.

My experience of South Africa is this, that the people of South Africa are desirous of peace — that people will co-operate and that the people will not tolerate anybody in South Africa to separate them, and therefore, gentlemen, I think it is a matter for mutual congratulation that the day has dawned when we shall be free to talk and to take off our coats and do the spade work.

There are other big questions before South Africa. We have passed our childhood and we are on the verge of great national development which must be based on sound principles. The time for idle talk has passed and time for action has come.

As to what we have done as a party, and are going to do, particularly, I would point out what I think ought to be done in order to strengthen the foundation of South Africa and to strengthen the White population of South Africa in peace; the party we are forming today must be a party with a great, broad line of policy. We must not be afraid to incur debt liabilities, but we must take steps to develop South Africa as best we can — and therefore on absolute business lines, we ought to borrow sufficient money to achieve that object.

We shall, therefore, in the first place, in the portions of South Africa where rainfall is plentiful, endeavour to buy up such portions of South Africa which will be suitable to start large settlements.

Secondly, in those parts of the country in which the rainfall is not large, but which are fit for the support of man and beast — in those parts we must systematically set about boring for water, and there also start settlements on Crown and other suitable land which may be purchased by the Government.

Then there is a third point. The Government must, wherever possible, construct large dams and lead the water out of our larger rivers for the irrigation of still more ground for the establishment of settlement. The question is asked where shall we get our labour. Well, if we put our heads together we shall solve the problem. Because if we get that problem solved, and if we import White labour into South Africa, one would be able eventually to make good settlers. But I should like to say this to avoid misunderstanding. When we talk about irrigation schemes and labour colonies in South Africa, and there being English and Dutch in South Africa, who would like to go on those settlements, that it must be understood it is not going to be a question of sustaining every poor man in South Africa, because I say, and I say it to my sorrow, that there are many in South Africa who will not help themselves, and we are not going to help such. Therefore, the criticism levelled at this scheme that we were going to keep up the system of distributing doles, will meet with disappointment. I say, gentlemen, that in all the schemes the Government have only one object, and that is to help those people who are prepared to help themselves.

In the wake of agricultural development will follow commercial development. A commission has been appointed and we are waiting for its report. In every case the policy of the Government is one of protection for such industries which have the right to exist in this country. We intend that South Africa shall in the future not only be a country of agricultural development, but also one of industrial development. We shall endeavour to effect our purposes by legitimate support from the Government.

There are many big questions to solve, and one of the most important is that of South African defence. We who have arrived at manhood ought to appreciate and accept our responsibilities in this matter. The British Government has repeatedly warned us that the burdens now resting on England's shoulders were becoming too heavy for her to bear and that we should look to ourselves for our own defence. The time has arrived to act and we are prepared to accept our responsibility. The position of affairs throughout the world is unsettled and we must not run the risk to become the sport of fortune. The draft Defence Bill will be published shortly, and I hope it will have your hearty support. I say that out of the material we have at our hands in the two races in South Africa we ought to be able to raise the finest defence force in the world — a force which will be an ornament to South Africa.

It is impossible for me to touch at this stage on all the big questions, and I will, therefore, proceed and address a few words to you on the programme before the Congress. You will be familiar with the programme, which is before you, and you will doubtless know that during the last session of Parliament a number of our friends came together and drafted these principles published in the form in which they are before you.

Now, I will say, and doubtless you will agree with me, that there are a number of faults in that programme. There are a few points which as far as I can judge ought to be entirely eliminated, and that we should like to see done. I think the basis on which we should approach this matter is that we should appoint a committee which in the course of our deliberations will go through the constitution as published, and report on it. Where we have a large Congress such as this it is an exceedingly difficult matter to touch on all the small points of difference, and I am going to make an appeal to you not to let these smaller points of difference stand in the way of co-operation. What I want the Congress to do is to get the big principle got through first. The smaller points in connection with these principles are very likely numerous, and we can from time to time change them as the people desire. Therefore I ask you, gentlemen, let us adopt the principle first. Do not let the smaller matters stand in the way of forming our big party.

The first question, therefore, which you will have to answer will be this: Are you going to co-operate with us to establish that big South African Party? We have intended that the name of the party should be " The South African Party ". We have now arrived at that line in history that we want to establish something which is going to stand firmly and permanently. The smaller points are generally the stumbling-blocks which I and my colleagues laid before the public during the last elections. You will agree with me that we pledged our honour to carry that programme into effect. We are, therefore, as a party and as a Government pledged to carry out that programme. Therefore we should select a committee out of our midst to discuss these matters, and I trust that all of you who are here and wish to propose any amendments will hand these to that committee.

Gentlemen, friends, and brothers, if we do not take advantage of this golden opportunity today to make of South Africa a happy and prosperous country where we could all live mutually in peace, happy and in harmony, and if that is not done then, brothers and friends, we must assuredly fall back on the bitter and racial bitterness and then we shall have dissention and strife, instead of harmony and peace, and then we shall begin to break down instead of building up. But I say, God will not have this. This Congress, representative of every part, and of every section as this community, is ample proof that with the hearts of everyone of the community is the sincere desire and wish to exclaim: " One country, one people, one God." Gentlemen, I have very great pleasure, before I sit down, to propose the following resolution:

" This Congress being convinced of the necessity to have an organisation for the whole of the Union for the advancement of principles and the interests of the South African Party, resolves to form the South African Party, organised with the manifesto and draft constitution, published by General Botha as its basis."

GENERAL J. B. M. HERTZOG[1]

GENERAL HERTZOG addressed the Congress in Dutch. Speaking afterwards in English, he said: Now, gentlemen, I cannot promise to repeat verbally what I have said in Dutch, as that is impossible, but I think I can promise you this, that as far as the spirit of it is concerned, you shall

---

[1] Speech by General Hertzog at the South African Party Congress, Bloemfontein, Reported in the *Star,* 23 November 1911.

have it as faithfully as I possibly can do it. Let me thank the English people present here — I should not say English gentlemen, but English fellow-South Africans — I thank them most heartily for giving me the opportunity of saying here what I have said over and over again to my fellow-Dutch-speaking citizens of the Union. We stand today on the threshold of starting a young South African nation on its course. The South African spirit prevails in South Africa, but what it has lacked was the really necessary step to meet one another and to take one another's hands conjointly to co-operate in building up the future of South Africa. In the past we have had our little organisations, Dutch-speaking for the most part, and our English fellow-citizens have stood too often apart, feeling perhaps a little strange to everything that occurred during the near past.

Quite right. Every one of us appreciated that. What I have felt for a considerable time past, and what I fought for, is this, that the time has arrived for us South Africans, no matter whether we are Dutch-speaking or English, to see that we recognise this fact that so long as we stand apart, and try to get good (*sic*) by different means we must expect that the greater part of that which we as a nation have to accomplish, will not be done by us. This afternoon we have taken a resolution which shows that we are really not only conscious that we have to work together — not only that we have to work together, but that in spirit we have to be one in South Africa. We have shown that by what we have taken on ourselves today — namely, to do away with and to say farewell to those old organisations which have helped us to make history in South Africa in the past. Those organisations had become dear to us, and it is with regret that we have to say farewell to them. And that shows all the more the earnestness with which the Dutch and English-speaking peoples are prepared to co-operate for the future — that we may say we are prepared to let all that go, and see a new organisation come into existence whereby we shall act as one man — and I cannot help repeating what I heard yesterday as soon as possible.

General Louis Botha, in his speech yesterday morning, made a statement that the Executive of the Orange Free State had given him the assurance that they would take steps to have the Education Act laid on the table of the Provincial Council in conformity with the majority report. Gentlemen, let me tell you this, that is not a step which was lightly undertaken by the Provincial Council authorities in this Province. That was not a step which either I or anybody else undertook with a light heart. The law may have been disliked, but let me give you this assurance that to the people for whom this law was called into existence to preserve their rights that law was very dear; but the people in this Province said — and I speak on behalf of the people of this Province — that they had taken that step on account of the sincerity shown, by which they felt that the welfare of South Africa was bound up, not with the Dutch or English-speaking citizens of the country, but with the existence of co-operation of

56

both races together. And it is for that reason that the Executive has given its consent and has pledged its word to see that we shall have that law brought into such form as is desired by both sections.

Well, gentlemen, I tell you that is the spirit in which I and the people of this Province intend to co-operate with our English fellow-citizens. I can only hope that when we go back we shall be animated not by small considerations of detail, but by the spirit and tone of the South African people, both English-speaking and Dutch-speaking.

GENERAL J. C. SMUTS[2]

GENERAL SMUTS then addressed the meeting in response to repeated calls. He was received with great enthusiasm. It had not, said General Smuts, been his intention to say anything at all on that occasion, especially after the speeches made on the previous day by General Botha and President Steyn. To his mind, they had expressed so fully and clearly what were undoubtedly the principles which should guide them in South African politics that it was unnecessary to add one word. Still, as they had done him the honour of electing him to the head committee, he would say just a few words.

He had to confess that he had come to the Congress with a certain amount of misgiving. They had been told by the Opposition Press, which took great interest in their affairs, that at that Congress the party would go "bust". Well, they had come from all parts of South Africa and from all sections of the people, and they had a gathering unprecedented in the history of South Africa. He would only say this: Let them not make an end with the enthusiasm displayed. They had only begun their campaign. Enthusiasm and motive power had been shown, but uphill work lay before them in the formation of a great South African Party, to which right-minded people, all true South Africans, could belong and could belong cordially. But such a party organisation all over South Africa would require a great deal of spade-work.

Still, the old party organisations they had were organisations with long and distinguished records. People were attached to them and to their traditions. But with regard to those organisations and traditions and the attaching of people to them, he would say what he had said regarding the attachment there was to old Colonies and to their traditions — others would take their place. New organisations would fully and adequately take the place of old organisations, and they would form a great association to which all right-minded people in South Africa could belong. He was not a particularly strong party man, but he knew that if anything was worth having it was worth fighting for and fighting hard. He knew

2 Speech by General J. C. Smuts at the South African Party Congress, Bloemfontein. Reported in the *Star*, 23 November 1911.

that the forces against him, the forces that worked in a spirit opposite to the South African spirit, were powerful in South Africa, and they would have to work hard to form a South African Party. The people saw that union was only the first step in a great movement which was going to build up a great country and a great nation in South Africa. The real work, both of union and party, still lay before them, and it would be hard work which had to be done. He had some experience of it while he had been in the Government.

The speaker then proceeded to emphasise the difficulties in the Government's path. There were many persons in the Government — men of great standing in South Africa, old men who had grown grey and some of whom had lost their hair in the service of South Africa. They also had young men, perhaps too impetuous and full of energy. They had a very mixed team. They had men who had not worked before in politics, who had their own views on South African questions and, therefore, as General Botha had told them before, they could not in a Ministry such as theirs always have full unanimity. They had men of strong minds who were determined to fight for their own opinions — as opportunity arose. They would sometimes see differences of opinion, but if there was one thing which they were all imbued with, and which they would carry out, it was the South African spirit, and that was what they wanted to be tested by. There might be slight or larger points of differences, but they would find that every man in the Government, whether he came from the Cape, Natal, or the interior, was determined to build up South Africa on a basis which was purely and truly South African in spirit.

PROGRAMME OF PRINCIPLES[1]

1. THE SOUTH AFRICAN PARTY acknowledges the Divine guidance in the destinies of nations, and recognises the obligation to take into account the religious character of the people of the Union and to maintain religious freedom for everyone

2. Its political object is the development of the South African spirit of national unity and self-reliance,[2] through the attainment of the lasting union of the various sections of the people, the advancement of this national unity, based on maintaining the existing rights and liberties, and it calls upon all sections of the population, all churches and religious societies to co-operate in the building up of the South African nation.

3. In regard to the Constitution and South Africa's relations to the British Empire, the South African Party embraces the following principles:

(a) The people of South Africa do not desire to limit their future political development as a free people and leave the door open for

---

[1] As revised by Congress in 1930 and issued by the Head Office, Pretoria, February 1931.

[2] In the Afrikaans text the word " selfstandigheid " is used, which may also be translated as " independence ".

the evolution of that freedom under Divine Providence. They recognise at the same time that any far-reaching change in our form of Government can only rest, just as the establishment of our present Constitution at the National Convention, on the broad basis of the united will of the people, i.e. on the co-operation of all sections of the White population, and not merely on a parliamentary majority.

(b) With a view to giving effect to the strong desire of the people for peace and unity, and having regard to the sharp division of opinion on constitutional questions, it is accepted that it is not in the best interest of South Africa to agitate for any change in our form of Government as laid down in the Constitution, and that our Constitutional development shall be left to the natural course of circumstances.

(c) No obligations or responsibilities towards other parts of the British Empire or other countries shall be undertaken which are contrary to the interest of South Africa, which derogate from the existing status of South Africa.

(d) In the application of the above fundamental principles no distinction of race as regards the European population is recognised, but all who wish to co-operate on this basis are welcome in the ranks of the party.

4. For the development and furtherance of the progress of country and people the South African Party advocates the following measures:

(a) The just and equal treatment of all parts of the Union.

(b) The maintenance of the fundamental principles of the South Africa Act, and the avoidance of all causes of estrangement and misunderstanding between the various sections of the people.

(c) To ensure the advancement of the people by means of an educational system which will take into account the various requirements of the people and conditions of the country.

(d) The adoption of an equitable and judicious system of taxation, which will have due regard to the development of the natural resources of the country.

(e) The necessity for economy in the administration of the country.

(f) The development of agriculture and stock farming as constituting the permanent resources of the country.

(g) The promotion of commerce and industries, and of the exploitation of the mineral resources of the country.

(h) The encouragement of desirable European immigration, and the prevention of Asiatic immigration into South Africa.

(i) The conviction that all questions affecting Native policy, should be approached by the White people of South Africa, in a broad spirit of co-operation between parties, and in the endeavour to secure for

Native races their natural and distinct development, and to ensure that in the building up of South Africa all grounds for future discord between White and Black shall be avoided.

(j) The maintenance for South Africa as part of the British Empire of an adequate system of national defence.

(k) The improvement of the conditions of labour, and securing to White labour its fair share in the agricultural and industrial development of South Africa.

(l) The promotion of an impartial, economical and effective administration of justice.

(m) The maintenance of public health and morals.

5. The South African Party is founded on these principles and appeals to the people of South Africa to co-operate with a view to ensuring that practical effect be given to them.

3

GENERAL J. B. M. HERTZOG AND SOUTH AFRICAN NATIONALISM

SPEECH AT GERMISTON, 5 DECEMBER 1911[1]

GENERAL HERTZOG analysed the different elements which, in his opinion, formed South African society. He said they must look facts in the face. They had two streams of life in South Africa. On the one hand were the old Dutch-speaking South Africans right through the country. They had the true South African feeling, and for them there was no other country. That portion of the people had its own national life and national spirit, but it was only a portion of the nation in South Africa. Then they had the old English population in South Africa. That portion of the English-speaking population had, like the Dutch people, been long in the country and they felt themselves at home in this land. They also had no other country. They formed a very large portion of the English-speaking people of South Africa. But there was a third class in South Africa. It was formed of persons who were not yet what he (the speaker) called South Africans. It was a class which was here with good intentions, but it had not made itself at home, and had not, as yet, joined the ranks either of the old Dutch or of the old English portions, and it felt that it was ready to shake the dust of the country off its feet whenever those things from which it drew benefits existed no longer.

He was only drawing their attention to facts. The last class which he had referred to was to be found in every young country to which people flocked. The people forming it had always a strong feeling for their motherland and wished to return to that land. These people were South Africans from a legal point of view and they had the franchise but these things did not give them the national spirit or help them to enter into the national life. Up to a short time ago — up to the National Convention — though they had two strong South African teams, both with the true South African spirit, these had not worked together, and had not been able to work together in order to create one South African national life. The English stream had gone one way and the Dutch stream had gone another. But, fortunately, one of the good consequences of the war had been that they were now placed in such a position that the opportunity existed for these two streams to fuse, and what was the result today?

Nobody could deny that at the South African Party conference in

[1] The *Star*, 8 December 1911.

61

Bloemfontein the other day the two streams of old English and old Dutch had arrived at a stage at which they had agreed to lead their national South African life together. (In his English-spoken summary later in the evening General Hertzog said in this connection: " The streams still flow, though a good deal of the one has been diverted into the course of the other.") In Parliament they saw that real South Africans, whether Dutch or English, had absolutely decided to form a true national South African spirit and life.

Now he came to the other element — the element which regarded South Africa as a strange country. He did not wish to say who belonged to this party, but would rather say that they were all people to whom the national spirit was strange. Let them consider the influence of party politics. The party system was a splendid thing to forward personal interests. The causes which had in the past stood in the way of South Africa becoming one nation were now being used to strengthen party politics and to keep English-speaking people away from the Dutch. If they wanted a national spirit it must be Dutch and English. He reminded them that during the elections the cry of " Vote British " had been raised. If his memory served him right, Sir Percy Fitzpatrick had always been using that. That was a proof of the truth of what he had been saying about party politics.

SPEECH AT NYLSTROOM, 5 OCTOBER 1912[1]

H E D W E L T on the language agitation, and said he would go out of his way to meet the English section, provided no sacrifice of principle were involved. The Dutch were the least aggressive people in the world. At the show he noticed everything was in English, though to say the least of it half those present and interested were Dutch-speaking. Would not, if circumstances had been reversed, the English section have claimed half a share? Nobody could abandon the people's language rights without stigmatising himself as a traitor. The English section did not need his advance[2] with regard to their language. That was why he confined himself to Dutch. They were all equals, and the Dutch people would not yield one inch on the question of practical equality of language, for he was not an advocate of mere form.

The address of welcome had mentioned national ideals. Well, it was just on this question that the fight between the Nationalists and Unionists was being waged. He and his were South Africans first of all. The paramount question to him always was, what are South Africa's interests? The Opposition had started a farcical campaign in order to infuse life into a child whose existence was almost despaired of. Colonel Byron had ac-

1 The *Star*, 5 October 1912.
2 Advocacy?

cused him of wanting to make the Africander "boss". Colonel Byron was quite right, for he (the speaker) would continue to work for the dominance of the Africander in South Africa. He would always fight against Colonel Byron and foreign adventurers of his kidney being the people's trustee. For years that had been South Africa's misfortune. Dr. Smartt was today no more an Africander than when he first set foot here. Some people became imbued with the South African spirit the day after they landed. But some people were not likely to become Africanders in 100 years. Colonel Byron was one of them, and always compared the Government of this country with Australia to the former's disadvantage. Why did not Colonel Byron take a single ticket journey to Australia?

Proceeding, General Hertzog attacked the Opposition for its attitude on immigration, and said that 663 immigrants had cost the Transvaal £1,350,000 since 1902. This was not the end of it, and did not include the value of the Crown lands given them. Two hundred and twenty-three had entirely failed and £210,000 were irretrievably lost to the Exchequer. At this rate £2,000,000 a year would have to be allowed for immigration in future, because surely the Opposition would take nothing less than 1,000 immigrants annually. No, they would have to build up the country as one built a house, putting one brick after another in its exact place, and not dump immigrants down on the country as one dumped bricks from a Scotch cart, because that would not build a house.

The political fight was no longer between English-speaking and Dutch-speaking South Africans, but between those two on the one hand and foreign, mostly English-speaking, adventurers on the other. The Natal people were Africanders, and the Opposition would make no headway in Natal. In 1910 the people might have assimilated the Opposition, just as a farmer might put bastard sheep among his "mofschapen",[3] but once the separation had been made complete by such things as the "Vote British" cry, re-union became increasingly difficult. He would continue to speak on such like subjects as long as the Opposition spoke in its present vein.

[3] Pure bred merino sheep.

SPEECH AT SMITHFIELD, 14 OCTOBER 1912[1]

REFERRING TO his Nylstroom speech General Hertzog said it was the policy of the Government that the South African (Africander) should be "baas" everywhere in South Africa. He should be "baas" politically in the Administration and in the schools. The Government to which he belonged was a South African Government. He had said that South Africans should be "baas" at Grahamstown, Port Elizabeth,

[1] Extract from speech at Smithfield, as reported in the *Star*, 14 October 1912.

Uitenhage, and many other places, and the sentiment had been heartily welcomed. Colonel Byron was the first to object to it.

Only one person had the right to be " baas " in South Africa — namely, the South African. He could understand that statement was not in accordance with the policy of the Opposition, because there were few South Africans in the Opposition. There were a few misled men, but still true. Sir Percy Fitzpatrick was much upset at the doctrine of " Good South African and foreigner ". What he (the speaker) did say at Nylstroom, was that the people had become conscious of themselves as a nation. They felt their own power. They had reached national manhood, and they felt that South Africans and not strangers should rule the country. Formerly they had been governed by people who were not South Africans, and who would never become South Africans. Now that they were capable of ruling themselves they would no longer allow themselves to be ruled by those who were not South Africans. That was what he had said at Nylstroom, that Colonel Byron need not worry about the South African being " baas ".

He would be. He would not allow himself to be governed by foreign fortune-seekers (" fortuin zoekers ") like Colonel Byron. He (General Hertzog) did not know why Sir Percy had taken offence at that, for no one could deny — certainly not Colonel Byron — that in the sense intended he is a stranger in South Africa, for he came from elsewhere. He (General Hertzog) had used the word "fortuin zoeker ", and if anyone liked to translate it " adventurer " he could not help it.

Sir Percy thought it a pernicious doctrine that South Africa should be governed by South Africans. Was it pernicious that England should be governed by the English? Sir Percy could not pretend that he (General Hertzog) meant only the Dutch when he said South African. Grahamstown knew he did not, Port Elizabeth knew he did not, Uitenhage knew it, and even Nylstroom knew that he had referred to all South Africans. In the same speech he had said that the journey of Sir Thomas Smartt and his confreres to Natal was useless, because the Natalians were South Africans. They had only to meet them to see that they were as good South Africans as the Dutch-speaking people. He (General Hertzog) had said South Africans should be " baas " but he wished to draw no line between the South Africans and the outsiders.

That was the policy which Sir Percy had said was pernicious and appealed to the prejudices of ignorant, superstitious people. He could assure Sir Percy that among the people so described were many as well educated as Sir Percy and many who had a great deal more common-sense. He (General Hertzog) had said Sir Thomas Smartt was not a good South African and that Colonel Byron was a fortune-seeker. He meant that they had come to South Africa to seek their fortunes and had not yet become South African in feeling. As regards the Leader of the Opposition, he thought a man who was really a South African would not have advised that the Constitution of the Cape Colony should have been suspended. The least that could be said of a man who did that was that he was not a son of the people whom he served.

Speaking of the Opposition generally, General Hertzog said it was ridiculous the way in which they appealed for sympathy. Arguments they had none. If they had convinced South Africa of anything it was the unfruitfulness of their intellects. The only thing they prided themselves on was the support of the Government — where the Government was right. That was not difficult. "The difficulty is to be right ourselves and to get others to support us." The Opposition had expressed not one original thought and had shown no initiative. They simply trotted forth overworked platitudes and made pathetic appeals *ad misericordiam,* or else they tried to arouse suspicion. The outburst that had followed Nylstroom he could only ascribe to suspicion, to a desire to cause nervousness, and to work on the feelings of the public, especially the English-speaking public. If any one deserved the name of criminal those people did who wished to gain sympathy in that way. There was absolutely nothing in his Nylstroom speech to which any South African could take exception. People like those who lived on the Rand, who came to the country to make fortunes and then leave, would be frightened of the speech, because they felt that their influence was in danger of being lost. There was, of course, nothing wrong in coming to South Africa to seek one's fortune, but what he did object to was these people ruling the country as against South Africans. Against that he would protest.

SPEECH AT DE WILDT, 7 DECEMBER 1912[1]

GENERAL HERTZOG addressed a meeting at De Wildt Halt, on the Rustenburg line, today. In regard to the question of national development of languages, he said, a small storm had broken over his head, but he did not mind these storms so much so long as he achieved his object. He did not agree with the opinion that the task was an ungrateful one, because there never had been a question on which the Dutch people had been so unanimous as on the language, and he had enjoyed the greatest support not only from Dutch-speaking South Africans but also from English-speaking South Africans. The language question, however, was only part of the great question of South African nationalism.

A storm had been caused by what he had said at Nylstroom, where he had stated that the day had come when the South African spirit would come to the top, and that that spirit would declare itself unwilling any longer to have South Africa ruled by those people who were not imbued with the proper South African spirit. People had expressed indignation at that because it would exclude from the Government those people who were not South Africans.

[1] Extract from speech at De Wildt, as reported in the *Star,* 7 December 1912.

He stood by what he had said at Nylstroom; if they wished to see South Africa ruled in the interests of the country it should be ruled by people imbued with the South African spirit. He understood the report of Sir Thomas Smartt's reply to this to mean that he (Sir Thomas) was in the first place an Imperialist and in the second place a South African. If that was Sir Thomas Smartt's meaning it had fully proved that he (General Hertzog) had been right in what he had said that Sir Thomas Smartt was not a true Africander.

Imperialism was important to him (General Hertzog) only when it was useful to South Africa, to its land, and to its people, and when it was not serviceable he had respect for it from a distance, but as a South African he had little to do with it, and when it was contrary to the interests of South Africa and the interests of the people of the country then he was a distinct enemy of Imperialism. "I am prepared," General Hertzog continued, "to let my future as a politician depend on that. That is my feeling, and by that I stand. Imperialism is important to me when it is in the interests of South Africa, and when any question of that kind is to be dealt with, then it will always be my duty to ask myself: Is the solution of this question in the interests of South Africa? And if it is to the detriment of the country then it is my duty to have nothing to do with it."

In regard to a contribution to the Navy, he said it had been stated they were not prepared to fulfil their obligations, but he knew that wherever South Africa was concerned the people were always prepared to fulfil their obligations to protect their interests. They had not allowed themselves to be led away by what they had seen in the papers and by what was said from political platforms for political purposes. If they had done so they would perhaps already have given 20 or 30 Dreadnoughts to the Imperial Government. The Government felt that when the country's affairs had to be dealt with they should not allow themselves to be influenced for sentiment or jealousy. Because the Malay States had given one Dreadnought it was ridiculous to say that South Africa must also give one. It was the Government's duty to consider everything carefully in the interests of South Africa, and for that reason they had so far refrained from all this sentiment, but when the time came South Africa would be ready to do its share for the protection of its own interests in the first place and of the Empire's interests in the second place.

All this noise had been started by a few thousand of interested people in the first instance; that was not simply his opinion, but if they read a book by Hobbs and others they would see what really lay behind the shout of "Empire, Empire". The great capitalists were interested in it, and they started it, and then the matter was taken up by those in this country who had political interests. They tried to raise a feeling with the object of keeping Dutch and English-speaking Africanders apart. Most of those people were hard put to it to get recruits for their political party, and every month they got something fresh to widen the breach which they considered should exist between Dutch and English-speaking people, and those were the people who said: " Hertzog is busy preaching racialism." That is simply because they wished to see racialism exist, and if they could get him (General Hertzog) to preach it, then he would be of the greatest assistance to them. He repeated what he had said at Nylstroom that to an Africander Africa comes first, and as Africanders they should in the first place be governed by Africanders. If that was racialism then he was prepared to go to any part of South Africa to preach that doctrine.

General Hertzog proceeded to urge the necessity for the creation of a South African nationalism. He was not one of those who always believed in protesting his loyalty. People, eventually, did not believe those who kept on doing so. As regarded conciliation he had nothing to conciliate, as he had not done any harm to anyone. He felt that it was his right and duty to urge the importance of South African nationalism to the Dutch-speaking people, and if ever the day came when he enjoyed as much confidence on the part of the English-speaking population as he did from the Dutch then he would also preach his doctrine to them. He was sometimes misunderstood, but these misunderstandings would pass and the day would come when they would all realise they were Africanders aiming to achieve the same object.

4

THE NATIONAL PARTY

GENERAL J. B. M. HERTZOG, 7 JANUARY 1914[1]

AFTER PRAYER by the Rev. Mr. Postma, General Hertzog addressed the Congress, and in the course of his remarks, said he wished to explain what led to the holding of this Congress. At the last Provincial Congress the Executive had been instructed under certain eventualities to take such steps as might seem necessary. In the circumstances which had arisen the Executive had invited delegates from other Provinces to attend and the Executive felt extremely gratified at the response received. On 8 October the Executive decided that unless a satisfactory solution was arrived at at the Congress[2] in Cape Town another Congress should be called to take such steps as would have the effect of the people securing the rights to which they were entitled. Whether or not that had the effect of disturbing the unity of the South African Party this Congress was one of the most important that could be called. When the South African Party was formed the Provinces had to make many sacrifices, but they should now ask whether they should also sacrifice compensations which had been given.

They would have to decide whether they could any longer remain in a party which, by the actions of those who represented it in political life, had shown that the principles on which that party had been formed and which were most dear to the people were not going to be put into effect. They could not allow the party to become the coffin of their national ideals, but if they decided not to remain in the party then there remained something else to be done. They had openly to express their aims and ambitions. Had it not been for the vagueness and designed ambiguity of the principles of the South African Party the people would never have been in the position in which they were today. If they wanted unity then it could not be achieved by giving up principles, but by an open expression of the fact that they stood for their national principles which they would not sacrifice. What they should aim at here was to lay down firm and sound principles.

As to the status of the Congress he wished to emphasise that this was not a Congress under the statutes of the South African Party. The position they occupied was that of a great interprovincial vigilance committee guarding the principles of the party. If they decided to secede,

1 Speech held at National Party Conference, Bloemfontein. The *Star*, 7 January 1914.
2 South African Party Congress.

68

then it did not follow that there was secession. It meant that this Congress was of opinion that members should resign from the South African Party and should form another party. The co-operation of all Provinces was essential if they wished to achieve the ambitions they stood for.

The Rev. Mr. Foster,[2] of Rustenburg, at this stage interrupted the speaker, and asked the Congress to declare itself a Conference of members of the South African Party, the result of which would be that people from the other Provinces would have the right to vote and speak.

General Hertzog replied that this would not be in order. He suggested that Senator Charles Marais be elected chairman.

This was agreed to.

A Free State delegate raised the point of legality, stating that if the decision of Winburg was set aside and the delegate was allowed to represent the minority they did something which was wrong.

After a few words by the Chairman, General Hertzog proposed a vote of condolence with Mrs. Fischer and with Mrs. Brain in their sad bereavements. He said Mr. Fischer and Mr. Brain had devoted their lives to the service of the Free State. They had the greatest respect for both those men, and the names of Mr. Abraham Fischer and Mr. Brain would always be remembered by them as great friends of the country.

The motion was adopted in silence, all those present remaining in their seats.

A committee to arrange the agenda was then appointed, and the Congress adjourned for half an hour.

[2] Read Vorster.

PROGRAMME OF PRINCIPLES[1]

1. THE NATIONAL PARTY represents the national conviction and aspirations of the South African people within the Union, and strives to develop and realise this conviction and these aspirations to the utmost blessing of the country and its people.

2. The party acknowledges the guidance of God in the destinies of countries and peoples and seeks to develop the people's life along Christian national lines.

3. The party recognises the necessity of fostering a strong sense of national autonomy and expressly declares that the interests of the Union and its people should be put before those of any other country or people.

4. The position of the Union in regard to its relationship towards the United Kingdom, resting on the good faith of two nations, is unequivocally

[1] Programme of principles as approved of by the special congress of members of the South African Party, Orange Free State Province, held at Bloemfontein, 7-9 January 1914. Published as a pamphlet by *Het Volk Drukkerij*, Potchefstroom. Translated from the original Dutch by the present editor.

recognised by the party. It is convinced that the maintenance of a cordial understanding between the Union and the Empire depends on a meticulous avoidance of any act whereby the political liberty of the people of the Union might be curtailed or restricted or whereby any of the liberties of the country or its Government might be withdrawn from the immediate supervision or control of the people of the Union.[2]

5. The party recognises the just claims of the people of Union to mutual respect and free enjoyment of all that belongs to a people in respect to language, history, religion, customs and morals. By encouraging a feeling of true appreciation of these qualities the party strives to develop a sense of national worth and of a healthy national character.

6. The party recognises that the promotion of the spiritual, national and material welfare of the people is the duty and calling of the State. It is convinced that that calling may only be exercised by means of an impartial and conscientious official view of the rights and privileges of every part of the population, guaranteed by the Constitution.

7. The party recognises the right of every inhabitant of the Union to have the official language which is his own, acknowledged in public offices or in the public service everywhere in the country, and to be served in that language by Government officials. The party declares, therefore, that the appointment of officials who do not possess the necessary knowledge of both official languages, is a negation of the rights and interests of the inhabitants.

8. As the maintenance of its rights and liberties is the first duty of a people, the party recognises the necessity of increasing the people's knowledge of the rights and liberties guaranteed to it by the Constitution as a free and autonomous people.

9. The party is convinced that the basis of the welfare of South Africa rests on the unity of the European population in a spirit of dedication to South Africa and of mutual esteem of and loyalty to their fellow-citizens, and further, that the achievement of this goal should be sought by firmly demanding that each section of the population be accorded its own rights.

10. The party believes that the achievement of its declared aims must be sought along the following lines:

Education

(a) The party acknowledges the duty of the State to supervise education and to see that every child, according to opportunity and talent, shall receive instruction based on sound psychological and national principles

---

[2] In view of the resolution of the Imperial Conference of 1926 the party in 1927 amended article 4 as follows:

"The National Party accepts the resolution by the Imperial Conference at its 1926 session. It aims at the maintenance of our sovereign independence, recognised thereby, and the autonomous exercise of State functions. In accordance herewith the National Party declares itself opposed to any tendency, action or policy implying the curtailment or limitation of our liberties. It undertakes to combat any such tendency, action, or policy by all justified means."

so as to enable it to take an honourable place in society. At the same time it recognises the right of the parents to choose the direction in which such instruction should be imparted in regard to the moral and religious education of the child. This principle applies to secondary and higher, as well as to primary, professional, technical and general education. Without wasting public funds the party is in favour of an educational system, organised in such a way as to allow every part of the country to share in the benefit of higher and lower education, and to provide a sufficient, capable and reasonably well-paid staff of teachers.

Agriculture, stock-farming, industry and commerce
(b) By recognising agriculture, stock-farming, industry and commerce as the principal sources of the country's permanent material welfare, and their development and encouragement as the best way of promoting the country's durable economic independence.

Labour
(c) By recognising the worth of the labourer and by always keeping a watchful eye on everything concerning his happiness and welfare, and to take the necessary steps in connection therewith. The party believes that this aim may be achieved by securing—

(1) labour conditions of such a nature as to ensure to the self-respecting citizen of a suitable and happy sphere of work,
(2) a feeling of confidence and sympathy between employer and employee,
(3) confidence in the sympathy and impartiality of the Government, and in the sincere interest in and care for the interests of the workers, with a proper concern for the interests of the employers,
(4) a feeling of satisfaction amongst workers in regard to the present and confidence in the future.

Immigration
(d) Immigrants of European descent and of good character who are prepared to throw in their lot with the people of the Union, are welcomed by the party, but the party is opposed to the systematic importation of immigrants by the Government at public expense, as long as the necessary assistance to settle citizens of the Union on the land is not forthcoming.

The Natives
(e) In our attitude towards the Natives the fundamental principle is the supremacy of the European population in a spirit of Christian trusteeship, utterly rejecting every attempt to mix the races. The party further aims at providing the Native with the opportunity to develop according to his natural talent and aptitude.

Asiatics
(f) By protecting the European as well as the Coloured and Native

population against Asiatic immigration or competition and by refusing to extend any already existing rights of Asiatics.

Finance

(g) By a national financial policy, that is to say:

(1) by keeping a watchful eye on the country's expenditure and income and, particularly, by insisting in Parliament on a sound control of finance.
(2) by a system of taxation in accordance with the paying capacity of the taxpayer and through which the natural sources of the temporary wealth of the country will be sufficiently mobilised in order to promote the country's permanent welfare.
(3) by making provision whereby the sources of State income originating from the exploitation of minerals and other temporary wealth of the country, in case of their eventual exhaustion, will be sufficiently replaced by new sources of income of a durable kind.

National Defence

(h) By recognising our duty as a people to create an efficient system of national defence on land and sea in order to protect the country and its interests, and by promoting a defence system in accordance with the people's national autonomy.

Sunday

(i) By recognising the duty of the Government, with due regard to the principle of sovereignty in each sphere, publicly to respect and maintain the Sunday as a day of rest.

Organisation

(j) By not allowing members of the Government to serve on the Head Committee, as in conflict with the true interests of the party.

11. In order to defend the above principles and to apply them in practice the National Party desires to maintain itself as an independent political group. It prefers not to fuse with any other party which is based on principles in conflict with its own. The party is prepared to co-operate with any other party when and in so far as similarity of aims gives occasion to it, but, in such a case, the co-operating parties shall remain independent from each other, in order to be free of each other as soon as the similarity of aims no longer obtains.

12. As soon as and as often as is necessary the party shall decide on and publish a programme of action in which is summarised the party's demands in regard to legislation in practice. In as far as principles are concerned, these demands shall be based on the existing articles which, as a programme of principles, shall be the political constitution of the party.

5

THE SOUTH AFRICAN LABOUR PARTY

PROGRAMME OF PRINCIPLES[1]

1. THE CONTROL of the credit and the financial policy of the country through the creating of a State bank.

2. The promotion of manufacturing industries in the Union as far as natural resources are available. State assistance to any industry, either through a premium or a protecting tariff, accompanied by proper safeguards:

(i) To the consumer against exorbitant prices; and

(ii) to the worker against wages inadequate to maintain civilised standards of living.

3. The promotion of the development of agriculture by the encouragement of co-operative effort and organised research.

4. The encouragement of government and municipal enterprise in the supply of public necessities.

5. Taxing the unimproved value of land and more particularly that in the possession of Land Companies; and the application of the principle that where mining rights are held, granted by the State, they should either be exercised or automatically revert to the State.

6. The discouragement of the movement of Natives to the European centres and the encouragement of the development of the Natives in suitable Native reserves.

7. The protection of Western standards against the encroachment of Asiatic competition and generous financial provision to encourage Asiatic emigration from the country.

8. A vigorous system of education providing for free primary and secondary education for every child and for free University education for every student who passes the prescribed examinations.

9. The institution of Wage and Conciliation Boards and of the principle of the eight-hour day in industrial and commercial institutions.

10. The prohibition of contract labour whether for Europeans or Coloureds.

11. The institution of high age pensions and State insurance against weakness and unemployment.

12. Equal rights for women.

[1] Extract from the Manifesto of the South African Labour Party, published in 1910.

6

HERTZOG-CRESWELL PACT

CRESWELL TO HERTZOG, 12 APRIL 1923[1]

My dear Hertzog,

It is clear that any co-operation between our respective parties, however narrow or wide in scope, is certain to be made the subject of hostile propaganda by the South African Party and its Press. So I suggest that it would be as well to put on record the actual facts of the position.

You and I have, on several occasions, discussed the present political situation quite candidly, informally and without prejudice, and I think that the substance of these conversations can be correctly summed up as follows:

(1) We found ourselves broadly in agreement in our view that the present Government acts as though dominated by the conviction that the interests of this country are best served by its taking what may be termed the "big financial" view of our serious internal and financial problems. Its policy is not only injuring the present welfare of the country but is seriously jeopardising our destiny as a civilised people. The necessity to combat this trend of policy, which has been growing continuously more pronounced in recent years, is largely the cause of the common opposition of our parties to the present Government and the party supporting it.

(2) We next examined whether there was any legitimate basis upon which we could recommend co-operation between our parties, at all events in so far as elections were concerned. It is clearly undesirable to facilitate the election of Government candidates on a minority vote by splitting the anti-government vote.

(3) The most difficulty in the way of any such co-operation being effective is the fact that, quite irrespective of the real views and intentions of yourself and your party, the South African Party propaganda has inoculated numbers of the English-speaking section of the people in many parts of the country with the belief that if your party achieved power you would at once set about trying to "cut the painter" and establish a republic — the old secession bogey, in fact, of the 1921 election.

To a lesser degree, possibly, a few dwellers in the country districts have been induced to believe that the Labour Party is a Bolshevik group

---

[1] Published in the *Star*, 21 April 1923.

74

whose dearest wish is to decapitate or otherwise maltreat all owners of property — or some other such absurdity. As the former point was successfully drummed into the public mind at the last election, it is most important to disprove it. At the same time you must remember that in common with the bulk of Labour's supporters, I am as you know unalterably opposed to any " cutting of the painter."

I pointed out that this is a matter upon which the great majority of English-speaking South Africans are very sensitive and that an essential condition for any such election co-operation being effective was an explicit declaration on your side to reassure them that their votes at the next general election would not be used contrary to their desires in this matter.

In this regard you said that while no member of your party could be expected, any more than any member of the Labour Party, to renounce his freedom to express, inside and outside of Parliament, any views he may hold on this or any matter, you were able to give this explicit undertaking to electors at the next general election, viz. that in the Parliament that will then be elected, should a Nationalist Government come into power, no Nationalist member of Parliament will use his vote to upset the existing constitutional relationship of South Africa to the British Crown. We are agreed that under these circumstances we could quite properly recommend to our respective parties election co-operation on the lines indicated in paragraph 2 of this letter. This co-operation would indicate that we both appreciate the urgent necessity for the next Parliament to devote itself singlemindedly to domestic measures required to promote the prosperity of the country upon lines more congenial to its people than those at present followed.

(4) Pursuing our discussions we recognised that the logic of facts would compel the taking up of measures which both parties would probably, in principle, support. But we also recognised quite fully the differences which today exist between our parties, not only in political outlook, but also, probably, in the racial and other prejudices which influence large numbers of habitual party supporters, and we were agreed that in any election co-operation that may take place in any constituency it should be understood that the candidate of whichever party, if elected, would owe allegiance to his own party and no other, and that any votes given to him by supporters of the other party, should be given on this clear understanding.

I think that the foregoing correctly expresses the substance of our conversations and I suggest that if this is confirmed by you we should send this correspondence to the Press.

Yours very truly,
F. H. P. Creswell.

HERTZOG TO CRESWELL, 19 APRIL 1923[1]

MY DEAR CRESWELL,

In answer to yours of April 12, I am glad to be able to reply that I entirely agree with your suggestion of offering for publication the statement containing the results of our exchange of ideas on the matter of co-operation between our respective parties at the next general election.

I have carefully considered the statement submitted by you, and as it truly sums up the substance of our conversations I have nothing further to add except to give my full confirmation, which I hereby do.

Yours very truly,
J. B. M. Hertzog.

[1] Published in the *Star*, 21 April 1923.

MEMORANDUM BY COLONEL CRESWELL[1]

IN APRIL 1923 the correspondence was published in which General Hertzog and I, after consulting our Parliamentary colleagues specified the terms of the agreement for the next election which we recommended to our respective parties. That agreement comes to an end at 8 p.m. on polling day except in so far as the Nationalist Party is bound by its pledge in respect to the constitutional question.

In terms of the agreement elected candidates owe allegiance to their own party and to no other. Such is the formal position today after the election. The Labour Party must therefore immediately and without delay determine its attitude to the new Parliament.

In the exercise of our freedom as a party we must realise very fully that that freedom must be used with a full sense of our responsibility to the country. And in order to make clear how, in my opinion, we shall best discharge that responsibility I propose as briefly as possible to trace how the present situation has been arrived at.

The publication of the correspondence referred to in April 1923, was the commencement of a great change in the political situation which had been in progress ever since. Reckoning, as they so often asserted, that any co-operation between the Nationalist and Labour Parties was impossible, the South African Party thought itself safe for a long period in power. It tried hard to prevent the ratification of the agreement by the conferences of the respective parties. It failed in this as it failed in Parliament, and at the elections, because its members mistook not only the effects of the Pact on the attitude of the two parties towards one another, but also the attitude of the public to the Pact.

[1] Immediately after the general election of 1924 and quoted by Margaret Creswell, *An epoch of the political history of South Africa in the life of Frederic Hugh Page Creswell*, pp. 97-101.

76

The relationship between the two parties, established by the Pact, induced on the part of each a desire to give ear to and to understand the viewpoint of the other party in a way it had never previously done. This resulted in a growing co-operation in Parliament in a number of matters of practical politics — notably on the Conciliation Bill and other matters affecting industrial life. So far as the public is concerned this growing understanding and co-operation between two parties which, whatever their differences, represent a great many people whose interests are rooted in South Africa, was viewed not with aversion but rather with a growing hope. The hope was that it would lead to a Government in which the interests of the people would always come first. The thoroughly cordial and intimate co-operation of supporters of both parties at the election was in fact an expression of this earnest hope that the " Pact " afforded a way of escape from governments and parliaments eternally dominated by big business interests. I believe that the big bulk of Labour supporters share that earnest hope.

The country is tired of political jugglery and manipulation. It has had three general elections in four years and has at last got away from the rule of the South African Party and from the powers behind that party. It looks to the Nationalist and Labour Parties to give it a rest from the turmoil and unsatisfactory rule from which it has suffered, and to try and promote general good feeling and well-being. If, owing to any selfish or unreasonable attitude on the part of either of the two parties, its hopes are disappointed and it is plunged into another election in a year or two with the risk of the return of power of the South African Party, it will not forgive for many years the party deemed responsible for this disappointment.

I am therefore certain that in the new Parliament it will be the duty of the Labour Party, no less than of the Nationalist Party, to do its utmost to prevent a breakdown of the present co-operation, consistent, of course, with no repudiation of principles. When one contemplates the practical work that has been done to try and get the country out of the state of depression and unemployment into which the policy of the South African Party has flung it, and also the main lines of practical policy on which the two parties broadly agree, this task, although difficult, should not be beyond our powers if there is a reasonable desire on both sides to forbear from treading on one another's corns. That is the position that confronts us in the immediate future.

Now the question will very likely arise (and it is in relation that this Memorandum is written): Can our task be best performed by shouldering some of the responsibility of Government if invited to do so, or will it be more easily and well done by holding aloof?

1. I will first view the question from the standpoint of the ordinary difficulties of parliamentary work.

If we hold aloof it will certainly be much, very much, more difficult to avoid a breakdown of friendly co-operation. Let us take an instance of what is likely to be of constant occurrence. A measure is brought into the House after being considered by the Cabinet. The Cabinet, without the benefit of the advice of a representative of Labour, comes to a certain decision. When it is discussed in the House, the Labour Party desires some comparatively serious alteration. Let us suppose that at first the Government yields. The Nationalists will certainly be jeered at each time they do so by the South African Party opposition and Press. And in course of time they will, if this is of constant occurrence, feel that they are losing prestige with their own supporters. Each time such an incident occurs it will make it more difficult to obtain a like concession next time and will make a breakdown more likely. A great deal of this will undoubtedly be avoided if, before measures are determined on and made public, the Cabinet through the advice of a Labour element in it is able to shape it so that such conflicts are reduced to a minimum.

2. Next let us take it from the standpoint of the administration. It must not be forgotten that for seven months in the year Parliament is not sitting. Without the help of the Labour Party colleagues the Government is certainly more liable to do things which will "tread on the corns" of the urban industrial population than it would do if it had colleagues who are more closely in touch with that population than is the Nationalist front bench. On this ground our holding aloof will again greatly increase the difficulty of avoiding a premature breakdown.

3. There is a further weighty reason why my judgment is against holding aloof if the new government make their offer on conditions that we can reasonably be expected to accept. It is this. The "Pact" has received the support it has done very largely because the people of both races look upon it as going a great way to get rid of the old South African Party and the business method of dividing us by playing upon our race feelings. If the Labour Party holds aloof the Government will be composed entirely of men of the Dutch section of the people. With the best will in the world to avoid being at all racial, that very fact will inevitably re-arouse those race jealousies which had been the main obstacle to the Labour Party's progress and to the progress of the ideas for which it stands. The situation will be one which will be a tremendous strain on the Labour Party in Parliament, all of whose members are from the English-speaking section, and the strain would, I fear, lead to a breakdown before very long.

A purely Nationalist Government, forced by the aloofness of the Labour Party to find support elsewhere, would naturally try and get this from the Dutch section of the South African Party and this would accentuate the difficulties.

4. A further consideration arises from varying opinions in the Nationalist Party itself. In this, as in every party, there are some who are more conservative and some who lean to more advanced views. If Labour holds aloof the balance will swing to the conservative elements in the House more than if Labour did not hold aloof. This again would make

the position more difficult and precarious and with a watchful opposition backed by a powerful Press might play into the hands of the South African Party and render more probable that party's expectation of getting back to power in a year or two.

5. I now look upon the position from the standpoint of the Nationalist Party and its leader. There are certain things that stand out in the history of the co-operation of the last 18 months.

First there is the thoroughly straight and loyal way they have played the game both inside and outside the House. There has been a real desire to try and meet our point of view in a number of measures which have been before the Parliament. We have no right to put this down to mere electioneering tactics and the fact that they ask us to share the responsibility of the Government, if they do so, will be an assurance of their desire to try and meet us halfway in the future where they can.

Secondly there is the fact that they have, without a doubt, very greatly appreciated finding that there is a large section of the English-speaking people with whom they have been able to co-operate with cordiality and in good faith and this has certainly had an inestimably good effect throughout the country. Their position in the new Parliament, like ours, will be one of great difficulty. They have very little first-hand knowledge of the facts and the problems of industrial life. I express my own conviction, founded on some knowledge, when I say I am very sure that they earnestly desire to do the right thing for the people.

With the difficulties confronting them and although they are anxious, as we are, that the hopes of the people shall not be disappointed and are conscious of the difficulties of steering through a Parliament in which they do not command a majority, should not we, in their place, say something of this kind:

"You people have helped us to get rid of the South African Party. We have shown we want to meet, where we can, your point of view. With the best will in the world we cannot do this as well if you hold aloof as we could if we had on our inner councils representatives of yourselves who had the first-hand knowledge which we have not got."

And should not we start on our job with less cordial feelings and so increase the chances of a breakdown, if the other party just held aloof and said "No. You must take the responsibility and we will look on and criticise".

For all these reasons I am clearly of the opinion that if we are asked to do so on terms that give us sufficient influence, and with the assurance that the main policy and measures of the immediate future are such as we feel we can honestly offer co-operation, it is then our duty, both to the country and to our supporters and ourselves, not to shirk the responsibility but to accept it. In saying this it must of course be understood that the Labour Party must retain its separate and distinct organisation. Indeed, in such circumstances it is more essential that our organisation in the constituencies should be rigorously kept up to full strength.

In conclusion let me say that after having given much thought to the matter I am quite certain that those are entirely wrong who think that by holding aloof they will enable their party to avoid responsibility for unpopular actions by the new Government. The Government will only be kept in power by our support as the balancing factor. The South African Party and its Press will take very good care to keep this fact constantly before the public. And if there is one certain thing, it is this: When the next general election takes place the electors will hold us responsible, by having kept the Government in power, for every unpopular act committed by them.

The difference between holding aloof and being represented in the Government will be that, in the former case we shall be blamed by the public for things we had no opportunity of preventing and that in the latter case we shall have the best chance of using our influence inside to prevent things being done for which, if done, we shall be blamed by the electors.

7

NATIONAL AND SOUTH AFRICAN
PARTY COALITION 1933

DIARY OF GENERAL J. B. M. HERTZOG[1]

MONDAY, 30 JANUARY 1933 Conroy[2] came and told me there was much talk in the Lobbies and that it was his intention to ask me at the caucus meeting next morning whether I could tell the caucus how I felt about the question of co-operation. The next morning, Tuesday 31 January, the Chief Whip Malan came and told me officially of Conroy's intention. At the caucus meeting, therefore, the question was put to me, and my reply in brief, was: I have no doubt, as I have already told my colleagues, that we should not leave unanswered the invitation of Smuts in the Assembly to co-operation, or rather his offer of it, and that I would invite him to a discussion of the question of co-operation to see in how far it was possible, and in the following way. I would, I said, issue a statement of a general nature containing conditions — which I named — which would be an essential basis of any agreement for co-operation in the Cabinet. On publication of the statement I would send a special copy to Smuts and inform him that I sent it in view of his speech in the Assembly and the invitation it contained.[3] I then indicated to the caucus the necessity of not leaving Smuts's invitation unanswered, as otherwise it would later be used against us at the elections and it would be said that we had refused the hand of friendship, and Smuts could not be blamed if he now made common cause with the Natal Devolutionists and Federalists, thus giving the Afrikaans language and Afrikanerdom an irremediable blow. I emphasised that we could not win the next election, relying upon our own strength, as the National Party would have to do in the circumstances, and that by rejecting his offer we would drive Smuts into the arms of these people and of Roos,[4] and they would compel him after the election, as they had already said they would do, to give Natal the necessary measure of federation to banish the Afrikaans language from Natal.

---

[1] Quoted by C. M. van den Heever, *General J. B. M. Hertzog*, Johannesburg, pp. 243-247.
[2] Edwin Conroy, National Party, M.P.
[3] 24 January 1933.
[4] Tielman Roos, former Transvaal Nationalist leader, at this time agitating for a " National Government ".

There was much uneasiness among the members, for apart from the fact that Dr. Malan had made propaganda among them, he made it clear that he was opposed to my view. After talk for and against, the caucus decided — I did not wish to intervene further in the discussion — to ask me to come to the caucus the following week with a " clear proposal ".

In the meantime it was clear to me that, with the obvious division of opinion in the Cabinet and also in the caucus, it would not be advisable for me to comply with this request, and that the time had come for me simply to take action as leader and obey my own feeling that it was desirable in the interests of the party and so fulfil my obligation. It was clear to me that by seeking a decision from the caucus or even from my Nationalist colleagues in the Cabinet, I would give the impression that I wished to shift my responsibility as leader to investigate what might be in the interests of the party on to my fellow-Ministers of the caucus. I decided, therefore, to proceed with the issue of a statement in the spirit indicated and send a copy to Smuts. If Smuts indicated that he wished to discuss it with me, I would meet him, and if it led to anything acceptable in the interests of the party, I would place it before my Nationalist colleagues and also before the caucus, and if there was division in either about accepting what I should recommend, I would appeal to a joint congress of the National Party, to whose decision I would submit — provided, however, that someone else would have to take my place as leader.

I thereupon summoned my Nationalist colleagues, including Dr. Malan, to my office and informed them of my intention and that I would immediately proceed to draw up the necessary statement and would invite them to assist me with their advice.

Tuesday, 7 February — yesterday — I appeared before the caucus and informed them of my decision. I told them that I regarded it as imperative that we should get the co-operation of Smuts and the South African Party and that if we went to the polls on our strength nothing could avert defeat which would in the circumstances be a calamity for us, for Smuts would be compelled to close the breach in his party between the jingo section and the Afrikaner section and would thus be obliged to comply with the demands of the Devolutionists and Federalists of Natal and therefore to sacrifice Afrikanerdom and the Afrikaans language to them. The people would not forgive us for that; therefore I felt that I could not neglect to do my duty merely because Dr. Malan or the caucus might disagree with me. The people would rightly say that I should have appealed to them before deciding to submit the caucus or my colleagues. I therefore felt compelled to act as leader and act as I had indicated.

Great uneasiness — strong opposition, which now and then threatened to become sharp. Dr. Malan addressed the caucus. He was against a statement, no matter how complete, as suggested by me; and was against coalition — for that is what it would be in principle. Our Afrikaans language rights, etc. would suffer thereby.

I informed the caucus that the statement would be given to the Press that afternoon for publication the following morning and that I would send a copy to Smuts.

In the afternoon there was general excitement among members of the Assembly and talk of resignation by Dr. Malan and a break away. Several people came to see me to get information. I pointed out to them that Dr. Malan had no reason to cause a split as nothing would be done before the congress had given its approval to what I might propose in regard to co-operation, and that he, just as much as I, was bound to submit to the decision of the congress.

Wednesday, 15 February. Feeling, I gather, somewhat subsided, but still running high. The statement appeared this morning. Handed Smuts a copy yesterday with a letter. In the afternoon *circa* 6 o'clock I received his answer that he was prepared to discuss the matter.

This morning at 11 o'clock we two met here in my office (in Parliament). The interview very friendly and promising. He handed to me for consideration a typed document containing his statement and consisting as to one section of general principles and as to the second portion of what may be called a programme of action for co-operation. Agreed that Smuts, Duncan,[5] Havenga[6] and I should meet next time — to be fixed by me — for discussion of points. I informed him that whatever we might do would be of provisional nature to be approved eventually by the Party Congress. He was in entire agreement. He hoped, however, that we would conclude negotiations as quickly as possible to avoid undesirable influences as far as possible; and that after the reconstruction of the Cabinet we should proceed at once to an election. At the election each of the parties would retain the seats it had and agreement would be reached about the others. I told him I wished to retain Colonel Creswell in the Cabinet and would like to provide — by ambassadorships *inter alia* — for Ministers who might fall out.

General Smuts's of 14 February read: " I have read the statement sent to me today with your letter. The object of the motion I introduced was the constitution of a Government in which the two parties, after coming to agreement on principles, should participate on a more or less equal basis and in which — although each would retain its identity — they would co-operate cordially on a previously determined basis of national policy. I gather from your statement that its purpose is to prepare the way for the consideraton of such a proposal, and if that is so, I should be glad to discuss the matter with you further."

17 *February.* Smuts and I, supported respectively by Duncan and Havenga, met in my office (Parliament) and discussed my statement and *inter alia* the conditions of co-operation mentioned therein. Everything appeared to go well and to be promising. Some amendments were suggested, viz. in condition (1) that before the words " national principles "

5 Mr. (later Sir) Patrick Duncan, one of the leaders of the South African Party.
6 Mr. N. C. Havenga, Minister of Finance in General Hertzog's Cabinet.

should be inserted the words "South African" and that in condition (2) the last two lines concerning the flag should be reworded so as to include a reference to the Union Jack. Re the clause or condition concerning Native affairs Smuts had serious objections. He did not wish any legislation on this matter to be introduced so long as co-operation lasted. Havenga and I could not agree to this. Smuts also thought the second last paragraph of his typed document on the Provincial Councils should be included in ours. We intimated that we were not unwilling to consider the matter, but that it could not be included in the form he proposed. After one or two small matters, we adjourned.

Monday, 20 February. Met again in my office. Clearly no other obstacle in our way than the condition on Native question. Various amendments suggested, but none acceptable — either to me or to Smuts. We parted feeling that this might prove an insuperable difficulty, as both Havenga and I took the view that we could not jettison this condition. Duncan expressed the hope that we would not allow the matter to suffer shipwreck.

Tuesday, 21 February. Havenga and I again met Smuts and Duncan. Native condition as framed by me aroused serious opposition from Smuts's side. Smuts eventually requested that he and Duncan withdraw to discuss the matter and see if a formula could be found. They withdrew and *circa* 5.30 my secretary brought a draft addendum from Smuts containing a proposed addition to condition (VI) as proposed by me. I discussed it with Havenga, Pirow,[7] Grobler[7] and Kemp.[7] Grobler objected. He feared the non-co-operators among us would represent to the public that we had abandoned finding a solution of the Native problem within a reasonable time. Havenga, Pirow and Kemp were emphatically of my opinion that Grobler's objections were not well founded and that we should not break off negotiations on that account, for there was nothing new in Smuts's proposal but merely a statement of what was implicit in my proposal.

[7] Ministers in General Hertzog's Cabinet.

8

THE UNITED SOUTH AFRICAN NATIONAL PARTY

PROGRAMME OF PRINCIPLES[1]

I. THE PARTY acknowledges the sovereignty and guidance of Almighty God in the destiny of peoples and countries, and desires the development of the people of South Africa along Christian-national lines, without prejudice to the right of the individual citizen to freedom of thought, conscience and religion.

Its object is the development of a predominant sense of South African national unity, based on the equality of the Afrikaans-speaking and English-speaking sections of the community, coupled with the recognition and appreciation by either section of the distinctive cultural heritage of the other.

To this end, it seeks to unite in political co-operation all who, whether hitherto members of the Nationalist or South African Parties, or standing outside of both those parties, are prepared to endorse the party's aims and principles, and to accept in good faith the obligations arising therefrom.

II. The party takes as its starting point the seven points of co-operation between the South African and Nationalist Parties, and on the basis thereof sets forth its aims and principles as follows:

1. *Principles and Spirit of Government*

(*a*) The Government of the country shall be conducted on a basis of South African national principles and in a spirit of South African national independence in harmony with our sovereign independent status, as confirmed by the Statute of Westminster, and the Status of Union Act, 1934.

(*b*) It shall be the aim of the party to ensure, in the Government of the country:

(i) The realisation of the national aspirations and convictions of the people of South Africa, with the motto, " South Africa First ";

(ii) The achievement of full national unity in a spirit of devotion to South Africa, and of mutual confidence and goodwill, as the necessary basis of our spiritual and material welfare;

(iii) The promotion of a healthy feeling of national pride, based on the fullest appreciation of the nation's spiritual and cultural heritage in

---

[1] As adopted by the inaugural congress of the party, 5 December 1934.

all its bearings, and the protection of the rights of every section of the population therein.

2. *Constitutional Position*

(*a*) The unitary basis of a United South Africa shall be maintained intact as laid down in the South Africa Act, and no authority or right in conflict therewith, or capable of being applied in conflict therewith, shall be granted to any province or provinces.

(*b*) The status of the provinces shall be maintained, with the extension, when necessary, and subject to the provisions of sub-section (*a*) hereof, of provincial powers and functions within the framework of the South Africa Act.

(*c*) The maintenance is affirmed of the existing relationship between the Union and the British Commonwealth of Nations and co-operation with its members, subject, however, to there being no derogation from the status of the Union, and no assumption of external obligations in conflict with its interests.

(*d*) While the party stands for the maintenance of the present constitutional position, no one will be denied the right to express his individual opinion about or advocate his honest convictions in connection with any change of our form of Government.

(*e*) Without derogating from the provisions of the Union Flag Act, or from the place therein assigned to the Union Jack, the authority and power of the Union shall continue to be symbolised by our National Flag.

(*f*) The rights and privileges guaranteed to each section of the people by the Constitution shall be impartially maintained and safeguarded.

3. *Equal Language Rights*

Equal language rights in respect of the Afrikaans-speaking and English-speaking sections of the population shall, in practice, in so far as the State is concerned therewith, be exercised and maintained in all respects, and in every part of our national life within the Union.

4. *Agricultural Policy*

(*a*) While the interests of the various sections of the population will all equally enjoy the attention and the care of the Government, the maintenance and welfare of a healthy rural population will be the subject of special effort and application.

(*b*) By the application of a progressive land settlement policy, the establishment on a sound basis of an independent, self-maintaining class of small landowners will be promoted.

5. *Social Policy*

A proper standard of living will be assured to the workers, and the existing " civilised labour " policy will be maintained. The contentment and welfare of the workers will be further promoted by instilling a sense of common interest and mutual goodwill between employer and employee; by stimulating confidence in the Government's impartiality, and in its concern for the interests of the workers; and by improving, wherever practicable, wages and conditions of labour, with a view to the workers' status and standard of living.

6. Native Policy

(a) An earnest endeavour will be made to arrive at a satisfactory solution of the Native question along lines which, without depriving the Native of his right of development, will recognise as paramount the essentials of European civilisation.

(b) It is recognised that a solution of the political aspect of this question on the basis of separate representation of Europeans and Natives, or otherwise, being fundamental in character and not having hitherto been a matter of party division, should as far as possible be sought through agreement and should be left to the free exercise of the discretion of the individual members representing the party in Parliament.

(c) The recognition of the Natives as a permanent portion of the population of South Africa under the Christian trusteeship of the European race is accepted as a fundamental principle of Native policy, together with the definite avoidance of race intermixture, and the promotion of a spirit of goodwill and mutual confidence between the two races as being in the best interests of South Africa.

7. General Economic Policy

(a) The maintenance of confidence in the economic future of the Union will be ensured by the protection of its currency as well as of its capital assets and resources, which serve to promote the progress and development of the land and its people.

(b) The two great primary industries, agriculture and mining, will be recognised as the foundations of the country's permanent welfare, which is to be reinforced by the concurrent development of commerce and manufacturing industry in such manner as will best promote its stability and self-dependence.

(c) A sound and equitable financial policy will be followed, having regard to the necessity for economy in administration, the fair distribution of the burden of taxation, and the application, as far as may be equitable, of the country's wasting assets in such a way as to promote the development of its permanent resources and to ensure its economic stability.

(d) On economic grounds it desires to unite all sections and classes that enjoy the right of existence, into a solid people's union, with a feeling of safety, and in a spirit of mutual trust, solidarity and joint national responsibility.

(e) It therefore endeavours to create such economic circumstances which will ensure to every section a fitting livelihood and that everyone, and particularly the economically weaker sections, shall be protected against any exploitation.

(*f*) In this spirit the party declares itself decidedly against any policy which has for its object the tendency to advance class warfare, or to sacrifice any interests of the people in favour of organised capitalism.

III. For the furtherance and development of its aims and principles the party stands for the following:

1. The just and equitable treatment of all parts of the Union.

2. The maintenance by the State of the principle of the public observance of Sunday as a day of rest, with due regard to the liberty of the individual citizen in the domestic sphere.

3. The recognition of the duty of the State to supervise education in a manner which will ensure a national system, based on sound psychological and educational principles; and the full recognition of the rights of parents, more especially in regard to the moral and religious training of their children.

4. The maintenance of public health and of a high standard of public morality.

5. The encouragement of desirable European immigration with the assurance of equality of treatment in the Union, it being understood that a State-financed system of immigration under existing conditions is not desirable.

6. The protection of the European, the Coloured and the Native population against Asiatic immigration or competition, while recognising and maintaining existing rights of Asiatics born or legally domiciled in the Union.

7. The assurance to all the peoples of South Africa, White, Coloured, and Native of fair and equal justice, of impartial administration, and reasonable opportunities for material and spiritual progress.

8. The maintenance of an adequate system of national defence, conceived with due regard to the status and situation of South Africa, and to its requirements for protection against hostile attack.

IV. Whenever and as often as may be found necessary, the party shall declare and publish a programme of action which shall contain the demands for practical legislation. These demands shall, in so far as principles are connected therewith, rest on the basis of the foregoing clauses, which constitute the political charter of the party.

THE DOMINION PARTY
OF SOUTH AFRICA

PROGRAMME OF PRINCIPLES[1]

T H E   N A M E of the party shall be " The Dominion Party of South Africa."

The party stands for:

1. *Constitutional*

(*a*) The maintenance of the British Empire as a united whole with common aims and interests, and the securing of the Union's part therein with status as a Dominion of the British Crown, with the full measure of self-government provided in the South Africa Act of 1909.

(*b*) Opposing all movements to resolve the component parts of the Empire into Sovereign States.

(*c*) Fostering a policy whereby the Government of the Union in the exercise of its rights and opportunities of advising the Crown on matters of common interest, shall promote community of action throughout the Empire in defence, diplomacy, trade and commerce, and shall frankly accept the obligations as well as the benefits that flow from Empire partnership.

(*d*) Securing throughout the Empire the status of a British subject — that is, a subject of the King of Great Britain and of the Dominions beyond the seas — to each and all who owe allegiance to His Majesty the King.

(*e*) The amending of the Status Act and Seals Act to bring the Constitution of the Union into harmony with the foregoing objects, and to restore the terms and conditions of the Covenant of Union, the South Africa Act of 1909.

2. *Co-operation Within the Empire*

The establishment and maintenance of friendly relations in trade and commerce, and in all matters affecting our common welfare by consultation and co-operation with all Governments in the Empire, and, as a part of this policy, the system of reciprocal Empire preferences, includ-

---

[1] Approved at First Annual Congress, held in Durban, 29 to 31 October 1934. Published as pamphlet.

ing those secured to and granted by the Union, to be expanded. No foreign state to be automatically admitted to the benefits of such preferential system, nor granted subsidies or favoured treatment to the detriment of the mercantile marine of the Empire.

3. *Language Equality*
The preservation of equal language rights as prescribed in the Act of Union, i.e. the right of every South African, including every Government servant, to use either or both official languages at his option, save in so far as the use of the second language is an essential qualification for the work on which he may be engaged.

4. *Governor-General*
The principle that the office of Governor-General should be dissociated from party politics of the Union, and that his appointment should be made by His Majesty the King as part of his personal prerogative.

5. *Defence*
(a) The recognition that the defence of the Union and of its naval and aerial communications, including the maintenance of Simon's Bay as an essential link in such communications, can only effectively be undertaken if it forms part of the larger operations for the defence of the whole Empire.

(b) Collaboration with the Imperial Defence Committee.

(c) An adequate contribution by the Union of South Africa towards the upkeep of the Royal Navy.

6. *Social Policy*
(a) No racial discrimination of any kind between citizens of British and of Dutch descent in South Africa, and a fair treatment shall be accorded to all races and classes in the Union.

(b) An advanced and broad policy of social betterment to secure social justice for all workers, European and non-European.

(c) A scheme of unemployment insurance, the production of more wealth and its wider distribution among all classes by the concentration of national energies on profitable enterprise and the training of all classes for participation therein.

(d) The recognition of the basic right and duty of every South African to earn a living, and the conduct of the country's affairs in such a way that work is available for all.

(e) The recognition of the obligation on the part of the State to secure the provision of sufficient food, clothing and housing for the whole population.

(f) A reduction in the cost of living, and the prevention of artificial scarcity in the necessities of life caused by internal rings and combines, and by the excessive exportations of food products, which increase the burdens of the local consumer.

(g) The immediate and continuous alleviation of unemployment by using every effort to develop industry, including mining, coupled with the restoration to the land of those who have been driven therefrom by economic stress.

(h) The elimination ot slums, with the provision of additional housing accommodation with financial assistance from the State administered through local authorities.

(i) The improvement of old age pensions and better administration of the existing Acts.

(j) The investigation of the position of pensioners' widows who at present are not provided for.

(k) The principle that the welfare of the returned soldier, and of the dependants of those who lose their lives in war shall be a charge on the State.

7. Public and Railway Services

(a) The maintenance of the rights and privileges of public and railway servants.

(b) The right of association and the development of cordial co-operation between service organisations and the Government.

(c) An unceasing struggle against all forms of political favouritism in public service appointments and promotions, and against nepotism and jobbery in these appointments.

(d) The regular periodical publications of all persons appointed to the public service.

(e) The maintenance of a scrupulously non-political Railway Board and Public Service Commission to secure the confidence of all members of the services within their jurisdiction and act in conformity with the provisions of the South Africa Act of 1909.

8. Education

(a) The complete divorce of all political influences from the educational system.

(b) A reform of the education system of the Union with the object of providing methods of education which will more adequately equip all citizens for the work which they may be called upon to render to society.

(c) Closer attention to the needs of the growing child and directing his education to be more in harmony with the needs of current employment.

(d) The provision of an education which will enable the agricultural population to undertake the task of developing agriculture.

(e) The furnishing of more facilities than at present exist for industrial, technical and vocational education.

(f) Adequate salary scales and equitable conditions of employment for all teachers.

9. Rehabilitation of Agriculture

(a) A scientific survey of the agricultural and pastoral possibilities of the country which is necessary for the rehabilitation of the farming community on a sound economic basis and the absorption on the land of many of those who have been driven from it.

(b) Measures of defence against drought in all farming districts and Native areas, including extensive schemes of afforestation in suitable areas, and a general policy of soil and water conservation which will enable the countryside to carry a larger population at a higher standard of living.

(c) Reversal of the present tendency of excessive State interference with agriculture and the encouragement of a greater spirit of self-reliance and independence.

10. *Industrial Policy*

The encouragement of South African industries by means of:

(a) A reasonable customs tariff, with due regard to the interests of the consumers.

(b) The exploration of facilities for encouraging the establishment and development of approved new industrial undertakings.

(c) The stricter supervision of the various determinations of the Wages Act and the more rigid enforcement of penalties for the deliberate evasion thereof, the composition of such Wages Boards to be strictly non-political.

11. *Freedom of Speech*

Complete freedom of speech and of the Press and the strict non-political control of broadcasting.

12. *Asiatics*

(a) The maintenance of restrictions of Asiatic immigration.

(b) Opposition to the further penetration of Asiatics amongst the European and Native population.

(c) The encouragement of repatriation of Asiatics.

(d) Stricter supervision of Asiatics in commerce and industry, especially in regard to wage determinations.

13. *Child Welfare*

The encouragement, co-ordination and proper control of child welfare.

14. *Immigration*

A systematic immigration policy to attract settlers from other portions of the Empire, who by their energy and capital can add to the development of our national resources, and to this end the provision of reduced passages, the selection and training of settlers and facilities for the acquisition of land under the Land Settlement Acts.

15. *Mining Policy*

(a) The completion of the geological and scientific survey of the mineral possibilities of the Union, with a view to rendering assistance to prospectors and others in the discovery and development of fresh sources of supply of precious and base metals.

(*b*) The recognition that the prosperity of the country depends upon the successful carrying on of the mining industry in all its phases, and that further facilities be granted for the opening of new mines by amendment of the law wherever necessary, thus enlarging the scope for additional employment and profitable investment of capital.

(*c*) A more equitable system of mining taxation with the object of encouraging the introduction of new capital.

(*d*) The better regulation and modification of railway rates as applying to all classes of mining, as policy of stimulating greater production and utilising the Union's enormous resources in coal and base metals, and consequently commanding the expansion of markets at present hampered by excessive railway rates.

16. *Provincial System*

(*a*) The maintenance and extension of the rights and powers of the Provincial Councils, and particularly financial rights in conformity with the provisions of the South Africa Act.

(*b*) Encouragement and extensions of local self-government in all its aspects.

17. *Public Transportation*

(*a*) The revision of the control and working of our transportation systems whereby cheap and efficient transport of all classes of goods and passengers can be assured.

(*b*) The elimination of political influence in the practical working of the railways and harbours of the Union, and in the putting into fuller operations of Sections 125, 126 and 127 of the South Africa Act of 1909.

(*c*) The encouragement of effective cheap road motor transport as far as possible by private enterprise regulated in the public interest.

18. *Taxation*

The adoption of a fair, just and impartial scheme of taxation throughout the Union, with due regard to the ability of the individual to pay.

19. *Native Policy*

(*a*) The retention of the Cape Native franchise as provided in the South Africa Act, 1909, until such time as a general and effective policy has been evolved, for the representation of Natives throughout the Union, and subject to prior consultation with the Natives of the Union.

(*b*) The placing of relations between the European and Bantu races on a stable basis which will ensure the predominance of White civilisation in the Union.

(*c*) The raising of the economic condition of the Natives.

(*d*) The training and appointment of administrators and police adequately qualified in Native languages and customs.

8

(*e*) The recognition that the provision of remedies for White unemployment, the prevention of slums in urban areas, the provision of adequate lands for Native occupation and instruction and assistance in the proper use thereof are essential and interdependent questions at the root of the economic relations between the European and Bantu races.

10

THE NATIONAL PARTY
OF SOUTH AFRICA

PROGRAMME[1]

1. *Character and Purpose*

1. The party acknowledges the sovereignty and guidance of God in the destiny of countries and seeks the development of our nation's life along Christian-national lines, with due regard to the individual's freedom of conscience and religion.

2. (*a*) Its purpose is to promote and to safeguard the welfare of South Africa and her people, in so far as this can be done by political means. It therefore seeks to inculcate and foster a vigorous consciousness of national autonomy and independence, as well as a strong sense of national unity. This unity is to be founded on a common and undivided loyalty and devotion to South Africa and her interests, on mutual trust and on the recognition of the equal rights of both Afrikaans- and English-speaking citizens coupled with mutual appreciation of each other's cultural contributions.

(*b*) It stands for the just and equal treatment of all parts of South Africa, and for the impartial maintenance of the rights and privileges of every section of the population.

3. The party strives to realise the national aspirations and convictions of the people of South Africa, under the motto " South Africa first ". It will also promote a healthy national self-respect based on a full appreciation of the spiritual and cultural possessions of the nation in all their various forms, and founded on the protection of the rights of each section of the population.

4. With these objects in view the party seeks to unite in political co-operation all who are prepared to subscribe to its aims and principles and to accept in good faith the obligations arising therefrom, on the understanding that nobody may become a member of the party unless he is willing to put the interests of South Africa in all circumstances above those of his race or his land of extraction or of any other country.

---

[1] Revised programme taken from 1952 Constitution.

II. *Political Status and Future*[2]

5. The party is founded on the unequivocal recognition that South Africa is a sovereign, independent State, which possesses every right, and, on its own authority, can exercise all the functions of a state in the fullest international sense.

6. It undertakes to maintain this independence faithfully and to oppose by every permissible means any interpretation, tendency, action or policy contrary to or threatening such independence, and also to remove any inconsistency hampering the fullest realisation of that independence.

7. It will thus ensure that the Government of the country is carried out on the basis of South African national principles and in the spirit of national autonomy as a free, sovereign and independent nation.

8. The unitary basis of a united South Africa, as laid down in the South Africa Act, will be upheld, and no power or right in conflict with or which can be applied in conflict with that basis will be granted to any province. The party also declares itself in favour of retaining the provincial system, for the present.

9. The party acknowledges without reservation the right of the nation to change its form of Government or State by constitutional means at any time, if it considers it to be in the country's interests.

10. It is convinced that the republican form of state, separated from the British Crown, is the form best adapted to the traditions, circumstances and aspirations of the South African nation, and is also the only effective guarantee that South Africa will not again be drawn into Great Britain's wars.

11. While the party thus declares itself in favour of the attainment of this form of state, it recognises at the same time, however, that a republic can be established only on the broad basis of the national will, and with the faithful observance of the equal language and cultural rights of the two sections of the European population. Accordingly it stipulates that this constitutional change can be brought about only as the result of a special and definite mandate from the European electorate, and not merely by a parliamentary majority obtained as the result of an ordinary election.

---

2 The following new articles were added by the provincial party congresses in 1957; the others were re-numbered:

Art. 8: The party accepts the point of view that South Africa as a sovereign independent state has the status and the right to take the above-named steps whether it is a republic or not and irrespective of whether it is a member of the Commonwealth or not.

Art. 12 (*b*): The party considers that proclamation of a republic and withdrawal from the Commonwealth are two separate questions which need not be answered at the same time, and that in regard to the second question it should be judged and decided at any definite time according to the relative circumstances and South Africa's interests and situation internationally.

III. *National Flag*

12. The party declares emphatically that it views the national flag as the only exclusive symbol of our South African nationhood and of the constitutional authority and power of the Union.

IV. *Economic Independence*

13. The party urges the promotion of South Africa's economic independence and the expansion of her trade relations in all directions, as far as her own interests can be served thereby. It declares itself opposed to any policy or action tending to prevent or retard such development.

V. *Immigration*

14. The party welcomes the strengthening of the European population by the immigration of desirable persons, provided that the interests of the established population are taken into consideration, but it does not favour a system of immigration at State expense. Furthermore it urges that the State should take the necessary steps to ensure that no undesirable person enters the land, and that immigration be limited to those elements which can readily be absorbed by the South African nation and which cannot be considered a burden or danger to the community.

VI. *Equal Language Rights and Co-operation between the European Races*

15. The party desires to foster a spirit of mutual trust and co-operation between the European races. It will thus ensure that equal language rights for the English- and Afrikaans-speaking section of the population are observed in practice and maintained in every way in all spheres of South African national life where the State is concerned or is able to exert influence. The principle of bilingualism will therefore be applied faithfully, not only in the various departments of the Civil Service, but also in all parts of the Provincial Administration and in all public administrative bodies in State or State-aided institutions.

VII. *Relations with the Non-European Races*

16. As a basic principle of its attitude towards Natives and Coloureds the party recognises that both are permanent parts of the country's population, under the Christian trusteeship of the European races. It is strongly opposed to every attempt which might lead to the mixing of European and non-European blood, and strives to cultivate a spirit of goodwill and mutual trust between Europeans and non-Europeans, as being in the best interests of South Africa.

In accordance with this principle it desires to give the non-European races the opportunity to develop themselves, each race in its own field, in both the material and spiritual spheres, in keeping with their natural

97

gifts and abilities. Furthermore the party assures them fair and just treatment under the law and in the administration of the country.

It also declares itself in favour of the territorial and political segregation of the Native, and of separation between Europeans and non-Europeans in general and in the residential and — as far as is practicable — in the industrial spheres. In addition it wishes to protect all groups of the population against Asiatic immigration and competition, among other means by preventing further encroachment on their means of livelihood and by an effective scheme of Asiatic segregation and repatriation.

VIII. *Co-operation Between Employers and Employees*

17. In the economic spheres the party desires to knit together people of all sections and levels having a right of existence so as to provide security and foster a spirit of mutual trust, solidarity and joint national responsibility. It therefore strives to create economic conditions that will ensure a proper livelihood for each section and which will protect all, particularly the economically weaker section, against exploitation in any form. Accordingly the party declares itself emphatically opposed to any politics or policy calculated or tending to promote class strife, or to the sacrificing of any national interest for the benefit of organised money powers.

18. In general the party aims at arousing a true interest in and concern for the interests of the workers, on the part of the Government and the people, with the due consideration for the employers' interests. The worker will be ensured a proper livelihood, and in order to raise his status and standard of living, and to promote his welfare and contentment, the party will endeavour :

(a) to inspire a feeling of community of interests and mutual regard between employer and employee;

(b) to improve wages where necessary, and working conditions so as to give every citizen the opportunity to enter a suitable, satisfying and assured field of work;

(c) to guard workers in South Africa against competition from labour sources outside the country;

(d) to give efficient protection to the civilised worker in general against replacement by uncivilised labour forces, and in particular to protect the European worker from being forced out of the sphere which he is entitled to occupy in view of his position and the standard of living expected of him.

IX. *General Economic and Financial Policy*

19. General.—The two great primary industries, agriculture and the exploitation of the mineral resources of South Africa, are recognised as the foundation of the country's lasting material welfare. This welfare should also be promoted by an accompanying development of commerce

and secondary industry such as to perpetuate the progress and independence of the land.

X. *Agriculture*

20. While the interests of the different sections of the nation will all enjoy equal attention and care from the Government, the existence and welfare of the rural population will be the object of particular endeavour and concern. The application of a progressive settlement policy will aid the healthy introduction of an independent and self-sufficient class of small landowners. The party envisages an independent and prosperous farming community and thus urges powerful State encouragement and support for the agricultural industry in all spheres, among other means, by satisfactory protection against foreign competition and against exploitation by the middleman, as well as by an efficient system of marketing, farming, credit and agricultural education.

XI. *Mining and General Industry*

21. The Mining Industry.—The party desires to encourage the exploitation of our mineral resources in every way, with due consideration for the welfare of the worker and for the State's claims to its rightful share in the country's mineral wealth.

22. Secondary Industries.—The party wishes to encourage the vigorous growth of all secondary industries capable of sound progress, among other means by providing satisfactory protection, taking into consideration the interests of the domestic consumer, by an efficient credit system, and by internal and external marketing.

23. Financial Policy.—The maintenance of confidence in South Africa's economic future will be guaranteed by the protection of its finances as well as of the capital assets and resources which aid the progress and development of the country and its people. A healthy and just financial policy, that will take into account the necessity for thrift in the administration, will be pursued. This will be accompanied by a fair division of the burden of taxation, and the employment — as far as possible and in accordance with circumstances — of the country's temporary assets so that they will serve to develop its permanent resources and perpetuate its economic stability.

XII. *Education*

24. The party considers it the duty of the authorities to supervise education and ensure that every child receives instruction in accordance with its talents and opportunities, and based on healthy educational and national principles. It thus urges that in carrying out this duty the Christian-national basis of the State should be taken fully into account, as well as the right of the parent to determine in which direction such education should be given as regards the ethical and religious development of the child.

XIII. *National Health*

25. The party envisages the introduction of a comprehensive and efficient system for the protection and advancement of the nation's health.

XIV. *Public Morality*

26. The party recognises the duty of the authorities to respect and preserve the Sunday as a day of rest in the public sphere, to oppose all unchristian practices in the national life, and to maintain a high moral code, at the same time taking into consideration the freedom of the individual citizen in his own sphere.

XV. *Defence*

27. The party envisages the maintenance of an adequate system of national defence, drawn up in accordance with the independent status and position of South Africa and with its need for protection against enemy attacks.

XVI. *Application of Principles*

28 In order to apply and defend these principles in practice, among other means by legislation and at election time, the party maintains itself as an independent political group, organised on a federal basis, and will determine its programme of action from time to time on the basis of its programme of principles. The programme of action must not conflict with any of these principles.

XVII. *Alteration of Principles*

29. This programme of principles contains the common principle of the National Party organisations in South Africa which have joined the Federal Party, and is not to be altered by their congresses except in consultation with one another through the medium of the Federal Council.

11

THE UNION FEDERAL PARTY

PROGRAMME[1]

1. *National Aim*

To create in South Africa opportunities for people of all races to enjoy fullness of life and liberty under the protection of the law, to enable our country to play an honourable and constructive part in world affairs and to promote Western Civilisation among the peoples of South Africa.

II. *The United States of Southern Africa*

A long-term policy for Southern Africa is essential.

We shall seek ultimately to provide a Constitutional structure and way of life acceptable to neighbouring states, colonies and protectorates as a basis for a future Federal Union of the States and Territories of Southern Africa.

III. *To Reshape within the Act of Union the Present quasi-Unitary System to one of Federal Union*

To entrench the material elements of the contract of Union and, within that framework, to reshape the present quasi-Unitary system to one of Federal Union by redistribution of powers from the Central to Provincial Governments, giving a far greater measure of autonomy to the Provinces, especially in matters which directly concern the life of the citizen, the general principle of which found an earlier expression in the Hollander Memorandum.

IV. *The Right of Provinces in given circumstances to determine their own futures*

We shall work for the maintenance and assertion of the right of the people of any Province of the Union, in the face of any actual, attempted or projected violation of the letter or the spirit of the Constitution, to remain a part of the Commonwealth of Nations under the Crown; a Province so as to act in the following amongst other eventualities: A weakening of our allegiance to the Crown; the setting aside of the Entrenched Clauses; the denial of the testing power of the Courts; the abolition of the Provincial Council system or the reduction of Provincial powers; the

[1] The *Natal Mercury*, 11 May 1953.

101

abolition of full protection or of recognition of the equal rights of both official languages.

V. *The State and the Citizen*

The maintenance of a Western democratic form of Government and of Parliamentary institutions; the protection of the basic liberties of the people and the freedom of the individual, and of his right to appeal to the Courts against any arbitrary act of the Executive; the retention by Parliament of direct control over, and the limitation of the Executive's powers; the elimination of all forces of totalitarianism whether Fascist or Communist.

VI. *Racial Accord*

The promotion of racial accord among Europeans with unyielding resistance against any attempt at the domination of one group by the other.

Racial harmony between European and non-European is as essential as that between European and European; a progressive rather than repressive non-European policy in line with Western traditions and Christian teachings on race relationships.

VII. *Non-European Policy*

The abandonment of fear as the guiding principle, and the adoption in its place of courageous policies, offers the only hope in the field of non-European affairs. The policies that have so far been pursued hold out no genuine prospect of permanently peaceful relationships among the peoples of South Africa.

We believe that the immediate aim in the field of non-European affairs should be the rapid improvement of living conditions, welfare services, education, and economic opportunities; thus striking at the roots of crime, disease and political discontent.

We adhere to the principle that the franchise already extended to the non-European should in no way be curtailed or by any means rendered less effectual. The South African-born non-European should be accorded a right of expression in the organs of Government, commensurate with his degree of civilisation, as follows:

(*a*) The present system of limited group representation of Natives to be maintained and an interim period of group representation of Indians on a system similar to that accorded to Natives to be initiated.

(*b*) Subject always to due safeguards against disproportionate representation of any one section of the non-European population, the long-term policy to be taken in steps over a considerable period of years, is the ultimate placing of those non-Europeans who have passed suitable tests of a high standard, upon the common roll of voters.

We recognise the fact of increasing economic integration of the non-European peoples in the economy of South Africa.

We accept the desirability of residential and social segregation between Europeans and non-Europeans, to be obtained on a fair and equitable basis and wherever possible by the encouragement of voluntary population movements through housing and town planning schemes designed to that end and to the establishment of the foundations of a sound family life.

We believe that those Natives who have attained a high degree of civilisation should be entitled to exemption from those laws designed for the protection of backward peoples.

We stand for the recognition of all South African-born people, Coloureds, Bantu and Indians, as members of the greater South African community.

12

THE LIBERAL PARTY OF SOUTH AFRICA

PROGRAMME[1]

1. The name of the party is the Liberal Party of South Africa.

II. *Principles*

(i) The essential dignity of every human being irrespective of race, colour or creed, and the maintenance of his fundamental rights.

(ii) The right of every human being to develop to the fullest extent of which he is capable consistent with the rights of others.

(iii) The maintenance of the rule of law.

(iv) That no person be debarred from participating in the Government and other democratic processes of the country by reason only of race, colour or creed.

III. *Objects*

(i) Equal political rights based on a common franchise roll.

(ii) Freedom of worship, expression, movement, assembly and association.

(iii) The right to acquire and use skills and to seek employment freely.

(iv) Access to an independent judiciary.

(v) The application equally to all sections of the population of the principle of compulsory, State-sponsored education.

(vi) The right to own and occupy immovable property.

(vii) The right to organise trade unions and other economic groups and associations.

The party will employ only democratic and constitutional means to achieve the foregoing objects, and is opposed to all forms of totalitarianism such as communism and fascism.

---

[1] Taken from the Policies of the Liberal Party of South Africa, issued as a pamphlet, Cape Town, 1955.

13

THE PROGRESSIVE PARTY
OF SOUTH AFRICA

PROGRAMME[1]

1. The maintenance and extension of the values of Western Civilisation, the protection of fundamental human rights and the safeguard of the dignity and worth of the human person, irrespective of race, colour or creed.

2. The assurance that no citizen of the Union of South Africa shall be debarred on grounds of race, religion, language or sex, from making the contribution to our national life of which he or she may be capable.

3. The recognition that in the Union of South Africa there is one nation which embraces various groups differing in race, religions, language and traditions; that each such group is entitled to the protection of these things and to participate in the government of the nation; and that understanding, tolerance and goodwill between the different groups must be fostered.

4. The maintenance inviolate of the Rule of Law.

5. The promotion of social progress and the improvement of living standards through the energetic development of a modern economy based on free enterprise, whereby the national resources of men and materials can be fully utilised.

6. The promotion of friendly relations with other nations, more particularly the members of the Commonwealth and those who share with us the heritage of Western Civilisation.

Constitution and Franchise Proposals

The party regards our present flexible, highly centralised Constitution as entirely unsuited to South Africa, whose inhabitants comprise a plural society consisting of several racial communities. A Constitution of this kind may work well enough in a homogeneous society such as that of Great Britain in which deep-rooted constitutional conventions operate; but in a plural society such as ours it enables any group which happens, for the time being, to command a Parliamentary majority to dominate and to exercise unchecked power over the others. This inevitably causes,

[1] Main principles and policies adopted at inaugural congress 13-14 November 1959, Johannesburg. Issued by the Party's Public Relations and Publicity Department, Johannesburg.

among the subject communities, growing frustration and hostility which threaten the very existence of civilised society in South Africa.

The party is, therefore, profoundly convinced of the need for a reformed Constitution, which will contain adequate safeguards for each of our racial communities against domination by any other, will accord to each a share in government, will guarantee the fundamental human rights and liberties of the individual, irrespective of race or colour, and will decentralise legislative and executive power in the interests of a reasonable degree of provincial and local self-government.

Regarding such a reformed Constitution as alone capable of providing a political framework for inter-racial co-operation, Congress states its achievement to be a major objective of Progressive Party policy, and requests the National Executive to appoint a commission of experts to consider and report upon detailed proposals for such a reform along lines best calculated to achieve the following aims:

(1) To establish conditions which will enable the peoples of South Africa to live as one nation in accordance with the values and concepts of Western Civilisation.

(2) To enable suitably qualified citizens of a defined degree of civilisation belonging to any population group to participate in the government of the country, according to their ability to assume responsibility, through the holding of public office and through registration on a common electoral roll for election of members of the House of Assembly, with special provision for the representation of persons not so qualified.

(3) To provide constitutional safeguards through a reform of the Senate and/or otherwise to prevent the exercise of unchecked power in order to dominate any other group, White or non-White.

(4) To decentralise legislative and executive power by devolving on the existing provinces, or any other provinces into which the Union may in future be delimited, and any additional provinces, comprised of neighbouring territories that may in future join the Union, such powers or functions as need not be exercised by the central Parliament and Government in the interests of the peace, safety and welfare of the Union as a whole. The Commission to consider in this connection:

(a) the form, generally, of the government of the provinces;

(b) the effective protection within the provinces of the rights of racial groups;

(c) the financial relations between the central government and the provinces.

(5) To guarantee, by inclusion in the Constitution of an entrenched Bill of Rights, the fundamental human rights and liberties of the individual, such as freedom of religion, speech and association, equal protection of the laws, and also the equal status of the official languages.

(6) To ensure the maintenance in South Africa of an independent and learned judiciary, impartial justice and the rule of law.

The party further urges that the Commission have due regard for the necessity for obtaining the widest possible degree of national acceptance of the proposed reformed Constitution, and therefore requests that it make recommendations in regard to the summoning by a future Progressive Government of a National Convention, representative of all racial communities, to consider proposals for constitutional reform and to recommend to Parliament, for enactment by it, a reformed Constitution for South Africa.

Economic and Labour Policy

We stand for the energetic development of a modern economy based on free enterprise.

Economic and Labour Policy should be directed to the conquest of poverty by increasing the National Income, maintaining a high and stable level of employment and hence improving the living standards of all sections of the population. To this end, a positive programme to ensure the fullest utilisation of our human and material resources should be undertaken. This envisages—

(1) The expansion of the home market by increasing the productivity and purchasing power of all workers.

(2) The expansion of the export market through the lower costs consequent upon such increased productivity.

(3) That the State will supplement the activities of private enterprise by undertaking such public works as are necessary to maintain a high level of employment and will encourage the development of a rapidly expanding economy by providing basic services which private enterprise cannot supply, e.g. soil reclamation, water conservation, electricity and other power, certain transport services, scientific and technological research facilities.

(4) Anti-cyclical budgeting and the determination of financial, monetary and fiscal policy to maintain a high level of employment and to encourage the maximum flow of investment capital from both local and overseas sources.

(5) The encouragement of industrial development by reasonable protection of economic and potentially economic industries, especially against unfair competition from countries where the standard of living is lower than in the Union.

(6) The recognition that while the decentralisation of industry may be a desirable aim under certain circumstances, the location of industries should be determined predominantly by economic considerations, with due regard for the needs of areas where the gold mining industry is declining.

Note: We believe that the full economic development of the Union can be achieved only if our country is regarded as a single interdependent economy. We recognise, however, that special measures will have to be taken in attacking the economic problems of the underdeveloped areas.

(7) The removal of restrictions which prevent the free mobility of labour and the establishment of a nation-wide network of labour exchanges operating on a voluntary basis.

(8) The development of a stabilised urban labour force which can develop into a responsible urban non-White middle class and of a settled agricultural labour force.

(9) The provision of adequate facilities for the education and technical training of industrial and agricultural workers of all racial groups to enable them to undertake more skilled occupations.

(10) The repeal of the job reservation provisions of the Industrial Conciliation Act and the institution of an enquiry, with a view to lifting other restrictions which prevent the employment of non-Whites in certain occupations. Such relaxation would allow industry to take full advantage of technological changes while the opening up of employment opportunities for non-White workers with the subsequent expansion of the demand for goods and services of all kinds must redound to the benefit of all sections of the community.

(11) The protection of wage standards by the implementation of the "rate for the job" principle, irrespective of colour or sex. No undercutting of wage rates by workers prepared to subsist at lower standards will be permitted.

(12) The restoration of the freedom of the trade unions; the inclusion of skilled and semi-skilled Africans in the definition of " employee " in the Industrial Conciliation Act; and the recognition of Trade Unions established for unskilled African workers under the control and guidance of the Department of Labour, until such workers have learned to undertake the responsibilities of collective bargaining.

(13) The institution of a comprehensive enquiry into the family cost-of-living position of the lower income groups, with a view to the introduction in any area or region of a minimum unskilled wage below which no person should be employed, allowance being made for wages in kind.

(14) The extension of the range of social security benefits to provide adequate protection to workers, particularly to the lower income groups.

(15) That we hold it to be the business of government to steer the economy between the twin dangers of inflation and deflation. Heretofore South African governments appear to have known no cure for the one save the evils of the other. We believe that success in this task of achieving buoyancy with stability is essential if an economy based on free enterprise is to function in the national interest.

108

(16) Finally, that only by co-operating in the economic field with other territories in Africa and by fostering closer economic ties with our neighbours can isolation and poverty for all be avoided.

The Urban African

(1) Recognition of the permanence of urban African communities.

(2) Discouragement of the migratory labour system and the creation of a settled, stable urban and rural population living under normal family conditions.

(3) Abolition of the pass laws and influx control, accompanied by provisions such as housing, labour bureaux and other measures designed to improve the economic and social conditions and consequently the stability of the African urban and rural population.

Resolution on Identification of Citizens

The policy of the Progressive Party is to repeal the existing Population Registration Act and to institute a simple and equitable system of identification applicable to individuals of all races.

The Social, Residential and Amenity Aspects

The party accepts that economic integration is an established and permanent fact. It regards this as being in the interests of all the people of this country. It recognises, however, the social conventions which have grown up in South Africa over a long period and respects the desire of individuals to reside among and associate with people of their own race. It will not, therefore, force residential or social integration upon anyone, but equally it will not deprive people of different races of their freedom of association.

In accordance with its principles, the party will:

(1) Repeal the Group Areas Act, and amend or repeal other relevant Acts.

(2) Allow persons of any race to acquire and occupy for industrial and commercial purposes, property which has been zoned for these purposes.

(3) Make provision for the members of the different race groups to realise their desire to live amongst their own people.

(4) Allow freehold title to all.

(5) Prohibit the compulsory removal of individuals or groups on racial grounds.

(6) Recognise the right of individuals to freedom of association, and rescind laws limiting participation in Churches, Universities, professional trade and other voluntary associations to members of one particular race group.

(7) Meet the reasonable wishes and needs of the different race groups for the provision of separate amenities or services.

109

9

The Republic

The party believes that the interests of South Africa demand internal peace and external security, and that both would be gravely endangered by a republic such as envisaged by the Nationalist Government. Congress is, therefore, resolutely opposed to such a change, and the party will accordingly campaign against it.

Only when internal peace is guaranteed through a constitution which protects the traditions, language, culture, way of life and share in government of all sections of our population, and only when external security is protected through ensured membership of the Commonwealth, in which South Africa should play a positive and responsible part, can a change to republicanism be considered without real danger to South Africa.

When these conditions are fulfilled, and if the matter is then still an issue in South Africa, it will have become one of preference, rather than principle and, at that stage, the people of South Africa should choose the form of government which they prefer. No change of this kind should be made, however, without the assent of a substantial majority of the electorate at a referendum of all registered voters.

Education Policy

The party, believing as it does in the maintenance and extension of Western Civilisation, has as the objects of its education policy the following:

(a) the fostering amongst all the citizens of South Africa an appreciation of the basic tenets of that civilisation;

(b) the development of the individual to the full extent of his capacity in order that he make the maximum contribution to his own welfare and to the nation to which he belongs;

(c) the promotion in the children of each group of an understanding and appreciation of the cultures, traditions, backgrounds and aspirations of the other groups, thereby fostering better relationships amongst the people of South Africa.

Availability and Type of Education

Acknowledging education to be one of the most important factors in the life of the nation, the party will strive to ensure that education of the highest possible standard will be made available to all in South Africa.

The aim of the party will be:

(1) to provide adequate facilities for free primary and secondary schooling;

(2) to extend progressively the provisions for compulsory school attendance as the facilities become available;

(3) to ensure that technical or University education will be available to those who would profit from such education. Provision will be made for bursaries or loans for deserving students to assist them to attend such institutions for higher education.

While the party will make provision for separate schools for the children of the various racial groups, it believes that there should be no basic difference in the type of education which will be received by those groups comprising our population. Education should, at all times, be free from party political bias.

Parental Choice and Type of School

The party recognises the fundamental right of the parent to determine the medium of instruction of his child.

While not derogating from the right of the parent, whenever it is practicable to select the type of school in which his child should be educated, the party will encourage the establishment of parallel and dual-medium schools.

The party acknowledges the valuable contribution that private schools have made to education in South Africa and it will assist such schools to fulfil the important role they have to play in our educational system.

Control of Education

While making provision for the maximum degree of consultation and co-operation between the various authorities responsible for education, the party is convinced that the interests of primary and secondary education can best be served by making such education the responsibility of the Provinces of the Union. The party will repeal the Bantu Education Act and the " University Apartheid " Act.

Teachers

Recognising the necessity for an adequate number of suitably trained teachers, the party will:
(1) ensure that adequate facilities are provided for the training of teachers;
(2) raise the prestige, status and economic position of the teaching profession, thereby encouraging a greater number of suitable persons to take up teaching as a career.

Universities

The party recognises the right of the Universities in South Africa, although assisted financially by the State, to full academic autonomy.

Freedom of Conscience

All Professors and lecturing staff at our Universities and all teachers at State schools, shall enjoy complete freedom of conscience.

SECTION III

THE DEVELOPMENT OF CONSTITUTIONAL INDEPENDENCE AND THE SYMBOLS OF NATIONHOOD

1

SMUTS'S HIGHER STATUS

MR. TIELMAN ROOS[1]

THE PRIME MINISTER had spoken of the British Empire consisting of free sovereign States. Would anybody dare to say, asked Mr. Roos, that Imperial statutes had no binding force upon the Union of South Africa? If they had any binding force, it was untrue to say that the Empire consisted of free States. He would ask the Prime Minister, when he replied, to tell this House whether Imperial statutes had any binding force whatever in the Dominion of South Africa. If he ventured to tell the House that they had no binding force, then they would know that, as far as he (General Smuts) was concerned at all events, he believed in the doctrine which he preached. Another development which would flow from that would be that, without the consent of this Union, no Imperial Garrison could be sent to South Africa. He (Mr. Roos) admitted that under the Constitution there was nothing to prevent an Imperial Garrison from being sent to South Africa, but there was everything to prevent it if the British Empire consisted of absolutely equal sovereign States. " We were determined to see," the Prime Minister had said, " that that recognition was given to us, but we were equally anxious to see that nothing was done which would loosen the ties which bind together the British Empire." If, Mr. Roos argued, we were a sovereign State in the same sense in which the United Kingdom was a sovereign State, if we must only answer for our deeds to the League of Nations, then that meant that the British Empire was to a very large extent dissolved. His contention was that nothing had happened to change the relations of the different Dominions to the United Kingdom, and that all these fine-sounding phrases were meaningless.

The Union Parliament was not able to pass laws repugnant to Imperial statutes. Had the right of the Imperial Parliament to pass legislation affecting South Africa been repealed? Such doctrines as had been enunciated in the House were dangerous to inculcate in South Africa unless they were true. Were Imperial statutes not in force today in South Africa? Supposing, went on Mr. Roos, all the Dominions excepting South Africa ratified the Peace Treaty, would the Treaty then not be ratified? South Africa

---

[1] Speech by Mr. Roos (National Party). This, and the following three are extracts from speeches held in the House of Assembly during the debate on the ratification of the peace treaty of 1919. The *Cape Times*, 9-11 September 1919.

did not come into the Treaty as a sovereign State, but only as an entity of the British Empire. South Africa never made war and could not make peace. None of our puny efforts would be able to let us say that we were at war when the Empire was at peace. He cordially accepted the principle of the League of Nations, but South Africa was not a separate member of the League but only as a member of the British Empire, for only self-governing and fully independent countries could become members of the League. The statement that South Africa was fully independent was caused by the looseness of the language used by General Smuts. There was one point he (Mr. Roos) was prepared to state which might be of very great value as regards the future of South Africa. If a sufficient number of important people asserted that a thing was a custom of the British constitution, that change in the constitution might follow these statements, but we could not become independent off-hand by the statement of any statesman, however important he might be. He would vote against the Peace Treaty with the greatest of pleasure, although he did not think his vote or the vote of that House would make any difference whatever.

DR. D. F. MALAN[2]

DR. MALAN went on to deal with the status of the Union, and said it was not at all clear to him that a change had taken place in that status. The Union's status could have been made clear if it had been laid down that every nation forming the League must have a certain status.

The League of Nations had not laid it down that only independent self-governing countries could be members. In fact, a country like India, without even a responsible government of its own, was admitted as a member. That reminded him of the well-known saying that the existence of bad coin depreciated the value of all coin. Thus the admission of countries like India depreciated the value of the membership of other countries. Possibly admission to the League meant the eventual absolute freedom and independence of all members.

It was not clear to him at all, however, that all members of the League had the right in international affairs to vote as they pleased, even independent of Britain. As matters stood, however, it would appear to him that the name of Britain being mentioned as a unit, the stamp of dependence was for ever placed on the Dominions. The document before the House said that at the Conference the King was represented by General Smuts on behalf of South Africa, by Mr. Hughes on behalf of Australia, etc., but it said that Mr. Lloyd George and Mr. Bonar Law represented Britain and the Dominions across the sea, not the United Kingdom. It did not seem to him that the status of the Union was any higher than before. All that had occurred was that the Government of Britain had

2 National Party.

agreed that the Dominions should be consulted, but in the League of Nations the Empire was as one whole. Consultation was all very well; but it also meant placing all kinds of responsibilities and burdens on the Dominions. If South Africa's status had been raised, it should be made clear that they had been given the right of self-determination. He asked the Prime Minister definitely to reply to the question whether, seeing that England had the right to divest herself of the Colonies, the Dominions had also by the vote of the majority the right to separate from England? Only if that were so could they call themselves Sister States on a footing of equality.

GENERAL J. B. M. HERTZOG[3]

R EGARDING the higher status which they were told that South Africa had achieved, Mr. (*sic*) Hertzog asked why there was this mystery about the matter. Surely the higher status did not lie solely in the honour which Ministers had had of signing the Peace Treaty. It undoubtedly had been a great honour to those Ministers — but what of South Africa? General Smuts had spoken of South Africa's status of equality with Britain. Did it mean that South Africa stood on a basis of absolute equality with Britain, that both had a common King? All the people wanted to know was not how great was our status, but how great was our freedom. He asked for a clear reply as to what South Africa had been given, and he repeated his request of eight years ago that the Minister should not continue on his course of deception and misleading — why should the people continually be kept in ignorance? He asked the Minister to give a clear reply: had South Africa the right to decide its own destiny just as England had that right?

The Minister should not speak in parables, he should make clear what he meant. By his present actions he was making South Africa suspicious and creating the impression that Dutch South Africa was trying to deceive English South Africa. It was owing to Ministers not playing openly and not laying their cards on the table that suspicions had been created, and that suspicion had been passed on to the Nationalist Party.

Mr. Hertzog proceeded to say that he did not propose making any personal attacks — although he realised that there were many members behind the Prime Minister who felt hurt at whatever he said, feeling the false position in which they found themselves.

Dealing with the reply given by Mr. Lloyd George to the Nationalist deputation, Mr. Hertzog said that Mr. Lloyd George had stated that in 1908 the Free State had had the right to become free again and declare itself free. Instead of doing so, however, the Free State had entered Union. In regard to the objections of other nations to the Dominions of the Empire joining the League of Nations, Mr. Hertzog said that objection was not to South Africa or the Dominions being free, but their

[3] Leader of the National Party Opposition.

117

objection was that the Dominions should be members if they were not free, if they were dependents of Britain. General Smuts dare not say, he challenged him to say that South Africa was free to get away from Britain if it so desired. He (Mr. Hertzog) asked General Smuts to say exactly what our freedom meant; he asked him to play his cards openly, and only then would the suspicion disappear.

Mr. Hertzog went on to express gratification that neither he nor his party had had anything to do with the war or its fruits. He felt convinced, however, that the freedom of South Africa as it existed before 1914 was done with. South Africa would be inveigled into all kinds of European difficulties, but the people would not rest until all the rights which stood to be sacrificed today had been restored.

GENERAL J. C. SMUTS[4]

THERE WAS no misconception among British statesmen as to what the position was and it was on that basis that matters had been agreed to in Paris. Regarding the League of Nations, General Smuts said a question had been put whether South Africa had exactly the same advice and the same representation on the League of Nations as Britain. The question was in the affirmative absolutely and independently of England, and he hoped it would not take many months ere South Africa's representation on the League would be announced. It was incorrect to say that in the League the Empire was regarded as a unit. The Empire was regarded as a group, but South Africa had exactly the same rights and voice as England, although England was a permanent member of the Central Council. At the same time South Africa could be elected to the Central Council. For that they had to fight hard, as it was considered by other countries that the day might come when one of the Dominions would be so elected and that England would then have two votes.

On the question whether South Africa could, if so pleased, separate from the British Empire, General Smuts said that question in regard to South Africa's self-determination had been put to Mr. Lloyd George, who had replied[5] that the Union of South Africa rested on a great pact which could not be disturbed by the one-sided decision of one party to the pact. General Smuts quoted from Mr. Lloyd George's reply to the Nationalist deputation, that the disruption of the Union could not be agreed to. He

---

[4] Prime Minister and leader of the South African Party.

[5] Letter to General Hertzog dated 5 June 1919, extract from which reads: "*Finally I would point to the status which South Africa now occupies in the world. It is surely no mean one. As one of the Dominions of the British Commonwealth the South African people control their own national destiny in the fullest sense. In regard to the common Imperial concerns, they participate in the deliberations, which determine Imperial policy, on a basis of complete equality.*" (Quoted by Dr. D. F. Malan in *Afrikaner-Volkseenheid*, pp. 62-63.)

believed that Mr. Hertzog and his co-deputants had rendered a great service to South Africa in getting that reply from Mr. Lloyd George. General Smuts quoted further from the reply of Mr. Lloyd George against any sectional choice for disruption. Mr. Hertzog had addressed his query to the highest authority, where he had received his reply.

Constitutionally, the Union Parliament was the legislative power for the Union, and the doctrine that the British Parliament was the sovereign legislative power for the Empire no longer held good. The question whether the British Parliament could bind the Union by any laws it passed could easily be answered. The British Parliament could, without the consent of the Union Parliament, not pass any law binding South Africa, without a revolution.

MR. ROOS: Would it be legal?

GENERAL SMUTS: "It would be unconstitutional." That was the position which would be recognised by any authority. The Union Parliament was the only legislative power, as regarded South Africa, and no other body could pass laws for South Africa without South Africa's consent, without causing a revolution. As regarded the question of status, General Smuts said that until last year British Ministers had signed all documents and dealt with all matters affecting the Dominions. But a change had come about in Paris, when representatives of the Dominions had, on behalf of the King, for the first time signed that great document on behalf of the Dominions. The change was that in future the representatives of the Dominions would act for the Dominions. This precedent had now been laid down for the future. The British Constitution was most elastic and the precedent might bring about the greatest changes. Where in the past a British Minister could have acted for the Dominions, in future Ministers of the Union would act for the Union. The change was a far-reaching one which would alter the whole basis of the British Empire. In future all parts of the British Empire stood on exactly the same basis. (General Hertzog: In the past you would have been put in prison for saying that.)

General Smuts, continuing his speech in reply to the debate, said that great self-governing Dominions had of late years received greater and greater legislative powers, so much so that if the British Parliament were today to pass legislation in regard to the Dominions it would be a revolutionary action. He had explained on the previous day that as the result of the Conference in Paris the Dominions in future would in regard to foreign affairs, deal through their own representatives. The Dominions of the Empire would in future, therefore, stand on a basis of absolute equality. The British Empire would, therefore, be a league in which all the Dominions would be on an equal basis as regarded their Governments. The Prime Minister repeated that in the League of Nations all the Dominions, with England, would stand on an equal footing, and would be recognised as such. The only difference would be that England would be a permanent member of the Central Council. Therefore in future all parts of the Empire would equally be consulted in matters of war and peace.

If a farce was being enacted in this House of Parliament then the same farce was being enacted in the British House of Parliament and in the Houses of the various Dominions. He could quite understand why General Hertzog did not appreciate that position which had been arrived at in Paris and he could sympathise with his nervousness that he (the Prime Minister) might be arrested by his colleague the Minister of Justice. He would have thought that General Hertzog and his friends would have rejoiced at the new status which had been arrived at. The allegations of misleading and deception were totally unfounded and were unworthy of this House. Why, asked the Prime Minister, was there this feeling of distrust? It was because among one party there was an absolute obsession as to this complete secession. He would not go any further on that point. The word secession was an evil thing. They knew what it had led to elsewhere. They knew how in America millions of lives had been sacrificed on the altar of secession.

For South Africa there were two courses open — one a course of upbuilding and mutual co-operation. That was the course on which they were today. The other course was the one on which they had travelled in the past — the course of blood and tears. He had for three years fought for the cause of the republics — he had fought from the one corner of South Africa to the other for that cause. That was in the days when the greatest shouters of secession today were nowhere to be found. That was in the days in which the republics had done their utmost for their cause. What had that great struggle led to? It had led to Vereeniging, and by the decision arrived at at Vereeniging they wished to stand.

" We did our duty in those days and we wish to stand by our word of honour," continued the Prime Minister. " Had we not done our duty in these days we might want to have another try. The path of secession is a path which must lead to a broken South Africa, a discredited South Africa, with the Native population outnumbering the White population. Only along the road of co-operation can we hope to continue our present course of progress, honour and prosperity. Along that course there lies a great future for us. Along the other we can hope for nothing but misery."

Proceeding, General Smuts drew an analogy between the two deputations which had gone to Europe from South Africa. The one deputation had gone with the instructions and authority of this House. The results of the actions of that deputation were recorded in the annals of history. The results of that deputation were that South Africa today stood on a footing of equality with the other nations of the world. What had the other deputation led to — the secession deputation? It had led to Mr. Lloyd George's reply, which hon. members were acquainted with. He held that the secession movement had led to nothing but misery and bitterness in South Africa. It was due to that movement that his words of peace and conciliation had been received with bitterness and distrust.

120

2

TITLES AND HONOURS IN
SOUTH AFRICA

Mr. Arthur Barlow (Labour Party): I move[1]—

That in the opinion of this House an address should be presented to His Most Excellent Majesty the King in the following words:

" To the King's Most Excellent Majesty.

Most Gracious Sovereign.

We, your Majesty's most dutiful and loyal subjects, the House of Assembly of the Union of South Africa in Parliament assembled, humbly approach your Majesty praying that your Majesty hereafter may be graciously pleased to refrain from conferring any titles upon your subjects domiciled or living in the Union of South Africa or the mandated territory of South West Africa.

*

Mr. Speaker read a letter[2] from His Excellency the Governor-General as follows:

" Governor-General's Office,
Cape Town,
6 July 1925.

The Hon. the Speaker of the House of Assembly,
Cape Town.

Sir,

I have to inform you that the Address of 26 February from the House of Assembly regarding the grant of titles to British subjects domiciled or living in the Union of South Africa or in South West Africa has been laid before His Majesty the King, who was pleased to receive it very graciously.

I am, Sir, your obedient servant,
Athlone, Governor-General."

[1] House of Assembly, Debates, 24 February 1925. Motion adopted after debate by majority of 71 to 47, 26 February 1925.
[2] House of Assembly, 7 July 1925.

3

SOUTH AFRICAN NATIONALITY AND FLAG

DR. D. F. MALAN, 25 MAY 1926[1]

THE BILL is certainly — and I say this without fear of contradiction — the most important Bill which has been introduced into this House for many a year. At the same time, in spite of what has been said to the contrary, or might be said to the contrary, I consider it to be one of the most urgent. The Bill has got nothing to do, at least it has got nothing directly to do, with the material welfare of the country. It has no direct connection with what is generally called "bread-and-butter politics", important and necessary as "bread-and-butter politics" may be in its place. On the other hand, it has to do with the nation itself. It has to do with the very existence of the nation as a separate entity. It has to do with the unity of our national life and sentiment. It has to do with our national status and the recognition of our national status by other nations of the world. It has to do with what is more than material possessions, with what is, after all, even more than our fatherland; it has to do with the soul of the nation.

As the title shows, the Bill consists of two different parts. The first has to do with the definition of South African nationality; in other words, it has to do with a legal recognition by ourselves, and for the legal information of other nations, that we exist as a South African nation. The second part, which is based on the first, and is a logical result of the first, has to do with the establishment of an outward and visible symbol of our independent nationhood, and our national status. It has to do with the binding together of all sections of the people in one common sentiment. It provides, in other words, for a South African national flag.

I wish first to deal with the first part of this Bill, that part which has to do with the definition of South African nationality, and here I shall begin by trying to remove a misconception which, on the part of the ignorant, is only natural. There are some who consider that this Bill defining South African nationality in some or other way affects the franchise; that, by conferring South African nationality on a person, we

---

1 Speech by Dr. Malan (Minister of the Interior) in the House of Assembly on the occasion of the introduction of the South African Nationality and Flag Bill, 25 May 1926.

do, *ipso facto*, confer on him the right to vote. There is nothing of the kind. Franchise rights only exist by virtue of our franchise laws, and not by virtue of the fact that we are South Africans. If franchise rights are to be conferred on people who do not possess them today, or if people who today possess franchise rights are to be deprived of them, then that could be brought about only by the amendment of the existing franchise law. It is certainly advisable in general that our South African nationality law, if this is passed into law, should be brought into harmony with our franchise laws, or our franchise laws brought into harmony with our South African Nationality Act, but there is certainly no necessary connection between the two.

What this measure which I now propose does, is merely to make clear to ourselves and to foreign nations what a South African citizen is; in other words, it makes clear as to who belong to the South African nation, and who do not. During the course of this session I introduced a Bill, which has been passed both by this House and the other House,[2] to define the meaning of "British subject", and in that way to distinguish the British subject from aliens. This Bill which I am introducing now is complementary to the Bill which has been passed. It makes clear what is meant by a South African citizen, and it proposes to distinguish between a South African citizen and foreigners, and at the same time to distinguish between a South African citizen and other British subjects who are not South Africans.

This brings me to another misconception which I think I ought to remove. There may be some who think — and I have heard that opinion expressed — that this Bill, if it is passed into law, does away with British nationality; that if we are South African citizens, as defined by this Bill, we would no longer be British subjects. Of course, there is nothing of the kind in the Bill. A British subject as defined by the British Nationality Bill, which was passed into law only a short time ago, means a subject of H.M. the King, and nothing more than a subject of H.M. the King. As H.M. the King is also King of South Africa in the same way as he is King of Great Britain and Canada and New Zealand, and other Dominions, every South African citizen is also, *ipso facto*, a British subject; but at the same time every British subject is not a South African citizen, and does not belong to the South African nation. In other words the Bill proceeds upon the basic assumption that while all British subjects, wherever they may live, acknowledge the same sovereign, as citizens of the separate Dominions or parts of the British Empire, they have their own distinct and independent nationhood; or, to express it still differently, the Bill is a practical recognition of the fact that the Dominions and Great Britain are sister states, existing on a footing of equality with each other.

In connection with this point, I may further say that the definition of South African nationality as proposed by this Bill has a direct bearing

2 Act 18 of 1926.

on the recognition of our status by foreign nations. Since the signing of the Treaty of Versailles, we have had considerable difficulty with foreign nations as far as the recognition of our status is concerned. As signatories of that treaty we are members of the League of Nations, and, as members of the League of Nations, we have a right to take part in international deliberations; but this has been our experience, that when we come to these international conferences, we are looked upon, not as guests coming to such a conference to which we have been invited in our own right and dignity, but as coming there — in the opinion of foreign nations — merely as followers in the retinue of another nation; and for that reason we are turned back from the front door, and we are sent round, if we are to get admission at all, to the back door. We are slowly, but we are surely, overcoming this humiliating misconception and prejudice, and with the help of the British Government, Locarno has certainly been, and will in future be, of very material assistance to us to overcome that misconception and prejudice.

But how can we expect a foreign nation to recognise our status and our international rights if they do not know, and if they cannot know, legally at least, with whom they have to deal; if legally there is no such thing as South African nationality; if, legally, as a nation, we do not even so much as exist? Apart from the recognition of our status, the matter is one of considerable practical concern. It is one of practical concern to us in our domestic administration. As hon. members will know, the question is asked of every individual in the country, when the census is taken, to what nationality he belongs, and there is a good deal of uncertainty as to what a person must fill in as a reply to that question. At one time it was taken that everyone who was born in South Africa could fill in that he was a South African. A good many understood the question quite differently, and though they were not born in South Africa they filled in that they were South Africans. The same uncertainty has existed also with the taking of the census this year, and this year only those who were born in South Africa after Union were asked to fill in as their nationality South African. Now this Bill, when it is passed into law, will make an end to that uncertainty with regard to the nationality of persons living in South Africa.

Further, we have certain rights in connection with our membership of the League of Nations which it is impossible for us, under existing circumstances, to exercise. As hon. members will know, we may nominate as signatories to the Treaty of Versailles and as members of the League of Nations, a judge or judges on the panel of judges sitting in connection with the International Court of Justice; but the law in connection with that particular point requires that the judge nominated by a particular member of the League of Nations shall be a national of that particular country. Because we have got no South African nationals, we have been excluded from the exercise of this right that we have. This is a point which has weighed so much with the Dominion of Canada, that they have preceded us in the passing of a Canadian nationality law, and what we are doing today in attempting to pass a law of the same nature, we do on the example of the oldest and largest Dominion.

But, and further, South Africa has got interests abroad which can only be properly cared for and safeguarded if we pass a law of this nature, if we define South African nationality. We are not so cut off from the rest of the world as we were formerly. South Africans continually go abroad, not only to travel, but to settle abroad, and while they are still connected with us, while they still consider their domicile is in South Africa, and while they still think that they belong to our South African nationality, as they conceive it, they look to us to protect them and care for their interests. We have recognised this in connection with Angola only this session. We have passed on the Estimates a sum of money to have to send to Angola a Union agent to take care especially of the interests of South Africans who are settled there and have been settled there for quite a considerable period. We have hundreds of students who have gone from South Africa to continue their studies in other countries, and they are scattered in all parts of the civilised world, and in some cases they have come into contact, and sometimes into conflict, with the immigration laws of different countries. All of us will think of the immigration laws of the United States. But while that is so, there exists no legal definition of what a South African citizen is. We issue passports to persons who have been born and bred in South Africa and who belong to us, and when they take leave of our territorial waters we cannot say for whom we are responsible, and for whom not.

Further than that, we have Union ships which continually anchor in foreign ports. We have great material and commercial interests connected with our trade, through our own Union ships, with foreign countries. The nationality and the status of these ships and those who are on board is not defined. When they come to foreign ports they are either merely British, or their status is altogether undefined. If this Bill is passed into law, we define what South African nationality is and what a South African national is, and these will become properly defined, and if this Bill is passed into law it will incidentally establish to a large extent the natural consequence of it; that is, extra-territorial jurisdiction.

Coming to the details of the Bill, I wish to explain that this Bill proceeds on the same lines as the Canadian Act. Every person who is born in South Africa and is a British subject who has become one by being born under the British flag, by annexation or naturalisation, is considered a British subject. Every person who is a British subject who has been settled in the country for at least two years will be considered to be a South African. If anybody leaves our shores and settles abroad, he will be in a position to remain a South African, and his children can remain South Africans, if they choose to remain so. South African nationality will be lost only when a person relinquishes his domicile in South Africa when he goes abroad and renounces his South African nationality, or he assumes alienage in another country; or when he becomes a national of Great Britain or any other Dominion.

I come now to the second part of this Bill, namely, provision for a South African national flag. The reason why we make provision in this particular Bill dealing with the definition of South African nationality is because these two provisions, of a South African national flag and the definition of South African nationality naturally belong to each other. I shall not agree to the passing of the one without at the same time agreeing to the passing of the other.

A flag is not a mere cloth; a flag symbolises national existence, a flag is a living thing; it is the repository of national sentiment. A flag is able to create the greatest enthusiasm; a flag is able to move to tears; a flag can stir the deepest springs of action, and it can inspire to the noblest efforts. For a flag a nation can live; for it it can fight and it can die. For that reason there is nothing in the life of a nation which is so powerful as a unifying factor whenever there are different sections composing that nation as a national flag. Without a common national flag that symbolises the existence of that nation in inspiring that nation to a common and noble effort, without such a common national flag, no nation can live.

South Africa has got the misfortune — no, sir; it is not a misfortune, but a deep tragedy — that it has no flag of its own. South Africa contains within its bosom different races speaking different languages, and having different traditions, and to a large extent having different ideals. South Africa, more than any other country in the world, has got on its shoulders the task — the almost impossible task — to unify and cement through one common bond. What makes the task so much greater and so very much more difficult is that through its great, but at the same time tragic, history, the different races of South Africa have drifted apart, and have at times even shed each other's blood. This the races of South Africa realise today — that they must stand together, and they stretch out their hands to each other.

But South Africa has got no common symbol of its common nationhood. There is no South African national flag to unite them in one common sentiment and in one common brotherhood. There are flags in South Africa — perhaps we have got too much of it — but the practical effect of the flying of these flags in South Africa is not to unite, but to divide, and I have stated here on a former occasion that it is the usual thing in South Africa that whenever there is a function in which English-speaking South Africans are more particularly interested the flag that is flown is the Union Jack, and considering the history of a large section, all the other sections of the population are *ipso facto* excluded. On the other hand, whenever there is a function in which Dutch-speaking South Africans are more particularly interested — something which has to do with their history and traditions — a flag is also flown, but it is either the Vierkleur or the old Free State colours, and *ipso facto* the other section of the population is excluded.

126

All this may be quite wrong, and probably it is, but nevertheless it is a fact, and we as practical politicians must look facts in the face. It is difficult in any case to fight history as history is remembered by a section of the people, or remembered by an individual, but it is absolutely impossible to fight symbolised history — history symbolised in a flag. The present position is a matter of divided sentiment in South Africa and, therefore, of divided nationality. It is certainly bad enough, but the position becomes much worse when we think of it that the absence of a South African national flag, one common South African national flag, and the presence of two or more other flags, which practically have the practical effect of dividing the people — that that position darkens and confuses every other position in the country.

South Africa is a land of great, and we may say, of terrible problems. We have had our racial conflicts in this country in the past. We have to do with racial questions in the country. We have problems here which are so great that we may say, on the solution of these problems depends the maintenance of our civilisation of South Africa. And to solve these problems, it is essential, in the first place, that we shall judge in connection with these problems on their merits, and in the second place, in the solution of these problems that we shall have racial co-operation, and whenever a problem of that nature is brought forward, then the question of the flag or one of the flags is brought forward, and it at once darkens and confuses the issue, and drives the races of the country into different camps. It has been said and probably will be said again in this House when the matter is discussed, that the problem of securing provision for a South African flag is not an urgent one. Probably it is the most urgent and most fundamental of our problems.

The Bill does not raise the flag question. There is a flag question in South Africa, and we cannot get away from it. All the Bill proposes to do is to settle the flag question. In settling the flag question, we settle the race question, we facilitate the settling of all the other problems and questions in South Africa. The Bill which I now propose is settling the flag question on the only lines on which it can be practically and reasonably done. Unfortunately, this Bill, as far as at least the second part is concerned, is not the result of agreement. There was a hope, especially after the assurance given last year by the hon. the Leader of the Opposition, that we could come to an agreement on this point, but these expectations, this hope, have been dashed to the ground. And after the experience which we have had — I speak for myself here — there is little chance of ever coming to an agreement on this question — with the Opposition, I mean.

For me and for my colleagues, and I may say for the parties which sit on this side of the House, the fact that no agreement has been reached or can be reached with the Opposition in future, does not settle the matter. We consider that the question is of such importance and of such urgent importance that, in the first place, we wish to have agreement, and we shall still do what we can in future to get agreement on this point; but if we cannot get common agreement among all sections of the population with regard to this matter, then we say it is better to have a flag without agreement — in spite of disagreement — than to have no flag at all. And it must be simply our look-out on this side of the House to see that what we propose is practical and reasonable.

When we faced this question of securing a South African national flag, we realised that there were two requirements which we had to consider. The first is that that flag shall be such a one that it is possible for it to be a common flag for both sections of the population and that it shall not remind the two sections of the population of their past differences, but should unite them for the future in one common sentiment and one common nationality; and the second requirement which we considered was that that flag should be a correct representation of our constitutional position.

The attitude of the representatives of the South African Party on the negotiating committee[3] was that, in any case, the flag shall include the Union Jack. It is true that, at the same time, they were also willing to include the old republican colours, but I think they will agree with me when I say they were willing to include the old republican colours in that flag merely to make the inclusion of the Union Jack more acceptable to the other section. And the agitation which has arisen as a result of the breakdown of these negotiations very clearly shows that one thing is insisted upon, and that is the inclusion of the Union Jack in that flag.

I think that hon. gentlemen generally, on all sides of the House, will agree that, knowing South Africa as we do; knowing the history of South Africa as we do, and the associations connected with the Union Jack for a large section of the population, that any flag in which the Union Jack was included would not be acceptable to a large, perhaps to the larger, section of the country. I think that hon. gentlemen on the other side, when they think impartially on this matter, will say in connection with this sentiment which I express, that we on our side of the House are more able to interpret the feelings of the Dutch section of the population today. If they had been able to interpret the sentiments of the Dutch-speaking South Africans in the country they would have sat, not on that side, but on this side of the House.

But let me come to the proposal which was made by hon. gentlemen on the other side. They not only insisted on the inclusion of the Union Jack, but were willing to combine with the Union Jack the colours of the old republics. Apart from what I have already stated, there is more than one objection against that. It is certainly not constitutionally correct.

What is the constitutional position of South Africa as a dominion? What is the constitutional position today in connection with what is today called the British Commonwealth? There exists no such thing, even though

---

[3] A committee appointed after the session of 1925 and representing the National, South African and Labour Parties in order to negotiate a settlement of the flag issue which was first raised in Parliament in 1925.

it is often so called, no such thing as an empire, and that has been stated, for the information of the hon. member for East London[4]—that has been stated, over and over again, in speeches in the country, by his own leader. There is no such thing as an empire, because an empire implies one State. There is no such thing as a subjection of one part of the so-called empire to another part. What exists today is nothing more than what is, I should say, most correctly expressed by the expression — community of British nations, a community of British nations which are free to hold together or free to divide and free to go each its own way. An authoritative statement has been made in regard to this constitutional position some years ago in these words: " It was now common ground, and we gladly accepted the position that there was no kind of authority in practice, whatever there might be in theory of constitution; that the Parliament and the peoples of the United Kingdom claimed any longer to exercise over the Parliaments and the peoples of the Dominions."

And he goes further, to say: " The day may come, unless certain other steps are taken — that one dominion in foreign policy may go the one way and the others may go another way."

This has been stated by no less a person than Lord Milner, when he was a very prominent member of the Lloyd George Cabinet. It is not a leader of national opinion in one of the Dominions. This sentiment has been expressed by an English Minister and it so happens that it was expressed by the man who can be considered above all others as a high priest of imperialism. If, under these circumstances, when each British Dominion has got its own national existence, its own independent nation-hood, the Union Jack, the flag of one particular portion of the Empire is included in that national flag, it is not sufficient; it is not a correct representation of the constitutional position.

But there is one other objection against the proposal which has come from the other side of the House, and it is that if we adopt a flag in which the Union Jack is included and at the same time the colours of the old republics, then the two races in this country will not stand, as they re-presented it, on an equal footing with each other. We must not forget that in such a flag the Union Jack is a living flag and the flags of the old republics represent something that is dead. It does not break with the past. It reminds of the past and it reminds of the past in such a way that whether it is right or whether it is wrong it is in any case a fact that to a large section of the population it will stand for domination and for conquest and defeat.

On the lines which this Bill proposes to deal with the flag question, we shall have a flag for South Africa, and that flag shall be an altogether new design which shall look to the future and shall not look to the past; and at the same time to give a correct representation of our constitutional position, we are willing to have the Union Jack, the flag of the Empire, and to display the Union Jack officially on all occasions which are intended

4 The Reverend Mr. Rider.

specifically to represent or to indicate our relationship to the British community of nations.

This proposal can be looked upon, that is if we are considered, as we are considered by many people, to represent the Dutch-speaking section of the population; this proposal can be looked upon as a double concession on our part. In the first place we were willing to give up the representation in the Union flag of the old republican colours. I said that these republican colours stand for something that is dead, but that which is dead is not dead in the sense that it is not enshrined in the heart of hundreds and thousands in this country and therefore if it is not represented at all in the Flag of the Union of the future, then something is really actually given up. So far as we are willing to adopt an altogether new design we have already made a concession, but further, if it is so, as we represent, that we are the party standing for secession; that we do not wish to recognise in any way that we belong to the British Commonwealth, then by adopting a clause in this Bill in which we specifically make mention of the relationship between South Africa and the British Commonwealth of Nations, in agreeing to display on certain occasions the flag of the Empire, is that not a concession that is worth something to our English speaking South Africans?

It has been said that we stand for a Dutch-speaking South Africa. Thus we have made in this proposal a double concession. I do not consider it a concession. I consider the whole proposal is nothing more than the only practicable and reasonable proposal we can make.

So much for the proposals we have put before the House. Since the breakdown of the negotiations there has been started an agitation for the inclusion of the Union Jack. Considering the history of the country and the sentiments of the people, that agitation comes down to nothing else than a point-blank refusal on the part of sections of our English-speaking compatriots to make any allowance for the feelings of their Dutch-speaking South Africans. While they are unwilling to make any allowance for the feelings of their fellow South Africans, they accuse those who stand for this practicable and reasonable proposal of stirring up race hatred and in that way insult them. I am speaking more particularly of certain newspapers. I cannot conceive of anything more unworthy or unpatriotic but perhaps that is not so much the fault of the people themselves. It is more the fault of those on whose shoulders the responsibility rests to enlighten them, and who have not enlightened them correctly in regard to this matter. I need only point to the fact that the papers generally which stirred up this agitation have systematically concealed from the public the second part — and a very material part — of this proposal. The official display of the Union Jack on certain occasions.

With more information given to the people I am certain that after this agitation there will come a revulsion of feeling that will sweep away misconceptions and put to shame those who have misled the people. We feel on this side of the House that in view of that agitation more information to the country is necessary, and it is for that reason that it has been decided not to proceed further this session with this Bill. But when I say that we are not going to proceed further this session, I say it on the definite understanding that early next session we are going to proceed with the Bill, and that the flag which on that occasion will be brought up will be a flag on the same general principle on which the present proposals rest — that is to say it shall not include the Union Jack and it shall not include the republican colours. It will be an altogether new design.

As far as the particular design which is contained in this proposal is concerned we are not wedded to it. It has been represented that this flag which is proposed is nothing more than a disguised Vierkleur. This flag has been designed by an Englishman[5] who has lived for many years in South Africa — an Englishman who has identified himself with South Africa and is a true South African. He is an Englishman who is a student of history; he knows and understands the history and sentiments of the people and for that reason there could be no objection to the flag. He has explained that in drawing up his design it never entered his mind that this is a disguised Vierkleur. In any case if there is this objection that it looks too much like the Vierkleur we are willing to drop it, and we shall certainly drop it, and we shall try as much as possible during the recess to get as much agreement as is possible in regard to this question and to create such machinery that we shall come to the very best possible selection of a flag as I have described in general principle. But this must stand fast — we must have a national flag, a South African flag, and we shall have it. In securing that flag we shall not look to the extremists on the one side or the other side.

Let me tell hon. gentlemen opposite that the extremists on both sides want no flag at all or a flag in which the Union Jack is included. The extremists on their side say — we don't want a South African national flag, we want the Union Jack because it stands for conquest and subjection. If we eliminate the Union Jack then we shall eliminate something that would remind us that we are not free in this country. We shall not look to extremists on either side. We shall look in regard to this matter to the great volume of moderate opinion in the country, and in proceeding any further we shall make an appeal to the moderate opinion in the country — we shall make an appeal to all true sons of South Africa.

5 Professor Eric Walker of the University of Cape Town.

GENERAL J. B. M. HERTZOG, 25 MAY 1926[1]

I AM ONE of the old republicans who, in 1902, had to surrender their flag, and I must say that everyone who left Vereeniging went away with

1 Extract from speech by General Hertzog (Prime Minister) in the House of Assembly, 25 May 1926. *House of Assembly Debates.*

the feelings so well represented by Senator Reitz in his poem at the time, a poem which later and still today hangs on the walls of thousands of households. I read a few lines of the poem taken from an English newspaper. That is the spirit in which we took leave of the old flags at Vereeniging. That is the spirit in which everyone of us still carries them about in our hearts, but they lie buried, " consecrated to the past ". Now I ask, was there a difference all this time between the Dutch-speaking and the English-speaking people in South Africa? While the English-speaking had their Union Jack, what did we have? What did I and my fellow republicans have, what have I today, what have they today? The Union Jack? I have not the least feeling against the Union Jack. I bear just as little feeling against it as any other flag, whether the tricolor of Holland or the Stars and Stripes. But the Union Jack — let us look facts in the face — the Union Jack means nothing more to me than that when I see it I say — It is the flag of a great people, a glorious flag of a great country.

But I say the same when I see the Stars and Stripes, or even when I look at the flag of little Holland. The feeling, on the other hand, which inspires me and that I read in them is nothing more than the feeling of recognition of a great people, nothing more than the reading of the history of a people entitled to its flag, but in which I have no share. The Union Jack stands for Great Britain; that is the flag of Great Britain, the flag of the subjects of Great Britain, and if the subjects say that they attach great value to it, and that they appreciate it very highly, then I say that I can understand that very well. From what I have felt and what I still feel today towards the flag of that small country — the Free State — which no longer exists, I can well understand what the feelings of those subjects are. But now I ask my friends not to forget that since 1902 I have had no flag. Let us look facts straight in the face. The Union Jack is actually the flag under which I stand. It is, indeed, the flag under which I enjoy my citizenship and can enjoy it, but if it is said that it is my flag then I say — No; it is not my flag.

In the proper patriotic sense of the word, it can never be my flag. That is the case with thousands. Let us not be hypocritical, but acknowledge frankly that of the Dutch-speaking people who vote for hon. members of the Opposition there are not 10 per cent who feel differently from me on this point. It is a fact. When Union came everyone of us felt that we ought necessarily to have a flag which would not only be a flag for the English-speaking in South Africa, but also for the English and Dutch-speaking in South Africa. The hon. member for Standerton (General Smuts), the Leader of the Opposition, does he not have that feeling? He was one of the first to acknowledge it and to say from the public platform that we must have a national flag for South Africa. Hardly had Union come about when he did that. Thereafter the South African Party passed a resolution that we should have a flag. Women and men of the Dutch-speaking population stood actually as one in favour of it that we should have our own national flag in South Africa. That was all an admission

132

that the Union Jack was not our flag, and could not be our flag. But circumstances prevented effect being given to that. What is, however, the result of that condition of things? Every time there is a difference about great problems — yes, sometimes it need not even concern great problems — the English-speaking in South Africa go and shelter themselves under the shadow of the Union Jack and call out only one thing — The Union Jack is in danger.

On that basis we can never become a people. It is impossible that in that way we can ever hope to obtain that unity of spirit which is so absolutely necessary for a people to be filled with if we want to have unity. That cannot be, and yet while on the opposite side in eloquent speeches such as that of the hon. member of Caledon (Mr. Krige) to which we have listened, a plea is made for us to become one people, we all the time maintain the great and weighty means which has always been used as an instrument to divide our people into two. It is time that an end came to that and therefore I say that we can no longer go on as in the past attaching the interests of the country and the people to something by which it may be ruined. The danger is too great to leave it to mere chance.

I want to call the attention of my English-speaking friends to the fact that they want co-operation with the Empire. Now I say that we can get that in the best way — yes in the only way — by allowing the Dutch-speaking Afrikanders to feel that they are not merely a people banished, outside the bounds of a common nationality. That is what they feel and that is the result of the position in which they have been since 1902, and it will be so as long as that condition continues, and if we want hearty and fervent co-operation, then the removal of that condition should be one of the most essential things. I and other Dutch-speaking people belonging to the old republics feel that. Whether the hon. member for Standerton (General Smuts) as a philosopher calls it the " inferiority complex " makes no difference to me. It is a fact, and it does not matter what we call it. The fact is that I and many with me, more or less strongly feel that those who represent the minority of 1902 still have that feeling continually with the floating of the Union Jack over South Africa. I can assure the hon. member for Standerton that not 5 per cent of the Dutch-speaking Afrikanders, yes not 1 per cent, take up the philosophic view that the hon. member today wanted us to take as the proper one to be held. You want me to cherish respect for the Union Jack. Let me honestly say that I, just as much as anybody else on the opposite side of the House, also want everyone of the Dutch-speaking Afrikanders to have respect for the Union Jack, but then not as the flag of South Africa, but as the flag of Great Britain, as a flag of a great nation with a glorious history; but you cannot get me to have respect for a flag which you fly over me and which came there under the circumstances in which the Union Jack came.

I have during the period since 1902 always tried to have no feeling whatsoever against the Union Jack, and I think I can honestly say that I have not the least feeling of enmity against that flag. Let me say again: I want that flag to be respected because I am convinced that when there is respect, we in South Africa will be better able to see how much it is in our interests to work together heartily in friendship with the country whose flag it is. One will not get that respect by putting the Union Jack on the National Flag of South Africa, and I will presently say why.

Before I do so, let me say that this morning it was asked by the hon. members for Standerton (General Smuts) and Yeoville (Mr. Duncan): "Why will you Dutch-speaking people not be satisfied with the Union Jack and with the republican colours on the flag?" If by that is meant that the Transvaal Vierkleur, the Free State flag and the Union Jack must be on our national flag, then I only want to say we cannot help feeling that the flags of the republics are dead. They have been buried and what we feel for those flags is only the feeling of sentiment, love and respect, to which we have a right as towards phases of the past. Do not please ask me therefore to place a dead body alongside of a living power. I as well as others feel that that would not be honest. Then there are other people, men like the hon. members for Standerton and Yeoville, who think that we can be satisfied with the Union Jack as a flag on the National Flag of South Africa, and then by a mixing together of colours of which some belonged to the old republican flags make the people of South Africa think — There you have the Vierkleur.

I could reply that in the colours of the flag design there are no less than two colours which the Union Jack also has. I only say what I already said this morning by an interjection to the hon. member for Standerton. If it is as hon. members opposite think that Dutch-speaking South Africa must accept it, then I regard it as an insult, because it is nothing but a piece of fraud. We should have the same right to say to the English-speaking people in South Africa — Be satisfied with the flag containing two colours of the Union Jack.

We must not trifle with the matter because it is very important. I have longed from the bottom of my heart and still long that we as parties should be unanimous about the matter. Unfortunately that does not appear to be attained. Now I want to show why we cannot be satisfied with the Union Jack on the National Flag of South Africa. I think in any case it would be fatal now. There was a time when I actually had it under consideration, but I now say that even if I at that time had favoured it, it would be fatal after what has occurred. After what has occurred one can simply have no feeling of love and sympathy towards the National Flag if the Union Jack is on it. The way in which the Sons of England have acted — let me say not all, but some of them — because I believe and trust that the large majority of them are men who are just as anxious as we are, to solve the matter — and the way in which they have been supported by certain newspapers makes this impossible. I am sorry that a newspaper of the importance of the *Cape Times* can so lower itself as to write the article which appeared in its issue of 21 May. I will make a few quotations from it here and there:

"Yet squabbles perpetually break out between the two main parts of our European population; and, again and again the squabble comes because a small minority of the Dutch-speaking people cannot forget the past. They cherish hatred as though it were a treasured national possession. They yearn for symbols of their momentary political predominance. To gratify their sectional passions they are willing to go to any lengths; and the more heavily they can trample upon the traditions and affections of their English-speaking fellow citizens the better they seem to be pleased. No thought of the welfare of South Africa restrains them. And rather than give any least concession to the sentiment of South Africans of British birth or descent, they have no scruple about riding roughshod over the most earnest appeals made to them by their English-speaking Labour allies."

Then the article says further: "The Labour section in the Pact will swallow anything so long as the Pact Government can be kept in power." Later it is said: "Are the Nationalists incapable of the same respect for the Union Jack? The demand that the Union Jack shall be excluded from the South African flag suggested irresistibly that they are. They cannot forget, nor can they forgive. Inveterate hatred rises in them at the sight of the Union Jack and they demand that the flag of South Africa shall register and perpetuate this hatred . . . and their chosen members of Parliament loll on the back-benches almost literally spitting venom whenever the Union Jack is mentioned."

I am going to utter a word of criticism. I leave the matter there but I wish to say that in that page and in other newspapers a challenge has gone out to Dutch-speaking South Africa which Dutch-speaking South Africa dare not refuse to take up. The challenge must be accepted. I shall not allow that such expressions shall be used in future, because when we had the opportunity we did not take the necessary steps to prevent it.

Now I ask the question — What is the whole question before the House? It is to obtain a national flag, and what the national flag should contain is mentioned in what the Minister of the Interior has told the House, subsequently was intimated to the hon. member for Standerton and later again to the joint committee. The committee accepted that. The basis on which the national flag should be tested was as follows: Firstly that there should be a national flag; secondly, that the national flag should be an expression of our independent South African national existence; thirdly, that it should be an expression of our common national existence; and fourthly, that it should stand as a symbol of our acknowledged national status. There cannot be the least doubt of it that it is a sound basis on which our national flag should be judged. I am therefore not surprised that that basis is taken by the hon. member for Standerton and was approved by the joint committee.

Now I want to ask how far that test has been complied with, and to give a reply to the question, I want, shortly, to go into the four points. In the first place we must have a national flag for South Africa. Is the Union Jack going to comply with that requirement? Will a flag with the Union Jack make it actually a national flag? The hon. member for Yeoville (Mr. Duncan) says that it would be an expression of a wider conception of our citizenship outside the Union, of a wider citizenship with the other Dominions and England. But then I ask my hon. friend if that is what we want. Do not let us confuse our flag with the Empire flag. Let the Empire flag exist for anyone who wants to form part of the Empire. But the South African flag stands for South Africa.

In the second place the flag must be an expression of our independent South African national existence. Now I say to my English friends — Put your Union Jack on the flag, and you will get exactly what I have just said, viz. that the flag for the Dutch-speaking portion of the population will not stand for independence, but for subservience. We cannot get away from that. We must look it in the face.

In the third place, the flag must give expression not only to our independent South African national existence, but also to common South African national existence. Then I ask my friends what they want me that I should have in common with them if the Union Jack was incorporated in the flag? To them the flag has been a symbol for over 200 years, although the flag only came much later. To them the flag is a symbol, but the Dutch-speaking part of the people is no part of the people to whom that flag is a symbol. Where, therefore, is the expression of a common national existence?

The fourth requirement is that the flag should be the symbol of our agreed national status. What is our agreed national status? Is it necessary that after what we heard in 1919 and often thereafter from the hon. member for Standerton (General Smuts) — that we were free and on equality with Great Britain — for me to say any more about it? Now you come and want to put the flag of Great Britain on our national flag. Why? Let me say this to my English friends: Examine yourselves well, ask yourselves why you want that, and you will have to acknowledge that with 90 per cent it is the hankering after, the longing after, the floating of the flag of Great Britain over the Union. The hon. member for Yeoville (Mr. Duncan) was only half-way through his speech when this began to come out. Let me say that I appreciate his speech, but he had not gone far when he let it out that the end in view was that the flag should not only stand for us, but also as a portion of something. At once the inferiority came out, and I say that we must not lose it from view. That is why we want the Union Jack not to be in the South African flag. I say that the Union Jack will get more recognition from me and my friends than it has today if we have our own flag. The expression of our national status is one of the requirements in the declaration approved by the hon. member for Standerton and by the committee, and the inclusion of the Union Jack in the flag is not consistent with that.

I want to tell you this further, that it is our duty, both of my hon. friends opposite, as for us here, to see that the Dutch-speaking, as well as the English-speaking people concerned in this matter, attain unity as soon as possible; but if we cannot get unity, we shall have to take the step, we shall have to undertake to get a flag, and in these circumstances the English-speaking part of the people have no more right to demand the Union Jack than others, who think that it reminds them of inferiority, have to demand that we shall have a flag without the Union Jack. That is the point, I think. The Dutch-speaking people have just as much right to demand that the Union Jack shall not be in the flag as the English-speaking have to insist that it shall be so included. And if one has just as much right as the other, I say it is the duty of the Government and of us who are in earnest about this matter to say, as it is such a great question between the two sections of the population on which they greatly differ in opinion, views and feelings, that the Government must intervene. Then it is the duty of the Government to take up and judge the matter sympathetically and impartially. But when the Government has reached the point of being able to say that this party is wrong and the other right, I say the Government is obliged to take action on the lines of those who are right. And when we, as a Government, come to Parliament and say and acknowledge that those Dutch-speaking and English-speaking people who say that it is not necessary for the Union Jack to be contained in the flag are right, then it is no more than our duty to give the necessary assistance, to give and do justice to those who are in the right.

Hon. members opposite cannot blame us on any ground whatsoever. It can only be said that the English-speaking part of the population have rights which the Dutch-speaking part do not possess. If the Dutch-speaking part of the population have the same right, why, then, is there this excitement, this abuse and this suspicion of English people such as the Minister of Defence, who have not one drop less English blood in them than hon. members opposite. I have learned from more than two years' intimate co-operation with the members of the Labour Party that they are just as anxious as I and other hon. members opposite that a solution should be found in a healthy spirit which will lead to something useful to South Africa. It is not worthy to try and make political capital out of a great national matter.

Let me say that I have received many telegrams, amongst others one of which I want to make special mention from the South African chairman of the British Empire Service League, Sir William Campbell, on behalf of his society. I appreciate the telegram most highly. I will read it: " While the league is non-political and non-racial, and embraces in its membership those of both races whose feelings with regard to the design of our national flag must necessarily vary, the league is obliged also to do everything possible to make the Union a great and contented nation, and for this reason would earnestly ask you to consider the desirability of not forcing on the country a flag which is unacceptable to any section, but rather still to strive to find a design which will be acceptable to all, in which endeavour I would assure you of the loyal assistance of the league."

That is what I appreciate, and I hope the " Hear, hears " of hon. members opposite are a sign that they are just as prepared. It is for this reason, because I know that there are people, many here in this House, who feel like that, that I think we are much closer to each other if we can only get away a little from the political atmosphere, which puts us in hostility towards each other. Because I know that, I and my colleagues say that we should wait another year. I thought, however, that I ought not to allow the opportunity to pass to at any rate honestly and frankly let my hon. friends opposite know what was going on in me, and what was going on today in all the Dutch-speaking people of South Africa. Dutch-speaking South Africa is not an enemy today of the English-speaking people. I assure the House that the Dutch-speaking people are just as anxious as the English-speaking can ever be to have a South African people, and the Dutch-speaking people will only ask — Let us no longer stand in a position of inferiority in South Africa.

I hope my hon. friends opposite will clearly understand that we cannot go on year after year postponing the matter, and we think that we shall be able next year to put the Bill through. As for us, I cannot say otherwise than that it is our intention to put it through, but I do not think it is desirable that we should go into the matter further now. I thought it advisable that both sides should have an opportunity of talking about the matter, and I do not think that either side has need to be ashamed of what has been said.

GENERAL J. C. SMUTS, 25 MAY, 1926[1]

WE ARE DEALING with a very grave subject, and a very difficult subject, and we have to discuss it in such a spirit that we may eventually come to a conclusion. We are not going to decide it today. We shall not be finished with this question today, nor will the people of South Africa be finished with the question today, and we must discuss it in such a spirit that it may be possible for us to come to an amicable understanding hereafter. I am, therefore, sorry that the Minister used language and made statements which will make it very difficult to continue the debate in a calm spirit and to find a workable solution. Some of the statements he made I must repudiate at once — some of the statements he should never have made.

---

[1] Extract from speech by General Smuts (Leader of the Opposition) in the House of Assembly, 25 May 1926. *House of Assembly Debates.*

There is, for instance, the arrogant statement that they on that side of the House represent the Dutch-speaking people of this country. The Minister knows, as everybody in this House knows, that it is not only a mere exaggeration, but is untrue and it is not helpful. The cause we have at heart is not helped by statements of that kind. The Minister says that if they did not represent the Dutch-speaking people we would not be in Opposition. That is not true. The Minister sits there, and hon. gentlemen sit there, with the help of the Labour Party, who are not Dutch-speaking, so he has no reason whatever for making that statement.

There is another statement that he made which I think very wrong, out of place and entirely untrue — it is that in what has happened over this Flag Bill the English-speaking section of the people have shown that they are not prepared to make any allowance for Dutch feeling.

Dr. D. F. MALAN: I said a section of the English-speaking people.

GENERAL SMUTS: The meetings of protest which are being held all over the country are not merely taken part in by the English-speaking section of the South African Party, but also by the English-speaking section of the party opposite. I don't want us to import unnecessary feeling into the debate, but fairly and frankly to recognise facts. The facts are clear and patent, that the English-speaking section as a whole take up the same attitude on the question of the flag. I think the Minister has used language which he should not have used as a patriotic South African, and, besides, it is untrue.

Another statement he continually made I also repudiate — that is that there is an agitation in the country which has been worked up. I do not think so.

AN HON. MEMBER: What about the leading article in the *Cape Times* this morning?

GENERAL SMUTS: I could quote some leading articles in other papers. The Minister, if he has been following the Press on the other side, must have known that the newspapers are using somewhat violent language, and not on one side only. The Government Press have used as violent and strong language as can conceivably be used. I say let us view the matter calmly and quietly, and not make charges against each other which will make a solution impossible. I shall do my best to deal with the subject in that spirit.

The committee which dealt with the matter from both sides of the House really defined the position of parties on this question, and let me just repeat very briefly what happened there. The Minister today has taken the same line in the speech which he has just made to us. On that committee the representatives of the South African Party took this line, that for the future flag of South Africa to command the affection and respect and the loyal adherence of the people of South Africa, it ought to embody both the old republican colours and the Union Jack. The representatives from the Government benches took the line that there should be an entirely new design, which would be a break with the past, and that position they maintained up to nearly the end of the negotiations and the conferences that took place.

Finally, they came forward with this proposal which the Minister considers as a great concession, that in addition to this entirely new design for the South African flag, there should be in the Bill a clause for the display of the Union Jack on certain occasions which would be relevant to the Imperial connection. The Minister has said today that he looks upon that as a great concession. The concession did not prove acceptable, because it was felt by the representatives from our party that there was nothing in the concession. What are the occasions — I thought the Minister would tell us — what are the occasions when the Union Jack would be seen in South Africa?

The only occasion I could think of was Empire Day, which is one of our holidays. I have been thinking over this matter, and to my mind no other occasion presents itself as suitable under the terms of this Bill for the flying of the Union Jack in South Africa, and the result would be this, that the great concession, which the Minister refers to, to English feeling in South Africa, would mean that there might be one occasion in the year on which the British flag might be seen in South Africa, and even that occasion might disappear.

(The Minister of Defence interjected a remark.)

GENERAL SMUTS: I am afraid the Minister is right in his interjection. If this Bill were to go through, you would see the Union Jack more often than before.

However, that was the issue between the two parties in the committee. We stood for a combination of these two things from our past, the old republican colours and the Union Jack, and the representatives of the Government took up the line that there should be an entirely new departure, an entirely new design, as a symbol of our nationhood in the future. That was the honest difference of opinion between the two parties, and that is the difference of opinion still. The Minister has announced that he is not proceeding with this Bill, but that next session he will proceed with a Bill on the same principles, that is, an entirely new design in which the Union Jack will not be found, so that it is clear from the Minister's statement that the Government will continue on the lines that they pursued in the committee. I can only say that we see no reason whatever for departing from the attitude which our representatives took up in that committee.

We think there is no solution of this flag question except by means of the combination of the old republican colours and the Union Jack, and we feel that on those lines the solution can be found, and will be found. The Minister says that that will not be constitutionally correct. I do not follow that argument. Why should the flag of this country not represent the constituent sections of its people? After all, the Union Jack itself is of that character. The Union Jack, which is the flag of the British Empire, represents the constituent sections that came into the united state of Great Britain and Ireland.

MR. TIELMAN ROOS: Ireland has got a separate flag.

GENERAL SMUTS: Yes, the Free State of Southern Ireland.

COLONEL D. REITZ: You (the Government) will turn this country into a Southern Ireland?

GENERAL SMUTS: I want to argue the position on the facts, and I say this, that it is to my mind perfectly correct constitutionally that we should have a flag which should represent the different sections of the people and their past, and the traditions which they bring from the past. I take up this position, which differs *in toto* from that taken up by the Minister. He looks upon the old republican flags as dead; he looks upon them as having been defeated and washed out, except from our hearts. I believe that these flags are a great reality in South Africa. The Minister complains that on many occasions, festive occasions in the interior, you will see the Transvaal Vierkleur or the Free State Vierkleur.

AN HON. MEMBER: Unofficially.

GENERAL SMUTS: Unofficially, but it is there.

GENERAL HERTZOG: You can have the Union Jack also.

GENERAL SMUTS: Yes. These are facts. These flags have not been stamped out, they have not been killed; it is not a case of death.

GENERAL HERTZOG: Nor will the Union Jack be killed!

GENERAL SMUTS: No, that is just what I would say to the Prime Minister. There is no case of anything being killed. This is a case of recognising the past, the honourable past of both peoples. I take up this attitude, we have our flag which was settled immediately after Union in 1911. I have never held the view that that is the permanent flag of this country. But I say this, that I shall feel it very deeply if we adopt for South Africa a flag which does not contain the old republican colours.

GENERAL HERTZOG: I would look upon it as an insult.

GENERAL SMUTS: The Prime Minister says that a flag for the Union which contains the old Vierkleur, he would look upon as an insult.

GENERAL HERTZOG: No, excuse me, I say the colours. That is a different thing.

GENERAL SMUTS: It only shows the difference of mentality in this country. I say this, whatever the Prime Minister may say, and whatever his feelings may be on so intimate a subject, I would feel it very deeply if the flag for which I fought, and which symbolises to me the great past of South Africa, should be buried for ever and done with.

AN HON. MEMBER: That's clever!

GENERAL SMUTS: No, it is not clever. We have a document in the interior, President Kruger's last letter to the Boer people, which I look upon as his last will and testament to the Boer people, and in that letter appear his last words of advice shortly before his death. His words were these —

Soek in die verlede al wat daarin skoon en goed is, en skep daarna u ideaal vir die toekoms. (Seek in the past for what therein is good and noble, and create from that your ideal for the future.)

As far as I am concerned, I should like to live up to that testament,

141

and I would like the people of South Africa to live up to those words of one of our greatest statesmen, and when we come to settle a flag for our future, I would like to embody in it what the Dutch-speaking people of the interior look upon as one of the good and noble things from our past.

The Minister may think we can lightly break with the past. We cannot do it. A nation is a living thing, the past is linked with the future, and you can only go to the future if your roots are in what is good and noble in the past. I say this, that as regards our old Vierkleur flag, I would like to see it embodied in the flag of the future. The same feeling prevails among the English-speaking people with regard to the Union Jack. The Minister is very wrong when he says that that flag stands for conquest and subjection. I am sorry he said that. He said that it is looked upon in that way. I say to the Minister that that is a wounding thing which he said, because nothing is more untrue than that.

Mr. N. C. Havenga: It is a fact.

General Smuts: I am awfully sorry to hear that from the Minister of Finance. The hon. the Minister feels like that because he suffers from what has been called the " inferiority complex ". There are people in South Africa who always think that they are being treated as inferiors. Many of our Dutch people seem to suffer from this — inferiority complex. It is an unworthy complex. We are not treated as inferiors, and I do not look upon anybody in South Africa as superior to me or my people; I look upon the Dutch people as fully equal to the best there is in the world, and the Dutch-speaking section in South Africa are equal in every way, mentally, morally and otherwise, to the best in the English people. When the British section of South Africa ask for the inclusion of their flag, they do not intend to lord their superiority; they do not intend to show that they are the victors and that we are the subjects in South Africa. They have the same feelings as we Dutch-speaking people have, and that is that we do not want to surrender the sacred and noble symbols of our history and our traditions. We are not going to make a break. Let us respect that feeling. I have that feeling myself, and I respect the British people, my English-speaking fellow-citizens, for that similar feeling which they have. If the Minister ever wants to get a united flag in South Africa — and I hope we shall come to it — we shall have to respect that feeling. He is making a great mistake if he thinks he can simply break with the past, and he makes an equal mistake if he thinks he can break with the English-speaking past. No, we shall have a flag, but it will be a flag by agreement.

The good that has been done by our thrashing this out in that little committee and in the country at large is this, that we are getting to a measure of agreement, for which I am grateful; not agreement on the lines the Minister has foreshadowed, but on other lines, and I think wiser, and more statesmanlike lines. I have heard a great deal of criticism levelled against my friends from Natal. It is said they are jingoes.

Our friends in Natal and elsewhere have been blamed for setting going a great agitation in the country. They have not. There is a deep, genuine, spontaneous feeling moving among certain sections of the people, and it is only the part of statesmanship to recognise that. We are like a wise physician; we see the symptoms, we see the facts before us. It is no use applying logical formulas or theories to a situation like that. A wise statesman recognises the facts. It is not a case of jingoism; it is genuine strong feeling. Members in this House from Natal — the so-called jingoes — have come to me and they have said — General, we are prepared to take the old Transvaal Vierkleur if the Union Jack is accorded a place on it.

That does not sound to me like jingoism, like treading on the feelings of the other part of the population. That does not sound to me like the intolerance which the Minister has accused a section of the British people of. No, to my mind, it shows that we are ripe for a solution of this question on sane and wise lines. The discussions we have had may do some good in this way, that we are shown a line of approach, that we are coming together, that we want to embody in our future flag the symbols that both of us bring from the past. Let that be our formula — not exclusion, but inclusion. That is the wise line which the British people took in settling their national flag. I think on these lines we shall get consent, and we shall have a flag which we will take to our future as a symbol of South African unity and co-operation, and not as one of division and disunity.

To my mind the question is soluble, and I would appeal to members on all sides of the House to set aside the partisan feeling which has crept into this subject. It was inevitable that when you raised a question like this in the atmosphere which does still exist in South Africa, and in the atmosphere which has been worked up politically in recent years, that partisan feelings should enter and that bitterness and violent language would be used, but I say this, that we are the high court of the nation who should look on these questions with a calm and judicial mind; we should take a different view, and we should look the facts in the face and recognise that it is possible for us to have a national flag on which the vast bulk of the people can be agreed; and let that flag be our old republican colours from the interior and let us have on it a representation of the Union Jack.

HON. MEMBERS: Never.

GENERAL SMUTS: There is the intolerance; that is what raises suspicion, when hon. members in this House show this feeling of utter exclusion of anything that savours of the British connection.

AN HON. MEMBER: A century of wrong.

GENERAL SMUTS: We have seen it followed by a century of justice. I do not see how we can serve the cause of the Boer people by forever raking up the past and the bitterness of the past. The Vierkleur should be no cause of bitterness to the English-speaking people in South Africa, and it is not. The Union Jack should be no cause of bitterness to the Dutch-speaking people. I, therefore, say, if we cannot agree on these lines, if English and Dutch will not treat each other on a fair basis of equal treatment and justice, then it will be very difficult for us to come to any national flag.

The Minister may flatter himself that he can achieve a flag by compulsion, but it will not be the flag of this country. The more he passes it by majorities of this House the more he will see the excluded flag flying in this country on every occasion. The position of the South African Party in this matter is perfectly clear. We want to see justice and fair play done to both sections of the people of this country. We have, for the last 15 or 16 years, been trying our best to build up South Africa on a basis of equal justice to both sections, and as far as we, as a party, are concerned, we shall never submit to seeing injustice or violence done to the feelings or rights of any section in this country. I think the Minister is acting wisely in dropping the Bill for the present, and I hope before he comes forward with a new Bill next year, and before he brings forward a Bill on the lines he has adumbrated today, he will give the subject very careful consideration, otherwise he will find next year the position far worse than it is this year, and he will find himself checkmated by the strength of public opinion much more conclusively next year than this.

The Minister has discussed this South African nationality on the assumption that it has something to do with our status abroad. It has nothing to do with our status abroad — nothing in the least. It is an internal question, and certainly can have no influence or effect whatever on our external status. How it is going to affect us internally I do not quite see either. I have been studying the Bill to see in what way this new citizenship affects the rights and duties of citizens inside the country. I fail to see exactly what is the relation of British citizenship — for which we passed a Bill only a few weeks ago — in this country, and South African citizenship. The Minister may, perhaps, make it plain to us, but to me the position seems to be that in South Africa you cannot be a South African without being a British subject. That seems to be the basis of this Bill — it is the very nature and essence of this Bill. You must be a British subject before you can be a South African. So long as this is recognised, the fear that people have that this Bill is revolutionary in its first part falls away. I do not think we should have any difficulty about this part of the Bill.

I have nothing further to add, except that I do most sincerely trust that the Government and the parties behind them will give this matter the very gravest consideration before they fling this apple of discord again before the people of this country. Let us have a united flag, but if we have another attempt made on these disastrous lines which have been followed by the Government this time, we shall see an even worse disaster than we have seen this time.

4

HERTZOG'S EQUAL STATUS

THE BALFOUR DECLARATION, 1926[1]

T H E Y A R E A U T O N O M O U S communities within the British Empire, equal in status, in no way subordinate the one to the other in any aspect of their internal or external affairs, although united by a common allegiance to the throne and freely associated as members of the British Commonwealth of Nations.

[1] Formulated by a committee with Lord Balfour as chairman and ratified by the Imperial Conference, October 1926. It was embodied in the Statute of Westminster, 1931, which, in its turn, was given a place in South Africa's Statute Book by the Status of the Union Act of 1934.

GENERAL J. B. M. HERTZOG, 16 MARCH, 1927[1]

Y O U H A V E T O make up your minds which it is going to be. Whether you are going to be a member of an empire State of which no subordinate part can have sovereign freedom, or of so many sovereign free States united in voluntary co-operation, or associated as the British Commonwealth of Nations. Let me say that the Imperial Conference gave a decided and final answer to the question. The Imperial Conference definitely rejected the view of the Empire held at the time by the hon. member for Standerton[2] and the hon. member for South Peninsula,[3] in favour of the existence of so many free sovereign peoples freely united in mutual co-operation towards the rest of the world with a view to mutual benefit. The Imperial Conference, therefore, acted very clearly according to the formula of the hon. member for South Peninsula.

It made up its mind which it was going to be, dependence or complete independence.

The Imperial Conference disposed of the question of sovereign independence, and by its decision once and for all gave a final and unequivocal decision in favour of sovereign independence. It seems to me that the

[1] Extract from statement by General Hertzog (Prime Minister) in the House of Assembly, 16 March 1927. *House of Assembly Debates.*
[2] General Smuts.
[3] Sir Drummond Chaplin.

145

hon. member has submitted to this decision. I heartily congratulate him thereon, and I also wish to express my pleasure at the way he has shown in his speech that he fully appreciates and values the good and beneficial results of the decision of the Imperial Conference. I say in all earnestness and honesty that I congratulate him on it. But he will understand now when I say that I am sorry that he, at the same time, felt himself obliged to detract from the good work of the Imperial Conference. I can quite understand why he did so. The great significance of the declaration of the Imperial Conference is, of course, just as clear to him as to anybody else in, or outside of, the Empire. It is clear to him also that the declaration also contains a decision against which it is futile for him or his party to any longer resist. He therefore felt obliged to accept the decision, but in view of the speech three months before to his constituents, he had now to make it appear as if he had always held that opinion, even from that time. That is why we find the lame remark at the beginning of his speech, where, in view of the declaration of the Imperial Conference, in a deprecatory way he says the following: "Most of us thought this was already the position, and was fully recognised in England and the Dominions."

I should like actually to be told by the hon. member who are included in the words — most of us. Is it his leader, the hon. member for Standerton, the hon. member for Yeoville (Mr. Duncan), or the hon. member for Illovo (Mr. Marwick) with the Natal members? Who are most of us? I should like to know that. The statement. "Most of us thought this was already the position" would not have sounded so stupid if it had not come from the hon. member or his party. From me, or from the Nationalist Party, it would have come quite naturally, because ever since 7 December 1912, I have never preached anything else about our status than the doctrine now recognised in the declaration of the Imperial Conference. On the other hand, the South African Party, with its leader in the van, has never done anything else but deny and oppose that doctrine. What is more, it is precisely the preaching of that doctrine by us, and by me, and, let me say, the denial of it by the hon. member for Standerton and his colleagues in the Cabinet, which led to the crisis in 1912 by which the South African Party ceased for good to exist, i.e. the old South African Party. It is due to that that the hon. member for Standerton sits there today, and I here. Otherwise, we should have both sat there or both here.

GENERAL SMUTS: I am quite content to sit here.

GENERAL HERTZOG: Precisely. Nor did I say that the hon. member was dissatisfied. I only mentioned the cause.

GENERAL SMUTS: You will not always be sitting there either.

GENERAL HERTZOG: I shall not, nor do I wish to. It has nothing to do with the matter. The whole question is what brought about the split between him and me. It was nothing less than his heresy because the Imperial Conference, if it did anything, has finally killed the idea of the hon. member for Standerton about the Empire in 1912. The

146

statement of the hon. member for South Peninsula is therefore deplorable, because if he is right, then practically nothing of any State importance or significance was effected by the declaration of the Imperial Conference. If that is so, if the old feud has not been settled, and if that declaration is so ambiguous that we must take it that it allows the feud of the past (from 1912 to 1926) to continue, than I want to ask my hon. friend to bear in mind what it will mean and must mean to the maintenance of the Empire to which he attaches so much value. Let him think of that.

I could not imagine anything more damaging to the sentiment within the Dominions, not only here in South Africa, but in all the Dominions, towards the Empire, than if it were said today that that declaration of the Imperial Conference has left undecided the whole question whether we belong to an Empire-State or not. Fortunately, I am fully convinced that that is not so. The Imperial Conference completely settled that question, and decided against my hon. friend there, and I recommend him to accept it and to put up with it. No, I feel that the hon. member well knows that his denial of the importance of what was done by the Imperial Conference is a mere subterfuge, to save him from the dilemma in which he has been placed by the policy of his party in the past, and by the speech which he made to his constituents three months ago.

If anyone were to ask me now what the Imperial Conference had done, what was to be said to its credit, than I must say that it is not difficult to give an answer. In the first place, it made an authoritative declaration about our national status. I repeat that it made an authoritative declaration about our national status. That had never been done before, alhough I find from the records in my office that the hon. member for Standerton in 1921 himself made an attempt to obtain a declaration from the Imperial Conference of that year.

AN HON. MEMBER: He surrendered.

GENERAL HERTZOG: Yes, that is quite right because he never brought it up before the Imperial Conference. Before he got so far, he became afraid for some reason or other.

SIR THOMAS SMARTT:[4] That is not usually his custom.

GENERAL HERTZOG: The hon. member for Fort Beaufort (Sir Thomas Smartt) was also there. Can it be that he restrained him? Is that possible? I accept that he did not do it, but nevertheless I half think that the hon. member for Fort Beaufort knew of the point. Why does he say that he made an attempt? And if there is anything which makes me smile and convinces me of the injustice which took place on such occasions and in such debates, then one can find in the records the eloquence with which the hon. member for Standerton debated with himself the desirability and necessity of obtaining such a declaration, and then to read that five years thereafter, on 18 September 1926, the

4 Successor to Dr. L. S. Jameson as Leader of the Unionist Party.

same member who was so eloquent went about on the platforms in the country, and eventually went to the town hall of Johannesburg, and there speaking in connection with my statement in Cape Town, that I was going to England to insist there on such a declaration?

GENERAL SMUTS: What declaration?

GENERAL HERTZOG: The hon. member knows well enough, because he must have read my speech, to refer to it in his speech. But I will repeat what I said. I am not afraid. I said on 6 September: "I notice that an idea has got abroad that at the Imperial Conference in October it is my intention to ask that we shall have a written constitution regulating our national and international status. I wish at once to say that I shall do nothing of the kind. The Union being a free and independent State, nothing more is to be gained by committing that to writing, but what I shall urge is that the necessary steps shall be taken for our national status, equal to that of Great Britain and any other of the Dominions, and entitled to international recognition, shall be so published and declared to the world, that we shall no longer have men like Mr. Patrick Duncan pretending ignorance and, through their ignorance, causing irreparable injury."

But let me return to my friend's eloquent declaration in 1921, and compare it with what he said in September 1926, viz. — " We know " (continued General Smuts) " what a declaration like that means ".

I should like the hon. member for Standerton (General Smuts) to tell me in what respect the declaration that he wanted to obtain differed from the one I suggested. That would be very interesting. I have my suspicion, but I should very much like the hon. member to tell me. Then he goes further: "It has been felt in this country and Great Britain that a declaration such as General Hertzog has adumbrated means the break-up of the British Empire."

And this is the same hon. member who recently went about from platform to platform on his pilgrimage through the country, and what did he do? He said that he and his party are the men who always stood for the sovereign independence of South Africa to prevent the British Empire breaking up.

Let me honestly acknowledge that the British Empire has been broken up by the declaration of the Imperial Conference, but it is the Empire of the hon. member which has been broken up. It is that Empire State into which with that group-unity idea he wanted to push us and make us subordinate appendages. That is the Empire which has quite rightly been torn asunder, but how then can the hon. member still come and tell us that he and his party were always protagonists of an independent sovereign South Africa? What does he say more? He says that I have now come back from the Imperial Conference and have been converted to his belief. Really, anything more ridiculous and insincere I can hardly imagine.

But, as I said, the first thing that was done at the Imperial Conference was that an authoritative declaration was made about our national status, a thing which has never yet been ventured upon by any previous Imperial Conference. I think that that at least is something which can be placed to the credit of the 1926 Imperial Conference. But, in the second place, the Imperial Conference, in the declaration, in clear language acknowledged our independent sovereign national freedom, and, as I have already said, the Empire policy of the hon. member for Standerton (General Smuts) is entirely defeated.

But in the third place, the declaration at the same time contains the settlement of a weighty political issue for the Dominions. I have already pointed out that people like the hon. member for Standerton, and his party in this country, were up to that time the protagonists of an authoritative Empire to which the Dominions, at any rate as far as foreign policy on important points was concerned, would be subordinate. And with that Empire idea, the Nationalist Party and I would have nothing to do, and we would not meddle with the existence or creation of such an Empire. We always persisted that the Dominions, by virtue of their self-government, had a claim to complete sovereign independent freedom, and that issue was settled once and for all by the Imperial Conference.

As to South Africa, the decision of the Imperial Conference was favourable to the doctrine preached by me, and against that held by the hon. member for Standerton (General Smuts) and his party. Well, one can easily understand from this the anxiety of the hon. member for South Peninsula (Sir Drummond Chaplin) and, I may also say, the hon. member for Standerton (General Smuts) to find an escape from their past, by saying: "Most of us thought that this was already the position, and was fully realised in England and the Dominions."

Let me say that the hon. member for Standerton and his party have completely forgotten their former doctrine. They have quite forgotten the policy the hon. member followed for so many years, and let me say again that I sympathise with them, because to hopelessly defeat a healthy party, such as the South African Party was in 1912, on an Empire policy, which was subsequently declared to be null and void, is really no small matter. I can therefore well understand that an escape is today sought from that position, but let me add that I am very glad that at any rate in this connection we have obtained a united sentiment and conviction, united feeling over a question which in the past gave rise to much that was utterly injurious to our country as well as to our people, and I am convinced that if we want to be a prosperous people and a happy people, then the more we can avoid further disputes on questions relating to our national freedom, the more we are agreed on that, are honestly at one, and convinced that we are a sovereign free people, the more it will do us good as a people.

It will also further be the best thing for what hon. members opposite appreciate more then I do, viz. what they call the Empire. I say again, appreciate more than I do, because with regard to the Empire, I have never yet, since De Wildt, departed from what I stated there, and I could repeat again now what I stated there. The Empire is only useful to me as far as it is useful to the people and the country. If it is useful to South Africa, and I think hon. members opposite will be much more prepared to concede this than in 1912.

GENERAL J. C. SMUTS, 16 MARCH 1927[1]

WE ARE BUSY with a matter which, of all, is the most important to this country. Our status has been a matter of grave difficulty and contention in the past. We want to deal with it on its merits, and in a judicial spirit, and if we can make the work of the conference the beginning of a new departure in South Africa, and make it the lever to lift ourselves from the deep ruts of the past, let us do so, and don't let us pursue the old spooks in the old spirit. I want to approach the work of the conference in that spirit. I don't want to make charges; I don't want to refer to any party aspects of this question, but I want to discuss some of the national aspects of the work which was done by the conference.

Let me say this. In my opinion this conference has rendered a great service. The report of the conference is a great document, a most valuable document, which we all ought to be very grateful for. I go further. So far as the Prime Minister took part in the work, I think the gratitude of South Africa is due to him for the share he took in that work. I do not think it is fair to the component parts of the Empire, or to the other statesmen who took part, that we should represent it as if it was his work alone.

GENERAL HERTZOG: I hope I have never said anything of that kind.

GENERAL SMUTS: No, the Prime Minister has never said so.

MR. T. BOYDELL[2]: Then why suggest it?

GENERAL SMUTS: It has been repeatedly suggested and stated. It is unfair. I think this conference has done important work, and work for which we have every reason to be grateful. Let us be clear about what it is. Do not let us misrepresent the work or exaggerate it, let us view it in the proper light, because, if we misrepresent this work — and the result which has been achieved — and exaggerate it, there is sure to be a reaction afterwards. The work is good enough to stand on its own merits. It need not be misrepresented or exaggerated. The Prime Minister was, perhaps unconsciously, in his statement misrepresenting the work of the conference.

Let me mention two cases. My hon. friend, the member for Peninsula (South) (Sir Drummond Chaplin) asked months ago. "Will General Hertzog tell us what he means by independence?"

---

1 Extract from speech by General Smuts (Leader of the Opposition) in the House of Assembly, 16 March 1927. *House of Assembly Debates.*
2 Minister of Labour.

As far as this report is concerned the word " independence " is carefully avoided. The question addressed by the hon. member for Peninsula (South) to the Prime Minister is not, in direct terms, answered in this report.

GENERAL HERTZOG: Do you mean the declaration does not also mean we are independent?

GENERAL SMUTS: I will come to the declaration just now. I do not want the Prime Minister to say anything that might have a tendency to misrepresent what took place. It is a significant fact that all through this document, which defines our status, the word " independence ", over which we have fought a battle royal in South Africa for all these years, is carefully avoided. There was more sense in the question addressed to the Prime Minister by my hon. friend than the Prime Minister is willing to admit.

When the House rose for dinner I was dealing with some of the statements made by the Prime Minister which, I feared, might lead to misunderstanding. I want us to be perfectly clear and explicit about the work of the Imperial Conference, and the results, so far as they affect us. Now there is another matter raised by the Prime Minister, which I want to deal with at once, as I am afraid it also might lead to misunderstanding of the position. The Prime Minister said that it had been the position of this party and especially of myself, that the Empire was or should be a sort of super-state, that there should be a super-state, a super-organism which had or should have authority over the Dominions, that this had been the position taken up by members on this side of the House, and by myself in especial — that there should be, or that there was, such a super-state in the Empire.

I do not want to enter into controversial matters now; nothing is further from my mind; I want tonight to steer clear of all matters of controversy, and see how far we are in agreement on the great matters which have arisen in connection with the last Imperial Conference, and I am bound to say this: That I have never held such a view in all the years that I have spoken of the Empire — and I have given the matter a great deal of thought. Nowhere, as far as I can remember, have I expressed the view that there should be a super-state in the Empire, to which the component parts should be subordinate. On the contrary, I have always said that there should be a union of free and equal states within the Empire, a small league of nations. From the beginning, I have always held that view, and it is my view still, nor do I know that members on this side have ever held any other opinion. There has been, there should be, no super-state. It is a misunderstanding on the part of the Prime Minister. The Prime Minister has for years laboured under this obsession, that some evil-minded persons, some persons with dangerous aims in the politics of the Empire, were trying to establish a central authority to which the component parts of the Empire would be subject. I do not think there has been any such policy.

151

GENERAL HERTZOG: Is not that the inevitable result of your group Union idea?

GENERAL SMUTS: No, the group unity is nothing more than consultative unity.

DR. D. F. MALAN[3]: Read your Glasgow speech again.

GENERAL SMUTS: Oh, my Glasgow speech? I have made many speeches, and, of course, one may sometimes say a thing which is capable of various interpretations, but I thought this matter out in my own mind years ago, and, so far as I am conscious of any opinions on the subject, I have always consistently held this view, that there must be a new form of free government in the world, that the Empire might be the beginning of such a form of government, not a government by subjection, but a government by consultation, a government which would be a free union of equals. And those ideas I expressed in regard to my conception of the Empire. I fought the idea of imperial federation. Hon. members know, it is on record, as somebody said at the time that I had torpedoed imperial federation, simply because I have stood for this other alternative of free and equal union. And later on, when I had the opportunity to push this further idea home, I did my best to have it established in the central conception of the League of Nations. Do not let us get side-tracked in this debate. What I have stood for is what this conference has declared, and I am very glad it has been done.

MR. N. C. HAVENGA: That was not the generally accepted idea.

GENERAL SMUTS: No, perhaps not. I may say, in reply to what the Minister of Finance has said, that these are very difficult matters. Unless you are a constitutional lawyer, unless you have had great experience of the working of political institutions, you cannot expect people to understand these matters clearly. What I say is that there is no new departure in this report, that the committee of the Conference of Imperial Relations purported to make no new departure. What they meant was, so far as it was possible without laying down a formal constitution for the Empire, to express as clearly and succinctly as possible the actual practice which had grown up, and to follow that up by the removal of anomalies, historical anomalies which everybody admitted should be removed. I made an attempt some years ago to have some of these anomalies removed. The Prime Minister referred to a document which he has found amongst the papers in the Prime Minister's office. I made a gallant attempt; there was no idea of "Hands-upping". That is an opprobrious term which the Prime Minister should not apply to me. He knows that it does not fit me. Why apply it?

GENERAL HERTZOG: I only used it on the suggestion of somebody else.

GENERAL SMUTS: No, circumstances were against me. The Prime Minister was right in his speech at Pretoria when he did not speak in bitterness, as he did this afternoon. Circumstances were against me in those days. Great changes have taken place, not so much in South Africa

Minister of the Interior.

152

as in other parts of the Empire. The Prime Minister met a different body of colleagues in the conference from those whom I met. The Prime Minister may take it from me that it is largely due to the fight that I put up for these new ideas that they had gained ground in the Empire. There were more people willing to do things in the new light than there were years ago when I made my abortive attempt. There was no running away, not in the least.

Now, I want us to understand what has been done, because I think the work done is good enough and great enough to stand on its own merits, without exaggeration, and without misrepresentation. The Imperial Conference purported to express in formal language and in deliberate language what was the practice, and to remove anomalies, and they have done that in a way for which I give them every praise. Do not let us today give any occasion for the idea that some revolutionary change has taken place in the Empire. If you do that, it will recoil on you. Let people understand that this is the evolution which has been going on for a number of years, and to which expression, perhaps final expression, perhaps not, but to which formal expression has at last been given. That expresses the truth, and do not let us make people understand in the backveld or in any other part of the world that there has been a sort of somersault in the Empire, that there has been a revolutionary change — there has been nothing of the kind.

If you look at the report itself you will see that this is what it purports to do, and what it purports to express. The report of the sub-committee in imperial relations opened with the statement that they could not, nor intended to, write a constitution for the Empire. They meant to recognise facts and put them in black and white, and they then proceeded to write down the formula which has been accepted as the new status. We have all read it; we are all pleased with it, and we all think it expresses the true position as it has developed and exists in the Empire. Then they go on to say that this has been an evolution. The point that has been reached is the climax of an evolution that has been going on, and they say that there have been several alternatives which have been ruled out. They mention imperial federation, and they state the only alternative left was by way of autonomy for the Dominions, and they make the further statement that every self-governing member of the Empire is now master of its own destiny; there is no distinction; in fact, it is subject to no compulsion whatever. They state this, not as a new principle, but as a fact.

MR. HAVENGA: A fact which many people would never recognise till now, especially in this country.

GENERAL SMUTS: Yes, but that is the value of this report. I agree with the Minister. The value of the report is that it is an explicit recognition of fundamental facts and existing practices, and that it removes doubts and suspicions. The report goes on, after a reference to India, to say that there are still existing administrative, legislative and judicial forms which are not formally in accord with this position and which have to be reformed, and they go on to mention what I call the historic anomalies and they provide machinery for the reconsideration of these with a view to their subsequent removal; the whole underlying idea of the report being this, that it expresses what exists in fact, but is sometimes subject to doubt, and also subject to historic anomalies. I find that this is the nature of the report, and I have been following with some care the statements which the principal actors have made about their work, and I want to quote to the House some of the statements made by some of these actors who were responsible for this document, as to what it purports to do, and what is the position as they understand it.

In the first place, let me take the speech of Lord Balfour, who was chairman of this sub-committee, at Edinburgh University, of which he is chancellor. He refers to the great work of the conference, and he asks this question: "What then was the change that has taken place?" That is the question which we are asking tonight, and what everyone has been asking. What is the change exactly brought about at the Imperial Conference? People ask themselves this, and the reply was far from obvious, because it never had been denied for many years that the Dominions were autonomous. I will ask hon. members to listen to this, because it is all-important to clear up difficulties that might arise hereafter.

"It has been explicitly stated by persons in authority, not, indeed, in any mere formal fashion, but what was even more impressive than a formal statement, it had been stated in the course of speeches as an accepted fact and stated before audiences which would certainly have expressed any objection had they entertained doubts on the subject."

The position of dominion equality had been accepted as a fact again and again. Then he goes on to refer to the war, and the great practical unity of the Dominions in the war effort they made. He refers to the peace treaty and the part played by the Dominions there alongside of Great Britain, and he winds up with this statement—

"At this moment when at Geneva the League of Nations meets, the representatives of the Dominions go there, of course, on equal terms with any other nation in the world."

He quotes this as existing practice—

"It is quite true that, as a matter of arrangement among ourselves, the representatives of the Empire are in constant and friendly communication. All their constitutional powers as members of the league are identical with the constitutional power of any other state in the world from the greatest to the smallest. Now, if that is so, and if it was so before the conference of 1926, what, you may perhaps say, was there for the conference to do? In the first place, I think this absolute equality of status was, perhaps, more obvious to the home country than it was to one or two at least of the Dominions."

Was he thinking of South Africa; was he thinking of the Prime Minister?

GENERAL HERTZOG: He was thinking of you and what you had said.

GENERAL SMUTS: Well, Lord Balfour is a deep man, and I am not going to probe into his thoughts. But evidently that was the practice, but there were some doubts and, in one or two of the Dominions there were questions. I have heard these questions too in South Africa.

He goes on to say that there were other small troubles, these historic anomalies and so on which were constantly being dragged in by constitutional lawyers and people who take a narrow view of the Empire.

MR. BOYDELL: And politicians.

GENERAL SMUTS: Yes, and the sort of politicians one comes into contact with sometimes. He says these survivals of defunct practice were all dragged to the front and were made the subject of criticism of the dominion status, implying that the status was unfair to the status enjoyed in the mother country —

" That was never held here, never I believe by thinking people. It was held, perhaps, in certain of the Dominions, and it was all-important that when the Prime Ministers met together last November that they should singly and severally in their collective capacity, give their authority to what we in this country have long believed to be a true doctrine, the doctrine of the equality of status."

That to my mind, sets out very clearly what the position was.

MR. HAVENGA: Apparently it was not in 1921 when you made your abortive attempt.

GENERAL SMUTS: The Minister is wrong. The question of equality of status was never questioned. The trouble was about the minor anomalies and forms, and the question was whether the time had come for these changes. I can assure my hon. friend that among thinking people in authority in Great Britain I have never found this doctrine questioned since 1917, when that resolution was passed about imperial federation. I had never heard this question of the autonomy of the Dominions and their equality with the Mother country questioned in any way. This is the statement of Lord Balfour, that the conference did not purport to do more than give expression to what they believed to be the actual position in the Empire, and I find the same position is taken up by the other leading actors. I have here a speech made by the Secretary of State for Foreign Affairs, Sir A. Chamberlain, a few days after the conference at Bristol, and this is what he says—

He had come from the conclusion of the Imperial Conference with the profound assurance that all which lay at the root of his father's policy was henceforth safe. Whatever might be the methods by which our unity expressed itself, in any time of stress or trouble the several self-governing nations of the British Empire would stand one and undivided before the world. Before the conference a certain anxiety pervaded the Empire as to what might be the result and consequences of it, but we have come out of the conference with a better understanding of one another than we had ever had. There had been the removal of suspicions, misapprehensions

155

and fears that His Majesty's Government here in Great Britain assumed an overlordship over the other free governments of the Empire which no British statesman for 30 years thought of claiming, much less of exercising.

It is this bogey which has become almost an obsession with the Prime Minister, that someone was trying to lord it over the Dominions.

GENERAL HERTZOG: It is strange that that should have been the feeling of Canada and Ireland as well as myself.

GENERAL SMUTS: Mr. Chamberlain says that one of the most solid and beneficial results of the conference has been to lay that ghost, and I hope the speech of the Prime Minister this afternoon is the last time we shall hear about this. Let the ghost lie; do not let us raise it again. No one wants the super-state, and no sensible person wanted it, or should have wanted it, and, therefore, let us lay it to rest and face the world as free men, and not as slaves labouring under some fear of subjection.

He goes on: " The nations had, in the intimacy of personal conference, not merely agreed upon a report, but had put ideas into a common stock, out of which each one had gained a greater appreciation, not only of his liberty, but of his responsibilities, a greater assurance that his liberties were not only safeguarded by the observation of these responsibilities, but could find the fullest development only in the close union of all, and the pursuit of common ideals and policy."

Sir Austin Chamberlain goes even further. He says not only was there this written result which we find as a formulation of status in the Empire, but there was an exchange of ideas; misunderstandings were removed, and all felt that in the continuance of the Empire, and in the pooling of resources and the sharing of responsibilities there would be the best prospect for each and all. Mr. Bruce, on his way to Australia, passed through Canada, where he made a number of speeches, and I find that at Ottawa he was reported to say this: " The result of the Imperial Conference created no new constitutional position. It defined clearly what had been the practice since the war."

I quote him simply to bear out this position I am stating—that this conference simply did their best to express the existing practice and position of the empire. Mr. McKenzie King, the Prime Minister of Canada, spoke in a similar sense in Toronto at a great party meeting: " No attempt was made to lay down a constitution for the Empire; the committee on imperial relations sought rather to formulate an authoritative sanction for rights which they contended should no longer be questioned."

On the same day he made a speech in which he tried to meet some of the criticisms of the Prime Minister of South Africa, who had been reported as making some statement about the Empire which had had an upsetting effect in Canada, and he tries to reply to it. The statement which was cabled as having been made by our Prime Minister here was: " General Hertzog said that the Empire signified to us nothing more than a mere name indicating our common adhesion, together with other peoples, to the Crown."

I do not know whether the Prime Minister made it, and I make no charge on the basis of this report. It was reported in the London papers that he had said: " The Empire is a mere name, and expresses nothing more than common adhesion to the Crown."

GENERAL HERTZOG: The Dominions, plus India and the other Colonies.

GENERAL SMUTS: Mr. McKenzie King referred to that unsettling cable, and I think that must be the cable, as far as I can make out; but he then replies to the statement at a meeting on the same day he had made the other speech already quoted. He said: " It looked to him as if General Hertzog had been trying to remove obstacles to imperial unity, and a wrong interpretation was placed on his words. The attitude of General Hertzog and President Cosgrave at all times suggested a desire for imperial unity. The report of the conference helped to clear the air of things that had been used by agitators at various centres of the Empire."

MR. BOYDELL: Unprincipled and untruthful agitators.

GENERAL SMUTS: It was true General Hertzog stated that the liberties of the people of South Africa were equal to those of Great Britain; but Canada was also unwilling to have Great Britain stand as a super-state . . .

Our Prime Minister made a similar statement in Cape Town on his arrival, when he said: " I have no fear of that Empire any longer." Quite right; the change has not been with the Empire, but with the Prime Minister. The Prime Minister went on to say: " And the reason why I have no fear of that Empire any longer is because of what has been done and achieved by the Imperial Conference. The Imperial Conference has done this, which I consider the greatest work which has even been done by any Imperial Conference — it has brought things to definite clearness."

Now I say, this, that all this shows that the Imperial Conference, instead of creating a revolution and making a new departure in the Empire, has been logically following the course which it and the Empire have always followed, stabilised the position by expressing clearly what has been the practice hitherto. We would be committing a great mistake, and we would be doing serious injury and opening the door to very grave mis-understandings in future, if we gave countenance to the idea in any form that more than that was done. I have heard it hinted and whispered all over the country that something wonderful has happened. Nothing more has happened than this, the position which existed before has been formulated in a report.

GENERAL HERTZOG: The position since when?

GENERAL SMUTS: At any rate, since the war, as both Lord Balfour and I have put it. Since the war, at any rate, that has been the position. I find that that has been perfectly clearly recognised here. When I came back after the war, I tried to put the position as clearly as I could to this country. I have made many speeches on the subject. Only on the eve of his departure for Europe, the Prime Minister quoted with approval

157

my formulation of the position, and said it could not be more strongly and better put, and he went on to quote with even stronger approval what Mr. Lloyd George has said years ago in the same sense.

Mr. Havenga: That was not accepted in South Africa as being the position.

General Smuts: I speak what is, of course, common ground.

Mr. Havenga: What, then, were we fighting about all the time?

General Smuts: I have been asking myself that question for months.

General Hertzog: Since 1912?

General Smuts: I rejoice that there has been this satisfactory conclusion to our long contention. I am not going to make any charges, because I should then fall into the same trap into which the Prime Minister fell this afternoon. This is not an occasion for wrangling and quarrelling, but an occasion for rejoicing. We have been divided as a people for years, and the principal bone of contention has been this constitutional question. I do not think the people of South Africa are going to be held apart by racial questions. It is the desire of every party to pull together, and it is the profound desire of the people of South Africa as a whole that they shall no longer be divided on racial lines. We who live here see the small troubles and the friction which arise from day to day, but they are passing. There is no doubt that there remains this stumbling-block on our future path — the profound differences in our attitude to the Empire and Empire questions generally. The differences have now been removed.

5

STATUS OF THE UNION

MR. OSWALD PIROW, 28 MARCH 1934[1]

I THINK EVEN the most determined opponent of this Bill will admit that the present constitutional position of the Union is no longer reflected by the South Africa Act. This is still the case, even if we add to and read into the Act of Union the provisions of the Statute of Westminster, e.g. no provision is made for what is undoubtedly the acid test of true self-government, namely, for the obligation on the part of His Majesty in South African affairs to be guided entirely by the advice of his South African ministers.

There may be members of the British Commonwealth of Nations who would be perfectly satisfied to piece together their constitution out of two British Acts of Parliament, supplemented by a number of conventions, either taken over from Great Britain direct, or inferred from the resolutions of the last two Imperial Conferences. In South Africa, unfortunately, experience has shown that constitutional doubts very soon become political issues — political issues, moreover, fought with extreme bitterness, and almost invariably along racial lines. A number of such doubts have arisen since the last Imperial Conference, and these doubts have been only partially settled by the Statute of Westminster. A considerable section of English-speaking South Africans want to know exactly where we stand as regards the other nations of the British Commonwealth of Nations, and with regard to the common allegiance to the Crown. For that reason they would like to see certain portions of the resolutions of the last two Imperial Conferences, or at any rate the Statute of Westminster, accepted by us as part of the law of this country. Similarly, the overwhelming majority of Afrikaans-speaking citizens are uneasy about a constitution which, in vital respects, might not be recognised by our own Supreme Court; in other words, since 1926, Union legislation defining our status has become inevitable. Some opponents of the Bill admit this, but say that there is no necessity to introduce legislation at this stage, when the Government should have its hands full with urgent social and economic problems. At the end of the session the general public will be able to judge whether the Government have lost any

---

[1] Extract from speech by Mr. Oswald Pirow, Minister of Railways and Harbours, during the debate in the House of Assembly on the Status Bill, 28 March 1934. *House of Assembly Debates.*

time in coming to grips with these urgent social and economic problems, but in any case there are two equally urgent reasons why the constitutional issue should be defined as soon as possible.

In the first place, we have at present a Government representing more nearly than any other Government in our history both sections of our population, and members of this Government are in complete agreement about every provision of the present Bill. In the second place, for the time being at any rate, there is no party warfare in South Africa. That will not always be so, and although we hope that future party divisions will not be on racial lines, the temptation to make a constitutional issue a racial issue will, in the future, be as strong as it is today. If we can settle our constitutional difficulties by means of legislation before new party alignments spring up, we may be spared in South Africa an incalculable amount of bitterness and strife.

There are some people who, whilst admitting that the Bill is necessary and the time opportune, insist that legislation of this kind should only be passed after the fullest consultation with Great Britain and the other Dominions. There might be something in this argument if the Bill contained a single principle which in one way or another has not been approved of by the last two Imperial Conferences and by the Statute of Westminster; in words, by Great Britain and all the Dominions. In any case, an objective study of the provisions of the Bill will show that there is not a single provision of the Bill which goes a step further than the existing constitutional position. The Bill sets out the present constitutional position of the Union, and nothing but the present position. Whatever legal or constitutional theories may be advanced on the wording of this Bill might equally have been advanced, and have in actual cases been advanced, long before this measure was drafted.

Coming now to the provisions of the Bill, we find that the preamble in itself should go a long way to satisfy the doubts of both sections of the community in connection with our present status. It is true that the preamble is not interpreted by a court of law, but its essentials are invariably reproduced also in this case in the body of the Bill, and in any case the preamble constitutes, for those who accept it, a moral obligation — as strong a moral obligation as any section of the Act. Now, in this preamble those who are concerned about our position in relation to the other members of the Commonwealth and to the common allegiance to the King, will find the Dominions, including, of course, South Africa, are described as autonomous communities within the British Empire, united by a common allegiance to the Crown. They will also find in the preamble a declaration that it is desirable to accept in South Africa, as part of the law of South Africa, the Statute of Westminster — a statute which refers to the Crown as the symbol of the free association of the members of the British Commonwealth of Nations who are united by a common allegiance to that Crown. On the other hand, that section of our population which is still sceptical as to the extent of our rights as a nation should be satisfied by the statement in the preamble which refers to our status as that of a sovereign independent state recognised as such by the Imperial Conferences and the Statute of Westminster. A reference to the provisions in the body of the Act shows that they bear out this contention in every respect. Objection appears to have been taken in certain quarters to the phrase " sovereign independence ". It is rather difficult to follow this objection, because the first of the seven points of coalition which were unanimously accepted by the country specifically lays down that our status is one of sovereign independence.

COLONEL C. F. STALLARD, 9 APRIL 1934[1]

THE HON. MEMBER for Kensington (Mr. Blackwell) has presented the subject as if he were talking about a law suit between the English and Dutch sections in South Africa and as a settlement of their long-standing differences. I hope nobody else will approach this question in that way. I am glad to think that the problem is not one to be dealt with in the tragic tones used by the hon. member. The problem is a simple one — what is it that South Africa wants: what mode of expression of thought will best turn into the language of a statute what we want; and the further problem, do we concede that any such language used can improve upon the position we now enjoy?

The question is really touching what is the fundamental basis on which our society is constructed. Do we want to have South Africa divorced from the rest of the Empire, or the rest of the Commonwealth, or do we want to have it interlocked as it is at present, or do we maintain that it is separate? Those are the questions which go to the root of these Bills, and unless we get a clear answer to them I do not think we can clarify the position before this House.

I understood the hon. member for Kensington (Mr. Blackwell) to say that there was a division in the Cabinet on the interpretation to be placed on these Bills, and that there would be if they are passed. I cannot pretend to have the legal knowledge that my hon. friend professes to have, but this is such a startling statement that I hope the Prime Minister,[2] and the hon. member for Standerton (the Minister of Justice[3]), will take steps to dispose of it at the earliest possible moment. If they will do so, I will willingly resume my seat and offer comments afterwards. My hon. friend, the Minister of Railways and Harbours,[4] has intervened, and he has shouldered the burden which one would have thought he might have been spared, having regard to the heavy nature of his duties with regard to rail-

---

[1] Speech by Colonel C. F. Stallard, Leader of the Dominion Party which was formed in the same year. *House of Assembly Debates,* 9 April 1934.
[2] General J. B. M. Hertzog.
[3] General J. C. Smuts.
[4] Mr. Oswald Pirow.

ways and harbours, and also with regard to defence. But we know his readiness to fill the breach, and he has filled the breach, and he has made a statement — a very concise one, and one we have had the opportunity of having a verbatim report of.

I hope there is going to be the greatest candour in discussing these Status Bills. If there is one attitude of mind which can be more detrimental to the country, as well as to Parliament, than another, it would be for us to think one thing and to say another, or for us to fail to be candid in the expression of our opinions. I have stated outside the House, and I want to say again inside the House, that my conception of the duty of a Member of Parliament is that he should express on all important public affairs the real and candid opinion that he possesses, and it will be bad indeed for parliamentary institutions if anything else prevails. I am so far from wishing these measures to be passed, at once, or at all, that I propose to move, as an amendment —

To omit " now " and to add at the end " this day six months ".

I know that this is not a mere delaying motion. It goes much further than that. I am convinced that the public is getting more and more anxious as the days go on about the contents and the meaning of the Bills, which have been put before them, and I am also convinced that even now at this stage the most profound ignorance prevails among the largest percentage of the population. That is due to the haste with which these measures have been brought before the country. I urge very strongly indeed that, even at this hour, this debate should be adjourned until a later date, to allow further time for discussion. I put a question to the Prime Minister today, which he was good enough to answer at short notice, which should go far to clear the minds of the public as regards there having been consultation and correspondence with regard to these Bills between the Government and other governments of the Commonwealth. The Prime Minister's reply has dealt categorically with that, and shows that there has been no consultation with regard to these Bills.

Mr. Walter Madeley: Certain stockholders have been protected.

Colonel Stallard: That is not consultation, but there was a suggestion made that English holders of South African stock, Union stock, should be protected in a particular way, and that was done — that, and that only.

The approval read by the Minister of Railways and Harbours before he introduced the Bill, to the effect that so far as the Crown was concerned the House was invited to express its opinion upon the measure, may impress people outside the House, who do not know the standing rules and orders, and the forms of this House, but it will not impress those of us who know that it is the ordinary form in the case of a Bill touching the prerogatives of the Crown, which is a condition precedent, under our standing orders, before a Bill of this kind can be discussed.

Now we are in a position, I think, to consider what are the merits of the measure which is before us. I am concerned, as I say, with the outlook from our point of view as South Africans, and with what is really to our interest and advantage. Do we wish to be members of the Commonwealth, or do we wish to be cut adrift? Do we consider that we are members of the Commonwealth in any sense other than that of allies, or of an alliance, or of a treaty, or an arrangement between us, or do we not? I think a great deal of misapprehension prevails as to what is in these Bills, and as to what is their intent and purpose. I deprecate very much indeed the fact that the Government did not see fit to consult with other Dominions with the same frankness as we are discussing the matter here in the House, for if the contention I hold is right that this Bill, one of a group of three — we cannot lose sight of that fact — that this Bill does profoundly alter our constitution, then certainly I say there should be consultation. If, on the other hand, the Prime Minister's contention is right that this Bill merely crosses the t's and dots the i's of the existing position, then I can understand the attitude of the Government, but if it does profoundly alter the position and alter the prerogatives of the Crown, and if it does give power to Parliament and the Executive to translate what has not been hitherto a sovereign independent State into a sovereign independent State, then I say that the case for consultation is made out 100 per cent.

It is decided in this Bill that we are in common allegiance to a common sovereign. How can that allegiance be common unless the powers of the Crown and the functions of the Crown are the same throughout the whole Empire? In striking at the prerogative of the Crown, and in diminishing it, you are striking also at the common quality of the allegiance that is owned thereto. Now I must say that I hold quite clearly, and always have held, the opinion that up to the present time we have had one Crown, that it was undivided, that it was, in its nature, indivisible, that the powers of the Crown were the same throughout each of the Dominions and in the old country, and that the advice tendered by Ministers in any of those Dominions was subject to the Crown in the same way as throughout the Empire.

Now the hon. member for Kensington (Mr. Blackwell) has spoken as though the limitation of the powers of the Crown to act by advice of the Ministers was something of a static nature, something that had already become crusted and become entirely a rule of law from which there would be no departure in Great Britain, and therefore the passing of an Act of Parliament to say that it should be so in South Africa, is merely recording an existing fact. To my mind, that loses sight of two very important features of the constitution under which we are now living. One is its flexibility. If you are going to cast into the form of a Bill all the implications, rules and conventions which affect one particular executive, or another particular executive, you are going to destroy the characteristic feature of the British constitution throughout centuries — one that has struck the attenion of every foreigner who has studied our constitution — not one through the centuries but has been struck by this, that without having a written constitution we have still been able to maintain continuity, clarity of thought and directness of action in every crisis that has arisen.

163

Mr. F. H. P. Creswell: What about the Bill of Rights?

Colonel Stallard: The example the hon. member gives me is surely an example of the other way, and it shows that in a time of crisis our constitution was just such as was completely adapted to introduce new ideas and limitations. The instance of the hon. member is entirely against the point of his interjection.

But I cannot stop to have a private war with the hon. member. I accept his point as giving me a very good illustration in the very opposite direction to which he is going. The flexibility of the constitution is the one thing we value, and is going to be struck at in this respect, and we are going to try to cast into the form of a written document the impression of what the present constitution is. I deprecate that very strongly indeed. I deprecate the diminishing of the prerogative of the Crown.

An Hon. Member: How is it diminished?

Colonel Stallard: I am going to tell you. The changes are profound and real. I know the Minister stated in introducing the Bill that there might be something in the argument used against it that the Bill contained no principle which, in one way or another, was not accepted by the two imperial conferences, and the Statute of Westminster or by Great Britain or any other Dominions. But he went on to say: "So uncertain was the matter that the Supreme Court might not accept it."

I confess that makes me alarmed. If the changes are so real and deep that you might alter what might be the decision of the Supreme Court now, what becomes of that contention? It is absolutely idle to do so. There are two or three matters in which the alteration goes very deeply indeed. Before I analyse those, I want to have a short word about the preamble. The preamble of this Bill, as the Minister of Railways and Harbours, may I say with respect, very properly pointed out, is a matter of great importance, and we have introduced here after a recital what our status is, a further matter introduced which is a reference to our position as a sovereign independent State —

Whereas it is expedient that the status of the Union of South Africa as a sovereign independent State, as hereinbefore defined, shall be adopted.

That is new language. This is absolutely new language. You will not find anything of "a sovereign independent State" in the Imperial Conference. You will not find one single word to justify that in the Statute of Westminster. Why introduce it? If it is a mere matter of dotting the "i's" and crossing the "t's", I ask, is it humbug, or is it done for a real purpose? I can only accept it is done for a real purpose, and to draw attention to the operative parts of that statute, so that in case of doubt a court may refer to the preamble in order to get an idea of what is meant. Where does it come from? It comes from the realm of controversy, not from the statute which has been accepted or anything else of the kind. It is a statement which comes from the depths of controversy and we have to give a special interpretation to it in order to come to the conclusion which the hon. member for Kensington (Mr. Blackwell) has done.

What is a sovereign independent State? It is a phrase no lawyer would have much difficulty in defining. It is a State which is in a position to do by itself anything it wants to do, with no other intervening influence or power at all. I want the House to regard it from this point of view, and others outside the House through what I am saying in the House. If we wanted deliberately to set out and make ourselves such a State, how would we set about doing it? What are the steps we should take if we demanded independence and cut the painter? There are two forms in which a Government acts; one is legislative and the other is executive. You would set about declaring the legislature as supreme and there is nothing to touch it, and the executive is responsible only to our own legislature and there is nothing that could touch it, anywhere else. When you had done that, what other powers could you give? Where you get an " i " and dot that and a " t " and cross that, would that give you greater power than that? I have thought over it, and I cannot find it. In this Bill that is done in the most deliberate and comprehensive language of which I can possibly conceive. The section says —

The Parliament of the Union shall be the sovereign legislative power in and over the Union and notwithstanding anything in any other law contained, no Act of the Parliament of the United Kingdom and Northern Ireland, passed after the eleventh day of December, 1931, shall extend or be deemed to extend to the Union as part of the law of the Union, unless extended thereto by an Act of Parliament of the Union.

I am glad hon. members agree with me on this point at any rate. That is a declaration of sovereign legislative power in the most unequivocal terms.

MR. STUTTAFORD: What does Parliament consist of?

COLONEL STALLARD: The King, the Senate and the House of Assembly. I am glad the mind of the Minister is working in tune with my own. We will see what the executive is. Hitherto executive powers have been vested in the King, and under the South Africa Act so it stands. Now, we are making a little amendment, dotting the " i's " and crossing the " t's ".

The executive Government of the Union in regard to any aspect of its domestic or external affairs, is vested in the King, acting on the advice of his Ministers of State for the Union and may be administered by His Majesty in person or by a Governor-General as his representative. Any reference in the South Africa Act and in this Act to the King, shall be deemed to be a reference to the King acting on the advice of his Minister of State for the Union.

MR. HAVENGA: Surely, you do not want it to be otherwise.

COLONEL STALLARD: I want this Bill altered in just a few ways, and if the Minister will co-operate with me we shall get together at once. The alteration here makes a most profound difference in the character of the

Crown. I am taking this as it stands literally and it was on this that I had to comment. I did not know at that time that any amendment was going to be proposed. As it stands here, executive government is now divested from the King and the power is, as it were, put into commission of the King in his council of Ministers of State. That is to say, when they advise he acts, and when they do not advise he cannot act.

MR. POCOCK: What is the position of Great Britain?

COLONEL STALLARD: The position in Great Britain is not that. In Great Britain, although the King does as a matter of fact, in ordinary practice, act only on the advice of his Ministers, he is not bound to do so. He has not done so on certain occasions in quite recent times.

GENERAL SMUTS: When?

COLONEL STALLARD: He did not do so in regard to the appointment of a Prime Minister when no recommendation had been made to him and in further matters with regard to the army, which probably the right hon. gentleman knows better than I do.

GENERAL SMUTS: I should like the House to know.

COLONEL STALLARD: Further, where the matter came up of the National Government, the action taken by the sovereign was of an active and not a passive character.

The Minister has met my criticism to this extent. He proposes now, so I understand, to say that where there is any conflict in the context between this and where it is indicated in the South Africa Act, that the actions of the Governor-General should be personal, he proposes to make an amendment which would allow the Governor-General, in terms of the existing law, to dismiss Ministers and to call for the assistance of somebody else, but in every other aspect of the prerogative, the King is tied, to act passively and not actively unless he has the consent of the Ministers.

As long as you have one government, whether in a dominion or in Great Britain, it is easy to find out what is required, and comparatively easy for the King to take action. In all cases, he may not do so, in some cases he does not do so, but in the ordinary course following the advice is in accordance with convention.

But what is the position created under the Statute of Westminster? It has created a fresh problem in regard to this. How does our constitution respond to it? The position created under the Statute of Westminster is that the King may receive conflicting advice from different sets of Ministers at the same time upon a matter which concerns more than one. The most outstanding instance is that of war and peace. It may also very readily be conceived as concerning the making or not making of a treaty. Other matters might arise connected with merchant shipping, status of ships and so on. It is possible for conflicting advice to be given on matters of South African interest, Canadian interest or United Kingdom interest which are not purely confined to one or the other. To my mind it is abundantly clear that this unwritten constitution which we are trying to put into a strait jacket meets the position absolutely. The Crown functions. It functions first by getting the utmost consultation possible. The King may then use advice, he may summon on a further meeting, but in the last resort if everything breaks down, the personal decision of the King controls the position.

If the King receives conflicting advice from different parts of the Empire, he is bound to neglect that advice in some shape or form. What is he to do?

GENERAL SMUTS: Give an actual case.

COLONEL STALLARD: The Minister will not take my point, which is that this has been created by the Statute of Westminster.

MR. OSWALD PIROW: You really ought to repeal the Statute of Westminster.

COLONEL STALLARD: I will not go as far as that. But this is the crux of the position. It is only in this way that a united front can be maintained where a common foe has to be faced. No one has been so responsible as the right hon. member for Standerton (the Minister of Justice) for showing the country the importance of the indivisibility of the Crown and of a single Crown. And we have listened and we have followed wholeheartedly in that respect.

GENERAL SMUTS: I never meant to make him an autocrat.

COLONEL STALLARD: No, the object of having an indivisible Crown is in order that you may present a common front to a common foe in time of crisis, and there is no question about our own domestic affairs where South Africa or Canada or Great Britain are concerned. There this question has presented no difficulty of any description. But that difficulty, if it arises, is not met by simply saying what this Bill says. You can say " Simonstown can be utilised by Great Britain in time of emergency, but South Africa itself is going to remain neutral ". Surely that would be an impossible position. It would profoundly alter the defensive power of Great Britain and the rest of the Empire if that were the position. Surely it is necessary for Great Britain and the Empire to know where they are going to stand — where they stand now, and where they are going to stand for all time. It is necessary to know that if we are involved in a conflict we shall stand with the rest of the Empire, and it should not be necessary to wait until a declaration of war takes place before the rest of the Empire shall know where South Africa stands. The Empire wants to know, and must know, whether it can, or cannot, depend upon Simonstown as a base in case of war. The effect of this Bill, if translated into law, will be in this respect to create the divisibility of the Crown, and to compel the King in certain aspects to depend on the advice tendered from South Africa.

What is the object of having a common king — it is to have a united front to be presented in time of crisis. That is what we are doing away with now. That result seems to follow, and it seems to be deliberately designed in this Bill to bring that about, and if it does do that, if it does create that divisibility of the Crown, then it has the effect of striking at anyone's status as a British subject.

MR. PATRICK DUNCAN[1]: What about the Statute of Westminster?

COLONEL STALLARD: The Statute of Westminster remains within the constitution as it now exists.

MR. DUNCAN: And where does this Bill go beyond it?

COLONEL STALLARD: This Bill goes beyond it by dividing the Crown and making a decision in one part of the Empire possible which may be diametrically opposed to a decision in any other part of the Empire.

MR. DUNCAN: You should criticise the Statute of Westminster.

COLONEL STALLARD: No, the Statute of Westminster does not do that, but under this Bill war may prevail in regard to one block of subjects of the British Empire, and peace in regard to another.

MR. DUNCAN: That can happen under the Statute of Westminster.

COLONEL STALLARD: There is not one section in the Statute of Westminster or in all the sections combined, which will give that result. There is not one word about independence in the Statute of Westminster. Actually, the legislative supremacy of the Parliament of Westminster is not departed from. It is treated as existing but to be used in a particular manner.

MR. DUNCAN: In what way?

COLONEL STALLARD: Well, with the consent and on the invitation of the Dominions concerned. And in regard to the executive power of the Crown, that is left untouched. And in regard to advice which may be tendered to the Crown, in that regard the Statute of Westminster confines itself to stating that in accordance with the existing practice advice may be tendered to the Crown by any Dominion, or by Great Britain. There is nothing whatever in the Statute of Westminster which diminishes the prerogative of the Crown. Now this Bill does. I cannot understand how anyone reading this Bill can say that the change from the present provision in the South Africa Act is not a very far-reaching one. I cannot understand how anyone can say that the executive power is still vested in the King. The Bill says that the executive power is vested in the King, acting on the advice of his Ministers, and any reference to the King shall be deemed to be a reference to the King so acting. Surely that is a very great departure from the existing position. Why is it done? If it is not for some purpose, then why does the Minister bring it in? Why not leave the South Africa Act as it stands? What is the object? I hope the Prime Minister and the Minister of Justice will give us a clear statement on that.

GENERAL SMUTS: It is the invariable practice.

COLONEL STALLARD: Then why the change?

GENERAL SMUTS: Because it is the practice.

COLONEL STALLARD: Why then the alteration in the South Africa Act?

GENERAL SMUTS: We want to bring the law into agreement with the practice.

[1] Minister of Mines.

COLONEL STALLARD: Has the practice been any different all these years?

GENERAL SMUTS: You asked me for a rational reason, and I gave it to you.

COLONEL STALLARD: It does not really answer my point. May I just deal with that a little further. It has been the invariable practice for the Crown to act on the advice of the Ministers in South Africa on South African affairs. It has been the invariable practice for the Crown to act on the advice of Ministers in other (parts) of the Empire. There are limitations to that, but let us accept for a moment that that is correct. We have now got the Staute of Westminster. Under that conflicting advice may be given. How does the alteration introduced by the Government meet the difficulties? It accentuates instead of meeting the difficulty.

GENERAL SMUTS: You must appeal to the Statute of Westminster.

COLONEL STALLARD: I accept the Statute of Westminster from A to Z completely and wholeheartedly. This cannot be built upon that structure. This is going far beyond it and far outside it. It is making it possible for the Crown, for the King, to act in one part of his Dominions in one way, and to act differently in another part of his Dominions. It makes it possible for a broken instead of an unbroken front to be presented in times of emergency.

MR. POCOCK: That is possible today. What about the Irish position?

COLONEL STALLARD: The Irish constitution is based on the Canadian constitution.

AN HON. MEMBER: I would like that.

COLONEL STALLARD: Yes, and there we have the spirit which would break up the whole of that living organism. It means that, instead of having an unbroken front, there may be a broken front presented to a common foe in time of crisis, and we may be split up into different portions. I believe that this possession of the prerogative is one of the greatest prizes which has been given to us. It is not something foreign which has been imposed on us nor is it an infringement of our liberty. It is a precious possession which we all have inherited, and we should be wilfully wasteful if we cast it on one side. It has been done for the purpose of creating a position of sovereign independence where the King, although he may be the same person, has one set of powers and duties in regard to South Africa and another set of powers and duties in respect of his sovereignty in other parts of the Dominions. I cannot conceive any more effective way of dividing up the rights of the Crown. It is because of that confusion of thought that there arises a threat to the position of a British subject.

Some people have talked as if I, or somebody else, had used the argument that our position as British subjects was threatened by the suggested removal of the qualification of being a British subject as one of the conditions of membership of the Union Parliament. I have never done anything so foolish. The threat to our being British subjects, however, is based on the dividing up of the Crown in respect to its sovereignty in

South Africa or elsewhere. From that angle the proposals in the Bill are a direct threat to our status as British subjects. I notice a tendency to substitute the words "British citizenship" for British subject. Why? A British subject means a person who owes allegiance to his Britannic Majesty. I do not know what the words "British citizenship" mean, because they have never been defined, but I take it they are meant to be used as indicating something which means allied. I hope that no alteration of that sort will ever be accomplished but that the words "British subject" will remain as the description of our status. The hon. member for Calvinia (Dr. D. F. Malan) has told us that the retention of the words is misleading. A good deal might be said for that in pure logic, for if I am right, and the Crown is divided and we owe allegiance to His Majesty in his capacity as King of South Africa, it is true in substance and in fact that the proposals in this Bill do contain a real and direct threat to our common status as British subjects.

MR. LAWRENCE: Do you say that we can divide the Crown if we consent to this Bill?

COLONEL STALLARD: I say the proposal in this Bill is to legislate to do that, but before you can legislate in that way, you have to get the consent of Parliament, which consists of the King, the Senate and the House of Assembly. There is a tendency to regard the prerogative of the King as a sort of private perquisite of His Majesty for him to be used at his own pleasure. Nothing of the kind. The liberties of the subjects depend on the prerogative of His Majesty. Because it is part of our freedom in its highest possible conception, that I am such a strong supporter of that prerogative, untouched and undivided. It is idle to say that we can do wrong, and that we are not sacrificing some precious possession we have in the ultimate hope that the King may impose his veto on it. South Africa does not want this Bill; it is not in the interests of the people; it has not been demanded by them and it is contrary to the hope expressed when coalition was formed, that we should cast on one side all controversial matters and concentrate on subjects pertaining to the material development of the Union. It is something which has stolen in on us against the wishes of the public.

GENERAL J. C. SMUTS, 11 APRIL 1934[1]

AT THE OUTSET I should explain that I have been prevented by circumstances from taking part in the debate at an earlier stage, but there are things which will best come from me, and I would like to state to the House and the country the view I take of this Bill and its provisions and their bearings. In the first place, I wish also to pay a tribute to the

[1] Speech by General Smuts, Minister of Justice, during the debate on the Status Bills in the House of Assembly, 11 April 1934. *House of Assembly Debates*

high level of this debate and the good spirit in which it has been carried on. The debate has been a credit to this House. I also wish to say how much I have appreciated the reception given to these Bills by the country generally. There is no doubt that these Bills have brought large sections of our people in South Africa up against a very difficult situation, and the way that our people all over the country, with a few exceptions, have viewed these Bills and accepted them is to my mind very creditable indeed to their intelligence and patriotism. There are certain exceptions, small areas of this country, in which there has been a tendency to work up an agitation, but that has been more due to newspaper action than to the independent action of the people themselves. I think on the whole the country has taken these Bills calmly, and I am sure that the debate which is taking place in this House, both by friends and by opponents of these Bills, will help to pacify and calm feeling, and to make people understand really what these Bills mean, what their import is.

A somewhat unfortunate impression has been created, partly by the Press. When I refer to the Press I must say this in fairness to the Press, that on the whole I think the Press has behaved magnificently in connection with this contentious matter, and when I refer to the Press I do not do so in a spirit of fault-finding. But a section of the Press has stated that there is something sinister in connection with the introduction of these Bills. It has even been suggested that there is some secret agreement between the Prime Minister and myself, and that we are on dangerous ground and have to tread very warily. I would remind the House that in the Governor-General's speech these Bills were announced. We said there, right at the beginning, that Bills were going to be introduced. And for what purpose? The language was important, because it was carefully considered at the time —

Bills would be introduced to bring the Union's legislation in harmony with the present constitutional position.

That was the intention announced in the Governor-General's speech, and that is the intention which we are trying to carry out in these Bills. No, sir, there is nothing to hide; there is nothing to shirk as far as I am concerned in these Bills. I am confident that we have an absolutely good case for these Bills, a 100 per cent case, and I am prepared to argue out the whole matter from beginning to end. I have from the very first moment taken my party into my confidence over these Bills. Before they were introduced into this House, I read them with my friends in caucus, and we discussed them carefully, in an earlier form and in their subsequent form, and the whole party, with a few exceptions, were quite agreed to accept these Bills. There were exceptions; my party has not been entirely agreed. It has been an old charge against us that we are not always in agreement, a very honourable charge, and at times I have had a very difficult job with some of my friends. And I had it here. But I know that they are honest and sincere. I know that some of them are severely troubled in their minds, and I for one am prepared to bear with them.

171

I only ask them to bear with me too. We discussed these Bills most fully in caucus before they were introduced, and I gave my party all the information at my disposal.

The suggestion has been made that these Bills come before this House in order to carry out certain promises which the Prime Minister made to the head committee of his party according to recent correspondence. I have already quoted the object of these Bills, and explained how they were introduced and announced on the very first day of the session, long before this correspondence took place, and I have stated, for the information of the country, how these Bills were dealt with by the Government. The Bills were originally drafted in the Prime Minister's office by the special legal adviser to the Prime Minister's Department, and they were entrusted to the Minister of Railways, as he seemed a more neutral person than the Prime Minister or myself.

We discussed these Bills, especially the Status Bill which is now before us, clause by clause, not once, but repeatedly, over and over again, until finally this Bill emerged in a form which was entirely new, and hon. members may take it from me that this Bill which we are now discussing in its present form is the Bill absolutely and truly of the whole Cabinet. You may say that if ever a Bill was drafted in Cabinet by the whole Cabinet, this is the Bill.

I may let the House into a further secret, and it is this, that some of the most contentious clauses, some of the clauses over which controversy has raged hottest, emanated from the members of the South African Party in the Cabinet. I say that in answer to my hon. friend when he says that the Bill represents an effort of the hon. member for Calvinia (Dr. D. F. Malan), and the members of the head committee of the Nationalist Party in the Cape Province. So far from that, these Bills are the work of the whole Cabinet. This Bill which we are discussing is the work of the whole Cabinet, and I assume the fullest responsibility for these Bills.

This matter has been going on for a long time, and these Bills have been for months under my personal consideration. I have searched my conscience, I have searched my legal knowledge, I have searched my experience of a lifetime in the working of constitutions, and I am satisfied that nothing is done here, and nothing is asked from the people of the country here, which ought not to be asked of them. We must bear in mind that there are some lawyers in the Cabinet, too, and men with a good deal of knowledge not only of the law but of the actual working of constitutions, which is an even more difficult matter; men of very good practical experience in these matters, and where we have come to an agreement, not as a matter of compromise but as a matter of trying to do the right thing, I think some weight ought to be attached to the immense experience and training in these matters which lies behind this Bill. Let me say this, and this is more important still — that the whole Cabinet was absolutely unanimous in their intention that nothing should be done but to express the existing constitutional position — that formula I read for the King's speech absolutely governed the whole situation as far as we were concerned. We had nothing to do with the controversies of the past, and with the controversies which have been raised on the floor of the House and in the country. Our object was simply to put into legal language, as far as human knowledge could do, the actual constitutional position as we understood it. No, there was no intention whatever to deal with contentious issues or to go a step beyond the existing position.

I have in writing the Prime Minister's promise that the points on which we had differed in the past would not be touched; that we would continue to differ on them. My hon. friend did not refer to that part of the correspondence. I do not think it was right for him to refer to the correspondence with the head committee without referring to the correspondence, which was far more important, which dealt with these matters. I had his promise, and we were perfectly agreed on that — that we never intended to raise those issues on this Bill. This Bill is a measure of common agreement on the vital issues of our constitution. I mention this because it is most important. The country should know it, the House should know it, and the future should know it — that there was no intention on the part of the Cabinet to go a step further than to express in legal language the existing constitutional position. And what is more, here we come to the House and we state that to the House and we state that fact to the country. My hon. friend the Minister of Railways and Harbours has done so; my hon. friend the Minister of Mines has done so, and my hon. friend the Minister of Education has done so. I am doing so, and whatever Minister here speaks in the debate will tell you that within our purview and intention as we view the matter, this Status Bill does not go one inch beyond the existing legal constitutional position of this country.

Well, that is very important for the working of this Bill in future. The light by which it should be interpreted is this governing declaration which is made here, which has been made by my colleagues and by myself, and on which we are unanimous. It is human to err; I do not say we have erred; but this is what underlies this Bill. It does not travel one inch beyond the existing position but states the position as we understand it, and as it is. If, in future, there are questions of interpretation, that is the governing principle. We understand this Bill to be merely declaratory of the present position, and it ought to be interpreted in future, and we ought to be guided in future, in that spirit. Now I think, in the light of this statement, the importance of which ought to be appreciated, there ought to be no difficulty. It is an idea which seems to be in some minds, and to which I am afraid expression has been given by the hon. member for Cape Town Gardens (Mr. Coulter), that there is some other object to be achieved by these Bills; that is entirely wrong. We simply wanted to express, as far as we were able, the existing position.

Now I come to this Bill itself. I am going to test the clauses of this Bill in the light of this declaration I have just made. What does this Bill say? It begins with a preamble which deals quite clearly and frankly with, and sets out quite fully, the whole position as it has developed since 1926. It starts with that basic declaration of 1926 — the Balfour declaration of 1926 — sets forth what happened subsequently, the Statute of Westminster, and in that way the preamble sets forth the whole position under our common law, that we have a system of states equal, autonomous, free, none subject to the other; that we are a free association in the British Commonwealth of Nations, and that we owe common allegiance to the Crown. The matter is followed up by a schedule, which sets out the Statute of Westminster — not only the operative clauses, but even the preamble of the Statute of Westminster, so far as it applies to South Africa. This Bill then goes on to make certain provisions, and I am going to mention under these provisions those which seem to be important and ought to be discussed in this House.

In the first place, we have the provision which says who our King is in the constitution.

MR. F. C. ERASMUS: And his heirs and successors.

GENERAL SMUTS: The present King is known and settled, and we extend the provision to his heirs and successors too, to provide for the future. There is no change in that and it has been the practice hitherto, and has been laid down in the South Africa Act of 1910. No change is made there. And surely it is a matter of great importance that we should have this solemn reaffirmation, in what will largely be our constitution in future, of the position of the Crown as existing hitherto, and as was laid down in the South Africa Act. Surely in the light of all the controversies which have raged in this country, it is a matter of profound importance that it should be done. No change is made. We are expressing once more for the present and for the future the existing constitutional position of the Crown. I look upon that as most important. This is the first important provision.

The second provision that is important deals with what is called here " the sovereignty of Parliament ". I submit, and hon. members will agree with me, that in this clause we do not travel beyond what is and has been the existing position both in practice and as laid down in the Statute of Westminster. I am not going to cover the position which my hon. friend, the member for Roodepoort (Colonel Stallard), and also the hon. member for Cape Town Gardens (Mr. Coulter) raised here whether there is still a residuary legislative power of the British Parliament. All that we say here in this provision of the Bill is this, that no British Act shall apply to this country unless it is covered by an Act of our own Parliament. There may be some residuary power left in the British Parliament. I do not know. It is not a matter that we need argue upon now, but we make the position perfectly plain as far as we are concerned, that is, that only an Act of our Parliament will bind South Africa in future. If there is a British Act and it has to have any relation to us, we must make it our Act. That is what is laid down here. Surely we are not travelling in the least beyond either the existing practice or the Statute of Westminster.

The Statute of Westminster uses the words " agreement and consent " but hon. members will understand that that is a vague expression. The question is: how is Parliament going to give its " agreement and consent "? We do it by Act and we lay down here that it is only by Act of our own Parliament that any law passed elsewhere shall apply to us. That is the Statute of Westminster and that has been the practice. I do not remember a single case since we had our constitution given us in 1910 where a British Act has been applied except by our own Act. Take a very important case which has special reference to us here, that is, the British Naturalisation Act. The Imperial Conference agreed that there should be a uniform Naturalisation Act throughout the Commonwealth. A model Act was passed in the United Kingdom and it was applied here to us by our own Act, just as we are doing in this Bill today. The practice of the law as laid down in the Statute of Westminster is carried out here and we do not in intention or in language go an inch beyond that.

Now we come to the executive Government, and that is the provision which the hon. member for Roodepoort (Colonel Stallard) has made the most of. It is provided that in executive Government, both in internal and in external affairs, the King acts on the advice of his South African Ministers. I ask whether that has not been the practice. There is only one answer to practice in this country ever since we received a constitution in 1910. There has never been any other way of acting. The King or the Governor-General as his deputy has always and invariably acted in the executive Government of the country on the advice of his Ministers. It has been our practice, it is the British practice. As long as there is a Government the King acts on its advice, and no innovation whatever is made here on the practice that has existed hitherto. It is the very nature of responsible government. Responsible government means that the King acts on the advice of his Ministers and if he did not, there would not be responsible government, there would be autocracy.

I am trying to prove my case that we have not travelled an inch beyond the existing practice and the existing law. These are the provisions, the really important and governing provisions, in this Bill — who is our King in South Africa, what is the authority of our Parliament and who is our executive Government? And I say that in the provisions laid down here, which were very carefully considered in the cabinet and drafted and re-drafted, over and over again, we have tried to express what is the existing position in practice and what has been agreed to at Imperial Conferences and laid down in the Statute of Westminster.

The hon. member for Roodepoort (Colonel Stallard) says we have travelled in two or three respects beyond the existing position. I am going to deal with the exceptions which he says we have made to the existing position. He says that where we use the words " sovereign independence " in the preamble, that is new, and travels beyond the existing position. There may be some difference of opinion as to the wisdom and expediency of using those words, but if you ask me the question whether we have the

175

right and are we right to call our present status by that name, then I have no doubt whether, and I think there can be no doubt. The whole position rests on that fundamental and governing declaration of the conference in 1926. It is set out here, in the preamble, and to my mind the most important part of that declaration, which is often overlooked and which I am afraid my hon. friend overlooked, is what I may call the equation between Great Britain and the Dominions. That is the governing thing. That was the most daring part of the declaration of 1926, to equate Great Britain with the Dominions. She is mentioned with them, she is lumped together with them, in this declaration. That I call the great equation of our Commonwealth, upon which our Commonwealth rests. If that equation is fundamental, if that is really what this great declaration of 1926 meant, then how can you conceivably argue that the Dominions are not sovereign international independent states, without denying that Great Britain, which is equated with them, has that status in the world?

It seems to me an utter absurdity, and it is only the unwillingness of some of my friends to face that situation that makes them boggle over this language. The British statesmen did not boggle over it. This formula was agreed to by the most powerful conservative government that Great Britain has ever had. This formula was drafted by two of the most able and experienced Ministers that England has ever had. Lord Balfour is especially associated with this declaration. Surely he was not the man to be caught napping, or to use words in absent-mindedness. He wrote down this formula, and the other man who was responsible more than any other, was the Lord Chancellor of that day, probably the most brilliant Lord Chancellor England has had in our generation, Lord Birkenhead. These were two of the brilliant men on the British side. Lord Birkenhead stood out amongst the Lord Chancellors of our day and was probably one of the ablest men to have held that position. Then we had Lord Balfour. His experience, wisdom and knowledge of the Empire was such as no one could question. These men were not afraid. These men wrote down the grand equation of the Commonwealth which equates Great Britain with the Dominions. Do not let us boggle over the words. If Great Britain is a sovereign international state, then by the laws of Euclid, by the laws of thought, the same thing can be applied to any of the Dominions. This was not only great statesmanship, but it was great faith in the future of the Empire, of the Commonwealth. These men knew the traditions of their race. They knew the essence of the British constitution, they knew and they had faith in the other members of the Empire and they did not boggle over the formula of equality. Do not let us do it. Although some of us may not like the word, some of us may hark back to the past and to what my hon. friend has somewhat ungenerously called the " Crown colony mentality " — do not let us here in this country do that. Let us have equal faith and equal pride in British institutions, and in the nature of the great group to which we belong, freedom, equality are the essence of it. I do not think we have made a departure there, except in the mere form of words. Nothing is implied in the words " sovereign independence " which is not implied by the whole full Balfour formula as written down. It has been pointed out in this debate that sovereign independence in the preamble is defined by those resolutions and declarations of the past. That is so. But I am not labouring that point. I think we are on safe ground by pinning our faith to that grand equation that was laid down in 1926 and which is the very foundation and will continue to be the foundation of the Empire. If there is to be any question of that equation, then it will be a bad day for our whole group.

Now I come to the second point which my hon. friend says is new. He says that in providing that the King in his government in South Africa acts on the advice of his Ministers, we have divided the Crown; he says that we have intended doing it and we have done it. He says that under the Statute of Westminster, the possibility arises of divided counsels, and therefore if the Empire has to be kept together on great critical and crucial occasions, there must be some authority to keep the Commonwealth together, and he says that we have taken that power away. He says we are binding the King, or his deputy in South Africa to act on the advice of Ministers here. He says the King can no longer exercise that prerogative of personal decision on critical occasions which will allow him to save the Empire. Now my answer to that is this. There is no such prerogative. I tried to push my friend for precedents on other occasions where the King had exercised that prerogative of personal action in cases of difference.

MR. NICHOLLS: Surely, although they have not arisen, they may arise.

GENERAL SMUTS: There is no such prerogative, and if there were such a prerogative left in England, then the British constitution would be an entirely different thing from what it is. The King would be an autocrat.

COLONEL STALLARD: The necessity may arise as a result of the Statute of Westminster.

GENERAL SMUTS: The hon. member has a quarrel to pick with the Statute of Westminster. I do not agree with him.

COLONEL STALLARD: I have no quarrel with it.

GENERAL SMUTS: The argument of the hon. member is this. The Statute of Westminster leaves the opening or creates the opening for divided counsels, and therefore the King must have this prerogative which will make united action possible. He must in the last resort take personal action and make a personal decision. I know my British constitution. I know it from the books, I know it because I have seen it work, and I have actually taken part in its working, and I can assure my friend that there is no such action possible for the King, there is no such prerogative. That prerogative stopped hundreds of years ago, it is a feudal prerogative, which goes back to the Stuart times or earlier. The King has no prerogative of acting on his own without the advice and countersignature of his Ministers. What is the prerogative of the King today? He has one undoubted prerogative, and that is to appoint his Prime Minister. We have all agreed that that is the King's prerogative.

177

MR. COULTER: He can dissolve Parliament and appeal to the country.

GENERAL SMUTS: I am inclined to think so myself but I just want to tell my hon. friend that there is no agreement about that. There is no agreement that the King can dissolve Parliament and dismiss his Ministry without their being first defeated in Parliament.

MR. COULTER: It was done in 1842.

GENERAL SMUTS: I qualify my statement on this point. I am quite sure that constitutional lawyers are unanimous in thinking that the King has the prerogative of appointing his own Prime Minister without consulting anyone. Sometimes he does consult, but he need not. There is the celebrated case where Mr. Gladstone resigned in 1893, and Lord Rosebery was appointed by the Queen as his successor without Mr. Gladstone being consulted. That appears from the correspondence which was published since. There is no question about that. It is customary for the King to consult his trained advisers, but he has undoubtedly the prerogative of deciding who the Prime Minister is to be, and the Governor-General here acts in the same way. But it is perhaps questionable whether he has the other prerogative.

That is the prerogative of the King. What else is there? You may say that he has the prerogative to veto a Bill passed by both Houses, but it is more than questionable whether that veto is still part of his prerogative. It has not been exercised, I believe, for more than 200 years, and if it is part of his prerogative, it is a dead prerogative. There is no prerogative on the part of the King to act on great occasions on his own. He cannot declare war on his own, he must act on the advice of his Ministers, and whatever proclamation is issued must be countersigned by his Ministers. He cannot make peace on his own. It is done on the advice of his Ministers. The King has no prerogative such as my friend there has suggested.

MR. NICHOLLS: There is no law against it, only practice.

GENERAL SMUTS: There is no such prerogative. My hon. friend says that a state of chaos would arise in a crisis. That has been the position and it may be the position again, but it does not arise. The British constitution rests on common-sense, it rests on wisdom, it rests on insight, it rests on great experience and on human nature and on none of these technicalities of law to which my hon. friend alludes. If the King did otherwise, he might lose his head as has happened before, or he would initiate a revolution.

MR. COULTER: Why should we have a Bill at all?

GENERAL SMUTS: With the evolution of the Dominions the British Government has agreed to that. They thought it wise to make this necessary far-reaching declaration in 1926 and after that they departed in the Statute of Westminster from the old practice of an unwritten constitution. There is no such prerogative, and if such a crisis were to arise we have only to rely on the innate sense of statesmanship, prudence and deep-seated sentiments that bind together our great group of nations, for there is no prerogative in law but only common-sense and human wisdom. These are the points of new departure which my hon. friend has mentioned. There is no such prerogative as he says we take away.

I would like to say a few words as to the points made by the hon. member for Cape Town Gardens (Mr. Coulter): he took a different line. He was also very strongly opposed to the use of the term " sovereign independence " and he also thought that there should be a central authority for the day of emergency. The King has no such functions in the British Empire and never will have; he is in quite a different position. The hon. member added another argument, that the South African Party has always stood for a clear position. We have fought secession, neutrality and a republic and all these things he thinks are wrapped up in this constitution. He says we are making a surrender of what we have stood for. I would say to him that I stand absolutely where I stood before. I have said so to the Prime Minister and he has agreed. We want in this document to lay down that broad basis of a constitution on which 95 per cent of the people are agreed. To my mind these things, secession, neutrality and the like are impracticable and academic. I do not believe that anything we can say in a constitution will settle our attitude or influence it when we come to the day of secession or to the day to declare our neutrality. These events, if ever they come to pass, would shake the whole British Empire and perhaps the whole world to its foundations.

It is futile. You may talk about these things in a debating way if you are a debating society, but men who have been through the ordeals we have been through attach no importance to formulae of words. Consider, for example, the position of the United States of America during the war. The United States did her utmost to keep out of the great war. She fought a presidential election during the war to keep out of it, and everybody was pledged to the full to keep out of the war; but in spite of all in a couple of months she was in the war. She could not maintain her neutrality. Whether it is neutrality or secession or any of these things, they will be decided, not by legal documents or the phraseology of a Bill like this, but by the ordeal of facts, of great events which might shake not only this country, but even the world, to its foundations. But sufficient unto the day is the evil thereof. Wise men leave these things alone.

There is nothing in this Bill which we are offering the people of this country to which I think any legitimate exception can be taken. I know the fears, I know the misgivings of some of my friends, but I give them my solemn assurance that, having studied these documents to the full, having given them as much attention as I can give them after a lifetime of experience in these matters, I find nothing in them that I cannot ask my people to ratify and to agree to. I go further, and I would say this here today, that this is the sort of settlement which, in the light of my experience, I would recommend my party and my people in South Africa to accept, because this is the sort of settlement that seems to me, and that always seemed to me, to make for the abiding peace of South Africa. Full sovereign status, freedom to the utmost without limit, but always in the group of comrades and friends with which we have marched hitherto in our history. Here you have it. This Bill gives us a full sovereign status and is intended to give that; but it also, at the same time, equally emphasises the other aspect of our position, and that is that we belong to a group of friends, a free world-wide association, and common allegiance to him, right through this great group, keeps it together. It seems to me that this is the sort of settlement which I would, if I were a dictator, dictate to South Africa. So far from betraying the position I have stood for, and the confidence of my friends, so far from doing anything that ought to shake their confidence, this is the sort of solution that, if it were in my power, if I were a dictator I would prescribe to South Africa.

MR. COULTER: Does our British nationality remain unimpaired?

GENERAL SMUTS: Absolutely. My hon. friend can accept the assurance which was given here the other day by the Minister of Railways, not only on the authority of his colleagues of his Government, but on the authority of the resolution that was passed by the last Imperial Conference, that our status as British subjects will not be touched except by common agreement.

MR. COULTER: I spoke of nationality.

GENERAL SMUTS: I ask my hon. friend not to quibble with me. I do not say he is quibbling, but I know there are turns and twists of phrases, and I do not want to be caught. I am simply pinning my faith to the language which is adopted in this document: " common allegiance to the King ".

MR. COULTER: I only want to make it clear that " common status " means " British nationality ".

GENERAL SMUTS: My hon. friend has the assurance of the Minister and of the Government that nothing will be done to touch that common status without common agreement, and there we may leave it. We may raise a fight over it, and he may then be alongside of me — one never knows. One never knows in this country what the next phase will be. But I have profound faith in this country, and I would ask my friends who do not quite agree with me to have faith in South Africa. I have quoted to them the case of the British statesman who had faith in what they call the " British Empire " — not only in their little island people, but faith in the whole group spread over the world; and I ask my fellow citizens here in South Africa: " Have faith in South Africa." After all, we have come grandly out of the struggles of the past — through all that South Africa has gone, and it has been tested as no other young nation has been tested in history. In our generation she has been tested to the utmost, and she has always come out with flying colours, and she is still moving forward. There has been no wreckage; there has been no fatal mistake by her people, but they have always been guided by sound sense — a nose, so to say, for the right; and I have the fullest faith that South Africa will continue like that. Do not fear. Do not look to phrases and to words, but look to the character of the people. They have struggled in the past, and have had controversies which seemed to shake the country. But again they have come together and have co-operated. They have done their duty on great occasions and have not let their country down. And I say, when we deal with a document like this, and launch into the dark future — a future which is darker for the whole world than for South Africa — let us have some faith in the people of South Africa — in their innate sense of what is fair and right, and in their wisdom and their practical statesmanship. The past has taught us that in that faith we do not go wrong. I appeal to my friends to accept the Bill in that spirit, and I appeal to the country also to do so.

I was profoundly moved the other night by what my hon. friend, the hon. member for Graaff-Reinet (Dr. Bremer), said about "nasietrots" (national pride). I know it goes very deep. To a large section of our people their pride is not only a national pride, but a personal pride. We shall never have peace in South Africa until we satisfy that. We must settle it once for all.

We have had two roots of division in the past; one root was racial, and the other was constitutional. The racial root is withering. More and more you see people fraternising, and doing away with the dead racial issues of the past. We shall continue to have difficulties and racial questions — all is not yet lovely in the garden. But the root is withering, as I say. Let us now cut the other root. I hope that this Bill will cut the root of the constitutional controversies which, for a generation, have divided South Africa and convulsed it to its foundations. In cutting it we are rendering South Africa the greatest service possible, and laying a sure foundation for the future. Unless we remove these fundamental causes of difference, we shall have no peace in this country. Do not think you will be able to discuss your economic questions in a fair and proper spirit. Do not talk about that, because over it all will be the poison of this controversy, this feeling that justice has not been done to the people of this country, that their status has not been recognised. Remove that, satisfy that feeling. It is a good and proper feeling, it is a human feeling of national self-respect, which nobody should resent. What we are doing here, and we are asking our friends who have that feeling, also to agree, is to confirm our friendship and our association with our group. I know that my English friends especially are profoundly attached to what is called the British connection. Whatever can he said in human language to affirm the British connection, is said in this Bill. That being so, and both sections of our population being satisfied and their aspirations being fairly met, let us accept this Bill. Let us not start a controversy among our people. Do not let us divide them, because we honestly mean to do the right thing by them, and to keep them together, now that we have brought them together. Let us accept this Bill, and give it to South Africa as one of the foundation stones of her future unity and strength.

6

THE POST-WAR CONSTITUTIONAL
POSITION

GENERAL J. C. SMUTS, 18 FEBRUARY 1948[1]

I WISH TO reply at once to the question asked by the hon. Leader of the Opposition. It is a straightforward question and requires a straightforward reply.

To begin with, I should like to say that in my opinion he is taking a too serious view of the actions of Lord Bruce and those of the House of Lords. Lord Bruce is a former Prime Minister of Australia, after which he was for a number of years Australia's High Commissioner in London, but he no longer holds that position. He is now a private person. Being a viscount, he is a member of the House of Lords, and as such he has raised this matter and put forward that proposal. The House of Lords discussed the question, but not as an authoritative body, but rather, as is usual in the House of Lords, discussed it by way of a first-rate debating point. The House here knows that the House of Lords is particularly fitted for such an occurrence. It is not an authoritative body. As far as questions of policy are concerned, the decision rests with the Government and the House of Commons. The House of Lords, however, consists of a large number of people with lifelong experience, of outstanding ability, of high prestige in all spheres of life, and they are the proper body to discuss the matter in broad outlines from a non-party point of view, and I am sure that Lord Bruce raised this matter there in such a spirit, and if they pass a resolution on anything, it is, viewed from a practical angle, in fact a decision of an academic nature.

The House should not forget that during the debate there, the British Government declared itself against the motion. Viscount Addison, who is the Leader of the House of Lords and who represents the Government and speaks on behalf of the Government, quite clearly stated in regard to this motion that the Government was opposed to it, that the Government considered it to be a retrograde step in view of the development which has taken place in the British Empire, and that it would not solve any questions, but would more likely give rise to greater difficulties. Viscount

[1] The Prime Minister (General Smuts) in the House of Assembly, 18 February 1948, answering the Leader of the Opposition (Dr. D. F. Malan) who referred to a motion in the House of Lords, introduced by Viscount Bruce, proposing the creation of a supreme council for the British Empire as a fixed permanent body with a permanent secretariat.

Addison spoke with authority, and with a background of much experience and knowledge of the matter, for he is well aware of the attitude taken up by the Dominions; the statement which he made there in connection with such a development as foreshadowed by Lord Bruce was therefore based on his authority as a member of the Government and on the experience he possesses.

The resolution was passed, but I would advise the hon. Leader of the Opposition and the House not to take it too seriously. The question has been raised from time to time. The Leader of the Opposition is quite right when he says that this is not the first time we hear about it. From time to time the question has been raised and discussed of how the various components of the Empire could be brought closer together, how to curb the tendency towards secession which exists, and to see how it will be most feasible to keep the surprising number of Dominions scattered over the whole world together in the general interests of the British Empire and the Commonwealth. It is an old problem which has often been discussed, and from time to time, as far as I can remember, it has also been raised even at Imperial Conferences; but the reaction there was always a negative one, because, as Viscount Addison remarked, it would mean a step of retrogression. The entire tendency and purpose of the development of the Empire of the Commonwealth lies in another direction. It tends more towards freedom, towards more authority and power for the various Dominions to which they attach much value, and which most of them will refuse to renounce or waive under any circumstances. That is the position, and therefore the hon. Leader of the Opposition views the matter in too serious a light.

As far as the point of view of South Africa and that of this Government is concerned, no doubt can exist. If the Leader of the Opposition should have had any doubts in regard to this matter, I shall remove them at once. I am absolutely opposed to the proposal, and the Government is entirely opposed to the suggestion made by Viscount Bruce. As Viscount Addison said, it would mean a retrogressive step. We have reached a position which was entrenched and laid down years ago in the Statute of Westminster, and today there is not the slightest chance to go back on that. That is quite clear. I know what are the views of the former members of Imperial Conferences. They held that view, at least the majority of them, and as far as the newer members are concerned, I believe that they will hold the same views, for we all know that the tendency among the more recent members was in the direction of total secession from the British Empire. That was also the tendency of the two Indian States which have now been added. Their tendency was to secede completely, but afterwards a compromise was arrived at; a compromise was effected under which they have been granted their independence under Dominion status, whilst still remaining under the British Crown, although they are totally free and independent with exclusive say in their own affairs. In spite of that, they are still under the British

Crown, but not under the British Government or the British Parliament; there is this symbol of unity for the whole Commonwealth under which they also come, and on those conditions they accepted the compromise. Their tendency right through, however, was to go still further, and I feel that if this question should be raised at an Imperial Conference, at a conference of Prime Ministers, the feeling which existed in the past against any steps such as the one now proposed by Lord Bruce will be much stronger still. I believe that the influence of new members on such a conference will be still more to the effect that it is best to leave the matter there and not touch upon it. I also think it is a wrong step; I do not think it is a progressive step. The co-operation existing in the Commonwealth today is based on discussions and consultations from time to time, on exchanges of opinion, but with a complete independence as far as the policy of each member of the Commonwealth is concerned. That is the position today, and that is the status of the members of the Commonwealth, and I do not believe that there is the slightest chance of abandoning that status; it would mean a retrogressive step. The greater the attempt to create a closer union in order to knit more firmly together the loosely connected entities, the greater will be the friction, the more pronounced will be the disunity, the stronger will become the tendency towards secession. I therefore do not take the resolution of the House of Lords seriously. I feel it is in the nature of an academic decision, as so many of the resolutions of the House of Lords are.

It is an excellent thing to have such a body; I cannot find fault with it. We have here, for instance, the Senate. The House of Lords discusses matters of public importance and passes resolutions, but if such a resolution does not tally with the policy of the Government, the Government is in no way forced to give effect to that resolution, for as hon. members know, the Government has not got a majority in the House of Lords. So even if they pass such a resolution, it does not take the matter any further, apart from being an expression of public opinion among the upper ten.

The question of a super State to which the Leader of the Opposition referred, is not a question we need worry about. It is being raised from time to time. The Leader of the Opposition was quite correct in his statement that under the stress of circumstances, under the heavy burden the world is suffering from and the danger of wars, the occurrence of which seems almost inevitable, there is much that can be said in favour of a world State, if such a thing were possible, which would eliminate the dangers now threatening the human race. That may still come one day.

DR. MALAN: UNO cured us of that idea.

GENERAL SMUTS: That only shows the difficulties one encounters on that road. If there were people who thought that the United Nations Organisation was a step in the direction of a world State, they have been taught by experience during the last two years that the result has been the exact opposite. Instead of the United Nations Organisation leading up to a world State, the result has been the opposite. Today it looks rather that the world is splitting up more and more. If there were any question of a world State there would not be one, but there would be at least two and perhaps three. Even the slightest attempt to move towards such a goal clearly shows that the actual development of the world goes in another direction.

I believe one of the mistakes which are being made in the world today is that people are driving towards a unity which is not based on realities. There is a diversity of outlook, of mode of living, of background and of views in regard to the future, which all work in a different direction which no longer correspond, and the people who today cherish a new world plan on the basis of unity forget to take account of the actual facts. The facts point in another direction, and that is the reason why I do not think we need worry about this resolution. We are facing very great practical problems in regard to the world position, enormous practical difficulties, and the people are looking for a way out, for a solution in the direction of a world State, are to my mind looking in vain. As the ordinary expression says, they are barking up the wrong tree. The facts point in another direction. They do not keep account of the fact that the actual development of the world goes in another direction. That is as I see the world position today. It is possible that there will be closer ties between countries in the world. It seems as if many States in Eastern Europe are prepared to forsake their independence and to become satellite States, thereby forming one large federal State in which they in fact lose their independence. Something of that nature is apparently taking shape and it is possible that as a counterpoise in the West, as a defensive measure and as a measure of self-preservation, another group of States will be formed, a group within which States will also be prepared to sacrifice a certain measure of their independence in order to save their countries from the position which has arisen in the East and from the danger threatening from the East. That is quite possible, for the position of the small nations of Western Europe, with their small, outstandingly brilliant populations which from time to time are crushed and trampled down by war, must be safeguarded. It is a position in which any possible measure must receive consideration, and quite possibly the idea which has been put forward lately, one can almost say during the last few days, of a Western union may well take root.

Dr. Malan: Surely that would not be more than a voluntary alliance.

General Smuts: But still it would mean that they come more closely together. Perhaps it will not be more than a voluntary alliance, but it will be the formation of the second group of States. It is possible that such a development will come about, in order to try and combat in that manner the serious dangers of another world war and the extermination of the human race. It is possible that something of that kind will happen, but the idea of a super State in the world is on the wane and the encouragement of the idea of such a super State is not in conformity with the

185

actual development in the world. The discussion may be interesting, but it is academical and to a certain extent it is not based on a proper foundation.

As far as we are concerned, we can continue along the road on which we are travelling and I do not think that either in South Africa or in certain other independent and sovereign parts of the British Empire many people will be found prepared to accept the idea propounded by Viscount Bruce. Our manner of consultation within the Commonwealth today works very well, according to my opinion. The British Government is prepared to keep in consultation with us even from day to day and from week to week, and if it is not done by way of cables, it is done by means of conferences and discussions with our High Commissioner. I do not believe it is necessary to adopt another method of consultation, and that idea of a council, even if it be merely an advisory council, proposed by Lord Bruce, is, in my opinion, unnecessary. Our method of consultation works well and we are more or less in the know of what is going on. We can put forward our viewpoint there and others can also do so, also the British Government itself; I do not believe that we need any new machinery. The more machinery, the more friction. That has been my experience and I therefore am afraid that the new machinery envisaged by Lord Bruce will lead to opposition, friction and misunderstanding.

The discussion we are having here today — and I agree here with the Leader of the Opposition — indicates that serious developments might result from the idea proposed by Lord Bruce. I therefore believe that we need not consider the idea of new machinery within the Commonwealth. It is wholly unnecessary and if it came to a point, it might even be dangerous. On behalf of the Government I therefore state unreservedly and clearly that we are against the idea of such a supreme council which would take the place of the existing method of consultation of which we make use.

7

THE NEW COMMONWEALTH

DR. D. F. MALAN, 11 MAY 1949[1]

A s I s a i d before my departure to Europe, the Prime Ministers' Conference which was to be held in London, was to be confined to one subject only. It was not possible at that stage to give more information in that regard. But that programme was adhered to. The only subject that was discussed at the conference was the position of India, the fact that India was to become a republic in the near future, and India's request, notwithstanding that event, to remain a member of the Commonwealth. This was the only matter that was discussed at the Prime Ministers' Conference. It is true that I had discussions with individual Ministers, more particularly with certain British Ministers, with regard to matters of importance to South Africa; but those discussions were outside the conference, they were entirely of an informal nature and I need not therefore make any reference to them.

The conference was faced with a specific problem, an involved problem and a delicate problem. The problem was this: One of the members of the Commonwealth had decided to change its form of Government and to declare a republic. That was not all. A unanimous resolution was passed at the same time in the discussions that were held in India by the Constituent Assembly, which was charged with the task of drawing up the constitution for the future, to the effect that India wished to remain a member of the Commonwealth in spite of the fact that it was becoming a republic. That was the problem with which the conference was faced. At the discussions two things were eliminated, from the nature of the case, and the first was that having regard to all the circumstances no attempt would be made to try to persuade India not to take the step it proposed to take, namely, that India should abandon the idea of declaring a republic. I say that from the nature of the case this was eliminated. In the first place there is the resolution that was passed unanimously by the Constituent Assembly and secondly there is the fact that the leaders of India had deeply compromised themselves with regard to this matter. Not only had they made promises to their own people in this connection, but they had committed themselves as far as this

---

[1] Extract from speech by the Prime Minister, Dr. D. F. Malan, in the House of Assembly, 11 May 1949. *House of Assembly Debates.*

matter was concerned in the eyes of the whole world, and it would have been useless in those circumstances to attempt to persuade India to retrace her steps. For that reason, from the nature of the matter, no attempt was made at these discussions to persuade India to abandon her intention of becoming a republic.

There is another matter that was also eliminated at the discussions and that was the possibility that India should steer a middle course, that is to say, that India should occupy more or less the same position in which Ireland is placed today, a country that was also a member of the Commonwealth but later withdrew and today stands outside the Commonwealth, but nevertheless occupies a position unlike that of any foreign nation. It was Ireland's wish to be outside the Commonwealth, but at the same time to remain associated with all the members of the Commonwealth jointly on a treaty basis. Any discussion with regard to this matter was eliminated because there was a definite request from India to remain a member of the Commonwealth and because she had previously intimated that that was her desire. Notice of that fact had already been given to the various Prime Ministers before their departure for London, that India definitely did not wish to occupy the same position as Ireland. She wanted either to remain entirely outside the Commonwealth, not associated with it, or to remain an ordinary member of the Commonwealth as hitherto. In those circumstances that possibility was also eliminated. I must say that when all the facts were placed before me before my departure by the Delegate of the British Government, Sir Percival Liesching, I personally came to the conclusion that it would be wrong and dangerous, particularly for South Africa, to think for a moment of accepting the second possibility to which I have referred, namely that India would be associated with the Commonwealth on a treaty basis, and I came to that conclusion for this reason that as soon as any country enters the Commonwealth on a treaty basis she is in a position where she is able to impose conditions and those conditions, in connection with India's relations with us, could cause great difficulties, especially for South Africa. In this respect the position of India differs completely from that of Ireland. Ireland is much closer to the members of the Commonwealth in many respects, perhaps in all respects, than India. The agreement between the members of the Commonwealth and Ireland affects the question of immigration, of citizenship, of the mutual recognition of citizenship, and it was on that basis that the agreement with Ireland was entered into, but it is clear to everyone that there is a great difference in the relations between India and the various members of the Commonwealth, jointly and separately. If we endeavoured to retain the association on a treaty basis we might plunge not only South Africa, but various other members of the Commonwealth into great difficulties. For that reason this possibility of a permanent association on a treaty basis was eliminated.

What remained therefore was just this: firstly there was the fact that

India proposed to declare a republic in the near future. I understand that the date on which this will be done has already been fixed, viz. 15 August. Then there was this further important fact that a request had definitely been made by India to the Commonwealth to remain a member of the Commonwealth, just as she had been in the past, even if she became a republic. The position is therefore that this definite question, this specific request, was put to the Commonwealth and it was necessary to give a candid reply to this straightforward question. The reply could only be " no " or " yes ". That was the problem that faced the conference.

Now I should like to explain from what standpoint I approached this matter as the representative of this House and as the representative of South Africa. In the first place, the reply to this question as to how I approached this matter was given by me, partly at any rate, when I had to make a statement of policy in the Senate before my departure. In that speech I think I explained the position with the greatest possible clarity at my command. The attitude that I adopted there was that the members of the Commonwealth were free and independent nations and that there could be no meddling in any way with that freedom and independence of the various members of the Commonwealth. Our policy is to protect the freedom and the independence of the separate members of the Commonwealth. That was the first point. The second point was that that freedom and independence of the separate members of the Commonwealth included the fullest right to determine their own destiny; it implied something that was mentioned years ago, a factor that played a great role in international or inter-Commonwealth discussions, namely, that every one of the separate members of the Commonwealth possesses to the fullest degree the right to determine its own destiny. That was the second point. But the third point was this, that as long as the Commonwealth remained faithful to its own character and as long as the Commonwealth did not impose restrictions on the freedom and independence of its members or closed the door to further constitutional development on the part of the separate members of the Commonwealth, so long would we in South Africa remain a member of this closer circle of sister-nations known as the Commonwealth. I adhere to the attitude that I had explained here on a previous occasion, and at the conference I also approached the whole question that was under discussion from this point of view.

The question that arose at the conference, the problem that had to be solved, was whether the conference should say " no " or " yes " to this specific request on the part of India to remain a member of the Common-wealth. Both possibilities and their implications had to be carefully considered. I think I am justified in saying that that was done at the conference not only by me but by all the other members. This matter was very carefully considered. Now I just want to say a few words with regard to each of the two possibilities that we could say " no " or " yes ".

I want to deal first with the possibility that we might have said "no" to India's request to remain a member of the Commonwealth notwithstanding the fact that she was to become a republic. What would have been the implications if we had said "no"? In the first place I want to say that if India had not made this request to us and had nevertheless declared a republic, the position would have been very simple; it would have been comparatively easy, as far as the other members of the Commonwealth were concerned. We might have said to India upon receiving notice that she intended to become a republic: "England, in relation to whom you were a subordinate State, granted you Dominion status; your Dominion status includes the right of self-determination; you have exercised your right of self-determination by deciding to become a republic, and since you have done so and you were entitled to do so, we have nothing further to say about it; we might say that we very much regret it but we cannot quarrel with you about your decision." We could only have added: "Leave the Commonwealth and leave with our blessing." That was all we could say and we might have added that we hoped that in spite of the fact that India was becoming a republic, she would in the future always remain a good friend of the Commonwealth and of the individual members. That would have been very simple and easy. But India put forward this request, in spite of the fact that she proposed to become a republic, to remain a member of the Commonwealth.

But the question that occurred to us was this, and it was a perfectly natural question: If we lost India as a member of the Commonwealth, a territory with a vast population of 400,000,000, would we lose India alone or would we lose even more? Well, I think everyone will agree that we would have lost India's goodwill. If India had not made this request to us to remain a member, then the position would not have been so difficult, but since she had made this request, if we refused to agree to her request then, from the nature of the case, it could only have meant that we would have lost India's goodwill, and it might have resulted in great harm, particularly in the sphere of trade, as affecting certain members of the Commonwealth, and not least of all Britain if we had lost India's goodwill. But apart from the fact that we would have lost India's goodwill, it would also have meant that if India could not be on friendly terms, as a fellow-member of the Commonwealth, with the other members of the Commonwealth — and every country must have friends nowadays — she would seek her friends elsewhere. Quite possibly she would look for friends in Asia and she would perhaps look for friends outside Asia. In this connection we must not lose sight of the position generally. As I said in the Senate before my departure, India is anti-Communist and in the present dangerous state of world affairs, that means a great deal to us. Asia — and I am thinking more particularly of China — is becoming more and more overwhelmed by Communism. If we lose the goodwill of India, if we lose the co-operation of India, then

190

not only the Commonwealth but the anti-Communist Western Powers will lose a foothold, an extremely important foothold, in Asia, and that may have a tremendous influence and prove a tremendous disadvantage in the dangerous world situation with which we are faced today. That is what we stood to lose and what we might certainly have lost if India's request had been rejected.

But there is yet another point of view which is important and which must not be overlooked. I refer more particularly to the position of the Commonwealth in the world. In recent years, certain parts of the Commonwealth have broken away. Ireland has left the Commonwealth. Burma has declared herself an independent republic outside the Commonwealth. Egypt is perhaps today further away from the Commonwealth than before. India has declared her intention to become a republic. The impression may easily be created in the world that the Commonwealth is disintegrating, that it is no longer a powerful force in a world in which we are facing a dangerous situation, in which there is the possible threat of war in the future, and the threat of aggression from Russia, from Communist countries; and that the Commonwealth will then be so weakened that it will no longer be a power in world affairs. The decision that was taken at this conference to allow India to remain a member of the Commonwealth was undoubtedly a decision that will give the world a different impression, and it will make the world realise that the Commonwealth is still a power in world affairs. It proves that the Commonwealth still exists with its various ties and that it is still intact. It was of the greatest importance that that impression that the Commonwealth was collapsing should be removed in the interests of everyone concerned. Those were the implications of saying " no ".

The only other reply that could be given as a candid reply to a straightforward question was to say, " Yes, let India become a republic if her people so decide, but let India remain a member of the Commonwealth as heretofore ". That was the reply, and the implications of that reply had to be investigated and considered. Well, in the first place, the implications of that reply were these: If a country like India, having accepted a republican form of Government, remained a member of the Commonwealth, it inevitably entailed a broadening of the basis of the Commonwealth. The Commonwealth would remain a Commonwealth, but its basis would have to be broader than has been the case hitherto. The other implication is that if a republic is allowed to be a member of the Commonwealth, it involves a change in the position of the Crown. India, by becoming a republic, has broken her ties with the Crown. The link with the Crown in the case of the other members of the Commonwealth has not been broken. The question arises what the position of the Crown is in those circumstances in relation to India which remains a member of the Commonwealth? These were the implications that had to be investigated and considered if the reply was to be in the affirmative, that India could remain a member of the Commonwealth.

Hon. members have seen the declaration that was issued towards the close of the Prime Minister' Conference. That declaration is self-explanatory. It means in the first place that the reply that was given to India was in the affirmative. Although India is becoming a republic she will remain a member of the Commonwealth. What is the significance of this in relation to other members of the Commonwealth which are not republics? In that respect the position remains unchanged. No change has come about as far as their position is concerned. It further means that we will now have this position in the Commonwealth. The King will form part of the Government of all the members of the Commonwealth, except in the case of India. In our own South Africa Act, the government of the country is described as consisting of the King, the Senate and the Assembly. That is also the position in the case of the other members of the Commonwealth, but in the case of India the King will not form part of the Government of India. He does not form part of India's constitution.

Another matter that arises from the declaration is this: The relationship of the individual members of the Commonwealth towards the Commonwealth as a whole remains unchanged, that is to say, any country that is a member of the Commonwealth retains the freedom that it has enjoyed hitherto in practice; the individual member of the Commonwealth is not bound by any policy laid down at the Commonwealth Conference or Prime Ministers' Conference, or at the Imperial Conference as it was known before. They bind themselves to consult one another and, as far as possible, to co-operate with one another. We can take it that to that extent they bind themselves morally. But nevertheless every member has the fullest right to differ from the other members and even to go so far as to oppose one another at international conferences; it has the right to adopt a different attitude as we have seen in the past at San Francisco, for example, in the case of Australia, and as we have seen time and again at international conferences. That freedom of every individual member of the Commonwealth remains intact, and that is of the utmost importance, because it means that the highest authority vests in the members of the Commonwealth themselves, and that every one of them remains a free and independent unit, a free and independent State. In no single case is the fate of any member determined from outside; it is not determined by another country as was the case years ago in the days of the Empire. It is not determined either by the various countries acting jointly or by any particular country from outside. Every member-state as the supreme authority in its own country, has its own destiny in its hands. That freedom on the part of every individual member of the Commonwealth in relation to the Commonwealth itself also remains unchanged.

There is another thing that remains unchanged and that is that there need not be any uniformity amongst the members of the Commonwealth with regard to such matters as immigration, or the granting of citizenship. This is nothing new. This has been the position for many years. South

Africa has its own immigration laws. Those laws differ completely from those of England. For example, England allows people from India, members of the Indian race, to enter England. There are no restrictions, but there are restrictions in South Africa. Restrictions of this nature are also imposed by other members of the Commonwealth. Australia adopts the policy of " White Australia ", that is to say, that Australia, just like South Africa, does not allow inhabitants from abroad, who are not Europeans, to enter the country. There is no uniformity between the various members of the Commonwealth. That position also remains unchanged. Every member of the Commonwealth has the fullest right to decide for itself what the composition of its population will be and to what extent it is prepared to grant or to refuse citizenship to others. That position, in any event, remains unchanged. That is the meaning of the declaration that was issued at the conference.

The declaration met with the approval of India. It was not difficult to get India to agree. Since she continues to belong to the Commonwealth as a unit in the Commonwealth, since she remains a member of the States forming an inner circle among the nations of the world, a community of sister-nations, she agreed that the King would continue to be recognised by India as the symbol, as it is put in the Statute of Westminster, of the free association of the various members of the Commonwealth. Those words which are used for the first time bring the position as it is up to date — the symbol of the free association of free and independent nations of the Commonwealth. That expression is used. In the declaration reference is made to the fact that whilst India remains in this inner circle, she will continue as in the past to regard the King as the symbol of the free association of independent and free nations belonging to the Commonwealth, and in that capacity as head of the Commonwealth of which India is also a member.

In connection with this matter, I had certain objections to the words " head of the Commonwealth ". My objection was this, that in describing the King as head of the Commonwealth it might give rise to misunderstanding in this respect that it may create the impression that there is a super-State; that the Commonwealth is a super-State and that the individual members of it are to a certain extent at any rate in a subordinate position.

I explained to the conference that it was necessary, particularly in the case of South Africa, that there should be no misunderstanding with regard to this matter, because in South Africa the Statute of Westminster had been submitted to Parliament for approval and because at that time there had been an important difference of opinion with regard to its interpretation. One school of thought maintained that the Statute of Westminster meant that the rights of the various members of the Commonwealth were tantamount to this that they had the right to secede if they wished to do so; that they had the right to remain neutral in the event of war, and in the event of any member of the Commonwealth being involved in the war; or that the Crown was not divisible; in other words, that one member of the Commonwealth — take South Africa as an example — would regard the King not only as King of South Africa and part of the constitution of South Africa, but would also regard him as King of England or other member-States of the Commonwealth. There was a difference of opinion with regard to the interpretation. That difference was of a serious and important character. Parliament was called in to take a decision in connection with this matter and at that time Parliament placed this interpretation upon it that there was no super-State either in name or in practice. This was a matter in regard to which there was a serious difference of opinion in South Africa, as far as this interpretation was concerned. We have come a long way since those days. I do not think there is any member in this House today, and I do not think there is anyone who is acquainted with the facts, who still maintains that there is a super-State or that we have not got the right to remain neutral or the right to secede. In the meantime that right to secede has been exercised by Ireland and it is now again being exercised by India and no one denies their right to do so. There is no one today who adopts that attitude, and I must say that I was pleasantly surprised to find at the Prime Ministers' Conference that there was not a single member at that conference who still accepted that erroneous interpretation that was placed upon the Statute of Westminster.

One and all emphasised that there is no super-State, that the Commonwealth cannot be described as a super-State and that those rights to which I have referred are part and parcel of the rights of every individual member of the Commonwealth. I was pleasantly surprised to learn this, but nevertheless, with a view to possible misunderstanding, I deemed it necessary to ask the conference to put that interpretation in black and white. This resolution was then unanimously passed, that where the expression " the King is head of the Commonwealth " is used, it must not be interpreted to mean that it alters any of the existing rights of the various members of the Commonwealth, and that the King — although he is indicated as head of the Commonwealth — fulfils no constitutional function as this.

I feel that the resolution that was adopted there has once and for all put this matter beyond any doubt and that this position will never be misinterpreted again in the future. I believe that this is the first time that the position has been stated authoritatively. The question was raised by me and others whether the declaration that was issued there required legislation; whether or not it would still have to be submitted to the various Parliaments by way of legislation in order to validate it. The legal advice that I obtained from our own side and the legal advice that came from the British Government which also had this matter gone into thoroughly, was to the effect that legislation was unnecessary. It was argued that that provision that the Commonwealth consists of a number of members freely associating with one another, and that the link between them would be their common allegiance to the King, did not form part of the Statute of Westminster, but that it was only the preamble; that the preamble must only be regarded as a declaration, and that the declaration of the Statute of Westminster could be replaced by this new authoritative declaration. In other words, no legislation is necessary to bring about this change in so far as the composition of the Commonwealth is concerned.

Now I should like to make a few general remarks, which I feel it is necessary to make on this occasion in connection with this matter. The first is that the trend of events in recent times has revealed a feeling of solidarity amongst the various members of the Commonwealth, that was probably not expected in the world outside and that probably surprised even members of the Commonwealth itself. That feeling of solidarity has been tested and it has stood the test. To begin with we had the case of Ireland. Ireland wanted to become a republic; nothing could stop her, and she eventually became a republic. This did not open the course that was eventually followed by India, perhaps because this course of action did not occur to Ireland and, on the other hand, it might not have occurred to the other members of the Commonwealth. For that reason it was simply accepted that Ireland, in becoming a republic, was placing herself outside the Commonwealth; that she would no longer be a member of the Commonwealth. But at the same time Ireland felt that she would like to remain associated with the Commonwealth, if not from inside, then from outside. An agreement was therefore entered into with Ireland in which it was stated on both sides — on the part of England and on the part of the other members of the Commonwealth — that Ireland was not to be regarded as a foreign country; that the Irish were not to be regarded as members of a foreign nation. What did this show? It showed that in spite of the fact that Ireland herself would remain outside the Commonwealth she did not lose her feeling of solidarity with the rest of the members of the Commonwealth; and all I can say is this, that if this course that India adopted and that has now been agreed to, namely to become a republic and yet remain inside the Commonwealth, had been held out to Ireland, I wonder whether Ireland would not have been a member of the Commonwealth to this day. But this matter has been disposed of. Whether the position can be changed is a matter in regard to which one can only speculate; we do not know what will happen. There is the case of India. In many respects India is not so close to the other members of the Commonwealth. For reasons of her own she decided to become a republic but the feeling of solidarity on the part of India was still so strong, in spite of all her real or imaginary grievances, that she decided simultaneously with the decision to become a republic, to apply for continued membership of the Commonwealth.

I say that the solidarity of the Commonwealth has been tested and it has stood the test. That has been demonstrated here in the clearest fashion. The question arises why that is so? That phenomenon — and it is a noteworthy and important phenomenon — requires an explanation.

The only explanation I can give is that in the first place there are common interests between the various members of the Commonwealth, and it is in that light that they see the position. Furthermore, they have a common or general outlook on life. There are some members who are closer to each other than others, but politically they have a common outlook; even in the case of India which is otherwise perhaps furthest removed from the other members of the Commonwealth, she has decided to model her constitution on the lines of the British constitution and our constitution in this country. In other words, India will be a republic but she will be a democratic republic and her method of Parliamentary government will largely remain the same as it was before. Moreover, as I have stated here before, India, like the rest of the world, is today taking her stand with the anti-Communist countries. She regards Communism in Asia or Communism which is trying to gain a foothold in India also, as a danger, just as we regard it as a danger. Well, there are common interests; there is a general common outlook. It was felt that the nations of the Commonwealth were standing together and that if at all possible they want to remain together.

But the main reason, in my opinion, why the Commonwealth can remain together, in spite of the changes and developments which have taken place, is that the Commonwealth has shown an ability to adapt itself to changing conditions in a changing world. In other words, what I have said here implies that it respects freedom, not only freedom for all the members jointly but freedom for every member as distinct from the Commonwealth. It has the quality of adaptability. We have seen that during our time in connection with South Africa as well. In our younger days most of us lived in this country under the domination of an Empire — a British Empire. That meant that the executive power was vested in one centre overseas. The remaining countries in the Empire were subject to the will and the domination of that one central authority. But during our lifetime we have also seen the British Empire transformed along peaceful constitutional lines into something else, a community of free independent nations, as far as the Dominions are concerned, linked together by certain bonds, but where the one Dominion, either with regard to its domestic or with regard to its external interests, did not occupy a subordinate position in relation to any other. The British Empire had such a degree of adaptability that it converted itself into something practically new. That same ability to adapt itself to new conditions in a changing world has been revealed again at this conference and in the decision taken there.

It has often been said — I believe my hon. friend on the other side of the House has often emphasised it in much stronger language — that the British Empire is not an organisation; that there is no such thing as a British Empire except England and her Colonies; that the Commonwealth is not an organisation; that it is a living organism and a living organism cannot continue to live unless it has the ability to adapt itself to new circumstances. And the fact that the Commonwealth has again shown that it has the ability to adapt itself and has shown that is not an organisation but an organism, made it possible for it to exist and to remain in existence in the past; it makes it possible for it to remain in existence today. If there had been any rigidity in the basis of the Commonwealth it would have collapsed long ago. This is a matter that must undoubtedly be taken into consideration in expressing an opinion with regard to the important step that was taken in this case. In other words, let me put it this way: where it has been necessary from time to time in the past to loosen the bonds holding the Commonwealth together, the Commonwealth has always succeeded in rising to the occasion.

What does that prove to us? The step that was taken at the conference goes to show that what is described in the preamble to the Statute of Westminster, namely, that the Commonwealth is based on a common allegiance, in other words, that all the members must — and in actual fact they do — recognise the Crown and form a link with the Crown, is not the only bond holding the Commonwealth together. I go further and say that it is not even the most important bond holding the Commonwealth together. I do not want to detract in any way from the value of the bond of common allegiance in certain cases. I do not want to detract in any way from the importance of the role that the King plays in some member-countries of the Commonwealth; but I do want to say with regard to the Kingship in England where the King is head of the State, where he is continually in touch with his people, where he continually comes into contact with them and is in every respect one of them, that the bond there differs from the bond elsewhere. I also want to concede that the Kingship in the case of some other member-countries of the Commonwealth is a unifying force. I refer more particularly to those members of the Commonwealth with a homogeneous population and a homogeneous population of British descent. I refer more particularly to Australia and New Zealand. I accept the fact that there the Kingship plays an important role in promoting unity.

But there are other member-countries of the Commonwealth that are in a different position. I take South Africa by way of example. The population of South Africa is not uniform. South Africa has a history which differs completely from the history of other members of the Commonwealth, and in these circumstances the Kingship cannot constitute the same bond of unity. I am not only referring to unity in relation to the world outside, but unity in this country, within our own borders. On the contrary, that link is frequently maintained at the expense of unity amongst your people.

That was the position in the case of Ireland. Ireland's circumstances were quite different from those of other States of the Commonwealth. For 700 years they struggled for their freedom. They have their whole history behind them. This led to discord in Ireland and unity was only brought about in Ireland when she took the step that she eventually took and when she severed that link. In the case of India one found the same thing. Whilst that outside link existed, the link with the Crown, India was unable to achieve unity. I am not referring now to India and Pakistan because there were other reasons that led to discord between them. But eventually India achieved unity again; I think this step that she has now at last taken in severing her link with the Crown has brought unity to India. The only conclusion that I want to draw from that is that the link of common allegiance to the Crown is not the only bond holding the Commonwealth together. There are other bonds as well — those I mentioned a moment ago — which are stronger than the bond of Kingship, and I think the present trend of events has demonstrated that most clearly.

I want to conclude on this note. What has been done in this case will not result in breaking up the Commonwealth; on the contrary it will build up the Commonwealth; it will preserve the unity and the power of the Commonwealth, and the impression that the world would have gained and undoubtedly did gain that the Commonwealth was in the process of disintegrating is now being removed. The unity of the Commonwealth, and with it its strength and its power in the world, has been maintained and, in my opinion, strengthened.

As far as South Africa is concerned, there have always been two schools of thought, not only in recent years, but for years and for generations, namely, the republican idea on the one hand and the other conception, on the other hand, that we must be linked up with a nation overseas. We have failed to reconcile those two standpoints and we will not and cannot succeed in reconciling them. But I can say this with regard to these opposing standpoints, that my opinion has always been — and I want to record it here — that the greatest unity will be obtained in the case of South Africa too when we become a republic.

I want to add to what I have said on previous occasions that at the present moment there are other issues, important issues of vital importance to this country in respect of which the population of this country — English-speaking and Afrikaans-speaking and members of all parties — hold the same view to a large extent. These are urgent problems that must be solved and in order to be able to do so, we must seek unity and stand together. But one thing is certain and that is that the declaration issued at this conference has brought us closer together than we have ever been before perhaps, as far as our different standpoints with regard to the constitutional position are concerned. There are some of us who are republicans; there are others who believe in the maintenance of the link with the Crown, but I make bold to say that in reference to one matter that that side of the House and this side of the House, all sections in South Africa, are agreed upon and that is that we want to remain in the Commonwealth if no restrictions are placed on our freedom; if our right of self-determination is not affected. Has there ever been such an opportunity in the whole political history of our country for many years for all sections of the nation to stand together? There is the danger of aggression from Russia; from the forces of Communism. What is our attitude? I assume that we are all agreed that it is a good thing that the Western Powers want to stand together, even in the military sphere, and that they have been able to form the Atlantic Pact. We on this side of the House have adopted the attitude that our sympathies lie with the Western Powers. We are anti-Communist and we want to throw in our weight with the anti-Communist countries. If this situation leads to war we cannot remain neutral. It has been said before and I believe that as far as external dangers are concerned we as a nation have never had such an opportunity of presenting a united front as on this question. Previous world wars have divided us. If a war breaks out in which we are threatened by the Communist danger, we shall be able to present a more united front than we have ever witnessed in this country, but whatever the future of South Africa may be in the constitutional sphere, however much we may differ with regard to the question of a republic, or the retention of the link with the Crown, on one point we are now agreed and stand together, and that is that whatever the circumstances may be we would like to remain in the Commonwealth for reasons that I have already indicated. I hope therefore that since the declaration of the conference was received with acclamation in England, even by the Conservative Party and even by Mr. Churchill, from whom one might have expected adverse criticism as Leader of the Opposition — but he offered no criticism; on the contrary he gave his whole-hearted support to this declaration — since it was received with acclamation, as far as we can judge, by other members of the Commonwealth, with an exception here and there, I hope that it will be possible to say the same of this House and of South Africa, and that this will be regarded as an important declaration that will tend to retain the Commonwealth as a world Power, a Power that will exercise tremendous influence in the interest of security in the present dangerous world state of affairs, and finally that it will also make a contribution towards bringing the population of South Africa closer together than we have ever been in the past.

8

SOUTH AFRICAN CITIZENSHIP

DR. T. E. DÖNGES, 10 JUNE 1949[1]

NATIONALITY LEGISLATION within, first the British Empire and later the Commonwealth of Nations has largely paralleled the constitutional development of the Commonwealth during the past 40 years, and I think it is very necessary for a proper study of the Bill that one should try to trace the development of nationality legislation during that period. That historical background naturally falls into four main periods. The first period is that lasting up to 1914 with the passage of the British Nationality Act of that year. This period may be described as the Single Code Period. There was only one body, the Parliament of Westminster, that could naturalise aliens with effect throughout the Empire. Apart from that, there were some forms of local naturalisation allowed in other parts. That period came to an end with the passage of the Act of 1914 which ushered in the second period, which one may aptly call the Common Code Period, to distinguish it from its predecessor, the Single Code Period. The object of the British Act of 1914 was to permit the Dominions to grant naturalisation with effect throughout the Empire. Hon. members will remember that the British Act of 1914 consisted of three parts. Parts 1 and 3 in terms of the constitutional position then existing were made applicable to all the parts of the British Empire. But part 2, which relates to the naturalisation of aliens, was only to have effect in a Dominion which adopted that part specifically in its own legislation. In fact, the various Dominions — not all of them but some of them — preferred to follow a different course. They were not prepared to accept the automatic application of parts 1 and 3, and to adopt part 2 specifically. What they did in most cases was to pass an Act consisting of all three parts in their own Parliaments, and differing only minutely from the parent Act of Great Britain. I think all the Dominions, with the possible exception of New Zealand, adopted that procedure. If the Dominions wanted to naturalise with full effect in terms of this new procedure, they could do so only on the basis of part 2, i.e., the Common Code, as it was called. This necessarily meant that any change in regard to the naturalisation of aliens, in

---

1 Extract from speech by Dr. T. E. Dönges, Minister of the Interior, in the House of Assembly, 10 June 1949, during the second reading of a Bill which was enacted as the South African Citizenship Act (No. 44 of 1949). *House of Assembly Debates.*

any part of the Empire, could only be made by altering part 2 uniformly and concurrently throughout the Empire.

That was the position under the 1914 Act and it was carried out in the way I have indicated for a number of years.

The third period one can more or less date from 1921. It lasted on and off until about 1947. If I were to give a label to this period I would say that it is the period of the Common Code plus separate nationality. In the supervening years, after the passage of the 1914 Act, the growing national consciousness in some of the Dominions was making its impact felt on the position created by the 1914 Act. Canada in 1921, and South Africa in 1927 provided for their own distinctive nationals. There was, in addition, during this period the Imperial Conferences of 1926 and of 1930, followed by the Statute of Westminster in 1931 and our own Status Act some years later.

Dealing with the position reached at the Imperial Conference of 1930 I may just indicate to hon. members how that Imperial Conference tried to reconcile the idea of the Common Code with the growing demand on the part of various Dominions for their own separate and distinctive nationals. One of the resolutions passed at this conference of 1930 was that—

It is for each member of the Commonwealth to define for itself its own nationals but that so far as possible those nationals should be persons possessing the common status, though it is recognised that local conditions, or other special circumstances, may from time to time necessitate divergencies from this general principle.

After the Statute of Westminster, of course, in 1931, the position had once more changed materially. The preservation of the common status of British subjects, as laid down in the British Acts from 1914 to 1922, as amended by the Statutes passed in 1923, 1933 and 1943, no longer depended on anything in those Acts of the British Parliament, but on agreement between the United Kingdom and the various Dominions.

MR. WATERSON[2]: Are you quoting from Berrydale Keith?

DR. DÖNGES: Various factors contributed to bring about the break-up of this system envisaged after 1922 and growing in body in the supervening years. There was, as I say, in practice a gradual breaking down of the Common Code and the common status during the years 1933 to 1946, and that was one of the facts that paved the way for the entry of the fourth period in the development of nationality legislation.

I would like to indicate to hon. members some of these factors that tended to break down the so-called Common Code.

MR. J. G. N. STRAUSS[2]: What are you quoting from?

DR. DÖNGES: I am not quoting from anything yet.

MR. STRAUSS: You were quoting a moment ago; you had a book in your hands.

DR. DÖNGES: Yes, I was quoting . . .

[2] United Party.

MR. STRAUSS: Don't be so shy about the author. Who is it?

DR. DÖNGES: I was quoting from Mervyn Jones on *British Nationality, Law and Practice*. He was also quoted with apparent approval by the Attorney-General of the United Kingdom when similar legislation was passed some time ago.

I do not think I can show this break-down better than in the words of Mervyn Jones at page 237—

Therefore in view of the legislative independence of the Dominions created by the Statute of Westminster, 1931, it became possible for those Dominions to adopt if they so desired, nationality laws which were not based on the common status, although it was part of the understanding that such laws would respect the common status. As shown by the official statements made at the Imperial Conferences of 1930, it was intended that, in practice, the nationality laws of all parts of the British Commonwealth would, so to speak, march together. "Dominion Nationality" would be a smaller group of subjects contained within the larger class of British subjects, and legislation regarding British nationality in this wider class would be the same throughout the Commonwealth. This position became, in fact. difficult to maintain . . .

The position that was envisaged in the 1930 conferences—

. . . this position became, in fact, difficult to maintain in an association of independent communities, each possessing Parliaments of their own with the widest legislative powers, and some of them with pronounced views on certain nationality questions, such as for example, the question of the nationality of married women. It was after 1933, mainly owing to differences of opinion regarding the nationality of married women that the system began to show signs of breaking down.

Then he quotes a number of instances in which various Dominions have been guilty of breaking down this so-called Common Code. In 1933 and 1934, the United Kingdom and Canada altered their laws to provide in certain cases for the retention of British nationality by women marrying aliens. In that way they broke out of the Common Code. In 1943 the United Kingdom again altered the neutralisation qualifications for certain aliens, extended the scope of the earlier amendment dealing with married women and altered the provisions of part 1 of the United Kingdom Act to enable certain persons born outside His Majesty's Dominions to claim British status. That was not all. In other countries similar deviations from the Common Code were adopted in practice. Notwithstanding recognition by Southern Rhodesia of some persons born there of alien parents or of locally naturalised British subjects before annexation (12 September 1923) as natural born British subjects, these persons remained aliens in the rest of the Commonwealth, although they were treated as British subjects by birth in Southern Rhodesia.

The Union itself is not free from blemish in this respect. In 1926 and again in 1932 they departed from the Common Code, but probably the major departure from the Common Code, as far as this Parliament is concerned, took place in 1942 when all minor children, including those born in the Union or elsewhere in His Majesty's Dominions, of automatically naturalised South West African Germans were deprived of their nationality under Act No. 35 of 1942. Under the nationality laws of all the other Commonwealth countries these children remained natural born British subjects with a common status, but in the Union they became aliens.

Canada went even further in 1946 in breaking down or contributing to the break-down of the Common Code. It was found in practice, as Jones has declared, that it was impossible to maintain the Common Code under the circumstances existing in the various parts of the Commonwealth. There were other forces also working in the same direction.

The conference of 1937 gave impetus to this movement. Again to quote Mervyn Jones—

Here General Hertzog (South Africa) proposed that the British Nationality and Status of Aliens Act, 1914, should be amended so as to confine the meaning of " British subject " to " subject of Great Britain ". This proposal was based on the argument that several reasons pointed to the desirability of each member state of the British Commonwealth having its own nationality law.

It is pointed out by the learned author that the result of this proposal, if adopted, would be a United Kingdom nationality, a Canadian nationality, etc. all belonging to the several states which are members of the British Commonwealth.

The writer continues—

(In 1937) the Government of the United Kingdom opposed General Hertzog's proposal on the ground that it would be the end of the doctrine of common allegiance on which the British Empire was founded. At the same time that Government agreed that, provided the common status was preserved, there was no reason why there should not exist, side by side with it, a dominion nationality law.

It is interesting to note that this suggestion made in 1937 has now been carried into effect as a result of the Conference of Prime Ministers in 1946, and I can only say that the suggestions made at the conference of 1937 have materially contributed to the procedure which has now been taken up in most of the members of the Commonwealth. As I say, this whole movement was continued and it was given direction and substance by the Conference of Prime Ministers in 1946 and the Technical Conference which followed it in 1947. Those two conferences were followed by legislation in the United Kingdom in 1948, New Zealand in 1948, Australia and Ceylon in 1948. It has already been preceded by legislation in Canada in 1946. It will thus be seen that of the main members of the Commonwealth, South Africa alone lags behind in legislation of this type.

But there is some advantage in not having been in the van. South

Africa can now pass the most up-to-date and constitutionally the most correct legislation of all the members of the Commonwealth. The recent Conference of Prime Ministers has written a new chapter in the history of the evolution of the Commonwealth from an Empire to a community of States bound together by common interests. Constitutionally it is no longer possible to talk of a common status. It is only possible to do so when there is either a common allegiance to one King, or a super-State; but since common allegiance is no longer an essential condition of membership of the Commonwealth, there cannot be a common subject-hood to circumscribe the common status; and since there is no question of a super-State, there cannot be a common citizenship. Constitutionally, therefore, there is no longer a Commonwealth subject or citizen. There are now, after the recent legislation in the various parts of the Common-wealth and after the recent conference in London, only citizens of Commonwealth countries enjoying preference within that community of States. South Africa's relation with the Crown still exists and is recognised in this Bill in the oath of allegiance, and South Africa's recognition of a Commonwealth founded on the free association of its member States is embodied in the preferential treatment which is accorded to citizens from such member States who wish to become South African citizens.

I want to make it perfectly clear that it is not this Bill which creates a new constitutional position. That is already there. The Bill merely gives expression to it. It is declaratory of that position which has been arrived at independently of this Bill. There are no doubt some people who do not like this development. There are always people who want to set any stage of our constitutional evolution in cement, who want to apply a constitutional strait-jacket to our development. There are, and I suppose there will be for a long time still, people who would keep South Africa in its swaddling clothes, when so many of its citizens desire to don the trappings of manhood. Such people there were in the past, and I dare say, like the poor, they will be with us in the future. Such people there were also in the other member States of the Common-wealth when this legislation was mooted there, and it is an interesting thing that there is a type which has its counterpart in the various parts of the Commonwealth. Fortunately in the other countries they were in the minority, and they were unable to make their countries unhitch their wagons from the star of constitutional life and development, and I trust that in South Africa that will also be the case.

MR. J. G. N. STRAUSS, 10 JUNE 1949[1]

WE ON THIS SIDE of the House do not take a back seat for any-body in this House or outside as far as our loyalty and love of South

[1] Speech by Mr. J. G. N. Strauss, Deputy Leader of the Opposition, in the House of Assembly, 10 June 1949. *House of Assembly Debates.*

Africa is concerned, and in the completeness and fullness of its freedom and the great desirability of having a distinct South African citizenship. But we prefer not to regard it, as the Minister said, as a passion. We prefer to regard it as a deep and pure love for our country, and we on this side would like to see a law which provides for a distinct South African citizenship.

We were very pleased when the Prime Minister came back from the recent Conference of Prime Ministers and made a statement with regard to his views of the Commonwealth. We rejoiced particularly when we heard him express the most strong and the most vigorous Commonwealth sentiments. We appreciated it all the more because we knew that he had not always adopted that attitude. Surely the Prime Minister does not deny that. We appreciated it in the spirit of a great authority that there will be more rejoicing in Heaven over one sinner who repenteth than over 99 just men who need no repentance. The Prime Minister came back and stated in Committee of Supply on his Vote—

Our policy is to protect the freedom and the independence of the separate members of the Commonwealth. That was the first point. The second point was that that freedom and independence of the separate members of the Commonwealth, included the fullest right to determine their own destiny; it implied something that was mentioned years ago, a factor that played a great role in international or inter-Commonwealth discussions, namely, that every one of the separate members of the Commonwealth possesses to the fullest degree the right to determine its own destiny. That was the second point. But the third point was this, that as long as the Commonwealth remained faithful to its own character and as long as the Commonwealth did not impose restrictions on the freedom and independence of its members or closed the door to further constitutional development on the part of the separate members of the Commonwealth, so long would we in South Africa remain a member of this closer circle of sister-nations known as the Commonwealth. I adhere to the attitude that I had explained here on a previous occasion, and at the conference I also approached the whole question that was under discussion from this point of view.

I do not want to quote further from the Prime Minister's speech. He spoke, as I have said, very strongly and very vigorously in favour of retaining the Commonwealth. Now we have heard from the Minister of the Interior quite a different interpretation of what took place at this Commonwealth Conference, quite different from what we understood the position to be. He told us, sir, that this Bill makes no change in the constitutional position; that the constitutional position was confirmed in London at the Prime Ministers' Conference. He tells us that there is no longer a common allegiance and therefore no longer common citizenship. After the way in which we rejoiced at the statement made by the Prime Minister we get this statement, which has caused a rude awakening, from the Minister of the Interior.

*　　*　　*　　*

The Minister has given a very full historical review of how the various statutes dealing with citizenship were passed in the various countries, and I do not have to traverse that ground again. I only want to point out that notwithstanding the events which took place, namely the Prime Ministers' Conference of 1946, the Committee of Nationality Experts who met in London in February 1947, Canada decided to retain the Act of 1946 which had been passed before either of those two events had taken place. The first point that I want to make on this Bill is a point with which I have already dealt to some extent, and that is that this Bill fails to incorporate the common clause, the key clause which was agreed upon at the conference of experts, and which appear in all the Acts of member countries of the Commonwealth. The Minister now tells us, of course, that the constitutional position has altered; that there is no longer any common allegiance and that therefore there can no longer be any common citizenship, and he spoke of the swaddling clothes in which we want to keep South Africa.

*　　*　　*　　*

We on this side of the House say that this common clause which was agreed upon should have appeared in this Bill. We say that this common clause which appears in all the other legislative measures — it appears in the British Act, as the Minister knows, the Act which was passed in 1948 — should have appeared in this Bill.

*　　*　　*　　*

The Minister now tells us that we are in a different position as the result of the Prime Ministers' Conference.

DR. DÖNGES: Don't you agree with your Leader?

MR. STRAUSS: I was referring to the provision with regard to common status, common citizenship, and I referred to the first section in the British Act which makes that quite clear. The Canadian Act has a similar provision in Section 26 which reads —

A Canadian citizen is a British subject.

And the White Paper on the British Bill is interesting. That says in paragraph four —

In 1946 Canada passed the Canada Citizenship Act. That Act in providing for the acquisition and loss of Canadian citizenship followed with certain modifications the provisions of the British Act for the acquisition and loss of British nationality. It also enacted that all

206

Canadian citizens were British subjects and all persons who were British subjects by the law of any other part of the Commonwealth should be recognised as British subjects in Canada.

This Canadian Act continued to recognise the common status of British subjects while departing from the common code system. The Minister has made a great deal about that. We do not object to that when that happens over a period. What we say is that the common status should be recognised by common citizenship throughout the Commonwealth; and we ask why there is this omission from the present Bill, an omission which does not appear in the Acts I know of, namely the British Act, the Australian Act and the Canadian Act. It is interesting to refer to the further two paragraphs that appear in the summary issued by the British Government. Paragraph five states —

It appeared to the United Kingdom Government that the question ought to be considered whether the citizenship principle introduced by the Canadian Act should be extended by agreement to the other Commonwealth countries. As a result of consultation with the Governments of this country (*sic*) a conference of experts met in London in February 1947, at the invitation of the United Kingdom Government. At this conference there assembled expert representatives from the United Kingdom, Canada, Australia, New Zealand, South Africa, Eire, Newfoundland, Southern Rhodesia, Burma and Ceylon . . .

It goes on to say in the next paragraph —

The United Kingdom Government has subsequently been in correspondence with the Government of Canada, Australia, New Zealand, South Africa, Eire, Newfoundland, India, Pakistan, Southern Rhodesia and Ceylon, and subject to what is said below with regard to Eire it is believed that legislation on the lines of this Bill will be acceptable to the other self-governing countries of the Commonwealth and is likely to be followed by legislation on similar lines in many of these countries.

Now, we know according to the speech of the Minister that South Africa is a notable exception. The Australian position is dealt with in the latest copy of the Journal of the Parliaments of the Empire, where Mr. Caldwell is quoted on page 615. He emphasised that the creation of an Australian citizenship in the Bill in no way lessened the advantages and privileges which British subjects who might not be Australian subjects would enjoy in Australia, that they would qualify for the franchise and have the right to be Members of Parliament and enter the public service. He went on to say —

A British subject who was not Australian born would be able to become an Australian citizen by a simple act of registration, but would not suffer in any way if he failed to do this. The " common code " had broken down, and the only means of maintaining the existing common status throughout the British Commonwealth was in the concept that citizenship of an individual member of the Commonwealth should carry with it common status. This was effected by Clause 7 (1) which provided that —

A person who, under this Act, is an Australian citizen, or by an enactment for the time being in force in a country to which this section applies, is a citizen of that country, shall by virtue of that citizenship be a British subject.

The section applied to the United Kingdom and Colonies, Canada, New Zealand, the Union of South Africa, Newfoundland, India, Pakistan, Ceylon and Southern Rhodesia. Now, we have to hear from the Minister this morning that all these countries that have provisions to that effect in their statutes are still in their mental swaddling clothes.

9

PRIVY COUNCIL APPEAL

MR. C. R. SWART, 8 FEBRUARY 1950[1]

IN THE EVENT of this Bill being accepted, which is my ardent hope and desire, it will be the fulfilment of a life's work for me. I trust that I shall be permitted to make just a few personal remarks, because ever since I entered public life and politics 27 years ago, it was one of the matters which I took up and wanted to see through. Throughout these 27 years it was advocated by me in Parliament as well as outside, and in this Parliament I attempted on several occasions to realise my desire. For me personally it will be a source of considerable satisfaction if this measure now succeeds, and I want to express the hope that we have already progressed so far on the road of South Africa that it will be accepted without opposition.

MR. BARLOW: Canada got in ahead of you.

MR. SWART: I am sorry that Canada should have been the first to put it through, but that is not my fault. Long before Canada began with it, I introduced in this House motions and Bills, and if hon. members who are now making interjections, had supported me, we would have passed it long before Canada. Since 1923, when I came to Parliament, I have advocated my case time and again and made positive efforts to have this measure accepted. As far back as 1935 I introduced a motion, when the General Laws Amendment Act came up for discussion, to give the Committee, by means of an instruction from the House, the right to abolish the appeal to the Privy Council. It was turned down. After that date I made various other attempts and then in 1937 introduced a Bill. It was also thrown out at that time. In 1947 I again introduced a Bill and it was again thrown out. The reason why it was not allowed at that time, was not because of any objection to the principle involved. There was no objection in principle, according to the speeches of responsible members. The objections to it at that time were merely of a temporary nature. It was said that the time was not opportune.

*   *   *   *

The first point I wish to make is that nobody doubts the right of this Parliament to abolish the appeal to the King-in-Council. Our South Africa

[1] Speech by Mr. C. R. Swart, Minister of Justice, in the House of Assembly, 8 February 1950, during the debate on the second reading of the Bill which was enacted as the Privy Council Appeals Act No. 16 of 1950. *House of Assembly Debates.*

Act and subsequent legislation as, for example, the Statute of Westminster provide that guarantee; but it is interesting, since Canada has been mentioned, to tell the House what happened there. In the year 1939, quite a few years after my efforts, a Bill was introduced in the Canadian Parliament and it was read a first time. Objection was made on the ground that it was doubtful whether the Canadian Federal Parliament had the right to abolish it. The question was consequently referred to the Supreme Court of Canada for a decision and the Canadian Court replied in the affirmative, namely, that the Canadian Parliament did have the right. It is interesting to read what Lord Jowitt said when he announced the decision of the Court — that is to say the decision of the Privy Council itself —

> It appears to their Lordships that it is not consistent with the political conception which is embodied in the British Commonwealth of Nations that one member of that Commonwealth would be precluded from setting up, if it so desires, a supreme court of appeal having jurisdiction both ultimate and exclusive of any other member. The regulation of appeals is, to use the words of Lord Sankey in the Coal Corporation case, a " prime element in Canadian Sovereignty ", which would be impaired if, at the will of its citizens, recourse could be had to a tribunal in the constitution of which it had no voice.

It is therefore an unquestionable decision that the sovereignty of Canada could be impaired if an appeal were made to a court outside Canada, in the constitution of which the people of Canada had no voice whatsoever. That Act, of course, has now been adopted by the Canadian Parliament. In South Africa we have the strangely worded Section 106 of our South Africa Act. It begins —

> There shall be no appeal from the Supreme Court of South Africa or from any division thereof to the King-in-Council . . .

Then it goes on to say —

> . . . except in certain cases where the Privy Council and the King-in-Council grant leave to appeal.

It was clearly the intention of the National Convention and of what we call the Constitution of the Union, to abolish the appeal to the Privy Council. I just want to read here what happened in a certain case when an appeal was made to the Privy Council. In 1920 there was the case of Whitaker versus Durban Corporation, and Lord Haldane laid down the principle as follows —

> One cannot read Section 106 of the South Africa Act, 1909, without seeing that the intention was to get rid of appeals to the King-in-Council, except such as, in the strict exercise of the prerogative, His Majesty would say that he would allow on some great ground.

For the next few years this was taken as the basis on which appeals to the Privy Council were allowed. It is vaguely stated here, when it says " on some great ground ", but that was the fixed principle. Then in 1934 while I was persistently advocating the abolition of this right, there was the case of the Pearl Assurance Company versus Union Government where an appeal was lodged on a minor legal point, namely, the question of compensation recoverable in terms of a penal clause in a contract, the so-called "Penal Clause in Contract", and the Privy Council actually allowed the appeal on that point. This again made it possible for practically an unlimited number of appeals to be made to the Privy Council. I know that the Government of that time — and I said so in Parliament — was disturbed by the new turn of events, and it was one of the reasons which compelled me at that stage to try to abolish the right of appeal to the Privy Council, because it clearly showed that there was a departure from the principle laid down by Lord Haldane in the previous case. At that time the then Prime Minister, namely the late General Hertzog, also replied to a question put by me and said that this case of the Pearl Assurance Company disturbed the Government, but he said that because the case was pending, it was not the right time to discuss the matter at that stage. He added that the matter would be considered as soon as a decision in the case had been given. As Prime Minister he felt, in other words, that this was an unfavourable turn of events, and he said that as soon as a decision had been given the Government would seriously consider the abolition; the reason was that an appeal had been allowed in a case which caused the Government some concern.

Since Union ten appeals against the decision of our Appeal Court have been heard by the Privy Council. In one case the appeal succeeded. But there were numerous other cases where leave to appeal was applied for; I am, however, not in possession of the figures. There is the danger that people may go there whether leave is granted or not. They go to the Appeal Court and saddle the other party with the expense involved in opposing the application. Therefore we must not only take those cases where leave was granted; we must also take the other cases where leave was applied for.

As I have already said, during my previous efforts the objection was raised that it was not the right moment, or else it was said that a case was pending and that the then Government did not at that stage want to go into the matter. Another objection was that such a Bill should not be introduced by a private member, but should be a Government measure. Fortunately as a result of the hurly-burly of politics I am in the Government today and in introducing this measure now I am not doing it as a private member.

Now, it is interesting to note what the attitude of the Leader of the Opposition (General J. C. Smuts) was at the previous attempt. I would like to quote what the hon. Leader of the Opposition said in the past in connection with this question. I am not talking now about the excuses made by him as to the reason why he could not accept it or why such a Bill could not be introduced. In 1936 he gave the following reply to a question —

In view of the fact that the Judicial Committee of the Privy Council is not versed in Roman-Dutch Law and of the possibility, while the right of appeal is retained, of great hardship being inflicted on persons of small means at the suit of wealthy litigants availing themselves of that right, the Government considers that the disadvantages of its retention clearly outweigh its advantages.

211

In 1947, in reply to my motion that the right of appeal to the Privy Council should be abolished, the former Minister of Justice, Mr. Lawrence, also explained his attitude. He said —

> Taking it as a whole one might say that so far as the administration of justice is concerned at the present time, there is no peculiar merit in having this slender right of appeal maintained.

I have many more examples of opinions which were expressed and which appear in the Hansard reports; they confirm this point of mine that the persons and leaders who voted against my motion, who voted against this effort of mine, did not base their objections on the merits of the case. They had other reasons. Whether those reasons were justified or not is not the point at issue. Their objections were not on the ground that it would be to our advantage to retain the right of appeal to the Privy Council. They admitted that it could be to our disadvantage and that it was unnecessary. They admitted that it was of no advantage to us.

The motives for this measure are very simple. In the first place I would like to say that we want to abolish the right of appeal to the Privy Council because we are a sovereign independent State, and it does not become us to allow an appeal to an overseas court. It is an anomaly, an anachronism. In the past there was some reason for its existence. But at present there is no reason for its existence. We have no control whatever over the constitution of that court of appeal, which functions overseas. Moreover, the Privy Council is not a court. It is an advisory Council to the King and for the exercise of his royal prerogative. For that reason the King thought it fit to appoint from the members of the Privy Council a judicial committee to deal with these cases. They submit recommendations in connection with cases on which His Majesty must give a decision — not that it makes any difference in practice. But that is the constitutional position. I would like to bring it to your attention that this committee is not necessarily bound by law or the principles of law. They are to advise the King, irrespective of whether it is according to law or not. That is not an assumption, as was proved in a case which was heard years ago and in which the persons who had to advise Her Majesty, said the following: it was the decision of Baron Park in re Ames (3 Moore 409) —

> We are not disposed to say that we ought to have recommended Her Majesty to have allowed the appeal, but we are not disposed to say that we have not the power so to have done . . .

Here the Privy Council gave a decision and admitted that it had given a wrong decision in terms of the law, but stated that it had the right to advise Her Majesty, irrespective of the fact whether it was according to law or not. I must say that this is something that happened in the remote past. It happened during the reign of Queen Victoria.

GENERAL SMUTS: Can you give us the date?

MR. SWART: No, I am not certain of the date, but it was during the reign of Queen Victoria. Today it is not of much practical use, but this is the position. They can submit any recommendation to His Majesty, whether such recommendation is according to law or not. If this is done, it may quite easily give rise to an absurdity.

In the second place I would like to say that this appeal to an overseas court might still be conceivable, and under those circumstances it might be justified, and that is if this overseas court was the most competent court. But the second point I would like to make is that it could be assumed without any reasonable contradiction that our Appellate Division is the most competent court in the whole world to adjudicate on South African Law. There is no doubt about that. The hon. the Leader of the Opposition also said so. We know that Roman-Dutch Law does not apply in England. Those judges of the Privy Council are not versed in Roman-Dutch Law, and it cannot be expected that they will be more competent than the judges of our Appeal Court. A few years ago a decision was in fact given by the Appeal Court in direct conflict with our law. I think I have mentioned it previously in a speech. But I think it is important enough to mention it here again. A case was heard in court and one of the best judges in Roman-Dutch Law, Sir Etienne de Villiers, gave the decision. It is not my intention to go into the details of this case, but I would like to read the decision. The point was whether a grandchild should inherit from the grandfather because her father had died before him. It was the case of Welsford v. Wright —

The Roman-Dutch rule has, therefore, clearly established, and if this court were free to decide the matter, in accordance with Roman-Dutch authorities, it does not admit of doubt that the grandchild Valerie would succeed to a share of the inheritance, as the testator's " children " are directly instituted as heirs. It seems, however, that the law was laid down in a different sense by the Privy Council in the well-known case of Galdiers v. Rycroft (17 C.S.C. 569 and 1901 A.C. 130) on appeal from the Supreme Court of Natal . . . This court is bound by that decision . . . In my opinion this court is bound by every decision of the Privy Council on the Roman-Dutch Law. In these circumstances the court must hold, though regretfully, that the grandchild Valerie is not entitled to any share of the inheritance.

Here we have a case where it is very clear. Anyone who has a knowledge of Roman-Dutch Law, realises that the Appeal Court had to give a wrong decision as a result of the decision of the Privy Council, and we are still bound by that decision. On a previous occasion I introduced a measure in Parliament to rectify this matter. It passed the Second Reading and the Committee State, but for some reason or other it was rejected at the Third Reading.

MR. TIGHY[2]: If this appeal is abolished, could it be rectified then?

MR. SWART: The Appeal Court will then be entitled to give another decision and that decision cannot be squashed by the Privy Council. I personally would very much like to see it rectified because at the moment this is a decision of our Court of Appeal and must remain so. I hope we will rectify this matter because it is unfair.

2 United Party.

MR. S. P. LE ROUX:[3] Could it be done in this Bill?

MR. SWART: No, not in this Bill but in the General Laws Amendment Bill. It is therefore not necessary to discuss any further whether our Appelate Division is the body best qualified to adjudicate on Roman-Dutch Law.

There are also additional reasons, but I have mentioned the two main reasons. There are, for instance, the additional reasons of distance and expense which have been mentioned by many members in this House. The Leader of the Opposition said that a wealthy litigant can go to the Privy Council but that the person of small means cannot go there. Mr. Merriman described this appeal to the Privy Council as " the plaything of the rich man ". There are various other reasons which I could advance here, but I think I have said enough. These two main principles form the basis of my point of view, namely, in the first instance that it does not become us in our present constitutional position as a sovereign independent State to allow an appeal to an overseas court over the constitution of which we have no control. In the second place we have in South Africa our own Court of Appeal which is best qualified to decide on appeal cases. Therefore, in view of the general constitutional ground of our sovereignty as well as for practical reasons we should take the step proposed in this Bill. We should take this step in the interests of our own judicature, namely, Roman-Dutch Law. Above all it is a question of the interest of South Africa in putting South Africa's interests first and in not being ashamed of our own judicial system and the application of that system by our courts. For that reason I would like to move that this appeal to the Privy Council be abolished and that our own court be made the highest Court of Appeal for our own cases in South Africa.

[3] National Party.

10

THE NATIONAL FLAG

MR. J. G. STRIJDOM, 1 FEBRUARY 1957[1]

I THINK THAT I am speaking on behalf of the whole House in saying that we have listened with the greatest interest to the speech of the hon. member for Hospital (Mr. Barlow[2]). Let me say this as far as his Bill is concerned. South Africa, as he has said, is a sovereign independent country, but, as he also indicated, a sovereign independent country which, in contrast with all other independent countries, occupies the peculiar position that we have two official flags, one being our national flag and the other also a national flag but the national flag of another sovereign independent country, namely Great Britain. It is difficult to imagine such a state of affairs in other sovereign countries such as Britain, for example. Can anyone imagine Britain accepting the flag of another country, in addition to her own national flag, or that the U.S.A. or Holland or Belgium or Germany would do such a thing? What then is the reason for the peculiar position that we have here? Those reasons are known to most of us but for the sake of clarity I want to deal with them briefly.

The fact that the Union Jack which flies in South Africa today is the flag of another independent country is, of course, due to the fact that South Africa is or was a conquered country and, as happens in all conquered countries, whether the conqueror be Britain or Germany or France, the flag of the conquered flies in that country. Similarly the Union Jack was flown in South Africa because South Africa was a conquered country. But after South Africa had become a conquered country and a Colony of Britain's, a very interesting development took place in the composition of the British Empire. Some of the Crown Colonies, as a result of legislation passed by the British Parliament, first developed into self-governing Colonies; and later on some of them, as the result of an agreement with the British Government, countries such as Canada, Australia and South Africa developed into sovereign independent countries, bound together in what was formerly called the British Commonwealth and what is now called simply the Commonwealth. *De facto* we in

---

[1] Speech by Mr. Strijdom, Prime Minister, on 1 February 1957, on the second reading of a Bill introduced by Mr. Arthur Barlow doing away with the Union Jack as one of the official flags of the Union. It was enacted as the Flags Amendment Act No. 18 of 1957. *House of Assembly Debates.*

[2] Conservative Party, formerly United Party member.

South Africa, for all practical purposes, attained independent status at the end of 1926. Juridically we attained it in 1931 when the British Parliament passed the Statute of Westminster.

Mr. Speaker, what would one regard as the logical and natural consequence of attainment of independent status by South Africa? One would have expected the disappearance of the Union Jack, which was the national flag of Britain, and which had flown over us because up to that stage we were subordinate to Britain. But it did not disappear, and there are reasons why it did not disappear, reasons which I want to deal with just briefly. I do not say that they are good reasons, but there are certain reasons. I ask myself — and this is a question which every stranger, who does not live in South Africa, would ask himself — why, when South Africa attained independent status, our people did not immediately celebrate with pride the attainment of independent status by accepting and hoisting the outward sign and symbol of that independence, namely a national flag of our own as the only flag of this country. Why, instead of that, did we have the struggle to which the hon. member for Hospital referred, a bitter and unpleasant flag dispute — let us admit it today — which lasted for a long time and which caused feelings in this country to run high and which eventually led to Act No. 40 of 1927 which gave these two flags to our country, namely the Union Jack which is the national flag of Britain, and our own national flag. And it then became necessary to attach to the Union Jack the meaning which the hon. member over there quoted, that is to say, that it would indicate the association of the Union with the other members of the group known as the Commonwealth of Nations. Principally — and let us admit it in all honesty, without reproaching one another, because there is not the slightest reason why at this stage in our history there should be any recriminations with regard to these things — principally because we in South Africa had two European groups who in respect of this matter adopted two diametrically opposed attitudes and who viewed this matter from two different angles, the one being the Afrikaans-speaking group, the conquered group, which naturally viewed the Union Jack and as a matter of fact the whole question of the independence of South Africa and the question of our own flag in quite a different light to the way in which our English-speaking fellow-Afrikaners viewed it. That was quite natural.

As against that there were English-speaking citizens of this country who naturally, in view of their history and perhaps for the very reason that we had another group here, namely the Afrikaans-speaking group, did not at that stage regard themselves as a separate South African nation, but who then still regarded themselves as part of the British nation and for that reason saw the Union Jack in the same light as the British people in Britain, that is to say, as their flag. Well, viewed in retrospect one can appreciate that. However disappointing it may have been to us, the Afrikaans-speaking section, that most of our English-speaking fellow-citizens in the years 1926-27 and thereafter adopted an attitude which so strongly conflicted with the attitude adopted by us with regard to the flag issue, I personally am convinced that what I have just said here was perhaps the main reason for their attitude at that time. Under different conditions today — we are no longer living in the year 1926, 1927 or 1931; we are now living in the year 1957, 30 years later — today under different conditions and looking back over the years calmly we, the Afrikaans-speaking section, can perhaps better appreciate the feeling of our English-speaking fellow-citizens in those days than we were able to appreciate it in the heat of the struggle, and I am convinced that the majority of our English-speaking fellow-countrymen in South Africa are also in a position today to appreciate with greater sympathy and better than they did in those days the feeling of the Afrikaans-speaking people in the country. This feeling on the part of the English-speaking people in this country in those days that they still formed part of the British nation and that for that reason Britain's national flag, i.e. the Union Jack, was also their flag, was so strong in the years 1926-27 that, as we all know, a rebellion was threatened if the then Government proceeded with its plan to give the Union one flag only, namely the national flag.

In view of this deep-seated feeling on the part of the English-speaking people of South Africa that they still formed part of the British nation and that they still regarded the Union Jack as their flag, therefore, the then Government, in those circumstances, entered into a compromise in order to meet the English-speaking section, and as a result of this compromise the Flag Act of 1927 was then placed on the Statute Book, which then, as the hon. member for Hospital has said, gave our country this system of two flags, namely a national flag as described in our present Act, and the Union Jack. The terms of that compromise have been read out by the hon. member over there. I do not want to quote them therefore. I just want to say briefly, in the first place, that the Union Jack was to be retained to indicate our association with the other Commonwealth countries; in the second place, that the Union Jack, together with our national flag, would be hoisted over the Houses of Parliament, the main Government buildings in the two capitals and in the capitals of the provinces and over the Government offices overseas. And that is a very important thing when one bears in mind that here a sovereign independent country was required to fly the flag of another country over its offices overseas. But that was part of the compromise. At this stage I want to ask whether there is any member in this House who can tell me, without prejudice and calmly, that he can imagine Britain, for example, flying the flag of another country such as the South African national flag, for instance, over her foreign offices, or that he can imagine Canada doing so? Even Canada and Australia do not do it. This provision, which is contained in our Act as a result of the compromise entered into in good faith at that time, is to be found in the legislation of no other country in the world, as far as I know. South Africa therefore occupies that illogical, inconsistent position.

The question now arises — and this is the question which the hon. member for Hospital raised — whether this state of affairs should continue. The question whether this state of affairs should continue was frequently raised after 1927. It was raised in this House in the course of various debates from time to time. It was frequently raised on public platforms, and the question was frequently raised in letters, in leader columns and in documents whether this state of affairs, this unheard of and illogical state of affairs, should continue, namely that South Africa should have two flags, that is to say, our own national flag and in addition to that the national flag of another country. This question was raised frequently and it was done after 1927 when this compromise was entered into, great changes took place in South Africa and the situation changed completely. Quite apart from other changes which came about after 1927, when for practical purposes we were already independent but were not yet juridically independent, the Statute of Westminster was subsequently passed in terms of which South Africa then became a sovereign independent country not only *de facto* but also *de jure* and in every sense of the word. This tremendous change came about after the flag agreement had been entered into in 1927, and this change inevitably exercised an enormous influence over the population as a whole. I make bold to say — and I do not think that any right-thinking person would contradict me — that gradually the fact that South Africa had become a sovereign independent country and was recognised as such throughout the world by all other sovereign independent countries, inevitably exercised an enormous influence over many of the English-speaking citizens of this country, in the first place with regard to their relationship with Britain and in the second place — and this is the most important aspect — their relationship with South Africa.

It stands to reason that the fact that together with us they were witnessing and participating from day to day in the exercise and implementation of our sovereign independent powers, brought home to them the realisation and the feeling which we had already had for generations, that they were no longer part of Britain or of the British nation but that, together with us, they formed the South African nation and that the independence of our nation could be symbolised by one flag only, namely by a national flag. Gradually the fact that since 1931 we had been a sovereign independent country, brought home to many of the members sitting over there and to the English-speaking section throughout the country the realisation that it was a completely inconsistent, illogical state of affairs for a sovereign independent country to allow the national flag of another country to fly as one of her flags. As a result of this course of events in the first place, and, in the second place, as the result of expressions of opinion which you, Mr. Speaker, and I and many of the members in this House have heard in recent years from English-speaking people, particularly from those English-speaking people in this country who were born here in the last 50 years and who grew up here and also many

others who settled here and adopted South Africa as their fatherland —
I say as a result of what we have observed and learned from them, I
have become deeply convinced and I think most people at least on this
side of the House — and I would say throughout the country — have become deeply convinced that over and above the Afrikaans-speaking section
of our people there is also today a very large section of the English-
speaking people, citizens of our country, who want only one flag for South
Africa. I say that in the opinion of the vast majority of our people, the
time is ripe to bring about this much-desired change, namely that South
Africa should have only one flag. I think that the vast majority of
people in South Africa are convinced — whether they all desire it, is
another matter, and I do not suggest that — I say the vast majority of
people in South Africa, even those who do not desire it, whatever their
reasons may be, are convinced of the fact that sooner or later South
Africa is going to become a republic. That, I think, is a plain as a
pikestaff.

MR. S. J. M. STEYN:[3] On what do you base that?

MR. STRIJDOM: That does not matter; I make that submission because
I want to come to my next point which has the greatest bearing on this.

Mr. Speaker, when South Africa becomes a republic this situation of
two national flags will naturally come to an end. In view of this, the
question has also been raised — and I myself raised that question —
whether this change as far as the two-flag system is concerned, cannot
stand over until such time as South Africa becomes a republic when the
issue will resolve itself. I myself raised that question, but as far as I
am concerned there are three reasons in particular, and very strong
reasons, why this change should be made now and should not be held
in abeyance until South Africa becomes a republic at some future date.
Let me mention those three reasons.

The first reason is that I believe that today the vast majority of the
White population, as I have put it and as the hon. member for Hospital
has put it, want this country to have only one flag. My second reason
for believing that this matter should be settled now and should not stand
over to be dealt with later, is that with a view to bringing about the
greatest degree of co-operation between the two White language groups,
English- and Afrikaans-speaking, with regard to the acceptance of this
principle of one flag, it is infinitely better to take this step now and not
later. Mr. Speaker, I put it that way because there are many English-
speaking citizens in our country today who share our desire as Afrikaans-
speaking people to have one flag but who are not yet convinced as to the
desirability of a republic but who, although they are not convinced on
that score, share our desire to have one flag for South Africa. And now
I say: Give these fellow-citizens of ours the opportunity to give practical
expression, without any strings, to their desire to vote with us for one

3 United Party.

219

flag for this country, namely a national flag, irrespective of whether South Africa becomes a republic sooner or later. The third reason that I want to mention is this: Mr. Speaker, a country's national flag, like its national anthem, is one of the strongest outward symbols of nationhood. Particularly in times of stress or on festive occasions and in times of great joy there are few things which so strongly promote that feeling of solidarity and patriotism in a nation as to see the flag of one's own country and to hear the national anthem of one's own country. Mr. Speaker, the acceptance of one national flag only must and will — I have not the slightest doubt in that regard — have a very beneficial effect in creating a feeling of unity between the two language groups in our country. It will strongly foster the concept of a common fatherland, of a common love for and loyalty towards that fatherland, and the realisation of a separate South African nationhood.

My feeling in this matter, with regard to the attitude of the English-speaking people in our country, is that the vast majority of them feel as we do, and that feeling is supported by the two leading English-language newspapers in South Africa, the *Argus* and the *Star*. They are the two leading English-language newspapers in this country, and I am convinced that in supporting this principle of one flag only for South Africa, they are interpreting the feeling of the vast majority of our English-speaking fellow-citizens.

Mr. Speaker, the placing of this Bill introduced by the hon. member for Hospital on the Statute Book of this country will be an extremely important milestone in the history of South Africa and of the South African nation. It will be like a new dawn breaking for us because what it is going to bring about, that is to say, a flag of our own which will serve as one of the symbols of our nationhood, in the years to come, will make an enormous contribution towards welding together into one nation these two language groups, just as the Americans, whatever the country of their origin, are Americans only today and not Hollanders or Frenchmen or Germans, etc. In the same way the acceptance by both language groups of one flag only for South Africa will be a potent factor in making us South Africans only, whether the country of our origin be Holland, Belgium, Britain, Germany or France. And that is what we all seek to achieve, that all people in South Africa should be South Africans only who will owe all their love and loyalty to this country only and who will no longer cling to another country overseas. I say that it will make South Africans of all of us, in spite of the retention by each language group of its own language, its own culture, its own religion and its own tradition; that should be no obstacle.

For these reasons I want to congratulate the hon. member for Hospital. Having regard to everything I have said here, I want to congratulate him warmly on his decision to introduce this Bill. The hon. member for Hospital is the oldest member in this House. In the years that I have known him, he has said very wise things at times. He has had a stormy political career; at other times he has said certain things which have evoked very sharp reactions. I want to say to him that of all the wise things he has ever done and said in this House, what he has done here today crowns it all. It is fitting that a member who has been a member for such a long time should, at his age, do this thing which is going to be a milestone in the history of our nation and which will usher in a new dawn for South Africa.

But, Mr. Speaker, having regard to the racial composition of our White population and in view of the difference of opinion which has existed in the past mainly between the two White language groups with regard to this matter, it is gratifying that this Bill, as the hon. member has said himself, has been introduced here today on his own initiative, without consultation with anyone, by him as an English-speaking member who took part in the flag struggle of 1926-27. This action on the part of the hon. member for Hospital will be conducive in the highest degree to co-operation in the future between Afrikaans-speaking and English-speaking where our common interests are involved, and that is why I want to congratulate him on this great service — and it is a great service — which he has rendered South Africa in introducing this Bill.

Mr. Speaker, the real significance and the value to our country and to our nation in the future of this Bill, and what it is going to accomplish, does not lie in the first place in what can be regarded as its negative effect, that is to say, the disappearance of one of this country's flags, namely the Union Jack, but in its positive effect, that is to say, the establishment of a sound, new set-up in terms of which South Africa will have only one national flag in the future, a flag which will be accepted by the vast majority of both language groups and will be accepted for all time to come — the principle of one flag only. To me it is a sign of a future in which firstly co-operation, secondly the concept of a common nationhood, and thirdly our common love for and loyalty towards our fatherland will constantly become stronger and stronger. Let me say this with the greatest emphasis, as I have frequently done in the past: These things are absolutely essential for the survival of our Christian White civilisation, for the survival of our White race in South Africa, and for the continued existence of our Western way of life here. I want to express the hope, therefore, as the hon. member for Hospital has done, that the great degree of unity which undoubtedly exists amongst the voters with regard to this matter, will also be evident from our deliberations in this House. Secondly I want to express the hope that as a result of our deliberations this Bill will be placed on the Statute Book without delay and as soon as possible during this session, and thirdly — and here I subscribe to every word the hon. member for Hospital has said in this connection — that in the discussion of this Bill on both sides we shall all deal with the matter objectively and on its merits, and that no one will do or say anything which may harm this great cause and ideal.

Mr. Speaker, this Bill, as the hon. member who has introduced it has

221

pointed out, contemplates no change in the form and design of our national flag. It simply lays down the positive principle that there shall be one flag only. There is a difference of opinion as we all know — and it will not help to hide the fact — amongst the public, although practically all of us agree that we should have one flag only, as to the form which that flag should take. There are many people in this country, young people in particular perhaps, who on many occasions sing the " Oranje, Blanje, Blou " (Orange, White and Blue) with great gusto, and there are many people of both language groups who in the course of years have developed a deep sentiment and love for the present national flag which has now flown over our country for 30 years. There are many other people in our country who want the present flag but who want the three small flags in the middle to disappear. There is a third group in our country who want the old Transvaal Vierkleur as the flag of this country. There is a fourth group who want the Free State Vierkleur as the flag of this country. There is a fifth group who want a combination of some of these flags as our national flag.

AN HON. MEMBER: And then there are people who want the Union Jack as our national flag.

MR. STRIJDOM: Well, if there are such people, there are very few of them. Similarly there may be other groups who want a national flag of a particular design. But I say that it would be very unwise to propose or to discuss any change in our national flag on this occasion. It could only cloud this whole issue and complicate the matter. This Bill, as the hon. member for Hospital has also said, has nothing to do with that. It merely seeks to lay down the principle that South Africa wants one national flag, and if this Bill is placed on the Statute Book our national flag will be the present national flag. Once this principle has been accepted and has been put into operation, the future itself will determine whether or not the present national flag is able to find an enduring place in the hearts of our people. Do not let us complicate matters on this occasion by discussing differences of opinion which are not relevant at the present time. What we are concerned with now is only this one important principle that South Africa should have one national flag only.

11

THE REPUBLICAN IDEAL

MR. J. H. H. DE WAAL, 21 MARCH 1927[1]

THE ACTUAL object of my rising is to deny a statement which came from the lips of the hon. member for Bloemfontein North (Mr. Barlow), viz. —

We are all of opinion that South Africa must remain an integral portion of the British Empire.

If statements of that kind remain unanswered then they create quite a wrong impression with the public outside. As for myself, I am not an imperialist, and never was. I shall never be one. I have been a republican since my childhood.

MR. JAGGER: Why did you not leave this country?

MR. DE WAAL: I should also have favoured a republic if I were a Hollander or an Englishman. I never could see why the head of a State should be appointed owing to his birth, instead of by virtue of merit.

THE REVEREND MR. RIDER: You are untrue to your oath.

MR. DE WAAL: In what respect? I fulfil my duties as a subject of the British King. But I have the right of pleading for the ideal of a republic, and I do it the more because I am a South African. The English members on the opposite side of the House cannot expect that South Africans should have the same predilection for the English King as they have.

MR. JAGGER: Who expects it?

MR. DE WAAL: I am glad that the hon. member understands reason and justifies my attitude. The King is the representative of imperialists in the first place. The majority of South Africans are not imperialists. A union of the White races of this country will never be able to take place while the eyes of one race are fixed on England, and of the other in South Africa. That union can only occur when all races are able to serve, respect and love the same head, and such head can only be a president. At any rate, it is not probable that the South African people, when it has to make a choice, will want a king. I, at least, elect for a republic.

[1] Statement by Mr. J. H. H. de Waal, National Party member, Deputy-Speaker and Chairman of Committee, House of Assembly, 21 March 1927. *House of Assembly Debates.*

I, however, thought that the hon. member for Lichtenburg (Mr. Roos) made a mistake at that time when he, so soon after the war, advocated a republic. I thought that it would be better if the development in that direction took place gradually, but the matter has been forced on South African people, especially on the two late republics. President Wilson and Lloyd George both stated that the reinstatement of the rights of small nations, which had been violated, was their slogan. If the representatives of Afrikanerdom had not at that time sent a deputation to England to ask for the restoration of the violated rights, they would certainly have been reproached by posterity. The Nationalist Party abode by the answer which their deputation had received, but continued the ideal of obtaining absolute independence. By that they meant, as I understood them, eventual separation from the British Empire. To me, and to many, it also meant the abandonment of the monarchical form of Government, in other words, the establishment of a republic.

The policy of separation did not, to my mind, mean a statement that we possessed the right of self-determination or sovereign independence. It did not, to my mind, mean equality with England inside the Empire. These rights we had had a long time, although the hon. member for Standerton[2] will not admit it. By separation from the British Empire I understood, I repeat it, separation from the Crown as well. That is how I originally understood the hon. member for Lichtenburg, who set the ball rolling. That also is why we did not want to be more closely bound to the Empire, and fought all the attempts of the hon. member for Standerton in the direction of closer union. We never incorporated separation in our programme of action. And today we are not making any active propaganda for it. But we want to see that the door is not closed for the realisation of the ideal.

The advocacy of that ideal has cost the Nationalist Party dear, because it kept them out of office for many years. My comfort, however, was that when the party once got into office — when once the pendulum swung in their direction — then it would take place ideal and all, and then we could, so much more freely, strive for its realisation. After all that struggle, the ideal is not now going to be sacrificed. The Nationalist Party has concluded an agreement with the Labour Party that, so long as the co-operation lasts, no motion will be introduced into Parliament in favour of a republic. The Nationalist Party will keep its word. Still more — even if the party did not have the co-operation of the Labour Party they would still not force the question on the Opposition. They only want to convince people. Only when we have convinced the majority of the English section of the desirability of breaking the bond with the British Empire — of course in a friendly way — can the great step be taken.

THE REVEREND MR. RIDER: That will never happen.

2 General Smuts.

MR. DE WAAL: We shall, of course, never be able to convince a man like the hon. member for East London City (the Reverend Mr. Rider). You cannot knock blood out of a stone. All Englishmen, fortunately, are not so unreasonable.

I thank the Prime Minister (General Hertzog) that he has obtained a declaration from such an authoritative official body as the Imperial Conference that we have the fullest right of self-determination. After that frank admission the Prime Minister feels, and so do I, more well disposed towards the makers of the declaration and less disposed to oppose them. The fact remains, however, that the ideal in favour of a republic still lives in our hearts. It is a little plant which has for good or ill been put in, and which must be cultivated and watered carefully until it is big. We cannot now allow it to die. I have thought it necessary to make this clear from my point of view in order to remove the impression created by the words of the hon. member for Bloemfontein (North), which I have quoted. I say the same as the hon. the Prime Minister: The British Empire is only useful to me as long as it is useful to South Africa.

What he obtained at the Imperial Conference is a milestone in our history of which we are proud, but it is only a milestone, not a goal.

DR. H. F. VERWOERD, 20 JANUARY 1960[1]

T H E N E X T problem which now comes within the realm of practical politics is the attainment of a republic in South Africa. It is therefore my intention on this occasion to ask for the confidence of the people of South Africa, as well as the confidence of this House, for the continuation of the application of that policy. With that end in view, I want to express certain opinions now in respect of our republican aim in the immediate future. I hope to make a very clear statement in that regard. In my opinion it is absolutely essential *inter alia* because there are all sorts of rumours in the English-language Press in South Africa as well as in other quarters in this country as to our alleged intentions. It has been alleged for example — I read it in yesterday's *Cape Times* — that it is our intention to hold a surprise election in regard to the republican issue in the second half of this year. In other words, certain allegations are being made with regard to the form in which the electorate will be asked to decide, as well as in regard to the time factor. The Opposition, with great self-complacency, have also been telling the people, even from public platforms, of the great dissension and uncertainty which are alleged to exist in the ranks of the National Party, in its caucus and in the Cabinet with regard to this matter. The United Party has been pinning its hopes on that. It has built its hopes on a foundation of sand.

---

1 Extract from speech by Dr. Verwoerd, Prime Minister, during the debate on the motion of no confidence. *House of Assembly Debates.*

I want to say in advance today that everything I propose to say here has the unanimous support of my Cabinet and the unanimous support of my caucus, and will, I have no doubt, also receive the full support of the National Party in this country. I want to add that I believe that it will also receive the full support of our other republican supporters in this country.

One of the problems with which one has to deal when one feels that the time for the realisation of this ideal is approaching, as I am convinced is the case, is this question in the first place: In what way should the electorate of South Africa be asked to take its stand in this regard? I want to say unequivocally that I do not believe that the decision should be obtained by means of an election. I want to announce therefore that this issue will be put to the electorate by way of referendum. The reason for selecting this method is that this concerns an issue on which the nation should be able to decide the future unhampered by other complications. We do not want the casting of a vote to be determined on party lines. I do not want to bind members of my party who do not wish to vote for a republic to do so. I do not know whether the hon. the Leader of the Opposition is going to try to make a party propagandistic matter out of this. I do not know whether the leader of the Progressive Party is going to try to make a party issue out of it. The Government, however, is going to have this issue put to the people of South Africa and, just as we do in this House when we leave something to the free vote of the House, the people will decide on their future, freely and genuinely. I do not believe, therefore, that an election in which the parties inevitably oppose each other, and in which the personalities of members (candidates) and of leaders play a role, is the right course. In making such a decision those factors ought not to play a role. I do not even want the question of confidence or no-confidence in a Government to be linked up with it. The Government is in power and will remain in power, so that nobody who votes a particular way need be afraid that in doing so he is throwing out his Government, and nobody who is not anxious to vote for the Government, need have the feeling that he cannot vote for the republic, although his love and his inclinations and his desires dictate that he should do so.

MR. EATON[2]: Will it be on a provincial basis?

DR. VERWOERD: I shall deal with all these points. The voting will therefore take place not by way of an election, but by way of a referendum.

There are various ways in which a referendum can be held. One possible method is to vote for a representative pro-republican in a large area or in a combined group of smaller areas, or for a group of pro-republicans in a province or in the country, or for an anti-republican or a group of anti-republicans. We reject that method because it also introduces the

2 United Party.

personal factor. We have chosen the method of a direct decision on this matter of principle: for or against a republic.

PROFESSOR FOURIE[3]: What sort of republic?

DR. VERWOERD: I appeal to hon. members to be patient. I do not propose to evade any question in this connection. I hope, therefore, that this is clear: The referendum will be on the straightforward question whether For or Against a republic. In order to permit of the organisational work in this connection, legislation will be introduced in this Session in order to make the ordinary election machinery available for such a referendum. Hon. members will recall that in the case of Natal, when the issue of Union was decided at the time, a special ordinance was also passed to permit of the use of the election machinery. That will be essential therefore. In order to be able to use this organisation in its present form, the referendum will have to be organised and the votes will have to be counted according to constituencies in the way in which elections are arranged at present. No persons and personalities and parties will be involved in the matter, however. The choice will be on the question whether for or against the republic. I do not know whether, in connection with the referendum, there is any other matter in regard to which there is still uncertainty.

MR. S. J. M. STEYN[4]: May I ask whether or not it is the intention to make available the results per constituency?

DR. VERWOERD: The figures in respect of every constituency will be made available, but the decision, in accordance with my party's constitution and in terms of the assurances which have always been given by my predecessors and by myself, will depend on whether there is a majority of White voters in favour of the establishment of a republic. Majority will mean a bare majority, even if it is one vote.

MR. S. J. M. STEYN: Both ways?

DR. VERWOERD: I hope the hon. member understands that it will be a majority decision, even though it is a majority of one only. In other words, if there is a majority of one in favour, then Parliament will have to take the necessary legislative action to establish the republic. If there is a majority of one against the republic, Parliament will not be entitled to take that step.

DR. D. L. SMIT[5]: Will the republic be within the Commonwealth or not?

DR. VERWOERD: I have asked hon. members to exercise a little patience. I am prepared to reply to all the questions. This is a question on which I had already decided to say a few words.

There is only one point in connection with the referendum which I think I should state equally clearly and that concerns the position of South West Africa in connection with such a referendum. There is a special relationship between the Union, consisting of its four provinces

3 Independent.
4 United Party.
5 United Party.

227

and South West Africa, but South West Africa is not a fifth province of the Union. The special relationship is between the independent monarchial state of South Africa and South West Africa and that relationship remains the same, irrespective of whether the independent state of South Africa is a republic or a monarchy. In other words, the relationship of South West Africa to the Union as far as the outside world is concerned is affected in no way whether we are a republic or a monarchy. It also means that the inhabitants, the voters of South West Africa, will not be able to take part in this referendum, however much we should like to have their majority of votes for the republic. I want to add in the most explicit language that this independent state of South Africa, whether it is and remains a monarchy or whether it becomes a republic, will not relinquish South West Africa. The link we have will remain or be extended, but as far as the voting with regard to a republic is concerned, I must say clearly that because of our constitutional relationship it is not possible to ask the inhabitants of South West Africa to take part in it, however much we should have liked to do so. It is in their own interests that this decision has been taken.

MR. H. G. LAWRENCE[6]: May I just put a question at this stage? Will the hon. the Prime Minister be good enough to inform the House whether he has decided who will constitute the voters who will be authorised to take part in the referendum? In other words, will the right to vote and to decide this issue be given not only to those who are on the White voters' roll but also to those who are on the Coloured voters' roll?

DR. VERWOERD: I have already stated clearly, as we have said throughout the years, that this issue will be decided by the White voters. The White electorate will decide the destiny of their South Africa in this respect.

The next question is when the referendum will be held. This concerns the timing of the referendum. I have already stated publicly and very clearly that it will not take place on or before 31 May 1960. In other words, this issue will not be confused in any way with our Union festivities. But at the same time I stated, and I repeat, that I do not consider myself bound and the Government does not consider itself bound in connection with any subsequent date. In saying that I am not suggesting that it will be held in the second half of 1960, nor am I suggesting that it will be in 1961 or 1962. The Government will choose what it considers in the interests of South Africa to be the best time to put this question to the electorate. It will, however, notify everybody timeously of the date on which the referendum will take place so as to give them an opportunity to think over the matter, although voters would be well advised at this stage to begin to consider the principle of this matter. The undertaking which I give here, therefore, is that the date will not be before 31 May. I make no announcement as to any subsequent date and no insinuations

6 Progressive Party.

228

and no inferences will be justified. I do promise, however, that when the Government considers the time proper and right, it will give timeous notice to the people of South Africa as to when the referendum will be held.

The next question that one should deal with at this stage, is what the nature of the presidency will be. I do know that it is on this very point that hon. members of the Opposition, for propaganda purposes, have tried to sow the seeds of dissension or have made allegations with regard to dissension. Perhaps they found some grounds for that in the well-known fact that many republicans are personally attached to the old republican system and to have the venerable position which the presidents of the Free State and the Transvaal occupied, including the method of their election. It is a well-known fact that there is a very strong feeling in our country for tradition and that also applies to that particular tradition. But at the same time it is the duty of all of us, when we have to take a decision on the destiny of our country, as it has developed hitherto, to look not only at traditions in connection with forms of government. It is also our duty to decide which form of government will be best under present-day circumstances. I think everybody realises that this country as it is today, with a much more heterogeneous population, with greatly increased State activities, with a much bigger and more widely distributed population, cannot simply accept the system of the republics of President Kruger and President Steyn as far as the presidency is concerned. In other words, the system under which the people elect a President who at the same time is head of the state and head of the government, is not suitable in these circumstances for the modern republic which South Africa would want to be. There would have to be a separation between the head of the state and the head of the government. Let me mention one argument which is of great importance, of greater importance even than the question as to whether the electorate should choose its President directly or indirectly. More important than that question is this question: How can the electorate retain its authority, its sovereignty? It has always been our attitude — a great struggle was waged in this regard not many years ago — that subject to the authority of the Almighty, the electorate must govern in that the electorate hands over this sovereignty to its representatives who exercise that authority for a certain period. Hence the reference to the sovereignty of Parliament. This basic principle of the sovereignty of Parliament exercised on behalf of the electorate is more important than any tradition, than any method of election, because in that way the electorate retains the power in its hands. When one introduces the other system under which the chief executive officer is at the same time President and Prime Minister, if I may put it in that way, it would be possible for this person to be chosen by the electorate in a certain way (that is to say, so that every vote has the same value) while Parliament is also chosen by the same electorate but in a different way (namely according to constituencies). Then there is always the possibility of a clash

229

between the executive authority and the legislative authority, because, as a result of the method of election, they may represent different trends. In that case there must be some means of resolving that clash, and, as is the case in the United States, the tendency usually is that the decision falls into the hands of the judiciary. When that happens there is either divided sovereignty or the supreme authority is placed in the hands of the arbitrator, but the electorate itself has become incapable of making its wishes heard unambiguously and carried out. Therefore, for the sake of the maintenance of this basic principle of the sovereignty of the electorate, as exercised by its representatives in Parliament, we undoubtedly prefer the method whereby the head of the state and the head of the government are two persons.

Then I want to add this: There were some people from time to time who believed that in order to obviate this possibility of a clash, the President could be nominated in some other way rather than directly by the people by means of a poll; that is to say, that he could be chosen according to the same method whereby a Prime Minister is chosen at the moment in this country. In other words, the Presidency could only be linked with the Prime Ministership. Against this possible method, however, there is something of fundamental importance to be said. In the first place it is a fact that the President will have to perform a special function. That function is to be the unifying factor in the national life, whatever the differences in the political sphere may be. This is an important function, an exacting function, a task which makes great demands upon the Presidency and upon the President's personality. No person, however good, however great, however strong, will be able in this South Africa of ours, as we know it today, to wage the political struggle on the one hand which the Prime Minister necessarily has to wage here and at the same time be able to serve as a unifying symbol and factor in the national life! In our country with its composition and problems as they are today that is simply impossible. Because of the significance of the Presidency, its unifying value in the life of the future united nation which we all desire so much, it is essential therefore that the President should be outside the political arena. In addition to that the Prime Minister's roots must remain in this Parliament. Not only must he appear here from time to time to defend executive policy, but he is continually accountable to Parliament. He must always be able to state his standpoint here; he must be able to give a lead here to his Government, and here he must always remain fully responsible to the electorate. No President, having other duties also and if chosen differently, would be able to comply with these demands. That is another reason why the separation between the head of the State and the head of the Government is unavoidable, and that is why we have come to this decision.

But there are also other reasons for it. One of them is this. The Prime Minister must necessarily take decisions, even when there are appeals from citizens against Ministerial decisions in regard to matters of a personal nature. The Prime Minister is the chief executive officer. He must necessarily sacrifice a certain amount of popularity now and then for Government decisions and refusals and he must be prepared to do so. But the Presidency cannot be exposed to the risk of having to sacrifice its unifying influence and esteem, just as little as the monarchy is exposed to it, by having to take this sort of decision which is the function of the executive authority. Consequently it is not desirable that the Presidency and the Prime Ministership should be linked, whatever the method of election may be. May I add this? The scope of the activities and obligations of a modern head of state and head of government are such that one can no longer expect all this from one person. We have the example of the United States where despite the most powerful support that one can get from an official corps and from co-executive officers, the task is such that the President is called upon to delegate executive powers to such an extent that he has very little or no connection with it. In terms of working capacity it is no longer possible in a modern state to cope alone in the main with everything.

The question may now be put to me: If the object of the Presidency is to perform a unifying task, if it is necessary that he should be held in high esteem, that he should remain outside the political arena, why not retain the monarchy then? My reply to that is the following: It is inherent in the monarchies of the Commonwealth that this person, however good and honourable he might be, is bound by bonds of birth to a different country. The fact that such a person is called the monarch of South Africa does indeed stress South Africa's independence as a completely independent State, but that does not take away the fact that the sovereign of South Africa, in terms of the monarchies of the Commonwealth, is always chosen from the heirs of the Royal Family in another State, Britain. It is not possible in a country with a population like ours (however much one may respect the sovereign of that other country, and however much one might honour him and fulfil the obligations as long as that person is also king of one's own country) to get away from the fact that this unifying effect is not there — particularly here where more than 50 per cent of the population have a different heritage from those stemming from the country having that sovereign. Such a person cannot have the same unifying effect as a man coming from the midst even of a heterogeneous people can have. The sovereign can and does have that effect in Britain, but the same person cannot fill that role for the whole of South Africa. The monarchy will always be the background for division. If we want to develop a common national sentiment we must have a Head of State who comes from our own midst and whom we respect. Now it would of course be ridiculous to select somebody from our midst and to make him a monarch. The Presidency is the obvious and logical fulfilment of the desire for national unity of the South African nation, under a Head of State born in this country. Therefore I say that this unified nation we all desire to have can be obtained

231

in one way only, namely through the kind of Presidency I have just mentioned.

Furthermore, I just want to say a few words about the status of the President, because here I wish to be very frank and I want to stress that I do not want to belittle the change and ostensibly facilitate the implementation of the function. I do not wish to bluff anybody by saying: " Oh, it is only the Governor-General called by a different title." Of course that is not so. It would be a mistake for people to say that becoming a republic merely means that the Governor-General is now called the President. What happens in fact is that a person is appointed who in respect of our state will enjoy the same high regard, as the head of the state, as that enjoyed by the presidents, heads of state or monarchs of other states. It is, if one may put it that way, the disappearance of the Governor-Generalship as the representative of a monarch, and the substitution for the monarch by a President with all the privileges a monarch enjoys. It is the monarchy which is being replaced by a republic. The monarch is replaced by the President. In other words, the status is not only high, but the functions also. He will enjoy not only the privileges which the Governor-General enjoys today in terms of the Union legislation, or which he has in the name of the Queen, but he will also enjoy the privileges which the Queen always enjoys, in addition to such extra privileges as the State may invest him with. Therefore I say that we are creating a position of high status and value. It may become a bond which will make it possible for us to become one nation and to set aside the division we had in the past. It is for that reason that I am today making an appeal, in all seriousness and with the greatest sense of responsibility, to everybody to co-operate and to achieve something which will put an end to the 150 years' struggle between South African nationalism and what is to some extent a foreign nationalism.

MR. LAWRENCE: Will the Head of State be appointed by the Government?

DR. VERWOERD: I am coming to that. In fact, that is my next point. My hon. friends should not be in too much of a hurry. They should really be in a hurry in regard to something else — to obtain a republic! The next question is: How is this President to be appointed? The reply to that is that this is one of the details. On that point Parliament will later have to deliberate and decide, but I am prepared to indicate what the possibilities are. One of the possibilities is that the Government will appoint that person. That creates certain problems — as the other methods also do — and certain objections will be raised. A second possibility is that he may be appointed by an electoral college consisting of the members of the House of Assembly and of the Senate — in other words, by the representatives of the people.

MR. RUSSELL[7]: The new Senate!

DR. VERWOERD: Yes, of course; not the Graaff Senate. A third possi-

[7] United Party.

232

bility is an even larger electoral college consisting of members of this House, the Senate and the four Provincial Councils. What Parliament in its wisdom will decide in this respect and what it will do in detail in implementing the decision given by the people, I do not want to anticipate now. I just want to indicate that it is my ambition to ensure that the President will enjoy the highest possible measure of acceptability and the highest possible status. Whichever method is decided upon, it should not be a method which makes the President personally the subject of dispute, but one which will really give satisfaction and which will most easily console those whose choice is not successful.

That brings me to the next question: What will the constitution of the republic be? We have already said that it will be a Christian republic, in the same way that today we strive to be a Christian state. In addition it has already been clearly stated that it will be a democratic republic. It has also been clearly stated already that it will be a republic in which the language and other rights of English-speaking friends as well as of the Afrikaans-speaking people will be fully protected. Therefore the general principles have already been stated clearly. We have also stated very clearly that we will retain the parliamentary form of government. In order to give hon. members an even clearer picture of how we see the road ahead, I however wish to add the following. The development of the Union of South Africa hitherto has been a continual changing of our original constitutional and other legislation in the direction of a republic. Right from the beginning we said that we were following the road adopted by Ireland. By that we meant that we were following the road of gradual development. The gradual development throughout the years since 1910 — and particularly when the National Party was in power to direct matters — was one of endless amendments and changes, each approaching more closely to a republic. Hon. members know that this was so in regard to our Status Acts. They know what happened in regard to our Flag Act. They know what we did in regard to abolishing appeals to the Privy Council. They also know what happened in regard to practices which were changed, for example in regard to our National Anthem. They know what happened in connection with our Citizenship Act. We never tried to conceal it. They were all steps towards a republic. One might almost say that our present constitutional composition, our present Union legislation even though it is sometimes in the form of various bits of amending legislation, already form a republican constitution, except in so far as the changeover from a monarchy to a republic has not been done yet. Therefore I say very clearly that I and my party regard our Union legislation, as we have it now, as almost completely amounting to republican constitutional legislation. When the people decide that the Union is to become a republic, certain changes will of course be necessary, including changes of a legislative nature, and in the new republican constitution all these changes that have been made over the years will have to be consolidated. In practice, however, most of these changes will be required in administrative practices and formulae. In other words, what I want to say is that there will be no radical changes in our parliamentary institutions or constitutional practices; that will not be necessary. All that will be necessary is the ordinary continuation of constitutional development which has always taken place on our road to freedom, which has always been the guiding principle of the National Party, and which is the only sober, realistic method of constitutional development for a decent nation which stems from Western civilisation. I therefore say that I see no reason why we cannot and should not ask for the full support of all people calling themselves republicans, including those who do so under the pro-republican clause in the constitution of the United Party.

There is a further question I have to discuss. It is whether the republic will or will not be a member of the Commonwealth. Hon. members know that the Programme of Principles of the National Party is very clear on this point. The Programme of Principles states the proposition that membership of the Commonwealth and the changeover from a monarchy to a republic are two separate matters, and that separate replies have to be given to these two questions. I have given a clear reply as to our intention to change the monarchy to a republic in South Africa. Now I am asked: What about the second question? Everybody should realise that one can give a reply to this question only shortly before that referendum is held. The reply one would give today, if one had to give it today, is not necessarily the same reply one would give in two or three years' time if in the meantime the situation were to change radically. For that reason it is clear that in terms of the constitution of my party I am not justified, nor would it be wise to do so, to give a reply on this point now. But I will make one promise, and it is a clear and unequivocal promise, namely that before this referendum is held the country will be told whether it will be the policy of the Government to remain a member of the Commonwealth, or not to remain a member.

I want to enlarge on this a little so that I may be clearly understood. It is the custom in many parts of the world today for nations to stand together to protect their mutual interests. We know of various groups of countries in Europe who have made alliances with each other, economically and in other respects. Each state joins such a group for the sake of its own interests. In other words, each of them becomes a member of such a group of states with a view to its own interests. Not (one of them is concerned with history (e.g. former conflicts) when deciding to take this step; it is not concerned now with anything else but the present interests of its country. At the moment, by being a member of the Commonwealth, we are also a member of a group in this way. This group really has just one characteristic differentiating it from the other groups, viz. that the Queen of England is called the Head of the Commonwealth for historical reasons, and without attaching any meaning to it. That is the symbol. The others have no nominal head or any symbol. One should in fact keep this difference in mind, but at the same time one should not exaggerate this difference. When the time for holding a referendum draws near enough to make an announcement necessary, we will therefore review the situation soberly, with particular reference to the three decisive questions. The first is what the position is in the countries of our partners in the group or club or society of nations, whatever one wants to call it. We shall particularly look at what the position is in Britain, because of its leading role in this alliance. Let me say this frankly, as being my personal standpoint: If the Labour Party in Britain were to come into power and were to form a socialist government revealing all the characteristics which it now reveals in opposition (viz. wanting to interfere in our domestic colour policy, opposing us economically — to boycott us and even to talk about kicking us out), I would seriously have considered taking the lead in no longer allowing South Africa to remain a member of the Commonwealth, because then the benefits of such membership as well as the friendly relations would have disappeared. I do not know whether such a state of affairs can be repeated there. We cannot see into the future. But that is an example of why I say that we must take into consideration particularly the position in Britain. Secondly, at that stage we will have to take into consideration the position within the Commonwealth. The Commonwealth itself is still developing steadily; amongst other things it is obtaining new members. I do not know what the nature of the Commonwealth will be in a few years' time. Nor do I know how the other members of the Commonwealth will influence its nature, to our benefit or to our detriment. But I do know one thing, viz. that it will be in the interests of South Africa to remain friends with Britain and also with the other countries in Africa. If a situation were to develop in which we can best retain our friendship with both of them by not being a member, but by negotiating with each of them on a suitable basis without quarrelling with anybody around one table, we would have to decide to do that. If on the other hand the contrary were to be the position, we would have to bear that in mind also. In other words, I am again merely giving an example without giving any indication and from which no inferences are to be drawn, of a second factor which will play a role in our deliberations at the appropriate time. A third factor is the basic one of the interests of South Africa. There may be other considerations than those I have just mentioned which may make it better for South Africa to be a member or not to be a member. Therefore all I am saying now is that before the referendum takes place we will announce what our conclusion is then, so that when somebody votes for or against becoming a republic he will know what action the Government is considering in this regard if it should receive the mandate.

The final point can be dealt with very briefly. It is the question of how the establishment of a republic will affect our relations with Britain.

My reply to that is this. Our policy is one of friendship with Britain and all other nations, but I particularly mention Britain because that is the country mostly affected by this change. I further stress that our friendship with Britain—the good relations between our two countries which at the moment are fortunately very satisfactory and to our mutual benefit — can only be strengthened if in our country we can eliminate anything which irritates and which is the result of our history. I believe that a Republic of South Africa and the United Kingdom will be good friends and co-operate smoothly in the economic and other spheres. Yes, I believe that they will be able to understand each other better, that they will be able to approach each other more easily, and even speak more intimately to each other, if there is no more suspicion in our country and if no more suspicion can be sown. Nationalist Governments in the past have always had the experience that when they tried to create good relations, the Opposition, which really desires to have such good relations, grasped at the opportunity to make political capital out of it by making it suspect in the eyes of its followers merely in order to put it out of power. That sort of behaviour will be something of the past in a republic.

The visit to South Africa of Mr. Macmillan in the near future stresses, as I have already said outside this House — and I said it with only the best intentions — how great the friendship can be between a potentially republican Government, and therefore later also between the Republic of South Africa, and Britain. Mr. Macmillan is under no illusions as to our republicanism. He was under no illusions, when he paid a friendly visit to Ghana, as to what they were thinking in regard to their republic. He is under no illusion as to what we have in mind in regard to friendship, although we are republicans, because I informed him along those lines. Therefore I say that I appreciate his decision to visit us all the more as being one of the greatest gestures of friendship and goodwill he is making to our country on behalf of Britain, being well aware of the possible future developments here.

Our aspirations are inspired only by the hope that eventually we will at least see the end of the disputes in regard to our constitutional future between the two language groups, so that we can become one united nation; and that in the economic sphere there will not always be the danger of the effects of these disturbing factors and the sowing of suspicion we so often have to the detriment of South Africa. In putting this question to the people, our endeavour will be to gain their confidence for everything we do, and above all, to give them a republic in which unity and the peaceful co-existence of our White population will be the main feature.

SECTION IV
THE INDIAN PROBLEM

1

INDIAN RELIEF

GENERAL J. C. SMUTS, 8 JUNE 1914[1]

THE MINISTER OF FINANCE (The Hon. J. C. Smuts) moved the second reading of the Indian Relief Bill. He requested members to approach such a thorny and difficult question in a non-controversial spirit. The House was now in a position to settle finally the Indian problem on a satisfactory basis, the recommendations of the Solomon Commission,[2] which inquired into the grievances of Indians, having been accepted as a solution by the Indian Government, and also, with one exception, by the Indian community residing here. He recalled the passing of the Immigration Act last session, and the agitation which followed it. Mr. Gandhi had raised four points on two of which it was possible for the Government to meet him. There were two other points on which is was impossible for the Government immediately after the session to meet the community's views.

One was the right of entry of the South African-born Indian into the Cape Province. In the Immigration Act of last year provision had been made that Indians entering the Cape Province from the other Provinces should be required to comply with a dictation test, and Mr. Gandhi desired that this restriction should be removed. The Government, however, pointed out that the point had been fully discussed during the debates on the Bill, and that the strongest exception had been taken to the proposed removal of the restriction, which maintained the restriction under the old Cape laws. The second question was the marriage question. In the Immigration Act of last year a clause had been adopted on the motion of the hon. member for Cape Town, Castle (Mr. Alexander) permitting the entry of a wife married according to polygamous rites, though the marriage was *de facto* monogamous. The Natal Division of the Supreme Court had, however, decided that it was not possible to recognise as legal a marriage celebrated according to polygamous rites. Administratively in the past there had been no difficulty in the matter, as the authorities had admitted one wife to every man.

MR. P. DUNCAN: Then why did they raise the question?

The Minister of Finance said that if he were to answer that question

---

[1] Speech by General Smuts in the House of Assembly, 8 June 1914. *House of Assembly Debates.*
[2] U.G. 16 of 1914.

it would take a very long time, and he did not think it was necessary to do so. It was a case that had presented some very extraordinary features. When it became clear that the Government could not satisfy the Indian community on these points the question of the £3 licence was raised. He did not intend to go in detail into that question, but he would say that it was impossible for the Government, when threatened with a strike, to make any concessions at all. Then followed a great deal of bloodshed and violence in suppressing the strike, and subsequently the Solomon Commission was appointed. It was assisted in its labours by a representative of the Indian Government, Sir Benjamin Robertson, whose services had been, as he could say from personal knowledge, of the very greatest value to the Commission. He had smoothed its work considerably, and had thrown light on many difficult questions. The Commission, it would be seen, had made 14 recommendations. To give effect to most of these it required merely administrative action, and here he would say that it was the intention of the Government to carry out the Commission's recommendations in their entirety, partly by legislation and partly by administration; and in this way to secure that peace which they were all longing for, that peace which was not merely of such importance to South Africa itself, but also to South Africa in her external relations. The points dealt with in the Bill included recommendations Nos. 1, 3, 4, 5 and 13 in the report.

The measure before the House dealt with recommendations 1, 3, 4, 5 and 13 of this Commission. The recommendations 3 and 4 dealt with the marriage question pure and simple. Recommendation 3, with which he would first deal, was as follows: There should be legislation on the lines of Act 16 of 1860 of the Cape Colony, making provision for the appointment of marriage officers from amongst Indian priests of different denominations for the purpose of solemnising marriages in accordance with the rites of the respective religions of the parties. Both in Natal and the Cape, as far back as 1860, a law was passed giving the Government power to appoint priests of Mohammedan belief. Although little advantage had been taken of the Act in the Cape, yet the Indian community claimed they should have the right to be married before their own priests. Section 1 of the Bill carried out this recommendation.

The next recommendation also referred to the marriage question, and was as follows: There should be legislation for the validation, by means of registration, of existing *de facto* monogamous marriages, by which are understood marriages of one man with one woman under a system which recognises the right of the husband to marry one or more other wives. Directions as to the mode of registration and of the particulars to be entered in the registry might be given by regulations to be framed under the Statute. This was a more difficult question for the Commission to deal with — the religious unions which were already existing among Indians in this country, but not recognised by South African laws. The Indians contended that an opening should be given for these unions, so long as they were monogamous, to be turned into legal marriages by a simple system of registration, which suggestion had been adopted. These people could go before marriage officers or magistrates, and when they had satisfied these officers that such a marriage did exist they could have it registered. This was to meet cases where a marriage already existed between man and wife. It was pointed out by the Commission that a marriage like that would not debar these people under their religious tenets from taking more wives. But those would not be legal marriages. Short of legalising polygamy, he did not see what more they could do. That was the most important and the most difficult question before the Commission, and in this connection Sir William Robinson rendered great assistance.

Since then representations had been made by Mohammedans, who were not quite satisfied and who said that according to their faith it was permitted to them to marry more than one wife, and by now giving an opening for only one marriage to become legal it seemed a great hardship, and one which the Indians wished to see removed. He (the Minister) argued the question, and they could not possibly satisfy him of any way of dealing with the claim they advanced. They mentioned the course that had been taken in Mauritius and he (the Minister) promised to go into the matter, but he had not received any information on that point, and so could not make a statement that afternoon. So among the Mohammedans there was not complete satisfaction with the report on this point, but so far as the Commission had been able to meet these people in a legal way the Commission had done so.

He would now come to the marriage question as it affected immigration, and the Commission reported as follows: Section 5 (g) of the Immigrants Regulation Act of 1913 should be amended so as to bring the law into conformity with the practice of the Immigration Department, which is " to admit one wife and the minor children by her of an Indian now entitled to reside in any Province or who may in future be permitted to enter the Union, irrespective of the fact that his marriage to such wife may have been solemnised according to tenets that recognise polygamy, or that she is one of several wives married abroad, so long as she is his only wife in South Africa." If an Indian was resident in South Africa, and wanted to bring out his wife and minor children, to which he was entitled in law, no inquiry would be made as to whether it was a legal marriage, but the inquiry would be: Were they married in the tenets of some religion? The man could only bring one wife. This would be found in Section 3 of the Bill, and thus disposed of the marriage question, which was a most difficult and important question.

He would now come to recommendation 13, which dealt with the question of domicile certificates in Natal. Under the old Immigration Law, the Natal practice was to issue domicile certificates, and these certificates when issued were conclusive as to the right of the holder to return to Natal. The system was abolished in the Act of last year, because it was found that in many cases these certificates got into the hands of wrong people. There were thousands of people entitled to these certificates, and the question was how to deal with them in such a way that no hardship would be constituted. The Minister then quoted recommendation 13, as follows: Domicile certificates which have been issued to Indians in Natal by the Immigration Officers of that Province, and which bear the thumb impression of the holder of the permit, should be recognised as conclusive evidence of the right of the holder to enter the Union as soon as his identity has been established. This was being followed.

This left one other point, and that was the abolition of the £3 tax in Natal. He did not intend to cover the whole history of the tax. Hon. members knew that this system of coolie labour was introduced many years ago. As the number of the Indians increased, it became a matter of concern as to what steps should be taken to get some of these people back to India. In 1893 a mission went from Natal to India, and the result was found in the law passed in 1895 — the law they were now concerned with. Indentured coolies, after they had finished their term of service and who did not wish to return to India nor to reindenture, could stay in Natal on the payment of a £3 licence. From the very start the law did not promise to be a success, and after five years another mission was sent to India to see whether it was not possible that the indentures should expire in India. The mission did not meet with success, and no change was made. The Indians claim that this tax should be abolished, and this was one of the questions the Solomon Commission went into. The Commission came to the conclusion that the claims of the Indians were fair and just and politic, and recommended the repeal of Clause 6 of the Act of 1895. This course was adopted in the Bill. The Commission pointed out that the tax was only payable by a small portion of the Indian population. The Commission pointed out that 11,000 males were at present liable to the tax and about 21,000 were still under indenture or had been reindentured. The Commission also pointed out that the Indian population was much larger, and that the people liable to the tax were the least able to bear the burden. When everybody paid a capitation tax such was easy to collect, but where only a small portion of a population paid, it became extremely difficult, because they could only collect through the machinery of the police. When a policeman wanted to make out that a man was liable to the tax, he must prove that he came to Natal after 1895, which was most difficult, and also that he did not come there as a free man, which was also very difficult.

From the very beginning this tax had been avoided in a wholesale fashion, and in 1905 the Natal Government passed a law by which no employer could accept the service of any of these people without making certain that he had paid the tax. That law had been on the Statute Book for some years, but had never been carried out. Just as it was difficult to collect the tax from the Indians it was found just as difficult to collect it by means of this amending law. The Commission pointed out that the position had become very serious indeed, because these people, in order to avoid the tax, wandered from place to place. The Commission advanced other arguments that told against the tax and finally came to the conclusion that the tax should be abolished. The Minister pointed out that the evidence as to whether the tax had the effect of inducing these people to return to India had been very conflicting, and the Commission was not satisfied that the tax had had any effect in inducing the coolies to return to India. The Commission suggested that the best course would be to repeal Section 6 of the Act of 1895, and the Minister pointed out that no other alteration was made in the status of Indians in Natal under this Bill. Clause 6 gave power to the Government to give free passages to any Indians willing to return to India, and renounce their rights of residence in South Africa. The object of the Government was to assist, in every way possible, to induce them to leave this country and go back to India.

He appealed to hon. members, especially those from Natal, to assist the Government in getting the Bill through this session. They had a unique opportunity of dealing with this troublesome question. It was a point which affected the whole of the British Empire, and he was sorry to say it was taking another form in one of the British Dominions. They had reached a stage after a long struggle when they could bring the whole matter to a conclusion, and he would ask members, especially members from Natal, to assist the Government on this occasion and so remove one of the most dangerous elements of discontent which at present beset them.

SIR AUBREY WOOLLS-SAMPSON, 8 JUNE 1914[1]

SIR A. WOOLLS-SAMPSON said he was very sorry he was not going to support the Government. The Indian community, under the advice and guidance of Mr. Gandhi, engineered a strike, and, to secure the support of the Indian Government and the sympathy of the British public, false statements of cruelty, coercion, and semi-slavery were cabled to every part of the civilised world. The Government of his country appointed a Commission presided over by one of the Judges of the Supreme Court to inquire into these allegations and to suggest remedial measures. Really it was the first duty of that Commission to nail down the falsehoods that had been circulated abroad in reference to the treatment of Indians by the White inhabitants, by the officials, and by the Government of this country. He regretted that in some instances this matter had received the support and countenance of a number of White men on the Rand, to whose everlasting discredit it should be said that whenever any question arose between the Coloured and White races in this country they could

[1] Speech by Sir Aubrey Woolls-Sampson, Unionist Party, during the debate in the House of Assembly on the Indian Relief Bill. *House of Assembly Debates.*

always on the slightest provocation discover more virtue in a coloured skin than they could in a white one.

In the course of their report, the Commission stated: " So far from assisting the Commission by placing before it the case for the Indian community for the redress of their grievances and by collecting evidence in support of the serious allegations of acts of violence committed upon persons sentenced to imprisonment in connection with the strike, the leaders decided on various grounds, which it is unnecessary to mention, entirely to ignore the Commission. The result was that not only was the Indian community not represented by counsel, but that, acting upon the advice given by Mr. Gandhi, no witnesses appeared to substantiate the charges of violence." Mr. Gandhi and his friends, despite the fact that an important Indian official had been appointed by the Indian Government to watch the interests of the Indian community throughout the sittings of the Commission, prevailed upon all his people not to give evidence, alleging mainly that he objected to the personnel of the Commission.

Mr. Gandhi's objection to the personnel of the Commission was a mere subterfuge. He was unable and so were his people to substantiate the charges which had been sent broadcast over the water, and he knew full well that their presence before that Commission would once and for all prove conclusively that they had engineered this strike on false premises entirely. The Commission was very anxious, if possible, to acquire some evidence with regard to these charges, and, as a matter of fact, an Indian named Sooker did appear before the Commission to tender evidence. The Commission pointed out, however, that the evidence that he gave was hearsay, but he stated that there was in the precincts of the court a man named Balbadhur who was himself one of the men who had been ill-treated after the strike. This man was brought before the Commission, and his complaint was that, after the strike, and on his return to the mine, he was assaulted by the compound manager. This was investigated, and it was found that the three witnesses whom Balbadhur had called before the magistrate to investigate the charge against the compound manager all denied any knowledge of the alleged assault, and thereupon the charge was withdrawn. The only single charge, therefore, that was brought to the knowledge of the authorities was proved conclusively to be founded entirely on bad evidence.

He (Sir A. Woolls-Sampson) now wanted to take two points. First, the question of the reliability of the Indians in their statements; and, secondly, whether they were justified owing to ill-treatment. As to the first point, the Commission said that it was well to draw attention to a fact which constantly confronted us in this country, and that was that the Indian community itself was in a great measure responsible for the stringency of the investigations which were made into applications of all kinds by the officials of the Immigration Department. That had been rendered absolutely necessary by the numerous attempts at fraud and impersonation which were constantly made by Asiatics. This (said the hon. member) went to prove that, as far as reliability was concerned, the Indian statements had to be accepted with very considerable reservation. He wanted to point out that in this instance there was nothing to justify the attitude adopted by the Indians, because this report went to prove that they were at that time well treated by those who employed them. The Commission quoted returns in regard to the number of coolies re-indentured, and added: " These figures are eloquent testimony to the good relations which exist between the coolies and their employers, to which reference has already been made."

The hon. member went on to say that this all went to prove conclusively that there was no ill-treatment in the case of the Indians in Natal, that this strike was engineered purely for political purposes, and possibly far more to serve a political purpose in India than it was in this country. It was made perfectly clear in reference to this £3 tax that when it was imposed it was imposed with the full consent of the Indian authorities, that it was imposed in the terms of indenture, and Sir Benjamin Robertson, who was the official appointed by the Indian Government, stated that, as far as it was possible to make this clear to the Indians, it was done, and that there could be no reasonable complaint on their part that we were imposing an unjust tax upon a number of people who were unable to pay it. "One thing, however, was clear " (the Commission reported), " and that is that all that could be done by the Government of Natal was done to explain the real position to them, and that it was upon the express understanding already set fourth that they were introduced into the Colony. It is equally clear that, whatever may be said about the coolies themselves, the Government of India, which may be regarded as standing in the position of guardians to their ignorant subjects, accepted and acquiesced in the provisions of Act 17 of 1895, which are embodied in the indentures, and that they, at any rate, were under no misconception as to the conditions under which the coolies were admitted into Natal."

At this stage he would like to refer to the disabilities under which we laboured by the presence of an overwhelming coolie population as we had it in Natal. When Europeans went to India, China or Japan, they took with them large sums of money, they established factories, industries and works of all descriptions and found employment for the poorer classes.

Proceeding, Colonel Sampson said that the Indian in Natal, in the course of his industry, employed his own people. He sent very little money abroad. He quoted from the report of the Indians' Grievances Commission and that the insurrection in Natal in 1906 had been brought about, it was said by the poll tax. He did not believe this, but nevertheless was of opinion that the withdrawal of the Indian tax would have a most injurious effect upon the Native mind and would lead to an agitation for the removal of the Native Hut Tax.

2

ROUND-TABLE CONFERENCE

DR. D. F. MALAN, 17 FEBRUARY 1926[1]

BEFORE YOU PROCEED to the other business of the House, Mr. Speaker, I wish, with leave, to make a statement on a matter of importance. As the House is aware, for a considerable time negotiations have taken place between the Government of India and the Government of the Union, in regard to the position of Indians in South Africa. These negotiations began shortly after I made a statement to the House last year, in which I intimated my intention of introducing at an early date legislation dealing with the Indian question in South Africa. These negotiations have proceeded until a very recent date. They have now reached a definite stage, and I may almost say have reached a certain measure of finality, and I think it is only right at this stage that I should inform the House as to what the actual position is today.

The first and the chief object which the Government of India tried to achieve through these negotiations, was the holding of the round-table conference on the position of Indians in South Africa. Though the scope of that conference, as was suggested by the Government of India itself, if it had been held, would have been restricted in a certain measure, yet, on the other hand, it is quite evident that the idea underlying the proposal was a discussion of the proposed legislation on the Indian question by this House, and especially the discussion of the Bill which I intimated to the House that I was going to introduce, a discussion between the representatives of the Union and representatives of the Government of India. The attitude which was adopted by us from the beginning in regard to this proposal — and to this attitude we have consistently adhered — was this, that this particular problem was a South African one, that it had to be solved by South Africa alone, and that it had to be solved with a view solely to the interests of South Africa.

Now we did not contend, and I think we would not have been justified in contending, that this attitude was inherently opposed to and, therefore, excluding any friendly conversations with an outside Government, but what we had in mind was, that if this conversation were to take place at all, then, while we on our part would be expected to make this concession if such a conference were not to turn out a failure, on the other

---

[1] Statement by the Minister of the Interior, Dr. D. F. Malan, 17 February 1926. *House of Assembly Debates.*

hand, there must be held out prospectively a counterbalancing advantage to the Union of South Africa. If we were called upon to make only concessions and there was no counterbalancing, then these conversations would not take place on an equal footing, and the people of South Africa would have a right to interpret these conversations as an interference in our domestic affairs from outside; and as far as we could gauge the opinion of the people of South Africa we had the right to say to the Government of India that any interference from outside in our domestic affairs would be tolerated neither by the people of South Africa as a whole nor by the bulk of the followers of any political party of the country. For this reason, and under these circumstances, we intimated to the Government of India that we were not in principle opposed to the holding of a round-table conference, but if we did hold one, then in the proposed discussions must be included this particular point, that the Government of India shall be asked to be willing to co-operate with the Government of the Union to assist the Government in making the scheme of voluntary repatriation more effective than it is. We more particularly thought of the possibility of holding out with the assistance and co-operation of the Government of India an additional inducement to the Indians to leave the country by holding out to them the possibility of an advantageous land settlement in India or adjacent territories. If the Government of India had agreed to include this particular point in the agenda of such a conference, the round-table conference, as far as we were concerned would have been held.

The Government of India, however, did not see their way to agree to a conference with only prospective concessions on our part without any prospective advantage, a conference which would be interpreted under such circumstances by the people of South Africa as not being held on an equal footing between the two different sides and as an intolerable inter-ference from outside in our domestic affairs. Failing a round-table con-ference, and with a view to making representations on our proposed legis-lation direct, the Government of India further approached us with the request to send a commission or so-called deputation to South Africa to inquire into the whole position of Indians here and to give to their own Government first-hand information. We on our side had no difficulty in agreeing to this request, especially as the Government of India undertook that the men they were going to send would be men of discretion, who would not come to South Africa as agitators and would not inflame by their presence here the mind of the Indian community and make in that way the problem which was already difficult, much more difficult. I am glad to say that the deputation has been in South Africa now for a considerable time and the Government of the Union has so far no com-plaint whatever against them. On the contrary the Government of the Union has every reason to be satisfied with the way in which they have acted in most difficult circumstances.

We went further in connection with this request, and we offered to the

Government of India that after the deputation had collected its evidence they should be allowed, in the name of the Government of India and of the Indian community in South Africa to lay the opinions of Indians before the select committee which would be appointed by this House after the second reading of the Bill. After receiving the preliminary report of this deputation the Government of India approached us with the further request not to proceed, at this stage at least, any further with our proposed legislation, but to appoint as a preliminary measure a commission, similar to the Asiatic Commission which went into the whole question in 1921, to make a fresh inquiry and to report to this House. Unfortunately we were not in a position to agree to this request. We pointed out — and I think quite justly — to the Government of India that, as a commission had made exhaustive inquiries into the whole problem as late as 1921, the position since that time could not have materially changed, and that it was unnecessary under these circumstances to have a fresh inquiry. We further pointed out that such a fresh inquiry would mean delay and would mean at least this, that during the present session we would not be able to proceed with our proposed legislation: and we pointed out that, in face of the impatience which existed in regard to the solution of this particular question, we had no right to tell them that we could accede their request.

So far, then, we had turned down two very important requests on the part of the Government of India, and under these circumstances we realised that a feeling was springing up in India and also among the Indian community in South Africa that we were forcing through this most important legislation, in which they were so vitally concerned, not only against the will of the Indian community and the will of the Government of India, but we were forcing through this legislation without giving them any proper opportunity to lay the case of the Indians before the Government of the country and before this Legislature. We felt that while this feeling lasted an atmosphere existed which was certainly not conducive to the successful solution of this most difficult and most important question. It was, therefore, we felt, necessary as far as possible to create an atmosphere of goodwill, an atmosphere which would be conducive to the successful solution of this question. Under these circumtsances we thought that this feeling must as soon as possible be removed, and the only way to remove this feeling was to afford an opportunity for wider evidence, less restricted evidence, to be laid before the Committee to be appointed by this House. Under the circumstances we definitely offered to the Government of India that we would propose that legislation of which notice had been given shall be referred to a select committee before the second reading. To this proposal we felt it was only right to attach certain conditions and safeguards. We felt it was necessary, because this was, under the circumstances prevailing in South Africa and in this House, an unusual procedure. It was unusual because the particular measure I introduced has certainly behind it to support it the volume of opinion in the country and as far as I can judge there is no great division of opinion in this House with regard to this matter. To refer it to a select committee before the second reading, we felt, would be an unusual procedure.

The conditions which we thought it was necessary to attach to this offer were, in the first place, that the Government of India should intimate that they would be willing to make use of this special opportunity offered to them; the second condition was that if they thought it necessary to lay any evidence before the select committee before the second reading such evidence should be brought forward by their deputation now in South Africa. Nobody else from India, either on their own behalf or on behalf of the Government of India would be allowed to make use of this special opportunity. The third condition was that the select committee appointed before the second reading would be required by this House to report within such a period as to enable this House to pass this proposed legislation during the present session. This offer, with the conditions, has been accepted by the Government of India.

To enable the House to judge of the spirit in which this particular offer was made and accepted, I ask permission to read to the House parts of the correspondence which has taken place recently, which has a more particular bearing on the points to which I have referred. On 5 February the following was dispatched —

While on the one hand my Ministers must regret their inability to accede to the request of the Government of India for a round-table conference or a fresh inquiry, they, on the other hand, fully realise the anxiety of that Government to place as fully as possible the case of the Indian community in South Africa before the Government of the Union. It is for this reason that they previously adumbrated the possibility of evidence before a parliamentary select committee by the deputation of the Government of India, now in the country, after the Bill shall have passed the second reading. Although reference to a select committee after the second reading will imply the maintenance of the general principles of the Bill, it will at the same time offer a very wide scope for evidence and will not even exclude evidence on such a fundamental question in which the Government of India is primarily concerned, as to whether the proposed segregation shall be voluntary or compulsory. To this suggestion which they have offered, my Ministers have thus far received no reply and they are consequently in doubt as to the existence of any difficulty on the part of the Government of India in accepting the same. If such difficulties should however exist on the ground of too great a restriction of the evidence, which the deputation might desire to bring forward, my Ministers would agree to propose the reference of the Bill to a select committee before the second reading, thus widening the scope for evidence so as to include the principles of the Bill. They wish it, however, to be understood that such a proposal on their part will be subject to the Government of India intimating their willingness to avail themselves of this opportunity, specially offered, to place evidence before the select committee, through their deputation now in South Africa, and further that it will be subject to the select committee being required to report to Parliament within such limited period as will enable Parliament to deal finally during the present session with the legislation proposed.

To this offer the following reply was received from the Government of India—

We are in receipt of your Excellency's telegram dated 5 February and would be grateful if you would be so good as to convey to your Excellency's Ministers our warm appreciation of the courtesy and consideration they have extended to us and to our deputation. While we cannot conceal from your Excellency our deep disappointment that your Excellency's Ministers have found it impossible to agree to either of the alternative methods put forward by us as best calculated to lead to a satisfactory solution of this problem, we recognise that our proposals have been given the fullest and most anxious consideration. We further understand that the offer now made to us involves a departure from normal parliamentary practice and procedure, and we see in this another proof of the desire of your Excellency's Ministers to find a solution of this difficult question. My Government are in the circumstances prepared to accept, subject to the conditions stipulated in your Excellency's telegram and to their observations in the succeeding paragraphs, the observations made by your Excellency's Ministers of an inquiry by a parliamentary select committee before the second reading of the Bill.

We note with satisfaction that the terms of reference to the committee will be sufficiently wide to include the considerations of the principles of the Bill, and we assume that it is the intention of your Excellency's Ministers also to allow the representatives of Indian opinion in South Africa an opportunity of presenting their case to the committee which we feel sure your Excellency's Ministers will agree could not fail materially to assist the committee in its task. As the Union Government are aware, our objections to the Bill are fundamental and are against the principles on which the Bill is based. We propose, therefore, to instruct our deputation to present case before the select committee in respect of general principles although it necessarily follows from our argument that we object also to the details of the Bill. We reckon that we realise that your Excellency's Ministers are anxious to avoid unnecessary delay, but we trust, in view of very grave consequences for the Indians which the proposed legislation must involve, fullest possible opportunity compatible with limitations laid down in your Excellency's telegram will be afforded for presentment of the Indian case. We are anxious that offer made by your Excellency's Ministers and our reply thereto should be published here with least possible delay and should be glad to know urgently by telegram when it is proposed to make these public in South Africa to enable us to arrange for publication here.

To this telegram we briefly replied as follows —

From His Excellency — My Ministers note with great pleasure and appreciation the readiness of the Government of India to avail themselves of the opportunity offered to them for the presentment of the Indian case through their deputation now in South Africa in accordance with the contents of my telegram of 4 February 1926. With reference to the observations in paragraphs 2 and 3 of your Excellency's agreement and for the further information of the Government of India, they desire to state that ample time will be given to the proposed select committee to hear and to consider evidence, and that the reference to the Bill to the select committee before the second reading implies that the Indian community in South Africa will, through their representatives, have the same opportunity and scope for presenting their case as will be accorded to the deputation from India.

With reference to the last paragraph of your telegram I am informed by my Ministers that they propose to lay on the Table of the House a copy of the correspondence between the Government of India and the Government of the Union with regard to the position of Indians to South Africa on Wednesday afternoon 17th inst. The Minister of the Interior will then make a statement in the House and move the reference of the Bill to a select committee before the second reading. My Ministers submit that it will be suitable if the publication referred to in your telegram could take place in India at the same time.

In accordance with the results of these negotiations I beg special leave of the House to give notice that Order of the Day No. 11 for Monday, 22 February 1926, second reading, Areas Reservation and Immigration and Registration (Further Provision) Bill will be discharged and that I shall move tomorrow that the subject matter of the Bill be referred to a select committee for inquiry and report, the committee to have power to take evidence and to call for papers, and that it be an instruction to the committee to bring up its report on or before Thursday, 1 April. In connection with this I beg leave to lay on the Table of the House now copies of correspondence that has taken place between the Government of India and the Government of the Union regarding this Bill.

DR. D. F. MALAN, 21 FEBRUARY 1927[1]

BEFORE PROCEEDING with further business, will you kindly allow me to make a statement on a matter of great importance to the country which I also owe to the House? In His Excellency the Governor-General's speech at the opening of Parliament it was announced that

---

[1] Speech by Dr. Malan, Minister of the Interior, 21 February 1927. *House of Assembly Debates.*

during the recess a conference had been held between representatives of the Governments of the Union and India on the position of Indians in the Union, and that a provisional agreement had been reached, which in due course would be laid before Parliament for their information and, if required, for their consideration. Shortly after the conference this agreement was submitted to and formally approved by the Union Government, and at the end of last week official intimation was received by us that it had now also been ratified by the Government of India. It was also agreed between the two Governments that the results of the conference would today be officially announced both here and in India in identical terms, and that immediately thereafter a more detailed and mutual summary of the conclusions of the conference should be laid upon the Table of this House and of the Legislative Assembly of India. I now proceed to read the communiqué approved by both Governments —

Communiqué approved by the Government of India and the Government of the Union of South Africa: It was announced in April 1926, that the Government of India and the Government of the Union of South Africa had agreed to hold a round-table conference to explore all possible methods of settling the Indian question in the Union in a manner which would safeguard the maintenance of Western standards of life in South Africa by just and legitimate means.

The conference assembled at Cape Town on 17 December, and its session finished on 11 January. There was in these meetings a full and frank exchange of views which has resulted in a truer appreciation of mutual difficulties and united understanding to co-operation in the solution of a common problem in a spirit of friendliness and goodwill. Both Governments reaffirmed their recognition of the right of South Africa to use all just and legitimate means for the maintenance of Western standards of life.

The Union Government recognise that Indians domiciled in the Union who are prepared to conform to Western standards of life should be enabled to do so. For those Indians in the Union who may desire to avail themselves of it, the Union Government will organise a scheme of assisted emigration to India or other countries where Western standards are not required. Union domicile will be lost after three years' continuous absence from the Union, in agreement with the proposed revision of the law relating to domicile, which will be of general application. Emigrants under the assisted emigration scheme who desire to return to the Union within the three years will only be allowed to do so on refund to the Union Government of the cost of the assistance received by them. The Government recognise their obligation to look after such emigrants on their arrival in India. The admission into the Union of the wives and minor children of Indians permanently domiciled in the Union will be regulated by paragraph 3 of resolution 21 of the Imperial Conference of 1918.

In the expectation that the difficulties with which the Union has been

252

confronted will be materially lessened by the agreement which has now happily been reached between the two Governments, and in order that the agreement may come into operation under the most favourable auspices, and have a fair trial, the Government of the Union of South Africa have decided not to proceed further with the Areas Reservation and Immigration and Registration (Further Provision) Bill. The two Governments have agreed to watch the working of the agreement now reached and to exchange views from time to time as to any changes that experience may suggest. The Government of the Union of South Africa have requested the Government of India to appoint an agent in the Union in order to secure continuous and effective co-operation between the two Governments.

Yes, that is the agreed statement. From the results as embodied in this communiqué just read, and in the more detailed summary to be laid upon the Table, it must be obvious that the conference fulfilled its difficult and responsible task in strict accordance with the spirit and character which this House and the country have been led to expect as the result of the preliminary negotiations, about which this House was fully informed last year. As hon. members will remember, it was then agreed that the conference to be held would not be such that the people of South Africa could justly look upon it as an interference from outside with domestic affairs, but that, on the contrary, both Governments will loyally co-operate with each other in the solution of the common problem. Throughout the conference there was a remarkable absence of the spirit of bargain. The decisions taken were arrived at solely and wholeheartedly, with a view to a comprehensive, effective and peaceful settlement. The results achieved cannot be therefore looked upon as reflecting a diplomatic victory in whole or any particular point for either side, but as the fruit of a common purpose, carried out in the spirit and by means of friendly collaboration.

It will also be obvious that the agreement which has been reached is more in the nature of an honourable and friendly understanding than of a rigid and binding treaty. By their decision not to proceed with the particular legislation which was contemplated last year, the Union Government have not in any respect or to any extent, surrendered their freedom to deal legislatively with the Indian problem whenever and in whatever way they may deem necessary and just. Nor, on the other hand, have the Government of India bound themselves, either permanently or for any limited period, to co-operate with us in any practical solution of our problem in the manner agreed upon. The position truly described is rather that both Governments have agreed upon a solution, which to some indeed may not seem ideal, but which is at least practicable and peaceful, and which holds out every hope of being effective, and that both have further agreed by means of mutual goodwill and co-operation to give this solution a fair and reasonable try.

The chief and most satisfactory method of dealing with the problem has obviously been found in an improved scheme of assisted emigration to be initiated by the Union Government with increased facilities and inducements and with proper safeguards against possible abuse. The most important feature of this scheme as well as of every other part of the agreement which has been arrived at, is that no stigma of racial inferiority is implied and that in fact such stigma has deliberately been removed where such may have been considered to exist in connection with the old so-called repatriation scheme. While South Africa's right to use all just legitimate means for the maintenance of Western standards of life remains untouched and absolute, and has, in fact, been reaffirmed, Indians who are willing and able to conform to these standards will be enabled to do so.

In so far as further restriction of immigration may be expected to result from the agreement, this will take place in strict accordance with the general provision which was formulated by the Imperial Conference in 1918 and is now in operation in connection with other Dominions and to which India herself was able to subscribe and in the carrying out of which she has found herself able honourably to assist. Further, if a three years' continuous absence from the Union would in future legally entail the loss of the right of domicile, it was agreed that such should be the case, not as a result of discrimination against Indians or any other race in particular, but as a result of an amended immigration law which will be of general application.

Under these circumstances there seems to be no reason why any section of the community should be otherwise than friendly disposed towards the working of a scheme which, if successful and effective, will go very far to ensure the peace and the happiness of the Indian community which will remain permanently settled in the Union and to establish lasting friendship and goodwill between the two great nations on either side of the Indian ocean.

In conclusion, I pay tribute to the members of Parliament, to the leaders of public opinion among the Indian as well as European community, and not the least to the Press and generally to the people of South Africa for the patriotic way in which they have assisted in the creation of that favourable atmosphere upon which the success of the conference was dependent and which was such a marked feature of its deliberations. Last year I ventured to make an earnest appeal for general self-restraint and co-operation, and the complete and whole-hearted response to that appeal has proved that it was not made in vain. Now that the results of the conference are known, the continuance of any curb on the public expression of views cannot be expected. But in a matter like this where sentiment can so easily be aroused and where any agitation of the public mind, either here or in India, can so easily wreck the best results of the conference, and the vital interests of South Africa, I know that with the fullest confidence we can once more rely on the good sense and the true patriotism, not only of this House, but also of all sections of the Press and the people of this country.

On behalf of the Government and the people of South Africa I also express our gratitude to the Government of India and to pay a tribute to the hon. leader and members of their delegation. The invitation from the Government of India, of which we availed ourselves during the recess, to send a representative deputation on a friendly visit to India, was prompted by feelings of genuine friendship, has afforded to the Government and members of Parliament a much valued opportunity of studying at first-hand conditions in India, and has been a potent factor in the creation of that atmosphere to which the success of the conference must be mainly attributed. The hospitality which the members of the deputation received from the Government and the people of India could not be surpassed. At the conference the hon. leader and members of the delegation displayed all that ability, sincerity and keen desire for a real and happy solution which inspired confidence and which belonged to the essence of statesmanship. I feel assured that both this House and the people will join in the fervent hope that the reward of their labours will be the inauguration of a new era of peace and friendship in the true interests of both, between our country and the country which they serve.

I lay on the Table a summary of the conclusions reached by the round-table conference on the Indian question in South Africa.

3

IMMIGRATION AND INDIAN RELIEF

DR. D. F. MALAN, 9 MAY 1927[1]

THIS LITTLE BILL was introduced by me for a double purpose. The first purpose is to amend certain existing laws. One is the Immigration Regulation Act of 1913, and the other the Indian Relief Act of 1914, which itself is an amendment of the Act of 1913; also the Asiatic Registration Act of the Transvaal and the Chinese Exclusion Act of the Cape Province. These laws have been in operation for quite a considerable time, and experience has shown that in certain respects they ought to be amended. There are certain defects — which are very evident. The other purpose for which I have introduced this Bill is to give effect to the agreement between the Union Government and the Government of India with regard to the position of Indians in the Union.

Most of these provisions in this little Bill are not new to the House. Some of them have been included in the Areas Reservation Bill, introduced by me last year, which was the subject of an inquiry by a select committee; and, as far as the agreement with the Government of India is concerned, that agreement has been exhaustively discussed in this House only recently. In any case, a summary of the conclusions of the conference embodying the agreement has been laid on the Table of the House, and hon. members are well acquainted with that summary. There is no general principle underlying the provisions of this Bill, and, therefore, the only thing I can do is to deal with the various provisions *seriatim*.

One provision has to do with the subject of deposits. It proposes to amend the Immigration Act of 1913. Deposits are required from immigrants to the country in cases of appeal. When they appeal they appeal to the Appeal Board, and the Government has security by deposits, against any loss. Further, it often happens that an immigrant appeals, but because it takes some time before the appeal is heard, he cannot be sent on by the vessel by which he arrived, and it is not always certain that he can be sent away soon if he loses his appeal. In the meantime he must be maintained by the Government, and in that case a deposit is required from the intending immigrant. Also, the shipping companies must give the Government security that while the ship is in port men will not be

---

[1] Speech by the Minister of the Interior, Dr. D. F. Malan, during the second reading of the Immigration and Indian Relief Bill, enacted as Act 37 of 1927. *House of Assembly Debates.*

left behind and come into the country illicitly, evading the immigration laws, but will be taken on board again and taken away by these vessels. The money deposited by these companies is forfeited in case these men should go ashore and not return. As the law stands at present, it is provided that the deposit shall be sufficient in the opinion of the Minister. This has always been interpreted that the immigration officer concerned can fix the deposit, but recently one of the courts — the Cape Provincial Division — held that the deposit must be fixed by the Minister in every particular case. Everybody will see that that makes the Act very difficult to work, because the Minister is not always in Cape Town. He may be in Pretoria, and not be acquainted with the circumstances. Therefore, we propose to amend this clause by making it competent for the immigration officer to fix the amount legally as he has done in practice in the past. The maximum remains at £100.

Another provision deals with appeals to the Appellate Division of the Supreme Court. It is rather strange that, under the existing law while there are in the Union three different appeal boards, no provision has been made for appeals to the Appellate Division. This has led to an impossible state of affairs. We find, for instance, that in one province a judgment has been given on a certain point which differs completely from a judgment given on the same point of law by the Provincial Division in another province. That has been the case on very important points. One point is whether the ward of an Indian could legally be introduced into the country. One division held that this was lawful; another division came to the conclusion that it was not lawful. That made it impossible for the department to administer the law in a uniform manner. In one province the order deeming all Asiatics to be prohibited immigrants was held to be illegal, while it was held to be legal by another division, and it was only casually that the matter was dealt with by the Appeal Court, whose decision saved the order. To prevent confusion arising in this manner, we propose that appeal shall be possible on a point of law from the provincial divisions to the Appellate Division.

Another provision of the Bill concerns deportations, and seeks to extend the grounds on which deportations may be effected. We add to the existing grounds incest, sodomy and aiding and abetting the introduction of immigrants in an illicit way as far as the law is concerned. It has come to the knowledge of the department that there are organisations for the introduction illicitly of immigrants into the country. We add to the penalty that people breaking the law in this way may themselves be deported.

There is another provision which makes it an offence to evade the immigration law and the immigration officers. At present if a prohibited immigrant only succeeds at the port or at any point of our extensive land borders in evading the immigration officer, then he is practically safe. Of course, he can be dealt with by the department when he is discovered, but discovery is very difficult, and it throws the onus on the department of discovering the prohibited immigrant and deporting him. We want a deterrent, and, therefore, we propose that evasion itself is an offence, and a prohibited immigrant, if he comes into the country, must report himself to an immigration officer within eight days.

A further provision concerns the entrance into South Africa of immigrants suffering from tuberculosis. At present, persons suffering from certain infectious diseases are regarded as prohibited immigrants. Persons suffering from tuberculosis are not *ipso facto* prohibited, and are allowed to enter with the permission of the Government. That permission is required, because every person suffering from tuberculosis is a potential source of danger, and the Department of Public Health protects the public against that danger by admitting such a person under certain conditions with respect to his movements and mode of life. To guard the Government against loss in such cases, it is usual to require from the tubercular immigrant a deposit in a bank, so that if he does not comply with the restrictions he may be sent back to the country whence he came at his own expense. Recently quite a number of cases have come to the notice of the department of persons coming to the country who have purposely given false information to shipping companies and to the Government on the forms they have to fill up on board ship, and in this way they have secured admission into the Union. As we did not know that they were suffering from tuberculosis, no deposit was required, and when they were sent back it was at the expense of the Government. As the Bill stands today the onus is thrown on the shipping companies, and if it is discovered according to this Bill anyone is suffering from tuberculosis and has given false information and has entered the Union without giving security to the Government, within six months he may be sent back at the expense of the shipping companies.

The shipping companies have objected against this provision and have sent a deputation to me to put forward their case. I have promised them that I am willing, in the committee stage, to move an amendment to the effect that if a person is introduced into the country suffering from tuberculosis, and it has not been brought to the notice of the port health authorities, then the shipping companies shall not be liable, if they can prove to the satisfaction of the port health officer of the Union that when the person entered the Union he was not suffering from tuberculosis, but that he contracted the disease after he entered the country. Another point is they shall not be liable, in the case of any particular passenger whom they suspect suffers from tuberculosis, and of which case notice is given beforehand to the port health officer, to the effect that they suspect that such a patient is suffering from tuberculosis, so that the port health authorities are enabled to examine themselves such a passenger and satisfy themselves as to the state of health of the passenger. The companies are fairly satisfied with this amendment which I am going to move in the committee stage, so that there is no reason, therefore, why it should not be accepted by the House.

SIR THOMAS SMARTT[2]: How can the captain of the ship know that a passenger is suffering from tuberculosis after the health officer passes him at the port?

DR. MALAN: There is a surgeon on board.

The other part of the Bill deals with the agreement between the Union Government and the Government of India. This agreement does not require much legislation. There is a good deal of the agreement which can be, and will be, carried out administratively. No legislation is necessary to secure, in connection with the assisted emigrating scheme, the co-operation of the Government of India. No legislation is necessary with regard to the Union of South Africa. The bonus under the agreement has been fixed by the Government for the future, administratively, and it is not a matter of law.

There are two points which must be dealt with legislatively. The first has to do with the further restrictions we place on the immigration of Indians into the country, and the other has to do with the conditions under which public money may be expended for the repatriation of Indians under the new assisted emigration scheme. As far as the further immigration of Indians is concerned, and the further restrictions against their entrance into the Union, I may explain that the position today under the Smuts-Gandhi agreement in the Indian Relief Act of 1914, is that Indians, who are themselves domiciles in the country, are at liberty to introduce into the country their wives and minor children under the age of 16 years, on condition that such Indians, when living in the country, shall only have one wife living in the country and shall not have children by any other living woman in the country. As I explained to the House on a former occasion, this opening left for the immigration of Indians is being abused to a large extent. We find Indians living in the country domiciled here only as individuals, but their home remains in India; then they introduce their minor children into the country, almost exclusively boys, simply for the reason of establishing a business domicile for these children, and as the law stands at present, these children, when they have once been here, even after they have become adults, as long as they live, they can always return under the existing law. Now that is a reason why there are being introduced into the country on an average 600 Indians per annum. On the one hand we spend a good deal of money every year to get Indians out of the country under our emigration scheme, and on the other hand Indians are, under the existing law, being continually introduced into the country to the extent of over 600 per annum.

MR. BLACKWELL[3]: Young men?

DR. MALAN: Yes, very few women, but mostly boys just under the age of 16. Now that was certainly not the intention of the legislation which was passed in 1914, and one of the results of the agreement to which we came recently with the Government of India is that as far as

2 South African Party.
3 South African Party.

259

we can judge, the further immigration of Indians will practically be stopped in future.

We have made two alterations. The first is that any Indian who has been absent from the Union — I am speaking of adult Indians — for three years successively will lose his domicile in the Union. We make that, as was explained before, of general application. Of course, as Europeans do not enter the Union as immigrants, because they are domiciled here or have a right of domicile in any particular Dominion (and enter the Union for the first time or repeatedly) simply because they can comply with the ordinary requirements of our immigration law, that will not in reality affect Europeans, but it will affect the Indians who, as a class, are deemed under the law of 1913 to be prohibited immigrants. After an absence of three years Indians will not be able to return to the Union unless they come to the Union as minor children of Indians who are domiciled in the country.

The other alteration is in connection with the introduction of minor children into the country. We have agreed that instead of the provisions of the Indian Relief Act of 1914 in regard to this point, we shall bring into operation the Imperial Conference resolution of 1918, which provides that the minor children of an Indian domiciled in any particular Dominion shall be allowed to enter that Dominion if they are accompanied by their mother, or if their mother is already domiciled in such Dominion. In other words, the principle which is laid down in that resolution is that minor children can be introduced into the Dominion only if not only the father is domiciled there as an individual, but the family as such. If this is brought into operation, according to the view of the delegation we had here from the Government of India and according to the view of our department, the number of minor children who will be introduced into the country will be reduced to a minimum. It will be very much reduced, so that practically in that way the further immigration of Indians from abroad will be stopped.

Further, the provision deals with the conditions under which public money may be expended in connection with the assisted emigration scheme. As I have explained on previous occasions, Indians who benefit under this scheme and who emigrate from South Africa to India or elsewhere with their families, will retain the right of re-entry into the Union on certain conditions if they return after the first year, but only during the second and before the end of the third year. If they remain away longer than three years they lose the right of re-entry. They cannot enter during the first year after their departure, so they must re-enter during the second or third year. As I have explained before, this is not a concession that we have made to the Government of India but it is a provision which is introduced with a view of making the emigration scheme more effective, but, of course, we must not forget that a large number of these Indians who wish to benefit under that scheme have been in this country for a considerable time. More than one-third of them have been born in this

260

country. Experience has taught us that the great objection on their part against going over to India is that on the day of their departure they must renounce the right of re-entering for ever into the Union. They know what they leave behind and they do not know what they will get on the other side, and in the uncertainty of their prospects they prefer to remain in South Africa. If this alteration is made it is expected that a very much larger number of Indians will avail themselves of the facilities for repatriation.

There are certain conditions attached to the expenditure of money on this assisted emigration scheme and in connection with those Indians who avail themselves of the facilities. In the first place, if an Indian avails himself of the repatriation scheme, if he has got a family in South Africa, that is to say a wife and/or minor children, he cannot go alone; he must take his family with him. Then if he returns within, say, the second or third year he cannot return alone or the members of the family cannot return individually even if some of them who left as minors became majors on the other side. If they return they must return as a group again. If they do return then all the money which was expended on them by the Union Government in connection with this assisted repatriation scheme, must be refunded by them on the other side, before they embark, and we will make provision on the other side for the receipt of the money by authorities there who will work in conjunction with the Union Government. No passport to any Indian will be issued by the Government of India for embarkation to South Africa unless all the money in such cases has been refunded.

I come to the amendments of the Asiatics Registration Act of the Transvaal. The amendments which the Bill proposes are of very minor importance. The one is to make it possible for Asiatics who leave the Transvaal to surrender their registration certificates. Very often an Indian wishes to leave the country for good, but no legal provision is made for him to surrender his certificate, and he may retain it, and we have found so far that it very often happens that he has sold it or made it over in some way to another Indian. The provision will now be made for the surrender in such cases in a legal manner of such certificates. Then there is a rather strange judgment — strange at least to the mind which has not got a legal bent — on the part of the Provincial Division of the Supreme Court of the Transvaal. That is, that even if it has been conclusively shown that an Indian had obtained his registration certificate fraudulently, it cannot be cancelled, and the fact that it cannot be cancelled gives him the right to live and remain in the Transvaal. Now that, of course, is something which ought not to continue; therefore, we make provision that in future if it is shown to the satisfaction of an appeal board or before a court that a registration certificate has been obtained fraudulently it can be cancelled, and such Indians deported from the country.

MR. CLOSE[4]: What decision was that?

4 South African Party.

DR MALAN: I cannot quote it, but I could tell later on.

Then there are certain hard cases of Indians in the Transvaal which we would like to meet. The Indian Registration Act of the Transvaal provides that an Indian can be registered, when between the ages of 8 and 16 years, by his parents. Now, after he has become 16 years, that is to say, a major according to the special law, he must register within one year, but if he does not do so within that year, he cannot be registered at all, and must be deported from the Transvaal.

MR. NEL[5]: Is that a good law?

DR. MALAN: Generally it is a good law, and we do not propose to alter that. All we propose is in cases of real hardship — where it appears to the Minister that it is really not the fault of that Indian — the Minister can issue a registration certificate of domicile. It is only to give discretion to the Minister in cases of real hardship, which ought to have been provided for.

MR. NEL: Where do these Indians come from that do not know the law?

DR. MALAN: Probably from Natal.

Then there is a small amendment to the Chinese Exclusion Act of the Cape Province, which, as hon. members know, was passed at the time Chinese labourers were introduced into the Transvaal. The Cape took alarm, and wanted to protect itself. That Act provides that every Chinaman — and there are only 2,000 altogether in the Union, and a great many fewer in the Cape Province — must be registered in the province. We do not propose to alter that, but the Act also provides that if a Chinaman should be convicted in a court of law for certain specified offences — amongst others, gambling — he must be deported from the country.

MR. JAGGER[6]: How about selling opium?

DR. MALAN: I think it is in the law — any offence. The Minister has no choice, and he must deport them. Only recently a case came before me which I thought a very hard one. And old Chinaman, I think 75 years of age, was convicted in a very trivial case — it was gambling. He had never been to China, or at any rate, the greater part of his life he lived in South Africa, and he had no relations oversea. The Minister had no choice whatever, but had to deport that man. The only alteration we now propose is to give the Minister the ordinary discretion he has in all other cases, and to give instructions, in such a case as I have mentioned, that the man shall not be deported. These cases will not occur very often, seeing that the number of Chinamen, especially in the Cape Province, is very small.

5 South African Party.
6 South African Party.

4

TRANSVAAL ASIATIC LAND TENURE

MR. J. H. HOFMEYR, 11 JUNE 1936[1]

THIS IS A select committee Bill. Some time ago I introduced a Bill which was referred to a select committee. That committee went into the matter very exhaustively. It took important and valuable evidence, and it gave much time and thought to the consideration of the details of the matter, and as a result it was able to bring out what is virtually a unanimous report embodying certain amendments of the original Bill.

It will have been noticed from the report of the select committee that while there were divisions in the select committee on three occasions, two of them touched on matters not in this Bill. Only in regard to one point actually in the Bill was there any division of opinion in the committee, so I am justified in saying that this Bill now submitted is to all intents and purposes a unanimous Bill from the committee. Having regard to the difficult nature of the problem, and to the divergent views represented on the select committee, I think that unanimity represents a very considerable achievement, and I should be failing in my duty if I did not express my thanks to members of the committee for the very conscientious and efficient way in which they tackled their difficult task. It is that fact and that unanimity which encourages me to hope that this House will be willing to deal with this Bill this session. I introduce it now because it is of considerable importance that it should be dealt with this session.

The House will remember that in 1932 legislation[2] was passed dealing with the problem of Asiatic land tenure in the Transvaal on a basis which envisaged a solution of the problem. At the same time, certain machinery was set up with a view to the solution of the problem. It was anticipated that the working of that machinery would take some little time, and therefore, as a transition measure, existing rights were protected until April 1935, when it was assumed that the new machinery would have functioned to the extent of making it possible to apply the solution envisaged by the legislation in 1932. Unfortunately, the machinery took rather longer to work, and it was necessary last year to extend that period of protection for another two years. That means that

[1] Speech by Mr. J. H. Hofmeyr, Minister of the Interior, 11 June 1936 on a Bill which was enacted as the Transvaal Asiatic Land Tenure Amendment Act No. 30 of 1936. *House of Assembly Debates.*
[2] Transvaal Asiatic Land Tenure Act No. 35 of 1932.

the transition period comes to an end early next year, and since it is very undesirable to leave this question continually in the air, I hope that we shall be able to pass this legislation this year, so that we shall be able to get the matter on a better footing when the transition measure legislation lapses by effluxion of time.

Before coming to the Bill itself, I should emphasise the point that this Bill deals primarily and mainly with the position of Asiatics and Coloured people on proclaimed land. The Bill, as referred to the select committee, dealt almost entirely with that aspect of the Asiatic land tenure question. It was only on that aspect that evidence was tendered, and the select committee in its report referred to that fact, and went on to say —

Your committee therefore did not feel itself able to come to any conclusion in regard to the Asiatic question in general in relation to other parts of the Transvaal. For the consideration of this question it would appear to be appropriate that a further inquiry by way of a select committee during next session or otherwise should take place.

Before dealing more specifically with the Bill, I think, with a view to the understanding of it, I should just, without going into undue detail, indicate something of the background. I think I can best do that by referring to four landmarks in this field of our legislation. First of all, there is the law of 1885, the old republican law, No. 3 of 1885, as re-enacted in its final form in 1887. The important clauses of that law were paragraphs (b) and (d) of Clause 2, where it was said that Asiatics firstly could not be owners of landed property in the republic save only in the streets, wards and locations which the Government shall, for sanitary purposes, point out for habitation, and secondly, that that Government shall have the power, for sanitary purposes, to fix streets, wards and locations for habitation. That, of course, applies to the Transvaal as a whole. No restriction was imposed on Asiatic occupation, but it was implied that Asiatic ownership should be possible in streets, wards and locations pointed out for habitation and nowhere else. Those were the underlying principles of the law of 1885.

The next landmark is provided by the gold law, which was a law of gradual growth, but which one may take as finally enacted in 1908. There we have a law dealing not with the Transvaal as a whole, but primarily with certain parts of the Witwatersrand. The underlying principle of the gold law in regard to this matter of Coloured occupation was a drastic restriction in respect of occupation as well as ownership on the gold-fields. The vital clauses of the gold law in this regard were Sections 130 and 131. Section 130 dealt with land held under mining title, and Section 131 with proclaimed land generally. That was the general scheme of things under the gold law. But that restriction of Asiatic occupation under the gold law was absolute neither in scope nor extent. Not all the Witwatersrand falls within the scope of the gold law, and not all classes of Coloured occupation were forbidden by these two sections as passed in 1908. From the very beginning, therefore, there has been a certain amount of quite legal Asiatic and Coloured occupation, and there has even been a certain amount of legal Asiatic and Coloured ownership, but because there was this legal occupation and because of the difficulty of interpreting in practical details the terms and the scope of the gold law restrictions, illegal occupation grew up alongside of legal occupation, and for lack of machinery no effective steps were taken to check it. And there was also alongside of the ownership of which I have spoken by individual Asiatics, another method of ownership, ownerships through Asiatic companies and through European trustees acting on behalf of Asiatic companies. That position has gradually developed on the Rand.

Then we come to the third landmark, the Act of 1919. That Act was passed with a view to liquidating the position created by this growth of illegal occupation alongside of legal occupation. It was based on the so-called Smuts-Gandhi agreement. Its primary purpose was to legalise occupation then existing of Asiatic traders on the basis of vested rights as referred to in the Smuts-Gandhi agreement. In effect that law gave the Asiatic traders then in occupation protection in respect of that occupation with the right to move anywhere within the same township. That was the purpose of the law of 1919. And that purpose was fulfilled. But I think it would be correct to say that alongside of that purpose there was also a further intention which was not fulfilled. The further intention was to say: thus far and no further. It was intended that that illegal occupation having been legalised, there should be no further illegal occupation, and the select committee indicated that it contemplated that by suggesting that a register should be framed of those who were in legal occupation. That recommendation was not carried out, and therefore the position remains that there was no effective check and that illegal occupation continued and was extended.

Then we come to the fourth landmark, the law of 1932, for which the Leader of the Opposition[3] was responsible, and which marked a considerable advance in dealing with this problem. That law, in the first place, extended the scope of the gold law restrictions, by bringing in certain areas which had previously not been subject to those restrictions, and secondly, it extended the scope of these restrictions in so far as it made them more complete, made them cover more classes of Asiatic and Coloured occupation. That was the first point in that Act. Secondly, sir, the law of 1932 set out to deal with the ownership of land by Asiatic companies, and European trustees to which I have referred, purporting to recognise vested rights, but for the rest seeking to put an end to that system.

Then I come to two more important points. In the first place the law of 1932 initiated a new way of dealing with those who have tacitly been allowed to enter into illegal occupation, and that new way

[3] Dr. D. F. Malan.

of dealing with them was embodied in Section 131 (*a*) of Act 35 of 1908, which empowered the Minister of the Interior, after consultation with the Minister of Mines, to exempt certain areas. Secondly, with a view to controlling illegal occupation, it was laid down that a certificate for a trading licence could only be issued to a person in legal occupation, and there was also inserted into the law of 1919 a clause which allowed a certificate, issued under Section 131 (*a*) of the gold law, to be evidence of legal occupation. The underlying principles of that legislation were first of all to set aside areas where Coloured and Asiatic people might live and trade with some measure of security, and secondly to make it possible to take effective steps to prevent illegal occupation outside the areas so set aside.

Those were the main trends of the legislation of 1932, and those trends were followed up by the appointment of the Feetham Commission with two main purposes, first to make recommendations as to the areas to be set apart, and secondly to compile a register of legal and illegal occupation. The commission has gone into its work completely and thoroughly, and has presented us with some very valuable reports. In the course of its investigation it found that certain points needed rectification in the legislation. It made recommendations and the Bill I introduced was first framed. It is that Bill which is now before the House in a revised form. In all its essentials this Bill purports to extend the advances initiated by the 1932 legislation, and at the same time its proposals are based on principles which go back to the original legislation.

5

ASIATIC LAND TENURE AND INDIAN REPRESENTATION

GENERAL J. C. SMUTS, 25 MARCH 1946[1]

IT IS UNNECESSARY for me to emphasise the importance of this Bill. That is appreciated on every side of this House, and all over the country. But it would be clearly undesirable to over-emphasise the importance of this Bill. There is a movement abroad to exploit the international implications of this Bill, to magnify its consequences from that point of view, and I am afraid that an attempt is being made to frighten and stampede the public of this country in regard of this measure. I am the last person to minimise the importance from an international point of view of this Bill, but essentially it is an internal measure. Essentially it is an attempt to provide social peace and the good ordering of our society here in South Africa, and we are not going to be frightened by any movement, any propaganda, which may be intended to frighten the people of this country.

The Bill has been represented as being an insult to India, as a challenge to Asia, almost as a challenge to world opinion. It is nothing of the kind. It deals with an internal question which affects the peace and the good order of our society in South Africa. It is essentially, whatever might be the implications in other directions, a domestic question for us to solve, and if we were not to tackle this question, which has drifted for many years, and it is allowed to drift further, we may drift on the rocks. We may then come to a stage where this question will become a first-class international issue, and the intention now is to prevent it from becoming such. We have examples in other countries of similar situations having been allowed to drift until only force and vast suffering could settle them. We had the case of the Germans in Sudetenland. We had the case of German communities in Hungary and Russia, who finally now have to be repatriated to their countries of origin at vast expense and at the cost of enormous suffering. We want to prevent that and to establish an order of things here in South Africa under which the various communities in our society can live peacefully and quietly together, and this can only be done in some such way as we are attempting to perform it by means

[1] Speech by General Smuts on the second reading of the Asiatic Land Tenure and Indian Representation Bill, 25 March 1946. *House of Assembly Debates.*

of this Bill. My point is that South Africa is responsible for its own society, for its own internal peace and good order, and no efforts from abroad, no efforts from anywhere to secure foreign interference, and to exercise pressure on our plans for solving this question will deter us or have any effect. This matter arises out of a great historical mistake that was made in South Africa many years ago.

We are now, at long last, attempting to limit the mischief of that mistake, and we in this House, in dealing with this very difficult and important question, must view it in that historical perspective. This is an old question, and we are the innocent victims today who have to deal with it today, and deal with it in the spirit of justice and fair play all round. The introduction of indentured Indian labour into Natal in 1860 to solve the labour troubles of the sugar planters there has had consequences which none foresaw. We are the later generations of innocent victims, both Indian and European, who have to deal with this question, and we shall both have to make our contribution. It will not be solved in a one-sided way. Both European and Indian will have to make their contribution in solving this question. This Bill is intended to formulate the contribution which each will have to make in dealing with the question.

I have spoken of the historical perspective of this Bill. I may remind the House of another aspect. Forty years and more after this mistake in Natal, a similar mistake was made in the Transvaal in the introduction of Chinese labour in order to solve the labour problems on the gold mines. If that attempt had succeeded the future of South Africa might have become hopelessly compromised. The situation may well have deteriorated beyond repair. The whole trend and orientation of South Africa might have been altered. Instead of being a European community looking to our Western culture, we might have established an Asiatic orientation and the whole future of South Africa might have taken a different course. I think it is not least the merit of the late General Botha — and I assisted him — that with his great efforts this attempt was nipped in the bud, and South Africa was saved from a situation even more menacing than the introduction of Indian labour into Natal 45 years earlier. I remember the good service of Colonel Creswell, on that occasion, but above all I remember the attitude of the British people themselves. The British people took up the cudgels on this question. Hon. members will remember that historic general election in England at the end of 1905, which gave quietus to this attempt to introduce Chinese labour into the Transvaal. The British people felt that it was a case where they had to interfere, and to interfere very positively, and the result was that this additional menace to our South African society never came to fruition. Mr. Speaker, today an appeal on humanitarian grounds is made to the British public, an appeal which goes very deep and very far, and I would ask my English friends in Natal, in this country and abroad, in Britain, to remember this historical perspective of the whole question, and I would ask them not to be stampeded on general humanitarian grounds, but to remember the real fundamental issues at stake, and once more to do what they did 40 years ago, and keep the position of our Western Civilisation safe here in South Africa. That is all we intend in this Bill — fair play and justice to our Indian fellow citizens, but we do not want to change the structure of South African society and to have conditions here which may in the end jeopardise the structure on which we have built. Neither European nor African culture would be assisted or fostered by such a development. We do stand here also for human rights. We are determined to discharge our humanitarian duties in a fair way to all sections of our community, and to the Indians also, but we maintain that we must preserve the European orientation of our society, and not switch over to the Asiatic. That is the fundamental issue in this Bill; that is what we intend in this Bill. If we fail, if we do not pass this Bill now, I am afraid the failure may well affect the future of South Africa. I make the most earnest appeal to hon. members to be helpful in putting this Bill through as soon as possible.

The Bill itself, although it is long, although it looks involved and complicated, is a simple one. It rests on a few simple principles and has a simple structure. It deals with the land question, in Natal mostly, and with the political status of the Indians in Natal and the Transvaal. In both these respects, both in the land clauses of this Bill and the political clauses, we are not breaking new ground. We are following a well-known South African principle, we are following practices and principles which have been approved here in Parliament, practically unanimously, and which we regard as essential to the structure of our complex society in South Africa. Fundamentally the principle of separate land tenure and residence, and of separate political representation for Indians are the same here in this Bill as in the case of the Natives, and the Native legislation which is already in force in this country. Although there may be variation in details, fundamentally the structure which we intend to establish here for the Indian community is very much the same and rests on the same principles as that which we have already laid down in connection with our Native population. I want hon. members to bear that in mind. In the difficulties which surround this question and all the complexities which have to be met and seem almost insoluble, we have finally gravitated towards the old solution which was found for the Native question, and which, I submit, can really be applied to our Indian population also. I do not see how they can consider that as an insult to them, rather is their objection an implied insult to the Native population in this country. No insult is intended, and no new principles are laid down. We are simply applying old well-tried principles to the case of the Indians.

The Bill consists of two chapters. The first chapter deals with the land question, the second with the question of political rights. I wish to make it quite clear that in the view of the Government these two provisions, the land clauses and the political clauses, are inseparable. The scheme is one whole and it would not be possible, and the Government could never agree, to one part being passed and the other being dropped.

We insist that this Bill shall be passed as a whole and if it is not passed as a whole, it falls away. No other course is possible. As I have said, both sections of our population, European and Indian, must make their contribution to the solution of this question. The Indians came here innocently. We are the innocent sufferers from mistakes made generations back. If there is to be a fair solution, both sides must do their best to help in the solution, and make some sacrifices in order to establish a fair basis for the future. It is the solution we have adopted in the case of Natives, and it is a solution which is proposed here. We took away land rights, we limited land rights, but we thought it absolutely necessary in that connection to give a political status to our Natives, and not to treat them as a disfranchised minority. In the same way here we are taking away rights, we are taking away rights from Indians in Natal, and just as we did in the case of the Native population, we should give them in all fairness a political status, a voice in the affairs of this country, a platform on which they can speak for themselves and protect their own interests. I say the two parts of this Bill are inseparable. It is almost a matter of course. I think it is necessary to emphasise it in this Bill. I know there is a strong feeling in favour of the land clauses of this Bill, but it cannot be allowed that these clauses of the Bill should be passed, that this part of the Bill should become law, without the other part also being put on the Statute Book.

Before I come to the clauses of this Bill, let me deal briefly with the old history of this matter. I have referred to the coming of the indentured Indians to Natal in 1860. It did not take a long time before doubts and misgivings began to arise in Natal. Whilst the sugar planters no doubt were satisfied with the labour they got, the rest of the civil population in Natal were getting more and more disturbed over the consequences and conditions. Problems grew up from the very early stages of this new departure from Crown policy. In 1885, at the same time as legislation against Indian land holding was passed in the Transvaal, a commission was appointed in Natal to go into these difficulties which had arisen. I mention this merely to show how early difficulties were felt, and the population of Natal were becoming restive because of the policy which had been adopted.

Shortly after Union, in 1911, partly owing to the insistence of the new Government of the Union, and partly owing to the action of the Indian Government themselves, the indentures were stopped, and since then we have had no indentured labour, but the difficulties and consequences of what had gone before were continuing to be felt and to increase. One commission after the other was appointed in order to probe into these questions and problems. Hon. members will remember the Lange Commission which sat here in 1921 and collected very valuable evidence on all these problems, and as a result of that commission the first Class Areas Bill was introduced into the Union Parliament during 1923. In 1924 the South African Party Government was defeated, and their successors, the

Nationalist-Labour Government, once more had to take more or less the same course and introduce another Bill very much like the Bill of 1923. At this stage, I may say, it was felt unanimously by every section of the European population that the position was becoming unendurable, and that some solution had to be found, and where one party had made the proposals, another party, apparently opposed to them on almost every ground of policy, had to adopt practically the same course.

At this stage, when the second Class Areas Bill was introduced by the new Government, the Government of India came forward with a proposal. They said they had a proposal to make for solving this question. They had proposals to submit, and they asked for a round-table conference in South Africa at which their proposals could be discussed. Well, we know what the proposal was. It was a proposal for the repatriation of Indians from Natal, and if that was accepted, it would be the best solution if it were possible even today, but it did appear the way out of the vast trouble in 1927. The Cape Town Conference was held and this proposal was thrashed out there and was accepted. It had good support, and the first year the repatriation of Indians with financial assistance from this Government was a success, and then reports came back from India from those who had returned to their motherland that their conditions there were far worse than here and that they were happier in South Africa, with the result that this effort at repatriation came to practically a dead stop, and nothing further could be done. Thereupon the Indian Government asked for another conference, the Conference of 1932, in order to explore other means of settling South African Indians outside South Africa. The attempt was made once more to thrash out this question, and investigations were made in America and in Asia in regard to settling South African Indians elsewhere and for their expatriation from South Africa, but nothing came of this effort, and the result is the question remained just where it was. The difficulties increased. A new commission was appointed, the Broome Commission, once more to go over the whole ground and see what could be done, and we know more or less the history of the Broome Commission. It made a number of reports, it made three reports. The first report was not unsatisfactory, but the second report, made in 1943, was of so alarming a character that Parliament thought fit at once to take action and, as hon. members will remember, the so-called Pegging Act was passed in 1943 to call a halt, to put a stop to what was going on in Natal. It appeared that on a very large and rapidly increasing scale properties were being bought up in the heart of Durban by Indians, and the fear that Durban might lose its character and become an Indian town became so intense that the Government and Parliament felt bound to take action, and the Pegging Act was passed.

We are today at the point where this Pegging Act itself is going to expire, at the end of this month, and if that Pegging Act were to expire, and the further purchase of property were allowed, you might have chaos on a larger scale than ever before in South Africa, and the position has therefore become one of great urgency, and there is a great necessity to pass legislation which will take the place of the Pegging Act and not only stop the difficulties with which that Act was intended to deal but to settle the Indian question on a more or less permanent basis for the future. In spite of the passage of the Pegging Act the Broome Commission went on with its inquiries, to see on what lines a permanent solution of the question could be obtained. The Pegging Act was looked upon as an interim measure, a temporary measure, to stop the evil which had grown up, but a permanent solution had still to be found, and that commission went on with its inquiries. It went on until quite recently, and the final result had been quite unsatisfactory. No solution has been found. We are therefore at this stage in a position where we have ourselves to evolve a solution of this question. The various inquiries that have been made, the various attempts at solving this problem, have all failed, and we have now to start *de novo* and find out what is the best solution, and the Government, after very careful inquiry, has prepared the Bill which lies before members of this House.

From the Broome Commission there emerged two recommendations I want to deal with; the one was that Indians should be enfranchised, that they should get political rights and that they should be on the common roll with the European population, but that the particular franchise given them should be a loaded one. That proposal was what was commonly called the common loaded franchise. The Indians would be part of the general electorate of the country, they would vote in the same constituencies, they would have the same members of Parliament, but they would have a loading of their franchise. It would be a higher franchise and very much higher qualifications would be demanded than in the case of the Europeans. That was their first proposal, with which I shall deal presently. Their second proposal was for holding a round-table conference once more, finally. These are practically the only two suggestions of any note which have emerged from the Broome Commission.

There is another historical matter to which I want to refer very briefly, and it is this. Whilst the Broome Commission was continuing with its inquiries and its attempts to find a solution, the suggestion was made to me, mostly from Indian representatives, that another way of reaching a rapid solution could be found. There was very grave objection on the Indian side to the continuance of the Pegging Act. We had to prolong it once or twice, and the feeling was very strong among Indians that every effort should be made to bring the Pegging Act to a termination as soon as possible; and a suggestion was made to me that a solution might be found on the lines of separate residential areas in Natal, a sorting out of the population, so there would not be this mixture in occupation and residence of the two sections of the population which had led to all this friction. It was represented to me at that time that along these lines of separate residential areas a solution might be found of the trouble in Natal and a solution that might guide our course for some considerable time. I thought it worth while exploring this solution, and in the Pretoria Agreement of 1944 an attempt was made to formulate this proposal in proper form and to submit it to the Provincial Council. The idea was that the Provincial Council in Natal should deal with this question as mostly an Indian question and should have power to establish different areas for the European and Indian communities, and that this higgledy-piggledy residence of people together in the same areas, which had led to all the friction, should be put a stop to. In these negotiations the Indians insisted on one point, and it was this: that whereas they were not averse to this separation of living quarters, they were averse to what they called compulsory segregation, that is that they should by law and by compulsion be forced to live in areas set aside entirely for non-Europeans. What they wanted was free areas, that free areas might be set aside where they and others, Europeans and others, might abide and live together. They did not want Indian locations. They did not want separate areas for themselves alone which they thought would be too much like racial segregation and to which they had the strongest objection. They did not object to separate areas being set aside provided these areas were free areas, uncontrolled areas, wherein Indians, along with others could reside. That was a point on which they were strong. Another point on which they had very strong feelings and insisted most strongly was that the purchase and ownership of land should not be interfered with, that it should not be restricted, and indeed should not be dealt with at all.

MR. J. G. STRIJDOM[2]: Was it that in addition to separate areas they should also have neutral areas?

GENERAL SMUTS: These are neutral areas. The neutral areas would be separate areas where Indians and others should abide and live. They were very strong on these areas, not merely Indian areas but free areas and that they should have the right to abide in these particular areas anywhere in Natal. The agreement was made that this matter should be put before the Provincial Council, and the Provincial Council when it came to deal with this scheme agreed in principle to the Indian proposal but insisted that it should apply also to ownership and purchase of land, that if there was to be a restriction in regard to residence there should also be a restriction of ownership. The Indians have insisted there should be no bar, no restriction on them owning land anywhere in Natal. But the Provincial Council would not accept that and introduced additional clauses which also applied a restriction on the ownership of land. In this way the Pretoria Agreement could not be carried out. There were other legal difficulties which resulted from the restricted jurisdiction of the Provincial Council in these matters, and the Pretoria Agreement fell through, and we had to start *de novo*. I mention this matter of free

2 National Party.

areas here because it seemed to me something very much like a part of our Native legislation. Hon. members will remember that our Native land legislation proceeded on these lines, that whereas there were scheduled areas set aside entirely for Natives, there were also what were called released areas, areas which were not so set aside, in which Europeans and Natives could continue to go and live together. The Indian idea seemed to me to approximate very much to the idea of released areas which we have already adopted for the Native population, and the solution we have found here makes use of this motion of free areas to be set aside. I will come to that just now.

I just want to impress on the House this fact, that all through these difficulties every attempt was being made by the Government to find a solution of these troubles. It must not be thought this Bill now before the House is a bolt from the blue, that this measure has not been thought over and inquired into from every aspect. All through these years, and even in the war years, when we were pressed with very grave and difficult questions, the Government kept in touch with the Indian population and kept in touch with the European population there. Conference after conference was called. There was not a section of the community which was not consulted and every effort was made to explore the position and find a solution, and it is only as a result of all these efforts that were made during those years of trouble that we come now to this solution which we have before us.

I want to deal very briefly with these three questions to which I have referred, the two questions recommended by the Broome Commission — the loaded common franchise and the round-table conference — and this question of Indian ownership and free areas, because they are all three important for this Bill.

Let me begin with the round-table suggestion as a way out. The suggestion there is that we should once more, as in the case of the Cape Town Agreement, call in representatives from the Indian Government for a round-table conference and explore the solution. To me that does not seem a feasible way out for many reasons. For one thing it is too late now. We are at a point where the Pegging Act expires this month. There is no time any more for lengthy explorations through a round-table procedure. Nor does it seem to me that such a round-table conference will come to any solution. It is not like the case of 1927 where the Indian Government came forward with a definite proposal of repatriation or finding some other place where South African Indians would go to. There is no definite suggestion at all there. It is solely a suggestion for a round-table conference where we shall try to find a solution. To my mind the likelihood of such a conference being a success is most remote, and we shall only spend a great deal of time over this question and in the end reach no solution, and after such a failure of the round-table conference the position will be worse than it is today. Another difficulty about the round-table conference at this stage is that any solution come to which

274

the European population do not like will be looked upon as coming from Indian inspiration. The difficulties against any such solution would be increased, the opposition would become greater, and looking at this matter as one which is urgent and calls for a practical solution, it seems to me the holding of a round-table conference between the South African and the Indian Governments is a council of despair. It must lead to failure. It will only involve loss of time, and in the end the position will be worse than today.

But there is stronger ground. There is the ground of principle; and it is this. This is essentially a domestic question for South Africa. It is a question of our own internal affairs. These Indians, the vast bulk of them, more than 80 per cent of them, are South African citizens. They insist on it, they are South Africans. And how can we, under such circumstances where the people concerned, Europeans and Indians alike, are South Africans, where the whole situation is domestic, a South African internal situation, how can we call a conference with another government to help us in finding a solution? It seems to me we would be departing from a clear ground of principle which is the only one we can stand on. Once we depart from that sure ground of principle, where we do not assert our own authority in our own home on matters of a domestic character it seems to me we are lost. You do not know what is going to happen. Our Indian citizens will have to make up their minds whether they are South Africans or whether they are Indians, whether they are citizens of South Africa or whether they are citizens of India, in calling in the intervention of another government to assist them. But as things are today, with Europeans and Indians both citizens of this country, trying to find some way of living together in this country, it seems to me it would be a clear departure from fixed principles on sure foundations if we were to invoke the assistance of another government to help us. The Indians have pointed to the Cape Town conference, and the Cape Town Agreement, as a precedent against the attitude I have taken up. My reply to that has been this, that in the first place the Indian Government came to the Cape Town conference with a proposal they had to make. They had a solution they wanted to discuss. And no one would debar a proposal of that kind. If we have any difficulty and some other friendly government wants to make a suggestion along which they think the difficulty can be removed we are only too willing to listen to them.

In the case of the Cape Town conference the Indian Government had some definite proposal to make which they wanted to discuss, a proposal which was accepted and which worked for some time. There was another difference in the case of the Cape Town conference. In those days India was not represented here. The Indian Government was entirely unrepresented here. There was no Indian Agent, there was no High Commissioner. There was nothing. And there was really no way for the Indian Government to talk to us and consult with us except perhaps through the intermediation of the British Government. Today the position is entirely different. India, since the Cape Town Agreement, has had an Agent-General here, and it is represented today by a High Commissioner. If the Indian Government wishes to say anything to us it has its right, as is the right of any other government, and it can do so through its diplomatic representatives here, and a round-table conference is entirely uncalled for under those circumstances. The Indian Government can put before us through its diplomatic representative whatever proposals it likes in regard to this question or any question, and so long as our domestic jurisdiction is not violated we are prepared to listen to such proposals. Today they can do it, and a round-table conference is quite uncalled for.

The other matter I wish to refer to is the question of the loaded franchise. We cannot find a solution by way of the round-table conference. Can we find a solution by way of the common loaded franchise which the Indian Government favours, which the Broome Commission has recommended and which the Indians very strongly insist on? The Indian people in South Africa do not want to be treated as a separate entity. They want as South African citizens to be treated on the same basis and in the same way as the rest of our people. They want the same political system, the same constituencies. In view of the Indian numbers in Natal, they are prepared to have a loaded franchise, that is, to have a higher franchise qualification fixed for them than for Europeans, but they do not want a separate system. That proposal has been most definitely rejected by the people of Natal. They will not look at it, and along those lines a solution is not possible. Even if it were feasible, even if it were desirable, it is not possible, the people there will not have it. But there are other objections to it. The people of Natal say: Look at our numbers, even if we have a loaded franchise what is our future? Look at the population figures; how can we endure the menace of the future and of what may happen when we know the franchise may be changed from time to time? There may be a loaded franchise now, but will that remain for ever? And they will not look at the question of a common franchise with the Europeans.

MR. A. BARLOW[3]: Will the communal franchise remain for ever?

GENERAL SMUTS: I am just putting the practical objections there were against the Indian proposal of the loaded franchise, and I said as far as Natal is concerned it is no solution at all, because the European people there simply will not accept it, and to my mind it is a matter of principle.

I think we have decided, I think South Africa has decided once and for all, that our complex society will be dealt with on separate lines. We have done it in the case of the Natives, and we are going to do it in the case of the Indians. Any other system, I think, will lead to endless friction. You will never get it through Parliament in this country, you are simply attempting an impossible solution. It will not be accepted by the people of South Africa, apart even from the people of Natal. That is the system which has been accepted with regard to the Natives, and if

3 United Party.

we have to live in peace here together in South Africa it will have to be the accepted policy in the case of the Indians. No, the loaded franchise will not do. But there is another argument in this case which in my opinion is very strong. The Indians say this separate political system for them is an insult, and they will not accept it. But it is the Indian system. It is the law in India. India is working today under a constitution framed for India which recognises separate communities. There is a separate system working in India. The whole social system is one of segregation in India. I am not arguing whether it may or may not be a mistake, but I am quite entitled to argue from the actual situation in India today. The Indian Parliament has not a common franchise, but a community franchise. The electorate is divided into communities. The numbers of members are apportioned separately, and the electorates vote like that, and I think it does not lie in the mouth of Indians to say a separate system, a communal system in South Africa, will be an insult to them. It is not an insult to India. It is not an insult to our Natives here that we have such a system. Why should it be an insult to them? To my mind I think that largely disposes of the objection they have made against this proposal. We cannot look for a solution to a common loaded franchise. It is not practical politics in this country, and it is not necessary either. It is unwise. It does not fit in with our South African scheme of things. So both those recommendations of the Broome Commission, also supported by the Indians and the Indian Government, have to drop, and we have to proceed on lines of our own.

Let me say a few words on this question of property. The Indians have insisted, and still insist most strongly, there should be no restriction on their right of buying and acquiring and getting an ownership of land anywhere in Natal. They are prepared to compromise on the question of residence. They are prepared to have separate residential areas to which they will be restricted, but they will not accept a restriction in regard to ownership. I thought at first a solution on those lines might be explored. That is what underlay the Pretoria Agreement, that we should leave the question of ownership as too difficult, that we should leave it alone for the moment and simply deal with this question of living together in mixed areas, which had led to very much friction and which would lead to more friction. But the Provincial Council in Natal said they would have nothing of such a solution, that if there were to be separate residential areas, if there were to be a restriction on residence in Natal, there should be a restriction of ownership, and that Indians should not be allowed to buy land wherever they liked. And I must say there is a good deal to be said for the European point of view in Natal. Looking to this question as a long-range problem, and seeing what the effects would be if Indian ownership were unlimited, and Indians were unrestricted in buying land, but were only restricted in residence, I can see that in the long run it must break down. If a person may own land there, but cannot live there, it is essentially an untenable position, a position which in the long run will not be justified and will break down. And knowing the methods that are in vogue in South Africa for circumventing laws, it seems to me that it would be quite easy to circumvent a law like that. Take the ordinary case. Our law provides and will continue to provide that a European resident can have his servants with him. We have that now, and cannot prevent it. One can conceive of a case where an Indian buys land, and is the owner of the land, but cannot live there himself; only a White lessee can live there. The Indian gets a dummy White. We know the system. It is well known in the Transvaal. He gets a dummy White who brings his servants there, Indians, and in the end the provision against residence falls away unless the question of ownership is also dealt with.

It became clear to me, after giving the subject all possible consideration, that we want something that will work, something that is not a mere expedient, and if we want that we shall have to be pretty thorough in dealing with this question, and we shall have to deal not only with the residents, but also with ownership, with the result that in this Bill we deal with both. We restrict residence and we restrict ownership, and they are both restricted to these free areas. In Natal, outside of these free areas, it is not free to an Indian in future either to get occupation or residence, or to buy land. That is restricted to these, what in the Native Acts are called released areas. It is restricted to these free areas where he or anyone else can buy land and reside. That is the provision made in this Bill. We have not got reserves as we have in the case of the Natives, but we have the free areas provided for in the Native legislation, areas in which Indians and others can live. The rest is barred to the Indians, and is left for the European population only. Let me just add that the system which I have sketched applies to the future. We do not touch the *status quo*. That would be an impossibility and lead to problems which are quite insoluble, and only time can solve it. But we are calling a halt to this evil of mixed residence and ownership. We stopped that system and say that for the future Indians shall not buy land and shall not reside or acquire leases except in these free, uncontrolled or released areas.

Mr. J. G. Strijdom: What about your exemption clauses?

General Smuts: These are the exempted areas. Now let me deal with this question. In regard to the *status quo*, we leave that alone. We do not touch vested rights. With regard to the future, this setting aside of exempted areas takes place. I will return to this point in a moment, but let me just say that part of the work in connection with these free areas has already been done, and in the schedule of this Bill hon. members will find, both in Durban and round about Durban, these free areas laid down in the schedule. The schedule also includes a free area in Pietermaritzburg where a measure of agreement has been obtained, and in regard to Glencoe and Port Shepstone, where there has been complete agreement, and there is no opposition. In regard to Durban we rely on the evidence which has been gathered by the Broome Commission — they went fairly fully into these matters — and the evidence which was gathered by the Post-war Works Commission under Mr. Mitchell, who is now the Administrator. That Commission has gone pretty fully into the areas surrounding Durban, and the Bill follows the result of their work, that of the Broome Commission and that of the Post-war Works Commission. The schedule follows these recommendations, which are incorporated in the Bill. We have, therefore, four separate areas in Natal included in this schedule, the area in and around Durban, the area in Pietermaritzburg, and the other areas at Glencoe and Port Shepstone. But of course the Bill applies to the whole of Natal. The restrictions must apply right throughout Natal, not only to the urban areas but also to the rural areas, and it will be necessary to go through the work which has not yet been done by either of these Commissions, and that work will have to be done, and for that purpose a board is constituted in this Bill, a mixed board consisting of two Europeans, two Indians and a European chairman, which will continue with this work and settle further areas which have to be demarcated as free or exempted areas in Natal. In this respect the Bill differs from the structure of the Native Acts. When we dealt with the Native legislation we have a complete picture before us. All the areas had been gone into by the Beaumont Commission and could be included in the Bill. But in the case of the present Bill, by reason of the urgency of our legislation we could not wait for all this research and demarcation to be completed. We put into the Bill the work which has already been done in regard to Durban and the other places mentioned, but the rest of Natal still has to be surveyed by the board.

DR. D. F. MALAN: Has the board full powers?

GENERAL SMUTS: The board has full powers to make recommendations to the Government. Just as the Broome Commission this board will investigate on the spot questions as to the reservation of areas and limits, and the inclusion of what into the areas. They will make recommendations to the Government and the Government will act thereon.

Mr. Speaker, it seems to me that we are thus, in effect, getting as close to the recommendations of the Native Acts as we possibly can. If we had had time to complete all the investigations and to demarcate all these areas, and to have put them into the schedule to the Bill, we would have done so, but we did not have time, nor have we time now, and therefore, because of the urgency of the occasion we have stereotyped what has been done, and we leave it to this board to complete the investigation in future.

There is one other matter which this board will have to deal with. It will be necessary to consider particular cases where transfer of property or transfer of residence may be permitted outside of these released areas, and that work will continue to be done by this board. Hitherto this work has been done merely by the Minister of the Interior. Under the Pegging Act it was similarly the *fiat* of the Minister of the Interior which was final in questions of transfer or residence or ownership. The Minister of the Interior had a free hand in Natal. Under this Bill, the Minister simply becomes the final authority to decide, but he is advised by this board in regard to any changes which may be made outside of the scheduled areas. That will have to be done. The position, then, is this, that in Natal in future there will be under this Bill, when it becomes law, in regard to the future determination of areas, a separation of areas. Natal will be left to White residents and White ownership. Certain areas will be marked out as free or exempted areas, where Indians may buy and live in future; and not Indians alone, but also Whites and Natives They are free areas, free to all. You will therefore have these free or released areas, just as you have them today under the Native legislation. But the rest of the country cannot be penetrated. We shall therefore prevent this penetration which has been going on, and which has instilled this fear in Natal, and created the crisis with which we had to deal in the Pegging Act. In this way we think that we will get nearer to a reasonable solution of this land question. The Indians will have a fair scope still. In the scheduled areas set aside for open occupation and purchase they will have a good chance of prospering.

DR. MALAN: Will the urban areas be included in the free areas?

GENERAL SMUTS: Urban and rural areas are treated alike. Everywhere in future there will be separate free areas where Indians, Natives, or Europeans can buy and live together.

MR. J. J. SERFONTEIN[4]: There are no separate areas for Indians?

GENERAL SMUTS: No, we did not adopt the principle of having separate areas where only Indians can live, because they have the most violent objection to that form of segregation. We mark out in Natal certain areas where Indians can buy and live in future, but not they alone. They object to living alone. I think this system is quite workable and it is accepted in Natal as the solution of this problem of penetration which has inspired them with so much fear. I am sure that it will leave a good scope to the Indian population to expand and to develop and that justice will be done to them substantially whilst this fear of penetration which has obsessed Natal will be removed, and that we will have our Indians living peacefully in Natal in separate areas.

Mr. Speaker, I have finished with the land clauses of the Bill so far as they concern the Province of Natal. I only want to add one word to what I said, and it is this. It is an appeal to Natal members to accept the schedule. Naturally in a matter like the schedule which deals with the free areas set aside where Indians together with others may reside and purchase, many small details may be included which may lead to differences of opinion and to opposition. We had the same situation when we dealt with the schedules to the Native Bills in 1936. There is an infinity of matter on which people may differ and interests may clash.

4 National Party.

I would appeal to hon. members from Natal to accept those schedules. They are framed on close investigation by the Broome Commission, by what I call the Mitchell Commission, and on all relative evidence, and I do not think we can improve on them. I do not think we can get anything better. Two of those areas are approved by both Indians and Europeans. The other two may not be in the same category, but we have acted on the best available evidence, and if the Bill is to get through we must accept those schedules as I hope they will be accepted.

Now I come to the political rights and status which it is proposed to confer on Indians under this Bill. The main question I have argued, and the Government has settled, that is there shall be for Indians a separate franchise, a separate electoral roll and separate constituencies. This separate system follows the Native model. All therefore that remains is to demarcate the necessary constituencies, the electoral areas under the Bill. The Government has decided that three constituencies should be given to the Indian community in Natal and in the Transvaal, and that the electors in these two provinces shall be considered together and shall be divided into three equal constituencies. The Indians in the two provinces are lumped together. In the Transvaal the Indians form too small a community to be an electorate by themselves. As members know, the Indian population of Natal is approximately 220,000 or 230,000 and in the Transvaal it is only something like 25,000, and they will therefore see the disparity is very great, and when we come, not to population but to people entitled to vote, to electors, the numbers will be very much smaller still, and the Transvaal will not have by any means sufficient voters to form a constituency. They have to be lumped with Natal and the Indians in the two provinces will be equally divided into three constituencies under this Bill. These will return the representatives of the Indians in the House of Assembly.

In the Senate a different scheme is arranged, and there it is again proposed to follow the model of the South Africa Act. The three constituencies for the Assembly will be lumped together as one constituency and will return one Senator. The second Senator will be nominated by the Government on the lines of the South Africa Act, for his knowledge and experience of Indian matters.

MR. E. R. STRAUSS[5]: Will these representatives be Europeans?

GENERAL SMUTS: I am coming to that. That will be the representation in the House of Assembly and in the Senate, three elected members in this House, one elected member for the Senate and one nominated Senator.

Now we come to the Provincial Council. The Transvaal being too small for an electorate it drops out and cannot get a member of the Provincial Council. If we did give one the number of electors will be so small compared with a European constituency in the Transvaal that it would be a ridiculous matter, the difference would be too glaring, and would be sufficient for very serious criticism. A Transvaal urban constituency con-

[5] National Party.

sists of something like 9,000 to 10,000 voters and the Indians in the Transvaal scarcely number a couple of thousand, so the difference would be so great that a separate constituency for the Indians cannot be justified, and we are left with Natal, where it is proposed to give two elected representatives in the Provincial Council for Natal. Two constituencies will be arranged in that way. These members so elected, members of this House and of the other House to be so elected or appointed, will follow the scheme of the South Africa Act. In the South Africa Act a colour bar is drawn for Parliament and only Europeans, as members know, can be members either of this House or of the Senate. That is the scheme in the South Africa Act, and if that is followed, we are not making any change there.

We follow the South Africa Act once more with regard to the Provincial Council in Natal. There is no colour bar as regards representatives in the Provincial Council, and if we had to restrict the Indian representation in the Province of Natal to Europeans we would have to change the South Africa Act and introduce a new colour bar, which we are not doing. We are leaving the situation exactly as it is in the South Africa Act.

Mr. J. G. Strijdom: How can you say it?

General Smuts: Yes, I am simply stating the case as it exists under the South Africa Act and as it is law today. We apply the same system that is inaugurated there: Europeans for Parliament, no colour bar drawn for the provinces, and as a matter of fact we know a provincial councillor in the Cape . . .

Mr. J. G. Strijdom: What about Natal?

General Smuts: There is nothing at all to prevent them. Dr. Abdurahman was a member of the Provincial Council.

Mr. Bowen[6]: So was Mr. Reagon.

Mr. J. G. Strijdom: Does the Prime Minister mean to say that up to now, quite apart from this present Bill, a Native could have been a member of the Natal Provincial Council?

General Smuts: Yes, if he was a voter he could be a member. Now, that is the position in the South Africa Act, the position as it existed hitherto, and as we follow it here. The position of these Indian representatives in Parliament will be exactly the same as that of the Native representatives, i.e. they have the same rights and privileges subject to certain reservations. For example, an Indian Member of Parliament will not be able to vote for a Senator. The Indian Provincial Councillors in Natal will not be able to vote for a Senator. These are the reservations made in the South Africa Act and there is no change. The scheme remains the same. The position therefore is quite simple. In regard to the electoral arrangements, we constitute these new constituencies both for the Senate and the Assembly, and also for the Provincial Council in Natal, and we follow the scheme as laid down in the South Africa Act. It is quite a simple and straightforward position once the decision is taken, to give political representation, and about that there should be no question

6 United Party.

at all. We ought to do something. The European population, in view of the presence of the Indians in Natal, should make concessions. Both sections should make their contribution, and I think it is just and fair that this step should be taken, otherwise we will simply be taking away rights, and giving nothing in return, and leaving the Indian community as an unrepresented section of our community. I do not think that that will be justified. I think the time is overdue for making this change. Probably the change should have been made at the time the Native Bills were passed, but it was ripe to do it, and now that we are dealing with the Indian question on a broad and comprehensive basis, I think that step should be taken.

I now pass on to the clauses, the provisions of this Bill affecting the Transvaal especially. They are somewhat intricate and technical, and I think that they should be dealt with in committee, and not in the second reading. They enter into a number of questions. There is, for example, the position of Indians under the gold law on the gold areas in the Transvaal. That has been a very difficult and intricate matter. Changes were made in the gold law from time to time. Finally, some years ago, the Feetham Commission was appointed to straighten out the tangles that arose. Some of these tangles have been removed, but some still remain, and we are left with the balance of the Feetham Commission's difficulties. Beyond that we have a number of what may be called evasions. The laws dealing with land tenure in the Transvaal have been continually evaded, and we have had the Murray Commission — and I believe other commissions too, but more specifically the Murray Commission — which went into these cases, and made certain recommendations, and the clauses in the Bill in so far as they affect the Transvaal, are intended to carry out the recommendations of the Murray Commission. These clauses deal with forms of evasion such as White dummies who are used to evade the law. We have to deal with companies. A combination of companies was formed in order to deal with this land question, and to evade the law. This was very cleverly and successfully done. The Murray Commission has dealt with these cases, and made certain recommendations which are embodied in the Bill. There is the question of the controlling interest. That is dealt with here, and similar things that have arisen through attempts to evade the law. These attempts will in future be defeated and the original intention of our legislation carried out if these clauses are accepted. The original Act applying to the Transvaal, as hon. members know, was Act 3 of 1885, which forbade Indians from holding, occupying or owning land in the Transvaal, except in areas pointed out by the Government. Now, that is a matter which also requires elucidation, and in some respects amplification to straighten out the difficulties, and this Bill deals with that also. I hope we will deal with it successfully. I do not think that I need go into particulars because no doubt these matters will be dealt with more effectively in the committee stage.

I just want to say one word about purchases of land by Indians in the Cape Province. Complaints have been made to the Government recently from various quarters that the door having been closed to indiscriminate purchasers in the Transvaal and in Natal, there are very clear indications of attempts being made in the Cape to penetrate here and buy land. I just want to utter a warning note to our Indian friends in the Cape to be careful about this. The Indians precipitated the crisis which led to the Pegging Act. But for the large-scale penetration into Durban during the war, our troubles might have been much lighter, and milder. But these purchases, these acts of penetration, led to the Pegging Act which in turn has led to this Act. So one thing leads to another, and at every stage our burdens increase. I would just warn my Indian friends not to provoke undue irritation of the position at the Cape.

MR. J. G. STRIJDOM: That is a pious hope.

GENERAL SMUTS: No, it is a warning. These are not pious hopes. We have warned before and you have seen what the results have been when the warnings were not heeded.

MR BARLOW: Why not stop Europeans from selling to Indians?

GENERAL SMUTS: How can we? I do not think we will overload this Bill with the problems of the Cape. The problems in the Cape are not too serious, and on the whole the position here is satisfactory. Let sleeping dogs lie. Our Indian community here have been unprovocative to a degree. In the Cape the Indians have really set an example to the Indians in the rest of the Union. That being so, I think we would be making a great mistake if we attempted to overload this Bill with a fresh problem.

MR. E. H. LOUW[7]: The Indians from Natal will buy ground in the Cape.

GENERAL SMUTS: That is exactly what I am warning against. If they do, fires will be lighted here also. There will be the same fear here, and some future Government may find itself in the same undesirable position in which I am today. I am just uttering these warnings here, and I hope they will be heeded.

Mr. Speaker, I have stated that the Bill is urgent, and the urgency is due to the expiry, almost immediately, of the Pegging Act. I would appeal to hon. members to speed up the passage of this Bill. The Government hopes that it will be unnecessary to send this Bill to a select committee. We can thrash out such difficulties as we have about it here in the House. If this Bill goes to a select committee it will take time, and it may not even pass. It certainly will not pass within the time at our disposal, and I therefore would appeal to hon. members to assist the Government in a very difficult problem which concerns South Africa very vitally and to put this Bill on the Statute Book, and thereafter let us see how best to deal with the problems which will arise. I think it affords an opportunity for making a new start. From the point of view of some it may appear to be harsh. From the point of view of many others we may appear to be giving more political rights to Indians that we should. I say that on the whole it lays down a broad basis on which better relations can be built up in future,

7 National Party.

and I make my appeal to all sides of the House to be helpful, and place this Bill on the Statute Book, and thereafter build on it as a basis for the future.

So much for this Bill. In spite of present Indian opposition to this Bill I have no doubt that the time will come, and it may come pretty soon, when Indians in Natal will recognise the solid advantages to be derived from this measure. Ever since the 'eighties of the last century the position of Indians in Natal has been surrounded with misunderstanding, friction, and antagonism, until it has become almost intolerable. Whatever rights the Indians in Natal enjoyed, were enjoyed under protest, and they have never had any sense of security. The time has come to let the Indian know exactly where he stands. This Bill seeks to establish a sound foundation on which the future may be securely built. There need be no friction between the various sections of the community in future.

But the passing of this Bill does not mean that all mistakes will be obliterated, and that all the needs of the Indian community will be met. The Government must see to it that the Indian gets a square deal in every direction, even beyond the field covered by this Bill. His crying needs today are housing, health, employment and education. It must be left to Government policy to see that these needs are met as far as possible. After the Cape Town Agreement of 1927 the office of the Commissioner for Immigration and Asiatic Affairs was established. In connection with the uplift clauses held before the Indian community the idea was adopted that his office would act as a liaison between the Indians and the several Government Departments. Unfortunately that never came to fruition. The post of Commissioner of Asiatic Affairs was created, but no machinery was ever brought into operation whereby the Indians could get a square deal in all respects. It is the intention of the Government now to secure that this office is properly organised in order that the needs of the Indians may be carefully watched and duly attended to by the authorities concerned, central, provincial or local. There is much that must in fairness be done, and it is incumbent on the Government to see that the several authorities charged with their respective functions do what is necessary for the welfare of the Indian people throughout the country. If the provincial and local authorities do not measure up to their responsibilities, it may be necessary for the central government to consider legislation or to take any other action. This is a matter for the future, after it has been seen how all concerned react. The Government has particularly in mind the establishment of an advisory committee, not the board envisaged in this Bill, but the committee consisting of interested voluntary workers on which Indians and Europeans will be represented and which will advise the Government on all matters pertaining to the welfare of the Indians, through the Commissioner for Indian Affairs. Such a committee would inquire into the avenues of employment, etc., and co-operate with the central, local and provincial government in matters affecting housing, social welfare and other amenities. Education, health and social services would

285

be amongst the major issues, and generally it would advise the Government on any matter dealing with Indians. In this regard it is not the intention to deprive the Indians of any rights or privileges enjoyed by them today. They will still have the right of access to any Department or Minister as at present, but it cannot be seen in what other way the interests of the Indians can best be served.

It is very necessary for the Government to know at all times what the actual position is. There must be someone whose job it is to see that the policy of the Government is carried out. It is principally for this reason that it has been decided to have this body falling under the Minister of the Interior. For all these years the real issues have been obscured by this one major issue of the relations between the Indian and the rest of the population of the Union, bound up with the question of land tenure in Natal and the Transvaal, so much so that the real practical needs of the Indians were neglected. The time has arrived to liquidate this big outstanding account and to settle once and for all this question of where Indians can live permanently and not be the playball of various interests and politics, but where their foundations for future happiness may be laid. The Indians must have adequate and fair opportunities, especially in regard to these four main requirements of housing, health, employment and education.

DR. D. F. MALAN, 25 MARCH 1946[1]

THE PRIME MINISTER in his speech this morning began by pointing out that this Bill he is introducing is of the very greatest importance. I do not think there is anyone who will dispute that. He also stated that he thinks the country in general has been deeply impressed by it. He followed up by saying that on the other hand the importance of this measure must not be over-estimated, and must not be over-stressed. The reply I want to give to that is that it is very difficult to emphasise too greatly or to estimate too highly its importance. It is very difficult to over-estimate it. My opinion is, and I think there will be many in this House on both sides who will agree with me, that if we consider the importance of this Bill, its implications and its far-reaching, sweeping nature, that in the ten years that have elapsed since 1936, when we adopted the Bill in connection with the demarcation of areas for Natives and their representation in Parliament, no more important or more far-reaching Bill has come before this House.

But what I wish to point out further is this, that in connection with the treatment of the subject and the manner in which it has been presented and carried through this House, we have every reason to be dissatisfied. Not only members on this side of the House and on the other

[1] Speech by Dr. Malan, Leader of the Opposition, during the debate in the House of Assembly, 25 March 1946. *House of Assembly Debates.*

side of the House, but I think the country as a whole has every reason for dissatisfaction. In the first place, it is the intention that this measure, which is of so far-reaching a character, should be put through this House in a week's time, less than a week, and it is the intention of the Prime Minister also to drive it through the Other Place in a single week. The Rt. Hon. the Prime Minister has earned for himself the reputation in the course of years, especially in respect of legislation affecting the non-European population, of generally following delaying tactics. This is never the time to tackle the matter or to tackle it as radically as is proposed. You must postpone it, and things will solve themselves, and the trend of events in the course of years will themselves show how they must be solved. Consequently, take your time. He has earned the reputation of using an expression which no other statesman in South Africa has employed so frequently or brought into effect so frequently, " Let things develop ". In South Africa this has really become proverbial in its use in reference to the Prime Minister. But now the Prime Minister has come completely into conflict with these tactics and his policy of the past, and he wishes to bring an important matter such as this, with its far-reaching implications, before the House and to drive it through the Assembly in all stages and through the Senate in all stages in a single week. And how much time have we this week? On the first day on which it has been presented here there will be, with the exception of the leaders of the various parties and groups in this House, very few members who will be able to take part in the debate. Tuesday and Friday are private members' days, and they cannot be devoted to this subject, except for a short period. Consequently, this subject must be settled, and driven through all the stages in this House, today, Wednesday and Thursday. I say that we have every reason to be dissatisfied in respect of the manner in which the Government is dealing with a measure of such a drastic nature.

But we have also reason to be dissatisfied in reference to another point, namely, the indecision that the Prime Minister and his Government evinced in connection with the subject over a considerable period right to the end. Through the Speech from the Throne the Prime Minister let it be known that he was bringing up legislation of this nature. Shortly afterwards he made a statement in this House in connection with it. In reply to a question that I put to him not so long ago, he stated what would really be the contents of this Bill, and how far it would go. But since that time — it is only a short while ago — he has changed front on an extremely important point. He stated in this House that there would be representation of Indians in the provincial councils of both Natal and the Transvaal. Not that I do not agree with him not including the Transvaal now. I agree with that, but this circumstance indicates how the Government was groping around in reference to this matter, and adopting an indecisive attitude to the very last. How much time have they had? Two Pegging Acts were adopted in the course of recent years.

In 1939, that is seven years ago, a Pegging Act was passed in connection with the Transvaal, and in 1943 there was another in connection with Natal. Both were temporary measures. Why were they of a temporary character? Because the Government said: We want to solve this problem both in the Transvaal and Natal; these are big problems, we want to devote our attention to the subject and we shall come before Parliament with legislation of a permanent character. They had seven years in the case of the Transvaal and three years in the case of Natal. But right to the end the Government floundered round so that the country asked what the Government was really going to propose. I think we have reason to be dissatisfied with that floundering and indecision of the Government in connection with so important a matter.

There is yet another subject on which we have reason to be dissatisfied and that is that the Rt. Hon. the Prime Minister does not intend, and apparently did not intend to refer this Bill, which is of so important and sweeping a character, to a select committee. Bills have already been introduced into this House which did not possess one-twentieth of the importance of this radical measure, but the Government came and agreed, or themselves proposed, that before the second reading of the Bills was taken they should be referred to a select committee of this House. This Bill, I say, putting it at the lowest is twenty times as important as the Bills to which I have referred. It contains a new principle of a far-reaching nature; the franchise is now given, the individual franchise, to non-Europeans in the northern provinces. This has never previously happened and I think it is a matter which touches the foundations of White South Africa. It touches an agreement that was entered into, a compromise that was arranged, between two conflicting standpoints and principles, when the Union was accomplished. Now the Prime Minister comes and for the first time he proposes in this Bill that the franchise shall be given to non-Europeans in the northern provinces, with the exception of course of the Free State.

GENERAL SMUTS: In Natal the Natives can get the vote.

DR. MALAN: An opening has been left for the Natives to be enfranchised, but how many are there? The Governor-General had the right to allow the franchise to non-Europeans or Natives in Natal, but this has long since become a dead letter. The number who have thus been admitted to the franchise is so small as not to be worth mentioning.

MR. H. G. LAWRENCE[2]: On a separate roll.

DR. MALAN: That makes no difference. In practice the franchise does not exist for Natives in Natal. It affects the point the Prime Minister has mentioned here, that he is not altering the position under the South Africa Act when he proposes that two Indians can be elected as members of the Provincial Council in Natal. He stated that Indians could have been elected in the past. But hitherto the Indians in Natal have not had the franchise, and if Indians had been elected for the Provincial

2 The Minister of Justice.

Council then the European voters would have elected them. No European voters would have elected Indians to sit in the Provincial Council of Natal. It is only Indians who have the franchise who would have done that, but the Indians had not the franchise. This is a reason for dissatisfaction — that the Government has not referred to a select committee of the House an important Bill such as this, as one would have expected they would, where the various representatives of the various parties in the House could consult one another on the subject. He is pushing it through as a Government measure without the House having the opportunity to discuss it thoroughly through a select committee.

This Bill is entirely comparable with the Bills that were first presented to the House in 1936, and later to the Joint Sitting of both Houses of Parliament. Those Bills were also comprised of two parts, as the Prime Minister has already mentioned here. The one was a delimitation of areas just as is happening today in connection with the Indians. The other related to the representation of Natives in the Assembly and in the Senate. But how was that matter in connection with the Natives dealt with? Before the Joint Sitting of both Houses of Parliament in 1936 a joint select committee of both Houses of Parliament was appointed. The joint select committee did not only sit as long as it was possible to do so during the Session of Parliament, but it also utilised the recess, and they did not do it in one year, but the select committee devoted for several years its best attention and all its powers to it. This is the way in which a similar matter was approached and dealt with ten years ago. Now the Prime Minister comes and without having a select committee of this House, he seeks to drive this Bill through the Assembly and through the Senate in a few days.

But what I wish to add is that I consider there is every reason to expect that in connection with this important and far-reaching and very drastic measure it would be so tackled, it would be so treated in this House and outside this House to keep it above the pressure of party politics. I myself nineteen years ago, as Minister of the Interior, had to deal with this Indian problem. The difficulty at that time was not so great and so urgent as now, but the question was there and I shall read from the statement how I took up the matter, a statement that I made in 1932 in this House, and this is the spirit in which not only I individually but also the Government to which I belonged took up this subject and tried to solve it. It is a statement I made on 5 April 1932. It was made after a conference had been held with representatives of the Government of India to consider whether the Cape Town Agreement that had been entered into five years previously had worked or not, whether it should be continued or not, and whether anything else should be done to make it operative again, because as the Prime Minister has said, for a few years it went well and large numbers of Indians were repatriated, but after that the matter virtually became moribund. I then made the following statement in this House—

In conclusion I wish to place on record the welcome and significant fact that it has been found possible for representatives of both sides of this House to associate themselves with each other in the conference negotiations.

As the responsible Minister at that time I invited the Prime Minister, who was then Leader of the Opposition, to take part in the conference or to send representatives to the delegation that the Union Government had appointed to meet the deputation from India. The Prime Minister appointed the late Sir Patrick Duncan and Mr. Heaton Nicholls, who represented the Opposition there—

In principle this does not signify a new departure as for a considerable time past it has been demonstrated on various select committees that the general outlook of the different parties on the Asiatic question is fundamentally the same and that co-operation on non-party lines was therefore eminently practicable. On the other hand the country will not fail to appreciate the importance of this further step which has now been taken by which political parties have deliberately associated themselves with each other in a common responsibility in order, for the country's sake, to keep an important national question out of the arena of party strife. The Asiatic question is to my mind pre-eminently one where the public interest demands the co-operation of every section of the community in an atmosphere of self-restraint and calm deliberation. The path which we have so far successfully followed I propose to continue in the future. Even at this stage therefore I wish to assure the House that when the investigation of the possibilities of overseas settlement, to which both Governments have agreed, is completed and when the whole position will have to be reviewed in the light of that report, I shall once more invite to our councils and to our assistance those representatives of the Opposition who co-operated so cordially with us at the conference.

I say this is the way in which at that time we dealt with the matter and I think it is the right way to deal with it. I am glad to be able to say that even today I look back with thankfulness to the time when that matter was dealt with and when I proposed nothing that had not been laid before the select committee of the House, or on which the other side of the House at that time was not consulted. The result was that all the decisions of the House at that time in connection with the Indian question, and there was a whole series of them, were taken with the approval and the concurrence of the House — there were two or three exceptions — with the approval and concurrence of all the members of the House. Therefore I repeat that we have every reason to be dissatisfied that the Government has chosen an entirely different way to deal with this matter.

In reference to the attitude of the Indians I wish to identify myself completely with what the Prime Minister has stated, that the Indians must decide once and for all whether they wish to form a part of the permanent population in South Africa, or whether they are a foreign element here who have their national home in another country, and that they accordingly have the right to feel that in matters affecting them they may make an appeal not to the Government of this country but to make an appeal against the policy of this country to an external government. This is a matter that the Indians must decide in the first instance. If they decide, as is apparently now the case, because they are making an appeal to governments overseas, and if the report published yesterday morning is correct, they are prepared not only to make an appeal to the U.N.O. but to the individual governments of Russia, France and China — I maintain that if this is their attitude then they are not entitled to the consideration in this country that every section of the permanent population has from the Government If this is their attitude, then we cannot do otherwise than regard them as a foreign element in the country. Then we must also regard them as a responsible speaker in the Legislative Assembly in India described them, as Indian citizens. Not only is it necessary that the Indians themselves should come to a final decision on this question and act accordingly, but it is also a matter on which we should have clarity. Let me say at once that my viewpoint was, when I had to deal with the matter as Minister of the Interior, that I should take up the attitude which at that time was correct, namely that a portion of the Indian population in South Africa belonged to the permanent population because they were born here. But another section was not in that position. They were born in India. They always had their children educated in India and then they returned to our country. They also maintained their connection with India, and it was also said they felt more at home there than here. For that reason the repatriation scheme was an effort we made to return to India those Indians who actually, on their own admission, were aliens in this country. That was the viewpoint. But after this repatriation scheme was exhausted it appeared, and I think it is today the case, that probably 85 per cent to 90 per cent of the Indians in South Africa have been born in South Africa. In India they are aliens. Consequently I take up the attitude that they form portion of the permanent population of South Africa.

This gives us a right — a right to demand that they shall not seek assistance from another government overseas in reference to legislation that is introduced here and that affects their interests. It is our right to demand that this shall not occur. We do not permit it in the case of other sections of the population and we cannot permit it in their case. On the other hand this imposes an obligation on us. If they form part of the permanent population the bounden duty rests on us to treat them as a permanent part of the population and to solve this question on a basis that is just. That is the standpoint I take up. I can only say that if our standpoint is right I do not say that there should not be a representative of India — the Agent-General — in South Africa. He can be here, but then he should be here not for the interests of those Indians who reside here as inhabitants of this country. He has nothing to do with them. Their interests are a domestic matter, and it is a matter for our Government, and he has nothing to do with it. He should be here for general matters affecting the interests of India, just like the ambassador of any other country. He cannot take up an exceptional position here.

I come now to the Bill itself. As the Minister has said, this Bill consists of two parts. The first part of the Bill wishes to bring about separation in the possession of land and of occupation in Natal. It is necessary, as the Prime Minister has explained, as a result of the penetration that has taken place on such a large scale and at such a tempo, that the White population in Natal — and the Prime Minister is absolutely right in thinking this — regards this as a menace to their position. Let me say at once that apart perhaps from some details I now wish to discuss we agree with that part of the Bill. Thus we are going to support that section of the Bill. We live in South Africa in a country where there are various races, races which in many respects differ widely from one another not only in regard to their level of civilisation but also in other respects. There is only one way — I cannot see any other — in which these various races in South Africa can live together in peace, without there being friction and incessant friction, without the one section or the one race contemplating the other as a danger to it and to the country, and the one way is that we should have colour bars in the country. Without colour bars in the country we cannot have that condition of peace and that feeling of security here. But with those colour bars in this country we must, as I have already said in connection with the permanent parts of the population, so conduct ourselves that they will be treated justly and have a future in the country.

What other course can be struck to accomplish that purpose? Has anyone yet presented any other effective policy in regard to this matter? Yes, the Minister of Finance,[3] a colleague of the Prime Minister, announced his policy on the eve of the introduction of this Bill. In Johannesburg on the occasion of a graduation ceremony he gave an address in which he expounded his policy very clearly on this subject. He regarded colour bars as just a disclosure of prejudice on the part of those who instituted them. They were the breeding ground of the prejudice that existed. If that prejudice, as the Minister of Finance described it, and if those colour bars which have been instituted as a result of it, are removed in South Africa then nothing must be left of them. You cannot do away with some and allow others to remain. If this happens, then there is only one outcome of the matter, and that is the downfall of the White race in South Africa. There are no two opinions on that. The Minister of Finance on a previous occasion — I remember it and perhaps other hon. members recall it as well — said to us: Yes, but there is one exception, there must be social dividing

[3] Mr. J. H. Hofmeyr.

walls, there must be social separation. For the rest in every respect there must be equality of treatment, but it is right that socially we should not mix as Europeans do with Europeans, and the Minister of Finance said it was a question of training and education; the White population must be trained to maintain the dividing line. To that I say that you cannot have any social separation in this country or in any country and maintain it without there being separation in other spheres. Without separation in other spheres you cannot maintain social separation in the country. Look at Cape Town. Here you have equality in almost every sphere. There is nothing to divide the one from the other. What happens in regard to social separation under such conditions? I will say nothing further about that. Just look around in Cape Town and then you will see a signpost for the whole of South Africa, a warning of the logical application of the way the Minister of Finance has indicated. If we follow that road logically then we come to the outlook and the attitude of Dr. Philip, Van der Kemp and Read,[4] who lived in the days before the Voortrekkers. If the doctrine or the attitude of the Minister of Finance is carried out consistently and applied, then I say not many years will elapse before a great part of South Africa will follow the road of which we have a warning here in Cape Town; it may take a longer or shorter period, but eventually South Africa will have no other future than that of a third-rate South American half-caste population. It has no other future.

I come now to the second half of the Bill, the political representation of the Indians in the Assembly and the Senate. In reference to this matter the Prime Minister has stated that the two parts of the Bill are inter-dependent and cannot be separated, or he does not intend to separate them. Why does he do this? He does this with an eye on the attitude of the Indians. He is attempting to secure their co-operation to give them something as a substitute in order to satisfy them. He has an eye on India and perhaps on the British Government with a view to appeasing them. That is why he is doing this. But has he succeeded? Is the British Government satisfied; is India satisfied, and are the Indians in our own country satisfied, either with one part of the Bill or with the other part of it? If it was his intention to shape the Bill in this way so that it would secure satisfaction and co-operation then I say that from the start it has hopelessly miscarried. It has already failed hopelessly, but for this failure he has made the White race here in South Africa pay the price through this Bill.

The first question that we wish to put in connection with political representation is this, and we must regard the matter in the light of the reply to it: How does this representation that the Prime Minister wishes to give the Indians affect the colour problem as a whole? In South Africa we have not to deal only with the Indian problem. We have to

---

[4] Of the London Missionary Society, and regarded as champions of the rights of the non-White people.

deal with the colour problem to the fullest extent — Natives, Indians, Coloureds. How is the colour problem, as a whole, affected by this measure if we put it through? There can be only one answer to that, and it is that if this Bill should ever prove a solution to the Indian problem it at the same time creates in the broader sphere of the colour problem as a whole greater problems and greater dangers than even this Indian problem, even without this Bill today. I shall tell you how: Those three sections of the colour problem are, as I have stated, an inter-dependent whole. If you break down the dividing wall at one place it is ever so much harder to protect it at another place. It is like a dam. If you break the wall at one place the whole wall is affected and the whole dam is affected. It is the same with this problem. It was unfortunately left as an unsolved problem in 1910 with the accomplishment of Union, and because the question was then left half open, or not solved at all, you had for the first 36 years after that a continuous nibbling at this Bill. It was taken in hand fragmentarily and subsequently it had to be tackled again and no progress was made, while the position became worse and worse. Now I say: Push through this Bill which is a fragmentary solution of the colour problem in general, solve the problem in this way and look at the reactions which of course will follow immediately. The Indian population, to whom three members in the Assembly are given — we shall leave the Senate for the moment — number 250,000 in all the provinces. The Indians in the Cape enjoy the franchise, and consequently they do not fall under this. In the northern provinces there are still fewer. The 250,000 get three members here in the Assembly. I say, what is the reaction to that? Have you forgotten that a large number of Coloured people live today in the northern provinces?

MR. BARLOW: It is a very small number.

DR. MALAN: There are Coloured people in such numbers that they constitute a problem in certain areas. The Minister of Lands came along only a short time ago with settlements for Coloured people in a part of Natal. He wants to have the right to establish such settlements for Coloured people everywhere in the northern provinces. I should say that they would be immediately entitled to ask: " If 250,000 Indians have three representatives in Parliament, though the Indians are the most recent arrivals in South Africa — it is a new element in the population here — why should the Coloured people in the northern provinces remain unrepresented?"

MR. BARLOW: Because there is hardly a single one.

DR. MALAN: They have not the franchise there. They have not the parliamentary franchise, and immediately there arises what you have hitherto had in only a small degree, namely a new and serious problem.

But more than that. Here you have the Native population. They are represented here in Parliament by three members. If the Indians with a total of 250,000 altogether in the country get three representatives in the

Assembly, what do you imagine will be thought that will arise naturally in the minds of the Native population? They number 8,000,000, and these 8,000,000 who form part of the permanent population of the country must thus be placed on an equal footing with the Indians, who only number 250,000 and who also receive three representatives. Thus you at once create a feeling of injustice amongst the members of the Native population, and they will demand that they should have not three but 30 representatives, if they are to be placed on an equal footing with the Indians. This is also going to complicate the whole question of South West Africa. South West Africa, it is hoped, is going to be incorporated in the Union. There, too, it is also a question of the franchise. What representation will be given to them here in Parliament? And the problem is: Can you exclude the Coloured population there — and it is a large Coloured population — from the franchise when you are giving the franchise to 250,000 Indians to whom you have given three seats in Parliament?

You see what serious consequences, what new and greater problems than we have had hitherto will arise as a result of this measure. In other words, give that representation in the Assembly to the 250,000 Indians, and then I say this country will have a halter round its neck and it will not easily get rid of it, especially if that idea of the Minister of Finance takes root which regards as prejudice, and something to be abolished, that herrenvolk feeling, that feeling of superiority on the part of the Europeans. How can you after that refuse the new demands that are made? As regards Natal, I can only say that I will not go into that. Natal is represented here, and Natal can speak for itself. I can only say that the principle that is introduced there is a new principle in practice. It is not a question of theory, it is a question of practice. It will simply not remain at that. If the Indians have the franchise for the Assembly and for the Senate, and they have the franchise for the Provincial Council of Natal, can you, with any justice, deny them the municipal franchise? You cannot do that. You cannot possibly do that, and therefore it will also have its further applications in that connection, and if you cannot apply it there you will simply cause greater difficulties than the difficulties which will be eliminated by this Bill.

Just one other point, and it is this: The way in which this representation is given — I am still confining myself to the Assembly — creates a tremendous change in the character of our Parliament as representatives of the people. It creates a tremendous change in the character of our Parliament, especially if we take it with the change that is brought about by the introduction of the Native legislation in 1936. Let us reflect for a moment what the position will be if this Bill is adopted. In this Assembly there will be sitting a bloc of six non-European representatives. I say it is a bloc. I do not say that they will always, as might be expected, vote together. It is a bloc; but I am also referring to the fact that these six representatives are on an entirely different basis to the other members who are sitting in Parliament. Under what arrangement do they sit here?

They sit here solely to represent race interests. We do not sit in Parliament and we are not elected on the basis of race. We are elected, no matter to what party we may belong, to represent the general interests of the country. We are sitting here because we hold certain views, on which we differ amongst ourselves, on national problems in general. We represent our constituencies, the voters who have sent us here. But we represent South Africa as a whole, all of us. But that is not the case with those who represent the Natives, and it will not be the case with the representatives of the Indians, and as this is so — you recognise it is the case when Parliament dissolves all our seats fall vacant with the exception of those of the Native representatives and the representatives of the Indians; these do not become vacant; they remain — and now with a bloc of six, and especially as the parties in this House always stand more or less at equal strength, what is going to happen then? You will be calling in the representatives of the non-European population in South Africa to be the arbiters as between European and European. You call them in to umpire between European and European in this House, and in order to do this you place them in an exceptionally privileged position.

We cannot retain our seats when Parliament dissolves. We have to go to the country and submit to the judgment of the nation, but those six are not subjected to the judgment of the people or the verdict of their constituents. They sit tight there in their seats for five years. They have no responsibility on general national questions to the people as a whole. In other words, this position may arise there is a big problem over which there is a difference of opinion in Parliament; the Government decides to go to the country on that question; it has not a big enough majority, or it suffers defeat by a few votes, and it decides to place the matter before the country and ask the people to give an answer either that the Government should stay or that the Government should fall. The people give their answer but the majority is not too big. Then that answer given by the people, that decision of the nation in this great and serious and pressing national problem is stifled subsequently by that bloc of six in Parliament. I say that is an utterly impossible position that is being created in this way, and accordingly I move the following amendment—

To omit all the words after " That " and to substitute: " this House declines to pass the Second Reading of the Asiatic Land Tenure and Indian Representation Bill until the Government gives an assurance that it will take the necessary steps to refer to a joint committee of both Houses of Parliament for consideration and report the solution of the colour question in all its aspects upon a basis of separation, including the Indian, Coloured and Native question; such committee to have power to draft and recommend such draft Bill or Bills as may be deemed necessary; and further, with this end in view, that the operation of the Trading and Occupation of Land (Transvaal and Natal) Restriction Act, 1943, amended according to the demands of existing circumstances, be extended for a further period of two years, viz. to 31 March 1948."

6

REPRESENTATION OF INDIANS
AND NATIVES

DR. D. F. MALAN, 20 JANUARY 1948[1]

I MOVE—

That, in view of all the circumstances, this House is of the opinion —

(1) that representation of Indians in Parliament does not serve the purpose for which it was intended and is harmful to the interests of the people, and that Chapter II of the Asiatic Land Tenure and Indian Representation Act, 1946, should accordingly be repealed;

(2) that the Representation of Natives Act, 1936 should be amended —

(a) so that Natives shall have representation in the Senate only and not in the House of Assembly as at present, as recommended by the joint committee of both Houses in 1935, and

(b) to provide for the abolition of the Natives' Representative Council and the substitution therefor of representative Native governing bodies for the various Native territories set up on the basis of tribal and language affinity and with powers of government under European trusteeship granted gradually in relation to the degree of development of the groups concerned and their ability to bear responsibility for self-government; and;

(3) that the offer of the Prime Minister to the Natives' Representative Council as set out in his official statement of 14 October 1947, viz. to eliminate all European representatives from that Council and to transfer paramount powers to it in both European and Native territories, is wrong in principle, will infinitely aggravate the danger of Communism in South Africa and will, if carried into effect, be fatal to the security of European civilisation as well as to a sound understanding between the races. This House accordingly requests the Government to take the necessary steps to give effect to this view, and considers that by failing or refusing to do so, the Government will lose the confidence of this House.

Mr. Speaker, the motion appearing here in my name refers, as will be clear, to the colour policy which in our opinion should be adopted for the future in South Africa. The motion takes into account that, as far as the present and future colour policy is concerned, we find two different schools of thought in South Africa; two different trends which are pursued

---

[1] Speech by Dr. Malan, Leader of the Opposition, in the House of Assembly. *House of Assembly Debates.*

by members in this House, and, to be more specific, one by hon. members on this side of the House and the other by hon. members of the Government and those that follow them. The motion is an attempt to obtain clarity, more clarity in regard to this matter, so that not only members in this House, but also the people outside, can give a proper verdict in regard thereto. We on this side of the House hold our manifest and clear conviction and policy in regard to this matter. What is contained in this motion is not our complete colour policy. Our complete colour policy will, when the election takes place be laid before the people in a lucid and definite form. I can give hon. members the assurance that we have completed our work in connection with that matter. It is not a matter which has still to be thrashed out. Our point of view is definite and clear as far as we are concerned, and when and how the matter will be put before the people is our own affair. In that respect we shall follow our own judgment. It will be done at the proper time and it will be done unequivocally. That is the one school of thought which exists.

In opposition to us is the other school of thought, namely the one of the Government and of the followers of the Government. In regard to their policy today, no actual doubt exists, at least not in my mind, and I think also not in the minds of most people in this country. These two policies are in direct opposition, differ radically on important aspects, and as far as this motion is concerned, there is only one choice in regard to the differing aspects of the two schools of thought. A choice exists, but it is a choice which will indicate very clearly the difference between the different trends which are represented by the one and the other side of the House. It is very necessary that we should obtain clarity in regard to this matter. As I said before, the people will ultimately decide this matter, the people will ultimately hold their fate in their own hands, and it is imperative that the people should understand the difference between the one and the other side. I just want to say at this juncture that the course which is being pursued by the Prime Minister, and especially by the Deputy-Prime Minister[2] who until recently was the Minister of Finance, is fatal in my opinion, and I think in the opinion of the larger section of the people. I want to go further and maintain that if the policy which the Government has adopted and with which it is apparently still continuing today is to be proceeded with at the pace at which it has been during the past year or few years, it will not take another 25 or 30 years before the composition of this House will to a large extent have been radically altered in such a way that at least in this House the non-European population of the country will dominate.

There was a time when this House agreed that in regard to this colour problem the policy which was laid down at the coming into being of the Union should remain intact, that as far as the three northern provinces were concerned the franchise would not be extended to the non-Europeans in those provinces.

2 Mr. J. H. Hofmeyr.

298

MR. BARLOW: Who wants to extend it?

AN HON. MEMBER: Your party did so.

DR. MALAN: That standpoint has been departed from. Two years ago that standpoint was departed from in this House. There was a time, and not so very long ago when members in this House, including — I ought to mention it — the former Minister of Finance, the present Deputy-Prime Minister who then also said that he was in favour of equality as far as political rights are concerned, and also advocated equal rights in the industrial and economic field, nevertheless held that there was one thing which he did not favour, and that was social equality. He, and I may say all members of this House as far as I can judge, felt that way, whatever may have been the difference of opinion in certain respects in regard to the principle of equality in other spheres of life. What do we find today? An agitation has been set afoot, a strong movement which as far as one can judge is gathering momentum, aiming at the abolition of all colour bars in every sphere of life, including the colour bar in social life. A few days ago we even had a statement by nobody less then a Senator who is the mouthpiece of a growing section in our country, and who merely reiterated what another Senator who had been overseas in connection with the colour problem had said again and again with the utmost emphasis: Down with all colour bars, down with the colour bar also in social matters. Today one hears this, and one hears it in circles where one never expected it in the past.

I have emphasised more than once that in regard to this matter on which the two schools of thought diverge, on which they differ radically, that the people should be called in as arbiters at the general election. The people hold their fate in their own hands. That is not the way which I originally chose myself. That is not the road I would have liked to tread in regard to the colour problem, because I realise that this colour problem does not affect one or the other party only — it affects not only one section of the European population, but the future of White civilisation and the position of the White race in South Africa. For that reason, I considered that it would be best to keep this colour problem out of party politics.

MR. HEYNS[3]: That has always been our policy.

DR. MALAN: I am pleased to notice that hon. members on the other side of the House support this sound principle. But two years ago I made an attempt in this House — is their memory so weak? — I made an attempt not once, but twice, by moving a proposal in this House that this matter should be lifted out of the normal party political struggle, and that, as happened in 1936 or prior to 1936, a joint committee of both Houses of Parliament should be appointed to conduct a thorough inquiry in regard to this problem. Not only that, but I also proposed that such a committee should include all the parties of this House, all the political sections representing the people. That motion, which I introduced two years ago, was rejected twice in succession and unanimously by the other

[3] United Party.

side of the House. What happened thereafter is that the solution of this problem — and a start was made by way of the Indian problem — was forced through this House by the Prime Minister. He dealt with it purely and solely from a party political angle, and he forced it through by means of a party political majority. In regard to the colour problem, he in any case had not the right to do this without the people having given him a mandate to that effect. This House was elected on the basis of another issue, a very specific question, namely, that during the course of the war the people were asked, seeing that after all we were at war, whether the war should be continued in the same way by the present Government.

AN HON. MEMBER: And the people gave their reply.

DR. MALAN: Yes, the people gave their verdict, but they gave a verdict on that one particular question, and not on the other one.

The question I want to ask now is this: What right did the Prime Minister have, what right did the Government have to abuse the majority they obtained in that way in this House, trying to solve the other problem here and to solve it in their own party political way — a problem which is of vital importance to our people? It affects the entire future of the people. What right did the Government have to tackle that problem and solve it in that way? The Government not only abused the position into which special circumstances had placed it, but as far as this matter is concerned the Government committed a breach of faith towards those who supported it at the elections on quite a different issue. In regard to this question, the colour policy which should be followed, we have here the members of the South African Party[4] who, as far as this question is concerned and especially as far as the Indian problem is concerned, are diametrically opposed to the Government, and those members assisted to bring the Government in the position in which it finds itself. Then there is the Labour Party. As a result of this issue which was put before the House two years ago by way of the Indian Bill, the Labour Party split, and a section, an important section of the Labour Party, did not agree with the Government on this colour problem. But that is not all. I go further and maintain that there are quite a number of members on the Government benches who support the Government, but who in fact do not agree with the Government on its approach to the Indian problem, and on the Government's colour policy in general. There is the Trades and Labour Council, the trade union organisations. In general they supported the Government in its war policy. What, however, became evident at the last congress of the Trades and Labour Council at Port Elizabeth? That the trade union organisations had been ruptured from top to bottom. And the reason for it? They split on this one subject of the future colour policy. That is the actual position in our country. That is the opinion held by the people, and I ask from where did the Government obtain the right in those circumstances to simply continue with a majority which is

[4] Formerly the Dominion Party.

obtained on that other issue, and to solve this problem along party political lines without consulting the people in regard thereto?

When my motion had been rejected twice in succession — my proposal to keep this matter outside and above the party political arena, and to make it a broad national issue, to find a solution of this problem for the people in general and to consult all political parties in the country — when that motion had been rejected, I told the Prime Minister: In regard to this matter I now can see no other road open to me than to appeal to those who stand above the Government and above this House, namely, the people. The people will decide their own fate. I cannot follow any other road. I then clearly stated that at the next general election we would have to appeal to the people.

I have already said that the Government has already chosen a definite line of policy and that it is trying to drag the country in that direction along party political lines. At the time I drafted this motion, before giving notice of it in this House on Friday last, on the facts which we were dealing with at that time alone it would have been justifiable to introduce this motion; those facts were a sufficient ground for bringing this motion before this House. Since that time, however, I have been strengthened in my conviction. I am now going so far as to maintain that in view of what has happened since, no more opportune time and no more suitable motion that the one I am now moving could be brought before this House in connection with our general colour policy.

I wish to refer to two matters. The one is the statement by the Government, a solemn declaration in the Speech from the Throne, in which the Prime Minister with the utmost clarity made it known that certain proposals he had made and which were of vital importance as far as the colour problem is concerned, would be proceeded with, and that he had already committed himself to it; that he was merely waiting for some further consultation with the Natives' Representative Council which will be newly composed within a couple of weeks. The other event I wish to mention is that a reshuffling of the Cabinet has taken place, and one of the outstanding aspects in this connection is that the former Minister of Finance, now the Minister of Mines, received official recognition as Deputy-Prime Minister and Leader of this House.

HON. MEMBERS: Hear, hear.

DR. MALAN: That "Hear, hear", sounds rather unconvincing, and it sounded to us as if there is a lack of cordiality amongst members on the other side, who fully realise what the implications and the meaning of that change are. In the past it was said that there was no certainty at all that the Minister concerned would be nominated as the successor of the present Prime Minister. He himself time and again made statements that it was not so sure that he would be designated. Now he has been appointed in the most conspicuous manner — when the present Prime Minister goes he will be his successor, and if he should not become his successor it will amount to a direct smack in his face. I therefore say that in view of

301

these facts, we now know more definitely than ever before what the colour policy of the party on the other side is going to be, because we know very well what that Minister stands for. He is honest enough to state his opinion on the public platform and in this House in regard to the colour problem. He does not mince matters. He said that if we wanted to make political capital out of what he said in this House, we would be free to do so. That can only have one meaning, and that is that the present Government has tied itself as a Government and as a party to the possible future Premiership of the former Minister of Finance, provided the Government gets a fresh mandate from the people at the next election. This can only mean one thing and mean it clearly.

I again want to ask the Prime Minister what right he has in these circumstances to tackle the colour problem along political lines and to try and solve it by adopting a certain policy without having received a mandate from the people? Who has given him the right to shackle his party to the possible Premiership of the former Minister of Finance, and by implication to his policy?

Now I want to deal briefly with the three different points which form the basis of this motion. My first proposal is to repeal the provisions in regard to Indian representation in this House, which appear in the enactment passed two years ago. The reasons which I advance is that that legislation, in so far as it refers to the representation of Indians in Parliament, has proven itself to be useless and does not serve the purpose for which it was intended and is, as I express it in my motion, harmful to the interests of the people. I want to emphasise the fact that this legislation was brought before the House two years ago in the Asiatic Land Tenure and Representation of Indians Bill, without, as far as I am aware, anybody having asked for it. It was an entirely uncalled for piece of legislation. Furthermore, I want to point out that, if it is intended as a solution of the Indian problem in South Africa, it has entirely missed its mark. It did not have the slightest effect on the general attitude and disposition of the Indian population towards the Government of the country, towards the laws of the country, towards the measure of segregation laid down in that Act aiming at the prevention of penetration by Indians in European areas. It has not in the slightest way brought about a change in their attitude. On the contrary, they continued to defame South Africa in the eyes of the Government of India which eventually even resulted in a boycott against South Africa. They went further and laid a charge against South Africa at UNO and they succeeded in obtaining a conviction against South Africa by that organisation, a conviction which is still standing today. It has not been repealed. It is a conviction against South Africa, which has made South Africa into a condemned party, almost into a criminal, in the eyes of the peoples of the world, not merely in regard to the Indian question, but also in regard to the colour problem in the country in general, even as far as it is based on tradition. As a solution of the Indian problem, and an attempt to placate the Indians, it has been a complete failure and has missed its mark.

302

But that is not all. It is not merely what the Indians have already done. In a few days' time, I believe in four days' time, as has been announced, the Indians of Natal intend to penetrate into the Transvaal. It is their intention to simply transgress the long-established and recognised law of South Africa, an enactment which has been in force since 1913, and simply to provoke South Africa in regard to that Act. Is there anybody who can maintain that this legislation of two years ago has been a solution to the Indian problem, and that as such it has been of any use whatsoever?

I go further and maintain that this piece of legislation which was passed here two years ago, and which we should now like to see repealed, was not a compromise between the Union Government and the Indians in regard to the solution of the Indian question. It was a compromise and it was stamped as such by the present Minister of Mines when he discussed this matter here in the House. He said that it was a compromise — but a compromise with whom? Not an agreement between the Indians and the Government but a compromise between one section of the Cabinet and one section of the party on the one hand, and himself and those who followed him, on the other. In other words, that piece of legislation was forced through this House with no other intention than that it should be a piece of party political legislation in order to enable the party on the other side to present a united front in this House. The will of the people had to give way for those party political considerations. The Deputy-Prime Minister did not leave the slightest doubt in regard thereto. That is the reason why he told the Government and afterwards told this House that this Indian legislation would be put before the House as a matter of compromise with him and that consequently no amendment would be accepted. The discussion of this matter would not be limited. The convictions of the members might be what they were, but he insisted that nothing should be added and nothing should be taken away from the legislation. This is a compromise which was agreed to in view of the political interests of the party on the other side and not in view of the interests of the people.

As I pointed out on that occasion, this measure of legislation very deeply and very seriously affects the general colour policy of the country. In the first place we have the aspect that that legislation was considered by the Prime Minister and by the Deputy-Prime Minister to be merely a first step in a certain direction. Still more explicitly, he said that this was the beginning of a return to the Indians of all the political rights which they had enjoyed in the past and which in the course of time had been taken away from them. He very clearly said: We do this to start with, and then we shall go further and try to give municipal franchise to the Indians in Natal. That was the commencement; it was the forerunner of all the other things which would have to follow, and the Prime Minister attempted to give municipal franchise to Indians in Natal. He tried to give the Indians the municipal franchise in Durban, but Durban called together the municipal voters in order to take a decision on the matter, and with a majority — as far as I can remember of at least 12 to one — Durban rejected it. All this shows that the Government with this legislation and with its implications and consequences which were predicted at the introduction of the Bill, did not in the least represent the will and the opinion of the people. On the contrary, they proceeded with it in the face of the feeling and conviction of the loyal province of Natal and of the most loyal town in that loyal province, viz. Durban. On that occasion I also said that this legislation is affecting our whole colour policy. We have 250,000 Indians in this country. According to the qualifications laid down in the Act, the number which would have received the vote would have been much smaller, and that small number of Indians now has the right to elect three members to sit in this House. I then asked: What are going to be the consequences in regard to the other non-European sections in the country? In the northern provinces we have 100,000 Coloured persons. They belong to this country; they are not strangers or foreigners who have come here from other countries, and if that little band of Indians who came here and who are still so closely linked to India, get three representatives in Parliament, how will we be able to refuse the franchise to the Coloured people in the northern provinces?

Moreover, we have 8,000,000 Natives in this country. If the Indians are to be represented in this manner by three representatives in this House, will not the Natives argue that when a small number of Indians have three representatives, the 8,000,000 Natives, according to that standard, must have at least 30 members; I said that an agitation in that direction would be set afoot. What I predicted at that time has literally come true. Even the innocent and well-disposed Bunga of Transkei has passed a solemn resolution demanding that the representation of the Natives in this House, especially in view of the representation which is being given to the Indians, should be increased and should be increased very considerably. That agitation came about. For that reason I maintain that the time is overdue when we as a House of Assembly should retrace our steps, and admit the futility and harmfulness of that legislation which was passed without any mandate from, or consultation of the people, and which was passed for party political purposes, and that the sooner we repeal that legislation, the better it will be.

I now come to my second point, and that is the revision, which I ask for, of the solution of the Native problem which was found, or rather was not found, in 1936. That legislation must be revised, and I am not alone in regard to this matter and the opinion that it should be revised, for the Prime Minister clearly indicated in the Speech from the Throne, and he furthermore clearly indicated in the offer which he made to the Natives' Representative Council, that the legislation which was passed at that time must be revised and must be revised very considerably. That legislation — and I want to use a strong expression — has proved to be a failure. It has become apparent that it has been a failure in all its aspects, and that is the reason why revision has now become necessary. What I ask for here is on the one hand the abolition of two bodies, two institutions, which came into being as a result of that Act. The one is the abolition of the direct or communal representation of Natives in this House, so that the Natives will in future be represented, not in this House, but solely in the Senate, as was laid down in 1936.

The second one is the abolition of the Natives' Representative Council itself. I first want to deal with what I mentioned last, namely the abolition of the Natives' Representative Council. I am in the fortunate position that in 1936 I, as the Leader of the then Opposition against the Coalition Government, pointed out, and as strongly as I could warned against the danger of that legislation and the consequences which it would have. At that time — you may read it up if you want to, in Hansard, in the report of the Joint Sitting of both Houses of Parliament — I pointed out that this calling into existence of the Natives' Representative Council was creating something which we had not in this country before, and which in reality did not exist; that is to say, it would create a unified Native nation in this country. There is no such thing as a unified Native nation in this country. We have Native groups in this country, and those Native groups differ from one another as far as their traditions are concerned, as far as their tribal relations are concerned, as far as their language affinities are concerned, and there is every reason to take that into account in your legislation, and there is every reason, when such a large unified Native nation does not exist, not to call one into being by means of legislation. I pointed out that this was a far-reaching effect of the Act which was then passed. I furthermore stated that this Natives' Representative Council would become a hot-bed for agitators. I furthermore pointed out that they would not be satisfied with the position which was given to that Council by the enactment, but that they would come with demands, that they would want more powers, and that, instead of that body removing the Native question out of the realm of ordinary party politics in this country, it would make the Native question more acute. Those predictions have become true to the letter. It has become a hot-bed of agitators, and one Minister of Native Affairs after the other emphasised this fact, which was borne out by their experience. They started putting forward demands and making greater and greater demands, until they ultimately arrived at a point of view which encouraged them to demand the removal of all colour bars in the country, and if that were not done, they would go on strike — and they did go on strike — and that solution came to nought. It was a hopeless failure to try and find a solution for our Native problem along these lines. I now ask, in view of those facts, that the Natives' Representative Council should be abolished. That Council does not solve the Native problem, but has merely aggravated it.

Furthermore, I ask here for the abolition of the representation of the

Natives in this Parliament. In asking that, I am not asking anything which is not fair. When I ask that, I ask it for two reasons. The first reason I mentioned at that time, and it has already been mentioned before. I went to the trouble of reading up what I said in 1936 in this House in connection with the matter. I said that the attitude of the representatives of the Natives in this House was going to be determined by the attitude of those who had elected them. Their attitude would be determined by the attitude of the Natives' Representative Council. In this House they would be nothing but the mouthpiece of the views accepted by the Natives' Representative Council, and the fiercer that Council would agitate and the greater the demands put forward from that side would be, the more would we find that same attitude on the part of the members who represent Natives in this House. They even went further in this House, and they did not confine their activities to the purpose for which they had been elected, viz. representation of Native interests, but they went further and became the champions here of the Indians with whom they had nothing whatever to do, and they appeared here as the authorised representatives of all non-Europeans in the country. The work they do is therefore different from that for which they were elected. But what has happened? The Indians went and complained to India and the representatives of the Natives in this country supported those complaints, not only by speeches which they made in the country in connection with the matter, but by sending a deputation there to lay a charge against South Africa in India, and one person who is a member of the Senate even went so far as to go to the United Nations Organisation in America and accuse South Africa there, as if our country were the worst criminal among all the nations on earth. I say that on those grounds I am fully justified in asking, since that representation has also taken a different course from that originally intended, to ask that the representation in this House should be abolished. I ask again: Am I demanding something unfair? Is this a matter merely of party politics on our side?

Parliament and the Government of those days followed the sensible way I suggested two years ago in connection with the solution of the Native problem, a way which the Prime Minister rejected almost with scorn, and that is to lift the Native problem and its solution out of the arena of party politics and to place it into the hands of both Houses of Parliament and into the hands of all the representatives in this House. That road was followed. And what was the result? The result was that the committee which was appointed by both Houses of Parliament came to a conclusion and put a recommendation before this House and drafted a Bill which was put before both Houses at a Joint Sitting. What was their recommendation? Their recommendation was that the Natives should be represented only in the Senate and not in this House. That was the joint wisdom of the two Houses of Parliament, and that was the joint wisdom of the representatives of all parties.

GENERAL SMUTS: Opinions were sharply divided about it, and that is why it was dropped.

DR. MALAN: I shall explain further what the history was. The importance of that Bill No. 1 of 1936 is of so much more importance, because the then Prime Minister, General Hertzog, a few years before had given his opinion on what should be done, and he had proposed that the Natives should be given representation in this House.

MR. BARLOW: Yes, seven.

DR. MALAN: That is what he proposed.

MR. BARLOW: And there are only three today.

DR. MALAN: But the combined wisdom of the two Houses of Parliament was mobilised and the combined wisdom of the representatives of all parties, and they said that what the Prime Minister had suggested some time before was an impossible blending of two separate principles. The one is equality, and the other is segregation, and it would be fatal to try and solve the problem in that manner, and they set aside what the Prime Minister had in mind before, and they came to this House with the recommendation that there should be no representation of Natives in this House, but only in the Senate. That greatly reinforced the justification for the attitude I took up in 1936 in regard to this matter. The point of view adhered to by the joint committee at that time was also my point of view, and what I am asking here today is not at all unfair. I say: Let us revert to the sound policy of both Houses of Parliament and the joint policy of all the parties in this House. That is what I am proposing here today.

There is also a positive side to this motion. We want to give representation to the Natives. We want to establish institutions for the Natives in accordance with their degree of development and their ability to take their government in their own hands. We have had the example of the success of a scheme of this nature and its solution: We have the Bunga in the Transkei with which the Natives were satisfied, and in which, to a large extent, they had the government in their own hands, where they could live their own lives as part of the Native population in this country belonging together by reason of tribal and language affinity; and the evidence has always been — and it was also their own evidence — that they were happy. Instead of progressing in that direction and also extending that system to other areas and on the same basis, you simply go on and establish again a black nation. You are going further along that road. What we want is not suppression. The assertion that we follow a policy of suppression is untrue. We follow the principle of trusteeship, and a trusteeship which grants the Native an opportunity in his own area to live his own life and there to develop himself according to his capacities, to his competency and ability.

Just a few words about the last point I have mentioned in my motion and that is the offer which the Prime Minister has made to the Natives' Representative Council and which he has published officially and to which he also referred in the Speech from the Throne last Friday, and to put it into practice he is merely waiting until a few weeks' time when the

307

Natives' Representative Council will be constituted and he can consult them further about the matter. I must say that I was very surprised when I read that official statement by the Prime Minister, more in particular in view of the failure — which he himself admitted — which took place in regard to the Natives' Representative Council. He is continuing along the same road, instead of admitting the failure of his previous steps which went in the wrong direction. That offer by the Prime Minister has the same defect as the legislation of 1936. It calls into being one Native nation by means of a general representative council for all Natives in the country, however much they may differ from one another in tradition, in tribal organisation with separate characteristics and separate languages. He puts his seal of approval to the calling into being of one unified Native nation in this country, something which does not in fact exist. I must grant the Prime Minister the credit, if there is any credit in it, that this is not a new idea as far as he is concerned. It is an idea which he cherished many years ago. But at that time he was afraid of public opinion and for that reason he did not put it into practice. As far back as 1920 when the Native policy came under discussion in this House he said: "That conference of Natives, which is called together from time to time, should be further developed and ultimately it should become a Native Parliament." That he said in 1920. The speech he made in 1936 emphasised practically the same idea. We have now arrived at the position that what he at that time could not get the people to agree to, he is now trying to achieve by means of a majority which he obtained for other reasons, to force through, without consulting the people and for party political ends, a measure which will call into being a Native parliament, as he called it himself on a previous occasion. If the Prime Minister believes that this is going to be a solution of the colour problem and the Native problem, then I must say that I cannot regard him as anything else but a senseless and inveterate optimist. That will not solve the colour problem in this country but will merely aggravate it to a very serious extent. Does the Prime Minister believe that what he is now offering to the Natives will put a stop to their demands and insistent demands for further concession? No, it will not put a stop to it but will on the contrary encourage them owing to the success they have achieved, to make further demands.

What their further demands will be we already know. The Deputy-Prime Minister in the absence of the Rt. Hon. the Prime Minister overseas, wanted to make one further attempt to make the Natives' Representative Council resume its functions and to make them abandon the strike which they had commenced. The Deputy-Prime Minister met them. A report of the meeting was given and he did his very utmost to explain to the Native representatives there what the present Government had already done for them and what it still intended doing in the future. The Natives listened to him and told him that they would give their reply afterwards. What was the reply? The reply was: You have misunderstood us, we do

308

not really know what you are after; you came to tell us how much our conditions under the present Government have been improved; that is not what we want; we want nothing but the abolition of every colour bar in this country and we insist on being the equal in every respect of the European. And thereafter they continued with their strike. Does the Prime Minister believe that he will now satisfy them with his concessions? Not for a single moment. They know what they want and they will continue even more than in the past, also as a result of the concessions made, to make greater and greater demands. The body which he now wishes to call into being and to invest with such powers will very soon incite dissatisfaction and the making of all sorts of claims not only among the Natives in the Native areas, but also among the Natives who have become detribalised and who live in European areas. Just imagine, that body will obtain powers also in regard to urban Natives, the urban Natives in municipal areas. If those Natives are dissatisfied with what a municipality does or omits to do, where will they go to? To the municipality? No, to the Natives' Representative Council, and the location inhabitants in the various municipal areas will be incited by the Natives' Representative Council to make all kinds of impossible demands. Instead of solving the Native problem and facilitating it, you are going to aggravate it and make it immeasurably more difficult.

Finally I want to say that in my motion I mention that this offer by the Prime Minister will aggravate the Communist danger in South Africa, and that he will be assisting the Communist agitators in the country and will be assisting them considerably. That there is a Communist danger today has been admitted by the Prime Minister himself.

Towards the end of the previous session he stated in this House that a Communist agitation has taken root in the country and he said that the doctrine of Communism was a diabolical gospel. I am pleased that he sees it today. He did not always see the light when we saw it. At that time he had blindfolded himself. I now want to ask this: Can he supply the Communists with a better instrument in this country than a Natives' Representative Council with powers in the Native areas and with powers in the European areas, a Natives' Representative Council which creates a Black nation and then represents that Black nation? Can he place a better tool into the hands of the Communists?

We know the methods of the Communists. The method is to start from Russia and establish Communist Parties in the various countries. They are now doing so openly. The Comintern allegedly no longer exists. The Cominform I believe, the International propaganda office, which is in contact with the Communists in the various countries, aims at revolution. What was discovered in Canada? An inquiry was instituted there and a report was submitted which created an enormous sensation in Canada and throughout the world. The same thing happened in the United States of America. They discovered that spy services exist in the various countries and they aim at the encouragement of internal troubles in those countries and instigating revolution in those countries in order to prepare the way for a war which may possibly come. Does the Prime Minister want to make us believe that South Africa is an exception as far as that is concerned? They have excellent chances in South Africa with the Native population we have here and they can incite the Native population against the European population. Here they have a better opportunity to prepare a revolution than in many other countries of the world, and what does the Prime Minister do?

We notice that in some countries not only are Communist Parties being created, but even preliminary government machinery in order to be able to take over the reigns of government, as for instance in Greece. Now the Prime Minister comes along and creates a body, the Natives' Representative Council, as he defined it in his offer to that body. He calls into being a body representing all the united Native peoples and he grants them certain rights. I want to ask where Stalin and the Communists can look for a better instrument, a better means of ultimately achieving their aim in South Africa?

We are here as a responsible body, we have to decide here about the White civilisation in the country and about the position of the White man. We carry that responsibility and the people outside will call us to account in regard thereto, and all I ask is that in discussing this matter, it should be evident that we realise that responsibility.

7

CONFERENCE BETWEEN INDIA
AND SOUTH AFRICA

DR. D. F. MALAN, 31 AUGUST 1948[1]

AS FAR AS the Indian problem is concerned it is the first subject on
which he put a question, and he asked whether we were going to negotiate
with the Government of India. The question whether or not we shall
negotiate was brought up at the last General Assembly of UNO. The
resolution taken on that occasion by UNO is really that it was left to the
Union of South Africa and India to contact each other and in that way
to bring about a solution of the differences between them. This question
can be mentioned: Do we intend to treat with the Government of India
in regard to the differences that exist between us? My reply to that is
this: We are in fact prepared to do so; we do not mind holding a round-
table conference with India, but certainly not in such a way as to be tantamount to the intervention (" inmenging ") of India or of any other power
outside South Africa in our domestic affairs. I think that the then Minister, the hon. member for Salt River (Mr. Lawrence) who was at the last
General Assembly, gave an assurance that such negotiations would be
started; but when further questions were put to the Rt. Hon. the Leader
of the Opposition, who was not there himself but nevertheless took the
responsibility, about how such negotiations were proposed by him, his
answer was this (I gave special attention to his reply): That he is prepared to hold a round-table conference with the Government of India, but
on the basis of the conferences held in 1927 and 1932. If he wants negotiations with the Government of India, on that basis, I have no objection
to make.

At that time I was the Minister mainly responsible in this matter. I
myself drew up the documents that were exchanged between our Government and the Government of India, and I was chairman of the conference
that was held in Cape Town. I took good care that those discussions
would not in any way imply interference on the part of another country
with our country's domestic affairs. Accordingly, we only assented to our
having conversations with each other if it was to our country's advantage,
in so far that from the outset we could be assured that South Africa
would be able to gain something for itself at such discussions, and what

---

[1] Extract from speech by Dr. D. F. Malan, Prime Minister. *House of Assembly
Debates.*

we could gain was clearly set out beforehand as conditions, and these were that India should help us by way of assisting in connection with repatriation with a view to effecting an appreciable reduction in the Indian population in South Africa, if this was possible; and the whole of the negotiations and the Cape Town Agreement were based on this, that we would, with India's assistance, have repatriation, a thing we never previously had. That agreement which signified the suspension for a period of five years of legislation that we contemplated on the Indian question was an experiment. It was so described. I can also say this about it, that it did not tie our hands; even in the interim we could adopt such measures on the Indian problem as we deemed necessary. Only, as long as that agreement lasted, we were to advise India in advance of our proposals in reference to the solution of the Indian problem, in order that they might have an opportunity of making such representations to us as they considered necessary or desirable.

If a round-table conference can be held on that basis, and the Rt. Hon. the Leader of the Opposition has said that he is prepared that there should be one on that basis, I have no objection to it. I have no objection to advising the Government of India that should they again desire conversations on that basis we are agreeable, but on the clear understanding that it does not imply nor can it in such circumstances imply, outside interference in our domestic affairs.

SECTION V

CAPE COLOURED
REPRESENTATION

1

NATIONAL PARTY POLICY

DR. D. F. MALAN, 19 FEBRUARY 1936[1]

I WOULD LIKE to take the liberty of moving the following amendment to the motion[2] which is now before the joint sitting —

In line 2, after " Natives " to insert " and for the separate representation of Coloured people "; and in line 5, after " Natives " to insert " and Coloured people ".

If the amendment is passed the motion will read as follows —

That leave be granted to introduce a Bill to make special provision for the separate representation of Natives and for the separate representation of Coloured people in Parliament and in the Provincial Council of the Province of the Cape of Good Hope, and to that end to amend the law in force in that Province relating to the registration of Natives and Coloured people as voters for Parliament or a Provincial Council; to establish a Natives' Representative Council for the Union; and to provide for other incidental matters.

The effect of this amendment is that if the action contemplated therein is taken we shall have a Bill before this joint sitting not only for the separate representation of Natives in Parliament, but also for the separate representation of another group, namely, the Coloured people. I would like to make it quite plain at once, that in saying that I do not mean by it that by legislation of this kind any amendment will be made in the existing qualifications for the franchise on the part of Coloured people. In my opinion the existing qualifications will remain as they are. But I do not mean by this — I say it to remove all misunderstanding — that the Coloured people and the Natives should be taken together as one group, and be represented in Parliament as a joint group. What I mean is that there should be two separate groups acknowledged by the Bill for the purposes of the representation in Parliament, or rather let me say three separate groups, namely Europeans, Coloured people, and then the group (Natives) for whom provision is being made in the Bill now before us.

I would also like to say here why I am bringing up this matter for discussion on this occasion. The reason is that if we want to make any

---

[1] Speech by Dr. Malan, Leader of the Opposition, during the Joint Session of both Houses of Parliament, 19 February 1936.

[2] Introduced by General Hertzog, 14 February 1936, for leave to introduce a Bill for the Separate Representation of Natives.

amendment in our existing Acts in the direction I have indicated, then as far as I can judge it will have to be done in the same way as has been done in connection with Natives, i.e. a Bill to give separate representation to Coloured people will also have to receive the approval of the two Houses sitting together in a joint sitting. I would also like to explain that if the amendment is passed, then it need not delay the Bill which is now being moved, or the one which may still be introduced. The matter or matters which have to be dealt with during this session of Parliament need not be delayed, and for the reason that the Bill which is now being moved in connection with Natives draws the line between Coloured people on the one hand and Natives on the other. If the Bill, in the form that I am now suggesting, is passed, then there will be another border line required, and it is a border line at the other end of the group with which I am more particularly concerned here, the border line between the Coloured people and the Europeans.

Now, so far as this is concerned we know that preliminary work in that respect has already been done, by Bills already introduced into the House. But even apart from that the dividing line is in the ordinary legislation today in our administration of the country, and is already working. We have discrimination between White and Coloured people. In the franchise qualifications there are certain qualifications which apply to Coloured people and Natives, but those qualifications do not apply to Europeans. Therefore a clear line has already been drawn there, and not only there. The franchise has been granted to the European woman, but a line has been drawn between the European woman and the non-European woman. That is on the Statute Book. It is actually in force, and as far as we can follow the position up to the present it has never yet, so far as I know, given rise to any difficulty anywhere. Therefore if a select committee were to be appointed to implement the proposed Bill in the way I have indicated in my amendment, namely to make provision for separate representation in Parliament for Coloured people as well, then there is no need for it to lead to trouble, and no time worth mentioning need be spent on it, so that there need not be any delay of any kind in connection with this Bill which the joint sitting intends to pass. Now in introducing this amendment I would like to call to mind that the question of the Coloured people has already, from the start, been regarded as a part, an essential part, of the colour question in general in our country, with regard to representation in Parliament as well. In 1927, or even before that time when the Prime Minister brought up this so-called Native question, he gave this House the assurance time and again, and the people in the country as well, that the Native question and the question of the Coloured people had to stand together. On the occasion of his speech at Smithfield, he said very clearly that the Native question could not possibly be solved without the solution of the question of the Coloured people as well.

On the introduction of legislation by him it was regarded as dealing with questions that were inter-related. But not only that. Parliament itself regarded the matter in that way, and not only the House of Assembly, but both Houses of Parliament, and accordingly when a Joint Committee of both Houses of Parliament was appointed, instructions by way of a resolution of both Houses were given to that Committee to take into consideration both the Native question as well as the question of the Coloured people, and to make a report on them to both Houses. The position, as I understand the matter, is this, that the Government did not in any way carry out that mandate of the Joint Committee. So far as the Native Bill was concerned, the Joint Committee of both Houses made a report which was approved of — I think I am entitled to say so — by an overwhelming majority of the members, but it was removed from the Order Paper and the Government introduced a different Bill. The work of the Joint Committee which was done on the instructions of both Houses of Parliament over a period of nine years — two years on the instructions of the House of Assembly alone, and seven years on the instructions of both Houses — that work has simply been rejected by the Government. It is simply being entirely pushed aside, or practically pushed aside so far as the fundamental principle thereof is concerned, and the Government is introducing different legislation.

But so far as the question of the Coloured people is concerned, the Government has gone still further. While the Joint Committee of both Houses was sitting the Government notified them, by message, that it did not intend to proceed with any legislation in connection with the Coloured persons' question, and the Committee just assumed that in the circumstances its deliberations with regard to that question would be futile. Not only was the mandate of Parliament ignored by the message which was sent to the Joint Committee, but the mandate of Parliament was thwarted.

I would also like to say a few words on the matter itself, which I have brought up for discussion by way of my amendment. The first idea I want to express is the following: What it provides in so far as the representation in this House or in Parliament and in the Provincial Council of Coloured persons as a separate group is concerned, is nothing else than the logical sequence of existing legislation and of the new Bill which is now being moved in connection with the Natives. If we were to declare the Coloured people as a separate group for purposes of representation in Parliament, then we are not declaring anything new, then we are not introducing a brand new principle into our legislation, but then we shall be carrying through to its logical conclusion a principle which has already been acknowledged by legislation. It is, in fact, true that there is a distinction between Natives and Coloured people. To a great extent the Natives are still closely connected with their tribes. The Coloured people no longer have any tribal connection of that kind. It is indeed true that the Natives have their own territory in our country, which has been granted to them. There are reserves which already exist, and which it is proposed to extend. It is true that the Coloured people have no such reserves in our country,

317

no reserves which have been or can be granted to them. To that extent it is true there is a distinction, but that does not prevent our legislation for all that regarding the Coloured community as a self-contained and separate group which is dealt with separately from the Europeans. Just to mention a few of the things. So far as education is concerned, a clear line is drawn. You have schools for Europeans where Coloured persons are not admitted. You have schools which have been established for Coloured persons only, and where it is not possible for a European child to be admitted. The existing Act, the South Africa Act, has prohibited Natives from having a seat in the House of Assembly as well as in the Senate. In the same way it is prohibited for a Coloured person to have a seat in the House of Assembly or in the Senate. The Act which prohibits Natives obtaining the franchise in the northern provinces, also in the same way prohibits Coloured persons from obtaining the franchise there. So far as this is concerned, we have franchise qualifications, and as I have already shown, there is a clear dividing line drawn between the qualifications of Coloured voters and the qualifications of European voters. The Coloured voter has to comply with certain qualifications with which the European voter need not comply. The same also applies in the case of women's franchise. The European woman has the franchise, but the Coloured woman is excluded from it. Even this Bill which is being moved, and about which the Prime Minister has already made a statement, proposes that in the Provincial Council the Natives shall be represented by additional members, but that there also those Natives will be represented only by Europeans, and not by non-Europeans. Accordingly, there also you have the same distinction between the same groups, and so far as our legislation goes it is quite clear that we are not introducing a new principle when we classify the Coloured voter in a separate group, but that we are simply introducing this amendment, which is a logical application of what is already in existence and already acknowledged by our legislation.

But there is another matter that I want to emphasise, and it is this. Why is this Bill in connection with Natives being introduced in this joint sitting? It is because it is intended to establish such a relation between the races in the country, between the European race and the Native race, that you will also in future eliminate the colour question so far as they are concerned, from our party politics. You must arrange such relations between the races that the race question, the colour question, can be eliminated from our party political struggle. That is deep down so far as this matter is concerned, the actual intention of the Bill as far as I can see. But now my contention is this, that if the Native question is solved on this basis, and according to the Bill which has been moved, the one according to the Bill that is proposed and the other according to the Bill which will be moved in the place of it, then you have not yet attained that object. Then you have not eliminated the colour question from our political struggle. Everybody knows the history let me say of the last few years, or more particularly of the present year, and when he remem-

318

bers the by-elections that are being held and the political speeches that are made on various platforms, and even the difficulties that have arisen inside of the United Party at its congresses, then he will admit that it has more to do with the question of the Coloured people than it has to do with the Native question; and when we have solved the Native question then the other one will remain just as it is, and we ought for the same reason why we wish to solve the Native question, as Parliament and the mover intended it, to solve the question of the Coloured people, and to establish such relations that we shall be able to eliminate from our political struggle the question of colour in general in connection with the Natives and in connection with the Coloured people. And now the only way to do so, as far as I can see, is to go forward on the lines which our legislation has already taken; carry it out to its logical conclusion, and obtain for the Coloured people, as a separate group of their own, its representation in Parliament. Now we must, in connection with this matter, when we have to decide what the right thing to do is, allow ourselves to be guided by experience, so far as experience has been gained in other countries in this connection. The proposition that I want to lay down is this, that the question has caused no trouble in countries which are acknowledged as aboriginal countries, just let us say as Black men's countries, because the Europeans that are there are in a great minority, and the Europeans do not, in the last resort, have the ambition of governing the country to the exclusion of the aborigines who lived there. One example of that, I should say, is the Dutch Indies, where the Dutch Government from the very start, allowed no land to be owned by Europeans. Except in towns where they were carrying on business, Europeans could not own any land in the Dutch Indies. The land belonged to the aborigines, and according to the proclaimed policy of the Dutch Government they are engaged there in training up the aborigines in the public service and also in other ways, as quickly as possible for them to take over entirely the administration of that country on their own shoulders. It is a country which is admitted not to be a White man's country, and that it cannot be made a White man's country, and there no difficulty occurs. There are countries, on the other hand, which are regarded as White men's countries, and the population of aborigines is so small that it is not worthy of mention, and there also the question furnishes no difficulties. There the measure that I am proposing is not necessary either. One has a country like Australia where there actually is an aboriginal population, but that population does not obtain and does not need to obtain any representation in the legislative body as a separate group. But there are other countries where the solution that I am suggesting is actually applied. Let us take a country like Kenya.

In Kenya there are three distinct races which are all three represented in the Government of the country. There are the Europeans, who regard the country, at any rate to a great extent, as a White man's country. Then you have the Indian population there as well as the Native population. After all kinds of difficulties have arisen in connection with the question, and deputation after deputation had been sent to England, the solution was ultimately arrived at to give representation in the Legislative Council of Kenya to a certain number of Europeans, to a certain number of Indians, and a certain number of Natives. The representation of the Natives is small at the moment, but in proportion to their development the representation of their group will be increased; but there is one of the Dominions, namely New Zealand, where there is worthy of mention a considerable Maori population. New Zealand has years since arrived at the solution to give the Maoris their own separate representation in the New Zealand Parliament. And with what result? The result has been very happy. The result is that the friction between the races there in consequence of the colour distinction has become much less. Everyone is in his own group, and everyone remains in his own group, and we find, on the whole, that the best relations exist there and the best co-operation. I say we should allow ourselves to be guided by the experience of other countries. In the United States of America where there is a Coloured and Negro population worthy of mention, the same principle has been followed which still prevails in South Africa now. Can one say that the position there has been improved by their all having been placed on the same voters' roll? Can one say that the relations between the European and the Coloured elements have been improved there? No, just the reverse. The evidence is that the friction between the races has become much more serious, and there are areas, in the states, the southern states, where the Negro or the Coloured person actually has the franchise nominally, but where he dare not exercise it. If they get separate re-presentation and if they form their own group, then I am certain of it that they will bring about much improved relations, as is the case today in New Zealand.

We must allow ourselves to be led by the experience of other nations, and we must also allow ourselves to be guided by our experience here in South Africa. We have noticed here how in other than political matters there used formerly actually to prevail the state of affairs that you still find in political matters, namely that Europeans and Coloured people were regarded as one group, and it had ill-fated results. Not only for Europeans, but also for the Coloured people, and especially as regards the relation between the two. We had it in educational matters where there were originally schools for both. The solution that was arrived at was a separate school for each, each separate from the other. That has been to the advantage of both. We had it in ecclesiastical matters, not only in one church but in all churches where Europeans and Coloured persons sat together on the same church benches. That only gave rise to friction, and not only to friction but what possibilities were there for the Coloured people to stand on their own legs? They had to be satisfied with the back benches, and they always had a stamp of inferiority put on to them until, under the lead not of a Dutch-speaking, but of an English-speaking

320

Afrikaner, the principle of separate churches was laid down, and that had the best results for both races, and for the relations between the two races. Instead of competition, instead of friction, there came about on the side of the Europeans active assistance to the Coloured persons for raising themselves up in the world, and of standing on their own legs. And I say that if one is going to carry out the same principle, which is a sound principle, in political life, then the friction will disappear, and then the feelings of humiliation so far as the Coloured persons are concerned, will disappear. The Coloured person will get better control of his own interests in the Legislative Assembly than is the case now. Today he gets promises when an election campaign is proceeding, but when the election is over he is forgotten. He will be able to promote his interests better, and instead of friction we shall have co-operation, not only in political matters, but active assistance will also be given, and good relations will arise between the two races instead of friction. It is a sound principle, and it is the logical application of what we already have, and it is an element in the solution of our Coloured people's problem, which ought not to be dropped at this stage.

DR. T. E. DÖNGES, 25 APRIL 1951[1]

T H I S   B I L L of which I now move the second reading has a two-fold origin and a two-fold purpose. It primarily has its origin in the racial composition of our population, which is unique in this world, and in the determination of the White electorate of South Africa to perpetuate the White race in South Africa, in the interest not only of South Africa and the world, but also in the interest of the non-Europeans, as well as of the Europeans in our own country. It therefore constitutes part of the Government's apartheid policy. It is a further instalment in the carrying out of the mandate handed to this Government by the electors in 1948.

This Bill, however, also has its origin in the evils and dangers, actual as well as potential, to the Europeans as well as the non-Europeans contained in the existing system, evils which in the course of years have become more and more pronounced. This Bill, therefore, represents an effort to lay down a new political system, to devise a system which on the one hand will ensure the maintenance of White civilisation, and on the other hand will release the Coloured people from a system which in the past has been of no practical value to them and has had nothing but demoralising effects on their character, and has acted disruptively in their relationships with the White section of the population. That, Mr. Speaker, is briefly the two-fold purpose of this Bill, and I now wish to develop those two aspects somewhat further.

---

[1] Extract from speech by the Minister of the Interior, Dr. T. E. Dönges, in the House of Assembly, on the second reading of the Separate Representation of Voters Bill, 25 April 1951.

The racial composition of this country is well known to everybody. We have close on 9,000,000 Natives in this country, 1,000,000 Coloureds, 300,000 Indians and about 2,750,000 Whites. Ever since the introduction of representative government in South Africa the fear of political domination by the non-Europeans has hung like a dark cloud over this country. Responsible persons in the different provinces have to the best of their ability taken steps to tone down that danger as much as possible. Some have done so in a direct fashion, as for instance the Free State and the Transvaal. Others have devised formulas aiming at achieving the same object in an indirect manner — as in Natal for instance. The Cape has from time to time also made its contribution, in order to reduce as much as possible what it regarded as a danger. Of all the four original colonies, however, the Cape has been least concerned about the position, judging by the legislative steps taken to cope with it. After Union the danger was dealt with from time to time by a series of steps, which it is not necessary for me now to enumerate, the principal one of which, however, was taken in 1936 by the passing of the legislation of that year.

The potential danger of the Coloured vote, has however, persisted. Our position in South Africa is different from that of a country where there is a small Native population, as, for instance, in New Zealand. The mixed population which one finds there cannot by intermarriage with an indigenous population increase to such an extent as to endanger the ratio of the White population as against the Native population. The existing ratio is 17 to one.

For the same reason it will in the circumstances probably be possible in the course of time to have the mixed breed which may spring up there, absorbed by the Whites. In South Africa, however, the position is entirely different. Here we must always have these close on 9,000,000 Natives in the background. It is not just primarily the natural increase of the Coloured population which presents the greatest menace, even though that too is a situation which has to be taken into account. Potentially, therefore, the natural increase of the Coloured vote may constitute a menace to White South Africa, but the danger lies mainly in the fact that we have this tremendous Native reservoir which by intermarriage may potentially be responsible for the number of Coloured people in this country increasing. The possibilities are almost unlimited; in practice, even if it is not always legal, this does happen, especially while the Coloureds have no realisation of their own independent existence and have not developed any pride in what is their own. That possibility is also added to by the steady detribalisation and urbanisation of the Native population coupled with a depreciation in their self-esteem and their own pride. These are dulled by their continuous contact in the towns with the Coloured population. That is the position as far as this one aspect is concerned. We have a situation here which is unique in this world and in those circumstances we have to maintain White civilisation; and I say again, Mr. Speaker, this White civilisation must be maintained not in the interests only of the White people of South Africa, but I believe it is just as much in the interests of the non-European population of South Africa, and in the interests of the general good of South Africa itself that White civilisation here should be maintained.

It is no use telling us that we must wait until such time as the problem has unfolded itself to its full force and extent. Let me just remind hon. members that a former Parliament in 1936 considered this matter to be sufficiently serious — even though the number of Native voters on the electoral rolls of the Cape was only slightly over 12,000 — to convince it that we must take precautionary measures in regard to this matter. Steps were taken at the time and the position was not allowed to develop to such an extent as to render the solution so much more difficult. Consequently even in the circumstances prevailing in 1936 we were faced with a position which caused many people to feel concerned so that important steps in this respect were taken. In 1936 when there were only slightly over 12,000 voters on the Native voters' rolls in the Cape Province, there were people who realised how important this matter was, and I think it is apt to quote what a man like Mr. B. K. Long[2] had to say about it . . . (Interruptions) I might perhaps remind hon. members opposite of the fact that he was one of them in those days. He sat on the same benches with them.

This is what Mr. B. K. Long said about the Native vote, and this was in 1936 —

In some Cape constituencies, by that time, the Native vote had increased substantially and White candidates for election to the Union Parliament had practically to prostrate themselves to solicit these Native votes. Whichever candidate managed to secure them was more or less certain to be elected. This touting by White candidates for Native votes in Cape constituencies was very repulsive to Europeans not only outside the Cape Province.

That was the position when the total of Native voters on the voters' roll was only 12,000, and it is for that reason that I say that in matters of this kind we must face up to the potential danger, and a responsible Government and State must see to it that proper precautionary measures are taken, measures which will be timely, and that there is no waiting until the situation has developed to such an extent that it is difficult to carry out any steps of this nature.

I now come to the second part of what I have mentioned here and of what I want to develop somewhat further. The Coloured vote in the Cape has always been a sham and a fraud as far as the Coloured people are concerned. It has in actual fact not given them anyone to plead their cause in this House. During election time their vote has been canvassed in an improper manner, just as Mr. Long stated had happened in connection with the Native vote. All kinds of promises were made to the

---

2 *In Smuts's Camp*, Oxford University Press, 1945.

Coloured man at election times. Coloured voters were taken to the polls in Packard motor-cars, but the day the elections were over, the Coloured man was completely forgotten — and was left without practically any representation in Parliament. All promises made to him were conveniently forgotten.

DR. L. STEENKAMP: And does not the Nationalist Party forget its promises as well?

DR. DÖNGES: This Bill, on the contrary, has been introduced for the purpose of giving effect to an election promise which was made in 1948. The Coloured vote had been turned into a political football. It had been exploited by unknown forces which pretended that they controlled that vote and that they were prepared to promise it to a political party in return for certain rewards. I need not repeat my quotation of what Mr. Long in this connection said about the old system. It seems to me that hon. members opposite are aware of it.

MR. DU TOIT: It is ridiculous.

DR. DÖNGES: The hon. member should beware lest he become autobiographical.

DR. A. H. JONKER: And your party bought votes from the Coloured people at Kraaifontein.

DR. DÖNGES: For the moment the question of which side did it does not concern me. I am not accusing either side. But if hon. members opposite think that the cap fits them, by all means let them wear it. I am pointing to the evils attaching to that system, and if hon. members opposite get so fidgety about it, then it would appear to me that the cap fits them. Consequently, those unscrupulous leaders in their own group, and those political agents, have abused the Coloured people's votes — not for the good and in the interest of the Coloured people but in the interest of those corrupt leaders and of those political parties. The value of this vote has only been theoretical and imaginary to the Coloured man as an individual and as a community. It was a shadow and it had no substance.

MR. A. BARLOW: Who said that?

DR. DÖNGES: As the hon. member wants to know who also said it, I would refer him again to what Mr. Long wrote in his book. This is what he said —

I doubt very much in any case whether the vote, on the same register as the Whites, hasn't really been a curse to the Coloured people. It has given them an illusion of power which has never been anything but an illusion. They would have much more real influence in Parliament if they had direct representatives of their own there, as the Natives have. There are the germs of genuine representation, on a considerable scale, in that system, much as it has been condemned and denounced. The Coloured vote, in the same constituencies and on the same register as the White vote, has been little but a sham for all the years that it has existed. There is no future for it. Nothing is more certain than its disappearance as soon as it threatens to outnumber the White vote in any constituency, or to be strong enough to elect a candidate of its own to Parliament. It is getting near that stage now, and the day of its end is almost in sight. Apart from a shock to their dignity, the Coloured people will gain far more than they lose when it is abolished and something more genuine, if less superficially impressive, takes its place.

The former hon. member for Gardens (Mr. Long) who used to be editor of the *Cape Times* is not the only one to have written these things; nor is this all that has been said. There are other serious disadvantages connected with the old system, and among others there is this, that on account of this fear of political domination by the Coloured people, or even fear of wider political powers for the Coloured people, and the effect of such wider powers on the maintenance of White civilisation, even those who were well disposed towards the Coloured people, were unwilling to do their utmost for the educational, cultural and economic uplift of that section. On account of the fact that there was this fear in their minds of political domination, they felt that every step they took for the uplifting of the Coloured people was a step which would lead to the downfall of the White community. It is because of that that even the well-disposed White man refrained from doing what he could have done — it is because of fear of that political domination. Now it may be said that this was an imaginary fear. Whether it was an imaginary fear or not, that fear definitely existed in the minds of people, and it is a psychological fact which must be taken into account. It is for that reason that we say that if we stabilise the political rights of the Coloured people on a basis which will remove that fear, the White man will be more prepared than in the past to exert himself to uplift the Coloured people physically, economically and culturally. That is the position as far as the Coloured people are concerned. That is the position if one looks at the matter from the point of view of the Coloured people.

There is, however, a wider point of view as well which we have to assume. We must not only take account of the Coloured people in a matter of this kind. Apart from the fact that the franchise, the vote, has had no real significance to the Coloured people, as Mr. Long has shown, we must also take into account the fact that the existing system has detrimental effects on the country as a whole. The exercise of the Coloured man's franchise under the present system has caused continuous friction between him and the European, and between Europeans and Europeans among themselves. There has been continuous rivalry for their votes between the Europeans and between them. There has been continuous rivalry for registration. Attempts have been made to get people, who are not qualified, put on the voters' roll. Attempts have been made to get people who have been registered in that way removed from the rolls if they did not possess the necessary qualifications. There has been a continuous state of ferment, and this condition has caused trouble and friction. At every election the position has become worse, and it is a position which has been humiliating to the European, offensive to the Coloured and harmful to both.

Furthermore, in a constituency where the composition of the electorate was such that the Coloured voters could be the arbiters between the parties, we can well understand that it was self-evident that a feeling of aversion developed among the Europeans. They realised that not only did the Coloured people decide which party was to be elected in that particular constituency, but, in addition, they were the people who could determine which candidate was to secure the party nomination. In such conditions one can understand the sense of friction which such a state of affairs created between the Europeans among themselves, and between the Europeans and non-Europeans. These are not imaginary arguments. This is the experience of people with knowledge and experience of conditions in the Cape Province. Those who have taken an active part in politics can testify to it if they want to be honest.

I say that if the present system under which the Coloureds exercise their political rights is prone to these defects, defects which are detrimental to themselves, and also to the country as a whole, then surely that system needs to be reformed in the interest of the country as a whole, as well as in the interest of the non-Europeans and the Europeans separately. Such a reformed system will then have to comply with certain demands and conditions. If we want to turn it into a system which will not contain disadvantages for the non-Europeans, then it has to comply with certain conditions and certain demands, and the following are the requirements which I want to lay down.

I say that the reformed system must comply with certain requirements. In the first place it must be a system by which the relationship between the European and the Coloured people is improved by removing the points of friction or which eventually become the matter of fact, is part of the general policy of apartheid. One of the underlying principles of apartheid is to remove the points of contact which are the points of friction or which eventually become the points of friction. This also applies to political points of contact, just as it applies in any other respect. I say that the points of contact which can become points of friction must be removed as far as possible. A second demand with which the reformed system has to comply is that it must enable the Coloured man to exercise his political rights to a greater extent in his own interests, and in the interest of the country, than what the existing system allows him to do. The third demand is that it must lift the Coloured vote out of the party-political sphere, out of the position in which it is today where it is the football of political parties.

There is a fourth demand with which such a new system has to comply, and that is that it has to remove the abuses which have crept into the old system, and that it must also remove the evils attaching to the old system in respect of both the Europeans and Coloured people. The fifth demand is that the new system must place the Coloured vote beyond the zone of fear, so that the European can advocate the uplift of the Coloured community, and can promote it without having to entertain the fear that he is making a noose for his own neck. In other words, the menace of domination, no matter how improbable it may be considered to be, must be removed. It must be clear that stability is being achieved, and I say that only if those requirements are complied with, only then will a system such as that which we are now proposing in this Bill be a real improvement.

Now let me come to the system contained in this Bill to see to what extent it complies with the demand. It is not difficult to devise a system which will comply with the demands, because as a matter of fact such a system was adopted in principle years ago in connection with the Natives in relation to whose franchise these same evils and dangers prevailed. I just want to say a few words now about the principle of separate representation in itself. It is interesting, Mr. Speaker, to study the arguments of the South African Native Affairs Commission from 1903-1905, and to compare these with arguments which have for a long time been adduced in respect of Coloured people, and which in regard to them are just as true as they were in regard to the Natives at the time when this report was written. I refer to paragraph 441 —

> The Commission arrived at the conclusion that the possession of the franchise by the Natives under the system existing in the Cape Province, which permits it being used in a spirit of rivalry with an antagonism to the European electorate, which makes the organised Native voter the arbiter in any acute electoral struggle between electoral parties, and which as the Native voters increase numerically will enable them to outvote the Europeans in certain parts of the country, is going to create an intolerable situation and is an unwise and dangerous thing.

That same argument is applicable to the Coloured vote. At the stage when this recommendation was made, and even thereafter, at the time of the coming into being of Union, the number of Native voters was very small — only one quarter of what the Coloured vote is today. But these facts, which are stated here are not just what Mr. Long says today about the Coloureds; these are facts which in the past 50 years have been the experience of this country. These things are still just as true today as they were in those days. I turn over to paragraph 442 —

> On the other hand the Commission recognised that it was unnecessary and impracticable to take away the franchise from the Native where they already had it. All that is needed being to change the manner in which it should be exercised.

And then they go on to say that this should be done throughout the country, and not in just one part. This was the Inter-Colonial Commission. And then they went on to say —

It is likely to be advantageous to the State, and conducive to their contentment to give them the same privileges as elsewhere in South Africa; provided this can be done without conferring on them political power in any aggressive sense, or weakening in any way the unchallenged supremacy, and authority of the ruling race which is responsible for the country, and bears the burden of its government.

MR. RUSSELL: The burden of government?

DR. DÖNGES: Yes, Mr. Speaker, that is a burden which hon. members opposite are only too anxious to undertake. And then it goes on —

Having arrived at these conclusions, the Commission had little difficulty in deciding upon the system which it would recommend for adoption in order to attain the objects in view . . . The central idea of the scheme, in favour of which there is entire unanimity between the members of the Commission, is separate voting by Native electors only for a fixed number of members to represent them in the legislatures of the country, with the same status as other members; the number and qualifications of such members to be settled by each legislature; the number not to be more than sufficient to provide an adequate means for the expression of Native views and the ventilation of their grievances, if any, and not to be regulated by the numerical strength of the Native vote . . .

I shall tell the House a little later who the people are who say this. In the meantime I just ask for hon. members' attention so that they may hear the facts. Then they go on in the next paragraph where they say this —

Among the results hoped for from the change are:

I only want to quote a few of these —

The avoidance of racial strife, on the inevitableness of which under the existing system in the Cape Colony the Commission has already dwelt.

The freeing of all questions affecting the betterment of the Natives from any considerations of consequent increase in their political power, and from the resulting hostility to measures conducive to their progress and improvement on the part of any Europeans otherwise friendly to the Native cause.

The direct representation of Native views and interests by members elected by the Natives themselves, and by them alone, which has never hitherto been the case.

And so it goes on, and then the Commission anticipates an objection which may be made. It says that some people will raise the argument that even if there are a number of representatives of the Natives in Parliament, there will be rivalry among the parties in Parliament for their support — their support will be courted by the various parties, and in regard to that objection the Commission says this —

It is true that there will still be political influences at work among the Natives, and party candidates will still compete with each other for their votes, but the Commission has sufficient confidence in the political sagacity of the Natives to believe that they will not become the mere tool of parties, but will speedily realise their responsibilities and, appreciating their opportunity when returning a member for themselves, will choose that member wisely.

(Interruptions.) I assume that these interruptions constitute a general vote of no confidence in the members representing the Natives —

The votes of their members in the respective legislatures will still count in a division and will be sought for by contending parties but, whatever party triumphs may result from their votes, there will not arouse such racial hatred as must come in time from the system which makes the Native voter a political dictator in local elections.

Now let me tell the House who these people are who have signed this report, who have unanimously made these recommendations, and hon. members will see, if they need any proof, that the principle of separate representation does not mean any injustice; they will find proof of that fact in the statement of these people. The chairman of that Commission was Sir Godfrey Lagden; among his members he had Colonel W. E. Stanford, he had a man like Sir Thomas Scanlen and a man like Sir Herbert Sloley. These are all people of whom one can say that they were Liberals, but even they actively recommended a system of separate representation for the Natives, because they considered this to be in the best interests of the Natives.

I am only using this analogy as proof of the fact that separate representation in itself was not regarded even by recognised Liberals and friends of the Natives as inappropriate or as degrading for non-Europeans, but that it was recommended as being in the interest of those non-Europeans.

This Bill now before the House does not go as far as that, nor is it in every respect comparable with the 1936 Act, but the system of separate representation is a common ground for both the recommendations of this commission and also for the legislation which was introduced in 1936, and it is for that reason that I say that this system of separate representation is a system very strongly recommended by these two separate bodies, viz. the South African House of Assembly in 1936 and the 1905 Commission, that it was regarded by both these bodies as acceptable for the non-Europeans.

Now let us pause for a while at the 1936 legislation. The hon. member for Claremont (Mr. S. F. Waterson) who spoke here the other day said that what was objected to was the question of method. Let me ask hon. members opposite this. This 1936 legislation embodied a system of separate representation. Is that system something detrimental, or something pernicious to the non-Europeans? Is it something immoral? If it is immoral then surely it cannot be remedied by being agreed to by a two-thirds majority. Hon. members are entitled to say that it is the method which is wrong, but then they must not come and say that there is some-

329

thing wrong with the content of this legislation, because if they do say that, then they belie, they condemn their own action in 1936 when they voted for the content of legislation which embodied the same system of separate representation. It cannot be argued that these people who were members of this commission, or that those who voted for the Bill in 1936, were people who in principle would be prepared to accept a system which would do anything that was unjust to the Natives of South Africa. Just as little can that be said about the separate representation which prevails in New Zealand today. The principle, the system, is identical, although naturally there are many differences between the legislation in New Zealand and the legislation embodied in this Bill before the House.

I want to say just a few words about the position in New Zealand. In New Zealand under the 1852 Constitution the Maoris had in theory identically the same franchise as the Europeans, but in practice, according to an official document —

. . . they remained virtually unrepresented until 1867. In 1867 the Maoris were given four representatives and some of them who owned land individually obtained a sort of double vote.

MR. BARLOW: The Maoris sit in Parliament.

DR. DÖNGES: That, however, was abolished in 1893, and I am very sorry that the interruptions of the hon. member for Hospital (Mr. Barlow) were not also abolished in that year. Some of the Maoris were then given the right to come on the European voters' rolls, but that provision was also abolished in 1896. Today the position in New Zealand is that the Maoris have separate representation. In a House of 80, they have four representatives, the same number as they were given in 1867. They have their own representatives there. Those representatives are Maoris themselves, or rather let me say they can be Maoris. That is how it is applied there, but I am speaking of the principle of separate representation. The representatives of the Maoris in New Zealand are elected in the same way as the representatives of the Europeans, but they are not elected on the same day. The election for the four Maoris takes place on a different day from the general election for the White representatives, and a Maori of mixed parentage can, if he so desires, have his name put on the Maori list or on the European list, but if a half-Maori again marries a Maori, then he has to go back onto the Maori list. That is the principle which is applied there.

In regard to the system of separate representation, we have three instances before us. We have that of the Inter-Colonial Commission of 1905, which I have mentioned. We have the example of the position in New Zealand; we have the example of what our own Parliament did in 1936, and I contend that those three examples prove that the system of separate representation does not constitute an injustice either to the Europeans or to the Coloureds. As regards the content, therefore, it cannot be regarded as assailable. In regard to the method, I have already on two previous occasions stated that this Bill does not clash with Section 35 even if that section should still be of full force and effect. Consequently, also as far as method is concerned, it is thoroughly constitutional.

I want to add just one further argument to those which I have already put forward, and this is the considered opinion of a man of very high repute in the whole of the Western Province, a man who as the result of his lifelong residence in the Western Province has acquired a special knowledge of Coloured affairs and who therefore is in a special position to be able to speak with authority on a subject such as this. I refer to ex-Judge H. S. van Zyl, and I just want to state what he said after his years of experience — he is not a man who has lived in the Free State or the Transvaal but a man who has grown up and lived here in surroundings where the greatest concentration of Coloured votes is found, and this is what he said —

Therefore, the removal of Coloured voters from the Common Roll, even without a two-thirds majority, would, in my opinion, be in accordance with the spirit of the Act of Union.

Here we have an authority whom I am sure hon. members opposite would have liked to have quoted themselves. I have now saved them that trouble. I have quoted it. What makes it extremely bitter to hon. members opposite is the fact that these, actually, are words which were recorded in a Press interview with the *Cape Times*. I really think that this is an instance of " adding insult to injury " as far as hon. members opposite are concerned.

Now I want to come to the main points of the Bill itself. First of all I want to point out that the Bill does not touch any voter's qualifications for the franchise. If hon. members opposite read the Bill they will see that there is nothing in it touching the franchise qualifications. Nobody today on the voters' roll for the House of Assembly or the Provincial Council is deprived of the franchise, and anyone who in future obtains the requisite qualifications will be entitled to be placed on the voters' roll. The basis of division between European and non-European voters which exists today will continue. This Bill does not introduce a new basis of classification. It is the identical basis of classification which has always existed so far. The existing voters' roll of the Cape Province, which as hon. members know, consisted of three parts, is now split into two. That is all that happens, and the individuals whose names appear on one list will now vote only for their own representatives in the same way as those whose names are on the other list vote for their own representatives. Every group has its own Members of Parliament to represent that group in Parliament. The number of representatives is more or less in accordance with the number of voters in each group. On this basis the Coloured people get four representatives in the House of Assembly and one in the Senate, and the Europeans fluctuate in number in the House of Assembly, dependent on the Union quota.

The ratio between the European representatives and the Coloured representatives in the House of Assembly will remain constant, 150 to 4.

The number of 150 has been pegged under the South Africa Act, and that is why the number of four is also being pegged down. This is a very important provision in order to secure stability because otherwise if there were the possibility of a change we would again be transferring to another sphere the likelihood of such friction and discord as has prevailed in the past. It is exactly in order to remove this constant friction that we are now pegging the ratio and as the number of White representatives is limited, so the number of non-European representatives is also limited.

The powers of these four representatives in the House of Assembly will be identical to those of the 150, except that they will not be members of the Electoral College for the election of Senators, and this of course is right, because in practice it means absolutely nothing to them under existing circumstances. Under no conditions, even if they have the right to be members of the Electoral College, would they be able to elect a single Senator. As a result of their numerical strength they are not able to elect a single Senator. But they are compensated for this by the appointment of one Senator, and this is considered necessary in order to give them a direct mouthpiece in the Other Place. In the Provincial Council of the Cape the Coloured people will have two representatives, and the existing position under Section 70, sub-section (2) of the South Africa Act will be maintained here. That is all we are doing here in regard to the question of who can represent them in the Provincial Council. We must, however, remember that the right to vote for the election of members of the Provincial Council has never been an entrenched right in the South Africa Act. The franchise for the Provincial Council is not protected under Section 35, and it is for that reason that the number of members they will get in the Provincial Council will not be identical to what they will get in the House of Assembly. I also just want to point out that the ratio which they will have in the Provincial Council, viz. two out of 59 in actual fact is proportionately a larger representation than they will have in the House of Assembly, viz. four out of 163.

Then, their representatives in the Provincial Council will have the same powers as other members of the Provincial Council, except, as I said, that they will not be members of the Electoral College for Senators. The compensation which they are to be given in place of that, will again be in the form of the appointment of one Senator to look after their interests in the Senate. In Natal the Coloured people who are at present registered will retain their franchise but no new ones can qualify. This is in accordance with Section 35 (2) of the South Africa Act. But it is not only in accordance with that Section of the Act, it is also in accordance with the historical tradition of Natal which has followed the direction of the Transvaal and the Free State, and not that of the Cape. First of all, if hon. members will recollect, the Native, and subsequently, in 1896, the Indian too, had the franchise taken away from him in practice by legislation in Natal. Afterwards, this was also extended to the Municipal franchise in respect of Indians in the years 1922 and 1924. I do not want to say much about this aspect of the matter, because other members on this side of the House will go further into the historical tradition of Natal on the non-European vote.

Another important provision in the Bill is that in respect to the Coloured Council. The Council will consist of three nominated members to give representation to the three northern provinces, and of eight members to be elected by the four constituencies in the Cape. The difference between the Coloured Council and the old Coloured Advisory Council of the previous Government is particularly in two respects, and the first difference is that this Council will consist of people the majority of whom will be elected instead of all being nominated, as was the case in the previous Advisory Council. The second respect where it differs from the previous Council is that this Council will not have merely advisory functions. Provision is made, as hon. members will notice in the Bill, for them also to be able to have certain administrative functions. My ideas as to what those specific functions will be have not yet been crystallised, but I want to leave the opening, and the opening has been left and I hope that by means of the Council itself and by means of the Commission of Coloured Affairs we shall be able to get ideas which it will be possible to apply in order to give the Council a degree of administrative authority and administrative functions.

MR. BARLOW: That will be a colossal failure.

DR. DÖNGES: The hon. member has probably been asleep. The Coloured Advisory Council has, as he says, been a colossal failure, but it is no longer there. The hon. member has only just woken up to that fact. I definitely say this, that there is a great field for this Coloured Council in the sphere of housing, health and labour supply and the combating of social evils. If this Council is motivated by the right principles in respect of the uplifting of their own people they will be able to perform a very useful function. I am thinking, for instance, of such a serious social evil as drunkenness among the Coloured people. If this Council will make it one of its duties to devise means to combat that evil and to save their own people from the consequences of drunkenness, I think they will be able fully to justify their existence. I hope they will be able to do useful work in that respect.

Then finally there is the sub-department of Coloured Affairs. Here, too, we are still feeling our way. We have appointed a Commissioner of Coloured Affairs. We have been fortunate in securing the services of a man, who, I think, inspires general confidence. The underlying idea of that department is that of co-ordination. It will be a division which will be specifically concerned with Coloured affairs. The Council will make investigations; it will co-ordinate and it will have to sponsor the Coloured people with the various departments from whom the necessary assistance will have to be obtained. Under this system, which we are now introducing, there will therefore be three channels between the Government and Coloured population. The first channel is that of the representatives in the Senate and the House of Assembly and the Provincial Council. A second channel is the Coloured Council, and a third channel is the sub-department of Coloured Affairs. There we have the machinery. But whether that machinery is going to be successful or not will, to a large extent, depend on the attitude of the Coloured people themselves. If they want to avail themselves of that machinery, it will be there at their disposal.

MR. KAHN: They will not.

DR. DÖNGES: I know that many people have begun to think about these matters. I know that there are many who are no longer prepared to allow themselves to be led by the nose by individuals who have come here with foreign ideologies and who are looking after their own interests and not after the interests of the Coloured people. I know that some of them are still being misled, but I think — and I have proof of this — that there are many Coloured people who are beginning to look at matters in a different light and who realise that the true friends of the Coloured community are not always those who pretend to be their friends. In the past the Coloured Advisory Council devoted too much of its attention to political questions. It was intent on exploiting every possibility to secure political equality in this country, and that interfered with its usefulness, to a large extent. I hope that the new council will look more to the practical problems which will promote the welfare and the happiness of the Coloured community as well as the good relationship between themselves and the Europeans.

Those are, in general, the main traits of this Bill, and now in conclusion I want to make a few general remarks. From the arguments, from the grounds which have been adduced by me in the course of these debates, during the first and second and the third debates, I think there are five doctrines which we can now lay down as having been proved. The first is that the principle or the system of separate representation is morally unassailable. The second contention which I want to lay down is that the method applied to this Bill to make this system law in this country, is constitutionally in order in view of the fact that it does not clash with the letter of Section 35 and that it is in accordance with the spirit of Section 35 as testified by Ex-Judge van Zyl. The first proposition which I want to put forward is that in any case it is within the powers of this Parliament to lay down its own procedure, to pass a law the contents of which are morally unassailable. I feel that by rejecting the motion of the hon. Leader of the Opposition this House has unequivocally declared that this is the procedure it prefers, and which it proposes in order to get this legislation placed on the Statute Book. But there is a further proposition which I want to put forward, and that is that the great majority of the electorate fully support this Bill. It will be remembered that petitions were signed in 1938 when people were not yet as ripe for legislation of this kind as they are today. It will be remembered that a petition was presented by the Leader of the Opposition, the present Prime Minister, to which he referred the other day, a petition signed by more than 230,000

White electors of South Africa, many of them — I would almost say a large proportion of them — English-speaking electors. Now the hon. member for Cape Flats (Mr. Du Toit) comes here and also presents a petition. All that fuss, all those loudspeakers which paraded the streets to stir up people — after all those misrepresentations, only 100,000 signatures were secured.

It has also been proved by the general election of 1948 and the Provincial elections of 1949, not only by the figures recorded, but also by the proof which I brought forward the other day, that some of the most prominent people elected in 1948 elections have said farewell to that party, because they were not prepared to support this principle. I said that if that could be said about the green wood of that party, what then about the dried-out wood. There are thousands and tens of thousands among the United Party who support this Bill.

AN HON. MEMBER: And many of them sit in this House.

DR. DÖNGES: I do not exclude those United Party members who sit in this House. There is growing support for the measure among members of the United Party. One only has to read some of the letters which are published in the English newspapers today which state that the United Party should understand that the apartheid policy of this Government, and to wit, this Bill, has the support of a large section of their own members. It is not only among the Europeans that the Bill is supported to an increasing extent; among the Coloured people too, among those who are intelligent, and who do not take a prejudiced view of the matter, there are many who are beginning to realise that this Bill will mean a great deal more to them than the system under which they have been suffering all those years.

MR. KAHN: That is those who can be bribed.

DR. DÖNGES: They are the Coloured people who will not be deceived by men like the hon. member for Cape Western (Mr. Kahn). An artificial resistance is being built up today, and I contend it is nothing more than artificial. Look at the people who are inspiring this resistance, they are the Kahns, they are the Carnesons, they are the Gools and the Dadoos. They are the people who are applying their well-known technique in order to mislead individuals, to make them the dupes of their policy, and then in the long run, after they have followed the advice of those people, will have to pay the piper; it will not be those shouters who crow such a lot who will have to take the consequences, but the people who have followed their advice.

There is a fifth proposition which I want to put forward and that is that a moral obligation to the future of South Africa rests upon us to get this legislation passed. Under all the circumstances which I have enumerated I feel I can safely say that I agree with the late General Smuts, who last year in this House stated that this Government would be guilty of an act of fraud towards the electorate of South Africa if it failed to introduce this kind of legislation. I entirely agree with the then Leader of the Opposition.

As a Government we readily recognise our obligations to the Coloured community but that recognition does not give us the right to be indifferent or unfeeling towards the interests of the White community. If we look at their interests we also have to look at the interests of the White people, and even less does that recognition give us the right not to act in the interest of what we regard as being the cardinal interest in the whole of South Africa, viz. the maintenance of White civilisation in South Africa. We would be seriously failing in our duty, we would be failing in our moral duty, if we neglected to take the necessary steps to give effect to that highest interest.

It is with the definite conviction that this Bill is calculated to serve this highest interest of South Africa that I now have the honour to move the second reading of this Bill.

2

UNITED PARTY POLICY

PROGRAMME[1]

1. THE POLICY of the United Party in relation to the Cape Coloured people is based on the recognition of the special position which the Coloured people occupy in our multi-racial society and of the desirability of raising the standards and improving the living conditions of the Coloured people.

2. In regard to political rights, the United Party reaffirms the principle laid down by General Hertzog " that the Coloured people are not to be deprived of their existing political rights and (the United Party) will resist any proposals to change their franchise in a manner that would diminish these rights ".

3. In regard to economic status, the United Party will continue to foster wider opportunities for employment, and stands for the principle that Coloured people at the Cape shall not by reason of their race or colour be debarred from engaging in any form of industrial occupation or employment, and for the provision of facilities for their vocational training. The United Party will take steps to ensure that they will be provided with proper amenities in connection with their employment in factories.

4. In regard to social status, the United Party, recognising that the maintenance of social separation is in accordance with the desire of both Coloureds and Europeans, stands for the improvement and increased provision of housing, educational, social and health amenities for the Coloured people, in such a manner as to stimulate, on a voluntary basis, the development of separate Coloured residential areas, with powers of local self-government for such areas and the conduct of the various administrative, civic and other services in such areas by Coloured people themselves.

---

1 Taken from a pamphlet issued by General Smuts as Leader of the United Party as the declared policy of the party. Johannesburg, not dated, but probably 1949 or 1950.

THE MINISTER has gone out of his way to explain to us that this Bill means another instalment of the policy of apartheid. He has gone out of his way in his argument, at great length, to show the House that what is proposed to be done under this Bill is to segregate the Coloured people from the rest of our community completely as far as their political rights are concerned. That being so and particularly because the Minister has tried to show that separate representation for these people would involve no injustice — he said that it was " moreel onaanvegbaar "[3] — I would like to bring to the notice of the House the promises and the undertakings and the pledges that have been given by outstanding leaders of the other side to the Coloured people with regard to this very question of segregating the Coloured people. Sir, these pledges have been given in the past by the present Prime Minister, these pledges have been given in the past by the previous Prime Minister, the late General Hertzog, both when he was the Leader of the Old Nationalist Party, when the hon. the Minister of Finance (Mr. N. C. Havenga) was his colleague and his close supporter, and on other occasions. I think it is right, in view of the point made by the Minister, to indicate to the House the kind of promises that have been given and to show how completely hollow is the claim that there is morally nothing wrong with segregating the Coloured voter in this country. Let us call as the first witness, Sir, to give the lie to the claim made by the Minister of the Interior, the present Prime Minister, who said this—

The European, in the three Northern Provinces is accustomed to look with pity upon the Cape Province with its large number of enfranchised Coloureds . . . but by virtue of the fact alone that he (the Coloured person) has adopted the civilisation of the European and speaks the language of the European, and has the same interests to defend against the Native, he can also and will also, with proper enlightenment and sympathetic treatment, become the bulwark and the defence of the European and his civilisation. When the Northern Provinces will be struggling with anxiety against the dire consequences of the Native question, the Cape Province will be protected by the circumstances I have mentioned.

I hope the hon. the Prime Minister listens to these solemn words that he spoke. That is the pledge given by the Prime Minister: No segregation for the Coloured people. No, they speak our language, they live the same life as we do, no segregation for them. I think the Prime Minister will remember and I think the hon. the Minister of Finance will remember a pamphlet which was issued under the significant title of " Die Witman se Pand " (" The White Man's Pledge "). It was prepared by the late

---

[2] Extract from speech by Mr. J. G. N. Strauss, Leader of the Opposition, during the debate in the House of Assembly on the second reading of the Separate Representation of Voters' Bill, 25 April 1951. *House of Assembly Debates.*
[3] " Morally unassailable ".

Senator Langenhoven and J. H. Conradie, M.P. — I think he was the member who became Administrator, the late Mr. Conradie. This pamphlet was issued in 1949 (*sic*) on behalf of the Federal Council of the Nationalist Party and there we have this—

Except for an amendment which is being proposed by the North, the scheme of General Hertzog draws him into the orbit of the Europeans, so that a line of demarcation arises between the White man and the Coloured on the one hand and the Native on the other hand. The reasons advanced for this scheme are that the Coloured person has not, like the Native, preserved the language and the customs and racial identity of his aboriginal ancestors (the one side of his descent), but has accepted those of the White man as being more in accordance with his nature. As far as is possible in the circumstances he has identified himself with the Europeans; nowhere is he living apart; he does not feel that he has been separated; as far as a decent standard of living and behaviour and education are concerned he is approaching more and more those of the European.

And then these significant words which, as I hope, the hon. the Prime Minister will note and which, I believe, he will remember—

Their number is of decisive importance in quite a number of constituencies, but they have never yet made themselves felt in a separate racial policy or with separate racial consciousness. And he has his interests in common with those of the White man.

In other words, Sir, all these statements indicate very clearly that the old Nationalist Party, the Prime Minister himself individually, regarded the Coloured people of this country as being one with the White people politically, that segregation was to come but had to apply to the Natives — they had to be placed on the one side and the Coloured people and the Europeans had to be placed on the other side together, but not segregated politically, as the Minister of the Interior admits he proposes to do in this Bill.

MR. SUTTER[4]: Was Mr. F. C. Erasmus Secretary[5] then?

MR. STRAUSS: Well, I expect he had something to do with it. Then I have a few further revealing quotations from the speeches that were made during the joint session in February 1929, and here is one by the late General Hertzog who said this—

While the Native is one who is at home in the countryside, is one who lives tribally, and under tribal law, is also a stock farmer, and is, in addition, of a race which is entirely separated and has nothing in common, in language, or otherwise with Europeans, there is the Coloured person in our midst, right amongst the Europeans.

That is where the Coloured person stood according to late General Hertzog. And he continued—

[4] United Party.
[5] Secretary of the National Party in the Cape Province.

While the Native has his own language, the Coloured person has the European language as his mother tongue, stands practically on the same basis, surrounded by the same circumstances, and he practically breathes the same civilisation, and all that goes with it as the White man. To take that man therefore and to identify him from without by political action with the Native . . .

That is what the Minister now proposes doing —

. . . is to my mind completely in conflict with the interests of the Coloured people.

I now come back to the Prime Minister and I want to remind him of what he said during the joint sitting of 1929. He said the following, completely in contrast with what the Minister says he is now doing in this Bill —

. . . what we propose here is to draw a distinction, with the Natives on one side and the Coloured people on the other, as regards political rights, so that they shall share entirely in the Cape, and to a great extent in the Northern Provinces the same political rights as the European. That is what we propose, and what hon. members opposite are opposing in principle . . .

That is in Hansard, 1929. It will be up to the Prime Minister, whose words I have quoted, to say why he is in default today as far as those grave words are concerned, to say why he is not able today to suit his action to his words and why instead he is acting completely contradictory to the words that he uttered then. I come to the late General Hertzog, who spoke in 1936 at Smithfield, and I hope that the hon. the Minister of Finance will pay heed to what his late Leader said.

MR. HAVENGA: Yes, General Hertzog said that this leaves me without any honour now? (*sic*)

MR. STRAUSS: Well, Sir, I really don't know what to make of the Minister of Finance, because here I come, as is my duty, in view of the claims made by the Minister of the Interior, in view of the line taken by him, in view of what he proposes to do in this Bill, to which my hon. friend is a party — he is the main party — it is the Malan-Havenga agreement — I come along and quite objectively and dispassionately I quote a speech by the late General Hertzog and my friend's retort to that is: Because General Hertzog said that, you will say that I am without honour.

MR. HAVENGA: Not that you are going to say that. You have said so.

MR. STRAUSS: No, Sir, I am quite prepared to quote quite objectively what the late General Hertzog said and I am prepared to leave it to my friend's own conscience and I am prepared to leave it to his own judgment whether he will get up in this House and will tell us the reasons why he doesn't agree today with what the late General Hertzog said. I am not here to make personal accusations against my hon. friend. I think he will find, if he looked at everything that I have said, that I have a certain duty in this matter and I have dealt with the merits of this case. I am not concerned with him personally. He knows that.

I dealt with the matter as I saw the Minister's conduct. I have nothing against him personally, but I have to state the matter as I see it, seriously, in the interests of the country. Now, Sir, this is what the late General Hertzog said. My friend may not like to be reminded of it, but I have a duty in this matter —

The political activities of the purified politicians[6] not only mean a systematic incitement to dissatisfaction and dissension of certain classes of our populaton; it is also a deliberate incitement which ultimately can only lead to anarchism and anarchy among the unfortunates who become their dupes.

Nothing in their behaviour, however, is more detestable than the manner in which they are busy throwing overboard all sense of honesty in their attitude towards that section of our population which does not possess any voting value for them. There is a lack of sense of honour and magnanimity in this purified behaviour which gives rise to great despondency and which to us as an Afrikaans-speaking people is the more shameful because of the close link which exists between the leaders of the purified party and our churches. The same shameful lack of faith and loyalty to the given word is found with the purified population in their dealings with other sections of our population.

They are for instance today engaged in attempts to deprive the Cape Coloured person against his will and wishes of the right, which he has enjoyed all these years, to be registered on the same list with the Europeans, and that notwithstanding their repeated promises to the Cape Coloureds that they would maintain that right when we would succeed, as we have done, in segregating the Native.

He said that in 1936, immediately after the segregation legislation had been passed here at a joint sitting in 1936, and he then referred to the fact that the Government of the day had succeeded with the assistance of the Coloured vote to effect the segregation of the Native —

This unfaithful behaviour is only a result and expression of the general type of faithlessness which has characterised the leadership of purified nationalism since the first moment of its purified existence.

Originating from the impure atmosphere of untruth, faithlessness and political intrigue, this purified nationalism had from the first hour of its existence carried in itself the seeds of its origin. If, therefore, it is showing more and more infidelity and lawlessness in its actions today, it is merely obeying the law of heredity dictated to it by nature. Now my friend, the Minister of Finance, has heard the words, the

6 The reference is to Dr. Malan's National Party of 1936.

robust words, of a man of honour, his former Leader, the late General Hertzog. I leave it to him to deal with that. I prefer to make no comment. My friend has become very touchy about it and I leave it to him. I come to the other great speech that the late General Hertzog made, also at Smithfield. We remember those great, considered pronouncements that he had the habit of making in his own constituency, and I quote from his speech of 5 April 1938 —

A more serious breach of faith than the one of which these purified leaders of a purified party have made themselves guilty in this matter, can hardly be imagined. Their breach of the given word is nothing less than a blot on the fair name of the White man in South Africa.

There you have it. Those promises were solemnly made to the people and here we have General Hertzog's statement about this breach of faith, this breaking of the given word, this violation of the honour of the White man.

And he continues —

In other words, directly in conflict with the promise we gave the Coloured person when we needed his vote for the passing of segregation legislation for the Natives, we will now, after the Segregation Act has been passed, go along and apply both political and economic segregation against the Coloureds. What treachery, what infidelity.

I should like to hear what the Minister of Finance has to say about that —

What would become of the honour of the Afrikaner if it had to depend on the political morals of the purified party and its parliamentary leaders? All the election slogans elevated by the leaders of the purified party to the status of policy, are nothing but so many attempts to mislead the electorate, simply radiating insincerity, infidelity and unreliability, as is evidenced by the purified republican, purified Native and purified Coloured policies.

I know that the hon. the Minister of Labour does not like to hear these words, the words of a great man who had a notion of the honour and prestige and leadership of the European in this country. That cannot be said of the present-day Government. He continued —

It is typical of this election-time policy that it lacks all moral basis, and is, therefore, applied independent of any principle, moral limitations or obligations. This lack of moral restraint in the application of the purified policy is, as we have been assured, justified by the polling results. Whether it amounts to violence, untruth or breach of faith, the purified ethics do not worry about such things; the successful result in the interest of purified nationalism surely justifies anything.

Well, Sir, the hon. the Minister of Finance sits with the very people of whom these words were used by the late General Hertzog and, Sir, he is a party to bringing in legislation, which, as the Minister has openly stated today, has the undoubted object of segregating the Coloured people.

DR. DÖNGES: Segregating the Whites as well.

MR. STRAUSS: That is the kind of contribution that we get from the Minister of the Interior.

DR. DÖNGES: The trouble is that you can't answer it.

MR. STRAUSS: I know the Minister of the Interior has been very touchy whenever interjections were made and he exhibited a complete unwillingness to deal with questions. But I would like to come back to the Prime Minister and I would like to say that it is no wonder after the way that he changed his principles, that he went back on all he said, that the late General Hertzog was able to say of him these words on 23 March 1939, in this House. Some of my friends will remember. The late Prime Minister, General Hertzog, had quoted what the present Prime Minister had said, and as has been so often the case with my friend, the Prime Minister, when he hears these words, the recorded words from the past rising up against him, he finds it so strange that he could have uttered such words, that he often questions that he used them. He did it on this occasion. The late Prime Minister was quoting Dr. Malan, and then Dr. Malan interjected.

What is it? Are you certain that it is not an incorrect quotation? And the Prime Minister said —

No; it was from Hansard.

Dr. Malan: It is an incorrect quotation, a deceitful quotation.

The Prime Minister[7] went on to say this, Sir — that is the part that I really want to quote —

The Leader of the Opposition has always consistently been disloyal to every principle or big question which he and I, as long as we were working together, always stood for. He has consistently renounced them and it was for the same reason that I do not expect he will support what is laid down here in the summing-up of the policy of the Government, which is nothing less than the policy which the old Nationalist Party always and everywhere preached, not from 1924 but ever since 1917, and which policy the Leader of the Opposition got me more than once to explain in the Cape Province to the Coloured population. But as I have said, I am certain of it, he will deny it again. Very well, you see, as I said the other day, this sort of thing is very characteristic. The Leader of the Opposition is already becoming afraid of that beacon which he helped to put up during that period from 1913-14 to 1933.

Well, Sir, there you have a summing-up of the present Prime Minister by that great Afrikaner, the late General Hertzog.

MR. S. J. M. STEYN[8]: How true it is proven.

MR. STRAUSS: Yes, my friend might well say, "how true it is proven", and therefore, I say that it is idle for the Minister of the Interior to come in these sanctimonious tones and tell us that morally

---

[7] General Hertzog is meant here.
[8] United Party.

it is quite correct and quite in order to segregate the Coloured people politically from the Whites. I want to say this in all seriousness that a breach of these pledges amounts to the breaking of the word of honour of the White man to a section of the non-European people and I say that it is a serious thing to South Africa, it is a serious thing for the continuance of White civilisation when we come to a state of affairs where the non-Europeans will no longer be able to believe the pledged word of the European. I say that is a very serious thing indeed. These pledges were given not only by these great leaders, including the Minister of Finance, on his behalf by the late General Hertzog, outside in the country, but these pledges were given here in Parliament to the Cape Representatives who represented the Coloured people. The Minister of Finance, Sir, recognised how important it was that the White man should honour his pledges so that he would always be in a position of moral leadership, so that he would always be in a position that the non-Europeans would know that when the White man gives his word of honour that that would be his bond and he would stand by it. Because this is what he said in a speech at Colesberg on 5 April 1938 —

How fatal it will be when the European does not stand by his given word. You know how essential it is that the Native should respect the White man and rely on his word. It is pitiful that certain groups are now prepared for the first time in our history to exploit this problem for political purposes. The Afrikaner has always stood where the United Party stands today in connection with this matter.

Yes, Sir, at that time the hon. the Minister found himself in better political company than today. And in his speech at De Aar during that same general election, on the following day, 6 April 1938, he said the following —

Although the Nationalist members of the House of Assembly all voted in favour of these Bills . . .

There he refers to the purified Nationalist Party which at that time was under the leadership of the present Prime Minister —

. . . they now repudiate them and according to the manifesto of Dr. Malan, it appears that they even want to deprive the Native of the insignificant political rights which he still possesses.

And I think they still want to remove those rights. They still are of the intention to remove them, the political rights of the Native people, but, for the time being, they will not admit it. The other day when the hon. the Prime Minister was faced with having to reply to a question by the hon. member for Johannesburg (West) (Mr. Tighy) whether it was the Government's intention to remove the Native Representatives from Parliament, I believe his reply was that at the present time the Government had no intention of doing so. The hon. the Minister of Finance went on on that occasion at De Aar to say —

Because they do not carry the responsibility, the Opposition, . . .

344

of which Dr. Malan was the Leader at the time—

> . . . is adumbrating in connection with the Coloureds and other matters, a policy which is impracticable.

I would like to know now what has happened since then to make it possible to carry out this policy. The late General Hertzog used words very much to the same effect as the words used by the hon. the Minister of Finance then. He used these words in that speech of his at Smithfield about the " troubreuk "[9] of the White man's word to the non-Europeans. I will not refer to that again but he said also this about the necessity of the White man honouring his word to the non-European —

> The immediate consequences of such a policy is nothing but the stirring up of hatred, covetousness and strife amongst the people. In other words, the inevitable consequence of the policy of the Purified Party is national discord and civil strife. For the sake of a sound national life therefore I want to make an appeal today to the men and women of the Free State, nay, to all Afrikaner men and women, to maintain the high moral standard of our national life and to reject everything which is calculated to detract from the high standard of the Afrikaner character.

Those are great words and they substantiate the fact that the late General Hertzog lived up to the great words he spoke. He always had the courage and the conviction to carry out what he said. We ask ourselves as South Africans concerned with the future and the welfare of our country what is going to be the effect of this legislation. The hon. the Minister has tried to justify it on many grounds. He tried to justify it on the grounds that it was not only in the interest of the White people, but that it was also in the interest of the Coloured people themselves. I think that this legislation does nothing but bode ill for the future of South Africa. I can see that an action of this kind can only lead to the formation of a solid non-European bloc. It cannot be in the interests of the non-Europeans nor in the interests of the European people of this country. And that is so as we have already seen and has been stated by the newspapers in this country. We have seen that the non-Europeans today are doing what has never been done before in the history of South Africa They are forming a united anti-European bloc.

We read in the Press that the Transvaal Indian Congress has given its whole-hearted support to the Coloured people in the Cape in the struggle for the preservation of their existing franchise rights. We know that the Franchise Action Committee, backed by the South African Indian Congress, the African People's Organisation, the African National Congress, all Malay organisations, and we know also that the National Conventions Co-ordinating Committee has amalgamated with these other bodies. This amalgamation was announced on 3 March . . .

Now I hear the accusation at times that it is the Opposition that is acting in such a way that a non-European bloc is being formed in this

9 Breach of faith.

country. Well, we know where the truth lies. We know that it is the action, this very action of the Government, that is creating this united anti-European bloc. A warning was given on that score by the late General Hertzog who spoke in very clear terms on this matter. He said in 1929 —

I say that the European in South Africa will most deeply deplore it if he decides to drive the Coloured people to make common cause with the Natives. I assure you that this danger exists if we do not remove the injustice.

MR. DU TOIT: Who said that?

MR. STRAUSS: That was said by the late General Hertzog. He went on to say —

It is very clear to me that it was one of the most foolish attitudes the Whites could adopt to drive the Coloured people to the enemies of the Europeans — and that will happen if we repel him — to allow him eventually to come to rest in the arms of the Native. We know that in the past attempts were made and that they are still being made today, and that they cannot be advantageous to the Europeans and Coloured persons.

I hope that the hon. the Minister will note that legislation of this kind, according to the mature wisdom of the late General Hertzog, could have only one result, and that is to drive the people who, up to now, have been the friends of the Europeans, who have been the friends of the White people, to drive them into the arms, as General Hertzog said, of the Natives in this country. We have, once again, the statement of the Minister in charge of this Bill, that there is no disqualification, as far as the Coloured people are concerned, under Section 35 of the South Africa Act, and we have heard some curious sophistries which he would like to pass off as legal arguments in support of that assertion. No, Sir, the position is perfectly clear that there is a very substantial diminution, a very substantial deprivation, of the political rights of the Coloured people. I think that the Minister today has created the justifiable impression on my mind when he was speaking about that " groot swart wolk van gevaar van die Kleurlingstem " (a great black cloud of danger of the Coloured vote) and when he talked about taking steps to remove this question from the fear zone, namely, that he would be able to take steps under this Bill, to remove the fear of the most unreasonable White men in this country, and at the same time to do it without depriving the Coloured people of any of their existing political rights. If that is not the height of political hypocrisy, then I do not know what is.

After having listened to the Minister we certainly do know what is the height of political hypocrisy. We know now a good deal more than we did before he got up. Not only the hon. the Minister of the Interior, but the Prime Minister himself told us the other day in the plainest possible terms that there was disqualification. What did the Prime Minister say, Sir? The hon. the Prime Minister said this. He said: I admit that there is a relative diminution — " 'n relatiewe vermindering van regte ". And this is what he meant by that. He said that under this Bill in the future it would not be possible for the Coloured vote to give a decisive effect as between two White candidates in any constituency. (Time extended.)

I express my appreciation to the House, Mr. Speaker, for the extension, and I am all the more conscious of that in view of the fact that we have a limitation of time placed upon us, and I shall endeavour to put the remainder of my remarks as briefly as possible. Now that is what the Prime Minister said. He said that now in future it would not be possible under this Bill for the Coloured people by throwing in their weight for either the one candidate or the other, to create a decisive result. Now I ask any hon. member in this House who knows anything about elections, what other value has the vote than just that? What else is there in an election other than to put the one man in and the other man out? When the hon. the Prime Minister admitted that the other day he admitted everything there was to admit in connection with this matter. I saw a painful look on the face of his supporters when he made that statement so far as this Bill is concerned. I would like to know how it lies in the mouth of the hon. the Minister of the Interior or indeed in the mouth of the hon. the Minister of Finance who failed to get a ruling from the Speaker that the Bill did not amount to a disqualification.

MR. HAVENGA: I did not have to.

MR. STRAUSS: Now he denies that he wanted that ruling, but he failed hopelessly. He was hoping that that would be a way of escape for him out of his dilemma if the Speaker ruled to that effect. But the Speaker was not prepared to rule to that effect.

MR. HAVENGA: Why did you not get a ruling from the Speaker?

MR. STRAUSS: Let me say, Mr. Speaker, that I am far from being in the uncomfortable position in which my hon. friend, the Minister of Finance, is. I come back and I ask the Minister of Finance through you, Sir, what other value has the vote got than for a person to go to the polling booth in order to vote and to put the one candidate in and the other candidate out? And that is what the hon. the Prime Minister admits this Bill does. I have never heard such hypocrisy in my life before.

MR. SPEAKER: The hon. member must withdraw that expression.

MR. STRAUSS: I said it was hypocrisy ...

MR. SPEAKER: No, no, the hon. member must withdraw the statement that it was hypocrisy.

MR. STRAUSS: I withdraw that. What I wanted to say was this that I never knew before that such political hyprocrisy existed. We have heard speeches from the other side. We have heard speeches from the hon. the Prime Minister. We have read them We have not had the privilege of being present at all his meetings. I read one particular speech of his after the last Provincial Council elections when the Prime Minister was very much down in the dumps because his party had lost the constituency of Paarl. He made a speech then and he said they only lost it because of the existence of the Coloured vote.

347

And the members of the other side have gone from one end of the country to the other and have complained bitterly of this threat to White civilisation which is contained in the existence of the Coloured franchise.

And I would like him to explain to me how both these things can be true. How on the one hand they can proceed as the Minister claims they have done to remove all fear that White civilisation is in danger of being swamped by Coloured votes in the constituencies without diminishing any of the rights of the Coloured people. I would like him to tell me. That is what the Minister of Finance has to answer. I say it is idle for the Minister of Finance to get up in this House and tell us solemnly that there has been no change in his attitude and that his conscience is clear, I say what he owes to South Africa and what he owes to this House is to tell us how he justifies these things one by one and let him tell us the reason why his conscience is clear.

Mr. Speaker, I really am not impressed by the hair-splitting sophistry of the hon. the Minister of the Interior, not only on legal questions but also so far as the merits of this Bill are concerned. He told us for instance the other day in his sanctimonious way that it is better for the Coloured people to have four winners than 55 also-rans. If the hon. the Minister thinks that he impresses us by that kind of statement, let me tell him that we are able to see through that poker face and his statement as well. The real value of the Coloured vote up to now has been that they have been able to make their weight felt in a large number of constituencies, not in all 55 but at any rate in a large number of those 55 constituencies. Now he places them in a strait-jacket of four seats only.

MR. KAHN: May I ask the hon. member a question? Will the United Party restore this franchise if it gets back into power?

MR. STRAUSS: I prefer in this particular regard — I do not often do it and I do not like doing it — to follow the example of my hon. friend in charge of this Bill. (Interruptions.) My hon. friends should be patient and allow me to finish my speech and if they have any remarks to make they can get up and make them. What an interesting spectacle to see the gloating and the expressions of delight on the faces of the members of the Nationalist Party and the hon. Minister in charge of the Bill at the magnificent piece of work performed by their friend, the Communist member.

There is a great deal of disadvantage in these four members having to represent four constituencies for this whole vast area in the country and for the Provincial Council — I am only mentioning the point, I do not want to go into it — there will only be two members. How the unfortunate member will ever be able to cover that constituency and get in touch with his constituents to me seems to be a matter of physical impossibility. Under this Bill — I do not think the hon. the Minister mentioned that as one of the points — the Government can actually hold a general election and continue to govern the country indefinitely without even delimiting the four Coloured constituencies. That is a clause in the Bill. I do not want to go into the details of the next reason why we are opposed to this Bill, namely, that an analysis of the election promises, and the election results will show that the Government had no mandate from the people.

Perhaps I ought to say a word or two about that because the hon. the Minister has come forward and he has claimed that they have a mandate for this policy.

Let us see what the Government placed before the people in the general election. (Interruptions.)

Not only have we indicated on a previous occasion that in the general election of 1948 there was a majority of 120,000 votes for the combined Opposition parties as against the combined Afrikaner Party and Nationalist Party, but in the subsequent Provincial Council elections that majority had gone up to 160,000. But let us see what the mandate was that they got from the people. What did they place before the people in their election manifesto at the time?

I think the people have forgotten what the manifesto of their party said at the time. In the general election of 1948 and again, I think in March 1949, at the Provincial Council elections, these were the main points of their apartheid policy as put before the electorate. First and foremost was "Abolition of Native Representation in the House of Assembly". That was before the country — the abolition of Native representation in the House of Assembly. That is what my hon. friend says he has got a mandate for. The second point was: Separate representation for Coloureds in Parliament and in the Cape Provincial Council. The third point was: The Coloured to be represented by three European members in the House of Assembly. (The 1948 election manifesto provided that these three representatives would be elected by the Coloured Advisory Council, but the March 1949 manifesto simply provided that the three would be chosen by the Coloured people themselves.) The other main point was: The representatives of the Coloureds would not take part or vote in debates of confidence, declarations of war, or changes in political rights. That was their election manifesto.

Now the Malan-Havenga agreement and this Bill which is now before the House provides for four representatives in the House of Assembly, elected directly by the enfranchised Coloureds, no limitation on their debating or voting powers and no mention of abolition of Native representation in the House of Assembly. I say, I think the hon. the Minister ought to justify how he arrives at the specific mandate which he says they got at the general election. Now let me come to this point on which the late Mr. B. K. Long has so often been quoted because the attitude of this side of the House is that historically the Coloureds have not only earned their right to retain their vote as they have enjoyed it for nearly a century, but we say that the evidence of abuse is extremely limited and is most unreliable. Let us look at what the late Mr. B. K. Long said, which again my hon. friend the Minister of the Interior did not quote. This is what he said—

349

No responsible observer with practical experience of our politics would say that the proportion of our White population which is worthy of the franchise is anything but startlingly low.

MR. D. J. G. VAN DEN HEEVER[10]: Do you agree with that?

MR. STRAUSS: The hon. member over there asks me if I agree with that They quoted Mr. B. K. Long, and I am quoting Mr. Long back at them. But, Sir, I do not want to quote only the late Mr. B. K. Long, I want to quote again that great statesman, the late General Hertzog. This is what he said so far as this question is concerned —

Those of them who are educated have the right to say that they are civilised.

And note this—

There are some of them who lead a life which is sounder, better and more civilised than the life led by thousands and thousands of our own people. We can only hope that this concession will be a further incentive to the Coloureds in South Africa to see that they uplift themselves.

Now that kind of quotation from the late Mr. B. K. Long does not really advance the case on the other side, and I hope that in the future the hon. the Minister of Finance will prefer to follow the wise words of his Leader, the late General Hertzog, rather than shelter behind the words of the late Mr. B. K. Long. We on this side of the House say that there is no evidence to show that the Coloured vote is in any sense a real danger to White civilisation. On the contrary, our standpoint is that to deprive them of these rights is to drive them into the arms of the Natives, and in the words of the late General Hertzog that constitutes a real danger to White civilisation in this country.

Now the hon. the Minister has made a good deal of this Board he proposes to set up for the Coloured people and that that is some compensation for the rights which are being taken away from them. The submission of this side of the House is that it is nothing of the kind. We have had experience of representative councils for the Natives, but this is in fact not as much as the Native Representative Council is for the Natives. The Minister comes here and asks us to support this Bill, amongst other reasons because of this Board. He says he will give it administrative powers but he is not yet able to tell us what these administrative powers are going to be. He is waiting for some bright idea to come into his mind or into the mind of Professor du Plessis.[11] In the meantime he says we must support this Bill — we must give him a blank cheque. No, Sir, we on this side of the House say we have had experience of communal representation in the three Native representatives in this House and we say that there is a distinct danger in increasing the number of three that we already have, to seven as it will be if this Bill is enacted. If there is a bloc of seven communal representatives represent-

[10] National Party.
[11] The reference is obscure.

350

ing the non-Europeans of this country and if ever the day should come, as it may well come as the political parties are constituted in this House today, that that little bloc of seven members, perhaps with the help of a very left Labour Party, might hold the balance of power in this country it might be a bad day for South Africa.

If that ever happens, can you see those people for one moment allowing the state of affairs to continue? They will not only abolish the Native representatives, but they will also abolish the Coloured representatives. That exposes their political hypocrisy. For all these reasons we oppose this Bill. We say the Bill is totally unacceptable and we say it is a great danger to the continuance of White South Africa. We shall therefore oppose it with all the power at our command.

Now I have been asked what our position is with regard to the future. I have been twitted by the Nationalist Party and by their recent ally the former Communist member — I believe he is still regarded as a Communist by that side — what the United Party under present-day conditions in South Africa . . .

AN HON. MEMBER: Do you believe they will ever be returned to power?

MR. STRAUSS: I am glad to see that my hon. friend over there admits that the United Party will sooner or later be returned to power. (Interruptions.) I say that the United Party under present-day conditions has a very grave duty to perform to South Africa. This deprivation of political rights of the Coloured people is not nearly the sum total of deprivation of fundamental rights of citizens which has taken place under the regime of this Government. This deprivation of the political rights of the Coloured people is but an incident of the general, what I might also call wholesale, onslaught which has been made by this Government on fundamental human rights and human liberties. I do not have to detail them. We know what has happened in regard to legislation passed in this House recently. I do not want to criticise the legislation passed by the House but we do know that in the Suppression of Communism Act the right of free access to the courts has been taken away. We know of all the various encroachments on the rights and liberties of the citizens of this country. Now therefore the United Party's attitude is that when it is returned to power it will take the necessary steps to entrench in a new Bill of Rights in the Constitution the fundamental liberties of the people of South Africa. (Interruptions.) I do not know why people should be so curious of what the United Party is going to do because I indicated only the other day on the debate on the motion for leave to introduce this Bill that when the United Party is returned to power, we will rewrite into the Constitution the entrenched clauses which have now been taken out of our Constitution. The first fundamental right that we will rewrite into that Constitution is the continued equality of the two languages of our country. I see that the hon. the Prime Minister is not here now.

But my hon. friend will remember what he said as recently as 1948 about the question of the equality of the two languages. The question was put to him and he said what about the two-thirds majority that the Constitution provides for in regard to the language equality. He answered it and said, all that I can say is this: It does stand on an equal footing with the two-thirds majority in connection with the non-European vote. It falls into the same category so it stands in the same position. I would only say this in regard to the question of language equality, if it should have to be abolished on its merits, if that is justified, it will have to happen.

I say it is necessary after that statement, to rewrite an entrenched clause into our Constitution providing for continued equality of the two official languages. The other entrenched clause which should be rewritten into our Constitution is to safeguard the political rights of the Coloured people, and in the third place we should rewrite into that Constitution another fundamental right, which is the very breath of democracy, and that is the freedom of the Press, the freedom of the Press which has been gravely threatened by this Government. Our independent Press is being attacked by the Prime Minister, and practically every one of his Cabinet Ministers day in and day out, and therefore we shall have to entrench that freedom as well. We shall also have to entrench freedom of conscience and of religion; we shall have to entrench freedom of speech subject to the necessary safeguards to preserve democracy, and I think we shall have to entrench in future the position of the Union as a member of the Commonwealth of Nations.

If you will permit me, Sir, I want to state the remaining few points very briefly. I submit that that is one of the matters that ought to be entrenched, and I think the Prime Minister ought to support that step that I propose, because he has stated as recently as 1949 that every side of this House is in favour of the proposition that South Africa should remain a member of the Commonwealth of Nations.

MR. BARLOW: What about the sanctity of the law courts?

MR. STRAUSS: I am coming to that. I think we should also entrench the right of free access to the law courts. I think we should entrench the guarantee of their complete independence.

The United Party has stated that if the fight does not avail in this House, if this legislation is passed, then the question of the validity of this legislation will be tested in the law courts, and the Prime Minister has delivered himself on that issue.

He has stated quite categorically that if the law courts assigned to themselves what he referred to as the testing right, that would be a very serious thing indeed, and he referred to the crisis in the Transvaal Republic. Since the Prime Minister was allowed to make that statement, I submit that I have the right to reply to that, and all I want to say in reply is that in view of the threat to our law courts, that is one of the fundamental rights that ought to be entrenched.

There are only two more that I want to mention at this stage. The one is freedom of movement according to the law of the land, and the

352

other is freedom of lawful association. Those are fundamental rights that we as a party will aim at entrenching when we are returned to power in due course. I say that the political actions of this Government have made it abundantly clear that no fundamental right is secure if it stands in the way of the appetite for power that we see on the other side of the House, and, indeed, I say it in sorrow, that a new political virus has affected the party on the other side — not all of them perhaps but a great many of them — and some of their followers; that evil dictatorial virus that came over from Europe in the 1930's, has infected the people on the other side. As a result of that it will be the duty of the United Party to entrench these fundamental liberties of the people, and, Sir, it will be our aim to get the vast bulk of the people of South Africa behind our policy of entrenching these fundamental rights. We have learned to our sorrow that the word of honour, the pledged word, is no good any longer. It has been broken by these people and, therefore, the safeguard of entrenchment is necessary and the United Party pledges itself at entrenching these fundamental liberties of the subject in due course when it gets back to power.

3

LABOUR PARTY POLICY

MR. L. LOVELL, 25 APRIL 1951[1]

I HOPE THE HON. MEMBER who has just sat down will not take it amiss if I do not follow him into all the arguments with which he has just regaled this House. Speaking in the shadow of the guillotine, we have not much time in this debate. One of the questions I would like to deal with is an important one that was thrown across the floor of the House during the previous stages of this debate. It is the question which was put somewhat in this fashion: If it is immoral to rob the Coloured man of his rights, is it not immoral to do so by a two-thirds majority? That is the question which was asked by quite a number of members on the Government side.

MR. S. E. WARREN[2]: A two-thirds majority will not make it less immoral.

MR. LOVELL: The question can be put this way: Surely if robbery is a crime when committed by 51 out of 100 people, it is still a crime if it is committed by 66 people out of 100. This question contains a fallacy. It is a misleading question unless you follow it to its proper conclusion. The question whether the Coloured or the Native voters of the Cape, for example, should or should not retain their rights, was not regarded by all the parties to the National Convention as a moral issue but a political issue. Nor is this question as to whether the Coloured man should or should not retain his present rights regarded by all people at present as a moral issue. Some people do, but all agree that it is a political issue. For example, when the National Convention discussed this very question the Northern Provinces said that they should have no equality in Church or State, and the Cape said that they wanted political equality on the basis of a civilisation test. In other words, both the contending parties did not regard the issue as a moral one. Both agreed that it was a political one, and both came to a certain agreement regarding it. The Cape urged that the Cape Coloured voter should retain his existing rights in the Cape Province and that their view should not be overwhelmed except by a two-thirds majority. And what became a moral issue was not whether the Coloured man should retain his rights or not, but what became a moral issue among all the contending parties

---

1 Speech by Mr. L. Lovell, Leader of the Labour Party, during the debate in the House of Assembly on the second reading of the Separate Representation of Voters' Bill, 25 April 1951. *House of Assembly Debates.*
2 United Party.

was that these rights should not be taken away without a certain procedure being adopted, namely the procedure of a two-thirds majority. That was the contract of honour, if I may call it that, and that was the contract that imported into it the question of morality. After the 1909 Convention and the South Africa Act of 1910 this matter was taken further by members of the present Government, by people like the Prime Minister. The Prime Minister in 1925 gave certain pledges on the question of the Coloured vote. He said —

Die teenswoordige Regering sorg dat daar vir die Kleurling en vir Slamse geen kleurslagboom sal wees nie. (The present Government sees to it that there shall be no colour bar for the Coloured man and Malays.)

He also went on to say in March 1928 —

If I vote for the amended Bill as it now stands . . .

He was talking of the Bill to give European women the Franchise —

. . . I shall vote for the restriction to European women only. Then I come into direct conflict with the policy that I have hitherto published on platforms and most hon. members on this side also. That policy is nothing new. It is set out in the Native Bills, namely that a dividing line must be drawn between the Native and Coloured people and that the political rights of the White man shall be given to the Coloured people . . . personally I should like to give the vote to the Coloured women.

Then he went on to say in February 1929 —

In South Africa today a policy is being followed . . . of having the Europeans on one side and the non-Europeans on the other . . . What we propose here is to draw a distinction, with the Natives on one side and the Coloured people on the other as regards political rights, so that they shall share entirely in the Cape, and to a great extent in the Northern Provinces the same political rights as the European.

The point is this that where an hon. member of this House in the position which the Prime Minister then held, makes a pledge to the Coloured people in regard to their rights, then it becomes a moral issue when he tries to turn a somersault. That is when it becomes a moral issue. These quotations show very clearly that the hon. the Prime Minister gave a certain pledge or guarantee to the Coloured people, and the question of morality does not come into the picture, except in so far as he is not now carrying out that pledge or guarantee. When the hon. the Minister of the Interior moved the second reading of this Bill, no one could say to him that it was an immoral act as far as he was concerned. I have not yet heard him undertake to safeguard the rights of the Coloureds in the Cape, nor have I ever heard him maintain that the two-thirds majority in the entrenched clauses was valid. If I heard him maintain that, I might have accused him of being immoral in retracting his words. The question of morality does not arise in the case of the hon. the Minister of the Interior at all.

It does arise, however, in respect of the attitude of the Minister of Justice[3] and in respect of the hon. member for Uitenhage (Dr. D. G. Conradie) and in regard to the late Dr. Stals. There the question of morality arises in this way: Whereas one could not accuse them of doing anything immoral in proposing to take away the rights of the Coloured people in this Bill, one could charge them with immorality because they gave a pledge that they would not do it except by means of a two-thirds majority. It is in that fashion that you must answer the question in regard to the undertaking given by various people in this House. It is neither immoral for the hon. the Minister of the Interior to ask for these rights to be taken away or to say that the entrenched clauses are invalid. It is not immoral for the Minister of Justice to say that the rights of the Coloured people should be taken away but it is immoral on his part to attempt to do so, by a bare majority in view of the words which he used, when he said it is a matter of " good faith ", that these entrenched clauses would not be violated. It is all very well throwing questions across the floor of the House and saying that if it is immoral to take away the rights of the Coloured people, therefore it is also immoral to do so by a two-thirds majority.

On the question that was put to the hon. the Leader of the Opposition, both by the hon. the Minister of the Interior and the hon. member for Cape Western (Mr. Kahn), as to whether he would repeal this legislation if his party got into power, I was very glad to hear the reply of the Leader of the Opposition when he said quite categorically that he would, if he got into power, repeal this legislation. That is an undertaking which I am quite sure he will honour. The Labour Party approves of such a policy *in toto*. One thing that worries us is this. We do not know what festering sores, what wounds will be caused by this legislation. We do not know whether, if another Government comes into power, they will be able to deal with the bitterness which this Bill has caused. In so far as any alternative Government that comes into power has the power to heal those wounds, we will support them in doing so.

Mr. Speaker, the argument on the Government side has been more or less on the following lines. First of all, there is no disqualification of the Coloured voter. When you put forward counter-arguments to them to show that there is a disqualification . . .

MR. S. E. WARREN: Where are your arguments?

MR. LOVELL: I will give them to my hon. friend. The Coloured voter will no longer have any say in the election of Senators. He will be deprived of the right to vote against the Nationalist Government in 55 constituencies.

They say first of all that there is no disqualification and because there is no disqualification, they say that the entrenched clauses do not apply. Then they argue in this way. They say that if there is a disqualification,

[3] Mr. C. R. Swart.

the Status Act has done away with the entrenched clauses, and they say there is no moral obligation upon them to pass this legislation other than by a bare majority. Then they retreat into the last ditch, and they say that this is a matter of self-preservation. Once they come to that point, then of course, the question of justice, of morals and ethics, just does not mean anything at all. Obviously if you want to base your policy on the argument of self-preservation, it is a question of your life or mine, and the question of ethics does not come into the picture, as many members on the Government side have quite honestly said. Before you can invoke the principle of self-preservation, however, you must persuade reasonable people that that danger exists. But what is the danger, if you leave the Coloured voter in the position in which he now is?

MR. DU TOIT: They will lose the next election.

MR. LOVELL: That is the only danger. The great danger as far as the Nationalist Party is concerned, is that the United Party will get into power at the next election. It is not a question of White civilisation at all. In spite of all the arguments which have been advanced here, we know that the real issue is this: Can the Nationalist Party get into power at the next election, unless it removes the Coloured voter from the Common Roll?

I was saying that what is at stake here is not the preservation of White civilisation at all, but the preservation of the Nationalist Party. All they are fighting for is the preservation of the Nationalist Party. Why all these fears about White civilisation? The Coloured people represent less than half the population of the Europeans. We have never had any real trouble of any kind from the Coloured voter or from the Coloured population. They have stood with us both in war and in peace. How hon. members can say that they constitute a danger to White civilisation is beyond my understanding entirely. This Bill is based upon fear, whether it is an imaginary fear, or whether it is a stirred-up fear. What has happened to this country of South Africa? About 50 years ago, when we were a smaller group, situated at the bottom of a Black continent — that, I believe, is the popular phrase — with hordes of Blacks stretching from the north to the south, and we were in danger of being overwhelmed there were no people in those days who preached fear. President Kruger did not preach fear. Cecil Rhodes did not preach fear. The Europeans even indulged in the luxury of a war amongst themselves over a certain issue, although it also might have been said that they ran the risk of being overwhelmed by the huge Black masses stretching from the Nile to the Limpopo. This fear is initiated and is encouraged by the policy of the Nationalist Party. Afterwards they come to believe it and then they want to tell us that they need all these obnoxious measures in order to save White civilisation which is in no way threatened except by the Nationalist Party.

In conclusion, let me say this: This Bill is loaded with buckshot. It is aimed at the Coloured people, but in the end it will hit, as it has already hit the Constitution, the language rights and all the other rights that we hold dear in South Africa.

SECTION VI
THE NATIVE PROBLEM

1

NATIVE POLICY

GENERAL LOUIS BOTHA, 1 APRIL 1912[1]

H E D I D N O T wish to discuss the question of the Coloured people, but in regard to the Native question they were bound to act with the greatest caution. Some changes must be made, otherwise difficulties would arise. Were they to treat the races on a footing of equality, or must they try to find a solution which would give more satisfaction? To put them on an equality would never give satisfaction. He could not say that he had at present any solution of the question within view, but every responsible person would have to ponder the question, because it might be necessary to solve the problem at an earlier date than people generally thought. Personally, he thought that the solution would be found in the increasing of the rights of the Natives who must have a certain measure of self-government under White supervision in order that they might work out their own salvation and be treated justly. In a social sense the two races could never become one. Marriages between Whites and Blacks were impossible and would only lead to sorrow and mischief. The Natives should be improved on their own national lines.

GENERAL J. B. M. HERTZOG, 12 OCTOBER 1912[2]

A F T E R A R E F E R E N C E to various Acts of last session, General Hertzog proceeded to deal with Native affairs. He said he had not yet got to the bottom of the question, and before he did so he would consult his colleagues. He would deal with some essential points as they appeared to him. It was useless talking vaguely. If they did not now deal with the matter they would find that a fair solution in the near future would be impossible. When he said Native problem he meant the regulation of the relations between Europeans and Natives in the future through legislation in a fair and workable manner. They must meet the circumstances as they were at present. They could not legislate for all ages. At present relations between the races were unsatisfactory to the Natives and still more so to the Europeans, and if they went on as at present the country would not long remain White man's country. The Blacks suffered too.

1 Extract from speech, House of Assembly Debates, 1 April 1912.
2 Extract from speech held at Smithfield. The *Star*, 14 October 1912.

That was due to present circumstances. No one wanted a mingling of the races, and no one wanted the White man to be squeezed out of the country. On the other hand, a policy of repression or unfairness to the Natives would reflect on the character of the Europeans and would do harm.

Referring to the position in the country today, he regretted that the persons responsible were mostly Dutch-speaking farmers, who if they continued acting as they did, would prove the ruination of South Africa. He referred to their farming not with their own strength and brains, but with those of Natives. Kaffir-farming[3] would ruin the White man.

Proceeding to his suggestions as to a solution of the problem, the Minister asked if Europeans left the country what would become of the Natives? "Our destruction," he said, "would be theirs." For the good of the Natives, then, they must do something to assure the position of both races in South Africa. They must look not only to their own existence, but to that of the Natives also; but any solution must give the Natives an opportunity of developing along their own lines to obtain their rights as men. Any solution would have to provide the Natives with opportunity and leading.

The Cape system in the Native territories was the best so far as opportunity for Natives and the safety of Europeans were concerned. But the Cape system failed in not giving the requisite leading. In the Free State they were better in the latter respect, and the Free State would indeed act as a model in both connections except that in the Cape the Natives had greater opportunities. Those who championed the needs of Natives, men of strong conviction and transparent sincerity, did not like the Free State system, but he held that but for the leading of the Whites the Natives there would have no longer existed. In the Free State the pass system was objected to, but it was necessary for Natives themselves, as well as for the safety of Europeans. He was convinced that segregation with the separation of Black and White as was done in the Transkeian territories, was the only solution. There could be no talk of compulsion but they had to give the Natives an opportunity to go to any part of the country where they would be able to develop under proper leadership and to give the White men a chance of doing their duty to themselves without cheating either the Natives or themselves. Europeans would be forbidden to hold land in Native territories, and the only Whites allowed there would be those required by the Natives themselves. The Natives would then have a chance to work out their own salvation. In the White man's territory the Natives would not be able to do what they now threatened, namely, to squeeze out the White man from South Africa. The Natives would not be allowed to have land in the White men's territory, and thus he hoped kaffir farming would be stopped.

He wanted it to be clear that there could be no question of force, but

---

[3] The reference is to squatter labour.

if they were to reach his ideal they must take immediate steps towards it. They would have to provide places where the Natives could be removed to and similarly for Europeans. They would place Natives in those parts where there were already large masses of their compatriots, but the mixed districts, which they would ultimately have to do away with, would remain as at present. His scheme meant nothing less than defining the respective spheres of Blacks and Whites. He could not outline a complete scheme yet, but he could take the matter one step further. He would not exclude Natives from the fields of labour. They would be a source of strength if used legally and properly, but it must not be abused. Natives would be given the right to enter European territory in order to earn a living there. They had to consider the economic necessities of the country. He would place a complete scheme before Parliament and would welcome criticism.

2

THE NATIVE RESERVES

SPEECH BY MR. J. W. SAUER, 9 MAY 1913[1]

THE PROBLEMS arising out of the relations between Europeans and Natives were so complex and so difficult that one often despaired. The Bill only dealt with a phase of that large question, and he hoped the object aimed at would be attained, and that the bulk of the people affected by it would consider it as reasonable. That could not be done unless they had the interests of a large class at heart, and acted in a spirit of fairness.

Recently there had been a good deal of discussion on the question of segregation. Personally, he had never been able quite to understand what that meant. If it meant that there must be a complete separation between Europeans and Natives, so that they would not come into daily contact with each other, then it was an impossible proposal. The provisions proposed under the Bill were far less drastic than what some people meant by segregation, and, he hoped, far more feasible. He proposed in this Bill that the bulk of the two races, the European and the Native, should live in the main in separate areas — that was, that they should occupy and acquire land in separate areas. It, therefore, did not deal with those, and they were a very considerable number, who went to European centres to obtain work.

Section 1 of this Bill referred to the consent of the Governor-General having to be obtained under certain circumstances, and that implied a very important principle. Some people talked of provisions which would make it absolutely impossible for a European to acquire land in certain areas, and for Natives to acquire land in other areas. That seemed to him to be altogether too crude, and he thought that what they should have was not prohibition, but restriction, and the whole principle underlying this Bill was not absolute prohibition, but restriction. In Herschel, in the Transkei, and in locations in Bechuanaland, although some of these were Native areas protected by Act of Parliament, still the Governor-General or Government had the right to allow a European to acquire landed property there, or occupy it, and if that were not so, a large part of the business in those areas would come to a standstill. Therefore, he

---

[1] Mr. J. W. Sauer, Minister of Native Affairs, in the House of Assembly, 9 May 1913, during the debate on the second reading of the Natives Land Bill. Enacted as the Natives Land Act No. 27 of 1913.

could conceive that there might be cases in any of the Native areas where it might be desirable to allow Europeans to acquire land. These would only be individual cases, but it would be very necessary to provide for such cases. The first part of the Bill provided that, from the date of its commencement, no Native should purchase or hire from a European, and it also provided that no European could purchase or hire from a Native.

AN HON. MEMBER: In the areas?

MR. SAUER: No, that was all over the different provinces, excepting the scheduled areas. In the areas, other than the scheduled areas, the sale and purchase between Natives and Europeans was stopped. Europeans could not buy from the Natives, nor could the Natives from the Europeans.

The next provision was in sub-section 2, which said that if any person was in lawful occupation or if any person was in agreement of lease and was lawfully in occupation, he could not be moved until two things had happened. One was that the land upon which he was had been proclaimed a non-Native area, and until land had been pointed out to which he could be moved. This might be called a sort of provisional arrangement.

Then provision was made for the appointment of a Commission. It would be remembered that a Commission[2] was appointed in 1903 which had recommended that certain areas should be set aside by the Legislature within which only Natives should reside. It was proposed to appoint a Commission with very considerable powers, and this Commission was to report mainly on two things. It was to inquire and report on the area that was to be a non-Native area, that was the area within which no Native except with the consent of the Governor-General could acquire land. It would also have to report on the setting apart of additional Native areas. The proposals of the Commission would then be submitted to Parliament, and after Parliament had approved of them a Proclamation would be issued defining the areas. The effect of such a Proclamation would be that no Native could then purchase land in a non-Native area, and no person who lawfully occupied land at that time would be moved except an additional Native area had been proclaimed to which he might go. Section 6 provided that in the scheduled areas and the additional Native areas Europeans would be under the same disabilities with regard to the hire and purchase of land as Natives in non-Native areas, except that the Governor-General might in certain cases consent to such hire and purchase. Provision in this connection was also made in regard to municipalities. After a Proclamation had been issued proclaiming non-Native areas, provision was made that so far as municipalities were concerned, unless the local authority set aside lands where Natives could hire or purchase, the provisions of this Bill would not apply.

Dealing with the different laws with regard to the purchase and hire of land in the various provinces, Mr. Sauer pointed out that in the Free

2 The Lagden Native Affairs Commission, 1903-05.

State Coloured persons, which included Natives, could neither buy nor hire. There was some exception in regard to Coloured people who were lawfully married, and whose father or mother was White, and there were some exceptions in favour of bastards being allowed to purchase within municipal limits. That law in the Free State would remain after this Bill had passed. In the Transvaal the position was somewhat different. Prior to its annexation, and under the Convention of 1881, confirmed under the London Convention of 1884, Natives could buy land, but it had to be registered in the name of the Native Location Commission, and it was thought after the annexation that that would continue to be the law. An action at law, however, was brought, and the Supreme Court of the Transvaal pronounced that notwithstanding the Convention, but he (Mr. Sauer) thought, mainly owing to the annexation, that law no longer existed. In 1905 the Transvaal Parliament introduced a Bill which required that the registration of land bought by Natives should be in the name of the Secretary for Native Affairs. That Bill passed the Legislature, but it was vetoed by the Imperial Government. In the Transvaal, therefore, there were some limitations or restrictions. Under the Precious and Base Minerals Act of 1908 no Coloured person could own property within a diggings or township. Although theoretically the Native had the right to lease, there was a squatters' law which said that if a Native were allowed to lease he should not be allowed to keep more than a certain number of Natives on the land. But speaking broadly, the law in the Transvaal today was that a Native could purchase and hire land the same as a European. In Natal the law, speaking broadly, was the same as in the Cape. A Native could purchase and hire land.

At the Cape, generally speaking, the Natives had the same right as the Europeans to purchase or hire land. That, to some extent, had been modified by certain provisions in the Glen Grey Act.[3] In that Act a Native could not sell land which was acquired under the Glen Grey Act, and which could only be got by consent of the Government. He could not sub-let or sell the land under pain of forfeiting it. So there also the principle of restriction had been introduced. Here, too, like in Natal, broadly speaking, Natives could buy and lease land the same as other people. There were other small restrictions in the Native Locations Act, and another measure of a similar character — an Act relating to townships.

There was a very considerable difference between the laws. So far as the Free State was concerned, the right of purchase or lease would hardly be affected by the present Bill. So far as the Transvaal was concerned, it would put the law back to what it was prior to annexation, and so far as Natal was concerned the law would be considerably altered. As regarded the Cape, he had said that the law was practically the same as the Transvaal, but so far as this Bill went at present the provisions of this Act would not be applied to the Cape. When he first drafted this Bill, provision was made to include the whole of the Union, but he thought

---

3 Act 25 of 1894, Cape Colony.

that in dealing with a question of this kind it would be wise to have a uniform legislation over the whole of the Union. But his difficulty was this. Under the provisions of the South Africa Act anything touching the franchise rights of the Native could only be altered by a two-thirds majority. He saw the difficulties, and he decided for the present to leave that out of the Bill, though not without regret. It was first questioned whether this Bill would affect the franchise rights of the Native, and an eminent lawyer took the view that the provisions of the Bill would undoubtedly affect the rights of the franchise in the Cape, and the only way was to proceed in the manner prescribed by the South Africa Act. As to whether it should be applied to the Cape was a matter for the House to decide, and he would offer no unreasonable objection that would be likely to retard the progress of the Bill, and risk it not becoming law this session.

He would like to show the population and the distribution of the Native population, because that was how some of the difficulties arose. The population, according to the last census, of the whole Union, was 4,017,000. There were 508,000 in urban areas, and 3,508,000 in rural areas. It would be seen that the great bulk were outside urban areas, and it was fortunate it was so. Let them take the Cape. There were 113,000 within municipal limits, 1,145,000 in locations or reserves, 232,000 in service, 22,000 as squatters on land occupied by owners, 5,600 as squatters on land not occupied by owners, making the total population of the Cape 1,519,000. In Natal there were 35,000 in urban areas, 430,000 in locations and reserves, 57,000 on Crown Lands, 48,000 in service, and 261,000 squatters on land occupied by owners.

AN HON. MEMBER: White owners?

MR. SAUER: White owners.

AN HON. MEMBER: Throughout the Union?

MR. SAUER: No; only Natal.

Continuing, he said that there were 119,000 squatters on private land not occupied by owners — the absentee gentlemen.

AN HON. MEMBER: Crown land?

MR. SAUER: On private land.

Continuing, he said in addition to those he had given in Natal, there were 57,000 squatters on Crown lands as above stated. So in the Cape, they had 22,000 on land occupied by owners, 5,600 on land not occupied by owners. In Natal they had 380,000 squatters on private land, in addition to the 57,000 on Crown land. In the Transvaal there were 142,000 squatters on private land occupied by owners, 174,000 squatters on private land not occupied by owners, and to that must be added 65,000 squatters on Crown land, which made a total of nearly 381,000. In the Orange Free State there were 73,000 squatters on private land occupied by owners, 7,000 squatters on land not occupied by owners. It came to this, that the Cape, Natal, the Transvaal, and the Orange Free State had no less than 806,000 squatters on private lands, and the total number of squatters on private land and Crown land was 928,000. He was happy to say that a large proportion of these would not be affected by the Bill, as he would explain later on.

AN HON. MEMBER: Women and children?

MR. SAUER: Oh, yes — the total population. At least, I should hope so. If they took the land occupied by Natives, and the land not occupied by Natives, they would get the result more or less showing the distribution of the population. In the Cape there were 83,633,000 morgen of land, and the area reserved by the Government for Native purposes since the etablishment of the Cape as a Colony amounted to 5,975,000 morgen, and this worked out at 3.9 morgen per head of the Native population. Altogether there were 10,671,000 morgen in Natal, and the land reserved by the Government for Natives and in occupation at the present time amounted to 3,000,000 morgen or 3.1 morgen per head of the Native population. With regard to the Transvaal, he was afraid there was something of a falling off. The total area was 33,032,000 morgen, and the area reserved by the Government 882,000 morgen, which gave as the result .7 per head of the Native population. It was only fair to add that it would be somewhat more because the Transvaal had a very considerable proportion of Natives that came from various other parts of South Africa — from the Cape and Portuguese territory especially. Therefore the Transvaal would show better if they deducted the extraneous population of the Transvaal. Then as regarded areas reserved in the Free State for Native occupation they found that 74,289 morgen were so reserved out of a total area in the Free State of 15,243,000 morgen. This would give .2 morgen as the unit per head of the Native population. In the Transvaal the Natives were allowed to occupy land indiscriminately, and had done so to a far greater extent than in other parts of South Africa.

The total area of the Union was 142,000,000 morgen, and of that 9,932,000 morgen had been reserved in different places for Native occupation. In addition to that there were 240,000 morgen of land included in scheduled area in the Transvaal which had been acquired privately by Natives, and which had been occupied by them. This land had been acquired by them, and therefore had to be added to the scheduled area. The figures that he had given were to a large extent approximate, and the officials who had rendered infinite labour in this matter, had endeavoured to get as near to the totals as possible. The total amount of land which Natives occupied in South Africa, otherwise than in municipalities or in service, amounted to 10,843,000 morgen, practically going on for 11,000,000 morgen.

He would ask the House to give him its attention until he explained what was largely the crux of the matter, one of the most important features in this very difficult case. He had stated that there were 806,000 Natives on private property, and 122,000 on Crown land, altogether 928,000 squatters. When the Commission of 1903 — a most admirable Commission — sent in their report, they drew attention to the fact that

368

the squatting system in the different provinces, with the exception of one — and that was the good old sluggish Cape — was very unsatisfactory, and they recommended that the Cape Squatters Law should be adopted in the provinces. Subsequently the Cape adopted another law, which had put the Cape squatters in an entirely satisfactory position. The squatters were there because they had a legal right to be there. So far as the Cape was concerned a squatters difficulty did not arise. If the Bill came into operation these people would hardly suffer any hardship. It was the same with regard to Natal, although that province was not so well off as the Cape, as it had the great number of 381,000 squatters on private property, and 57,000 on Crown land, but there also they were legally entitled to be there. Whether there should be legislation upon the matter he would not go into now. The squatters in Natal were legally entitled to be there, just in the same way as those in the Cape. They could remain there until the area was proclaimed a non-Native area, and some land set aside where they could go to. In the Free State also they were legally in possession, and it was when it came to the Transvaal that the difficulties arose. In the Transvaal there were 316,000 squatters in addition to the 65,000 on Crown lands.

Now let him first deal with those upon the Crown lands, because that was comparatively a simple matter. Natives on Crown lands were there legally. They paid rent, and that rent put them in occupation. He could not say what notice might have to be given supposing the Government desires to terminate their residence there. All that was required was that adequate notice should be given so that these people might look around and find some other land. Now when he came to the 316,000 it was estimated that 100,000 were on what are called companies farms, and he might say that these were in unlawful occupation. Besides these, another 100,000 were in unlawful occupation, also on private land, making 200,000 in all in unlawful occupation. As regarded these, he would say that the Bill did not put them in any worse position. It did not make their occupation unlawful and, of course, the areas might be proclaimed non-Native areas, and therefore they would have to go, or they could be made to move. In the first place they were in no worse position, or they were just in the same unlawful occupation, as they were today. In the second place one of the objects of the Commission would be to make provision for cases of this kind, and there were various ways to make it. Either there might be additional Native areas in some other part, or they could go and see what ground could be appropriated for Native purposes.

There was a provision in the Bill giving the Governor-General, with the consent of Parliament, the right to do it. The position shortly was this, that, in the Cape they had practically no difficulties neither in the Free State. In Natal they were all there legally and they could only deal with them by proclaiming as a non-Native area where they were and making provision for them. In the Transvaal a large number were unlawfully there, they were unlawfully in occupation today, and provision was made in the Bill to meet cases of that kind in the manner he had stated, either by the expropriation of the land and leaving the Native there and declaring it an additional Native area or making an additional Native area somewhere else.

In this way in a large measure this question of the squatters could be settled. He was convinced that, in the interests of the Native it was well that the question of the squatters should be dealt with. Since it had been his business to inquire very closely into this matter he had felt that he touched a position that was going to arouse a state of feeling which it would be very difficult indeed to deal with. Therefore, he would say that, in the interests of those people who were largely entrusted to them, they should proceed to deal with this question and deal with it, he hoped, on liberal lines. Although many people were there illegally it would be very difficult indeed to deal with some of these people who were squatters on land which they and their ancestors had occupied for 60 or 70 years. That was the case in the Transvaal and in Natal. Some of them had been there from time immemorial, long before the White man. In such cases these people were only technically squatters, and they had a right to very full and fair consideration when they came to deal with them. The land owned by farmers amounted to the very small extent of 1,970 morgen.

As to the question of the purchase and hire of land, it was difficult to ascertain exactly what land had been privately acquired comparatively recently, because in the Deeds Office a man's colour was not registered or noted. He found, however, that there were 670,000 morgen owned in the different provinces privately by Natives. The Cape had 222,000 morgen, the Transvaal 178,000, Natal 144,000, and the Free State 127,000. He had a return laid on the Table of the House recently dealing with the period 1909-12, which showed that during that period Natives had purchased land aproximately of 162,512 morgen in the different provinces.

AN HON. MEMBER: Is that land held by Natives in trust?

MR. SAUER: The land held by Native trusts is not a scheduled area. This is land privately acquired by Natives.

Proceeding, he said that this question of the indiscriminate acquisition of land by Natives in different parts of South Africa was by no means a new question. The Commission appointed in 1903, representing the Cape, Transvaal, Orange Free State, Natal, Rhodesia, and the Protectorates, had upon it some of the most experienced Native administrators that we had had in South Africa, and some of them distinctly what some people called sometimes pro-Native men — none the worse, perhaps, for that. This Commission sat, and after taking evidence and considering the matter very minutely, they made certain recommendations. They said that they had " arrived almost unanimously at the conclusion that it is necessary to safeguard what is conceived to be in the interests of the

Europeans of this country, but that in doing so, the door should not be entirely closed to deserving and progressive individuals among the Natives requiring land, and have resolved as follows: That certain restrictions upon the purchase of land by Natives are necessary, and recommend: (1) That purchase by Natives should in future be limited to certain areas, to be defined by legislative enactment; and (2) that purchase of land which may lead to tribal, communal, or collective possession or occupation by Natives should not be permitted ". The Commission further resolved: " That whatever principles govern the settlement of the question of the purchase of land by Natives should apply equally to the leasing of land by Natives."

That Commission was not unanimous. The representatives from Natal had, he gathered, differed. As he understood, they were prepared to limit the prohibition in this case to purchase for tribal purposes, but they did not go so far as to prohibit the individual purchase. Colonel Stanford, a very eminent authority on Native questions, took the view that prohibition should be limited tribally.

In addition to that, they had a Departmental Commission consisting of some very able and experienced men at the Cape, and they came to the same view. They also expressed the opinion that they thought the time had come when indiscriminate purchase both by Natives and Europeans should cease. He had been in communication with some of the most experienced and prominent Native administrators of South Africa, and those with whom he had been in correspondence had entirely blessed the proposals set forth in this Bill.

The Commission set forth the reasons which influenced them in making the recommendations they did. In paragraph 192 of their report they more or less summarised their views on this subject, and, *inter alia,* stated:

If this process goes on, while at the same time restrictions exclude Europeans from purchasing within Native areas, it is inevitable that at no very distant date the amount of land in Native occupation will be undesirably extended.

There will be many administrative and social difficulties created by the multiplication of a number of Native units scattered throughout a White population, and owning the land of the country equally with them. Such a situation cannot fail to accentuate feelings of race prejudice and animosity, with unhappy results. It will be far more difficult to preserve the absolutely necessary political and social distinctions if the growth of a mixed rural population of land-owners is not discouraged.

The Minister went on to say that this was the view he had long held, that while Natives and Europeans in South Africa had lived here, and would continue to do so, their arrangements should be such that the social contact was reduced to a minimum. He believed in that way they would promote the interests and happiness of both sections. He

371

did not need to say that this was a matter for consideration of the Commission. He did not want to propose that the Native should neither purchase more land, nor did he say that he had enough land. All he said was that it would be wise to say that purchase by Natives among Europeans, and by Europeans amongst Natives, should be stayed. The future of the Natives, in his opinion, was unforeseen. They might say that their future was in the lap of the gods, but he was sure of this, that no measure that they took would succeed unless they had due regard to the interests of all the people, and he believed they would promote that to a large extent by their living in separate areas.

The principle was not a new one. In the Southern States of America people had begun to solve the question by sending the Negroes to Liberia, but the Negroes did not want to go, and the employers of labour were unwilling to lose their services. In some towns in the Southern States Negroes could not live, and in others they could not even sleep, but, thank God, we had not come to that. On the question of general separation, America had achieved no results. But we had done something better. In the European areas of South Africa, although there was no prohibition of or restriction on the sale or leasing of land in the Cape or the Transvaal, they had managed, to a large extent municipally, to separate Europeans and Natives. He did not think, however, that the Native locations were always a credit to the White man. But it was a great credit to South Africa that we had done so much as we had, and that we had respected the rights of the people in the scheduled areas. No White man, except by consent of the Governor-General-in-Council, could purchase land in those areas. Let them look at Glen Grey and at the Transkei. In the Glen Grey district they had introduced individual tenure. That had worked well, and the principle had been extended to the Transkei. In Glen Grey and in the Transkei the Natives had local self-government, and he said, without fear of contradiction, that no Natives of South Africa were so far advanced as those who lived under that system in Glen Grey and in the Transkei. We had practically in this country an illustration of the effects of the separation of the races.

Then there was the provision in the Bill which said that where Natives privately occupied land the Governor-General might arrange to acquire it and that individual tenure should be introduced and regulations framed, under which repayment could be made of the purchase price. Another provision was, where any number of Natives resided within a European area and it was thought undesirable that that should continue, the Governor-General had the power to make provisions for them outside the European area. Conversely, the right was given that land owned by Europeans in a Native area could be expropriated. These were the main provisions of the Bill. A Native was defined as a member of an aboriginal tribe or race of South Africa south of the Equator.

Mr. C. H. Haggar (Roodepoort): Must he be full-blooded or half?

Mr. Sauer: I do not think this is an occasion that we need to debate that.

Proceeding, Mr. Sauer said he was not at all easy about the definition. It was not an easy matter, and he had never seen in any legislation in South Africa a definition which could be called wholly satisfactory. They might have a Negro coming here from the Southern States of America or Liberia, and obviously these people should not be put in a better position than our own aboriginal Natives, for whom the vast majority of the people had kindly feelings; at a later stage he would endeavour to alter the definition.

He would like to point out the advantages of the Bill to the Natives. One very great advantage was the scheduled area, and thus the Bill would be the Natives' charter with regard to very large areas which would be reserved to them exclusively. He did not think that the area was sufficient, but if they were given that it would already be a long step towards doing them justice. The Bill also provided for individual tenure. Another advantage was that there must be additional Native areas. There was the further advantage that many social and other evils which resulted from the too close contact between Europeans and Natives would disappear.

He did not pretend to think or say, or believe that the Bill was going to solve the Native question. He heard many people, whom he called shallow-witted people, talk of solving the Native question. In America, where the European population was in the majority, the question was said to be insoluble. He was not one of those who believed too much in legislation, for legislation very seldom attained the anticipations of its authors. It was rather the invisible laws which would govern this matter — social, moral and economic laws, and all we could do was to aid or retard them. But he was sure of this, that the civilised race — the European race — must recognise that it may be difficult if not impossible to maintain its dominant position if these invisible laws were not obeyed.

He could not do better than conclude by quoting what Mr. Bryce, the late British Ambassador to the United States, had said. Mr. Bryce had observed: " The Negro is needed as a labourer, and the more he advances, the more useful is his labour to a country which urgently needs labour. To treat the Negro fairly and help him to progress is therefore the interest of the Whites." Then the late Mr. Henry W. Grady, of Atalanta, had said: " The problem of the South is to carry on within her body politic two separate races, equal in civil and political rights, and nearly equal in numbers. She must carry these races in peace, for discord means ruin. She must carry them separately, for assimilation means debasement. She must carry them in equal justice, for to this she is pledged in honour and in gratitude. She must carry them even unto the end, for in human probability she will never be quit of either."

373

COLONEL F. H. P. CRESWELL, 9 MAY 1913[1]

THE MINISTER in introducing the Bill, made certain remarks about the ideas of those who advocated segregation. He (Mr. Creswell) thought the party to which he had the honour to belong was the first party in this country which had the temerity to go away from the formula which was so dear to the other great parties, of one party advocating a firm and just Native policy, in contra-distinction to the other party advocating a just and firm Native policy. Their party had always advocated the separation of the races. Broadly speaking, their grounds were that they believed that if they had an uncivilised and a civilised people living cheek by jowl, they would find that the same code of laws and institutions which civilised people required for their development and well-being were unsuited and unfitted for an uncivilised people and if they adjusted their institutions and laws to suit the interests of an uncivilised people, it would be impossible for the civilised people to develop and expand in the country.

What they had advocated and did still advocate, was that the policy of this country, recognising that, should recognise also, that left to themselves, there would be a natural tendency for the separation of the two races, and what they had continually in that House, and out of it, opposed, had been those institutions which the hon. member for Fordsburg[2] had called attention to, which had sprung up, not in the interests of the Native people, but in the interests of certain classes of White people, which would enable the Natives to be used for the advantage of a certain class of White person, and forcing the Natives out of their own Native habits for the benefit of a comparatively small section of the White population. He need not remind the House how consistently they had advocated confining the difficulties to the Natives within our own borders by putting a stop to Natives coming from outside. He need hardly remind the House of the shocking state of affairs regarding the Natives disclosed in the statement made by the Minister yesterday. He believed, if they first of all confined the problem to the Natives within their own borders, and set aside cant of all kinds, and recognised that all these recruiting laws and indenture laws were not really in the interests of the Natives, but mainly in the interests of those who had secured the natural resources of this country, there would be less tendency to mix up the two races. He contended that if they recognised that many of these institutions which increased the point of contact were evil, that certain areas ought to be frankly administered in the interests of the Natives, and other areas frankly administered in the interests of the Whites, they would clear away many of the difficulties of their own creation, and see very much better in the future what the real difficulties of the problem were. This Bill, with all its defects, was a step in the right direction. That being the case, were the defects of the

---

[1] Extract from speech by Colonel F. P. H. Creswell (Labour Party) in the House of Assembly, 9 May 1913, during debate on Natives Land Bill.
[2] Mr. Patrick Duncan (Unionist Party).

Bill so great that it was necessary practically to oppose the passage of the Bill? That was what the amendment of the hon. member for East London[3] amounted to. Hon. members surely must have very short memories, because it was only a few weeks ago that they heard the hon. member for Fort Beaufort[4] criticising the Government severely upon the reference of another Bill to a select committee. The principle they held was that the Government should be a Responsible Government, and he would not support any proposal which was going to make a select committee of Native Affairs take the place of the Cabinet.

The Labour Party would vote for the second reading, reserving to itself the right to take full advantage of the opportunities it would have in committee of insisting on certain alterations being made in the Bill. They would not have any objection to referring the Bill to a select committee after its second reading, but their experience on select committees was not such as to encourage them to hope very much from that. The hon. member for Fordsburg had raised one very important point, who said that in the schedule a final arrangement was made of what territory should be a Native territory. That, however, was not his (Mr. Creswell's) view. He considered that the question of the gradual separation of the races would take many years to accomplish, and he could see no reason why, because the Bill was passed, there should never be any readjustment of these boundaries. One of his objections to the Bill was that it was not desirable to aim at a chequer-board sort of separation. The object of the Commission[5] in making recommendations for additional Native areas should be to aggregate all the Native areas in contiguity to one another, so that the Natives might have their own institutions and develop along their own lines. They had this system at work in Basutoland and in the Territories.[6] While the Europeans were undoubtedly the custodians of the Natives, they had an onerous duty, and it was desirable to divest ourselves of that responsibility. It should be the aim of the country to give the Natives their own parallel institutions.

GENERAL J. B. M. HERTZOG, 16 MAY 1913[7]

GENERAL J. B. M. HERTZOG said that, in the first place, he wished to congratulate the Minister of Native Affairs on the step he had taken in introducing this measure. Not that he regarded it as by any means sufficient, but he regarded it as a guarantee of what would come in the

3 Mr. Rider.
4 Sir Thomas Smartt (Unionist Party).
5 Later appointed under the Chairmanship of Sir William Beaumont.
6 The Transkeian Territories of the Cape which since 1894 had Councils with limited powers.
7 Extracts from speech by General J. B. M. Hertzog in the House of Assembly during the debate on the Natives Land Bill, 16 May 1913.

future. But he thought the Minister, at any rate, deserved credit for the step he had taken. Not that he agreed with him on all points, but the points where he disagreed were really more points of personal impressions and characteristics . . .

. . . He considered that it was as much in the interests of the White as in the interests of the Native people that a step such as indicated in the Bill should be taken. He held that the time had fully come for such a step to be taken. When they looked at the conditions prevailing in South Africa, then they must admit that they could not get away from the fact that there was friction in this country between the Natives and White people, or rather let him say between the rights and privileges of the Native and the White man . . .

. . . Everyone in South Africa who came into contact with the Native, where he most pressed on the White people, must admit that there was pressure. That pressure, and consequently that friction must increase and make itself felt more and more as time went on . . .

. . . During the short while he had the honour of being in charge of the Portfolio of Native Affairs he had received scores of letters from people in the Transvaal, who pointed out that farming was impossible where Natives and Europeans were next to each other. That naturally must have the effect of creating ill-feeling and bitterness, with the effect that it became more and more difficult for the Native and the White man to live in harmony, and as the number of Native landowners increased the friction must naturally also increase . . .

. . . The right hon. gentleman[8] had said that he did not consider it advisable for the Native to be restricted within certain divisions where he would be told to stop and have his property there. Unless they made such provisions he was convinced that they would never be honest towards the Native, and that they would never act honestly and straightforwardly towards him. There was no one in that House, he contended, who would dare tell him that today they were acting honestly towards the Natives. It would not blind him to hear people say " We are giving the Natives equal rights ". The fact was that so far they had always seen to it and would always do so, that in practice, whatever his rights on paper, the Native would not have these equal rights. " I am convinced that if my right hon. friend were asked to give his consent to the extension of the Cape franchise system to the rest of the Union, and that if the effect of such extension would be to give the Natives the majority in this country, he would not agree to do so. And if he were to agree to this, how many people in South Africa would agree? Let me appeal to the Cape members in this House and ask them whether they would be prepared to give absolute equality to the Natives and Europeans in South Africa? Would they accept a proposal to that effect, even if they knew that the result might be to give the Natives a majority? I am convinced that with per-

[8]Mr. John X. Merriman, a preceding speaker in the debate.

haps five exceptions at the utmost, every member would be opposed to such a step."

Proceeding, General Hertzog asked what effect this action towards the Natives must have on the minds of these people? There could be no doubt that the Native had not only a feeling of suspicion towards us, but he must also lack confidence in our honesty.

The right hon. gentleman had spoken of the education of the Natives and the civilising process they had undergone in the Cape. What did that civilisation mean and what did it amount to if the Native was yet excluded from taking part with the European in the latter's civilisation and the results of that civilisation? It was a great disadvantage to the Native and he must feel it to his soul — if he felt as we did — to be excluded from the privileges which the European people enjoyed, to be excluded from Parliament, to be excluded from the drawing-rooms, and to be excluded from ordinary contact. Under the present circumstances under which they were trying to help these Natives along, it could not be anything but detrimental.

Some hon. members had asked: "What about the civilised and what about the educated Native?" He repeated what he had said before and the same had been said by educated Natives in America: "The place of the educated Native is not among the White people, but among his own people." When in the Middle Ages an educated German came back from Rome, the centre of learning, had he felt any objections, had he felt degraded because he went back to his own people? The missionaries who were the best educated people, had to work among people who were just as barbarous and worse than the Natives were today. Today still they had missionaries from all over Europe. Did these people feel degraded because they lived among people of a lower stage of civilisation? Well, if it was not unbearable, not intolerable for the European, could it then be so intolerable for the Native to go back into the midst of his own people? After all, he (the educated Native) had bonds which tied him to his people, and these bonds would always remain. As a matter of fact, these educated Natives, notwithstanding their education, should feel more in common with the people of their own class than with the Europeans. What was written by American authors, such as Thomas and others? It had been tried there, too, to bring the civilised Negro into permanent contact with the White man, socially and otherwise. They knew how detrimental that state of affairs had been for the Europeans as well as for the Negroes. Negroes preaching in America on the subject had said, "We know it, the place of our educated Negro is among our own people". How could the right hon. member say that he wished the Natives to be educated if he did not wish the educated Native to have a chance of looking after that education, but asked him, instead, to come and sit with the Whites? It was unnecessary, he held, to give these educated people the option of living among the White people, because there could be no hardship for them to have to live among their own folks . . .

377

. . . It was in the interest of the Native himself that he should be segregated. Many people wanted the Native to have the vote. He emphatically repeated what he had said before, that in years and years to come the Native would not have more votes than he was allowed today under the Act of Union. Why not? Simply because they must take into account the feelings of the people, and these feelings would not change. Many people felt strongly on this matter. There was the hon. member for Tembuland (Mr. T. L. Schreiner), for instance. Many hon. members might agree with him that it was unjust that the vote was withheld from the Natives, and that it was to be regretted that the position was so, but, at the same time, they would point out that the interests of the White man must weigh heavily, and so heavily must these interests weigh, that they would say: " We are not going to give the vote to the Natives."

When they placed the Native in a separate territory they gave him an opportunity of developing, and his position would become stronger and stronger, and he would be able even to have a continually growing measure of self-government within that territory.

When the Minister of Native Affairs spoke about this matter, it seemed to him that he was of opinion that everywhere in the Union they should establish small locations. If they did that, he held, the Natives would have the greatest right to say, " You are doing us an injustice, because in these small locations it is impossible that we should ever be able to secure any substantial amount of self-government, whereas if we were placed in larger locations, we could have such self-government, as for instance, the Natives in the Transkei have ". Such a position would lead to satisfaction. They would not smart under any real or imaginary injustice as they did today. When a Commission was appointed as proposed by the Minister, he hoped that Commission would demarcate large territories where the Natives could go, and if that were not done they would never succeed in obtaining their object. Of course, if they had a certain amount of self-government, they would still stand under the control of this House. He wanted the European to feel that he was protected against a future danger, and that the Native was placed in a position where he could help himself to a position with sufficient power and authority as would conduce to his advancement.

3

NATIVES IN URBAN AREAS

GENERAL J. C. SMUTS, 6 FEBRUARY 1923[1]

THIS BILL was introduced to this House in the latter part of last
session but owing to representations being made from various quarters
that there should be further consultation and discussion on some of its
details, the Government decided not to proceed with the Bill, but let it
stand over for this session.

I need not point out to the House how very urgent the Bill has become
now. It is not the first time now, nor was it the first time last year,
that this matter was before us. Three years ago, when I introduced the
second reading of the Native Affairs Bill the Commission, which it was
proposed to set up in that Bill, would have for one of its first and most
difficult tasks the question of the better regulation and control of Native
areas. Even then three years ago this was considered one of the most
urgent and difficult questions which called for consideration and action by
this House. The Native Affairs Commission proceeded almost at once
after its appointment to deal with this matter. The Bill was drafted, and
was considered by the Native Affairs Commission, and they proceeded to
discuss the draft with local bodies all over South Africa, as well as with
representative bodies of Natives, and, in fact, as far as possible consulted
every interest throughout the Union in reference to the details of this
Bill. This had been going on for the last two years, and I will make
bold to say that no Bill has ever been introduced into this House which
has received such detailed consideration and discussion as the Bill now
before it. We have so far, Sir, succeeded in this House in keeping our
greatest political question out of the range of party politics. We have
really succeeded in steering clear of party politics whenever we approached
this fundamental problem in our life in South Africa, and in view of
the gravity of the subject, in view of the consideration which has always
been given; and will still be given when it goes to select committee, I
now urge that we discuss it here in this House from that larger point
of view, and not from any party or sectional point of view, which will
make the Native in this country understand that this is an impartial
attitude of ours when we approach the Native question of this country,

---

[1] Extract from speech by General J. C. Smuts (Prime Minister), in the House
of Assembly, during the debate on the Native Urban Areas Bill, reported in
the *Cape Times*, 7 February 1923. Bill enacted as Act 21 of 1923.

or any individual aspects of that question. Thus we shall not divide in this House on party lines, but will show that we are prepared to give it fair and impartial consideration. Consideration on these lines and in that spirit, whatever the result of this Bill may be, will help to foster a better spirit between the White and Native races in this country.

Before I come to the details of this Bill, let me say a very great change has come over South Africa within our own lifetime. I remember as a young man in this part of the country when I grew up here, it was a very unusual thing to see a Black man in this part of South Africa. We had our towns, and villages, we had our White population and Coloured people, who lived either among the Whites or on the fringes of the towns and villages, but the Native, except in certain harbours like working on the Docks, was a most unusual sight in those days. That was not so long ago when I was a young man. What is the position today? A complete change has come over South Africa owing to the economic development of the country, and owing to forces entirely beyond human control there has been a great flux, there has been a great influx of Natives from other parts of South Africa into towns like this and to other towns, and in fact the most tremendous social and political phenomenon of our day and our generation has been just this — the pressure of the Natives on the larger industrial centres of South Africa. The Native population has increased by leaps and bounds.

But the provision for their reception has not been made correspondingly, and today we are up against one of the most difficult problems in this respect in South Africa. No special means have been established for the reception of these people. No doubt there are locations in many towns in South Africa, many villages have their small locations, but for the influx which has taken place in the large industrial centres all over South Africa we have been entirely unprepared. The result has been that the Natives have gone into the towns, they have mixed with the rest of the population, they have not been segregated in their own areas next door, they have freely mixed with the rest of the population, and, Sir, the most lamentable results have ensued in consequence. Some years ago we had a Commission in this country which inquired into tuberculosis. The inquiry disclosed one of the most terrible conditions in South Africa, due very largely to this — due to this overcrowding of all sorts and conditions of people without any proper provision being made, without any sifting out, or any proper housing accommodation being provided.

We had another Commission, the Commission which inquired into assaults on women. That Commission made a similar report, showing that this lamentable situation which arose in South Africa was largely due to this intermixture of the population and the unwholesome conditions under which Native and White lived together. I need not paint the picture more than needs be; we know the effect of our neglect of dealing with this question has been that our White civilisation has been dragged down, that the Whites have suffered and the White civilisation in South

Africa, which we should hold up, has been degraded by the conditions of the present system. The Native, on the other hand, has suffered to an appalling extent as a result of this neglect. The Native has come to our towns unprovided for — innocent, untutored people, who often fall into the hands of criminals and pick up diseases and vice.

The result of all this neglect of our duty to deal with the situation has been harmful in the extreme both to the White and the Native population. Now this is a matter which has become more urgent, but it is not one which is beyond solution. There are aspects of our great Native question which appear to be almost beyond solution — questions so large and of which we know so little and over which we have so little control that they seem to be beyond all human control. But this question is not such a one. Although the question is difficult, housing and the urban control of Natives is manageable even at this late hour — if we undertake the task with energy and good will; and if the country responds — as I have no doubt it will — we may remove one of the biggest blots which is today resting on our civilisation. I am sure we can do so, and I hope we shall.

In dealing with this question, which has been delayed to some extent because legal responsibility has been shifted from one authority to another, hon. members, when they look at the clauses of the Bill, will see the various authorities which are referred to. In the first place, without doubt, responsibility, both moral and legal, rests upon the towns, the urban authority or the municipalities. The Native populations in the towns form just as much the people as the Whites do, and are there for the economic life of the town, and there is no doubt that, in the first instance, the responsibility for their care, control and proper condition rests on the towns. The towns can under our Constitutional system come under the purview of the Provincial Councils — which is the second authority. Above all is the Union Parliament and Union Government. The South Africa Act lays down, as hon. members are aware, that Native affairs as a whole shall be a charge to the Union.

We have, therefore, all the constitutional authorities concerned and all in their degree responsible for dealing with this matter. Hon. members will see that the Bill says that wherever necessary proper conditions by way of locations or otherwise shall be made by the town, and where a town through culpable or prolonged neglect does not do its duty, the Union Government will step in, and at the town's expense, do what the town should have done. Hon. members will see that it is laid down with regard to the establishment of locations that in the first place there shall be established in the necessary places a location for each town.

Of course, in most of the towns of South Africa they have these locations already, and I do not assume that under this Bill it will be necessary, even in a small percentage of cases, to take any special action; and these local authorities will find that this Bill exerts no pressure whatever. But there are places where the Native populations have increased out of all bounds, and for these cases it is laid down that locations must be established, or existing accommodation for the reception of Natives must be increased. Everything should be done to see that the Natives who are taking part in the economic life of a place are properly received and housed there.

Three distinctions are made in the first clause. It is laid down that there shall be locations of the ordinary type, that is, that a Native who has not emerged from barbarism and is accustomed to the most primitive form of life shall be housed much as he is housed now. But we have at this time of day to reckon with another situation as well — a situation amongst the Natives themselves. There are Natives who are no longer of a semi-barbarous type and have been taught and developed, and their housing conditions must necessarily be of a different character of those of the semi-barbarous Natives.

Members would see that the Bill made provision that either in the location or next door to it there should be what was called in the Bill a " Native village ", a place set aside where the better-class Native could live, the educated Native who had raised himself in the scale of civilisation, and it was not fair to ask that man to live in among the rest of his people who were still in a semi-barbarous state. In the Native villages there would be better houses, and very large arrangements would be made that the Natives would acquire their own plot of ground in the village, and put up their own houses.

" I hope," proceeded General Smuts, " that if this idea of better conditions for the better-class Natives takes root and develops, the result will be that in the end practically every Native, even those exempt under the Bill, will find it better and more convenient to go and live in the Native village, and in time they may have complete segregation of the Native population out of the White area, and living under their own conditions in the Native villages. If this Native village, which is one of the ideas contained in the Bill, is a success, then I am hopeful that this might be one of its far-reaching effects.

" The Natives would themselves see that it was better for them to go and live there, but to ask a Native, an educated Native, who, perhaps, has property in town, who is perhaps a professional man — a teacher or a trader — to go and live in among the semi-barbarous people, is not fair. At present we can only follow the practice which has existed so far, and that is to give exemption to these better-class Natives."

Then there was a third feature in the Bill in reference to the locations. Members would see that provision was also made for the establishment of reception houses, called " hostels " in the Bill, for the reception of Natives. The location would have its population, the population which was working in the town, either living in the village or in the location proper, but they would have what they had everywhere now in the big centres, a continually floating population of Natives who came for work and who got a pass or a certificate to look for work for a certain period.

Now there would be no accommodation for those people in the location; the location was already allotted and occupied by the people who were already working in the town. This floating population — which came and went and looked for labour and if it did find labour in the end it would get into the location, or if it did not find labour had to return to the place from which it came — this floating population had to be received in the meantime.

In Johannesburg they had established compounds, where those people could stay during the time they looked for work, and from which they returned again if no work was found for them. Those reception compounds would become, as they were called in the Bill, by the better sounding name " reception hostels." The two parts of the scheme were already in full working order in South Africa; they had the locations and in some of the big centres they had the hostels.

The novel part of the proposal before the House was that in regard to the Native village, and that had been put in, as he had explained, as a concession to the civilised Native who was moving on — and that Native did not like to go back to merge again in the semi-barbarous population.

GENERAL J. B. M. HERTZOG, 6 FEBRUARY 1923[1]

LISTENING TO General Smuts, he could have agreed with practically every word spoken by the right hon. gentleman, and he agreed that the position today was infinitely worse than it had been in the past. Without segregation they could not do justice, and they could not allow the present position to continue. The Prime Minister clearly saw to what the evil was due, and he clearly saw what the remedy was.

Why then had he not put his foot down, and pursued the course which he knew to be the right one? Had he done so, General Smuts would have tackled the problem of the Coloured man and laid proposals before the House simultaneously with the proposals respecting the Native. To him (the speaker) it was clear that the Native Affairs Commission had never received any intimation from the Government of the line along which it should work and make its recommendations to the House.

The Bill said that the Native would have the right to acquire land in the locations and also in the villages. They were dealing with land which, according to the law of 1913, was clearly White man's land, in which the Native could not acquire or rent land. But the Commission, without taking that into account, now enabled the Native to become a land-owner in such areas. Thus they were at once renouncing a principle which had been definitely adopted in 1913.

General Hertzog declared that on two grounds the Native was particu-

---

[1] Extract from speech by General J. B. M. Hertzog (National Party), Leader of the Opposition, as reported in the *Cape Times*, 7 February 1923.

larly hostile to the White man — the pan-African policy, on the ground of which the Native said the White man had no right in South Africa. On that point the Government and he and his party had always clearly answered: " We are here, and we are masters here." Another ground of hostility of the Native towards the Whites was that the White man had not always acted honestly and honourably by the Native. They were all guilty in that respect. He urged them to see that the election promises made to the Native were kept, and to beware lest they continued to give the Native ground for that contention. But now they told the Native that he could purchase land in the locations where he and his children could remain for all time to come. And if conditions should arise in days to come when, on the ground of public policy, it was found that the Native could not remain there, they would give the impression again of being guilty of breaches of faith. The Commission should have had its attention drawn to that principle so that the Native would have been given the opportunity of securing certain other rights, but it should have been made clear that on the White man's land the Native could only be a temporary resident.

Under the conditions laid down, the Native would ere long be demanding the franchise. The aspirations of the Natives would be awakened, and, as he had said before, nothing was more detrimental in South Africa than to give the Native the franchise. It would be detrimental and dishonest, because they knew that if they were to give him the franchise tomorrow they would take it off him again the next day.

For all those reasons he wished the select committee to give the Bill its most careful consideration. He agreed with the Prime Minister when he said that the whole question should not be dealt with from the party standpoint. They should deal with the question so that the Native should not be regarded as they heard from some, as a curse, but as an asset. And there was no doubt that he was an asset, and could be turned into a greater asset still.

They must regard the Native as a child, and they must be honest with him, treating him in such a manner that he looked upon the White men with trust and confidence. The Native had a culture which the White man did not understand; and they should beware that they did not shake the Native's belief in the culture and the civilisation of the White man.

4

REPRESENTATION OF NATIVES

GENERAL J. B. M. HERTZOG, 25 FEBRUARY 1936[1]

THE SUBJECT of the Bill which is now to be read a second time is
one which for the past 50 years and more has constantly received the
attention, and very serious attention, of the whole of the European population of South Africa. Ever since the day when in 1875, I think it was 1875,
the Cape Native was put on the voters' roll in the Cape Colony, it has
been a subject which was very anxiously considered and weighed by the
European population, and no wonder. If there are two things which have
always made the White population of South Africa feel very anxious, then
they are, firstly, the danger that there was of intermingling of blood, and,
secondly, the danger there was of being dominated by the Natives. I say
that it is no wonder, because ever since the first day that the European
came into contact with the Native it was found that, so far as numbers
were concerned, the Europeans were but few in numbers in comparison
with the millions, and possibly the millions more of Natives by which they
were surrounded. He, therefore, always felt faced by the question of the
mixing of blood, and if there was one thing against which the White population in South Africa, English-speaking no less than Dutch-speaking,
Dutch-speaking no less than people of any other race, should guard against,
it was the danger that the White population and its civilisation would be
dominated by a mixed civilisation of another race. That was always felt,
and it is still felt today.

I say it is a thing which was always very strongly felt, and is still felt
very strongly today. But in addition to that there was always the fact —
and let me here say at once that the European has always hitherto succeeded very well in preventing racial intermixture. It redounds to his
honour, and speaks very highly for him that notwithstanding all the temptation and all the causes which might otherwise have led to it, he was
nevertheless, able to keep his race pure in South Africa. But the second
thing that has always hitherto occupied him, and which is always deeply
felt still is the danger he runs of being overwhelmed eventually by the millions of Natives in the immediate and in the far-distant future. When in
1875 the franchise was given to the Natives in the Cape Colony on an

---

[1] Speech by General J. B. M. Hertzog (United Party), Prime Minister, on the
second reading of the Representation of Natives Bill in the Joint Session of
Parliament, 25 February 1936. *House of Assembly Debates.*

equal footing with the Europeans it was immediately regarded as the opening of the door to enable the Coloured population, that Native population of from 6,000,000 to 7,000,000 as against 2,000,000 Europeans, eventually to dominate the White population. If the Natives get the necessary education, and the necessary schooling, they must eventually get the upper hand if they only have the desire to take it. And no one can ever doubt about it that when the Native ever gets that upper hand at the ballot box, he will not omit to use it in his own favour. We must accept that, and it has always hitherto been accepted by the Europeans in South Africa.

You sometimes hear that the Natives are not a danger to the Europeans, and that it is shown by this, that during the past ten years they have not only made no progress, so far as the voters' rolls in the Cape Colony are concerned, but have actually retrogressed. That is no argument at all. The great fact which will always be decisive is: Can the Native eventually, whether in 50 years, or in 100 years, put himself in possession of the necessary qualifications for getting on to the roll? About that no doubt can exist. And as the Natives will number three times or twice as many as the Europeans, there can be no doubt that they will be able to dominate the Europeans. I say that since 1875 it has been felt by the European population that that putting of the Native on an equality with the Europeans at the ballot-box would sooner or later have to be taken into review. That was felt so strongly that, as we know, after the Second War of Independence,[2] immediately after the conclusion of peace, a Native Affairs Commission was appointed by Sir Alfred Milner to go into the whole matter, to inquire into it and to make a report as to what ought to be done. I do not want to go into that report here today, but yet I think that it will be a good thing if I just make a small quotation from it here. *Inter alia,* that report said (retranslation)—

The possession of the franchise by the Natives under a system which is in force in the Cape Colony and which allows it to be used in a spirit of competition with and opposition to the European voters, which makes the organised Native voter the deciding factor in any keen election fight between political parties, and which in proportion as the numerical strength of the Native voters increases, will enable them to outvote the Europeans in certain parts of the country, must inevitably create an intolerable position, and is an unwise and dangerous thing.

The commission went on to make recommendations, practically of the kind as are included in this Bill today, mainly of the same kind as are included in this Bill. Since that time the question with all its dangers has always filled the imagination of the European population, and we have constantly been engaged in South Africa in tinkering at it, and seeing what could be done. Unfortunately, I say unfortunately, up to the present feeling has always — in the first place as a result of the Second

---

2 The Anglo-Boer War of 1899-1902.

War of Independence — has always been such in our country that the two great sections of the European population could not manage to give their attention to this matter objectively, and in an impartial way, in order to see what should be done in connection with this question in the interests, not only of the European population, but also, in my opinion, just as much in the interests of the Native population itself. I say they were always hitherto too much obsessed with sentiments, as I have said, especially as a result of the Boer War, which prevented them considering the matter in the way it should have been considered.

But slowly we made some progress. The matter was taken up as most of us know, and as we can all remember a Bill was introduced in 1929 in a similar joint sitting of both Houses of Parliament, and that Bill was then rejected. But all the time everyone of us has always felt that even if we differed from each other, it would not take much longer, that there could not be much further delay in coming to a solution of this matter. Because not only was it a canker that was eating into the souls of the White population, but it was like a disease which inevitably had also to penetrate into the minds of the Natives, because as long as the Native exists in uncertainty of what his eventual lot is going to be so far as this question is concerned, we have always found, and we always shall find, that there are people who advise the Natives to take up a position directly in conflict with what the Europeans think should be done. That is done. We know that up to the present there have also been numbers of individuals amongst the Europeans who honestly thought that they were doing the right thing in recommending the Natives to act in opposition to what the Europeans thought ought to be done in connection with this matter.

But however many such Europeans there may have been, however innocent the Natives were from the point of view of their own interests, the fact remains that that kind of thing always kept their feelings going, and always made them more inflammable in proportion as the time went on. In the circumstances I think that we are right in rejoicing very greatly in this joint sitting about the state of affairs we have reached, about the measure of agreement that we have obtained, and of which we have reason to be proud. Nothing is a better proof to me of how much the interests of South Africa have often been kept in conflict, and possibly are still being kept in conflict, than the fact that now that the two great sections of the population, the English-speaking and the Dutch-speaking, have come to a time in our history when we can consider a matter like this calmly and quietly, that we, so far as this great matter is concerned, have arrived at such an amount of unity.

I now want briefly to inquire what is contained in this Bill. In the first place, it has already been felt for years, since Union, from the beginning, that the Natives could not be treated in one way in one province, and in a different way in another province. Here in the Cape Colony the Native got equal franchise rights with the European on the same basis and in the same ballot box. In Natal there was an amended form, which meant something on paper, but amounted to nothing in practice. In the Orange Free State and in the Transvaal there was none. We may say that there was no representation in those three northern provinces, of the interests of the Natives, in the legislative authority of the country. But one thing was very clearly felt, and that was that we could not go on, and have that large element of millions of Natives in our midst without them also having their interests represented in the legislative body of the country.

The second great thing about which I think we were all in agreement is that what was being done for one province should also apply to the other provinces, otherwise it would lead to a state of affairs which in its turn would give rise to a constant claim for further changes. We then sat as a select committee, and started from the point of view that in this country the same guiding principle should be accepted for all four provinces of the Union. Starting from that point of view we said, in the first place, that the Natives in South Africa should get representation for their interests only in the Senate, and that is what is being laid down in this Bill. As a principle it is laid down that the Natives from all over the Union, from all the four provinces, will all be put on an equal basis, and that they will get representation in the legislative body of the country, but they will get in the Senate, and not as was laid down in the Cape Act of 1875, in the House of Assembly of this country. That is the first point, Mr. Speaker.

But there were a few other points which were constantly such a rock of offence to the European population in South Africa, that we had to give our attention to them as well. One of them was that Natives were on the same roll, even if it was only in the Cape Province, but that they were put on the same roll as the White man, that they had to vote at the same ballot box, and for the same person as the White man, and that in the constituencies where there are Native voters, they all go together to the same ballot box with the White man. As I have said, that in itself was a thing which the White man could not agree with, because it opened the way, in his opinion and my opinion, to eventual domination by the Native in South Africa. But there was also a measure of social intercourse with each other, social intercourse which was inevitably caused by the way in which candidates were out to get the vote of the electors, to speak so as to please the electors, and by the way in which they went about with Native electors, a way which they would not have adopted otherwise. We all know that. It was a thing that went against the grain, and against the will of the Europeans, and I say it again, against the ideals of English-speaking as well as of Dutch-speaking people, that they should vote together, should vote jointly, be on the same voters' roll, that they should go together to the same ballot box, and that there they should both have their votes touted for when there was an election, and that was a thing which offended the feelings, because this free association caused by the joint voting allowed the position of the

White man in his opposition to miscegenation in South Africa to be weakened. Inevitably the easy intercourse, etc., was bound to lead to a considerable amount of social intercourse. The select committee, therefore, started from the point of view that it was not in the interests of the Native nor in those of the European to have that repeated, and, therefore, in this Bill it is laid down that the Natives will have their representation apart from the Europeans. They will have it in the Senate by representatives sent by them to the Senate, who will be elected separately from the Senators who are sent there by the Europeans. Those Senators will be voted for by a group of Natives, who are delegates of Natives to a Native college, and this Native college will vote for these Senators whom they send to Parliament. There is, therefore, here again a total and clear dealing with the Native separately, a separation from the White man, also in respect of sending, and the manner of sending members to the legislative body of the country.

With regard to the nature of the representation, the Bill lays down that there shall for the present be sent by the Natives of the Union to the Senate four Senators elected by themselves — one by the Transkei, one by the rest of the Cape Province, one by the Transvaal and the Free State jointly, and one by Natal. The four persons will be the persons who will be required to represent the interests of the Natives in the Legislative Assembly of the country. These four must be Europeans. But it was also found by the select committee that that would not be enough. When one notices the stage of development reached today by the Natives in South Africa, the select committee felt that the time had come for the Native to be brought into still closer contact with the whole of the legislative authority, not only with the Senate, but also with the House of Assembly of the country, in such a way that his interests will be respected, and that his interests will be laid before the legislative chambers of the country through the men chosen by them out of their own midst. The result was that the select committee recommended, and it has been included in the Bill, that there shall be a Native Council consisting of 22 members, 16 of whom shall be Natives, and six of whom shall be Europeans. So far as the 16 Natives are concerned, 12 will be elected by the Natives in the various circles who elect the Senators by the Natives themselves. Four Natives will be nominated from the four different circles, as representing the four different electoral circles, and they will be selected by the Government. There will, therefore, be 16 Natives on that Council, and in addition, there will be the six Europeans. One is the secretary of the department, and he will also act as chairman, and in addition to him five chief Native commissioners have been provided for; they will, therefore, be men who are well acquainted with Native affairs throughout the whole of the Union, men who can, therefore, be of great service in the deliberations that will take place. The Minister will have to lay down annually where and when the Council will meet, but the Council is intended to be in close touch with the legislative bodies, so much so that the Native Council is entrusted with the consideration of all matters affecting Native interests, especially those that affect Natives, and it is further entrusted with the duty of consulting and deciding on any matter which it thinks is or may be of importance to the Natives, and after deliberation the decision and report must be laid on the Table of both Houses of Parliament. In that way the Natives are, therefore, brought into direct contact, not only with the Senate where they have their direct representatives, but, so far as questions and views are concerned, that refer to their own people, they are put in a position to make themselves immediately felt in the House of Assembly as well as in the Senate.

It seems to me that this Native Council may be of far more value to the Natives — and so it will be — than what the Cape franchise would have been if it had been extended to the four provinces. It could not be otherwise. Here a really serious attempt is being made to see that the Natives are put in a position of bringing their complaints every year before the House of Assembly, and before the Senate, and in that way, it is clear to me, the European will immediately be reminded of his great duty as trustee for the Natives, as has never been the case before, and as never can happen under the Cape system.

Now I come to the Cape system itself. It was, of course, easy for the select committee to pass the resolution which I have put before this House, as long as it had to do with the three northern provinces. But it was a far more difficult question when we came to the Cape Province. There we had to deal with vested rights. The Natives here have the same qualification today of being put on to the roll as the Europeans, and of voting in the same way as the Europeans do. As I have already said, we at once said, " That cannot be ", for the reasons that I have given. Because with the large numbers of Natives in our midst, who may be qualified tomorrow or the day after, and put on to the roll, in comparison with the Europeans who are half as strong as the Natives, we could not take the course of thinking about placing the Natives in a position of being able eventually to overwhelm the Europeans. Well, what was to be done? Let me say this: the first Bill that I laid on the Table shows what we consider would be desirable to agree to, preferable to the one we have today.

But it is not a question of what is ideal. We could have ideal laws. I can assure hon. members I could lay many other Bills before the House that are ideal, but the question is — do we want to solve the question or do we not? We are concerned with practical politics. The people in the country want the sword which has been hanging over their heads all these years to be removed, and this is the only way of doing so.

I have always said since the first time I spoke on this subject, that we can settle the Native question naturally, but no one can deny that the greatest and the best way of doing it, and the way along which we ought to try to do it, is that we ought to get with us as many of the Natives and as many of the European population of South Africa as we possibly can. We could get a solution of the problem, but along a road which would immediately cause an agitation by which the

White population of South Africa would be split in two, and be like enemies in opposite camps, the one alone by itself, and the other with the millions of Natives behind it. I ask hon. members, and I ask the House what was our duty? No, I have always taken up that attitude, and in 1929 I said it. This question has over and over again been discussed with me, and we arrived at the decision to get the support of the Europeans to as large an extent as possible, but also to get the goodwill of the majority of the Natives with us, we would have to take care that we did nothing that the Native would regard as an action by which something was being taken away from him, by which an injustice was being done to him, and the European would have to feel that his conscience was satisfied with what was being done. It became clear to me that if we did not do that, then we should simply be causing a state of affairs in South Africa, which not only would lead to no good end, but which would more and more lead to conflict and dissension.

In the first Bill, which was laid on the Table of this Assembly we said: "Let us give the Natives seven members in the House of Assembly here." But this was subsequently reconsidered, and then it was altered to three. We then said: "Let us give the Natives three members." I thought at that time that three members would be enough if they were given in exchange for what the Natives have in the Cape Province today; the three members would represent the interests of the Natives, and I felt that if we did that we should be acting fairly towards the Natives. I felt we would then be able to say to the Natives: "We are acting fairly here, we are giving you more than you have today. Today you have not the right of sitting with the European; you cannot say 'That is my member who sits there, to look after my interests'. But in future you will actually be able to say, 'Those three members are sitting there to represent my interests.'" I thought that if we gave that to the Natives, then they could not complain much, but so far as the European population was concerned I felt that the European population also should have nothing to complain about. I felt that neither the church, nor any body, nor any person ought to be able to say that their consciences objected to the action taken. Our people say that you cannot amend anything in the present state of affairs, and you may not take away this or the other from the Natives. When people say that, I answer: "No, but then you are forgetting that there is very little legislation ever passed by which some right or other is not taken away, and you forget that there is no legislation which is ever passed by which this or the other thing is not amended."

There is one thing that I can say to the people who feel in that way. I respect their conscientious objection, I respect their feelings, but they must not forget that the Europeans have the fullest right of seeing that their continued existence in South Africa shall be secured. And when they appeal to me, as has sometimes been done recently, on the ground that it is not Christian, that it is in conflict with Christian principles, then I say: "Oh no, now I do not understand at all what you mean by Christian principles." Christian principles count for very much, and I hope that they will always count for very much with our people, but there is a principle of self-preservation for a nation, the principle which causes everybody to sacrifice his life in time of war, a principle which we abandoned in[3] the three years' war[4]. It is a sacred principle, a Christian principle, just the same as any other principle, and it stands equally high — I place that principle still higher, it is the only principle, that of self-preservation, of self-defence, by which humanity itself and Christianity itself will ever be able to protect itself. It may be said that the facts that I mentioned about our fear in regard to the future of the White man are not correct facts. That may be put forward, and then we can discuss it. But if you say that the European, when he says: "My safety demands that the Natives shall only get a measure of political rights, only in the way that is compatible with the White man and his civilisation in South Africa," if you say that it is unchristian to speak in that way, then I say that I do not agree with you. That is a principle that we have adopted, and accordingly we have said that the Cape Natives will get three members, i.e. the Natives in the Cape who have the franchise today, or will get it in the future. They will be put on a separate roll, and then they will be able to send three members, three Europeans, to the House of Assembly in future. By that I think full justice will be done to the Natives, and also to the Europeans, so far as their protection is concerned. Will the position of the Europeans be detrimentally affected by that? Just think of it, I do not believe that anyone at all will say that by giving the Natives three members in the House of Assembly, which will in future consist of 153 members, we shall be putting the Natives in a position of being able to overwhelm the Europeans.

I have already said that according to this Bill the Natives will send three European members to the House of Assembly. They will also retain that other right that they have to vote along with the Europeans for men who will represent them in the Provincial Councils. I said: "They will retain it." No, that is not quite accurate but in exchange for that they will get something similar to what they have in the House of Assembly. They will also get two White members in the Provincial Council of the Cape Province to represent their interests there. In this respect also the Natives will all go off the voters' rolls on which they are jointly registered with the Europeans. They will be placed on a separate list, and will vote separately. Their votes will have no influence on the election of an ordinary European member of the Provincial Council who is sent there by the Europeans. In that way the distasteful spectacle will stop which we have so often seen in the past, at our elections. I do not want to detain the joint sitting any longer. I, of course,

[3] Read: "Which made us enter . . ."—(Translation error in Hansard).
[4] The Anglo-Boer War, 1899-1902.

do not expect that I have convinced my hon. friend the hon. member for Roodepoort (Colonel C. F. Stallard) by what I have said this afternoon. I, therefore, expect, and will await the speech with interest, that he will speak on this subject, and I hope to answer him and others when the time comes. But I want again to say that we must not lose sight of the fact that the Europeans not only have rights but also duties, rights of their own and duties towards themselves. But then I also want to add something, and that is that the Europeans can also not forget that they also owe duties to the Natives. One thing I feel convinced of is that when this Bill becomes law, then not only the Europeans will feel relieved that the sword that has been hanging over their heads all these years has disappeared, and that they can, therefore, breathe freely, but the Europeans will also be thankful that now at last they are in a position of acting honestly towards the Natives. We cannot close our eyes to the fact that in the past we often felt that it was desirable to promote the Natives' interests, and to make them happier people; we felt that it would be of great importance to us with a view to the interests of the State to be able to help the Natives forward, but instead of doing that, we always put on the brake. Why? Because every time that the Natives took a step forward on the road of civilisation it was felt to be making the threat worse that he eventually would overwhelm us with his numbers. We were never honest towards the Natives; not deliberately, but because we were compelled to act in that way, we could not help ourselves as long as the sword was hanging over our heads. For that reason I feel that this Bill is of so much importance, although it is not the best. If I had had my own way I could have introduced a different and better Bill than the one of 1929, but we are not here to run after illusions, but to get practical results. For these reasons it is a real joy to me today, when I think that after the years of effort, after all the years of anxiety of the White population of South Africa, I am called upon to introduce a Bill here which is going to meet with the almost unanimous approval of this Assembly.

MR. J. H. HOFMEYR, 6 APRIL 1936[1]

I REGRET that I cannot vote for this Bill. I can hardly make that vote a silent one, and, therefore, I must ask the indulgence of the joint sitting to give my reasons for that vote. Circumstances have prevented me from doing so at an earlier stage, as I had fully intended to do. Those circumstances kept me away from this joint sitting during the whole of the second reading debate, and during the discussion of nearly all the vital points in Committee. I had intended to vote and speak

1 Speech by Mr. J. H. Hofmeyr, Minister of the Interior, during the debate on the second reading of the Representation of Natives Bill in the Joint Session of Parliament, 6 April 1936. *House of Assembly Debates.*

against the second reading. This Bill has emerged from the Committee practically the same as it was when read a second time. Therefore, I have no option but to vote and to speak against it now.

I used the word " regret " in all sincerity, I do very sincerely regret that I cannot, on this occasion, align myself with my leader, the Prime Minister's sincere desire to further the best interests of White men and Black in this country. I recognise that his knowledge and experience of Native affairs are far greater than mine, and that this Bill represents a life-work to him. I am most grateful indeed to him for his forbearance and his tolerance in this matter to an errant colleague. But for all that, there is a fundamental difference in this matter between my outlook and that which underlies this Bill. While that is so, I can do no other than oppose it, and I must do so regardless of what the political conse-quences for myself might be.

It is not the first time, Mr. Speaker, that a government of the Union has been divided on a franchise Bill. Five years ago the Prime Minister also introduced a franchise Bill for the enfranchisement of women. Two of his colleagues opposed that Bill at all stages. That Bill dealt with some 400,000 to 500,000 persons. This Bill deals with some 10,000 to 11,000 persons. But there is this further difference. By virtue of the seven points of coalition, those who entered into coalition specifically reserved to themselves the right to their own opinions in regard to this matter. The seven points contained this sentence —

This does not imply that an agreement has been attained in regard to the principle of separate political representation.

In the party programme again, that was stated to be a matter to be left to the individual party member. It was in that knowledge that some of us went into the present Government. It was with the knowledge of that fact that the country gave its endorsement to that Government. I claim today for myself that right to differ. But I want to make it very clear that in doing so I am neither directly nor by implication criticising anyone with whom I have been in agreement in the past but who today takes a different attitude from my own. I am merely asserting an individual right for myself.

I want to ask the joint sitting to view this Bill in its true setting. There is a right setting and a wrong setting in which this Bill can be viewed. Many hon. members have supported this Bill because they have viewed it against the background of its immediate predecessor, Bill No. 1. That is the wrong setting. The right setting in which to view this Bill is the two previous Bills of the Prime Minister, the Bill of 1926[2] and the Bill of 1929.[2] Those two Bills and this Bill represent a legiti-mate succession. The other Bill which I have mentioned, why, sir, that was left at the Prime Minister's doorstep by the hon. member for Roode-

---

[2] Earlier attempts by General Hertzog which did not get the necessary two-thirds majority of both Houses sitting jointly.

poort (Colonel Stallard) and by the hon. member for Zululand (Mr. Nicholls), and very gallantly adopted by him, fortunately only temporarily.

Let us look back upon those two Bills. The 1926 draft legislation provided for the representation of Natives on a communal basis to the extent of seven members in the House of Assembly. It provided for the representation in the House of Assembly of Natives in all provinces. It provided for the extension of Coloured representation to the north. It reconstituted the Native Council on a definite basis, making it a body meeting annually and giving it also legislative power. The 1929 Bill reduced the number of Native representatives in the Union House of Assembly from seven to three. It left the northern provinces to be represented in the House of Parliament only in the Senate. The 1929 Bill, therefore, from the point of view from which I am speaking, marked a retrogression on the Bill of 1926.

This Bill marks a further retrogression on the Bill of 1929 and that is why I want the Bill to be viewed in its true setting. Let me mention four points.

In the first place this Bill, unlike its predecessors, creates what is virtually a colour bar in the Cape Provincial Council. The right hon. Senator Malan on Friday quoted a letter written by Onse Jan in 1909[3]. He might also have quoted the fact that Onse Jan at that time protested, amongst other things, against the creation of a colour bar in the Union House of Assembly. We are now going further and we are creating a colour bar in the Provincial Council.

In the second place we are laying down a definition of " Native " which is going to degrade an ever-increasing number of Coloured people and place them for ever among the ranks of Natives.

In the third place, this Bill not only provides for a separate Cape voters' roll but it also provides for the immediate removal of all existing voters to that roll. To me that seems in conflict with the spirit of the Act of Union. If we look at Section 35 of the Act of Union, we find that there are two sub-clauses. The one deals with existing qualifications and says that any change in those qualifications leading to a restriction shall not be made except by a certain procedure. Existing qualifications are entrenched, but there is laid down a method by which they may be altered. But the second sub-clause of the same section lays down absolutely and in definite terms that as a result of any such change of qualifications no single Native already on the voters' roll shall have his name taken from that roll and in this case no procedure is laid down for an amendment. I contend that in this new provision in this Bill we are acting against the spirit of the Act of Union and I may say that I have very high authority for that statement of mine.

Then there is another point. It is now proposed to put up an entrench-

[3] Mr. J. H. Hofmeyr (Snr.), Leader of the Afrikaner Bond in the Cape.

ment of a two-thirds majority not only against any deterioration in the Natives' position but also against any improvement in the Natives' position. The National Convention did not think such a double entrenchment necessary. Why not? Because the White man was put in the constitution into an impregnable position. They thought there was no necessity to protect the White man. They did not think it necessary to protect the White man against the possibility of his own generosity. Today we are asked to do both. I have heard one of my friends say that it is only just and fair that, if we give entrenchment on the one side, we should also give it on the other, and that reminded me of the first recorded definition of justice. " Justice is the interest of the stronger." I am afraid it is from that conception of justice that a good deal of the support of this Bill is derived. I think it is clear then that this Bill is less acceptable than its predecessors.

I shall be told, however, that there is another side of the account — that this Bill creates a Native Representative Council. Let us remember that the 1926 Bill put on a definite basis the Union Native Council, making it in some respects a weaker, in other respects a stronger body than the body which we are now creating, giving it legislative powers, which we are not doing today. But apart from that, I want to say that I have always had hopes for this Native Representative Council, but I have always realised that everything is going to depend on the attitude towards it of Government and Parliament, during the first critical formative years of its existence; and when I consider the spirit in which these changes which I have been mentioning have been brought in the present Bill, when I think of the attitude of mind which underlies them, when I know how it has been said again and again that this Bill is only accepted for the present, when I realise that there will be powerful influences to make that Native Representative Council a futile body, then I find it difficult to maintain my hopes. I know that high hopes have been expressed during this session in regard to the Native Representative Council, but high hopes were also expressed in 1920 in regard to the Native Council created then. I find it difficult to discover ground for confidence that the hopes expressed at this time are not destined to similar discomfiture as were the hopes expressed in 1920. And so I again assert that this Bill is no more acceptable than its predecessors. It is called a compromise, but if we look back to 1926, then from the point of view of the Natives, it is the Natives who have done all the giving and none of the taking.

Let us see what this Bill does. The central feature is to give to the Natives an inferior, a qualified citizenship, a citizenship which has the marks of inferiority in clause after clause of this Bill and which bears the added stigma that whatever may be the advance of the Native in civilisation and education to all intents and purposes, he is limited for all time to three members in a House of 153. That surely is a qualified, an inferior citizenship. May I make my own position clear? I am not one of those who would necessarily stand or fall by the ideal of common citizenship as an absolute thing. I do not go with the right hon. Senator Malan to that extent. If we were starting with a clean sheet, I think it would certainly be possible to devise a system of separate representation in separate assemblies which would be fair and just and sound. I am not saying that it is impossible to do so even today. But we are not starting with a clean sheet. We are starting with the existence of a vested right which has been in existence and which has not been abused for more than 80 years. And I want to say this, that once franchise rights have been given and exercised by a section of the community, then no nation save at the cost of honour and ultimate security should take away those rights without adequate justification. The Prime Minister, when he substituted this Bill for its predecessor, either in definite terms or by implication admitted that fact. He admitted that you could not take away franchise rights without justification and that there was no justification today for that absolute removal of the existing Cape Native franchise rights. This Bill does not absolutely remove franchise rights but it does replace those vested rights by an inferior, a qualified right. I contend that the same principle applies in this case, and I say that no nation save at the cost of honour or ultimate security can take away these rights without adequate justification.

Well, we are taking them away and we are replacing them by a qualified and inferior right. We have then to ask, what is the justification for this proposal? Attempts have been made to answer that question. Some have sought to find that justification in terms of high ethical or political principle. Some have used those blessed word phrases, segregation, trusteeship, the Native developing along his own lines. The Native developing along his own lines — that means for most who use the words the same as the Native being kept in his own place. Segregation — well, what a thing of shreds and patches this Bill makes of political segregation, just as my hon. friend over there pointed out, territorial segregation has become a thing of shreds and patches. And as for trusteeship, I would only say this: I have always regarded trusteeship as implying that at some stage or another, the trustee is prepared to hand over the trust to his ward. I have yet to learn that the European trustee in South Africa contemplates any such possibility. And that being so, I find it very difficult to reconcile the use of the word trusteeship in relation to a Bill for which it is claimed that it is going to make South Africa safe for European civilisation.

But we are also told that we can justify this Bill because once the political question is removed the Native will receive better treatment. There will be more sympathy with their development. I know that that is sincerely meant, but I know too that, in the case of many people, that is simply a conscience-salving argument which they are laying to their souls. I say that because I have sat for five years in the Transvaal Provincial Council. There was no question of Native political representation there. There was no such bogey, but I know how desperately difficult it was to get any consideration whatever for any question of Native development. Let me put it concretely — before long, we shall have to face up to the question of the inadequacy of Native education. I wonder how many after the

397

first flush of enthusiasm over this Bill is passed, how many of those who support this Bill will be any more ready to repair the present inadequacy of Native education than they would have been if this Bill were not passed.

There is another justification adduced, and that is the justification of danger. We have heard so much, especially in the past, of the Cape Native vote being a danger. It is certainly not an immediate, urgent danger. In 1926 when the Prime Minister introduced a much more liberal Bill than this one there were 300,000 European voters on the roll of the Union and 16,500 Natives, but today there are 925,000 Europeans and 10,600 Natives. My department in 1933 and 1935 was instructed to do all in its power to get every qualified Native voter on to the rolls. In spite of that the figures dropped from 12,715 to 10,628 today. Today there are only 14 constituencies in the Cape with more than 250 Native voters. There are only four with a more than 10 per cent Native electorate. Surely there is no immediate urgent danger. But we are told there is that danger in the uncertain future, that danger of which my colleague, the Minister of Mines, was speaking. It is the fear of that danger which is the only real justification which has been advanced in favour of the act of deprivation in this Bill. Well, here I agree with my hon. friend the member for Wonderboom (Mrs. Malherbe), who said a wise and timely word on Friday when she declared that no sound policy can be based on fear. No sound policy can be based on fear, and if that is the only justification for this Bill, the only justification for this act of deprivation, the fear of what may happen in an uncertain future, then, sir, I say there is no adequate justification.

Well, sir, I object to the Bill for that reason. I object to it also because I regard, as I have always done, the principle of communal representation as an unsound one, and a dangerous one not least of all from the point of view of the European in this country. Communal representation of different races implies a divergence of interests, and in South Africa there is no real ultimate divergence of interests between Europeans and non-Europeans. There is a far greater community of interests in this land. We have on both sides a contribution to make to the welfare of South Africa, and the weakness of this Bill, from my point of view, is that it emphasises the differences, it stimulates hostility, and it pays no regard to the ultimate community of interest. After all, sir, this principle of communal representation is no new one. It has been tried before, and verdicts have been pronounced upon it before. Here I have what the Donoughmore Commission wrote about it in regard to Ceylon —

Communal representation, they said, was devised with a view to assisting the development of democratic institutions in countries of different races and religions, and in the hope of eliminating the clash of those various interests during elections. Unfortunately, the experiment has not given the desired results, but has had, if anything, the opposite effect. The representatives of the various communities do not trust one another. The introduction of communal representation into the constitution with good intentions, has had unfortunate results.

A year after, the Hilton-Young Commission in regard to East Africa wrote these words—

The surest foundation for a stable constitution is community of interests. The communal system where it has been tried has tended to accentuate differences and prevent the creation of a healthy political life.

The Simon Commission in regard to India similarly condemned it. They only allowed it to pass as a temporary expedient, in view of the deep religious cleavages in that unhappy land. What justification have we with these warnings before us for accepting and applying that system here? Surely we are deliberately accepting the worse course and incurring grave dangers for the future.

What, sir, is the chief objection to communal representation which emerges from these quotations? It is that it makes not for friendship, but for hostility. In the last resort, there is greater danger, there is more real cause for fear in this Bill than in anything we have today. By this Bill we are sowing the seeds of a far greater potential conflict than is being done by anything in existence today. Let me explain. To my mind, as I have always felt, the crux of the position is in regard to the educated Native. We have many educated and semi-educated Natives in South Africa. Many of them have attained to and many more are advancing towards European standards. They have been trained on European lines, they have been taught to think and act as Europeans. We may not like it, but there are the plain facts. Now what is the political future for these people? This Bill says that even the most educated Native shall never have political equality with even the least educated and the least cultured White or Coloured man. This Bill says to these educated Natives: "There is no room for you, you must be driven back upon your own people." But we drive them back in hostility and disgruntlement, and do not let us forget this, that all that this Bill is doing for these educated Natives is to make them the leaders of their own people, in disaffection and revolt. No, the introduction of this principle in this Bill will not make for peace and safety but for hostility and conflict and strife. I would put it in this way. This Bill is a Bill the acknowledged aim of which is the self-preservation of the European. It starts out from fear, and its underlying conception is the interests of the stronger. I do not believe that, in those circumstances, you can attain self-preservation. I do not believe that you can, in this country, have a safe Native policy which is not based on consent. I do not believe that we can assure the future of White civilisation in South Africa, save with the consent and the goodwill of the non-European people.

When I hear the Christian principle of self-preservation invoked in connection with this Bill, then I am reminded of the eternal paradox that whosoever will save his life shall lose it. It has been said recently, and I think we all acclaim it, " that the spirit of inequality and subjection in which the Peace of Versailles was concluded could only lead to great trouble. We are passing through days of division and strife, we have had them for years, and they are the result of that peace ". I can only hope that the same division and strife is not going to be the result of the spirit of inequality and subjection which is largely at the root of this Bill.

I said that this Bill is born largely of fear. I know people don't like that word. Let me be perfectly frank. It is a perfectly natural fear, it is a fear we all have whether we oppose or support this Bill. We have all got that fear of the White man being drowned in a Black ocean, and we have all got that fear of race mixture and miscegenation.

AN HON. MEMBER: A justified fear.

MR. HOFMEYR: No, it is an unreasoning fear, it is largely an illogical fear. Let me put this to my friend. We are told that political equality must make for social equality, and, therefore, for race intermixture. We are told that in regard to the Natives, but many of those who tell us that in regard to the Native have no fear at all of political equality in regard to the Coloured man. There, apparently, political equality will not make for social equality. I do not believe that the principle applies necessarily in either case, and I shall say why. Because the facts show that you get most miscegenation where you have White and Black people side by side, and where the Black people are kept in subjection. You get least race intermixture in such countries where the development of the Black people is encouraged and their race consciousness, their pride and their self-esteem are stimulated.

Let me give you the facts in South Africa. Here in the Cape we have a measure of political equality, which we have not got in the rest of the Union. Now take the figures in regard to offences against the Immorality Act for the last three available years. The figures in the Cape, where you have political equality were 3.2 per 100,000 of the Native population. In the rest of the Union where you have no political equality, they were 6.4 per 100,000, or twice as many. I have taken out the figures in regard to crimes of violence with sexual intent. In the Cape the figure is .6 per 100,000 of the Native population. I am now dealing with crimes of violence with sexual intent, committed by Natives on Europeans, and the figure in the Cape is .6 per 100,000 of the Native population. In the rest of the Union the figures are 2.4 per 100,000.

MR. C. R. SWART[4]: That proves nothing.

MR. HOFMEYR: No, sir, the fear is an unreasoning fear but, it is there for all that, and we cannot get away from it. It is that fact together with the sentiment based on tradition that is to a large extent behind this Bill. These are the facts that made the Prime Minister recede from the relative liberalism of the Bill of 1929 (which was) worse than the Bill of 1926, and made this Bill again worse than the Bill of 1929. And there is no finality. There is no more finality than there was in 1892, when Sir James Rose-Innes supported the Bill of that date because it might

4 National Party.

bring finality. That tide of reaction is still flowing forward. I know that those of us who are opposing that tide cannot hope to check it. The puny breastworks that we put up must be swept away, but I do believe that the mere putting up of those breastworks is going to accelerate the day when the tide will turn, as turn, I believe, it some day will.

Let me repeat then, I oppose this Bill. It is a Bill which replaces a vested right by a qualified and inferior citizenship, and which creates a system of communal representation. I oppose it because for that act of deprivation no adequate justification has been advanced. I oppose it because in that system of communal representation there are the seeds of hostility and strife, and I oppose it also because of those forces of reaction behind this Bill which, if left unresisted, are inevitably bound to do us greater harm than anything can do us today. I know perfectly well that I am speaking against the feeling of the overwhelming majority of this House. I know I am speaking against the feeling of the great mass of the people of this country, I know how my remarks will be described as " academic " and quixotic and unrealistic. I am accustomed to that. I can see all the adjectives that will be used. But these are matters on which the future must be left to judge. I expressed the belief that the tide of reaction will turn, and I base that belief on what I know of what is going on in the minds of some at least of the younger people in South Africa, especially in the universities. I believe that there is also a rising tide of liberalism in South Africa. It is mostly the younger people who are in the forefront of that tide. It is they who are the custodians of our future. And whatever we may or may not do today, it is by them that the ultimate issues in connection with this matter will have to be decided.

5

RACE RELATIONS POLICY OF THE NATIONAL PARTY[1]

A. INTRODUCTION

THERE ARE TWO distinct guiding principles determining the South African policy affecting the non-Whites. One line of thought favours a policy of integration, conferring equal rights — including the franchise as the non-Whites progressively become used to democratic institutions — on all civilised and educated citizens within the same political structure.

Opposed to this is the policy of apartheid, a concept historically derived from the experience of the established White population of the country, and in harmony with such Christian principles as justice and equity. It is a policy which sets itself the task of preserving and safeguarding the racial identity of the White population of the country; of likewise preserving and safeguarding the identity of the indigenous peoples as separate racial groups, with opportunities to develop into self-governing national units; of fostering the inculcation of national consciousness, self-esteem and mutual regard among the various races of the country.

The choice before us is one of these two divergent courses: either that of integration, which would in the long run amount to national suicide on the part of the Whites; or that of apartheid, which professes to preserve the identity and safeguard the future of every race, with complete scope for everyone to develop within its own sphere while maintaining its distinctive national character, in such a way that there will be no encroachment on the rights of others, and without a sense of being frustrated by the existence and development of others.

B. GENERAL GUIDING PRINCIPLES

IT IS THE primary task and calling of the State to seek the welfare of South Africa, and to promote the happiness and well-being of its citizens, non-White as well as White. Realising that such a task can best be accomplished by preserving and safeguarding the White race, the

[1] Pamphlet issued by the Head Office of the National Party, shortly before the end of 1947, in view of the general election in May 1948. Translated from the Afrikaans by Prof. I. van H. Fourie of the Dept. of English at the University of Potchefstroom.

402

National Party professes this as the fundamental guiding principle of its policy. Accordingly, the party undertakes to combat any policy, doctrine or attempt calculated to undermine or endanger the continued existence of the White race. Conversely, however, the party rejects any policy of oppression or exploitation of the non-Whites by the Whites as incompatible with the Christian character of our people and therefore unacceptable.

The party holds that a positive application of apartheid between the White and non-White racial groups and the application of the policy of separation also in the case of the non-White racial groups is the only sound basis on which the identity and the survival of each race can be ensured and by means of which each race can be stimulated to develop in accordance with its own character, potentialities and calling. Hence inter-marriage between the two groups will be prohibited.

Within their own areas the non-White communities will be afforded full opportunity to develop, implying the establishment of their own institu-tions and social services, which will enable progressive non-Whites to take an active part in the development of their own peoples. The policy of our country should envisage total apartheid as the ultimate goal of a natural process of separate development.

A standing advisory body of experts on non-White affairs is to be in-stituted. Education and juvenile care should be State-controlled. In con-nection with its racial problems, South Africa should tolerate neither outside interference, nor subversive propaganda sent abroad.

C. CHRISTIANISING POLICY

THE NATIONAL PARTY, anxious to stimulate active Christianising enterprise among the non-Whites, will gladly support the efforts of mission churches. Churches and missions, however, which frustrate the policy of apartheid or which propagate foreign doctrines, will not be tolerated.

D. THE COLOURED COMMUNITY

The position of the Coloureds

The Coloureds occupy a position midway between White and non-White. In their case the policy of the party is to apply total apartheid — that is, social, residential, industrial and political — between them and both the Bantu and the non-White communities. Intermarriage of Whites and Coloureds will be prohibited. The Coloureds will, in their established areas, be protected against unfair competition by the Bantu.

Political Representation

The Coloureds will be represented in the Senate by a White representative appointed by the Government by virtue of his special knowledge of the affairs of the Coloured community. The present undesirable system which gives the Coloureds in the Cape Province the franchise on the same voters' roll as the Whites, will be abolished, to be superseded by a system of representation which will grant them three members in Parliament. These will be elected by a Coloured Representative Council. They will not be entitled to vote on: (1) motions of confidence; (2) declarations of war; (3) amendment of the political rights of non-Whites. A State Department of Coloured Affairs will be instituted. In the Cape Provincial Council the Coloureds will be represented by three White representatives elected by the Coloured Representative Council. In the Cape Province a Coloured Representative Council will be instituted, consisting of representatives elected by the Coloureds with the existing franchise qualifications, the head of the Department of Coloured Affairs, and additional members appointed by the Government. In their own areas the Coloureds will elect their own boards to function within the framework of the bodies with higher authority.

Social and Welfare Services

Special attention will be given to the provision of social, health and welfare services which, by progressively enlisting the services of the Coloureds themselves, will eventually reach self-sufficiency in this respect. An educational system, congenial to the Coloured community, is being envisaged.

E. BANTU POLICY

General Principle

In general terms our policy envisages segregating the most important ethnic groups and sub-groups in their own areas where every group will be enabled to develop into a self-sufficient unit.

Bantu Territory

We endorse the general principle of territorial segregation of the Bantu and the Whites. More ground for the Bantu in terms of the Act of 1936 will only be granted after judicious consideration, but determined efforts will be made to encourage soil improvement and conservation in which the Bantu themselves will be induced to co-operate. A board of experts will be appointed to advise in connection with soil conservation in the Bantu areas.

The Bantu Reserves

The reserves should be the national home of the Bantu. There their educational institutions should be situated and there social services should be provided instead of the present practice of providing them in urban locations. Life in the reserves should be held in high esteem, giving leading members the prestige which will enable them to act as spokesmen for the Bantu. Opportunities for industrial enterprise will be created in order progressively to stimulate production and ensure stability, for which purpose planning boards will be formed.

Bantu in the Urban Areas

Aware of the problems connected with the influx of Bantu into the urban areas the National Party pledges itself to safeguard the European character of the urban centres and to provide strong and effective measures to ensure personal safety and the protection of property in a peaceful way of life. Separate residential areas will be allotted to the Bantu and congestion and slums will be prevented. The Bantu in the urban areas should be regarded as migratory citizens not entitled to political or social rights equal to those of the Whites. The process of detribalisation should be arrested. The entire migration of Bantu into and from the cities should be controlled by the State which will enlist the co-operation of municipal bodies. Migration into and from the reserves should likewise be strictly controlled. Redundant Bantu in the urban centres should be returned to their original habitat in the country areas or the reserves. Bantu from the country areas or the reserves should be admitted to the European cities or towns only as temporary employees, obliged to return to their homes after the expiry of their employment. For this purpose a convenient identification and control system will have to be devised.

The White Workers

The interests and employment prospects of the White workers in White areas will be protected. As far as is practicable apartheid will be observed in the factories, trades and industrial localities. Being opposed to the organisation of trade unions for the Bantu the party envisages a system of State guardianship in order to protect their interests.

Bantu Employment

A national system of employment control with a central employment bureau to administer the entire network, will be established with a view to achieving as flexible as possible a system of demand and supply of labour with a minimum of waste. This would imply thorough stocktaking of both the requirements and the labour potential in order effectively to divert the available labour into the various channels of farming, industry, mining and urban employment. All aspects of employment including that of migratory labour, should be thoroughly investigated.

Bantu Education

Education should be essentially Christian national in character adapted to the needs and the development level of the vast body of Bantu people. It should have a strong moral purpose and should inculcate national consciousness. It should be State-controlled, administered by a special department of the Department of Native Affairs. Financing Bantu education should be conducted in accordance with the cultural level and the economic capacity and requirements of the Bantu people, and should be more in proportion to their contribution to the national income than is the case at present. The Bantu are progressively to assume responsibility for financing and controlling their own education, under White supervision.

Social and Welfare Services

The Bantu are to be encouraged to develop social, health and welfare services, organised and conducted by themselves.

Political Representation

In addition to the three White senators appointed by the Government in accordance with the constitution and by virtue of their knowledge of Bantu affairs, we suggest additional representation in the Senate by four White representatives elected by the various Bantu Councils, these seven Senators forming a standing committee for Bantu affairs. These Bantu representatives shall not vote on: (1) motions of confidence in the Government; (2) declarations of war; (3) amendment of the political rights of the non-Whites. The present Bantu representation in Parliament and the Provincial Council will be abolished. The Native Affairs Commission will be replaced by a commission comprised of members with special knowledge of Bantu affairs. An efficient ethnological institute is also envisaged.

Bantu Self-Government

The party is in favour of a system of local government for the Bantu, more or less along the lines of the Bunga, which will uphold the authority of the tribal chiefs and enlist the services of educated Bantu. Such local councils are to be established in all the reserves with the prospect of developing into separate central councils for the different ethnic groups or sub-groups. Initially supervised by White officials, these councils will progressively be granted a measure of legislative and administrative self-government, in accordance with their growing ability to manage their own affairs, but compatible with the guardianship of the State. The Native Representative Council is to be abolished. Boards to be established in urban locations, however, shall have no prospect of developing into self-governing bodies. The system thus envisaged will eventually satisfy Bantu political aspirations more gratifyingly than the political rights in White areas as advocated by the United Party.

Administration

Reorganisation of the Department of Native Affairs is imperative in order to enable it to cope with its dual educational and administrative task. All Bantu interests and affairs should be administered by the Department of Native Affairs, with subordinate administrative branches.

F. ATTITUDE TO THE INDIANS

THE PARTY regards the Indians as a foreign element which cannot be assimilated in the South African set-up. Not being native to this country, they cannot expect more preferential treatment than an immigrant community. We accordingly have in mind the repatriation of as many Indians as possible, a first step towards which will be a thorough investigation of the feasibility of large-scale repatriation, enlisting the co-operation of India and/or other countries. This matter is of such urgency that South Africa should be prepared for a substantial sacrifice in order to finance such an undertaking. No Indian immigrants are henceforth to be admitted to the country. With the Indians still in our midst a definite policy of apartheid should be enforced between them and the Whites, and likewise as far as feasible between them and the indigenous non-White sections. The 1946 Act on Asiatic Land Tenure and Indian Franchise will immediately be amended to the effect that

(a) no representation in the legislative assemblies of the country will be granted to the Indians;

(b) separate residential areas will be allotted to the Indians, who will not be allowed to reside or possess property in White areas;

(c) Whites will not be allowed to reside, trade or possess property in Indian areas;

(d) as far as is feasible apartheid will be enforced between the Indians and the indigenous races;

(e) adequate compensation will be paid for properties confiscated in White or in Indian areas.

Trading facilities for Indians outside their own areas will be drastically curtailed. Eventually Indian traders in Bantu areas and locations will disappear, trade in such areas being the prerogative of the Bantu themselves. Migration of Indians from province to province will be put under restraint. The province of the Orange Free State should retain its ban on Indian immigration. The Cape Province should be effectively protected against Indian encroachment in trade and in the acquisition of property. Family welfare aid for Indians should be abolished. Our party will not tolerate subversive propaganda among the non-Whites against the Whites.

6

THE NATIVE POLICY OF THE UNITED PARTY[1]

1. IN ACCORDANCE with its programme of principles, the party stands for European leadership and authority and reaffirms the principle of Christian trusteeship towards the Native peoples as a permanent part of the population.

2. The party's Native policy is based on a recognition of the factual position, more especially—

(a) the difference between Europeans and Natives;

(b) the existence, in addition to the Natives in the reserves, of a settled Native population on farms and in urban areas.

3. The party is, therefore, not in favour of a policy of equality or assimilation and stands —

(a) for the maintenance of a policy of social and residential separation and the avoidance of race intermixture, and

(b) for the development, while taking account of the facts of difference referred to, of the Native peoples in their own and the country's interests.

4. Such development shall take place under European guidance

(a) in the Native reserves as the national and cultural base of the Native races, with a view to the increase of their carrying capacity, the spiritual and material advancement of the peoples dwelling there, the promotion of their progressive self-government, and the establishment of village centres provided with facilities for the development of appropriate handicrafts and industries;

(b) in European areas, both urban and rural, in such manner as will take account of the increasing part played by the Natives in the economic life of those areas, and more especially by the elimination of slums and shanty towns, and the creation, where necessary, of separate Native townships for permanent residence, provided with proper health, education, social and transport services, which shall progressively be administered by the Natives themselves;

(c) by the provision of the necessary training facilities to enable Natives to play their part in the service of their people.

[1] Extract from pamphlet issued by General Smuts as Leader of the United Party as the declared official policy of the party. Johannesburg, not dated, but probably 1949 or 1950.

5. In respect of Native political rights the United Party stands for the maintenance of the 1936 settlement, with the provisions made by it for the existing representation of the Natives by Europeans in the Senate and the House of Assembly, the Cape Provincial Council, and for the establishment of the Natives Representative Council. It favours, further, the development and expansion of the function and usefulness of the Council in relation to Native areas, under the general authority of Parliament.

6. The party also stands for —

(*a*) a system of labour registration and exchanges for the regulation of the flow of labour to the various areas and services requiring such labour, with due regard to the needs of agriculture.

(*b*) a system of regulated Native industrial organisation under government supervision, and

(*c*) the improvement and simplification of the Native Pass Law system.

While the party recognises the continual need for migrant labour in certain industries, it considers that in so far as Natives are required in industry, agriculture, or domestic service, and can be suitably accommodated in separate Native townships, or in connection with their employment, they should be free to take up such employment subject to the system of labour registration as referred to above.

7. In general, and as an overall objective, the party aims at maintaining and promoting goodwill and understanding in race relationships in the abiding interests of the country as a whole.

7

APARTHEID

GENERAL J. C. SMUTS, 16 AUGUST 1948[1]

MR. SPEAKER, in accordance with the usual practice in Parliament, this Budget debate is the proper place to raise large questions of Government policy. I propose to avail myself of that opportunity and to travel for a little while somewhat beyond the financial statement which has been made by the Minister of Finance. I do so in order to get some clarity on the Government's policy. At present the policy of the Government is most vague, and I think that before the House is called upon to vote supplies, it should know in broad outline what the Government's policy is on a number of large public issues now before the country. I know, of course, that this is a short session and very little legislation can be introduced during the session. Much will have to stand over until next year, but surely that does not prevent the Government from laying before Parliament and before the country a clear and convincing statement as to its policy on a number of these issues which are before the country.

I shall only raise a few points. I have limited time, as hon. members know, and no doubt hon. members on this side of the House will raise other points. I want to confine myself to a few specific issues, and I start with the issue which has raised the greatest hubbub in the country in recent months, i.e. the issue of apartheid.

During the last session of the previous Parliament this issue was raised here in this House, and we challenged the then Opposition at once to say what they meant by this word, to say what their policy was. We never had an answer. A promise was made that a commission would be appointed to define what apartheid meant, and there seems to have been some sort of commission appointed under the present Minister of Transport to go into this particular question. Some sort of report was rendered, but the question was left in the same darkness and obscurity in which it had been before, and we are just as far today from understanding what exactly is the Government's policy on this question as ever before. That is our position today.

During the election we had a wild turmoil in this country; we had mass propaganda such as we have never had in this country before, all centring round this issue of apartheid, but what it all meant we did not

[1] Speech by General Smuts (United Party), Leader of the Opposition, in the House of Assembly, 16 August 1948. *House of Assembly Debates.*

know. We had this wild storm raging over the country. We had the issue raised of a White South Africa, and the dangers that face future generations in South Africa. It was all a wild ramp which may turn into a " ramp "[2] in this country, but nowhere was the issue defined and was the exact policy of the Government stated. This was a slogan, a catchword, by which it was proposed to catch the vote of the country and it was wrapped in a mass of misrepresentations, such as we have never had in the political life of this country before. But there was no policy. It was only this wild confusion which raged all over the country, round a word which was not policy. I suppose it was not even meant as a policy. It was simply meant to befuddle the public mind and confuse the public and to make them vote blindfold over the most important and far-reaching and dangerous issue in this country.

MR. E. H. LOUW[3]: Has your Committee reported yet?

MR. C. R. SWART[4]: The Strauss Committee?

GENERAL SMUTS: We had something very tangible at the same time. We had the Fagan Report[5] and to me the most significant thing of all was this, that this report was scarcely referred to by the party which now sits on those benches. They simply by-passed this report. Here was the most searching inquiry which had ever been held in the history of South Africa into the question of Native policy. The report went into the figures; the report went into the statistics and into the facts. It traversed the whole area of the application of Native policy in this country and the vast problems which go with it. One would have thought that whilst we were fighting this election and we had this storm raging in South Africa, some reference would be made to this report which will remain one of the great public documents of this country. But not a word. Apartheid. Apartheid dominated the atmosphere by night and by day.

Well, sir, this country is faced with two practical issues in regard to this question of Native policy. The Government must decide, the country has to decide between these issues. The first is this: We may say that the Native reserves are destined to be and are to be, according to the policy of this country, the only home of the Native people of this country. That is a clear-cut policy. That we can understand. Send them to the reserves. The reserves must be their home and that is a solution of the Native question. I do not know whether that is the policy of the Government. I should like to know because it is a very important matter.

That is one of the alternatives before us, namely, the reserves, but if you adopt that solution you are up against vast difficulties. The first

---

2 Afrikaans for catastrophe.

3 Minister of Economic Affairs.

4 Minister of Justice.

5 Commission appointed in 1946 under the Chairmanship of Mr. Justice H. A. Fagan to report on certain aspects of Native policy. It reported in 1948 (U.G. 28).

difficulty is this, that you must have the land; you must have the soil; you must have the ground to accommodate and absorb the Native people of South Africa. According to the Fagan Report, at present the reserves which are already congested, which are already over-populated, accommodate only about 40 per cent of the Native people. Well, if we have to place the Native people, 100 per cent of them, on reserves, one can see what a land question arises before the country. We will have to double, we will have to treble the Native reserves of this country, and the practical question arises at once where is this land to come from? We do not know. All I know is that it is impossible even to carry out the mere modicum of expropriation which is involved in the Hertzog scheme, the Hertzog scheme of segregation. As the Minister of Native Affairs[6] will find out more and more, we are up against an insoluble proposition even to carry out the Hertzog scheme. Whether you go to the Transvaal or to Natal, or anywhere else, you find the farmers of this country, the land-owners of this country say: " Are we going to part with our heritage: Are we going to sell the land of our fathers? We shall not." Everywhere you are up against this stalemate in regard to this question; and therefore the policy of segregating and congregating our Native population as a whole in the Native reserves, is a policy which it is impossible to carry out in this country. If that is the apartheid which is contemplated then I have no difficulty at all in saying that it is an impossible policy, and it is not an honest policy because they know that it cannot be carried out.

And supposing that it were possible to carry it out what would happen? Supposing that we were to congregate our Native population in the reserves, and give them a fair chance and do our fair duty towards them, what is the industrial future of this country going to be? When industries start in the locations, in the reserves, and not as heretofore in our White areas, huge industries developing in the Native reserves based on cheap Native labour, what is going to happen to White South Africa, to White industrial South Africa? If this is the interpretation of apartheid — the segregation policy, the reserve policy, then you are up against something which is not only impossible, but which would be a deadly blow struck at the future of White South Africa.

What is the alternative? The alternative has been pointed out and has been advocated here by us on these benches, and has been affirmed after careful inquiry by the Fagan Commission, and it is that we shall go on developing tentatively very much on the lines on which we have been developing hitherto. The Native will come more and more into the White areas. The Native is not confined merely to the reserves at his home, but he is part and parcel of industrial South Africa. That is what has happened so far, and nothing can alter it. It has been the course of history for the past 100 years, and it will be the course of history for the next 100 years.

6 Dr. E. G. Jansen.

The Native has been integrated into our industrial system and into our economic system. He is our worker; he works on a lower level. He is not a competitor in that sense of the White man, but he is part and parcel of the whole which constitutes South African economic society, and the Fagan Commission was busy working out the problems which stare us in the face, the problems which arise from this situation — immense problems, problems such as this country has never faced before, such problems I suppose as no other European country has ever faced in the world. These are the problems staring us in the face and we have to solve these problems. We have to go in for what has been called the satellite village, the parallel township — not apartheid in that sense but side by side in our urban areas, in our industrial areas. You will have Black and White not far from each other, both playing their part in the economic activities and forming the integrated economic structure of this country.

It raises all sorts of difficult questions. You are taking the barbarian now into your system. It means education, it means housing, it means health — all those great social problems which afflict us not only in our White society but also in this larger set-up of Black and White South Africa. It also means that the Native has to be trained to a certain extent to play his part in this society. He has to become more efficient, he cannot remain simply a barbarian, working on the lowest level. He must be shaped into an economic instrument; he must be made economically and industrially efficient. For that purpose he must be educated also. Besides all this, you have the problem of teaching them the way they should go and helping them to look after themselves. The problem of self-government arises at once among them. If you have a Native township near to an industrial area you cannot simply run it with White officials — the thing does not work. It is not human nature, you have to train them to look after themselves. This question of educating them to look after their own administration is part of the whole problem that arises before us.

Mr. Speaker, this is the situation which the Fagan Report has put before the country with a force and with a convincingness such as I have never seen in any public document in South Africa. The late government declared that on broad lines they were prepared to carry out the recommendations of this report on these large issues. That was simply an affirmation of our policy. The question is what is our policy?

Mr. P. O. SAUER: I thought you were going to appoint a commission to work out your policy? The member for Germiston announced it — in fact, he would not be the chairman of it, somebody more important would be.

GENERAL SMUTS: We have our policy, it has been proved by this thoroughly impartial inquiry. We are convinced that in broad outline that is the line that should be followed in Native policy in this country, and not this other policy of apartheid, which means driving these people into the wilds to form locations of their own. We want to know what is the policy the Government is going to follow. I hope the hon. the Prime

413

Minister or the Minister of Native Affairs will tell the country, not in wild slogans and catchwords but in clear principle, which of these alternatives they are adopting as the Government policy. We must know this before we vote supplies; we want to know what the attitude of the Government is on this matter.

DR. D. F. MALAN, 16 AUGUST 1948[1]

I JUST WANT TO reply to one of the points put to me by the hon. Leader of the Opposition (General J. C. Smuts) and that is in connection with the policy of apartheid. The Leader of the Opposition said that he did not really know what was meant by apartheid. He says that we on this side do not know ourselves what is meant by apartheid, and that the entire election which we have had just recently took place without any explanation from us as to our policy and without any definition of apartheid from us. He says that we did not define it anywhere. If the Leader of the Opposition had not got into the habit of regarding everything affecting South Africa as things of minor importance, if for so many years he had not looked mainly at oversea interests instead of looking after the serious interests of South Africa, he would have known what we meant by apartheid, and in that case it would not have been necessary for him today to ask us to give a clear explanation of our policy. In connection with this matter, we have not only had discussions from time to time, but as a National Party we issued an election manifesto in which not only the negative side of the policy of apartheid was set out but also its positive side. Not only the negative side but also the constructive side of it was revealed in that manifesto in the clearest terms. How did the Leader of the Opposition conduct the election, if he did not even read that manifesto? Apparently his thoughts were elsewhere during all that time and not on the election.

If he asks what our Native policy is we have more reason to ask him what his Native policy is. During the general election, when an appeal was made to the people, this colour question occupied a prominent place. The question was repeatedly asked what the policy was of the Government which was then in power, and what did we get from him? The reply was given by more than one of his followers on the other side and by more than one of their newspapers, and that reply was that the Smuts Government had no colour policy. We are entitled to ask him what his policy is. The election is something of the past. Now suddenly the Leader of the Opposition awakens. Now he says that this is a matter which can no longer be postponed; a colour policy must be laid down at once for his party. He now says that they will take steps to make a statement as to their colour policy so that it will not be

[1] Speech by Dr. Malan (National Party), Prime Minister, in House of Assembly, 16 August 1948. *House of Assembly Debates.*

misunderstood by anyone. He now asks for an unambiguous colour policy and because it is such an urgent matter that policy must be given to the country immediately. The reply to that is, why so late in the day? Why did the people have to wait until after the election for a colour policy from the Opposition, the then Government?

Well, the hon. Leader of the Oposition wants to know what our policy is on this side of the House. I shall tell him first what it is not and then he may understand better what it really is. Our policy is not, as it has often been represented, a policy of repression. It has its negative side because apartheid in every respect is partly negative. One draws a dividing line. But apartheid also has its positive side. One can have justice done on both sides of the dividing line and lay down a constructive policy for both sides It is no reply to say that apartheid brings about repression.

In the second place, what our policy is not is this: We do not propose to carry on with any measure of the nature with which the Government came before this House in 1946, namely the measure in connection with the Indians, in terms of which the Indians would be given special representation in this House and in Parliament generally. That measure was not in accord with the views of this House, including those members who are today seated behind the hon. member on the other side. It was not in accord with the views and the convictions of any section of the European population in this country. It was not sought and desired by them. It was not even in accordance with the wishes of the Indians, and for that reason I introduced today for its first reading in this House, a Bill to repeal that measure. In any event, having regard to the views expressed by the followers of the hon. member on the other side, in the various parts of the country, as well as by their Press, we can only say that a bomb has fallen amongst them and that clearly illustrates the disunity which has come into existence in their ranks in connection with this measure. We may be starting with this policy of apartheid — because it is also the apartheid that we advocate — at the wrong end as far as they are concerned, but they cannot say that even during this session we are not going to do anything to give effect to our policy of apartheid. On the one hand we are continually reminded by them that here we have a session, and that we are not doing anything to give effect to the policy of apartheid, and on the other hand they complain that we are doing too much, as has already been done by their supporters in connection with the measure[2] just recently put into effect here by the Minister of Transport.[3]

Moreover, what our policy of apartheid is not is to give effect to the policy which was laid down by the Rt. Hon. the Leader of the Opposition when he was at the head of the Government, with the approval of his whole Cabinet, in principle, and that is to call into being, alongside

[2] Separate railway facilities in the Cape Peninsula.
[3] Mr. P. O. Sauer.

this Parliament for Europeans, a parliament for the Natives, and not only in the Native territories, but a Native Parliament which will exercise domination or power in the European areas as well. That is not our policy of apartheid, nor does our policy of apartheid mean, as the Rt. Hon. member wanted to make the House believe a moment ago, that we are going to eliminate all the Natives who are at present in the European areas and who come here to work and that we are going to send them all to their own reserves. That is a caricature of our policy of apartheid. There is no one on this side of the House who has ever advocated a policy of that nature, nor is it contained in our written policy of apartheid, our election manifesto.

AN HON. MEMBER: The "Kruithoring"[4] said so.

THE PRIME MINISTER: The Rt. Hon. member and the newspapers who support that side put up their own skittles and then try to knock them down.

Finally I just want to say this, that the policy of apartheid of this side of the House is not the policy adopted and followed generally, at any rate outwardly, not inwardly, by the ex-Minister of Finance on that side, the ex-deputy of the Rt. Hon. the Leader of the Opposition.[5] I mention that because according to his own statement a short while ago, it was announced that this well-known policy, as it is also recorded in Hansard, and as he set it out in this House, was set out with the detailed knowledge and with the approval of his leader.

MR. HOFMEYR: That is not what he said.

DR. MALAN: I say that we reject this policy and not only we on this side of the House reject it, but at the general election the people rejected it and that is why the other side suffered defeat at the election.

If you want to know what the positive side of our policy is, let me put it this way just briefly. In the first place, if we are going to take away anything from the Natives — and it is our intention to take away the representation which they enjoy in this House at the moment — then we want to give them something else which in our opinion is better for them, in other words, to call into being institutions for them in their own reserves, and to promote and further develop institutions of their own which will enable them to have a large measure of self-government and which will enable them at the same time to retain their own national character.

With regard to those who do not live in the reserves, just as little as the Europeans are allowed to live or to continue to live in the reserves without permits — Europeans can only live in the reserves under permit and they have no say in the Bunga[6] and in the other self-governing institutions in those territories — just so little should the Native who lives in the European area be given any greater privileges than that. And is there any injustice in that? Why should the Native not be here under per-

4 National Party organ.
5 Mr. J. H. Hofmeyr.
6 General Council of the Transkei.

416

mit; why should he have a certain amount of say in European institutions? Why should that not be withheld from him?

Furthermore, as far as the Coloureds are concerned, we do not want to deprive the Coloureds of representation in this House. We want to give the Coloured representation in this House, but through a better system than we have at present and that is to give them representation just as the Natives have it now. The Coloureds have no territories of their own. The Native has his own territory and his own national home.

A further measure which is essential is that we want apartheid as far as our educational institutions are concerned, more particularly in our universities. An intolerable state of affairs has arisen here in the past few years in our university institutions, a state of affairs which gives rise to friction, to an unpleasant relationship between Europeans and non-Europeans. If you want confirmation of that, you need only go to the universities and there you will discover what the position is. For that reason all the universities, as far as I know, except the Witwatersrand University, have broken away from Nusas[7] which was the strongest organisation amongst all the universities. That organisation has been banned from the universities. We do not want to withhold higher education from the non-Europeans, and we will take every possible step to give both the Natives and the Coloureds universities — and sufficient university-training as soon as we can, but in their own spheres; in other words, in separate institutions. I do not want to enlarge on this matter. There will be sufficient opportunity to discuss these matters further at a later stage.

I want to avail myself now of this opportunity to launch an attack in connection with the general attitude of the Opposition. There is one question in regard to which I want to approach them, not because it does us any harm but because it harms South Africa generally, in the international sphere as well, and that is the fact that they are continually bringing South Africa in discredit abroad, and particularly in connection with the change of Government which has taken place here.

7 National Union of South African Students.

MRS. V. M. L. BALLINGER, 16 AUGUST, 1948[1]

I HAD NOT INTENDED to apply myself at all in this debate to the general principles of apartheid. I had planned to confine myself to the practical application of this Budget to the people whom I represent. But the general issues have been raised on the highest level in the House this afternoon, and they have given rise to one or two declarations by the hon. the Prime Minister (Dr. D. F. Malan), which I feel deserve some more elucidation before this debate is concluded. I would be glad if the

1 Speech by Mrs. Ballinger (Native Representative, Cape Eastern), in House of Assembly, 16 August 1948. *House of Assembly Debates.*

hon. Minister of Native Affairs[2] would provide us with some of that elucidation.

I am referring not so much to what the hon. the Prime Minister said
about what apartheid was not, to which the other side clearly find it easier
to confine themselves, but with what apartheid is. I am concerned at the
moment with the hon. Prime Minister's insistence which has been continuous since the general election, that apartheid is not oppression. I am
concerned at the moment with his statement, which he apparently regards
as a positive statement in this connection, to the effect that apartheid means
— it is extremely difficult not to deal with this matter in negative terms —
no oppression. Let me try it from this angle. He says that the African
people will find their field of political advancement and their real avenues
of economic opportunity in the Native reserves. And he has explained
that outside these reserves, they will have no right which we would regard
as civil rights, while Europeans similarly will have no rights in Native
reserves except as temporary residents performing presumably administrative and commercial functions to be taken over in due course by the Africans themselves. On that basis, Africans would have no claim to rights
in the European area at all. That is how I understand the hon. the Prime
Minister. On the political side, he has made quite clear, that it is his
intention to abolish the present Native representation and to substitute
for it something in the nature of a Native Parliament in the Native
reserves.

Now if I am correct in interpreting the hon. the Prime Minister in this
way, I must confess his statements do not clarify the situation very much
for me, and I feel that they will have to be made fuller before they can be
put before the Native population. The hon. the Prime Minister really
dodged the main issue that has been put before him today. What are
the Native reserves going to be? What is to constitute the area of the
Native reserves? That is the question that was put to him by the Rt. Hon.
the Leader of the Opposition (General J. C. Smuts). It is the question
we have put to him on various occasions. And it is a very pertinent question. The fact is not disputed that at the present time those reserves can
accommodate only something less than 40 per cent of the Native population,
and that on a level on which they cannot maintain themselves at all except
with the continuous export of their labour. For the 60 per cent who are
outside those reserves, the hon. the Prime Minister has given us no future
whatsoever so far as I can see. I wish to put it to him as I see it. I refer
to his reiterated statement that he has been represented as intending to be
oppressive to the Native population. He says that is not so. Now there
are clearly various definitions of oppression as there are various definitions of apartheid. In my opinion oppression can be like apartheid, either
positive or negative. It can either be the subjecting of people to laws
and administrative restrictions that grind them down, that keep them on
the lowest economic and social level, or it can be simply complete neglect.

2 Dr. E. G. Jansen.

As I see it we are faced with both of those forms of oppression at the moment. I see the policy of the hon. the Prime Minister as he has stated it here in practical terms as positive oppression, as involving an economic condition in which the mass of the Native people must inevitably be ground down, must inevitably be economically and socially depressed. And I see the Budget which is the specific occasion of this debate as negative oppression, oppression by neglect. If the Native reserves can accommodate only 40 per cent of the Native population on a starvation basis now, obviously they can offer no hope and no foot-hold for the other 60 per cent, who are then placed in the position of being servants for the European community in the rest of the country, without any bargaining power whatsoever; since a man who has no hope cannot bargain for what he will receive from those who will give him a roof over his head in return for his accommodating himself to their wishes. In these terms the policy appears to me as simply and obviously a cheap labour policy. As such, in its long-term range, it is essentially oppression, and I do not see how anybody can defend it as anything else.

Now I have no wish to do the Prime Minister an injustice in this matter. I am extremely interested in the fact that the Prime Minister has again published his intention to abolish the present Native representation. In the circumstances it seems to me wholly inconsistent that members of his party should now be seeking to secure these seats. But I am not concerned about this inconsistency. I am simply interested to discover what, in practice, the Government's policy is to be and I shall welcome anything that will elucidate that. I have put the case forward as I see it in the light of my knowledge of the position of the African population under the land laws of this country, and I would welcome some explanation which would throw some light on the Prime Minister's urgent insistence that his policy will not in fact mean oppression for the African population.

DR. D. F. MALAN ON THE ENTRENCHED CLAUSES[1]

WHAT THE RIGHT HON. Leader of the Opposition supressed in presenting this subject is that this election was fought on this subject, but that this is not the only verdict that has been given on this matter. This subject was also before the joint select committee of both Houses of Parliament, and in that joint select committee (which was occupied a number of years on this question and on which representatives of all the parties in the House served) a resolution was taken. The joint select committee brought forward this proposal that was embodied in a Bill, that the Native franchise as existing in the Cape should be abolished; that the Natives should have no representation in the Assembly and that

---

[1] Extract from speech by Dr. D. F. Malan, Prime Minister, in House of Assembly 21 September 1948. *House of Assembly Debates.*

the only representation they would get, would be in the Senate. That was the result of this protracted consultation between both Houses of Parliament in the joint select committee in which all parties were represented. Judgment was given and it was a very authoritative judgment on this question.

The name of General Hertzog has been mentioned in this connection: that on that occasion he assented and eventually did not bring before the House the recommendation of the joint committee and that another Bill was eventually placed on the Statute Book, a proof that he was not in favour of this principle for which we now stand. Do you forget that General Hertzog himself after he introduced Bill No. 2 openly stated that Bill No. 1, namely that the Natives should have no representation in the Assembly, was the best.

MR. J. G. N. STRAUSS: But nevertheless he had it adopted by a majority of two-thirds.

DR. MALAN: In the clearest way he stated that Bill No. 1 was the best, and that too after he had introduced Bill No. 2. Now I repeat that the evidence that this is the right policy has been obtained by us in the judgment given recently by the people. We have it through the joint committee of both Houses. We have it from the mouth of General Hertzog, that this is the best for the people and for the country. I have emphasised that the abolition of Native representation in the Assembly is a policy that we have indeed laid before this House and before the people for approval, that it is the policy that the joint committee of both Houses of Parliament dealt with and that we have it from the mouth of General Hertzog himself that it is the best policy for our people.

I come now to the question of the two-thirds majority. What I laid emphasis on on a previous occasion and what I want to emphasise again is this. The first question on which we must have clarity is the legal question. It is asserted on the other side, again by the right hon. Leader of the Opposition, that it is a legal question and that we on this side of the House are preparing to transgress the law. Therefore we must have that question cleared up. There has been doubt on the legal aspect even amongst members who took part in the Budget debate. It was argued on that occasion that apparently there is a difference of opinion amongst jurists on this matter. So, as I said then, we want to reach finality and have it cleared up. But I have stressed, and I do so again, that we shall not take it upon ourselves to decide the legal question and to say whether that provision today is still legally valid. I then said that everything depended on it as far as we are concerned, that we want to have certainty and clarity on this point and that therefore we shall take the best legal advice.

Two findings are possible when the lawyers go into this matter. The one is that the two-thirds provision is still legally valid. If it is still legally valid and that is clear, then we on this side of the House, and no government have the right to trample underfoot that legal provision and commit an infraction of the law. We do not intend to do that. If the finding is that it was still legally valid then there is only one other way, namely, that we must have the policy approved by the people. We must do what is done in Australia and America, although their constitution is different — they are federal and we are a union — but we must do what they do, we shall have to go to the people. We shall have to go to the people with a referendum, to ask the people for leave to set aside this legal provision and to solve this question if necessary with a majority of less than two-thirds. Then there is only one way open to us, and that is to follow this course of action. I think I made that clear enough on the last occasion in this House.

But if the legal advice is different, namely, that the provision for a majority of two-thirds is no longer legally valid, then it has ceased to become a legal question and it has become purely a question of policy. This is the question of policy: that, bearing in mind all the circumstances, the Government of the day wishes to adopt such a policy, in the certain belief that the majority of the people are behind them, and that we are convinced. Then it is simply only a question of policy that we should agree to that, with circumstances having changed in the course of years, with new conditions having been created in the country which have made the colour question in general the most acute in our land, we should agree that as a consequence we are convinced that that policy must be carried out on the foundations we have laid down here. If we refuse to do so, if we should refuse to strike the course I have indicated, having regarded this as a question of policy, then we would be unfaithful to the people and to the people's highest interests. Then we would be betraying South Africa and European civilisation, and we are not prepared to commit this treason. Everything depends on whether this is a legal question; then we shall have to follow the policy that I have outlined here in connection with the two-thirds majority. But if it is not a legal question, if there is no question of breaking the law, we would be acting disloyally towards South Africa and we would be betraying the supreme interests of South Africa if we did not take action.

The question has also been raised: Yes, what about the two-thirds majority that is provided for in regard to language equality? All that I can say is this. This does stand on an equal footing with the two-thirds majority in connection with non-Europeans. It falls in the same category; both stand in the same position. I would only say this in regard to the question of language equality if it should have to be abolished on its merits, if that is justified, it can happen. If it can be shown to the country that on the merits it should be abolished, it can happen and it would have to happen. But now I want to say this in that connection. The question of the penetration of the Natives, their further and further encroachment on the Europeans so that more and more is equality coming about between Europeans and non-Europeans affects South Africa deeply. Our survival as Europeans depends on the solution of this problem. But, in the same way the future of South Africa depends on whether we preserve the principle of equality between one section and the other section of the European population, Afrikaans-speaking and English-speaking. And woe to the man who subordinates English language and culture or Afrikaans language and culture, the one to the other. He is playing false towards South Africa and its future.

GENERAL J. C. SMUTS[1]

I SHALL CONFINE myself only to one of these matters that have been raised, and no doubt other members on this side of the House will raise other points. I wish to come back to the colour policy, the apartheid policy of the Government. This policy has been very fully discussed in all its implications and it has been very fully analysed, and I think it had been brought down to two points which emerge from these discussions. The first is this — that the policy of apartheid is just a false and misleading catchword intended to exploit the colour prejudice of this country, to stampede public opinion and to make people believe that the policy of the United Party is one of equal rights and may lead to the downfall of White South Africa. That is the first point that has emerged from this discussion. The second point is this — that the intention is to do away with the political rights of the non-European peoples in this country. It has also emerged that this may involve tampering with the entrenched clauses of the constitution. I shall take this last point first.

I need not point out again, as has been repeatedly pointed out here, that the question of political rights of the non-European people in this country is one of the entrenched clauses of the South Africa Act, and that no bare majority such as the Government secured in the last election can deal with this most important issue. It is not merely a question of law, it goes much further. It is a question which was considered and it is on record that it was considered — one of the basic and fundamental conditions of the South Africa Act. Now, sir, what is curious is this, that this implication of the apartheid policy was never put before the people at the last general election. We heard on every platform, in all directions, this question of apartheid discussed as a matter involving the future of South Africa. But that most fundamental aspect of it, that the carrying out of this policy may mean tampering with the constitution, and by-passing the entrenched clauses of the South Africa Act — that, as far as my memory goes, was never laid before the people. I think that the people never realised what was on and what was at stake. Even here in this House it seemed during the early part of the discussion that people did not realise that this was really the ultimate issue in this great question.

[1] Speech by General J. C. Smuts, Leader of the Opposition, in House of Assembly 21 September 1948. *House of Assembly Debates.*

It was only in the course of the debates that gradually this issue emerged and once more confronted us with a situation very different, far more serious I may say, than that of apartheid itself. I say there has been no frankness, no fair dealing with the people of this country. When the Government started this policy of apartheid, and persisted with it on the basis of their small majority, they should have taken the people into their confidence and they should have said, We are up against the South Africa Act, we cannot go on with this policy; the people have not given us a mandate to carry it out, and we are not going on with it. Instead of that there has been a dubious, ambiguous policy pursued here. The Prime Minister (Dr. D. F. Malan) seemed almost not to have made up his mind yet what was the course which he was going to take in order to carry out this policy in these circumstances. I charge the Government with bad faith towards the people of this country. They should have told the country what this policy meant. If people had realised that this policy of apartheid may mean tampering with the constitution, may mean by-passing the sacred clauses of the South Africa Act, I think their attitude may have been very different.

Well, sir, as I say, it is on record that the National Convention looked upon these clauses as sacred and not to be tampered with. The Prime Minister says people may change their mind, one generation may not bind another. But it is the very object with which these clauses were put in, that they should be binding.

AN HON. MEMBER: For all time?

GENERAL SMUTS: That was the intention. But for that we would never have had Union, this united South Africa would never have come into being but for these clauses. Right through these last 40 years of these clauses nobody ever dreamt of by-passing these clauses. We hear about our sovereign position. It has nothing to do with our sovereignty. We may be sovereign but we may be bound by ultimate fundamental provisions in our Constitution. These safeguards were put into the Constitution originally just to meet a case such as we have today, where a snatch majority might intend to deal with a big national issue like this. The original intention was to meet such a case, and it is the very case which has occurred. All these 40 years these entrenched clauses of the Constitution have been looked upon as sacred and inviolable. It is only now in this revolutionary epoch, these unforeseen developments in this country, that we have a Government coming forward prepared to flout these provisions and to set them aside. Sovereignty has nothing to do with it. Our sovereignty as a nation has been recognised ever since the Statute of Westminster.

DR. MALAN: Democracy has something to do with it.

GENERAL SMUTS: No, democracy does not mean Fascism. We have been a sovereign country ever since the Statute of Westminster. But we accepted sovereignty subject to this condition. Parliament unanimously confirmed that the assumption of sovereign authority in this country will not touch those inviolable clauses in the constitution. That was in 1931. In 1934, when we passed our Status Act, confirmation was given to that condition, that we only accept our sovereign status under this condition, that these entrenched clauses shall not be violated. Nobody ever questioned these things, we looked upon these clauses as the bedrock, as the lifeboat of our constitution. So much so, in 1936, after the conferment of our sovereign authority, after it had been confirmed, and when the Hertzog legislation was brought forward in order to make the reform in the Native franchise and Native political rights, we still stuck fast to this provision. The Hertzog legislation of 1936 was put down in terms of the constitution. We did not by-pass these sacred clauses of the South Africa Act. It shows that all through these years people in this country have never had a doubt about this issue. Why fundamental changes should take place now at this date in this country today, why we should change our minds suddenly and scrap all this, I think is a matter which we should not contemplate for a moment. I think the people of the country, when they are faced with the issue, if it is put before them in all its gravity and seriousness, their attitude may be very different from what it was. Simply the bare catchword of apartheid was put before them. They must have an opportunity to pass judgment on this policy, on this re-volutionary departure, which the Government has brought before the country.

AN HON. MEMBER: It has been an issue for the last ten or 15 years.

GENERAL SMUTS: No, do not let the hon. member delude himself with these statements. I am therefore going to move an amendment. I want to pin down this House and concentrate the public attention of this country on this issue — that what is contemplated, what is involved now, is not merely the abstract catchword of apartheid, but what is involved is fun-damental change in the constitution of this country, a thing which we have never done before and which we did not contemplate doing in the future.

Apart from this very grave issue that arises on our constitution I would ask, as a matter of policy, is it wise, is it right for us to take away these very small rights which the non-Europeans have in this country? Their political rights are so limited, there is so little to it, that I should have thought it would be simple elementary political wisdom to leave the matter alone. Here you have three European representatives of the Natives in a House of 153 members. What is the menace, what is the danger? It seems to me that it is simply playing with enormous issues. Here you have millions of people entrusted to our care. They cannot speak for themselves, that is the little voice they have, that is all they have. We gaily and unconcernedly step over them, we almost stamp on them, and we walk across them and take away these small rights, or propose to take away these small rights that have been given to them. How can we face our own public opinion in this country? How can we face the public opinion of the world? How can we face the future of South Africa when we behave in this way to people that have been put in our charge as a

424

sacred trust? How can we defend ourselves? How can we with a clean conscience go forward to the future in such a way? I would therefore ask the House, and the people of this country, to be most careful. These people possess very small rights at present, and there is no question of their being extended in the immediate future. They may be extended according to the wisdom and the insight of those who follow us, but at present there is no such intention at all. The only matter we are faced with is the taking away of these few rights that they have. I think it is the height of folly.

Take the case of our Coloured people. Our Coloured people have always been considered as part, an appendage, of the European community. That has always been the case, it is our historic policy and outlook in this country. These people now, by tampering with their rights, putting them on a special roll, taking them off the common roll, are also going to be stampeded against us. I cannot conceive how any party, how any Government can be so foolish as to take a step of that kind. General Hertzog never took it. That was not his bequest to the country. In all the statesmanlike proposals he made, on which there were great differences of opinion but which ultimately were passed by almost the unanimous vote of this House, no such change was made. We left that alone. What are we going to do now? We are going to drive the Coloured people away from us. We are going to help to make a united front of all the colour in this country. We talk about a united front — we are making it. It is not the Communists that are making it, it is we that are driving them to it. I say a step like this that alienates our friends, people who really belong to us, from us, stirring up all this feeling, all this bitterness, all this despondent frustration, can only lead to one thing. They will all come together, you will have a united front, and that united front may be a Communist front. What is the use of our inveighing against communism when we are ourselves taking the most active steps in order to bring it about?

I am going to move the following amendment.

To omit all the words after " That " and to substitute " This House declines to pass the Second Reading of the Appropriation Bill before and until it receives an assurance from the Government that it will adhere strictly to the entrenchment provisions of the South Africa Act in respect of any proposals which it may submit for the abrogation or diminution of the existing political rights of the Native and Coloured peoples ".

So much for the one point I have raised — tampering with the political rights of the underdog in this country, of the people entrusted to our care, and over whom we are the guardians.

The other point was, I said, this misleading impression that has been created in the country by all this campaign of vituperation that equal rights is a policy of the United Party and that that policy will ultimately lead this country to its doom. It is so far-fetched to think that the United

Party, or any party, can be so stupid as that and embark on those policies, that it passes the wit of man. Our policy has always been different. Equal rights never has been our policy.

MR. C. R. SWART: What is your policy then?

GENERAL SMUTS: It is quite simple. Our policy has been European paramountcy in this country. Our policy has been not equal rights. We have never had any truck with equal rights. It is an abstraction forced upon us by our opponents. We stand and have always stood for European supremacy in this country. We have said that we have a position of guardianship, of trusteeship, over the non-European peoples in the country, and we must carry out that trust in the true spirit of exploitation but in a way which will justify our claim to be guardians of these people. We have never been in favour of equal rights. We have always stood and we stand for social and residential separation in this country, and for the avoidance of all racial mixture.

DR. MALAN: Is that your apartheid?

GENERAL SMUTS: To that extent of course. There is a great deal about apartheid which is common to all parties in this country. (Laughter.) They are amused about this, there is great amusement about it. The European people of this country, I think the other sections of the people too, have stood against this social or residential intermixture and all that it implies. If apartheid is taken in that social residential sense everybody is for apartheid. The Natives are for apartheid. The Coloureds are for apartheid, and so are we. We recognise the factual position in this country, that there are differences of race; it is not merely differences of colour, it is differences of race. And we also recognise that the great bulk of our Native people in this country live not in separate areas in territorial apartheid, but they live mixed up with us in European areas.

DR. MALAN: Nobody denies that.

GENERAL SMUTS: That is a factual position, and apartheid cannot be taken in any other sense. We have 60 per cent of these people living amongst us on our farms, in our cities and towns, and they will continue to live there. They have a right to be there, they have as much right as we have. There is no question of moving them territorially to reserves or any other areas. These are all common things between us, we do not dispute that. The hon. Minister of Native Affairs[2] said the other day that he could not even move these people to the Native reserves, that there will be no place for them; and we know that is so. All therefore we have in our Native policy today, and what our party stands for is this: Let us enlarge and develop these Native reserves and make them as attractive homes for the Native people who are there as possible. Let us have villages there, let us have amenities, let us have all the conditions which will make the reserves attractive and keep the Native people who are there and should be there within their own areas.

That is our policy, and of course it also involves this. As they become

[2] Dr. E. G. Jansen.

educated, as they make progress, we must see they are politically developed, that they can have a position of managing their own affairs in these areas. I think that is common ground too.

Mr. C. R. Swart: You are coming nearer and nearer to apartheid.

General Smuts: I do not see why the Government party should claim this, it has always been our policy.

With regard to the majority of the Native people who live in the European areas, they are economically necessary to those areas. They have lived there, they have the right to be there. Every day they work there and they are economically integrated with these areas. We cannot move them away. All we can do is to improve their lots, to prevent these eyesores, these abhorrent conditions which are now arising in the industrial areas in South Africa. Therefore, our party on this side of the House have advocated Native villages, satellite villages or towns in those areas, which will provide proper housing, proper health, proper education and other facilities in those villages alongside and parallel to the White townships. That is what we have stood for. I do not believe members on the other side of the House have a definite policy.

Mr. J. J. Serfontein: Do you approve of apartheid on the railways?

General Smuts: It has always been there, it has always been in the country.

Mr. J. J. Serfontein: In the Cape Peninsula?

General Smuts: Here it has been produced only as a provocative measure to set the Coloured people by the ears.

Mr. C. R. Swart: Are you against it?

General Smuts: They will never miss a chance of setting people by the ears and causing bad blood in order to score some petty political point.

Mr. C. R. Swart: Are you in favour of it in the Cape Peninsula, are you in favour of apartheid in the trains?

General Smuts: Is that the policy, is that what their apartheid comes to? (Laughter.) It is the smallness of this outlook, the bad human feeling, the desire to give pinpricks and irritate which I resent.

Mr. C. R. Swart: You cannot give me a reply to that simple question.

General Smuts: If I am for apartheid it is not in the spirit the Minister wants to carry it out. I think the only difference between us on this matter of making proper provision in the European area for vast masses of non-Europeans, the only difference between us is that it is a matter of greater urgency. We find that conditions are now pressing in on this country both on the Rand and in the Peninsula and in other parts of South Africa, which call for urgent attention, and we were taking the urgent action. We cannot wait any more. But what has happened now? All these improvements that were intended and that we were busy with have been slowed down. More inquiries are going to be started up. The establishment we have created is being dismantled.

Mr. J. J. Serfontein: Can you give us an example of one of the things you wanted to carry out?

GENERAL SMUTS: I think that is the policy we shall have to go in for, and that is the policy of the United Party, townships alongside of our White towns where the Native workers and others can be properly housed and can live under conditions which we can justify, conditions which will preserve their human dignity and make them feel they are men and not merely " skepsels ".[3] These matters have all been dealt with under the Fagan Report, which I consider one of the great State documents in this country. There may be some difference of opinion as to particular recommendations and I see that the hon. Minister of Native Affairs said that he reserved his opinion on particular recommendations of the commission but the analysis of the situation, the assemblage of the facts and figures and the setting out of the whole case, makes this, I think, one of the historical documents of this country. And the policy our party stands for, and has always stood for, is very largely expressed in the findings and the recommendations of that report. Our policy is as plain as a pikestaff and always has been.

Of course, there will always be a certain amount of migrant labour. The expansion of this country, the requirements of mining and other industries are such that even our Native population is not sufficient for our requirements. You know it on the farms, you see it in the cities, you see it in all the industries, you see it on the mines. We are going in for vast mining development in the Free State; we are warned there is no labour, that everything will be slowed down because of want of labour, and we shall continue to get a large amount of migrant labour both in South Africa and from beyond our borders to deal with situations like that. We shall there, too, have to see they are properly housed and decently looked after and that conditions from a human point of view are made as wholesome as possible. I think it will be necessary for us to establish institutions which will help to regulate this flow of labour for the various requirements of South Africa. There is a great clamour now amongst our farmers for labour. It is one of the greatest difficulties we are faced with. The shortage is not only in the towns and in the industries but equally on the farms, and we shall have to go in for a system of labour registration and exchanges which will regulate the free flow of labour to all the various needs and demands of the country. Those are the problems before us — not talking about railway compartments. These are the questions which lie on our doorstep and which South Africa calls for, and not these piffling things with which they trifle away their time in this country.

I think on great issues there is a great deal of consensus of opinion in this country already. And that is why I say that normally it comes down to political rights. I do not think there is so much dispute about the other things. Although they are too slow in grasping the development on our doorstep, in all that is fundamental I do not see

[3] Literally: " creatures." One of the euphemistic Afrikaans words for non-Whites.

much difference of opinion. But on political rights we contemplate this disastrous step which the Government wants to foist on the country and we say that our policy there, the policy of the United Party, is to stand by the *status quo*.

In 1936, after prolonged investigation, we for once got the people of this country in Parliament practically unanimous, and under happy conditions we could come together politically and produce there the settlement of 1936, the Hertzog settlement which stands and which we stand by. We see no reason to depart from it, to change the political representation, the political rights, small as they are, of the Native people and of the Coloured people of this country. As regards the Natives, we stand also by that somewhat unsatisfactory body, the Natives' Representative Council, which was established in that connection. Have that and improve it. It does not work very well. It is unsatisfactory, it is a debating society. The Natives' Representative Council today is largely a debating society with no responsibility, no work to do except talking, and, naturally, in a situation like that people will talk, people will criticise and go off the rails and be unsatisfactory. And therefore that is why we propose their position should be altered and improved. They should not be abolished, as proposed by the Government, but they should get a certain amount of authority to run their own affairs, to help in regard to the reserves, to have something to bite on, to have some job to do. No doubt they will make mistakes. That is the only way democracy works, by learning by its own mistakes.

After all, in the Bunga, such a body is already in operation, and I do not see why it should not be in operation over much of South Africa. Give the Native people and the Native leaders a chance and let them have some authority in regard to their own people. I think it will be a very grave mistake either to tamper with the political rights as they exist, or with this institution which we have established for the ventilating of Native opinion. The small position they have in the Parliament of this country let them keep; they are taxpayers, they are integrated with us on a very firm basis, let them have their say here too. And let us move forward to the future, not trying to break down what has been built up in the past, but gradually understanding, improving and removing mistakes, and in that way making the conditions of living together in this country for our various races and colours as easy as possible. That is our task, that is the great experiment in this country. Let us do our best to make it a successful experiment. It may go wrong. We will be the sufferers; we will suffer; we will pay. Therefore let us do our best to create a good human situation here and see that there is good feeling in spite of all this bitterness.

GENERAL J. C. SMUTS, 24 JANUARY 1950[1]

W E   H A V E   N E V E R been in doubt as to the real policy of this Government. They made it plain right through — their policy of apartheid, their policy of exploiting the feelings, the emotions of our people on the colour question in this country. At the last General Election they fought the issue before the country on the matter of apartheid, and they have never hesitated to say that they got a mandate from the country in this respect and that they were going to carry out that mandate. Well, that was renewed last year when the Provincial Elections were held, and the Government took part in that Election as if it were a General Election on the public policy of the country. Once more they said that they had their mandate, that they had won the Provincial Election on that issue and that they were going to carry out their apartheid policy, especially in its aspect of the political rights of the Natives and the Coloured people in this country. It was clear that that was the bedrock of the apartheid policy. Of course, it had much besides. It had much on which people in this country differed; it had much of a subsidiary character, but the real gist of the policy of the Government was the tampering with the political rights of the Native and Coloured people in this country, in spite of the constitutional provision of our law, in spite of everything in this country.

Now, sir, what has happened; where do we stand now? It has become quite clear that this policy was a fraudulent policy. It is not being carried out and it cannot be carried out; it cannot be carried out by that party, by that coalition and by the Government which is ruling the country today. They fought the last General Election on a false issue. They brought people under the impression that they could carry out that policy, and the event has proved now that they are unable to do so. They have had their warning. They had their warning at Brakpan[2] the year before last; they had their warning when the hon. the Minister of Finance[3] put his foot down — quite rightly and honourably — and said that he was not in favour of tampering with the South Africa Act in regard to the entrenched clauses. This was a warning. One would have thought that a Government fighting a general issue in this country of this far-reaching nature, would at any rate be at one, would be unanimous on the carrying out of that policy, but in spite of that warning that they had, in spite of the clear evidence that they were not agreed on this fundamental policy they went on.

Another warning came to them at Ladybrand, where the hon. the Minister of Finance said that he was not in favour of carrying out that policy with the majority that the Government has at present. Well, sir,

[1] Extract from speech by General J. C. Smuts, Leader of the Opposition, in House of Assembly, 24 January 1950.
[2] At a by-election.
[3] Mr. N. C. Havenga.

where are we? Here a General Election has been fought in this country on broadly the gravest issue that you could bring before this country. There is a coalition Government in power which claims to have this mandate, and what is the position? We are now warned by the leading members of this Government that they cannot carry out this policy. It is a very grave situation. I do not remember any such situation facing this country before. I say that the people of this country have been spoofed; they have been brought under the impression that apartheid in its political aspects can be carried out by this Government and by this party, and now on their own clear confession it is impossible to do so; they cannot do it. They were not able to do it last year and they will not be able to do it this year.

MR. HAVENGA: May I ask the Rt. Hon. the Leader of the Opposition when the Government had laid down that policy?

GENERAL SMUTS: Good Heavens! What was their mandate? The mandate was given to them in 1948, the mandate which was renewed at the Provincial Elections in 1949, and here we come and sit in this House, and we are told by the leading members of the Government, that is, by the Prime Minister and the Minister of Finance, that the policy cannot be carried out — and — of course, it cannot be carried out; it won't be carried out next year; goodness only knows when it can be carried out. This country, I say, sir, has been spoofed, has been misled. People all over this country, worked up under the emotions of this occasion, have been brought under the impression that they can have apartheid, they can have their heart's desire; they can see this principal aim and object of their party carried out. Where are we now?

DR. MALAN: You will have much of it this year.

GENERAL SMUTS: They will have a few particular arrangements, I suppose, on the railways or in the post offices, or elsewhere, but that is not the issue on which the general election was fought. That is not what was represented to this country as their apartheid policy. No, I think that constitutionally there can be no doubt that for any honourable self-respecting Government in the position of this Government, there is only one course, and that is to go, to resign. After all, this is a democracy; this is a democratic country; the Government rests on the will of the people, and when people have been misled, when people have been led up the garden path, and have been led by the Government to expect that this policy would be carried out fully in its political aspects, and they are then told by the Government itself that it cannot be done, there is only one course left and that is to resign. Let them go for another mandate; let them resign or let them go to the country once more for another mandate, and let the country express its opinion on it. We, on this side of the House, rejoice at this check which has come to the Government not from us; we have, of course, done our share in calling halt, in calling for caution and due moderation, but this comes from the Government itself. They have queered their own pitch;

they have made their own course impossible; it has come from them and we rejoice and we are glad that the people of this country have been given this pause and this opportunity to reconsider carefully once more what is happening in this country, what course we are pursuing, what object we are aiming at.

Let us have further consultation; let us have more time; let us give further consideration to a matter which is not merely one of party politics; that is the least important aspect of it. Its party political aspect is the least important; it is a question which affects the future of this country as no other political question in South Africa can affect it, and we are glad that there is this opportunity for further consideration. We rejoice at this position, but for the Government it is fatal. The Government cannot escape this conclusion that they have led the people up the garden path. They have made the people believe that they can see apartheid through in its political aspect, and they cannot do it. They have not been able to do it for one year, and a second year; they can wait for a third year and attempt to dig themselves in under false pretences but this policy on which they say they have a mandate from the people, they will not be able to carry out. Much harm has been done, sir, but so far the position is not yet fatal. The harm is not yet irremediable; there is still time, we are thankful, to consider the course before us and there is no doubt that in this pandering to the deep feelings of the people, this playing on the emotions of our people, the Government has started South Africa on a career which may have very far-reaching results. We see it already. We can see how this country is getting isolated, in spite of our attending conferences; we can see how South Africa, more than ever before, is getting isolated from the public opinion of the world.

There are two sides to this question. I know that our position is liable to be misunderstood abroad. I know that the position of South Africa on this colour question is a difficult one. It is very difficult to make people abroad understand our position, but what has happened in this country is this; this subject has been exploited. It has been published by the Government and their party in a way which can only do infinite harm to South Africa. Our best friends are nonplussed. We look around the world. I know the majority of people are inclined to be against us; but we have strong support in the world, we have strong friends who are inclined to stand by us. But will they stand by this apartheid policy of this Government, this policy on which the people of the country have been kept stretched out for the last two years? Will they stand by us there? No; we are alienating our friends, we are making the position of our friends very difficult. It is very difficult for them to keep on sympathising with us and supporting us while we are indulging in policies of this kind; policies which are the most difficult and dangerous in the whole world today. We make their position difficult, and we alienate their sympathy, and we make it impossible for

432

them to support us.

If there is one country in the world today which needs world support, which needs sympathy, it is South Africa. We are a singular experiment in the world. Here on this Black continent we are a small minority always trying to build up a European civilisation. We have done so with remarkable success. If we look back on what has happened over the last 200 years and more we have every reason to be grateful for the success which has been achieved. But we are the small minority on this continent, and one can understand the need for such a minority to have support far beyond its boundaries, world support, the support of reasonable people in other lands too. But by the policy we have now adopted or purported to have adopted as the official policy of this country, we make it almost impossible for us to have that sympathy, to have that support which can see us through in the days that are coming. If there is one country in the world that needs support in a case like ours it is South Africa. But the Government has made it very difficult for them to show sympathy with us — I am not speaking of UNO where the majorities are against us — I am speaking of countries, strong, powerful countries, who realise to a large extent our difficulties, we are making it impossible for them to stand by us. What has happened in South Africa? So far we have got on quite well. We have not publicised, we have not exploited those colour differences amongst us.

DR. P. J. VAN NIEROP[4]: Haven't you?

GENERAL SMUTS: I am sure I am not speaking for hon. members opposite when I say that, I am speaking for reasonable, patriotic South Africans who know the dangers of this question. Whether you read our past history, or the statements of our past leaders of both races in South Africa, you will everywhere find this element of caution, this element of reserve when they come to colour questions. Look at the publicity now being given to this matter in those countries and the results we see. It is admitted on all hands that there have never been such strained relations, such undesirable relations between White and Black in this country as exist today. There has been almost a revolution in public opinion. In these matters it is unbelievable that in the last couple of years there can have been such a setback to us, in so short a period, and it is largely due to such publicity.

It is due to this trying to exploit for party political purposes a subject that we should deal with very cautiously and with the greatest sincerity and reserve. It is largely due to that. And I say as long as the Government makes the foundation of its public policy this policy of apartheid, this policy of tampering with the rights of those who cannot speak for themselves, as long as they continue along that path South Africa is adopting a very dangerous course, and the sooner we can get them out of it the better. Whether you look at the situation abroad or in this country

[4] National Party.

you can see what a dangerous turn our public affairs have taken in recent years.

But I go further; it is not my only charge. I think this mentality of apartheid has affected hon. members opposite, has affected the Nationalists in this country especially, in a way which makes the danger far greater. There is no doubt that this outlook of apartheid is spreading beyond the colour question and a division is growing up among our European people which is almost as dangerous as that growing up between the colours in this country. If there is one thing which is fundamental and which ought to be fundamental with us, it is the consolidation of our European elements in this country.

8

BANTU SELF-GOVERNMENT

DR. H. F. VERWOERD, 27 JANUARY 1959[1]

THE LEADER of the Opposition[2] has alleged that we are violating the 1936 Hertzog agreement, as he described it. Furthermore he maintained that we are doing an injustice to the Bantu of South Africa by depriving them of a type of representation in Parliament and by merely replacing that representation by minor local boards. He made the accusation that this was a breach of faith and an injustice.

I now want to deal with the matter in this way. During the course of its history South Africa has developed a problem which has become more and more complicated. General Hertzog dealt with this problem on the basis that the White man would always retain supremacy in this country and that he could give a certain permanent opportunity to the Bantu to submit his difficulties to Parliament through a very limited number of White representatives. One could describe this system as an extremely limited form of junior partnership. General Hertzog regarded this as the conclusion of a period of development and as a final solution. But since 1936 tremendous changes have taken place amongst the Bantu themselves in our country. Throughout the world views as to the freedom and rights of people have changed and there have been tremendous developments in Africa as regards the granting of independence to States which originally had been under the guardianship of other States. We must give the situation in South Africa proper consideration in the light of these developments.

Now it is of no avail the Leader of the Opposition saying that we should simply go on as we have in the past, abide by the Hertzog agreement of 1936, and only make occasional minor changes to create greater satisfaction. We must examine what the result of these developments will be in the light of developments in Africa and in the mind of the Bantu. That is why the United Party cannot be trusted with the government of the country and why the National Party can be trusted. The United Party refuses to face that problem. They try to fob it off with words or by stating policies the consequences of which they refuse to accept.

---

[1] Extract from speech by the Prime Minister, Dr. H. F. Verwoerd, stating the policy of the National Party in the House of Assembly, 27 January 1959. *House of Assembly Debates.*
[2] Sir De Villiers Graaff.

They require of us that we should state the consequences of our policy in the far-distant future, but refuse to face even the immediate consequences of their own policy. I just want to add this in regard to the accusation of breach of faith. There have been members of the United Party, such as the hon. member for Constantia (Mr. Waterson) who have themselves said that the 1936 legislation has been a failure, that it has been made obsolete by later developments and that it should be changed.

I now ask why it is not a breach of faith to the Whites of South Africa to change those constitutional arrangements so as to give increased representation to the non-Whites in the Parliament of South Africa, but it is a breach of faith when we replace that system with a completely new system by which the Bantu is given a far greater control over his own affairs? Why is it not a breach of faith when the system is changed in such a way that the Whites are given relatively less power as against the non-Whites — greater powers for the non-Whites — but when the White man is to be given full authority only in his own areas and the Bantu will acquire full authority elsewhere in the course of time, it is a breach of faith? What would General Hertzog have done? Under the circumstances obtaining in those times he wished to be fair to the Bantu. Where a limited number of them in only one of the provinces had the franchise on the common roll and it was taken from them, he wanted to replace that franchise with something which he hoped would be of greater value. If that was correct, why is it wrong when we want to take away something today which they were given at that time and which they themselves today regard as unsatisfactory, which other members of the United Party have described as unsatisfactory and which is described abroad as unsatisfactory, in order to replace it with something positive which holds out great possibilities of development? Why is it a breach of faith when we want to give them something better than the 1936 legislation?

I am trying to visualise the great overall policy for South Africa and to compare it honestly with the policy of the United Party. South Africa is at the cross-roads: It must decide whether it is going to move in the direction of a multi-racial community with a common political society or whether it is going to establish total separation in the political sphere. The United Party says it accepts a multi-racial community, but in that community it nevertheless wants to maintain " White leadership with justice ". Its attitude is that it believes that the White man can retain control over the Government, the Cabinet and Parliament, but within that framework it wants to make all sorts of concessions to the non-Whites such as initially giving them a few more members in the Senate, or a reconstituted Senate, or certain types of guarantees in the Senate. United Party members have advanced all sorts of ideas as to how they want to grant the Bantu increased rights in Parliament. That is surely a fair description of the United Party's aims. I am not accusing the United Party of wanting to grant equality at once. I am not accusing it of wanting to have a common roll for everyone immediately with the consequential immediate domination by the Natives. I only say this: At the moment its policy is one of maintaining the leadership of the White man through discrimination, of hoping that he can always retain this leadership in this way and of only making minor concessions. As against that I say that that is a policy which it will be unable to maintain. It will be unable to maintain it because it must take into account the signs of the times. It is a type of partnership government which it is offering; perhaps the partners will have less powers than at the moment in Kenya, even less than at the moment in the Central African Federation, but nevertheless the Union will definitely be placed on the road of partnership by this policy. As a matter of fact, the British Government regards its conception of what it would like to see established as something which it also describes as partnership. They even regard the Basutoland Agreement, by which very small numbers of Whites have been absorbed together with a dominating number of Bantu into a Bantu Council, as a type of partnership with the Whites as a permanent junior partner. In the same way the United Party is moving along the road to partnership.

But the Bantu of Africa do not want that. Certain Natives in Ghana are demanding that in South Africa the Bantu should all be given a vote on a common roll, even if it is only done gradually. In other words, equal rights is the demand being made in order eventually to dominate South Africa. If they are given equal rights on a common roll they will want to and will be able to dominate the whole of South Africa to an ever-increasing extent. That is the unavoidable and inevitable final result of that policy, as we have already said so often in the past. That is in brief the policy of the United Party. That is how the National Party sees it with all its dangers. For that reason we tell the people of South Africa that we cannot govern without taking into account the tendencies in the world and in Africa. We must have regard to them. Our policy must take them into account. And we can only take them into account and safeguard the White man's control over our country if we move in the direction of separation — separation in the political sphere at any rate.

DR. J. VAN A. STEYTLER[3]: Is it practicable?

DR. VERWOERD: This question as to its practicability contains the old accusation of the United Party, and now as always I reject it. I believe that our policy, correctly understood, is practicable, and if the hon. member will listen to what I now want to say about the next stage, he will perhaps better understand this policy.

In the case of Basutoland the United Party Press welcomed the fact that Britain had allowed the Bantu people to move a certain stage forward in developing along their own lines. That is what it is and that is what hon. members opposite have praised. If Britain can establish something that the United Party describe as a Bantustan inside South Africa, and can do so with their blessing, and if their contention is that this develop-

[3] United Party. Since November 1959 Leader of the Progressive Party.

ment is inevitable and sound, why cannot the Union of South Africa, taking into account the ever-increasing desire for self-government which exists among the non-Whites, say: We are also taking steps to ensure that we adopt a policy by which we on the one hand can retain for the White man full control in his areas, but by which we are giving the Bantu as our wards every opportunity in their areas to move along a road of development by which they can progress in accordance with their ability. And if it should happen that in the future they progress to a very advanced level, the people of those future times will have to consider in what further way their relationships must be reorganised. I myself have already clearly indicated one of the methods which I consider will then be practicable. I have said that I take as a comparison the British Commonwealth of Nations where the various constituent members of the Commonwealth are not represented in the mother Parliament, but within which organisation there are still links — economic and otherwise — by which co-operation is possible without a mixed Parliament or government, whether of the country itself or of the federation, ever being established. I have gone much further in considering the future than the United Party has had the courage to do in considering the consequences of its plans because its members would otherwise have been obliged to admit honestly that the final result of their policy would be Native domination of all South Africa. I have adopted this attitude: Development cannot be prevented but the lesser danger is for the White man at least to control his own areas and to live in friendship with the Native areas, either as their guardian or as neighbours who have common interests with them and who therefore follow his leadership, without the White and non-White sitting in one Parliament or in one government.

Our attitude is that matters have now reached the stage, and that development has now reached the stage where we can proceed to the next stage in our positive plan of development. If the United Party had not blinded not only themselves, but the world as well, to the intentions of the Bantu Authorities Act, they would have understood us better today and would not have sat and jeered as they are now trying to do. For a change they could also try to have a great vision. But South Africa does not expect much of them; it places its faith in the governing party alone. I now say this: So many Bantu authorities have already been established, and so many regional authorities have already been established — yes, in a few instances territorial authorities are already functioning — that there is no doubt that by the time the period of office of the Native representatives expires, the territorial authorities will be in full operation in all the reserves. That will be the position, whether the development takes place on the basis of building up from the bottom as envisaged by the Bantu Authorities Act, or on the basis of a transition period, just as the Transkei itself preferred to establish a transition form of government rather than to wait for that stage when the final form would be established. In other words, our attitude is quite clear, namely that we shall soon reach the stage where the territorial authorities will be in operation, which is the stage at which both my predecessor[4] and I myself have said will be the time for taking the next step, namely to establish a clearer separation in the political field than exists today. We must then remove from the Union Parliament the remnants of a type of partnership policy which was envisaged as being the solution in 1936, but which the intervening 22 years have shown is inadequate and cannot be developed any further. In its place we must give the Bantu an opportunity to manage their affairs in their own areas. Indeed we regard the territorial authorities as independent bodies in the first stage of development. There are a number of unpopular control methods which the guardian exercises at the moment only in order to guide them along that road, but which will lapse as they advance from one stage to another.

The hon. the Leader of the Opposition has said today that there are certain matters in respect of which the guardian exercises control. I concede that there are matters over which the guardian retains control for the moment, but I have already said in introducing the Act that those methods of control will lapse in the course of time. I remind hon. members of the fact that precisely the same thing has happened in the case of Basutoland, about which they have been so full of praise. The High Commissioner there has a right of veto. The British Colonial Secretary holds certain powers of veto over their legislation and certain of their actions. Even in the case of the Federation, and particularly in the case of Nyasaland, Britain holds powers of a similar nature. There is nothing strange about the fact that here in South Africa the guardian, in his attempts to uplift the Bantu groups who have been entrusted to his care, must in various ways exercise supervision over them during the initial stage. When one studies the developments which have taken place in certain of the countries of Africa which have become independent, one asks the question whether it is not a pity that the guardian did not retain rather more control than he has.

When we introduce this legislation I therefore ask hon. members in the interests of South Africa not to concentrate attention — as they are doing — on the apparently negative aspect by only discussing the abolition of the Native representatives, and that alone. That is merely a subsidiary part of a supremely positive step towards placing the Natives on the road to self-government in their own areas. To be able to move along that road, it is inevitable that the other system should disappear. Otherwise they will be in continuous confusion as to where their future really lies. If we allow the Native representatives to remain in Parliament, whether in the House of Assembly, the Senate or the Provincial Councils, it will only result in confusion amongst the Natives and in the implementation of this policy. People then will not understand that (it) is the initial step along the road to separation. They will think, as the United Party want the people to think, that on the one hand there will be local councils

4 The late Mr. J. G. Strijdom.

and on the other hand representation in Parliament which can continually be increased. We must ensure that the outside world realises, and that the Bantu realises, that a new period is dawning, a period in which the White man will move away from discrimination against the Bantu as far as his own areas are concerned; that the White man is leading him through the first stage towards full development.

Leadership with justice, I said just now, is really a method of discrimination. It is a method by which one says: I shall remain master for ever, I shall suppress the other race for ever, but I shall discriminate " justly ". That is all that the so-called leadership with justice means. But when one says: We are no longer going to give the Bantu representation in the White Parliament because that White Parliament after all is the governing body of the White man in his own areas, but the White man with his Parliament will carry out his duties of guardianship over the Bantu in the Bantu areas and will give them the opportunity to develop fully in those areas, everyone knows what the future possibilities are. That is what the outside world praises when colonial powers give independence to territories. That is why England has been praised in regard to Basutoland. I therefore do not understand why we should be attacked in this respect. Surely the United Party is not going to persist in its accusations that we want to create Bantustans with consequent dangers to South Africa? After all they should then also criticise Britain because it has started with the creation of a Bantustan, a Bantustan of Basutoland, which they admit we will have to accept. If our neighbouring States are given greater independence under Britain's guardianship, why can there not be neighbouring States developing under our guardianship? But if developing takes place, within the limits of the ability of the Bantu to govern himself, under our guardianship in our Native areas — and I think the same method of development should be adopted in the Protectorates — we shall ensure that the relationships of these neighbouring territories in the economic and other fields are properly organised so that everyone can live together on a friendly basis.

After all, what is it that we are seeking in the first place in dealing with every problem of human relationships with which we are faced? Is it not friendship? When we say we want a republic, it is based on the principle of establishing closer ties of friendship with other countries. The United Party surely does not want to remain linked to Britain and have ties with Britain even though it militates against a section of the population entertaining a genuine feeling of friendship. What they desire with Britain is above all friendship, not ties. If the greatest measure of friendship can be achieved by both parties having their way, by the United Party having its way in that the bonds of friendship with Britain are strengthened and the National Party having its way in that the republic is established after which there will no longer be any suspicion attaching to such bonds of friendship — then everyone will have what they want. The same applies in Africa as well. In our dealings with the other countries of

Africa, we are seeking above all else for friendship. If we find we cannot gain this friendship in a certain way, let us say by establishing certain forms of diplomatic relations, but that we can gain this friendship by assisting one another in the scientific, economic and other fields, we should obviously adopt the policy by which the main objective, the gaining of friendship, can be achieved. The same applies to our own Bantu in South Africa. Friendship and good relations will not be achieved by giving them some say in Parliament through White representatives or even a few Native representatives. It will eventually result in a struggle between a majority of the one racial group and a minority of the other group. But that friendship can be achieved if the one group is allowed to develop towards exercising full control amongst its own people and the other group is allowed to acquire or retain full control amongst its own people. It is on that point which I wish to place all the emphasis : That our struggle is not in the first place destructive but constructive. We want to build up a South Africa in which the Bantu and the White man can live next to one another as good neighbours and not as people who are continually quarrelling over supremacy.

MR. M. D. C. DE WET NEL, 18 MAY 1959[1]

I WANT TO SAY that it is my deep and honest conviction that we have reached the stage where serious attention should be devoted to actually giving the Bantu the opportunity to manage their own affairs; because that is one of the elementary and the most moral rights to which every person is entitled. It is the legacy demanded by every nation in the world, and the Bantu eagerly demands it just like the White man and every other nation. Every nation in the world finds its highest expression and fulfilment in managing its own affairs and in the creation of a material and spiritual heritage for its successive generations. We want to give the Bantu that right also. The demand for self-determination on the part of the non-White nations is one of the outstanding features of the past decade. Outside Africa more than a dozen non-White nations have already obtained their freedom. In Africa it is the greatest phenomenon of the time. There are a number of people in Africa who have already received their freedom, and others are on the way to receiving it. This desire to manage their own affairs exists in the hearts of the Bantu population, just as it exists in the hearts of all other nations in the world. It is therefore our duty to approach these matters soberly and realistically. It is no use putting our heads in the sand and pretending to see nothing. We have to face the real facts. These matters

1 Extract from speech by the Minister of Bantu Administration and Development (Mr. M. D. C. de Wet Nel) explaining National Party policy during the debate on the second reading of the Promotion of Bantu Self-Government Bill in the House of Assembly, 18 May 1959. *House of Assembly Debates.*

lie near to the soul of the nation, and no safety valve in the world can smother them forever. The late Dr. Malan described it very pithily in this House once when he said that one might just as well try to stop the Southeaster with a sieve as to suppress the national sentiments of a nation. That applies to the Bantu also.

I say we must approach these matters soberly and with clear minds. If we close our eyes to them we are heading for self-destruction and death. People who are reckless in that regard are committing treason to their own people and digging the grave of the nation. We hear so many provocative remarks about Bantu nationalism and Black nationalism, but it is my conviction that there is nothing of the kind. If it exists, then there is also something like White nationalism. But what does exist in fact is hatred on the part of the Black man for the White man. That is the monster which may still perhaps destroy all the best things in Africa. But I want to ask whether this monster has not to a large extent been created by the White man himself? The fact that he has ignored the existence of national enmities[2], that he has ignored their own forms of government and that he has ignored their own cultural assets, has led to the growth of this monster, and that is the reason why we plead that this monster must not rear its head in South Africa. That is why we want to give them these opportunities.

Mr. Speaker, I want to say frankly that I believe in the existence of nationalism on the part of the Bantu population groups. We cannot deny it; it is there. Amongst the Zulus there is a feeling of nationalism which can serve as an example to more than one of us, but it is not a Bantu nationalism; it is their own racial nationalism, just as it exists amongst the White people of South Africa and of the world. I grant them that nationalism. If the White man is entitled to it, I ask what right we have to say that those people should not be entitled to it also? Let us be honest and fair. Moreover, nationalism is one of the forces which puts into motion the best things in the spirit of the human being. Nationalism is one of the forces which has led to the most beautiful deeds of idealism and sacrifice and inspiration. Should the Bantu not have it? It is the Nationalist who has learned to appreciate the cultural assets of other nations, and as someone once put it very strikingly, a Nationalist is the best citizen of the world. That is my belief in regard to this matter. For that reason I want to say this. It will always be my task to respect these things of the Bantu, but to assist them to develop it as something beautiful and something which is in the interest of South Africa. It is our task to provide the opportunities for developing these matters, so that we may have co-operation instead of racial clashes. To think that we can solve this problem by lumping together in one community everything which is Bantu is nothing less than a crime towards the Bantu. One of the good things contained in this Bill is that it formally recognises these national units among the

2 Entities?

Bantu, and to give them the right and to encourage them to continue along this road of national development.

· The question may be put in all fairness: Will it not be better, in the interest of South Africa, rather to continue building on the pattern we have now? I want to deal with a few considerations only.

In the first place, I stated the proposition that the overwhelming majority of the national groups in South Africa, including the Bantu, have rejected the ideal of a multi-racial community and have chosen separate development on their own. If we continued to build further on the present pattern, it would be nothing else but a negation of the will and the desires of the overwhelming majority of the population groups in South Africa, White as well as Bantu. In the second place we must be fair and honest and admit that the present state of affairs is very unsatisfactory to the Bantu and very uncertain for the Whites. If we continue building on the present pattern the position of the Whites will be very uncertain and the Bantu will not be satisfied. Let us remember that in this House there are three representatives who represent only the Bantu population of the Cape Province. The rest of the Bantu in South Africa are not represented in this House. Do hon. members want to tell me that the Bantu population takes no notice of that and that they are satisfied with it? It is an injustice which rankles in the minds of the Bantu in the other parts of the country. That is one of the main factors which engenders a spirit of suspicion and doubt regarding the honesty and the fairness and the justice of the White man. It is a political state of affairs which can no longer be tolerated. If hon. members want to be fair and logical, they should ask that at least the rest of the Bantu population in South Africa should be represented in this House on an equal footing with those in the Cape Province, and if they do that, I ask: Where will it end? We would then be setting in progress the same process which is being experienced in Kenya, Nyasaland and Northern Rhodesia today. We just cannot foresee the results of it.

In the third place, it is my honest conviction that these Bantu population groups can best be guided on the road to progress if their whole development is Bantu orientated, which means that all the administrative bodies from the highest to the lowest should be linked up and the whole of the Bantu population should be concerned in them. It must form part of the whole structure. The present pattern was White orientated, because it was coupled to the White man. The result was that there was a flight from the Bantu community. The developed Native no longer sought the satisfaction of his ambition to develop amongst his own people, but in the White areas. Surely that is a very sad state of affairs. There was a migration going on, not only of migrant labourers from the Bantu areas, but also of educated people from the Bantu areas, that most essential material for building up of a community. In my opinion every nation in the world is entitled to benefit from the efforts of its best sons and daughters and a policy which is calculated

443

to deprive them of it is immoral; it is human erosion. A policy like that cannot be tolerated. Such a policy is one of the chief causes of racial hatred.

In the fourth place, I am convinced in my mind that the expansion of the present system will have the result that the White population of South Africa will be dominated by the political power of the Bantu population. If this pattern is extended logically in future, I say that the White people will be dominated by the political power of the Bantu. Surely it must be a very stupid politician who cannot appreciate the logical consequences of this.

The present system of Bantu representation has really made no contribution in any way towards creating sound racial relations in South Africa. I challenge any person to deny that. All it has done is to increase racial tension. That is the only result which can today stand as a monument for those people, with few exceptions. If we extended the present system, what would the result be? It would create a racial hatred which South Africa simply cannot afford, because, in the course of years, we would then have a bitter struggle on the part of the White man to ensure that he is not ploughed under politically by the non-White groups of the population, but, at the same time, it must be remembered that if we accepted that principle today, then the Bantu would have to accept this Parliament as his Parliament, and he would then become involved in a struggle in which he would demand representation in this House on at least the same basis as the White man. That is the trouble which awaits South Africa, and I say that anybody who does not realise that, must be stupid. Mr. Speaker, if there are people who say that the Bantu will always be satisfied to be represented in Parliament by a few people, I say to them that they are living in a fool's paradise. No nation in the world would agree to it, and still much less the proud Bantu.

Reference has been made here to " White leadership with justice ". Mr. Speaker, this whole outlook is so unrealistic and childishly naïve that it amuses one. It is pathetic. Show me one nation in our modern history which would be prepared to agree to such a thing. Even the Bushmen rejected it in respect to the Bantu. Do members of the United Party want to tell me that the proud Bantu would agree to it? They can go and tell that story to political baboons but not to intelligent people. It is a hallucination!

Mr. Speaker, the African states are giving their reply today to this issue with which we are dealing. We are getting an object lesson with regard to this same issue in various territories of Africa. Are we politically blind or politically deaf? Are we going to learn no lesson from that? In places like Kenya, Nyasaland and Northern Rhodesia we saw that the British Government was prepared to go very far in giving the Bantu, on this same sort of basis, a say together with the White man in the government of the country, and what were the results? Did it produce peace? No, it created greater dissatisfaction. On this very same basis, they wanted to give greater rights to the Native population of other territories, and the result was simply that those people, once they had been given these rights, demanded that the sole say should be in the hands of the majority of the people. They are not going to be satisfied with anything less than the sole say. Why then should South Africa be an exception? No, Mr. Speaker, this political pattern does not create racial peace, but racial tension; it does not produce harmonious relations but clashes; it does not produce confidence but fear; it does not bring peace but strife; it does not produce order but chaos.

Mr. Speaker, in the light of South Africa's fundamental choice and standpoint, on the basis of our experience extending over generations, having regard to the salvation of South Africa and the happiness of all groups of the population, there is only one way — the traditional way, the way which is embodied in this Bill which I am submitting to the House for its consideration.

I want to pause for a moment to deal with the recognition of Bantu homelands. In the White Paper I put forward a few propositions which I do not want to repeat here, but I just want to make this submission again that in setting aside Bantu territories both before and after the establishment of Union, the object was not purely and simply to set aside land for them; the great object was to give that land to the various communities as their homelands. The object was not simply to set aside that land; the main object was to assist those communities with their development, to link them up with their land. This setting aside of land was undertaken not only by the British Government, but also by the Republican Governments. As from 1878 the Bantu territories of the Ciskei were deliberately demarcated by the British Government, and that was done in the region between the Great Fish and the Kei Rivers. The constituent parts of the present Transkei, with the retention of their identity as Bantu territories, were incorporated into the Cape Colony by means of a series of acts and proclamations as from 1879. In 1839 the Voortrekkers started with territorial demarcation in Natal, and that was continued by the British Government in 1843. Separate areas were demarcated and given to the Natal Native Trust in 1864. In 1897 Zululand proper, with the retention of its identity, was incorporated into Natal by legislation. In the Transvaal a start was made in 1853 with the granting of land to the tribes, and in 1881 a standing Native Location Commission started defining those areas. The republic of the Orange Free State, by means of grants and resolutions, also recognised Bantu areas. So, for example, in 1867, with a further extension in 1873, Witzieshoek was granted to two tribes, while in 1884 Thaba'Nchu was set aside for the Barolong. With the establishment of Union, the British Government kept the three large Bantu territories, Bechuanaland, Basutoland and Swaziland — which jointly represented one-third of the surface area of British South Africa, outside the Union and thereby indicated that these territories should be maintained as Bantu territories. After the establishment of Union the Union Government, by legislation, immediately entrenched as Bantu territories the areas which had been recognised by its predecessor as Bantu territories, and it did so by incorporating them in terms of the Native Land Act of 1913. But the Union Government did not leave it at that. Subsequently, a further 7,250,000 morgen of land were released for systematic addition to the Bantu areas and since then nearly 5,000,000 morgen of land have been added. But I say again that the main task was neglected, and that is the development which should have accompanied that. In the case of the Transvaal, the Free State and Natal the main object was perfectly clear.

I just want to pause for a moment to deal with the aims which it was intended to achieve in setting aside Bantu areas. The main aim was to create homelands for the Bantu. In the case of the Cape Colony there was a two-fold policy. The first aim coincided with that of the Transvaal and Natal, and the other was to establish a number of small locations which were to serve as a means of breaking up the tribes, of introducing civilisation to the Bantu, and, as an historian put it, as labour reservoirs for the Whites. Here we really had a difference between the opinion of the people and that of the authorities, but the mass of the population in South Africa regarded these areas as the homelands of the Bantu and the Bantu accepted them as such.

*

One of the fine things that we are doing in this Bill is to give formal recognition to the various Bantu population groups. That is a desire that we find on the part of all the groups of the population. In the short time during which I have had some dealings with them, one of the questions which has been put to me everywhere is this: "Can't you give us recognition; why are you tearing us asunder?" In this Bill formal recognition is being given to the existence of those population groups, but particularly to the process of national development by and in the population groups themselves. I think by this time hon. members will concede that you cannot start a process of development by simply linking it up with the White man's way of life. That would be nonsensical. No process in which the Bantu's dignity is not acknowledged can form the basis on which development can take place, and in refusing to appreciate his own system of government and his own rights we slight the dignity of the Bantu himself. But hon. members will also concede a second thing, Mr. Speaker, and that is that that process cannot be started by creating an artificial unit, in other words, by bundling all the Bantu together in one common society, as many hon. members on the other side want to do, because there are only two bonds which bind them together: The first is their colour and the other is their hatred of the White man. But there is something greater than that, something higher than that which binds people together, and that is their spiritual treasures, the cultural treasures of a people. It is these fine things which have united other nations in the world. That is why we say that the basis of our approach is that the Bantu too will be linked together by traditional and emotional bonds, by their own language, their own culture, their national possessions. I am convinced that for this measure I shall receive the gratitude of the Bantu throughout South Africa.

This Bill also gives the various population groups their own territorial authorities. That is very important. Where there are no territorial authorities as yet, a Territorial Council will be established in the meantime, but I am convinced that within a year or two all these matters will be disposed of.

But the most important consideration is that this Bill makes it possible for the Governor-General to transfer his legislative powers systematically to those Territorial Authorities. Because of the nature of our national structure it is not possible today to see this in clear perspective, but I am convinced that once these Territorial Authorities have all been established, and these powers have been systematically transferred to them, we are going to achieve excellent results. This is an act of faith in the Bantu such as we have never had before in South Africa, and it is something which is going to satisfy him and for which he is already very grateful today. I readily concede that many of these things will take a little time before they can all be arranged and before all these powers can be granted, but once all the Territorial Authorities are in operation, it is my intention to review this whole matter and to see how we can best shape it in the interests of every population group and in the interests of the whole of South Africa. But the Bantu himself will have to help in extending this system. He will be called upon to extend it, and that is one of the fine principles contained in this Bill, because now it will no longer be the White man who will be doing these things; it will be the Bantu himself.

In the second place I want to mention another important aspect, and that is that we envisage that the Bantu will develop his own courts. Let me put it this way: The Bantu has developed a very fine legal system which ensures a high degree of justice. That is why it has also been recognised by the authorities, but the mistake that was made was that no attention was given to the question of allowing the courts to develop together with the development of the community. It was looked down upon and jeered at. After all, according to the United Party it was just a court conducted by barbarians. Mr. Speaker, that is not fair towards the Bantu; it is not reconcilable with the general development of the Bantu. That is why this Bill provides for special attention to be given to this matter so that it will become possible for them to administer their own system of justice. They will be assisted actively to extend their own courts, and I anticipate that the time will come when they themselves will have their own supreme court in their own territories with their own judges on the Bench. I propose to give very serious attention to this matter.

But this Bill goes further. It holds out this prospect that the Territorial Authorities are going to look after their own education. I just want to announce that the Department of Bantu Education is ready, as soon as the Bantu Territorial Authorities are in operation, to place a large portion of the education in the areas concerned directly under the Territorial Authorities. That will mean that the Territorial Authority will exercise authority and control over all the school boards and committees in this area. In exercising that control it will have in its hands the most important means of building up its community culturally and economically. Just think what it will mean to the Bantu if he himself exercises control over his education. Welfare work and social services will also be placed under them in due course. We shall see to it that it takes place on a sound basis.

Then I want to mention another important matter and that is that in due course the Native Trust Lands will be transferred to the Territorial Authorities, a very important decision. It must not be forgotten that the land which has been set aside for them — 7,250,000 morgen — falls under the Native Trust. The Native Trust is responsible for the development of that land, etc. We now envisage transferring this land in due course to the Territorial Authorities. They will then be responsible for the proper conservation of the soil and its development, etc. I need only say this, Mr. Speaker, that when we look at the results which are being achieved at the present time, there can be no doubt that it would be in the interests of the Bantu and of South Africa as a whole to entrust that task to the Natives. It is a question of faith. They would be responsible for the allocation of that land and all that type of thing. Let me just say this: There are very few things which have caused so much dissatisfaction amongst the Bantu as the fact that the land which was purchased at the time — I refer to the land which was promised to them at the time by General Hertzog and of which a portion was bought — was placed under the Native Trust and not directly under the chiefs. Throughout the whole of South Africa I have heard this reproach. Under the system which is now being introduced it will fall under the Territorial Authority, which is a responsible body. This is an important step forward.

Then I want to mention another important principle which is contained in this Bill. Formerly the Governor-General could appoint or dismiss any chief at will. He will now be obliged to consult the Territorial Authority. I admit that in the past the Governor-General has always consulted the tribe, but the responsibility is now going to rest with the Territorial Authority. In this way it is being given status, it is being given the status in its own territory which our Government has in the territory of the White man. That is the basic approach in connection with this matter.

But there is another important principle embodied in this legislation, and that is that for the first time official links are being instituted between the Bantu territories and the Natives in the cities. For the first time! I admit at once that here we are facing a very great problem. I readily admit that there are many Bantu in the White areas. But I also want to make this further submission that very large numbers of those Bantu were not born in South Africa. There are many of them whose home is Basutoland. Do you know, sir, that there are approximately 1,000,000 Sothos in South Africa? Large numbers of them were born in the Protectorate of Bechuanaland, and Swaziland is the home of a large section. Do not let us overlook that factor. That is a factor which will have to be faced squarely sooner or later. But that does not detract from the fact that there are also large numbers of our own Natives in the cities, and that is a very important problem. The question which is frequently asked is this : What is to be their future?

Let me first say this — and in this regard I want to be explicit and clear. It must be quite clearly understood by the United Party and by the whole world that those Natives will never become part of the White community; we are not going to follow a policy which is going to lead to a common society in South Africa. Let us be perfectly clear and explicit on that point. But in the second place, I want to make this statement that the vast majority of those people have never lost their links with their own territories. I personally made some pilot surveys and the Tomlinson Commission[3] made a large number of pilot surveys over the whole country, and it was found that easily 80 per cent, if not more, of those Bantu had always retained some link or other with the Bantu areas. We are not faced here with a problem of displaced persons. Our practical experience has been that although a Bantu has been in the city for years, for perhaps two or three generations, he still knows where his tribe is, and you will be surprised to know, sir, how readily he is absorbed again into his tribe. Why do hon. members come along and make a mountain out of a molehill? The fact of the matter is that links will now be created between the Bantu areas and those people in the cities. I have no doubt that it will have a very salutary effect. It will also have a salutary effect on the moral standards of those people. It must not be forgotten that as far as customs, etc. are concerned, the Bantu in the cities constitute rather a loose population, and in those places where the different ethnic groups are already separately housed and where we have given them non-official recognition, it has already been shown that a new ideal has been created for these people, where they have their own links and their own mother-tongue and when we restore to them those emotional links which are of so much value to every nation in the world. I have no doubt that in this way we are going to create a very fine link as far as the whole Native population is concerned.

3 Appointed in 1948 by the Malan Government. Chairman: Professor F. R. Tomlinson of Pretoria University. Report under U.G. 61 of 1955.

Then I just want to say that in this process we should at least concede to the Bantu what the English people did not begrudge themselves. Let me just remind the House that the whole democratic system of the British nation was developed round the Royal house and the nobility. Let them deny it. It took years, but that is the position. Today every Englishman is proud of that democratic system. But it must not be forgotten that it is only since 1832 that that system has actually taken definite shape. Why then do we begrudge this same process to the Bantu? Here we have the same process. What is contained in this Bill is something that the Bantu understands, something that is integrated into his life.

But hon. members may ask perhaps why we do not carry on with this matter and leave alone the question of Natives' representation; why we do not allow the Natives' representatives to remain in this House; why we do not first complete the whole pattern and then consider thereafter whether we want to abolish the Native representation in this House. I just want to say that that is an attitude which can only be adopted by a person who has no knowledge at all of the Native. Any person who has taken the slightest trouble to make a study of the approach of the Bantu population to these matters, could never adopt such an attitude. Because in connection with this political issue, they have an axiom which runs as follows, that the idea of two bulls in one kraal never works. The Native does not want it; to him it is unthinkable. To have two political processes which are diametrically opposed to each other and which try to destroy each other, is something which the Native simply cannot understand, and he would regard that as the greatest dishonesty on the part of the White man. Sir, there are Natives who have asked me to abolish the Native representation immediately. If we want to be honest, then we must take into account the approach of the Bantu himself, and then we cannot start such a process; we must adopt the course that is acceptable and understandable and honest towards the Bantu population, a course which in their eyes is not a conflicting policy but which they regard as an honest policy.

The question may be put to me: What does the Native population think about this matter? How do they feel? I just want to say that after the introduction of this Bill I made it my business to make its contents known to all the Bantu population groups throughout South Africa. More than 3,000 copies of the Bill and of the White Paper were distributed amongst them. The full contents were also published in the journal *Bantu*, more than 30,000 copies of which were distributed. What was the reaction? The reaction was this, that I have here a large number of telegrams from all parts of South Africa, from all the important Bantu population groups, from Cyprian, from Victor Poto, from Botha Sigcau, from the Venda chiefs, from the Ciskei, etc. I have had telegrams from the responsible groups in every territory conveying their gratitude and congratulations and telling me to go ahead with this. And do you know, sir, that I did not have a single letter or telegram of protest? Do you know where I came across a protest? A moment ago at the entrance to Parliament, where there is a placard bearing the words " no taxation without representation ". The Black Sash!

MRS. BALLINGER: Hear, hear!

MR. DE WET NEL: I agree, but that is one of the great principles embodied in this Bill, because here it is envisaged that in the future they will impose their own taxes, and the time will come when all taxes in the Bantu areas will be imposed by the Bantu themselves. That is the only protest that I received. Everywhere the Bantu have acclaimed this as a new day and a new era which has dawned for the Bantu in South Africa. That is their approach to this matter.

The aims of this Bill could be briefly summarised as follows:

(1) It gives expression to the racial pattern and the philosophy of life of the people of South Africa in respect to the colour question. It is the product of a deep and honest conviction which flows from historical experience and which is based on the Christian principles underlying the approach of our people, because we do not begrugde those people what we claim for ourselves.

(2) It rests on the conviction that it will ward off those factors which may possibly plough the White man under, but at the same time it also creates the possibility for the Bantu to bring to the fullest fruition his personal and national ideas within his own population group. What we demand for ourselves, we do not begrudge the Bantu. Our approach is not simply negative but also positive.

(3) It converts the Bantu development which was formerly instituted under the direction of the White man, into a development which will be anchored in the Bantu community itself, a development in terms of which all the factors of nation and community building will be actively placed in the service of each group of the Bantu population, on the same lines as in the case of the White man. In this way the material and spiritual growth of the Bantu population groups will be set in motion, so that they will also be able to make a contribution to the eternal and lasting values of South Africa and of the world as a whole.

(4) It lays the foundation of a form of government in which all population groups, on a basis of honour and mutual respect, can be informed and consulted about the great problems of South Africa and where everyone's efforts can be harnessed in a spirit of mutual trust for the welfare of South Africa.

(5) It creates, I am convinced, a future of hope and expectation for all population groups in South Africa, a future of peace and security, not only for the White population of South Africa, but also for the Bantu population groups. Now every group will know in which direction it is moving. It removes the mists of doubt and uncertainty, which are the greatest cause of mistrust of the White man. Those mists of doubt and uncertainty have now disappeared. Everybody will know in which direction he is heading, and it is that certainty which gives man the greatest satisfaction.

(6) I am deeply convinced that this is the only basis on which a great and happy South Africa can be built for all population groups.

SIR DE VILLIERS GRAAFF, 18 MAY 1959[1]

I MOVE AS AN AMENDMENT (that) . . . this House declines to pass the Second Reading of the Bill because it, *inter alia,*

(*a*) aims at the division of South Africa into Black States and a multi-racial State, and if implemented, will involve grave dangers for all South Africans;

(*b*) is repugnant to principles of natural justice in that it removes long-standing rights without giving anything of substance in return, and leaves the Native population without any voice in the Parliament which governs them; and

(*c*) seeks to establish in the Black areas a system of government in conflict with Western democratic ideas, and will leave the millions of Natives permanently settled outside the reserves without any means of political expression whatever.

*

The hon. gentleman has said that he has forged a link between these people (outside the reserves) and their national units. But what does his Bill do? It deprives that section of the Native population throughout South Africa of the limited political rights which they have enjoyed hitherto. It replaces them with no new rights whatever. Instead of what they had, little as it was, the sole channel of political expression is going to be through something in the nature of a tribal ambassador called a representative, appointed by a Territorial Authority, in consultation with the Minister and subject to the approval of the Governor-General . . .

. . . The Natives of that national unit will have no other means of bringing their troubles to the attention of the electorate which elects this Parliament and decides whether they are going to be dealt with or not. The Press will not know about them. They will have no opportunity whatever of exercising pressure upon this Parliament in the event of their feeling that injustice has been done. They will not even have the right to get rid of the representative if they do not like him. Can one say that the Territorial Authority will really have any understanding and experience of the problems with which that Native permanently settled in the multi-racial part of South Africa has to deal? . . .

. . . The fact is that this Bill is based on a system of administration already standing very largely upon our statute books, based on a tribal

[1] Extracts from speech by the Leader of the Opposition, Sir de Villiers Graaff (United Party) during the debate on the Promotion of Bantu Self-Government Bill in the House of Assembly, 18 May 1959. *House of Assembly Debates.*

system which is not only largely outmoded, but which offers no real place for the educated, advanced, civilised Native who has sought to adopt the Western way of life as we know it. Nor has he any regard to the vast numbers of Natives who have lost their tribal affiliations. I know the hon. the Minister will tell us there are none. I can only tell him that I do not accept that evidence.

By destroying institutions of a Western democratic kind, and replacing them by what I would describe as tribal institutions, what this Bill is trying to do is to try and retribalise the Native who has already set his foot on the way to the Western way of life; something which is not only inadvisable, but, I believe, impracticable because the Native peoples all over Africa are reaching out for Western civilisation, and to deny that to them is merely to court trouble . . .

. . . What will the end result of all this be? Is this the sort of foundation upon which a modern, civilised, Western democratic institution is to be built up? To be built up in the future Black dominions of the hon. the Prime Minister? I say that it is not. I say what is much more likely is that this will bring about a reversion; a reversion to a system of primitive despotism of a kind which we knew in South Africa when the White man first came here; which we knew in South Africa amongst the Native peoples of that time, with all its attendant dangers to the whole population of South Africa. So much for the Bill. It is a bad Bill. But that is not all.

We reject this Bill not only because of its contents, but also because it is part of a pattern which we believe will lead to the destruction of South Africa and disaster for all its peoples. Because the inevitable result of this pattern must be the partition of South Africa into separate States. And I believe the hon. the Prime Minister knows that. I believe that he understands and accepts that that will happen. Why otherwise would he have referred to possible future relations between the emergent Black dominions and the Union of South Africa as we know it, by comparing it with the British Commonwealth of Nations? . . .

. . . One wonders what it is that has persuaded the hon. the Prime Minister to adopt this pattern. I believe that it represents his reaction to the march of events in Africa. It is quite true that originally the White people and the Native people in South Africa occupied different areas of the country, just as it is true that there were once no White people in South Africa at all. But the whole trend of South African history has been contrary to what the hon. the Prime Minister and his Government are trying to do at the present time. As late as the First World War the races in South Africa were still geographically so separated that statesmen of the calibre of General Botha, General Hertzog and General Smuts could have suggested that self-government in separate areas was a practical solution . . . But since that time the scene has changed. Modern South Africa has been built on a foundation of industrial development, which in its turn is dependent on Native labour to an ever-increasing degree.

These developments have rendered the thoughts expressed 30 and 40 and even 25 years ago very much out of date and one of the first people to realise that was non other than the late General Smuts, in a very important speech he made in the City Hall in Cape Town in January 1942 . . .

. . . Since those statements were made 40 years ago, times have changed, the pattern has changed and circumstances have changed. But this Government, under that hon. Prime Minister, seeks to ignore all these circumstances, and they seek justification for this policy which I have already shown is nothing more than a counsel of despair . . .

. . . He (the Prime Minister) has told us that he is doing so because he wishes to get away from discrimination. Discrimination is immoral. The present situation is not sufficiently moral for his liking, and therefore we must now embark on a course which can be justified on moral grounds. Well, let us test the morality of what the hon. gentleman proposes . . .

. . . Is it moral to condemn millions of Natives to live and work in areas for ever where they will never have any political rights at all? Is the disparity in agricultural and mining potential between the different areas such that it justifies the division of South Africa on moral grounds in the proportions indicated by this plan? Is it moral, while people are in the process of developing from a primitive state of society towards a higher degree of civilisation, to attempt to force them back into the primitive mould from which they are trying to break out? Above all, is it moral to arrogate to oneself the right to attempt to arrest the development of our Native people in the tribal stage of human society when similarly placed people throughout the world are reaching out for Western civilisation and are pressing irresistibly for the achievement of that civilisation, and to arrogate that right to oneself without consulting the people concerned? . . .

. . . In contrast to all this, the United Party have always held before the people of South Africa a different policy based on the facts of the South African situation and indicating a different road to be followed. That policy seeks above all the maintenance and the continued existence of the Union of South Africa as a united land in which the people of all the different races can build together harmoniously and in peace. That is basic and fundamental and that is one of the big differences between us. Hon. members opposite are prepared to fragment South Africa; we believe in keeping it one united land. We believe that in the Union the present leadership of the White race should be maintained, not on the basis of fear and selfish exclusiveness, but because — and this is a basic fact, too — the White race in South Africa is the bearer of Western civilisation. Therefore the maintenance of its leadership will depend on a sincere willingness and desire to share the fruits of that civilisation with those non-Whites who develop the capacity for accepting and carrying the joint responsibility for our future well-being on this sub-continent. It is quite clear that if you take account of the facts of the situation as they are at present, there is a long period of training in the ways and particularly

454

in the responsibilities of democracy which lies ahead of the vast bulk of the Native people. Only when they have had that training can claims to greater rights be entertained, and then only with the agreement of a decisive majority of the electorate.

In the long run, of course, the leadership of the White race in South Africa will depend on the moral quality of that leadership, the moral quality which the Prime Minister is throwing overboard in this Bill; and it should be remembered also that as the standard of civilisation of a community is raised, leadership will depend to an increasing degree upon numbers. Restrictive laws alone can never be a final solution . . .

. . . Therefore we stand for a positive approach to strengthening the position of the White race in South Africa. That is also fundamental, because we believe that a Native policy, to meet the present world situation and the situation on the African continent, cannot be divorced from a policy which will secure for the White man in South Africa a position of strength, so that justice done to the Native will not cause the White man to fear submergence and political and cultural annihilation.

Now, to give the White race that additional security we believe that positive action is necessary on three fronts. Firstly, our fiscal and social policy should be directed towards bringing about an increased birthrate amongst the European population . . . In the second place, we believe that this Government should assist large numbers of immigrants to come to South Africa rapidly. It is tragic that the propaganda of that side of the House has led some people to believe that immigration on a substantial scale may lead to unemployment in South Africa. That propaganda is based on the assumption that there is a limited amount of work in every society, and it ignores the fact that in an expanding economy immigration can stimulate development and create work . . . In the third place we believe that it is essential that the Cape Coloured community should be restored to its traditional status of an appendage of the White race. By their history, culture, language and religion they have been with us, the co-defenders of Western civilisation in South Africa. We must restore the Coloured people to the position where they will once again be our friends and allies in defending Western civilisation.

We recognise that for any policy to be successful it must gain the support and understanding of the broad masses of both the White and the Native people in South Africa. Hence it will be our determination to direct our attention towards determining the best methods of consultation with the non-White peoples and their leaders, and more particularly with the more responsible class of Native. We believe that bridges must be built, that contacts must be made and a climate re-established which is conducive to goodwill and mutual understanding, a climate which will never be attained by contacts limited to those at official level and the relationship of master-servant as we seem to have at the present time. It is against this background that we believe that representation of the Native people in the Central Legislature is essential; it is essential because

455

firstly good government requires a knowledge of the views of those governed, and secondly it will be impossible to get the co-operation of those to be governed, without giving them some measure of participation in the government of the country. Thirdly, only thereby will it be possible to check the inevitable tendency of those areas to break away, which the Prime Minister feels should get more and more autonomy.

I will immediately be asked what the form of that representation must be. The form of that representation must be, in general terms — I will deal with the specific provisions later — must be such as to enable Western civilisation and the leadership of the White race to be maintained and should be based upon the responsible class of Native whose recognition and emergence this party will actively encourage. And, sir, when I speak of a responsible class of Native, I speak not only of the educated man, the man with the big income; I speak of the man of good character, the man whom even the Minister of Justice wants on his side to help him to maintain law and order and I go further; I say that the extension of such representation to provide adequate political expression. can only be granted on the basis of the support of a decisive majority of the present electorate, and that it should be preceded by consultation between all those concerned, in order to ensure that there are adequate safeguards for the maintenance of White leadership. Sir, that is the general background . . .

. . . As immediate steps in the implementation of its policy the party proposes first of all the establishment of bodies at various levels through which the Native peoples will be able to maintain liaison with the existing instruments of government to ensure that Native opinion will be properly expressed and considered in public affairs as required by the national interest; secondly the granting of greater responsibility to the Native peoples in their own areas, both inside and outside of the reserves and it is recognised that since there are protected residential rights in the reserves it may be possible to grant the Native peoples in the reserves greater rights of self-government than those who are situated outside of the reserves, cheek by jowl with the European areas. We believe, thirdly, that the representation of Natives in all provinces in the Senate should be on the basis on which it exists at the present time, save that the number should be increased to six, and that in the election of those senators the more advanced and educated Natives, the responsible class of Native, will be given a special and personal franchise in the relevant electoral college. Fourthly — and here I know I will have the support of the Minister of Native Affairs[2] — we believe that the representation of Natives in this Assembly as it exists today in the Cape Province, should continue on that basis, and not only that, but that it should be extended on the basis of a separate roll to the northern provinces of South Africa. The separate roll is a constitutional safeguard which the public of South

[2] Read: Minister of Bantu Administration and Development.

Africa understands, and I know that on that basis I will have the support of the Minister and of gentlemen on that side of the House who were so keen to place the Cape Coloured people on a separate roll.

MR. P. O. SAUER[3]: May I ask you a question for clarification — a total of six or six for the province?

SIR DE VILLIERS GRAAFF: A total of six Senators for the Union. The Act of 1936 makes provision for two additional Senators, as the hon. the Minister would know. We propose that that provision be applied. Such representation to be by White Senators and White members of Parliament in the Senate and in the House of Assembly. In this connection I want to say at once that there is a strong body of opinion in favour of Natives and Coloureds being represented by people of their own race in this House and in the Upper House. But the policy of the United Party remains that they will be represented in this House and the Upper House by Europeans as in the past. Future Parliaments may decide otherwise, but that is not for us to comment on.

Sir, there are certain steps which one feels should be taken in the development of what I would call the responsible class of Native, both in the reserves and outside of the reserves. In the reserves we believe in extensive steps in the rehabilitation of the land and the industrial development of those areas, to some extent on the basis of the proposals made in the report of the Tomlinson Commission[4]. Sir, it is not necessary to re-discuss that matter; the whole matter was before this House earlier when we dealt with the Bantu Development Corporation Bill. But we believe that what is fundamental is that there should be a gradual extension of the right to individual ownership of land amongst the Native people in the reserves at the present time. In the urban areas we believe that there should be controlled home ownership for Natives in the areas set aside for them and that everything possible should be done for their economic uplift, in order to develop that responsible class of Native who will have an interest and a stake in the maintenance of law and order in South Africa. Both inside and outside of the reserves there should be an extension of the powers of the local government bodies; there should be an effective link between them and the European institutions of government, and wherever possible the elective system should be introduced and observed.

We feel that the general scheme which is envisaged here will restore harmonious race relations in South Africa and lead to a future co-operation between the various racial groups in South Africa . . .

. . . We believe that it will lead to future co-operation between the racial groups and the development of the common fatherland based on South African nationalism, rather than on African nationalism, and it will enable White leadership in South Africa to be retained by reason of

---

3 Minister of Lands.
4 Commission for the Socio-Economic Development of the Bantu Areas.

the growing strength of the White population and by virtue of a type of federal political system based on the representation of races, and not on geographical areas, in which constitutional safeguards would ensure that no group could oppress another. I want to say that we shall not be afraid to examine possible new constitutional arrangements which provide adequate safeguards to achieve the aims I have outlined, because we appreciate that this is not a static problem. It is a problem of human relations which is changing from day to day and which can only be appreciated as the result of close and continual consultation at all levels between the races. With this policy will go hand in hand a policy for the dynamic industrial expansion of South Africa, designed to raise living standards, to enable us to strengthen our European population and to win for South Africa the position of the industrial workshop of the Continent of Africa.

Tested against the criteria which I outlined when I first entered this debate, I feel that this policy will not be found wanting. It will enable us to win and hold the leading position on the Continent of Africa. It will place White leadership on a sure foundation. It will give our Native people cause and reason to become co-defenders of Western civilisation. It will build our real national strength on a South African patriotism shared by all the peoples of South Africa. I believe that that is the real difference between us and the hon. the Prime Minister. The hon. gentleman, beset by fears for which he has no answers, is preparing to dismember South Africa, while we, firm in our faith, seek always to build an ever greater South Africa where all the peoples placed here by Providence will be able to live in harmony and contentment.

9

PROGRESSIVE PARTY POLICY

DR. J. VAN A. STEYTLER[1]

FOR 300 YEARS the non-European has been in contact with the civilising influences of the White man in South Africa. For 50 years we have had a pattern developing in South Africa, a pattern of discrimination on the colour of a man's skin as the basis on which privileges and rights are accorded to him. For ten years we have had " baasskap apartheid ". And the political inquities perpetrated in the name of baasskap apartheid will take this nation and this country 100 years to live down.

Last year the hon. the Prime Minister, with his acceptance of the Bantustan concept as the basis of the Nationalist Party policy rejected, on behalf of the Nationalist Party, discrimination as the basis of political division. The hon. the Prime Minister said during the second reading debate, that he is according to the Bantu people the opportunity of developing to the maximum. His own words were " I am giving the non-Europeans, the Bantu people, the opportunity of getting on to the first rung of the ladder; whether they will reach the top will depend entirely upon their own ability. The hon. the Minister of Bantu Administration and Development said " Anybody who believes that the Bantu people will forever be subservient to other people in South Africa is living in a fool's paradise ". Therefore the Nationalist Party advances the concept of Bantustan.

Mr. Speaker, we have no quarrel with the Nationalist Party and with the Government in their search for a basis of non-discrimination on which political rights and privileges are accorded to the individuals in South Africa. But we reject completely the Bantustan cult because we believe it can never be brought into practice in South Africa. We believe that by virtue of the geographic distribution of the Bantu areas and the ethnic units, it is impossible ever to consolidate those areas so that they can form a homeland for the Bantu peoples. The Tomlinson Commission makes mention of the fact that there are 110 Bantu areas. In addition to that, there are 154 Black spots distributed over the length and breadth of the country, reminding me of the measle spots on the back of a child. If one listens to the speeches made in this House by

---

[1] Speech held by Dr. Steytler, Leader of the Progressive Party, on 20 January 1960. *House of Assembly Debates.*

hon. members opposite and if one goes into the speeches made outside, it is quite apparent that it is not the intention of the Nationalist Government to implement that policy. The Tomlinson Commission recommended that there is only one basis on which this can be made reality in South Africa, and that is if more land is bought for the Bantu people. The Government has said unequivocally that no more land in addition to the 1936 settlement will be acquired. In addition to that, a prerequisite to any idea of implementing Bantustans is the acquisition of the protectorates. As yet they do not form part of South Africa.

Our second reason for believing that it is impossible to realise this policy is because of the economic sacrifices that will be demanded from the South African nation. Once again the Commission recommended that £104,000,000 per annum should be spent over a ten-year period. The hon. the Prime Minister estimated that £30,000,000 would suffice. Other experts tell us that £1,000,000,000 might be necessary in order to realise this ideal. Our third objection is our doubt about the practicability of this policy on account of the racial distribution of our people. Even if by the wave of a magic wand this can become reality, what would be the position of the racial composition of our country? We find, too, that the Tomlinson Commission found that even if the entire scheme could be put into practice, which according to our way of thinking is an impossibility, the Whites will still be outnumbered by the non-Whites. The entire economy of South Africa will still be dependent on non-White labour. The non-White will still have a vice-like grip over the entire South Africa, because by virtue of the fact of his economic integration he has power which will put him in a position to demand all rights and privileges if he so chooses to do. That is the reason why we of the Progressive Party reject *in toto* the Bantustan concept. We believe that for all time to come South Africa will be a multi-racial country, and the choice before the people of South Africa is: How are we going to live together, because for nearly all time to come we will have White people, we will have Bantu and we will have Coloureds and we will have the Indian community, all part and parcel of the South African nation. The choice before the people is whether we are going to perpetuate our living on a basis, in the short-term view, of White domination, but as assuredly as we are gathered here today in the long term it will mean Black domination. Sir, it is our view that we can only maintain harmony and peace and co-operation between the various sections of our community if we discard colour as the only yardstick by which a man is accorded rights and privileges. We believe that after 300 years of civilising the non-White in South Africa it is incumbent upon us to recognise a civilised man when we see him. Therefore we say that we reject the separate roll as a basis on which a multi-racial country must be governed. We believe that there is only one way of doing it, and that is to place all qualified people on the Common Roll. We have come to that conclusion not only after a very extensive consultation with people, but also after going into all the evidence at our disposal, and with your permission, sir, I would like to quote some of that evidence.

The first one I would like to quote is General Smuts. In 1929 already at the Rhodes Memorial Lectures at Oxford he dealt with the Native problem of South Africa. I would like to quote an extract from his speech which has never before been quoted in this House. This is what he said —

> If we had to deal only with the tribal Native, the question would not be so difficult and the application of the general segregation principle to the particular case of political rights might be justified. Unfortunately very large numbers of detribalised Natives are spread all over the Cape. These urbanised Natives living amongst the Whites constitute the real crux of the problem as it is today. With the application of a strict educational, civilisation test it would probably be better to allow them to exercise their political rights along with the Whites.

Then we have at our disposal the findings of Royal Commissions which were appointed in the past to investigate in principle which of the two systems might be the better, whether the Common Roll be preferable or whether the separate roll might be the right one. In this connection we have the findings of seven Royal Commissions. The sum total of the findings amounted to this (that they had come unhesitatingly to the conclusion) that the communal representation is, as it were, a canker in the body politic, eating deeper and deeper into the vital energies of the people, breeding self-interest, suspicion and animosity, poisoning the new spirit of national consciousness and effectively preventing the development of a national or co-operative spirit.

Another one similar to that is the Indian Advisory Committee on Minorities. They reported —

> By an overwhelming majority we have come to the conclusion that the system of separate elections must be abolished in the near future. In our judgment this system has in the past sharpened communal differences to a dangerous extent and has proved one of the main stumbling-blocks to the development of a healthy national life.

I can also quote the 1950 Conference of the Federated Dutch Reformed Churches. They found the following:

> The system of direct representation of Natives in the Senate House of Assembly and Provincial Council must be considered a failure. Particularly during the past years the Natives did not evince a high sense of responsibility in appointing their representatives. The system of representation has up to the present been a source of contention between the interests of the Whites and non-Whites. Some Whites do not hesitate from playing up the interests of the two sections against each other. That is the cause of the ever increasing friction and contention between Whites and non-Whites.

The point here is that they are weighing the communal as against the

461

Common Roll system. Sabra said the same and just for the record I want to quote it also —

Supporters of the integration policy often claim that the granting of a fixed and limited number of representatives in the Europeans' Parliament should satisfy the Native population without creating any threat to the Europeans' dominance in the political sphere. Here it must, however, first be asked whether there are any reasonable grounds for presuming that the Native population will or can be satisfied with this type of representation in the long run, representation which clearly discriminates against them. Secondly, if the principle of group representation is adopted, how many representatives are to be granted to the Natives in the Assembly or in the Senate?

So we can go on quoting one finding after the other of expert commissions which have investigated the feasibility of the two systems, the Common Roll as against the separate roll. Not only that, but in the context of South Africa today we must remember that the non-White wants his rights. How can we justify not giving any rights or privileges to an educated, civilised man? We cannot justify it in the eyes of the non-White; we cannot justify it in the eyes of the world, and we cannot justify it in our own eyes. Mr. Speaker, I have no doubt that in the attempt of the hon. the Prime Minister in accepting the Bantustan concept one of the reasons that moved him towards that was the fact that not only were we losing the goodwill of the non-White in South Africa, but we were losing the respect of the outside world. Now there are many people who will say that should that be the case, how long will it be before the Whites are outnumbered on the Common Roll, that political power will go into the hands of the non-Whites. No, I do not wish to see that. All that I want to guarantee for South Africa is that when that day comes, and as sure as I am standing here it will come, no matter what Government is in power, I want to make sure that the people who govern my country must still be civilised people.

MR. SPEAKER: Order! I have granted the hon. member a lot of latitude, but there is a motion on the Order Paper which deals with the political rights of all South African citizens. Most of the arguments the hon. member has used can be used when that motion is under consideration.

MR. LAWRENCE[2]: On a point of order, may I point out that the hon. member's motion deals with a reform of the Constitution. Whereas admittedly the question of the vote is inherent in such a motion, I would urge that you allow the usual latitude to be given which is allowed to speakers on a no confidence motion.

MR. SPEAKER: No, I think I have given the hon. member a lot of latitude already.

DR. STEYTLER: I might mention, too, that these self-same fears of being swamped are being felt by the Whites in other parts of Africa where they have already had the Common Roll in practice for a number

2 Progressive Party.

462

of years. They have worked out a pattern there which, whether we like it or not, will have to be followed right throughout the African Continent. Now it might well be asked by hon. members what the qualification standards are going to be, and in this regard I would like to tell the House that we have appointed an expert commission.

AN HON. MEMBER: Who are " we "?

DR. STEYTLER: The Progressive Party. We have appointed the commission to go into the qualification standards to be laid down.

MR. SPEAKER: Order! What has that to do with the motion before the House?

MR. STEYTLER: I am coming to that.

MR. SPEAKER: But the hon. member must come to it immediately.

DR. STEYTLER: One of the reasons why we have no confidence in the Government is the fact that everything the Government does in relation to the non-Whites in South Africa, is done without any consultation whatever except through the Department of Bantu Affairs. We believe that if we have to live together with the non-Whites in South Africa, there is only one basis on which we can do it and that is that we must consult with them.

Co-operation does not only mean working together in factories. Co-existence does not only mean having sufficient to eat. It means more than that. It means that people who are ruled by laws must have a say in those laws. That is the reason why we maintain that the consultation which the Nationalist Party had in the past with these people is inadequate, and the only basis on which it can be done is by proper consultation and by giving those people the opportunity to voice their feelings.

It might be said, too, that with our policy the pattern of life that has developed in South Africa, residential separation and social separation, might disappear. I can assure this House that we have gone into this matter, too. We have consulted with people in all walks of life and we have found that that danger does not exist. I would like to refer the House to the position that obtained in South Africa before the Nationalists came into power. Did we have any Group Areas Acts? Did we have an Immorality Act? And yet after 300 years the White man is still a White man. We believe that that position will obtain for all time in South Africa, because it is not a law that guarantees the individual his identity. It is not the Group Areas Act nor the Immorality Act, nor all the other apartheid legislation, that is responsible for the White man still maintaining his identity. That is not the responsibility of the State or of a party. It is the responsibility of the individual. It depends entirely what value the individual ascribes to his race identity.

In this regard I might mention, too, that all the groups in South Africa are proud to be what they are. Like the White man, the Bantu, the Indian and the Coloured would like to retain their identity. One of the most dangerous signs developing in the country is the development of

463

group nationalism. We have the Bantu developing his own nationalism and that, too, is one of the main reasons that forced the Prime Minister to adopt his policy. You have the nationalism of all the other groups springing up, which sooner or later must clash. We believe that instead of having these various nationalities, races and groups developing their own nationalism, we should substitute for that a common patriotism towards South Africa. You cannot do that on the basis of the Nationalist Party policy. You can only do it when you give recognition to the individual on his merits and not on the colour of his skin. We believe, too, that one of the biggest enemies of South Arica is poverty. We believe that according to the basis of Nationalist Party policy it is an absolute crime after ten years of Nationalist rule that three-quarters of the South African population should still be living below the breadline. We believe that steps should be taken to give the individual the opportunity, which is a right that is his, a right that cannot be alienated, that he should be put into the position to develop his potentialities to the maximum. Therefore we believe that all people in South Africa should be given the opportunity to acquire skills so that they can improve their standard of living, so that they can educate their children, so that they can help to create the buying power of the South African nation. The time is long past where South Africa could afford the luxury of having the potentialities of 13,000,000 of her people lying dormant. The Progressive Party believes that if we want to develop in the way that we can, we must mobilise all our abilities, irrespective of the race or colour of the man. In that regard we believe that the restrictions put on our industry and on labour must be removed. We believe that a man has a right to sell his labour in the best market. (Interjections.) My hon. friends and many of our critics think that should we do that there would be chaos in the industrial centres of the country. I would like to refer the House only to one place, Port Elizabeth, where there never was influx control or pass laws until 1952, and yet it was the one city in which there was no trouble. Also that in Johannesburg after and during the war, despite the influx control and pass laws, parlous conditions developed, and with proper planning, with the stabilisation of labour in the rural areas, with the rehabilitation of the reserves and with proper housing and amenities in the industrial areas, all the so-called chaos will be removed.

We believe, further, that on this basis South Africa has nothing to fear for the future. Should we take all our people with us and give them hope, we need never fear any foreign ideology. It is essential that we should reject the present basis of our policies, because it is our destiny as the biggest nation in Africa that we should maintain our influence right throughout the African Continent. It is inconceivable to us how we can go completely and absolutely contrary to what is happening not only in Africa but right throughout the world. On this basis we can develop into the country that destiny wants us to develop into.

INDEX

INDEX

Note: (*a*) References that are obvious from chapter headings are not included in the Index. *Privy Council Appeal* is a chapter heading, therefore it does not appear in the Index as no reference to this subject is made elsewhere. References to political parties are given only when they occur in the Introduction.

(*b*) Although the words *African* and *Native* are also used (in practice and in the text) to denote the Black indigenous people of the Union, it was decided to use only *Bantu* in the Index, this being the current official name adopted in legislation. All general references are under *Bantu*; official names of commissions, acts, organisations, etc. appear under the name originally used, e.g. *African National Congress, Native Affairs Commission*.

469

470